# BASIC DOCUMENTS ON HUMAN RIGHTS

## THIRD EDITION

Edited by

### IAN BROWNLIE, Q.C.

*Chichele Professor of Public
International Law, Oxford*

CLARENDON PRESS · OXFORD

1992

Oxford University Press, Walton Street, Oxford OX2 6DP

Oxford New York Toronto
Delhi Bombay Calcutta Madras Karachi
Kuala Lumpur Singapore Hong Kong Tokyo
Nairobi Dar es Salaam Cape Town
Melbourne Auckland Madrid
and associated companies in
Berlin Ibadan

Oxford is a trade mark of Oxford University Press

Published in the United States by
Oxford University Press Inc., New York

First edition 1971
Second edition 1981
Third edition 1992

British Library Cataloguing in Publication Data
Data available

Library of Congress Cataloging in Publication Data
Basic documents on human rights/edited by Ian Brownlie.—3 ed.
Includes index.
1. Human right.  I. Brownlie, Ian.
K3238.A1B76  1992  323.4—dc20  92–9841
ISBN 0–19–825712–0
ISBN 0–19–825683–3

Typeset by Best-set Typesetter Ltd., Hong Kong

Printed in Great Britain
on acid-free paper by Biddles Ltd.
Guildford and King's Lynn

# CONTENTS

PART THREE

# CONTRIBUTION OF THE INTERNATIONAL LABOUR ORGANIZATION

PART FOUR

# CONTRIBUTION OF THE UNITED NATIONS EDUCATIONAL, SCIENTIFIC, AND CULTURAL ORGANIZATION

PART SEVEN

# DEVELOPMENTS IN AFRICA

PART EIGHT

# THE CONCEPT OF EQUALITY

PART NINE

# TRADE AND DEVELOPMENT

# PREFACE TO THE THIRD EDITION

THE object of this work is to provide a useful collection of sources on human rights in the form of a handbook. The editor is all too conscious of the problems of selection, and priorities are not easily established. Significant omissions there must be, since the collection is a handbook and not an encyclopædia. Amongst the omissions are the instruments relating to the humanitarian law of war and certain United Nations documents on the rights of minorities.

This edition incorporates the following new items: the Convention against Torture and Other Cruel, Inhuman or Degrading Treatment or Punishment, 1984; the Convention on the Rights of the Child, 1989; the International Convention on the Rights of All Migrant Workers and Their Families, 1990; the I.L.O. Convention Concerning Indigenous and Tribal Peoples in Independent Countries, 1989; recent Protocols to the European Convention on Human Rights; the European Convention for the Prevention of Torture, 1987; recent instruments relating to the Helsinki process; the Additional Protocol to the American Convention on Human Rights in the Area of Economic, Social and Cultural Rights, 1988; the Inter-American Convention to Prevent and Punish Torture, 1985; and the African Charter on Human and Peoples' Rights, 1981.

The Draft Convention on the Elimination of All Forms of Religious Intolerance, 1967, has been replaced by the Declaration on the Elimination of All Forms of Intolerance and of Discrimination Based on Religion or Belief, 1981.

The following items which appeared in the second edition have been excluded on practical grounds: the decision of the European Court in *The Sunday Times* case, 1979; the Declaration of Punta del Este, 1961; the resolution of the Lagos Conference on the Rule of Law, 1961; and the statistical data (The Widening Income Gap) in Part Nine.

Readers who are concerned to discover up-to-date and detailed pieces of treaty information should consult recent official publications or other official sources. In particular, it has not been possible in the present publication to record reservations made by parties to treaties and related information—for example, the acceptance of reservations by other States.

In conclusion, I express my gratitude to the following for assistance in obtaining documents and other data: Mr. F. D. Berman, C.M.G., Q.C., Legal Adviser, the Foreign and Commonwealth Office; Mr. Hugo Caminos, Assistant Secretary for Legal Affairs, Organization of American States; Professor D. J. Harris, of the University of Nottingham; Mr. Mark Neville, of the Human Rights Information Centre, Council of Europe; and

Mr. Kelvin Widdows, Office of the Legal Adviser, International Labour Office. I also gratefully acknowledge the courtesy and co-operation of Jane Williams, of the Clarendon Press.

*All Souls College*            IAN BROWNLIE
*OXFORD.*

PART ONE

# STANDARD-SETTING BY THE UNITED NATIONS ORGANIZATION

## INTRODUCTION

A MAJOR achievement of the draftsmen of the Charter of the United Nations was the emphasis of the provisions on the importance of social justice and human rights as the foundation for a stable international order. The Organization, and especially the General Assembly and the Economic and Social Council, has given impetus to the development of standards concerning human rights. The United Nations has undertaken both general propaganda work and the burden of drafting legal instruments containing detailed provisions.

The bodies most closely concerned with consideration of questions of human rights have been the Commission on Human Rights created by the Economic and Social Council, and the Division of Human Rights of the United Nations Secretariat. In addition there is a Commission on the Status of Women, and the Human Rights Commission has created two Sub-Commissions: on Freedom of Information and of the Press, and on the Prevention of Discrimination and the Protection of Minorities.

For further reference see Van Boven, in Cassese (ed.), *U.N. Law: Fundamental Rights*, 1979, pp. 119–35; *Bulletin of Human Rights*, Division of Human Rights, Geneva; *The Review*, International Commission of Jurists, Geneva (Biannual); *I.C.J. Newsletter*, International Commission of Jurists, Geneva; Schreiber, *Recueil des cours* (Hague Academy of International Law), Vol. 145 (1975, II), pp. 297–398; and see below, pp. 15–20.

Certain of the Specialized Agencies associated with the United Nations are also concerned with human rights, the International Labour Organization being the most prominent in this respect. On the I.L.O. and UNESCO see, further, below. The Specialized Agencies make periodic reports on human rights, which are forwarded to the Commission on Human Rights and other bodies by the Secretary-General of the United Nations.

The instruments reproduced in this section belong to the period of the United Nations, with the exception of the Slavery Convention of 1926. This has been included as a part of the existing controls on slavery.

# I. RELEVANT PROVISIONS OF THE UNITED NATIONS CHARTER

*TEXT*

## WE THE PEOPLES OF THE UNITED NATIONS DETERMINED

to save succeeding generations from the scourge of war, which twice in our lifetime has brought untold sorrow to mankind, and

to reaffirm faith in fundamental human rights, in the dignity and worth of the human person, in the equal rights of men and women and of nations large and small, and

to establish conditions under which justice and respect for the obligations arising from treaties and other sources of international law can be maintained, and

to promote social progress and better standards of life in larger freedom,

## AND FOR THESE ENDS

to practise tolerance and live together in peace with one another as good neighbours, and

to unite our strength to maintain international peace and security, and

to ensure, by the acceptance of principles and the institution of methods, that armed force shall not be used, save in the common interest, and

to employ international machinery for the promotion of the economic and social advancement of all peoples,

## HAVE RESOLVED TO COMBINE OUR EFFORTS TO ACCOMPLISH THESE AIMS

Accordingly, our respective Governments, through representatives assembled in the City of San Francisco, who have exhibited their full powers found to be in good and due form, have agreed to the present Charter of the United Nations and do hereby establish an international organization to be known as the United Nations.

## CHAPTER I
### Purposes and Principles

*Article* 1

The Purposes of the United Nations are:

1. To maintain international peace and security, and to that end: to take effective collective measures for the prevention and removal of threats to

the peace, and for the suppression of acts of aggression or other breaches of the peace, and to bring about by peaceful means, and in conformity with the principles of justice and international law, adjustment or settlement of international disputes or situations which might lead to a breach of the peace;

2. To develop friendly relations among nations based on respect for the principle of equal rights and self-determination of peoples, and to take other appropriate measures to strengthen universal peace;

3. To achieve international co-operation in solving international problems of an economic, social, cultural, or humanitarian character, and in promoting and encouraging respect for human rights and for fundamental freedoms for all without distinction as to race, sex, language, or religion; and

4. To be a centre for harmonizing the actions of nations in the attainment of these common ends.

*Article* 2

The Organization and its Members, in pursuit of the Purposes stated in Article 1, shall act in accordance with the following Principles:

1. The Organization is based on the principle of the sovereign equality of all its Members.

2. All Members, in order to ensure to all of them the rights and benefits resulting from membership, shall fulfil in good faith the obligations assumed by them in accordance with the present Charter.

3. All Members shall settle their international disputes by peaceful means in such a manner that international peace and security, and justice, are not endangered.

4. All Members shall refrain in their international relations from the threat or use of force against the territorial integrity or political independence of any State, or in any other manner inconsistent with the Purposes of the United Nations.

5. All Members shall give the United Nations every assistance in any action it takes in accordance with the present Charter, and shall refrain from giving assistance to any State against which the United Nations is taking preventive or enforcement action.

6. The Organization shall ensure that States which are not Members of the United Nations act in accordance with these Principles so far as may be necessary for the maintenance of international peace and security.

7. Nothing contained in the present Charter shall authorize the United Nations to intervene in matters which are essentially within the domestic jurisdiction of any State or shall require the Members to submit such

matters to settlement under the present Charter; but this principle shall not prejudice the application of enforcement measures under Chapter VII.

*Article* 10

The General Assembly may discuss any questions or any matters within the scope of the present Charter or relating to the powers and functions of any organs provided for in the present Charter, and, except as provided in Article 12, may make recommendations to the Members of the United Nations or to the Security Council or to both on any such questions or matters.

*Article* 13

1. The General Assembly shall initiate studies and make recommendations for the purpose of:

   (*a*) promoting international co-operation in the political field and encouraging the progressive development of international law and its codification;
   (*b*) promoting international co-operation in the economic, social, cultural, educational, and health fields, and assisting in the realization of human rights and fundamental freedoms for all without distinction as to race, sex, language, or religion.

2. The further responsibilities, functions, and powers of the General Assembly with respect to matters mentioned in paragraph 1 (*b*) above are set forth in Chapters IX and X.

*Article* 16

The General Assembly shall perform such functions with respect to the international trusteeship system as are assigned to it under Chapters XII and XIII, including the approval of the trusteeship agreements for areas not designated as strategic.

## CHAPTER IX
### International Economic and Social Co-operation

*Article* 55

With a view to the creation of conditions of stability and well-being which are necessary for peaceful and friendly relations among nations based on respect for the principle of equal rights and self-determination of peoples, the United Nations shall promote:

   (*a*) higher standards of living, full employment, and conditions of economic and social progress and development;

(*b*) solutions of international economic, social, health, and related problems; and international cultural and educational co-operation; and

(*c*) universal respect for, and observance of, human rights and fundamental freedoms for all without distinction as to race, sex, language, or religion.

*Article* 56

All Members pledge themselves to take joint and separate action in co-operation with the Organization for the achievement of the purposes set forth in Article 55.

*Article* 57

1. The various specialized agencies, established by inter-governmental agreement and having wide international responsibilities, as defined in their basic instruments, in economic, social, cultural, educational, health, and related fields, shall be brought into relationship with the United Nations in accordance with the provisions of Article 63.

2. Such agencies thus brought into relationship with the United Nations are hereinafter referred to as specialized agencies.

*Article* 58

The Organization shall make recommendations for the co-ordination of the policies and activities of the specialized agencies.

*Article* 59

The Organization shall, where appropriate, initiate negotiations among the States concerned for the creation of any new specialized agencies required for the accomplishment of the purposes set forth in Article 55.

*Article* 60

Responsibility for the discharge of the functions of the Organization set forth in this Chapter shall be vested in the General Assembly and, under the authority of the General Assembly, in the Economic and Social Council, which shall have for this purpose the powers set forth in Chapter X.

## CHAPTER X
### The Economic and Social Council

*Composition*

*Article* 61

1. The Economic and Social Council shall consist of twenty-seven Members of the United Nations elected by the General Assembly.

2. Subject to the provisions of paragraph 3, nine members of the Economic and Social Council shall be elected each year for a term of three years.[1] A retiring member shall be eligible for immediate re-election.

3. At the first election after the increase in the membership of the Economic and Social Council from eighteen to twenty-seven members, in addition to the members elected in place of the six members whose term of office expires at the end of that year, nine additional members shall be elected. Of these nine additional members, the term of office of three members so elected shall expire at the end of one year, and of three other members at the end of two years, in accordance with arrangements made by the General Assembly.

4. Each member of the Economic and Social Council shall have one representative.

*Functions and Powers*

*Article* 62

1. The Economic and Social Council may make or initiate studies and reports with respect to international economic, social, cultural, educational, health, and related matters and may make recommendations with respect to any such matters to the General Assembly, to the Members of the United Nations, and to the specialized agencies concerned.

2. It may make recommendations for the purpose of promoting respect for, and observance of, human rights and fundamental freedoms for all.

3. It may prepare draft conventions for submission to the General Assembly, with respect to matters falling within its competence.

4. It may call, in accordance with the rules prescribed by the United Nations, international conferences on matters falling within its competence.

*Article* 63

1. The Economic and Social Council may enter into agreements with any of the agencies referred to in Article 57, defining the terms on which the agency concerned shall be brought into relationship with the United Nations. Such agreements shall be subject to approval by the General Assembly.

---

[1] General Assembly Resol. 1991 (XVIII), B, para. 3, '*Further decides* that, without prejudice to the present distribution of seats in the Economic and Social Council the nine additional members shall be elected according to the following pattern:
  (*a*) Seven from African and Asian states;
  (*b*) One from Latin American states;
  (*c*) One from Western European and other states.'

2. It may co-ordinate the activities of the specialized agencies through consultation with and recommendations to such agencies and through recommendations to the General Assembly and the Members of the United Nations.

*Article* 64

1. The Economic and Social Council may take appropriate steps to obtain regular reports from the specialized agencies. It may make arrangements with the Members of the United Nations and with the specialized agencies to obtain reports on the steps taken to give effect to its own recommendations and to recommendations on matters falling within its competence made by the General Assembly.

2. It may communicate its observations on these reports to the General Assembly.

*Article* 65

The Economic and Social Council may furnish information to the Security Council and shall assist the Security Council upon its request.

*Article* 66

1. The Economic and Social Council shall perform such functions as fall within its competence in connexion with the carrying out of the recommendations of the General Assembly.

2. It may, with the approval of the General Assembly, perform services at the request of Members of the United Nations and at the request of specialized agencies.

3. It shall perform such other functions as are specified elsewhere in the present Charter or as may be assigned to it by the General Assembly.

*Voting*

*Article* 67

1 Each member of the Economic and Social Council shall have one vote.

2. Decisions of the Economic and Social Council shall be made by a majority of the members present and voting.

*Procedure*

*Article* 68

The Economic and Social Council shall set up commissions in economic and social fields and for the promotion of human rights, and such other commissions as may be required for the performance of its functions.

*Article* 69

The Economic and Social Council shall invite any Member of the United Nations to participate, without vote, in its deliberations on any matter of particular concern to that Member.

*Article* 70

The Economic and Social Council may make arrangements for representatives of the specialized agencies to participate, without vote, in its deliberations and in those of the commissions established by it and for its representatives to participate in the deliberations of the specialized agencies.

*Article* 71

The Economic and Social Council may make suitable arrangements for consultation with non-governmental organizations which are concerned with matters within its competence.

Such arrangements may be made with international organizations and, where appropriate, with national organizations after consultation with the Members of the United Nations concerned.

*Article* 72

1. The Economic and Social Council shall adopt its own rules of procedure, including the method of selecting its President.

2. The Economic and Social Council shall meet as required in accordance with its rules, which shall include provisions for the convening of meetings on the request of a majority of its members.

## CHAPTER XI
### Declaration Regarding Non-Self-Governing Territories

*Article* 73

Members of the United Nations which have or assume responsibilities for the administration of territories whose peoples have not yet attained a full measure of self-government recognize the principle that the interests of the inhabitants of these territories are paramount, and accept as a sacred trust the obligation to promote to the utmost, within the system of international peace and security established by the present Charter, the well-being of the inhabitants of these territories, and to this end:

   (*a*) to ensure, with due respect for the culture of the peoples concerned, their political, economic, social, and educational advancement, their just treatment, and their protection against abuses;

   (*b*) to develop self-government, to take due account of the political aspirations of the peoples, and to assist them in the progressive development of their free political institutions, according to the particular circumstances of each territory and its peoples and their varying stages of advancement;

(c)  to further international peace and security;

(d)  to promote constructive measures of development, to encourage research, and to co-operate with one another and, when and where appropriate, with specialized international bodies with a view to the practical achievement of the social, economic, and scientific purposes set forth in this Article; and

(e)  to transmit regularly to the Secretary-General for information purposes, subject to such limitation as security and constitutional considerations may require, statistical and other information of a technical nature, relating to economic, social, and educational conditions in the territories for which they are respectively responsible other than those territories to which Chapters XII and XIII apply.

*Article* 74

Members of the United Nations also agree that their policy in respect of the territories to which this Chapter applies, no less than in respect of their metropolitan areas, must be based on the general principle of good neighbourliness, due account being taken of the interests and well-being of the rest of the world, in social, economic, and commercial matters.

# CHAPTER XII
## International Trusteeship System

*Article* 75

The United Nations shall establish under its authority an international trusteeship system for the administration and supervision of such territories as may be placed thereunder by subsequent individual agreements. These territories are hereinafter referred to as trust territories.

*Article* 76

The basic objectives of the trusteeship system, in accordance with the Purposes of the United Nations laid down in Article 1 of the present Charter, shall be:

(a)  to further international peace and security;

(b)  to promote the political, economic, social, and educational advancement of the inhabitants of the trust territories, and their progressive development towards self-government or independence as may be appropriate to the particular circumstances of each territory and its peoples and the freely expressed wishes of the people concerned, and as may be provided by the terms of each trusteeship agreement;

(c) to encourage respect for human rights and for fundamental freedoms for all without distinction as to race, sex, language, or religion, and to encourage recognition of the interdependence of the peoples of the world; and

(d) to ensure equal treatment in social, economic and commercial matters for all Members of the United Nations and their nationals, and also equal treatment for the latter in the administration of justice, without prejudice to the attainment of the foregoing objectives and subject to the provisions of Article 80.

*Article 77*

1. The trusteeship system shall apply to such territories in the following categories as may be placed thereunder by means of trusteeship agreements:

(a) territories now held under mandate;

(b) territories which may be detached from enemy States as a result of the Second World War; and

(c) territories voluntarily placed under the system by States responsible for their administration.

2. It will be a matter for subsequent agreement as to which territories in the foregoing categories will be brought under the trusteeship system and upon what terms.

*Article 78*

The trusteeship system shall not apply to territories which have become Members of the United Nations, relationship among which shall be based on respect for the principle of sovereign equality.

*Article 79*

The terms of trusteeship for each territory to be placed under the trusteeship system, including any alteration or amendment, shall be agreed upon the States directly concerned, including the mandatory power in the case of territories held under mandate by a Member of the United Nations, and shall be approved as provided for in Articles 83 and 85.

*Article 80*

1. Except as may be agreed upon in individual trusteeship agreements, made under Articles 77, 79, and 81, placing each territory under the trusteeship system, and until such agreements have been concluded, nothing in this Chapter shall be construed in or of itself to alter in any

manner the rights whatsoever of any States or any peoples or the terms of existing international instruments to which Members of the United Nations may respectively be parties.

2. Paragraph 1 of this article shall not be interpreted as giving grounds for delay or postponement of the negotiation and conclusion of agreements for placing mandated and other territories under the trusteeship system as provided for in Article 77.

### Article 81

The trusteeship agreement shall in each case include the terms under which the trust territory will be administered and designate the authority which will exercise the administration of the trust territory. Such authority, hereinafter called the administering authority, may be one or more States or the Organization itself.

### Article 82

There may be designated, in any trusteeship agreement, a strategic area or areas which may include part or all of the trust territory to which the agreement applies, without prejudice to any special agreement or agreements made under Article 43.

### Article 83

1. All functions of the United Nations relating to strategic areas, including the approval of the terms of the trusteeship agreements and of their alteration or amendment, shall be exercised by the Security Council.

2. The basic objectives set forth in Article 76 shall be applicable to the people of each strategic area.

3. The Security Council shall, subject to the provisions of the trusteeship agreements and without prejudice to security considerations, avail itself of the assistance of the Trusteeship Council to perform those functions of the United Nations under the trusteeship system relating to political, economic, social, and educational matters in the strategic areas.

### Article 84

It shall be the duty of the administering authority to ensure that the trust territory shall play its part in the maintenance of international peace and security. To this end the administering authority may make use of volunteer forces, facilities, and assistance from the trust territory in carrying out the obligations towards the Security Council undertaken in this regard by the administering authority, as well as for local defence and the maintenance of law and order within the trust territory.

*Article* 85

1. The functions of the United Nations with regard to trusteeship agreements for all areas not designated as strategic, including the approval of the terms of the trusteeship agreements and of their alteration or amendment, shall be exercised by the General Assembly.

2. The Trusteeship Council, operating under the authority of the General Assembly, shall assist the General Assembly in carrying out these functions.

## CHAPTER XIII
### The Trusteeship Council

*Composition*

*Article* 86

1. The Trusteeship Council shall consist of the following Members of the United Nations:

(*a*) those Members administering trust territories;

(*b*) such of those Members mentioned by name in Article 23 as are not administering trust territories; and

(*c*) as many other Members elected for three-year terms by the General Assembly as may be necessary to ensure that the total number of members of the Trusteeship Council is equally divided between those Members of the United Nations which administer trust territories and those which do not.

2. Each member of the Trusteeship Council shall designate one specially qualified person to represent it therein.

*Functions and Powers*

*Article* 87

The General Assembly and, under its authority, the Trusteeship Council, in carrying out their functions, may:

(*a*) consider reports submitted by the administering authority;

(*b*) accept petitions and examine them in consultation with the administering authority;

(*c*) provide for periodic visits to the respective trust territories at times agreed upon with the administering authority; and

(*d*) take these and other actions in conformity with the terms of the trusteeship agreements.

*Article* 88

The Trusteeship Council shall formulate a questionnaire on the political, economic, social, and educational advancement of the inhabitants of each trust territory, and the administering authority for each trust territory within the competence of the General Assembly shall make an annual report to the General Assembly upon the basis of such questionnaire.

*Voting*

*Article* 89

1. Each member of the Trusteeship Council shall have one vote.

2. Decisions of the Trusteeship Council shall be made by a majority of the members present and voting.

*Procedure*

*Article* 90

1. The Trusteeship Council shall adopt its own rules of procedure, including the method of selecting its President.

2. The Trusteeship Council shall meet as required in accordance with its rules, which shall include provision for the convening of meetings on the request of a majority of its members.

*Article* 91

The Trusteeship Council shall, when appropriate, avail itself of the assistance of the Economic and Social Council and of the specialized agencies in regard to matters with which they are respectively concerned.

## II. PROCEDURE IN THE COMMISSION ON HUMAN RIGHTS OF THE ECONOMIC AND SOCIAL COUNCIL

The role of the Human Rights Commission in respect of complaints of human rights violations was minimal prior to 1967. Since that year three functions have been exercised:

(a) In 1967 ECOSOC adopted Resolution 1235 (XLII) which authorized the Human Rights Commission and its Sub-Commission on Prevention of Discrimination and Protection of Minorities 'to examine information relevant to gross violations of human rights and fundamental freedoms, as exemplified by the policy of apartheid as practised in the Republic of South Africa . . . and racial discrimination as practised notably in Southern Rhodesia, contained in the communications listed by the Secretary-General to [ECOSOC] resolution 728 F' and to 'make a thorough study of situations which reveal a consistent pattern of violations of human rights, and report, with recommendations thereon, to the Economic and Social Council . . .'.

The 'communications listed by the Secretary-General' consist of the list of individual petitions (complaints concerning human rights) which is distributed to Commission members before each session.

The powers given by ECOSOC Resolution 1235 (XLII) have been exercised in limited circumstances, that is, gross violations linked to general political situations in which a large number of United Nations Members were concerned, such as the policies of South Arica.

(b) Since 1967 the Commission on Human Rights has carried out a series of operational fact-finding activities with particular reference to South Africa, the territories occupied by Israel and the situation in Chile.

(c) In 1970 the Economic and Social Council devised a greatly improved procedure for handling communications (complaints) from individuals and non-governmental organizations relating to violations of human rights. The new procedure was established by ECOSOC Resolution 1503 (XLVIII), and calls for special examination.

The text of Resolution 1503 is set out below, together with the Resolution adopted by the Sub-Commission on 13 August 1971 on matters of procedure. The machinery set up by Resolution 1503 is complex. The object is to secure further examination (during the screening of communications) of those communications which 'appear to reveal a consistent pattern of gross and reliably attested violations of human rights and fundamental freedoms'. The procedure is in several stages, involving a working group of the Sub-Commission on Prevention of Discrimination, the Sub-Commission itself, the Commission on Human Rights and eventually an *ad hoc* investigatory committee appointed by the Commission.

Whilst the Resolution 1503 Procedure is a great improvement on what went on before 1970, the procedure has many drawbacks. A leading U.N. official (not writing in his official capacity) has commented: 'The procedure appeared to be very promising but due to many procedural technicalities, its time-consuming character and above all the inability or unwillingness of the Commission on Human Rights to act effectively, high expectations made way for strong disappointment. Although official United Nations documentation is silent on this score as a result of the rule of confidentiality, press reports reveal that the Commission on Human Rights saw fit to drop all cases (with the exception of the situations relating to the occupied territories in the Middle East and Chile, which were on the public agenda anyway), referred to it by the Sub-Commission': see Van Boven, in Cassese (ed.), *U.N. Law: Fundamental Rights*, 1979, p. 119 at p. 124.

The slowness of the procedure is partly due to the pressure of work. In 1976 54,000 applications were received: and the Sub-Commission was meeting only three weeks in the year. In 1979 the decision was taken to extend the sessions to four weeks in the year.

For further reference see: Van Boven, in Cassese (ed.), *U.N. Law: Fundamental Rights*, 1979, pp. 119–35; the same, *Netherlands International Law Review*, Vol. 15 (1968), pp. 374–93; Ermacora, *Human Rights Journal*, 1968, pp. 180–217; Marie, *La Commission des Droits de l'Homme de l'O.N.U.*, 1975; Schreiber, *Recueil des cours* (Hague Academy of International Law), Vol. 145 (1975, II), pp. 351–9; Humphrey, *American Journal of International Law*, Vol. 62 (1968), pp. 869–88; International Law Association, *Report of the Fifty-Fifth Conference*, 1972, pp. 539–624 (especially the reports of Humphrey and Schwelb).

## Resolution 1503 (XLVIII), 27 May 1970, ECOSOC

*The Economic and Social Council*

*Noting* resolutions 7 (XXVI) and 17 (XXV) of the Commission on Human Rights and resolution 2 (XXI) of the Sub-Commission on Prevention of Discrimination and Protection of Minorities.

1. *Authorizes* the Sub-Commission on Prevention of Discrimination and Protection of Minorities to appoint a working group consisting of not more than five of its members, with due regard to geographical distribution, to meet once a year in private meetings for a period not exceeding ten days immediately before the sessions of the Sub-Commission to consider all communications, including replies of Governments thereon, received by the Secretary-General under Council resolution 738 F (XXVIII) of 30 July 1959 with a view to bringing to the attention of the Sub-Commission those communications, together with replies of Governments, if any, which appear to reveal a consistent pattern of gross and reliably attested violations of human rights and fundamental freedoms within the terms of reference of the Sub-Commission.

2. *Decides* that the Sub-Commission on Prevention of Discrimination and Protection of Minorities should, as the first stage in the implementation of the present resolution, devise at its twenty-third session appropriate procedures for dealing with the question of admissibility of communications received by the Secretary-General under Council resolution 728 F (XXVIII) and in accordance with Council resolution 1235 (XLII) of 6 June 1967.

3. *Requests* the Secretary-General to prepare a document on the question of

admissibility of communications for the Sub-Commission's consideration at its twenty-third session.

4. *Further requests* the Secretary-General:

(a) To furnish to the members of the Sub-Commission every month a list of communications prepared by him in accordance with Council resolution 728 F (XXVIII) and a brief description of them, together with the text of any replies received from Governments;

(b) To make available_to the members of the working group at their meetings the originals of such communications listed as they may request, having due regard to the provisions of paragraph 2 (b) of Council resolution 728 F (XXVIII) concerning the divulging of the identity of the authors of communications;

(c) To circulate to the members of the Sub-Commission, in the working languages, the originals of such communications as are referred to the Sub-Commission by the working group.

5. *Requests* the Sub-Commission on Prevention of Discrimination and Protection of Minorities to consider in private meetings, in accordance with paragraph 1 above, the communications brought before it in accordance with the decision of a majority of the members of the working group and any replies of Governments relating thereto and other relevant information, with a view to determining whether to refer to the Commission on Human Rights particular situations which appear to reveal a consistent pattern of gross and reliably attested violations of human rights requiring consideration by the Commission.

6. *Requests* the Commission on Human Rights after it has examined any situation referred to it by the Sub-Commission to determine:

(a) Whether it requires a thorough study by the Commission and a report and recommendations thereon to the Council in accordance with paragraph 3 of Council resolution 1235 (XLII);

(b) Whether it may be a subject of an investigation by an *ad hoc* committee to be appointed by the Commission which shall be undertaken only with the express consent of the State concerned and shall be conducted in constant co-operation with that State and under conditions determined by agreement with it. In any event, the investigation may be undertaken only if:

(i) All available means at the national level have been resorted to and exhausted;

(ii) The situation does not relate to a matter which is being dealt with under other procedures prescribed in the constituent instruments of, or conventions adopted by, the United Nations and the specialized agencies, or in regional conventions, or which the State concerned wishes to submit to other procedures in accordance with general or special international agreements to which it is a party.

7. *Decides* that if the Commission on Human Rights appoints an *ad hoc* committee to carry on an investigation with the consent of the State concerned:

(*a*) The composition of the committee shall be determined by the Commission. The members of the committee shall be independent persons whose competence and impartiality is beyond question. Their appointment shall be subject to the consent of the Government concerned;

(*b*) The committee shall establish its own rules of procedure. It shall be subject to the quorum rule. It shall have authority to receive communications and hear witnesses, as necessary. The investigation shall be conducted in co-operation with the Government concerned;

(*c*) The committee's procedure shall be confidential, its proceedings shall be conducted in private meetings and its communications shall not be publicized in any way;

(*d*) The committee shall strive for friendly solutions before, during and even after the investigation;

(*e*) The committee shall report to the Commission on Human Rights with such observations and suggestions as it may deem appropriate.

8. *Decides* that all actions envisaged in the implementation of the present resolution by the Sub-Commission on Prevention of Discrimination and Protection of Minorities or the Commission on Human Rights shall remain confidential until such time as the Commission may decide to make recommendations to the Economic and Social Council.

9. *Decides* to authorize the Secretary-General to provide all facilities which may be required to carry out the present resolution, making use of the existing staff of the Division of Human Rights of the United Nations Secretariat.

10. *Decides* that the procedure set out in the present resolution for dealing with communications relating to violations of human rights and fundamental freedoms should be reviewed if any new organ entitled to deal with such communications should be established within the United Nations or by international agreement.

### Resolution of the Sub-Commission on Prevention of Discrimination and Protection of Minorities, 13 August 1971

*The Sub-Commission on Prevention of Discrimination and Protection of Minorities,*

*Considering* that the Economic and Social Council, by its resolution 1503 (XLVIII), decided that the Sub-Commission should devise appropriate procedures for dealing with the question of admissibility of communications received by the Secretary-General under Council resolution 728 F (XXVIII) of 30 July 1959 and in accordance with Council resolution 1235 (XLII) of 6 June 1967,

*Adopts* the following provisional procedures for dealing with the question of admissibility of communications referred to above:

(1) *Standards and criteria*

    (*a*) The object of the communication must not be inconsistent with the relevant principles of the Charter, of the Universal Declaration of Human Rights and of the other applicable instruments in the field of human rights.

    (*b*) Communications shall be admissible only if, after consideration thereof, together with the replies of any of the Governments concerned, there are reasonable grounds to believe that they may reveal a consistent pattern of gross and reliably attested violations of human rights and fundamental freedoms, including policies of racial discrimination and segregation and of *apartheid*, in any country, including colonial and other dependent countries and peoples.

(2) *Source of communications*

    (*a*) Admissible communications may originate from a person or group of persons who, it can be reasonably presumed, are victims of the violations referred to in subparagraph (1)(*b*) above, any person or group of persons who have direct and reliable knowledge of those violations, or non-governmental organizations acting in good faith in accordance with recognized principles of human rights, not resorting to politically motivated stands contrary to the provisions of the Charter of the United Nations and having direct and reliable knowledge of such violations.

    (*b*) Anonymous communications shall be inadmissible, subject to the requirements of subparagraph 2(*b*) of resolution 728 F (XXVIII) of the Economic and Social Council, the author of a communication, whether an individual, a group of individuals or an organization, must be clearly identified.

    (*c*) Communications shall not be inadmissible solely because the knowledge of the individual authors is second-hand, provided that they are accompanied by clear evidence.

(3) *Contents of communications and nature of allegations*

    (*a*) The communication must contain a description of the facts and must indicate the purpose of the petition and the rights that have been violated.

    (*b*) Communications shall be inadmissible if their language is essentially abusive and in particular if they contain insulting references to the

State against which the complaint is directed. Such communications may be considered if they meet the other criteria for admissibility after deletion of the abusive language.

(c) A communication shall be inadmissible if it has manifestly political motivations and its subject is contrary to the provisions of the Charter of the United Nations.

(d) A communication shall be inadmissible if it appears that it is based exclusively on reports disseminated by mass media.

(4) *Existence of other remedies*

(a) Communications shall be inadmissible if their admission would prejudice the functions of the specialized agencies of the United Nations system.

(b) Communications shall be inadmissible if domestic remedies have not been exhausted, unless it appears that such remedies would be ineffective or unreasonably prolonged. Any failure to exhaust remedies should be satisfactorily established.

(c) Communications relating to cases which have been settled by the State concerned in accordance with the principles set forth in the Universal Declaration of Human Rights and other applicable documents in the field of human rights will not be considered.

(5) *Timeliness*

A communication shall be inadmissible if it is not submitted to the United Nations within a reasonable time after the exhaustion of the domestic remedies as provided above.

## III. UNIVERSAL DECLARATION OF HUMAN RIGHTS, 1948

The references to human rights in the Charter of the United Nations (see preamble, Articles, 1, 55, 56, 62, 68, and 76) have provided the basis for elaboration of the content of standards and of the machinery for implementing protection of human rights. On 10 December 1948 the General Assembly of the United Nations adopted a Universal Declaration of Human Rights (U.N. Doc. A/811). The voting was forty-eight for and none against. The following eight states abstained: Byelorussian S.S.R., Czechoslovakia, Poland, Saudi Arabia, Ukrainian S.S.R., U.S.S.R., Union of South Africa, and Yugoslavia. The Declaration is not a legally binding instrument *as such*, and some of its provisions depart from existing and generally accepted rules. Nevertheless some of its provisions either constitute general principles of law (see the Statute of the International Court of Justice, art. 38 (1) (c)), or represent elementary considerations of humanity. More important is its status as an authoritative guide, produced by the General Assembly, to the interpretation of the Charter. In this capacity the Declaration has considerable indirect legal effect, and it is regarded by the Assembly and by some jurists as a part of the 'law of the United Nations'. On the Declaration, see Oppenheim, *International Law*, 8th ed., i, pp. 744–6; Waldock, 106 *Recueil des cours de l'académie de droit international* (1962, II), pp. 198–9; Verdoodt, *Naissance et signification de Déclaration Universelle des Droits de l'Homme*, 1964.

The Declaration has its own importance and cannot be regarded as having merely a historical significance. In particular many States are not yet parties to the International Covenants (see below). It is to be noted that Section VII of the Helsinki Declaration (see below, p. 391) includes the following passage:

'In the field of human rights and fundamental freedoms, the participating States will act in conformity with the purposes and principles of the Charter of the United Nations and with the Universal Declaration of Human Rights'.

The Universal Declaration is also given prominence in the Proclamation of Tehran. The Proclamation was adopted by a United Nations Conference on Human Rights: see the Final Act of the International Conference on Human Rights, Tehran, 22 April–13 May 1968, U.N. Doc. A/CONF. 32/41, Sales No. E.68, XIV 2.

## TEXT

### Preamble

*Whereas* recognition of the inherent dignity and of the equal and inalienable rights of all members of the human family is the foundation of freedom, justice and peace in the world,

*Whereas* disregard and contempt for human rights have resulted in barbarous acts which have outraged the conscience of mankind, and the advent of a world in which human beings shall enjoy freedom of speech and belief and freedom from fear and want has been proclaimed as the highest aspiration of the common people,

*Whereas* it is essential, if man is not to be compelled to have recourse, as a last resort, to rebellion against tyranny and oppression, that human rights should be protected by the rule of law,

*Whereas* it is essential to promote the development of friendly relations between nations,

*Whereas* the peoples of the United Nations have in the Charter reaffirmed their faith in fundamental human rights, in the dignity and worth of the human person and in the equal rights of men and women and have determined to promote social progress and better standards of life in larger freedom,

*Whereas* Member States have pledged themselves to achieve, in co-operation with the United Nations, the promotion of universal respect for and observance of human rights and fundamental freedoms,

*Whereas* a common understanding of these rights and freedoms is of the greatest importance for the full realization of this pledge.

*Now, Therefore,*

The General Assembly

*proclaims*

*This universal declaration of human rights* as a common standard of achievement for all peoples and all nations, to the end that every individual and every organ of society, keeping this Declaration constantly in mind, shall strive by teaching and education to promote respect for these rights and freedoms and by progressive measures, national and international, to secure their universal and effective recognition and observance, both among the peoples of Member States themselves and among the peoples of territories under their jurisdiction.

*Article* 1

All human beings are born free and equal in dignity and rights. They are endowed with reason and conscience and should act towards one another in a spirit of brotherhood.

*Article* 2

Everyone is entitled to all the rights and freedoms set forth in this Declaration, without distinction of any kind, such as race, colour, sex, language, religion, political or other opinion, national or social origin, property, birth or other status.

Furthermore, no distinction shall be made on the basis of the political, jurisdictional or international status of the country or territory to which a person belongs, whether it be independent, trust, non-self-governing or under any other limitation of sovereignty.

*Article* 3

Everyone has the right to life, liberty and security of person.

*Article* 4

No one shall be held in slavery or servitude: slavery and the slave trade shall be prohibited in all their forms.

*Article* 5

No one shall be subjected to torture or cruel, inhuman or degrading treatment or punishment.

*Article* 6

Everyone has the right to recognition everywhere as a person before the law.

*Article* 7

All are equal before the law and are entitled without any discrimination to equal protection of the law. All are entitled to equal protection against any discrimination in violation of this Declaration and against any incitement to such discrimination.

*Article* 8

Everyone has the right to an effective remedy by the competent national tribunals for acts violating the fundamental rights granted him by the constitution or by law.

*Article* 9

No one shall be subjected to arbitrary arrest, detention or exile.

*Article* 10

Everyone is entitled in full equality to a fair and public hearing by an independent and impartial tribunal, in the determination of his rights and obligations and of any criminal charge against him.

*Article* 11

1. Everyone charged with a penal offence has the right to be presumed innocent until proved guilty according to law in a public trial at which he has had all the guarantees necessary for his defence.

2. No one shall be held guilty of any penal offence on account of any act or omission which did not constitute a penal offence, under national or international law, at the time when it was committed. Nor shall a heavier

penalty be imposed than the one that was applicable at the time the penal offence was committed.

### Article 12

No one shall be subjected to arbitrary interference with his privacy, family, home or correspondence, nor to attacks upon his honour and reputation. Everyone has the right to the protection of the law against such interference or attacks.

### Article 13

1. Everyone has the right to freedom of movement and residence within the borders of each state.
2. Everyone has the right to leave any country, including his own, and to return to his country.

### Article 14

1. Everyone has the right to seek and to enjoy in other countries asylum from persecution.
2. This right may not be invoked in the case of prosecutions genuinely arising from non-political crimes or from acts contrary to the purposes and principles of the United Nations.

### Article 15

1. Everyone has the right to a nationality.
2. No one shall be arbitrarily deprived of his nationality nor denied the right to change his nationality.

### Article 16

1. Men and women of full age, without any limitation due to race, nationality or religion, have the right to marry and to found a family. They are entitled to equal rights as to marriage, during marriage and at its dissolution.
2. Marriage shall be entered into only with the free and full consent of the intending spouses.
3. The family is the natural and fundamental group unit of society and is entitled to protection by society and the State.

### Article 17

1. Everyone has the right to own property alone as well as in association with others.
2. No one shall be arbitrarily deprived of his property.

*Article* 18

Everyone has the right to freedom of thought, conscience and religion; this right includes freedom to change his religion or belief, and freedom, either alone or in community with others and in public or private, to manifest his religion or belief in teaching, practice, worship and observance.

*Article* 19

Everyone has the right to freedom of opinion and expression; this right includes freedom to hold opinions without interference and to seek, receive and impart information and ideas through any media and regardless of frontiers.

*Article* 20

1. Everyone has the right to freedom of peaceful assembly and association.
2. No one may be compelled to belong to an association.

*Article* 21

1. Everyone has the right to take part in the government of his country, directly or through freely chosen representatives.
2. Everyone has the right of equal access to public service in his country.
3. The will of the people shall be the basis of the authority of government; this will shall be expressed in periodic and genuine elections which shall be by universal and equal suffrage and shall be held by secret vote or by equivalent free voting procedures.

*Article* 22

Everyone, as a member of society, has the right to social security and is entitled to realization, through national effort and international co-operation and in accordance with the organization and resources of each State, of the economic, social and cultural rights indispensable for his dignity and the free development of his personality.

*Article* 23

1. Everyone has the right to work, to free choice of employment, to just and favourable conditions of work and to protection against unemployment.
2. Everyone, without any discrimination, has the right to equal pay for equal work.
3. Everyone who works has the right to just and favourable remuneration ensuring for himself and his family an existence worthy of human dignity, and supplemented, if necessary, by other means of social protection.
4. Everyone has the right to form and to join trade unions for the protection of his interests.

*Article* 24

Everyone has the right to rest and leisure, including reasonable limitation of working hours and periodic holidays with pay.

*Article* 25

1. Everyone has the right to a standard of living adequate for the health and well-being of himself and of his family, including food, clothing, housing and medical care and necessary social services, and the right to security in the event of unemployment, sickness, disability, widowhood, old age or other lack of livelihood in circumstances beyond his control.

2. Motherhood and childhood are entitled to special care and assistance. All children, whether born in or out of wedlock, shall enjoy the same social protection.

*Article* 26

1. Everyone has the right to education. Education shall be free, at least in the elementary and fundamental stages. Elementary education shall be compulsory. Technical and professional education shall be made generally available and higher education shall be equally accessible to all on the basis of merit.

2. Education shall be directed to the full development of the human personality and to the strengthening of respect for human rights and fundamental freedoms. It shall promote understanding, tolerance and friendship among all nations, racial or religious groups, and shall further the activities of the United Nations for the maintenance of peace.

3. Parents have a prior right to choose the kind of education that shall be given to their children.

*Article* 27

1. Everyone has the right freely to participate in the cultural life of the community, to enjoy the arts and to share in scientific advancement and its benefits.

2. Everyone has the right to the protection of the moral and material interests resulting from any scientific, literary or artistic production of which he is the author.

*Article* 28

Everyone is entitled to a social and international order in which the rights and freedoms set forth in this Declaration can be fully realized.

*Article* 29

1. Everyone has duties to the community in which alone the free and full development of his personality is possible.

2. In the exercise of his rights and freedoms, everyone shall be subject only to such limitations as are determined by law solely for the purpose of securing due recognition and respect for the rights and freedoms of others and of meeting the just requirements of morality, public order and the general welfare in a democratic society.

3. These rights and freedoms may in no case be exercised contrary to the purposes and principles of the United Nations.

*Article* 30

Nothing in this Declaration may be interpreted as implying for any State, group or person any right to engage in any activity or to perform any act aimed at the destruction of any of the rights and freedoms set forth herein.

## IV. DECLARATION ON THE GRANTING OF INDEPENDENCE TO COLONIAL COUNTRIES AND PEOPLES, 1960

The Declaration set out below was adopted by the United Nations General Assembly in Resolution 1514 (XV) on 14 December 1960. Eighty-nine States voted for the resolution and none against: but there were nine abstentions, viz., Portugal, Spain, Union of South Africa, United Kingdom, United States, Australia, Belgium, Dominican Republic, and France. The Declaration relates the normative development in the field of human rights to the rights of national groups, and, in particular, the right of self-determination. The Declaration, in conjunction with the United Nations Charter, supports the view that self-determination is now a legal principle, and, although its precise ramifications are not yet determined, the principle has great significance as a root of particular legal developments. See also the Declaration on the Inadmissibility of Intervention in Resolution 2131 (XX) of 14 January 1966, 5 *International Legal Materials* (1966), p. 374. Generally on self-determination see Whiteman, *Digest*, v, pp. 38–87; Brownlie, *Principles of Public International Law*, 4th ed., 1990, pp. 595–8; Rigo Sureda, *The Evolution of the Right of Self-determination: A Study of United Nations Practice*, 1973. Resolution 1514 (XV) is in the form of an authoritative interpretation of the Charter rather than a recommendation. For comment see Waldock, 106 *Recueil des cours de l'académie de droit international* (1962, II), pp. 29–34; and Jennings, *The Acquisition of Territory in International Law*, 1963, pp. 78–87. For earlier resolutions see Resolutions 637 A (VII) of 16 December 1952 and 1314 (XIII) of 12 December 1958.

The General Assembly established as a subsidiary organ a Special Committee on the Situation with regard to the Implementation of the Declaration on the Granting of Independence by Resolution 1654 (XVI) of 27 November 1961. This consisted at first of seventeen and later of twenty-four states. In 1964 the Special Committee examined situations and made recommendations in respect to fifty-five territories. In 1963 the General Assembly decided to discontinue the Committee on information from non-self-governing territories and to transfer its functions to the Special Committee. As a result, apart from the Trusteeship Council, the Special Committee is the only body responsible for matters relating to dependent territories.

## TEXT

*The General Assembly*

*Mindful* of the determination proclaimed by the peoples of the world in the Charter of the United Nations to reaffirm faith in fundamental human rights, in the dignity and worth of the human person, in the equal rights of men and women and of nations large and small and to promote social progress and better standards of life in larger freedom,

*Conscious* of the need for the creation of conditions of stability and well-being and peaceful and friendly relations based on respect for the principles of equal rights and self-determination of all peoples, and of universal respect for, and observance of, human rights and fundamental freedoms for all without distinction as to race, sex, language or religion,

*Recognizing* the passionate yearning for freedom in all dependent peoples and the decisive role of such peoples in the attainment of their independence,

*Aware* of the increasing conflicts resulting from the denial of or impediments in the way of the freedom of such peoples, which constitute a serious threat to world peace,

*Considering* the important role of the United Nations in assisting the movement for independence in Trust and Non-Self-Governing Territories,

*Recognizing* that the peoples of the world ardently desire the end of colonialism in all its manifestations,

*Convinced* that the continued existence of colonialism prevents the development of international economic co-operation, impedes the social, cultural and economic development of dependent peoples and militates against the United Nations ideal of universal peace,

*Affirming* that peoples may, for their own ends, freely dispose of their natural weath and resources without prejudice to any obligations arising out of international economic co-operation, based upon the principle of mutual benefit, and international law,

*Believing* that the process of liberation is irresistible and that, in order to avoid serious crises, an end must be put to colonialism and all practices of segregation and discrimination associated therewith,

*Welcoming* the emergence in recent years of a large number of dependent territories into freedom and independence, and recognizing the increasingly powerful trends towards freedom in such territories which have not yet attained independence,

*Convinced* that all peoples have an inalienable right to complete freedom, the exercise of their sovereignty and the integrity of their national territory,

*Solemnly proclaims* the necessity of bringing to a speedy and unconditional end colonialism in all its forms and manifestations;

And to this end

*Declares* that:

1. The subjection of peoples to alien subjugation, domination and exploitation constitutes a denial of fundamental human rights, is contrary to the Charter of the United Nations and is an impediment to the promotion of World peace and co-operation.

2. All peoples have the right to self-determination; by virtue of that right they freely determine their political status and freely pursue their economic, social and cultural development.

3. Inadequacy of political, economic, social or educational preparedness should never serve as a pretext for delaying independence.

4. All armed action or repressive measures of all kinds directed against dependent peoples shall cease in order to enable them to exercise peacefully

and freely their right to complete independence, and the integrity of their national territory shall be respected.

5. Immediate steps shall be taken, in Trust and Non-Self-Governing Territories or all other territories which have not yet attained independence, to transfer all powers to the peoples of those territories, without any conditions or reservations, in accordance with their freely expressed will and desire, without any distinction as to race, creed or colour, in order to enable them to enjoy complete independence and freedom.

6. Any attempt aimed at the partial or total disruption of the national unity and the territorial integrity of a country is incompatible with the purposes and principles of the Charter of the United Nations.

7. All States shall observe faithfully and strictly the provisions of the Charter of the United Nations, the Universal Declaration of Human Rights and the present Declaration on the basis of equality, non-interference in the internal affairs of all States, and respect for the sovereign rights of all peoples and their territorial integrity.

## V. CONVENTION ON THE PREVENTION AND PUNISHMENT OF THE CRIME OF GENOCIDE, 1948

This agreement was adopted by the General Assembly on 9 December 1948. Forty-three States signed the Convention and there have been 104 ratifications and accessions. The Convention came into force on 12 January 1961. The United Kingdom has ratified it: see the Genocide Act, United Kingdom Statutes, 1969, c. 12, in force 30 April 1970.

The text in various languages: *United Nations Treaty Series*, Vol. 78, p. 277; H.M.S.O., Misc. No. 2 (1966), Cmnd. 2904.

For further reference see Robinson, *The Genocide Convention*, 1960; Lemkin, *Axis Rule in Occupied Europe*, 1944; Anon., *Yale Law Journal*, 58 (1949), p. 1142; Whiteman, *Digest of International Law*, Vol. xi, pp. 848–74.

## TEXT

*The Contracting Parties,*

*Having considered* the declaration made by the General Assembly of the United Nations in its resolution 96 (I) dated 11 December 1946 that genocide is a crime under international law, contrary to the spirit and aims of the United Nations and condemned by the civilized world;

*Recognizing* that at all periods of history genocide has inflicted great losses on humanity; and

*Being convinced* that, in order to liberate mankind from such an odious scourge, international co-operation is required,

*Hereby agree as hereinafter provided:*

### Article I

The Contracting Parties confirm that genocide, whether committed in time of peace or in time of war, is a crime under international law which they undertake to prevent and to punish.

### Article II

In the present Convention, genocide means any of the following acts committed with intent to destroy, in whole or in part, a national, ethnical, racial or religious group, as such:

   (a) Killing members of the group;
   (b) Causing serious bodily or mental harm to members of the group;
   (c) Deliberately inflicting on the group conditions of life calculated to bring about its physical destruction in whole or in part;
   (d) Imposing measures intended to prevent births within the group;
   (e) Forcibly transferring children of the group to another group.

*Article III*

The following acts shall be punishable:

(*a*) Genocide;
(*b*) Conspiracy to commit genocide;
(*c*) Direct and public incitement to commit genocide;
(*d*) Attempt to commit genocide;
(*e*) Complicity in genocide.

*Article IV*

Persons committing genocide or any of the other acts enumerated in Article III shall be punished, whether they are constitutionally responsible rulers, public officials or private individuals.

*Article V*

The Contracting Parties undertake to enact, in accordance with their respective Constitutions, the necessary legislation to give effect to the provisions of the present Convention and, in particular, to provide effective penalties for persons guilty of genocide or of any of the other acts enumerated in Article III.

*Article VI*

Persons charged with genocide or any of the other acts enumerated in Article III shall be tried by a competent tribunal of the State in the territory of which the act was committed, or by such international penal tribunal as may have jurisdiction with respect to those Contracting Parties which shall have accepted its jurisdiction.

*Article VII*

Genocide and the other acts enumerated in Article III shall not be considered as political crimes for the purpose of extradition.

The Contracting Parties pledge themselves in such cases to grant extradition in accordance with their laws and treaties in force.

*Article VIII*

Any Contracting Party may call upon the competent organs of the United Nations to take such action under the Charter of the United Nations as they consider appropriate for the prevention and suppression of acts of genocide or any of the other acts enumerated in Article III.

*Article IX*

Disputes between the Contracting Parties relating to the interpretation, application or fulfilment of the present Convention, including those relating to the responsibility of a State for genocide or for any of the other acts enumerated in Article III, shall be submitted to the International Court of Justice at the request of any of the parties to the dispute.

*Article X*

The present Convention, of which the Chinese, English, French, Russian and Spanish texts are equally authentic, shall bear the date of 9 December 1948.

*Article XI*

The present Convention shall be open until 31 December 1949 for signature on behalf of any Member of the United Nations and of any non-member State to which an invitation to sign has been addressed by the General Assembly.

The present Convention shall be ratified, and the instruments of ratification shall be deposited with the Secretary-General of the United Nations.

After 1 January 1950 the present Convention may be acceded to on behalf of any Member of the United Nations and of any non-member State which has received an invitation as aforesaid.

Instruments of accession shall be deposited with the Secretary-General of the United Nations.

*Article XII*

Any Contracting Party may at any time, by notification addressed to the Secretary-General of the United Nations, extend the application of the present Convention to all or any of the territories for the conduct of whose foreign relations that Contracting Party is responsible.

*Article XIII*

On the day when the first twenty instruments of ratification or accession have been deposited, the Secretary-General shall draw up a *procès-verbal* and transmit a copy thereof to each Member of the United Nations and to each of the non-member States contemplated in Article XI.

The present Convention shall come into force on the ninetieth day following the date of deposit of the twentieth instrument of ratification or accession.

Any ratification or accession effected subsequent to the latter date shall become effective on the ninetieth day following the deposit of the instrument of ratification or accession.

*Article XIV*

The present Convention shall remain in effect for a period of ten years as from the date of its coming into force.

It shall thereafter remain in force for successive periods of five years for such Contracting Parties as have not denounced it at least six months before the expiration of the current period.

Denunciation shall be effected by a written notification addressed to the Secretary-General of the United Nations.

*Article XV*

If, as a result of denunciations, the number of Parties to the present Convention should become less than sixteen, the Convention shall cease to be in force as from the date on which the last of these denunciations shall become effective.

*Article XVI*

A request for the revision of the present Convention may be made at any time by any Contracting Party by means of a notification in writing addressed to the Secretary-General.

The General Assembly shall decide upon the steps, if any, to be taken in respect of such request.

*Article XVII*

The Secretary-General of the United Nations shall notify all Members of the United Nations and the non-member States contemplated in Article XI of the following:

  (*a*)  signatures, ratifications and accessions received in accordance with Article XI;
  (*b*)  Notifications received in accordance with Article XII;
  (*c*)  The date upon which the present Convention comes into force in accordance with Article XIII;
  (*d*)  Denunciations received in accordance with Article XIV;
  (*e*)  The abrogation of the Convention in accordance with Article XV;
  (*f*)  Notifications received in accordance with Article XVI.

*Article XVIII*

The original of the present Convention shall be deposited in the archives of the United Nations.

A certified copy of the Convention shall be transmitted to each Member of the United Nations and to each of the non-member States contemplated in Article XI.

*Article XIX*

The present Convention shall be registered by the Secretary-General of the United Nations on the date of its coming into force.

## VI. DECLARATION ON PROTECTION FROM TORTURE, 1975

On 9 December 1975 the United Nations General Assembly, by consensus, adopted Resolution 3452 (XXX), set forth below. Whilst General Assembly resolutions are not legislative in effect they provide evidence of the evolution of principles of general international law. The Declaration annexed to the resolution constitutes evidence for the view that the prohibition of torture is an existing principle of international law: see the *consideranda* in the preamble and note the terms of Article 2. On the relation between human rights and general international law see the *Barcelona Traction Case*, I.C.J. Reports, 1970, p. 3 at p. 32, and Brownlie, *Principles of Public International Law*, 4th ed., 1990, pp. 527–8, 598.

Further reference should be made to Resolutions 3448 and 3453 adopted by the General Assembly on the same date; and Resolution 31/85 adopted on 13 December 1976.

The adoption of the Declaration was the prelude to the drafting of a Convention against Torture (see the next item in this collection). However, it must be emphasized that the Declaration is declaratory of existing legal norms. The prohibition of torture is enhanced by the appearance of the Convention but the illegality of torture does not *depend* upon the existence of a Convention. The Resolution to which the Declaration is annexed refers to 'the obligation of States under the Charter'.

## TEXT

### The General Assembly

*Considering* that, in accordance with the principles proclaimed in the Charter of the United Nations, recognition of the inherent dignity and of the equal and inalienable rights of all members of the human family is the foundation of freedom, justice and peace in the world.

*Considering* that these rights derive from the inherent dignity of the human person,

*Considering also* the obligation of States under the Charter, in particular Article 55, to promote universal respect for, and observance of, human rights and fundamental freedoms,

*Having regard* to Article 5 of the Universal Declaration of Human Rights and Article 7 of the International Covenant of Civil and Political Rights, both of which provide that no one may be subjected to torture or to cruel, inhuman or degrading treatment or punishment,

*Adopts* the Declaration of the Protection of All Persons from being Subjected to Torture and Other Cruel, Inhuman or Degrading Treatment or Punishment, the text of which is annexed to the present resolution, as a guideline for all States and other entities exercising effective power.

## ANNEX

Declaration on the Protection of All Persons from being Subjected to Torture and Other Cruel, Inhuman or Degrading Treatment or Punishment

*Article* 1

1. For the purpose of this Declaration, torture means any act by which severe pain or suffering, whether physical or mental, is intentionally inflicted by or at the instigation of a public official on a person for such purposes as obtaining from him or a third person information or confession, punishing him for an act he has committed or is suspected of having committed, or intimidating him or other persons. It does not include pain or suffering arising only from, inherent in or incidental to, lawful sanctions to the extent consistent with the Standard Minimum Rules for the Treatment of Prisoners.

2. Torture constitutes an aggravated and deliberate form of cruel, inhuman or degrading treatment or punishment.

*Article* 2

Any act of torture or other cruel, inhuman or degrading treatment or punishment is an offence to human dignity and shall be condemned as a denial of the purposes of the Charter of the United Nations and as a violation of the human rights and fundamental freedoms proclaimed in the Universal Declaration of Human Rights.

*Article* 3

No State may permit or tolerate torture or other cruel, inhuman or degrading treatment or punishment. Exceptional circumstances such as a state of war or a threat of war, internal political instability or any other public emergency may not be invoked as a justification of torture or other cruel, inhuman or degrading treatment or punishment.

*Article* 4

Each State shall, in accordance with the provisions of this Declaration, take effective measures to prevent torture and other cruel, inhuman or degrading treatment or punishment from being practised within its jurisdiction.

*Article* 5

The training of law enforcement personnel and of other public officials who may be responsible for persons deprived of their liberty shall ensure that full account is taken of the prohibition against torture and other cruel, inhuman or degrading treatment or punishment. This prohibition shall also, where appropriate, be included in such general rules or instructions as are issued in regard to the duties and functions of anyone who may be involved in the custody or treatment of such persons.

*Article* 6

Each State shall keep under systematic review interrogation methods and practices as well as arrangements for the custody and treatment of persons deprived of their liberty in its territory, with a view to preventing any cases of torture or other cruel, inhuman or degrading treatment or punishment.

*Article* 7

Each State shall ensure that all acts of torture as defined in Article 1 are offences under its criminal law. The same shall apply in regard to acts which constitute participation in, complicity in, incitement to or an attempt to commit torture.

*Article* 8

Any person who alleges that he has been subjected to torture or other cruel, inhuman or degrading treatment or punishment by or at the instigation of a public official shall have the right to complain to, and to have his case impartially examined by, the competent authorities of the State concerned.

*Article* 9

Wherever there is reasonable ground to believe that an act of torture as defined in Article 1 has been committed, the competent authorities of the State concerned shall promptly proceed to an impartial investigation even if there has been no formal complaint.

*Article* 10

If an investigation under Article 8 or Article 9 establishes that an act of torture as defined in Article 1 appears to have been committed, criminal proceedings shall be instituted against the alleged offender or offenders in accordance with national law. If an allegation of other forms of cruel, inhuman or degrading treatment or punishment is considered to be well founded, the alleged offender or offenders shall be subject to criminal, disciplinary or other appropriate proceedings.

*Article* 11

Where it is proved that an act of torture or other cruel, inhuman or degrading treatment or punishment has been committed by or at the instigation of a public official, the victim shall be afforded redress and compensation in accordance with national law.

*Article* 12

Any statement which is established to have been made as a result of torture or other cruel, inhuman or degrading treatment or punishment may not be invoked as evidence against the person concerned or against any other person in any proceedings.

## VII. CONVENTION AGAINST TORTURE AND OTHER CRUEL, INHUMAN OR DEGRADING TREATMENT OR PUNISHMENT, 1984

This Convention was the sequel to the Declaration on Protection from Torture (see the previous item). The Convention was adopted by the General Assembly of the United Nations on 10 December 1984 and entered into force on 26 June 1987. Not less than fifty-five states have become parties. For the original text see U.N. Doc. A/RES/39/46; and H.M.S.O. (U.K.), Cmnd. 9593. There is also a European Convention against Torture (below, p. 383) and the Inter-American Convention to Prevent and Punish Torture (below, p. 531).

### TEXT

The States Parties to this Convention,

Considering that, in accordance with the principles proclaimed in the Charter of the United Nations, recognition of the equal and inalienable rights of all members of the human family is the foundation of freedom, justice and peace in the world,

Recognizing that those rights derive from the inherent dignity of the human person,

Considering the obligation of States under the Charter, in particular Article 55, to promote universal respect for, and observance of, human rights and fundamental freedoms,

Having regard to article 5 of the Universal Declaration of Human Rights and article 7 of the International Covenant on Civil and Political Rights, both of which provide that no one shall be subjected to torture or to cruel, inhuman or degrading treatment or punishment,

Having regard also to the Declaration on the Protection of All Persons from Being Subjected to Torture and Other Cruel, Inhuman or Degrading Treatment or Punishment, adopted by the General Assembly on 9 December 1975,

Desiring to make more effective the struggle against torture and other cruel, inhuman or degrading treatment or punishment throughout the world,

Have agreed as follows:

## PART I

*Article* 1

1. For the purposes of this Convention, the term 'torture' means any act by which severe pain or suffering, whether physical or mental, is intentionally

inflicted on a person for such purposes as obtaining from him or a third person information or a confession, punishing him for an act he or a third person has committed or is suspected of having committed, or intimidating or coercing him or a third person, or for any reason based on discrimination of any kind, when such pain or suffering is inflicted by or at the instigation of or with the consent or acquiescence of a public official or other person acting in an official capacity. It does not include pain or suffering arising only from, inherent in or incidental to lawful sanctions.

2. This article is without prejudice to any international instrument or national legislation which does or may contain provisions of wider application.

### Article 2

1. Each State Party shall take effective legislative, administrative, judicial or other measures to prevent acts of torture in any territory under its jurisdiction.

2. No exceptional circumstances whatsoever, whether a state of war or a threat of war, internal political instability or any other public emergency, may be invoked as a justification of torture.

3. An order from a superior officer or a public authority may not be invoked as a justification of torture.

### Article 3

1. No State Party shall expel, return (*"refouler"*) or extradite a person to another State where there are substantial grounds for believing that he would be in danger of being subjected to torture.

2. For the purpose of determining whether there are such grounds, the competent authorities shall take into account all relevant considerations including, where applicable, the existence in the State concerned of a consistent pattern of gross, flagrant or mass violations of human rights.

### Article 4

1. Each State Party shall ensure that all acts of torture are offences under its criminal law. The same shall apply to an attempt to commit torture and to commit an act by any person which constitutes complicity or participation in torture.

2. Each State Party shall make these offences punishable by appropriate penalties which take into account their grave nature.

### Article 5

1. Each State Party shall take such measures as may be necessary to establish its jurisdiction over the offences referred to in article 4 in the following cases:

(a) When the offences are committed in any territory under its jurisdiction or on board a ship or aircraft registered in that State;

(b) When the alleged offender is a national of that State;

(c) When the victim is a national of that State if that State considers it appropriate.

2. Each State Party shall likewise take such measures as may be necessary to establish its jurisdiction over such offences in cases where the alleged offender is present in any territory under its jurisdiction and it does not extradite him pursuant to article 8 to any of the States mentioned in paragraph 1 of this article.

3. This Convention does not exclude any criminal jurisdiction exercised in accordance with internal law.

*Article* 6

1. Upon being satisfied, after an examination of information available to it, that the circumstances so warrant, any State Party in whose territory a person alleged to have committed any offence referred to in article 4 is present shall take him into custody or take other legal measures to ensure his presence. The custody and other legal measures shall be as provided in the law of that State but may be continued only for such time as is necessary to enable any criminal or extradition proceedings to be instituted.

2. Such State shall immediately make a preliminary inquiry into the facts.

3. Any person in custody pursuant to paragraph 1 of this article shall be assisted in communicating immediately with the nearest appropriate representative of the State of which he is a national, or, if he is a stateless person, with the representative of the State where he usually resides.

4. When a State, pursuant to this article, has taken a person into custody, it shall immediately notify the States referred to in article 5, paragraph 1, of the fact that such person is in custody and of the circumstances which warrant his detention. The State which makes the preliminary inquiry contemplated in paragraph 2 of this article shall promptly report its findings to the said States and shall indicate whether it intends to exercise jurisdiction.

*Article* 7

1. The State Party in the territory under whose jurisdiction a person alleged to have committed any offence referred to in article 4 is found shall in the cases contemplated in article 5, if it does not extradite him, submit the case to its competent authorities for the purpose of prosecution.

2. These authorities shall take their decision in the same manner as in the case of any ordinary offence of a serious nature under the law of that State. In the cases referred to in article 5, paragraph 2, the standards of evidence

required for prosecution and conviction shall in no way be less stringent than those which apply in the cases referred to in article 5, paragraph 1.

3. Any person regarding whom proceedings are brought in connection with any of the offences referred to in article 4 shall be guaranteed fair treatment at all stages of the proceedings.

*Article 8*

1. The offences referred to in article 4 shall be deemed to be included as extraditable offences in any extradition treaty existing between States Parties. States Parties undertake to include such offences as extraditable offences in every extradition treaty to be concluded between them.

2. If a State Party which makes extradition conditional on the existence of a treaty receives a request for extradition from another State Party with which it has no extradition treaty, it may consider this Convention as the legal basis for extradition in respect of such offences. Extradition shall be subject to the other conditions provided by the law of the requested State.

3. States Parties which do not make extradition conditional on the existence of a treaty shall recognize such offences as extraditable offences between themselves subject to the conditions provided by the law of the requested State.

4. Such offences shall be treated, for the purpose of extradition between States Parties, as if they had been committed not only in the place in which they occurred but also in the territories of the States required to establish their jurisdiction in accordance with article 5, paragraph 1.

*Article 9*

1. States Parties shall afford one another the greatest measure of assistance in connection with criminal proceedings brought in respect of any of the offences referred to in article 4, including the supply of all evidence at their disposal necessary for the proceedings.

2. States Parties shall carry out their obligations under paragraph 1 of this article in conformity with any treaties on mutual judicial assistance that may exist between them.

*Article 10*

1. Each State Party shall ensure that education and information regarding the prohibition against torture are fully included in the training of law enforcement personnel, civil or military, medical personnel, public officials and other persons who may be involved in the custody, interrogation or treatment of any individual subjected to any form of arrest, detention or imprisonment.

2. Each State Party shall include this prohibition in the rules or instructions issued in regard to the duties and functions of any such persons.

*Article* 11

Each State Party shall keep under systematic review interrogation rules, instructions, methods and practices as well as arrangements for the custody and treatment of persons subjected to any form of arrest, detention or imprisonment in any territory under its jurisdiction, with a view to preventing any cases of torture.

*Article* 12

Each State Party shall ensure that its competent authorities proceed to a prompt and impartial investigation, wherever there is reasonable ground to believe that an act of torture has been committed in any territory under its jurisdiction.

*Article* 13

Each State Party shall ensure that any individual who alleges he has been subjected to torture in any territory under its jurisdiction has the right to complain to, and to have his case promptly and impartially examined by, its competent authorities. Steps shall be taken to ensure that the complainant and witnesses are protected against all ill-treatment or intimidation as a consequence of his complaint or any evidence given.

*Article* 14

1. Each State Party shall ensure in its legal system that the victim of an act of torture obtains redress and has an enforceable right to fair and adequate compensation, including the means for as full rehabilitation as possible. In the event of the death of the victim as a result of an act of torture, his dependants shall be entitled to compensation.

2. Nothing in this article shall affect any right of the victim or other persons to compensation which may exist under national law.

*Article* 15

Each State Party shall ensure that any statement which is established to have been made as a result of torture shall not be invoked as evidence in any proceedings, except against a person accused of torture as evidence that the statement was made.

*Article* 16

1. Each State Party shall undertake to prevent in any territory under its jurisdiction other acts of cruel, inhuman or degrading treatment or punishment which do not amount to torture as defined in article 1, when such acts are committed by or at the instigation of or with the consent or acquiescence of a public official or other person acting in an official capacity. In particular, the obligations contained in articles 10, 11, 12 and 13

shall apply with the substitution for references to torture of references to other forms of cruel, inhuman or degrading treatment or punishment.

2. The provisions of this Convention are without prejudice to the provisions of any other international instrument or national law which prohibits cruel, inhuman or degrading treatment or punishment or which relates to extradition or expulsion.


# PART II

*Article* 17

1. There shall be established a Committee against Torture (hereinafter referred to as the Committee) which shall carry out the functions hereinafter provided. The Committee shall consist of ten experts of high moral standing and recognized competence in the field of human rights, who shall serve in their personal capacity. The experts shall be elected by the States Parties, consideration being given to equitable geographical distribution and to the usefulness of the participation of some persons having legal experience.

2. The members of the Committee shall be elected by secret ballot from a list of persons nominated by States Parties. Each State Party may nominate one person from among its own nationals. States Parties shall bear in mind the usefulness of nominating persons who are also members of the Human Rights Committee established under the International Covenant on Civil and Political Rights and who are willing to serve on the Committee against Torture.

3. Elections of the members of the Committee shall be held at biennial meetings of States Parties convened by the Secretary-General of the United Nations. At those meetings, for which two thirds of the States Parties shall constitute a quorum, the persons elected to the Committee shall be those who obtain the largest number of votes and an absolute majority of the votes of the representatives of States Parties present and voting.

4. The initial election shall be held no later than six months after the date of the entry into force of this Convention. At least four months before the date of each election, the Secretary-General of the United Nations shall address a letter to the States Parties inviting them to submit their nominations within three months. The Secretary-General shall prepare a list in alphabetical order of all persons thus nominated, indicating the States Parties which have nominated them, and shall submit it to the States Parties.

5. The members of the Committee shall be elected for a term of four years. They shall be eligible for re-election if renominated. However, the term of

five of the members elected at the first election shall expire at the end of two years; immediately after the first election the names of these five members shall be chosen by lot by the chairman of the meeting referred to in paragraph 3 of this article.

6. If a member of the Committee dies or resigns or for any other cause can no longer perform his Committee duties, the State Party which nominated him shall appoint another expert from among its nationals to serve for the remainder of his term, subject to the approval of the majority of the States Parties. The approval shall be considered given unless half or more of the States Parties respond negatively within six weeks after having been informed by the Secretary-General of the United Nations of the proposed appointment.

7. States Parties shall be responsible for the expenses of the members of the Committee while they are in performance of Committee duties.

*Article* 18

1. The Committee shall elect its officers for a term of two years. They may be re-elected.

2. The Committee shall establish its own rules of procedure, but these rules shall provide, *inter alia*, that:

    (*a*) Six members shall constitute a quorum;

    (*b*) Decisions of the Committee shall be made by a majority vote of the members present.

3. The Secretary-General of the United Nations shall provide the necessary staff and facilities for the effective performance of the functions of the Committee under this Convention.

4. The Secretary-General of the United Nations shall convene the initial meeting of the Committee. After its initial meeting, the Committee shall meet at such times as shall be provided in its rules of procedure.

5. The States Parties shall be responsible for expenses incurred in connection with the holding of meetings of the States Parties and of the Committee, including reimbursement to the United Nations for any expenses, such as the cost of staff and facilities, incurred by the United Nations pursuant to paragraph 3 of this article.

*Article* 19

1. The States Parties shall submit to the Committee, through the Secretary-General of the United Nations, reports on the measures they have taken to give effect to their undertakings under this Convention, within one year after the entry into force of the Convention for the State Party concerned. Thereafter the States Parties shall submit supplementary reports every four years on any new measures taken and such other reports as the Committee may request.

2. The Secretary-General of the United Nations shall transmit the reports to all States Parties.

3. Each report shall be considered by the Committee which may make such general comments on the report as it may consider appropriate and shall forward these to the State Party concerned. That State Party may respond with any observations it chooses to the Committee.

4. The Committee may, at its discretion, decide to include any comments made by it in accordance with paragraph 3 of this article, together with the observations thereon received from the State Party concerned, in its annual report made in accordance with article 24. If so requested by the State Party concerned, the Committee may also include a copy of the report submitted under paragraph 1 of this article.

*Article* 20

1. If the Committee receives reliable information which appears to it to contain well-founded indications that torture is being systematically practised in the territory of a State Party, the Committee shall invite that State Party to co-operate in the examination of the information and to this end to submit observations with regard to the information concerned.

2. Taking into account any observations which may have been submitted by the State Party concerned, as well as any other relevant information available to it, the Committee may, if it decides that this is warranted, designate one or more of its members to make a confidential inquiry and to report to the Committee urgently.

3. If an inquiry is made in accordance with paragraph 2 of this article, the Committee shall seek the co-operation of the State Party concerned. In agreement with that State Party, such an inquiry may include a visit to its territory.

4. After examining the findings of its member or members submitted in accordance with paragraph 2 of this article, the Committee shall transmit these findings to the State Party concerned together with any comments or suggestions which seem appropriate in view of the situation.

5. All the proceedings of the Committee referred to in paragraphs 1 to 4 of this article shall be confidential, and at all stages of the proceedings the co-operation of the State Party shall be sought. After such proceedings have been completed with regard to an inquiry made in accordance with paragraph 2, the Committee may, after consultations with the State Party concerned, decide to include a summary account of the results of the proceedings in its annual report made in accordance with article 24.

*Article* 21

1. A State Party to this Convention may at any time declare under this article that it recognizes the competence of the Committee to receive and

consider communications to the effect that a State Party claims that another State Party is not fulfilling its obligations under this Convention. Such communications may be received and considered according to the procedures laid down in this article only if submitted by a State Party which has made a declaration recognizing in regard to itself the competence of the Committee. No communication shall be dealt with by the Committee under this article if it concerns a State Party which has not made such a declaration. Communications received under this article shall be dealt with in accordance with the following procedure:

(a) If a State Party considers that another State Party is not giving effect to the provisions of this Convention, it may, by written communication, bring the matter to the attention of that State Party. Within three months after the receipt of the communication the receiving State shall afford the State which sent the communication an explanation or any other statement in writing clarifying the matter, which should include, to the extent possible and pertinent, reference to domestic procedures and remedies taken, pending or available in the matter;

(b) If the matter is not adjusted to the satisfaction of both States Parties concerned within six months after the receipt by the receiving State of the initial communication, either State shall have the right to refer the matter to the Committee, by notice given to the Committee and to the other State;

(c) The Committee shall deal with a matter referred to it under this article only after it has ascertained that all domestic remedies have been invoked and exhausted in the matter, in conformity with the generally recognized principles of international law. This shall not be the rule where the application of the remedies is unreasonably prolonged or is unlikely to bring effective relief to the person who is the victim of the violation of this Convention;

(d) The Committee shall hold closed meetings when examining communications under this article;

(e) Subject to the provisions of subparagraph (c), the Committee shall make available its good offices to the States Parties concerned with a view to a friendly solution of the matter on the basis of respect for the obligations provided for in this Convention. For this purpose, the Committee may, when appropriate, set up an *ad hoc* conciliation commission;

(f) In any matter referred to it under this article, the Committee may call upon the States Parties concerned, referred to in subparagraph (b), to supply any relevant information;

(g) The States Parties concerned, referred to in subparagraph (b), shall have the right to be represented when the matter is being considered by the Committee and to make submissions orally and/or in writing;

(*h*) The Committee shall, within twelve months after the date of receipt of notice under subparagraph (*b*), submit a report:

(i) If a solution within the terms of subparagraph (*e*) is reached, the Committee shall confine its report to a brief statement of the facts and of the solution reached;

(ii) If a solution within the terms of subparagraph (*e*) is not reached, the Committee shall confine its report to a brief statement of the facts; the written submissions and record of the oral submissions made by the States Parties concerned shall be attached to the report.

In every matter, the report shall be communicated to the States Parties concerned.

2. The provisions of this article shall come into force when five States Parties of this Convention have made declarations under paragraph 1 of this article. Such declarations shall be deposited by the States Parties with the Secretary-General of the United Nations, who shall transmit copies thereof to the other States Parties. A declaration may be withdrawn at any time by notification to the Secretary-General. Such a withdrawal shall not prejudice the consideration of any matter which is the subject of a communication already transmitted under this article; no further communication by any State Party shall be received under this article after the notification of withdrawal of the declaration has been received by the Secretary-General, unless the State Party concerned has made a new declaration.

*Article 22*

1. A State Party to this Convention may at any time declare under this article that it recognizes the competence of the Committee to receive and consider communications from or on behalf of individuals subject to its jurisdiction who claim to be victims of a violation by a State Party of the provisions of the Convention. No communication shall be received by the Committee if it concerns a State Party which has not made such a declaration.

2. The Committee shall consider inadmissible any communication under this article which is anonymous or which it considers to be an abuse of the right of submission of such communications or to be incompatible with the provisions of this Convention.

3. Subject to the provisions of paragraph 2, the Committee shall bring any communications submitted to it under this article to the attention of the State Party to this Convention which has made a declaration under paragraph 1 and is alleged to be violating any provisions of the Convention. Within six months, the receiving State shall submit to the Committee written explanations or statements clarifying the matter and the remedy, if any, that may have been taken by that State.

4. The Committee shall consider communications received under this article in the light of all information made available to it by or on behalf of the individual and by the State Party concerned.

5. The Committee shall not consider any communications from an individual under this article unless it has ascertained that:

(*a*) The same matter has not been, and is not being, examined under another procedure of international investigation or settlement;

(*b*) The individual has exhausted all available domestic remedies; this shall not be the rule where the application of the remedies is unreasonably prolonged or is unlikely to bring effective relief to the person who is the victim of the violation of this Convention.

6. The Committee shall hold closed meetings when examining communications under this article.

7. The Committee shall forward its views to the State Party concerned and to the individual.

8. The provisions of this article shall come into force when five States Parties to this Convention have made declarations under paragraph 1 of this article. Such declarations shall be deposited by the States Parties with the Secretary-General of the United Nations, who shall transmit copies thereof to the other States Parties. A declaration may be withdrawn at any time by notification to the Secretary-General. Such a withdrawal shall not prejudice the consideration of any matter which is the subject of a communication already transmitted under this article; no further communication by or on behalf of an individual shall be received under this article after the notification of withdrawal of the declaration has been received by the Secretary-General, unless the State Party has made a new declaration.

*Article* 23

The members of the Committee and of the *ad hoc* conciliation commissions which may be appointed under article 21, paragraph 1(*e*), shall be entitled to the facilities, privileges and immunities of experts on mission for the United Nations as laid down in the relevant sections of the Convention on the Privileges and Immunities of the United Nations.

*Article* 24

The Committee shall submit an annual report on its activities under this Convention to the States Parties and to the General Assembly of the United Nations.

## PART III

*Article 25*

1. This Convention is open for signature by all States.

2. This Convention is subject to ratification. Instruments of ratification shall be deposited with the Secretary-General of the United Nations.

*Article 26*

This Convention is open to accession by all States. Accession shall be effected by the deposit of an instrument of accession with the Secretary-General of the United Nations.

*Article 27*

1. This Convention shall enter into force on the thirtieth day after the date of the deposit with the Secretary-General of the United Nations of the twentieth instrument of ratification or accession.

2. For each State ratifying this Convention or acceding to it after the deposit of the twentieth instrument of ratification or accession, the Convention shall enter into force on the thirtieth day after the date of the deposit of its own instrument of ratification or accession.

*Article 28*

1. Each State may, at the time of signature or ratification of this Convention or accession thereto, declare that it does not recognize the competence of the Committee provided for in article 20.

2. Any State Party having made a reservation in accordance with paragraph 1 of this article may, at any time, withdraw this reservation by notification to the Secretary-General of the United Nations.

*Article 29*

1. Any State Party to this Convention may propose an amendment and file it with the Secretary-General of the United Nations. The Secretary-General shall thereupon communicate the proposed amendment to the States Parties with a request that they notify him whether they favour a conference of States Parties for the purpose of considering and voting upon the proposal. In the event that within four months from the date of such communication at least one third of the States Parties favours such a conference, the Secretary-General shall convene the conference under the auspices of the United Nations. Any amendment adopted by a majority of the States Parties present and voting at the conference shall be submitted by the Secretary-General to all the States Parties for acceptance.

2. An amendment adopted in accordance with paragraph 1 of this article shall enter into force when two thirds of the States Parties to this Conven-

tion have notified the Secretary-General of the United Nations that they have accepted it in accordance with their respective constitutional processes.

3. When amendments enter into force, they shall be binding on those States Parties which have accepted them, other States Parties still being bound by the provisions of this Convention and any earlier amendments which they have accepted.

*Article 30*

1. Any dispute between two or more States Parties concerning the interpretation or application of this Convention which cannot be settled through negotiation shall, at the request of one of them, be submitted to arbitration. If within six months from the date of the request for arbitration the Parties are unable to agree on the organization of the arbitration, any one of those Parties may refer the dispute to the International Court of Justice by request in conformity with the Statute of the Court.

2. Each State may, at the time of signature or ratification of this Convention or accession thereto, declare that it does not consider itself bound by paragraph 1 of this article. The other States Parties shall not be bound by paragraph 1 of this article with respect to any State Party having made such a reservation.

3. Any State Party having made a reservation in accordance with paragraph 2 of this article may at any time withdraw this reservation by notification to the Secretary-General of the United Nations.

*Article 31*

1. A State Party may denounce this Convention by written notification to the Secretary-General of the United Nations. Denunciation becomes effective one year after the date of receipt of the notification by the Secretary-General.

2. Such a denunciation shall not have the effect of releasing the State Party from its obligations under this Convention in regard to any act or omission which occurs prior to the date at which the denunciation becomes effective, nor shall denunciation prejudice in any way the continued consideration of any matter which is already under consideration by the Committee prior to the date at which the denunciation becomes effective.

3. Following the date at which the denunciation of a State Party becomes effective, the Committee shall not commence consideration of any new matter regarding that State.

*Article 32*

The Secretary-General of the United Nations shall inform all States Members of the United Nations and all States which have signed this Convention or acceded to it of the following:

(*a*) Signatures, ratifications and accessions under articles 25 and 26;

(*b*) The date of entry into force of this Convention under article 27 and the date of the entry into force of any amendments under article 29;

(*c*) Denunciations under article 31.

*Article* 33

1. This Convention, of which the Arabic, Chinese, English, French, Russian and Spanish texts are equally authentic, shall be deposited with the Secretary-General of the United Nations.

2. The Secretary-General of the United Nations shall transmit certified copies of this Convention to all States.

## VIII. SLAVERY CONVENTION, 1926,
## AMENDED BY PROTOCOL, 1953

The Slavery Convention was signed on 25 September 1926 and entered into force on 9 March 1927. For the text in various languages: *League of Nations Treaty Series*, Vol. 60, p. 253; *U.K. Treaty Series*, No. 16 (1927), Cmd. 2910.

The Protocol of amendment was opened for signature on 7 December 1953, and the Slavery Convention as amended by the Protocol entered into force on 7 July 1955. For the text in various languages: *United Nations Treaty Series*, Vol. 212, p. 17; *U.K. Treaty Series*, No. 24 (1956), Cmd. 9797.

There have been problems in defining slavery and associated practices, and the position has been improved by the Supplementary Convention below, pp. 58–63. See, further, the I.L.O. Conventions concerning forced labour, below.

### *TEXT*[1]

*Article* 1

For the purpose of the present Convention, the following definitions are agreed upon:

(1) Slavery is the status or condition of a person over whom any or all of the powers attaching to the right of ownership are exercised.

(2) The slave trade includes all acts involved in the capture, acquisition or disposal of a person with intent to reduce him to slavery; all acts involved in the acquisition of a slave with a view to selling or exchanging him; all acts of disposal by sale or exchange of a slave acquired with a view to being sold or exchanged, and, in general, every act of trade or transport in slaves.

*Article* 2

The High Contracting Parties undertake, each in respect of the territories placed under its sovereignty, jurisdiction, protection, suzerainty or tutelage, so far as they have not already taken the necessary steps:

(*a*) To prevent and suppress the slave trade;

(*b*) to bring about, progressively and as soon as possible, the complete abolition of slavery in all its forms.

*Article* 3

The High Contracting Parties undertake to adopt all appropriate measures with a view to preventing and suppressing the embarkation, disembarkation and transport of slaves in their territorial waters and upon all vessels flying their respective flags.

---

[1] The preamble has been omitted.

The High Contracting Parties undertake to negotiate as soon as possible a general Convention with regard to the slave trade which will give them rights and impose upon them duties of the same nature as those provided for in the Convention of 17 June, 1925,[1] relative to the International Trade in Arms (Articles 12, 20, 21, 22, 23, 24, and paragraphs 3, 4 and 5 of Section II of Annex II), with the necessary adaptations, it being understood that this general Convention will not place the ships (even of small tonnage) of any High Contracting Parties in a position different from that of the other High Contracting Parties.

It is also understood that, before or after the coming into force of this general Convention, the High Contracting Parties are entirely free to conclude between themselves, without, however, derogating from the principles laid down in the preceding paragraph, such special agreements as, by reason of their peculiar situation, might appear to be suitable in order to bring about as soon as possible the complete disappearance of the slave trade.

*Article* 4

The High Contracting Parties undertake to adopt all appropriate measures with the object of securing the abolition of slavery and the slave trade.

*Article* 5

The High Contracting Parties recognize that recourse to compulsory or forced labour may have grave consequences and undertake, each in respect of the territories placed under its sovereignty, jurisdiction, protection, suzerainty or tutelage, to take all necessary measures to prevent compulsory or forced labour from developing into conditions analogous to slavery.

It is agreed that:

(1) Subject to the transitional provisions laid down in paragraph (2) below, compulsory or forced labour may only be exacted for public purposes.

(2) In territories in which compulsory or forced labour for other than public purposes still survives, the High Contracting Parties shall endeavour progressively and as soon as possible to put an end to the practice. So long as such forced or compulsory labour exists, this labour shall invariably be of an exceptional character, shall always receive adequate remuneration, and shall not involve the removal of the labourers from their usual place of residence.

(3) In all cases, the responsibility for any recourse to compulsory or forced labour shall rest with the competent central authorities of the territory concerned.

[1] 'Miscellaneous No. 11 (1920)', Cmd. 3448.

*Article* 6

Those of the High Contracting Parties whose laws do not at present make adequate provision for the punishment of infractions of laws and regulations enacted with a view to giving effect to the purposes of the present Convention undertake to adopt the necessary measures in order that severe penalties may be imposed in respect of such infractions.

*Article* 7

The High Contracting Parties undertake to communicate to each other and to the Secretary-General of the United Nations any laws and regulations which they may enact with a view to the application of the provisions of the present Convention.

*Article* 8

The High Contracting Parties agree that disputes arising between them relating to the interpretation or application of this Convention shall, if they cannot be settled by direct negotiation, be referred for decision to the International Court of Justice. In case either or both of the States Parties to such a dispute should not be parties to the Statute of the International Court of Justice, the dispute shall be referred, at the choice of the Parties and in accordance with the constitutional procedure of each State, either to the International Court of Justice or to a court of arbitration constituted in accordance with the Convention of 18 October, 1907,[1] for the Pacific Settlement of International Disputes, or to some other court of arbitration.

*Article* 9

At the time of signature or of ratification or of accession, any High Contracting Party may declare that its acceptance of the present Convention does not bind some or all of the territories placed under its sovereignty, jurisdiction, protection, suzerainty or tutelage in respect of all or any provisions of the Convention; it may subsequently accede separately on behalf of any one of them or in respect of any provision to which any one of them is not a party.

*Article* 10

In the event of a High Contracting Party wishing to denounce the present Convention, the denunciation shall be notified in writing to the Secretary-General of the United Nations, who will at once communicate a certified true copy of the notification to all the other High Contracting Parties, informing them of the date on which it was received.

The denunciation shall only have effect in regard to the notifying State,

---

[1] 'Miscellaneous No. 6 (1908)', Cd. 4175.

and one year after the notification has reached the Secretary-General of the United Nations.

Denunciation may also be made separately in respect of any territory placed under its sovereignty, jurisdiction, protection, suzerainty or tutelage.

*Article* 11

The Present Convention, which will bear this day's date and of which the French and English texts are both authentic, will remain open for signature by the States Members of the League of Nations until 1 April, 1927.

The present Convention shall be open to accession by all States, including States which are not Members of the United Nations, to which the Secretary-General of the United Nations shall have communicated a certified copy of the Convention.

Accession shall be effected by the deposit of a formal instrument with the Secretary-General of the United Nations, who shall give notice thereof to all States Parties to the Convention and to all other States contemplated in the present article, informing them of the date on which each such instrument of accession was received in deposit.

*Article* 12

The present Convention will be ratified and the instruments of ratification shall be deposited in the office of the Secretary-General of the United Nations. The Secretary-General will inform all the High Contracting Parties of such deposit.

The Convention will come into operation for each State on the date of the deposit of its ratification or of its accession.


Protocol Amending the Slavery Convention[1]

The States Parties to the present Protocol,

Considering that under the Slavery Convention signed at Geneva on 25 September, 1926 (hereinafter called 'the Convention') the League of Nations was invested with certain duties and functions, and

Considering that it is expedient that these duties and functions should be continued by the United Nations,

Have agreed as follows:

*Article I*

The States Parties to the present Protocol undertake that as between themselves they will, in accordance with the provisions of the Protocol,

---

[1] *United Nations Treaty Series*, Vol. 182, p. 51.

attribute full legal force and effect to and duly apply the amendments to the Convention set forth in the annex to the Protocol.

*Article II*

1. The present Protocol shall be open for signature or acceptance by any of the States Parties to the Convention to which the Secretary-General has communicated for this purpose a copy of the Protocol.

2. States may become Parties to the present Protocol by:

(*a*) Signature without reservation as to acceptance;
(*b*) Signature with reservation as to acceptance, followed by acceptance;
(*c*) Acceptance.

3. Acceptance shall be effected by the deposit of a formal instrument with the Secretary-General of the United Nations.

*Article III*

1. The present Protocol shall come into force on the date on which two States shall have become Parties thereto, and shall thereafter come into force in respect of each State upon the date on which it becomes a Party to the Protocol.

2. The amendments set forth in the annex to the present Protocol shall come into force when twenty-three States shall have become Parties to the Protocol, and consequently any State becoming a Party to the Convention, after the amendments thereto have come into force, shall become a Party to the Convention as so amended.

*Article IV*

In accordance with paragraph 1 of Article 102 of the Charter of the United Nations and the regulations pursuant thereto adopted by the General Assembly, the Secretary-General of the United Nations is authorized to effect registration of the present Protocol and of the amendments made in the Convention by the Protocol on the respective dates of their entry into force and to publish the Protocol and the amended text of the Convention as soon as possible after registration.

*Article V*

The present Protocol, of which the Chinese, English, French, Russian and Spanish texts are equally authentic, shall be deposited in the archives of the United Nations Secretariat. The texts of the Convention to be amended in accordance with the annex being authentic in the English and French languages only, the English and French texts of the annex shall be equally authentic, and the Chinese, Russian and Spanish texts shall be translations. The Secretary-General shall prepare certified copies of the Protocol, including the annex, for communication to States Parties to the Convention, as well as to all other States Members of the United Nations. He shall likewise prepare for communication to States, including States not Members of the United Nations, upon the entry into force of the amendments as provided in Article III, certified copies of the Convention as so amended.

## ANNEX
To the Protocol Amending the Slavery Convention Signed at
Geneva on 25 September, 1926

In Article 7 'the Secretary-General of the United Nations' *shall be substituted for* 'the Secretary-General of the League of Nations'.

In Article 8 'the International Court of Justice' *shall be substituted for* 'the Permanent Court of International Justice', and 'the Statute of the International Court of Justice' *shall be substituted for* 'the Protocol of 16 December, 1920, relating to the Permanent Court of International Justice'.

In the first and second paragraphs of Article 10 'the United Nations' *shall be substituted for* 'the League of Nations'.

The last three paragraphs of Article 11 shall be *deleted* and the following *substituted*:

'The present Convention shall be open to accession by all States, including States which are not members of the United Nations, to which the Secretary-General of the United Nations shall have communicated a certified copy of the Convention.

'Accession shall be effected by the deposit of a formal instrument with the Secretary-General of the United Nations, who shall give notice thereof to all States Parties to the Convention and to all other States contemplated in the present article, informing them of the date on which each such instrument of accession was received in deposit'.

In Article 12 'the United Nations' *shall be substituted for* 'the League of Nations'.

## IX. SUPPLEMENTARY CONVENTION ON THE ABOLITION OF SLAVERY, THE SLAVE TRADE, AND INSTITUTIONS AND PRACTICES SIMILAR TO SLAVERY, 1956

The Supplementary Convention was adopted by a United Nations Conference on 7 September 1956 and entered into force on 30 April 1957. One hundred and three States have become parties. For the text in various languages: *United Nations Treaty Series*, Vol. 266, p. 3; *U.K. Treaty Series*, No. 59 (1957), Cmnd. 257.

For further reference see Joyce Gutteridge, *International and Comparative Law Quarterly*, 6 (1957), p. 449; Schreiber, *Annuaire français de droit international*, 1956, p. 547.

*TEXT*

### Preamble

*The States Parties to the present Convention,*

*Considering* that freedom is the birthright of every human being;

*Mindful* that the peoples of the United Nations reaffirmed in the Charter their faith in the dignity and worth of the human person;

*Considering* that the Universal Declaration of Human Rights, proclaimed by the General Assembly of the United Nations as a common standard of achievement for all peoples and all nations, states that no one shall be held in slavery or servitude and that slavery and the slave trade shall be prohibited in all their forms;

*Recognizing* that, since the conclusion of the Slavery Convention signed at Geneva on 25 September, 1926, which was designed to secure the abolition of slavery and of the slave trade, further progress has been made towards this end;

*Having regard* to the Forced Labour Convention of 1930 and to subsequent action by the International Labour Organization in regard to forced or compulsory labour;

*Being aware*, however, that slavery, the slave trade and institutions and practices similar to slavery have not yet been eliminated in all parts of the world;

*Having decided*, therefore, that the Convention of 1926, which remains operative, should now be augmented by the conclusion of a supplementary convention designed to intensify national as well as international efforts towards the abolition of slavery, the slave trade and institutions and practices similar to slavery;

*Have agreed* as follows:

## Section I. Institutions and Practices Similar to Slavery

*Article* 1

Each of the States Parties to this Convention shall take all practicable and necessary legislative and other measures to bring about progressively and as soon as possible the complete abolition or abandonment of the following institutions and practices, where they still exist and whether or not they are covered by the definition of slavery contained in Article 1 of the Slavery Convention signed at Geneva on 25 September, 1926:

(*a*) debt bondage, that is to say, the status or condition arising from a pledge by a debtor of his personal services or of those of a person under his control as security for a debt, if the value of those services as reasonably assessed is not applied towards the liquidation of the debt or the length and nature of those services are not respectively limited and defined;

(*b*) serfdom, that is to say, the condition or status of a tenant who is by law, custom or agreement bound to live and labour on land belonging to another person and to render some determinate service to such other person, whether for reward or not, and is not free to change his status;

(*c*) any institution or practice whereby:

   (i) a woman, without the right to refuse, is promised or given in marriage on payment of a consideration in money or in kind to her parents, guardian, family or any other person or group; or

   (ii) the husband of a woman, his family, or his clan, has the right to transfer her to another person for value received or otherwise; or

   (iii) a woman on the death of her husband is liable to be inherited by another person;

(*d*) any institution or practice whereby a child or young person under the age of eighteen years is delivered by either or both of his natural parents or by his guardian to another person, whether for reward or not, with a view to the exploitation of the child or young person or of his labour.

*Article* 2

With a view to bringing to an end the institutions and practices mentioned in Article 1 (*c*) of this Convention, the States Parties undertake to prescribe, where appropriate, suitable minimum ages of marriage, to encourage the use of facilities whereby the consent of both parties to a marriage may be freely expressed in the presence of a competent civil or religious authority, and to encourage the registration of marriages.

## Section II. The Slave Trade

*Article* 3

1. The act of conveying or attempting to convey slaves from one country to another by whatever means of transport, or of being accessory thereto, shall be a criminal offence under the laws of the States Parties to this Convention and persons convicted thereof shall be liable to very severe penalties.

2. (*a*) The States Parties shall take all effective measures to prevent ships and aircraft authorized to fly their flags from conveying slaves and to punish persons guilty of such acts or of using national flags for that purpose.

(*b*) The States Parties shall take all effective measures to ensure that their ports, airfields and coasts are not used for the conveyance of slaves.

3. The States Parties to this Convention shall exchange information in order to ensure the practical co-ordination of the measures taken by them in combating the slave trade and shall inform each other of every case of the slave trade, and of every attempt to commit this criminal offence, which comes to their notice.

*Article* 4

Any slave who takes refuge on board any vessel of a State Party to this Convention shall *ipso facto* be free.

## Section III. Slavery and Institutions and Practices Similar to Slavery

*Article* 5

In a country where the abolition or abandonment of slavery, or of the institutions or practices mentioned in Article 1 of this Convention, is not yet complete, the act of mutilating, branding or otherwise marking a slave or a person of servile status in order to indicate his status, or as a punishment, or for any other reason, or of being accessory thereto, shall be a criminal offence under the laws of the States Parties to this Convention and persons convicted thereof shall be liable to punishment.

*Article* 6

1. The act of enslaving another person or of inducing another person to give himself or a person dependent upon him into slavery, or of attempting these acts, or being accessory thereto, or being a party to a conspiracy to accomplish any such acts, shall be a criminal offence under the laws of the States Parties to this Convention and persons convicted thereof shall be liable to punishment.

2. Subject to the provisions of the introductory paragraph of Article 1 of

this Convention, the provisions of paragraph 1 of the present Article shall also apply to the act of inducing another person to place himself or a person dependent upon him into the servile status resulting from any of the institutions or practices mentioned in Article 1, to any attempt to perform such acts, to being accessory thereto, and to being a party to a conspiracy to accomplish any such acts.

## Section IV. Definitions

*Article 7*

For the purposes of the present Convention:

  (*a*) 'slavery' means, as defined in the Slavery Convention of 1926, the status or condition of a person over whom any or all of the powers attaching to the right of ownership are exercised, and 'slave' means a person in such condition or status;
  (*b*) 'a person of servile status' means a person in the condition or status resulting from any of the institutions or practices mentioned in Article 1 of this Convention;
  (*c*) 'slave trade' means and includes all acts involved in the capture, acquisition or disposal of a person with intent to reduce him to slavery; all acts involved in the acquisition of a slave with a view to selling or exchanging him; all acts of disposal by sale or exchange of a person acquired with a view to being sold or exchanged; and, in general, every act of trade or transport in slaves by whatever means of conveyance.

## Section V. Co-operation between States Parties and Communication of Information

*Article 8*

1. The States Parties to this Convention undertake to co-operate with each other and with the United Nations to give effect to the foregoing provisions.

2. The Parties undertake to communicate to the Secretary-General of the United Nations copies of any laws, regulations and administrative measures enacted or put into effect to implement the provisions of this Convention.

3. The Secretary-General shall communicate the information received under paragraph 2 of this Article to the other Parties and to the Economic and Social Council as part of the documentation for any discussion which the Council might undertake with a view to making further recommendations for the abolition of slavery, the slave trade or the institutions and practices which are the subject of this Convention.

## Section VI. Final Clauses

*Article* 9

No reservations may be made to this Convention.

*Article* 10

Any dispute between States Parties to this Convention relating to its interpretation or application, which is not settled by negotiation, shall be referred to the International Court of Justice at the request of any one of the parties to the dispute, unless the parties concerned agree on another mode of settlement.

*Article* 11

1. This Convention shall be open until 1 July, 1957, for signature by any State Member of the United Nations or of a specialized agency. It shall be subject to ratification by the signatory States, and the instruments of ratification shall be deposited with the Secretary-General of the United Nations, who shall inform each signatory and acceding State.

2. After 1 July, 1957, this Convention shall be open for accession by any State Member of the United Nations or of a specialized agency, or by any other State to which an invitation to accede has been addressed by the General Assembly of the United Nations. Accession shall be effected by the deposit of a formal instrument with the Secretary-General of the United Nations, who shall inform each signatory and acceding State.

*Article* 12

1. This Convention shall apply to all non-self-governing, trust, colonial and other non-metropolitan territories for the international relations of which any State Party is responsible; the Party concerned shall, subject to the provisions of paragraph 2 of this Article, at the time of signature, ratification or accession declare the non-metropolitan territory or territories to which the Convention shall apply *ipso facto* as a result of such signature, ratification or accession.

2. In any case in which the previous consent of a non-metropolitan territory is required by the constitutional laws or practices of the Party or of the non-metropolitan territory, the Party concerned shall endeavour to secure the needed consent of the non-metropolitan territory within the period of twelve months from the date of signature of the Convention by the metropolitan State, and when such consent has been obtained the Party shall notify the Secretary-General. This Convention shall apply to the territory or territories named in such notification from the date of its receipt by the Secretary-General.

3. After the expiry of the twelve-month period mentioned in the preceding

paragraph, the States Parties concerned shall inform the Secretary-General of the results of the consultations with those non-metropolitan territories for whose international relations they are responsible and whose consent to the application of this Convention may have been withheld.

*Article* 13

1. This Convention shall enter into force on the date on which two States have become Parties thereto.

2. It shall thereafter enter into force with respect to each State and territory on the date of deposit of the instrument of ratification or accession of that State or notification of application to that territory.

*Article* 14

1. The application of this Convention shall be divided into successive periods of three years, of which the first shall begin on the date of entry into force of the Convention in accordance with paragraph 1 of Article 13.

2. Any State Party may denounce this Convention by a notice addressed by that State to the Secretary-General not less than six months before the expiration of the current three-year period. The Secretary-General shall notify all other Parties of each such notice and the date of receipt thereof.

3. Denunciations shall take effect at the expiration of the current three-year period.

4. In cases where, in accordance with the provisions of Article 12, this Convention has become applicable to a non-metropolitan territory of a Party, that Party may at any time thereafter, with the consent of the territory concerned, give notice to the Secretary-General of the United Nations denouncing this Convention separately in respect of that territory. The denunciation shall take effect one year after the date of the receipt of such notice by the Secretary-General, who shall notify all other Parties of such notice and the date of the receipt thereof.

*Article* 15

This Convention, of which the Chinese, English, French, Russian and Spanish texts are equally authentic, shall be deposited in the archives of the United Nations Secretariat. The Secretary-General shall prepare a certified copy thereof for communication to States Parties to this Convention, as well as to all other States Members of the United Nations and of the specialized agencies.

*In witness thereof* the undersigned, being duly authorized thereto by their respective Governments, have signed this Convention on the date appearing opposite their respective signatures.

*Done* at the European Office of the United Nations at Geneva, this seventh day of September, one thousand nine hundred and fifty-six.

## X. CONVENTION RELATING TO THE
## STATUS OF REFUGEES, 1951

The Convention was adopted by the U.N. Conference on the Status of Refugees and Stateless Persons at Geneva, 2–25 July 1951, and entered into force on 22 April 1954. One hundred and two States have become parties. For the text in various languages: *United Nations Treaty Series*, Vol. 189, p. 137; *U.K. Treaty Series*, No. 39 (1954), Cmd. 9171.

For further reference see Weis, *British Year Book of International Law*, Vol. 30 (1953), p. 478; the same, *American Journal of International Law*, 48 (1954), p. 193; the same, *Journal de droit international*, 87 (1960), p, 928; Grahl-Madsen, *The Status of Refugees in International Law*, 2 vols., 1966.

The Convention which follows is confined to those who became refugees 'as a result of events occurring before 1 January 1951'. This limitation is removed by the Protocol Relating to the Status of Refugees adopted by the General Assembly of the United Nations on 16 December 1966; see Weis, *British Year Book*, Vol. 42 (1967), p. 39 (text of Protocol at p. 67). The Protocol came into force on 4 October 1967, and not less than one hundred and three States are parties. For the text in various languages: *United Nations Treaty Series*, Vol. 606, p. 267; *U.K. Treaty Series*, No. 15 (1969), Cmnd. 3906. The text of the Protocol is not reproduced here: the changes it makes in Article 1A(2) of the Convention are indicated by square brackets.

*TEXT*

Preamble

*The High Contracting Parties,*

*Considering* that the Charter of the United Nations and the Universal Declaration of Human Rights approved on 10 December 1948 by the General Assembly have affirmed the principle that human beings shall enjoy fundamental rights and freedoms without discrimination,

*Considering* that the United Nations has, on various occasions, manifested its profound concern for refugees and endeavoured to assure refugees the widest possible exercise of these fundamental rights and freedoms.

*Considering* that it is desirable to revise and consolidate previous international agreements relating to the status of refugees and to extend the scope of and the protection accorded by such instruments by means of a new agreement,

*Considering* that the grant of asylum may place unduly heavy burdens on certain countries, and that a satisfactory solution of a problem of which the United Nations has recognized the international scope and nature cannot therefore be achieved without international co-operation.

*Expressing* the wish that all States, recognizing the social and humanitarian nature of the problem of refugees, will do everything within their power to prevent this problem from becoming a cause of tension between States,

*Noting* that the United Nations High Commissioner for Refugees is charged with the task of supervising international conventions providing for the protection of refugees, and recognizing that the effective co-ordination of measures taken to deal with this problem will depend upon the co-operation of States with the High Commissioner,

*Have agreed* as follows:

## CHAPTER I
### General Provisions

*Definition of the Term 'Refugee'*

*Article* 1

A. For the purposes of the present Convention, the term 'refugee' shall apply to any person who:

(1) Has been considered a refugee under the Arrangements of 12 May 1926 and 30 June 1928 or under the Conventions of 28 October 1933 and 10 February 1938, the Protocol of 14 September 1939 or the Constitution of the International Refugee Organization;

Decisions of non-eligibility taken by the International Refugee Organization during the period of its activities shall not prevent the status of refugee being accorded to persons who fulfil the conditions of paragraph 2 of this section;

(2) [As a result of events occurring before 1 January 1951 and] owing to well-founded fear of being persecuted for reasons of race, religion, nationality, membership of a particular social group or political opinion, is outside the country of his nationality and is unable or, owing to such fear, is unwilling to avail himself of the protection of that country; or who, not having a nationality and being outside the country of his former habitual residence [as a result of such events], is unable or, owing to such fear, is unwilling to return to it.

In the case of a person who has more than one nationality, the term 'the country of his nationality' shall mean each of the countries of which he is a national, and a person shall not be deemed to be lacking the protection of the country of his nationality if, without any valid reason based on well-founded fear, he has not availed himself of the protection of one of the countries of which he is a national.

B. (1) For the purposes of this Convention, the words 'events occurring before 1 January 1951' in Article 1, Section A, shall be understood to mean either

(a) 'events occurring in Europe before 1 January 1951'; or
(b) 'events occurring in Europe or elsewhere before 1 January 1951';

and each Contracting State shall make a declaration at the time of signature, ratification or accession, specifying which of these meanings it applies for the purpose of its obligations under this Convention.

(2) Any Contracting State which has adopted alternative (a) may at any time extend its obligations by adopting alternative (b) by means of a notification addressed to the Secretary-General of the United Nations.

C. This Convention shall cease to apply to any person falling under the terms of section A if:

(1) He has voluntarily re-availed himself of the protection of the country of his nationality; or

(2) Having lost his nationality, he has voluntarily reacquired it; or

(3) He has acquired a new nationality, and enjoys the protection of the country of his new nationality; or

(4) He has voluntarily re-established himself in the country which he left or outside which he remained owing to fear of persecution; or

(5) He can no longer, because the circumstances in connexion with which he has been recognized as a refugee have ceased to exist, continue to refuse to avail himself of the protection of the country of his nationality;

Provided that this paragraph shall not apply to a refugee falling under section A (1) of this article who is able to invoke compelling reasons arising out of previous persecution for refusing to avail himself of the protection of the country of nationality;

(6) Being a person who has no nationality he is, because the circumstances in connexion with which he has been recognized as a refugee have ceased to exist, able to return to the country of his former habitual residence;

Provided this paragraph shall not apply to a refugee falling under section A (1) of this article who is able to invoke compelling reasons arising out of previous persecution for refusing to return to the country of his former habitual residence.

D. This Convention shall not apply to persons who are at present receiving from organs or agencies of the United Nations other than the United Nations High Commissioner for Refugees protection or assistance.

When such protection or assistance has ceased for any reason, without the position of such persons being definitively settled in accordance with the relevant resolutions adopted by the General Assembly of the United Nations, these persons shall *ipso facto* be entitled to the benefits of this Convention.

E. This Convention shall not apply to a person who is recognized by the competent authorities of the country in which he has taken residence as having the rights and obligations which are attached to the possession of the nationality of that country.

F. The provisions of this Convention shall not apply to any person with respect to whom there are serious reasons for considering that:

(*a*) He has committed a crime against peace, a war crime, or a crime against humanity, as defined in the international instruments drawn up to make provision in respect of such crimes;

(*b*) He has committed a serious non-political crime outside the country of refuge prior to his admission to that country as a refugee;

(*c*) He has been guilty of acts contrary to the purposes and principles of the United Nations.

*General Obligations*

*Article* 2

Every refugee has duties to the country in which he finds himself, which require in particular that he conform to its laws and regulations as well as to measures taken for the maintenance of public order.

*Non-discrimination*

*Article* 3

The Contracting States shall apply the provisions of this Convention to refugees without discrimination as to race, religion or country of origin.

*Religion*

*Article* 4

The Contracting States shall accord to refugees within their territories treatment at least as favourable as that accorded to their nationals with respect to freedom to practise their religion and freedom as regards the religious education of their children.

*Rights Granted Apart from this Convention*

*Article* 5

Nothing in this Convention shall be deemed to impair any rights and benefits granted by a Contracting State to refugees apart from this Convention.

*The Term 'In the same circumstances'*

*Article* 6

For the purpose of this Convention, the term 'in the same circumstances' implies that any requirements (including requirements as to length and conditions of sojourn or residence) which the particular individual would have to fulfil for the enjoyment of the right in question, if he were not a refugee, must be fulfilled by him, with the exception of requirements which by their nature a refugee is incapable of fulfilling.

### Exemption from Reciprocity

*Article* 7

1. Except where this Convention contains more favourable provisions, a Contracting State shall accord to refugees the same treatment as is accorded to aliens generally.

2. After a period of three years' residence, all refugees shall enjoy exemption from legislative reciprocity in the territory of the Contracting States.

3. Each Contracting State shall continue to accord to refugees the rights and benefits to which they were already entitled, in the absence of reciprocity, at the date of entry into force of this Convention for that State.

4. The Contracting States shall consider favourably the possibility of according to refugees, in the absence of reciprocity, rights and benefits beyond those to which they are entitled according to paragraphs 2 and 3, and to extending exemption from reciprocity to refugees who do not fulfil the conditions provided for in paragraphs 2 and 3.

5. The provisions of paragraphs 2 and 3 apply both to the rights and benefits referred to in Articles 13, 18, 19, 21 and 22 of this Convention and to rights and benefits for which this Convention does not provide.

### Exemption from Exceptional Measures

*Article* 8

With regard to exceptional measures which may be taken against the person, property or interests of nationals of a foreign State, the Contracting States shall not apply such measures to a refugee who is formally a national of the said State solely on account of such nationality. Contracting States which, under their legislation, are prevented from applying the general principle expressed in this article, shall, in appropriate cases, grant exemptions in favour of such refugees.

### Provisional Measures

*Article* 9

Nothing in this Convention shall prevent a Contracting State, in time of war or other grave and exceptional circumstances, from taking provisionally measures which it considers to be essential to the national security in the case of a particular person, pending a determination by the Contracting

State that that person is in fact a refugee and that the continuance of such measures is necessary in his case in the interests of national security.

### *Continuity of Residence*

*Article* 10

1. Where a refugee has been forcibly displaced during the Second World War and removed to the territory of a Contracting State, and is resident there, the period of such enforced sojourn shall be considered to have been lawful residence within that territory.

2. Where a refugee has been forcibly displaced during the Second World War from the territory of a Contracting State and has, prior to the date of entry into force of this Convention, returned there for the purpose of taking up residence, the period of residence before and after such enforced displacement shall be regarded as one uninterrupted period for any purposes for which uninterrupted residence is required.

### *Refugee Seamen*

*Article* 11

In the case of refugees regularly serving as crew members on board a ship flying the flag of a Contracting State, that State shall give sympathetic consideration to their establishment on its territory and the issue of travel documents to them or their temporary admission to its territory particularly with a view to facilitating their establishment in another country.

## CHAPTER II
### Juridical Status

### *Personal Status*

*Article* 12

1. The personal status of a refugee shall be governed by the law of the country of his domicile or, if he has no domicile, by the law of the country of his residence.

2. Rights previously acquired by a refugee and dependent on personal status, more particularly rights attaching to marriage, shall be respected by a Contracting State, subject to compliance, if this be necessary, with the formalities required by the law of that State, provided that the right in question is one which would have been recognized by the law of that State had he not become a refugee.

### Movable and Immovable Property

*Article* 13

The Contracting States shall accord to a refugee treatment as favourable as possible and, in any event, not less favourable than that accorded to aliens generally in the same circumstances, as regards the acquisition of movable and immovable property and other rights pertaining thereto, and to leases and other contracts relating to movable and immovable property.

### Artistic Rights and Industrial Property

*Article* 14

In respect of the protection of industrial property, such as inventions, designs or models, trade marks, trade names, and of rights in literary, artistic and scientific works, a refugee shall be accorded in the country in which he has his habitual residence the same protection as is accorded to nationals of that country. In the territory of any other Contracting State, he shall be accorded the same protection as is accorded in that territory to nationals of the country in which he has his habitual residence.

### Right of Association

*Article* 15

As regards non-political and non-profit-making associations and trade unions the Contracting States shall accord to refugees lawfully staying in their territory the most favourable treatment accorded to nationals of a foreign country, in the same circumstances.

### Access to Courts

*Article* 16

1. A refugee shall have free access to the courts of law on the territory of all Contracting States.

2. A refugee shall enjoy in the Contracting State in which he has his habitual residence the same treatment as a national in matters pertaining to access to the courts, including legal assistance and exemption from *cautio judicatum solvi.*

3. A refugee shall be accorded in the matters referred to in paragraph 2 in countries other than that in which he has his habitual residence the treatment granted to a national of the country of his habitual residence.

# CHAPTER III
Gainful Employment

## Wage-earning Employment

*Article* 17

1. The Contracting States shall accord to refugees lawfully staying in their territory the most favourable treatment accorded to nationals of a foreign country in the same circumstances, as regards the right to engage in wage-earning employment.

2. In any case, restrictive measures imposed on aliens or the employment of aliens for the protection of the national labour market shall not be applied to a refugee who was already exempt from them at the date of entry into force of this Convention for the Contracting State concerned, or who fulfils one of the following conditions:

(*a*) He has completed three years' residence in the country.

(*b*) He has a spouse possessing the nationality of the country of residence. A refugee may not invoke the benefit of this provision if he has abandoned his spouse;

(*c*) He has one or more children possessing the nationality of the country of residence.

3. The Contracting States shall give sympathetic consideration to assimilating the rights of all refugees with regard to wage-earning employment to those of nationals, and in particular of those refugees who have entered their territory pursuant to programmes of labour recruitment or under immigration schemes.

## Self-employment

*Article* 18

The Contracting States shall accord to a refugee lawfully in their territory treatment as favourable as possible and, in any event, not less favourable than that accorded to aliens generally in the same circumstances, as regards the right to engage on his own account in agriculture, industry, handicrafts and commerce and to establish commercial and industrial companies.

## Liberal Professions

*Article* 19

1. Each Contracting State shall accord to refugees lawfully staying in their territory who hold diplomas recognized by the competent authorities of that State, and who are desirous of practising a liberal profession, treatment as

favourable as posssible and, in any event, not less favourable than that accorded to aliens generally in the same circumstances.

2. The Contracting States shall use their best endeavours consistently with their laws and constitutions to secure the settlement of such refugees in the territories, other than the metropolitan territory, for whose international relations they are responsible.

# CHAPTER IV
## Welfare

### *Rationing*

*Article* 20

Where a rationing system exists, which applies to the population at large and regulates the general distribution of products in short supply, refugees shall be accorded the same treatment as nationals.

### *Housing*

*Article* 21

As regards housing, the Contracting States, in so far as the matter is regulated by laws or regulations or is subject to the control of public authorities, shall accord to refugees lawfully staying in their territory treatment as favourable as possible and, in any event, not less favourable than that accorded to aliens generally in the same circumstances.

### *Public Education*

*Article* 22

1. The Contracting States shall accord to refugees the same treatment as is accorded to nationals with respect to elementary education.

2. The Contracting States shall accord to refugees treatment as favourable as possible, and, in any event, not less favourable than that accorded to aliens generally in the same circumstances, with respect to education other than elementary education and, in particular, as regards access to studies, the recognition of foreign school certificates, diplomas and degrees, the remission of fees and charges and the award of scholarships.

### *Public Relief*

*Article* 23

The Contracting States shall accord to refugees lawfully staying in their territory the same treatment with respect to public relief and assistance as is accorded to their nationals.

*Labour Legislation and Social Security*

*Article* 24

1. The Contracting States shall accord to refugees lawfully staying in their territory the same treatment as is accorded to nationals in respect of the following matters:

(*a*) In so far as such matters are governed by laws or regulations or are subject to the control of administrative authorities: remuneration, including family allowances where these form part of remuneration, hours of work, overtime arrangements, holidays with pay, restrictions on home work, minimum age of employment, apprenticeship and training, women's work and the work of young persons, and the enjoyment of the benefits of collective bargaining;

(*b*) Social security (legal provisions in respect of employment injury, occupational diseases, maternity, sickness, disability, old age, death, unemployment, family responsibilities and any other contingency which, according to national laws or regulations, is covered by a social security scheme), subject to the following limitations:

   (i) There may be appropriate arrangements for the maintenance of acquired rights and rights in course of acquisition;

   (ii) National laws or regulations of the country of residence may prescribe special arrangements concerning benefits or portions of benefits which are payable wholly out of public funds, and concerning allowances paid to persons who do not fulfil the contribution conditions prescribed for the award of a normal pension.

2. The right to compensation for the death of a refugee resulting from employment injury or from occupational disease shall not be affected by the fact that the residence of the beneficiary is outside the territory of the Contracting State.

3. The Contracting States shall extend to refugees the benefits of agreements concluded between them, or which may be concluded between them in the future, concerning the maintenance of acquired rights in the process of acquisition in regard to social security, subject only to the conditions which apply to nationals of the States signatory to the agreements in question.

4. The Contracting States will give sympathetic consideration to extending to refugees so far as possible the benefits of similar agreements which may at any time be in force between such Contracting States and non-contracting States.

## CHAPTER V
### Administrative Measures

*Administrative Assistance*

*Article* 25

1. When the exercise of a right by a refugee would normally require the assistance of authorities of a foreign country to whom he cannot have recourse, the Contracting States in whose territory he is residing shall arrange that such assistance be afforded to him by their own authorities or by an international authority.

2. The authority or authorities mentioned in paragraph 1 shall deliver or cause to be delivered under their supervision to refugees such documents or certifications as would normally be delivered to aliens by or through their national authorities.

3. Documents or certifications so delivered shall stand in the stead of the official instruments delivered to aliens by or through their national authorities, and shall be given credence in the absence of proof to the contrary.

4. Subject to such exceptional treatment as may be granted to indigent persons, fees may be charged for the services mentioned herein, but such fees shall be moderate and commensurate with those charged to nationals for similar services.

5. The provisions of this article shall be without prejudice to Articles 27 and 28.

*Freedom of Movement*

*Article* 26

Each Contracting State shall accord to refugees lawfully in its territory the right to choose their place of residence and to move freely within its territory, subject to any regulations applicable to aliens generally in the same circumstances.

*Identity Papers*

*Article* 27

The Contracting States shall issue identity papers to any refugee in their territory who does not possess a valid travel document.

*Travel Documents*

*Article* 28

1. The Contracting States shall issue to refugees lawfully staying in their territory travel documents for the purpose of travel outside their territory,

unless compelling reasons of national security or public order otherwise require, and the provisions of the Schedule to this Convention shall apply with respect to such documents. The Contracting States may issue such a travel document to any other refugee in their territory; they shall in particular give sympathetic consideration to the issue of such a travel document to refugees in their territory who are unable to obtain a travel document from the country of their lawful residence.

2. Travel documents issued to refugees under previous international agreements by parties thereto shall be recognized and treated by the Contracting States in the same way as if they had been issued pursuant to this Article.

## Fiscal Charges

### Article 29

1. The Contracting States shall not impose upon refugees duties, charges or taxes, of any description whatsoever, other or higher than those which are or may be levied on their nationals in similar situations.

2. Nothing in the above paragraph shall prevent the application to refugees of the laws and regulations concerning charges in respect of the issue to aliens of administrative documents including identity papers.

## Transfer of Assets

### Article 30

1. A Contracting State shall, in conformity with its laws and regulations, permit refugees to transfer assets which they have brought into its territory, to another country where they have been admitted for the purposes of resettlement.

2. A Contracting State shall give sympathetic consideration to the application of refugees for permission to transfer assets wherever they may be and which are necessary for their resettlement in another country to which they have been admitted.

## Refugees Unlawfully in the Country of Refuge

### Article 31

1. The Contracting States shall not impose penalties, on account of their illegal entry or presence, on refugees who, coming directly from a territory where their life or freedom was threatened in the sense of Article 1, enter or are present in their territory without authorization, provided they present themselves without delay to the authorities and show good cause for their illegal entry or presence.

2. The Contracting States shall not apply to the movements of such re-

fugees restrictions other than those which are necessary and such restrictions shall only be applied until their status in the country is regularized or they obtain admission into another country. The Contracting States shall allow such refugees a reasonable period and all the necessary facilities to obtain admission into another country.

## Expulsion

*Article* 32

1. The Contracting States shall not expel a refugee lawfully in their territory save on grounds of national security or public order.

2. The expulsion of such a refugee shall be only in pursuance of a decision reached in accordance with due process of law. Except where compelling reasons of national security otherwise require, the refugee shall be allowed to submit evidence to clear himself, and to appeal to and be represented for the purpose before the competent authority or a person or persons specially designated by the competent authority.

3. The Contracting States shall allow such a refugee a reasonable period within which to seek legal admission into another country. The Contracting States reserve the right to apply during that period such internal measures as they may deem necessary.

## Prohibition of Expulsion or Return ('Refoulement')

*Article* 33

1. No Contracting State shall expel or return ('refouler') a refugee in any manner whatsoever to the frontiers of territories where his life or freedom would be threatened on account of his race, religion, nationality, membership of a particular social group or political opinion.

2. The benefit of the present provision may not, however, be claimed by a refugee whom there are reasonable grounds for regarding as a danger to the security of the country in which he is, or who, having been convicted by a final judgment of a particularly serious crime, constitutes a danger to the community of that country.

## Naturalization

*Article* 34

The Contracting States shall as far as possible facilitate the assimilation and naturalization of refugees. They shall in particular make every effort to expedite naturalization proceedings and to reduce as far as possible the charges and costs of such proceedings.

## CHAPTER VI
### Executory and Transitory Provisions

*Co-operation of the National Authorities with the United Nations*

*Article 35*

1. The Contracting States undertake to co-operate with the Office of the United Nations High Commissioner for Refugees, or any other agency of the United Nations which may succeed it, in the exercise of its functions, and shall in particular facilitate its duty of supervising the application of the provisions of this Convention.

2. In order to enable the Office of the High Commissioner or any other agency of the United Nations which may succeed it, to make reports to the competent organs of the United Nations, the Contracting States undertake to provide them in the appropriate form with information and statistical data requested concerning:

- (*a*) The condition of refugees,
- (*b*) The implementation of this Convention, and
- (*c*) Laws, regulations and decrees which are, or may hereafter be, in force relating to refugees.

*Information on National Legislation*

*Article 36*

The Contracting States shall communicate to the Secretary-General of the United Nations the laws and regulations which they may adopt to ensure the application of this Convention.

*Relation to Previous Conventions*

*Article 37*

Without prejudice to Article 28, paragraph 2, of this Convention, this Convention replaces, as between parties to it, the Arrangements of 5 July 1922, 31 May 1924, 12 May 1926, 30 June 1928 and 30 July 1935, the Conventions of 28 October 1933 and 10 February 1938, the Protocol of 14 September 1939 and the Agreement of 15 October 1946.

## CHAPTER VII
### Final Clauses

*Settlement of Disputes*

*Article 38*

Any dispute between parties to this Convention relating to its interpretation or application, which cannot be settled by other means, shall be referred to the International Court of Justice at the request of any one of the parties to the dispute.

*Signature, Ratification and Accession*

*Article* 39

1. This Convention shall be opened for signature at Geneva on 28 July 1951 and shall thereafter be deposited with the Secretary-General of the United Nations. It shall be open for signature at the European Office of the United Nations from 28 July to 31 August 1951 and shall be re-opened for signature at the Headquarters of the United Nations from 17 September 1951 to 31 December 1952.

2. This Convention shall be open for signature on behalf of all States Members of the United Nations, and also on behalf of any other State invited to attend the Conference of Plenipotentiaries on the Status of Refugees and Stateless Persons or to which an invitation to sign will have been addressed by the General Assembly. It shall be ratified and the instruments of ratification shall be deposited with the Secretary-General of the United Nations.

3. This Convention shall be open from 28 July 1951 for accession by the States referred to in paragraph 2 of this Article. Accession shall be effected by the deposit of an instrument of accession with the Secretary-General of the United Nations.

*Territorial Application Clause*

*Article* 40

1. Any State may, at the time of signature, ratification or accession, declare that this Convention shall extend to all or any of the territories for the international relations of which it is responsible. Such a declaration shall take effect when the Convention enters into force for the State concerned.

2. At any time thereafter any such extension shall be made by notification addressed to the Secretary-General of the United Nations and shall take effect as from the ninetieth day after the day of receipt by the Secretary-General of the United Nations of this notification, or as from the date of entry into force of the Convention for the State concerned, whichever is the later.

3. With respect to those territories to which this Convention is not extended at the time of signature, ratification or accession, each State concerned shall consider the possibility of taking the necessary steps in order to extend the application of this Convention to such territories, subject, where necessary for constitutional reasons, to the consent of the Governments of such territories.

*Federal Clause*

*Article* 41

In the case of a Federal or non-unitary State, the following provisions shall apply:

(*a*) With respect to those articles of this Convention that come within the legislative jurisdiction of the federal legislative authority, the obligations of the Federal Government shall to this extent be the same as those of Parties which are not Federal States;

(*b*) With respect to those Articles of this Convention that come within the legislative jurisdiction of constituent states, provinces or cantons which are not, under the constitutional system of the federation, bound to take legislative action, the Federal Government shall bring such Articles with a favourable recommendation to the notice of the appropriate authorities of states, provinces or cantons at the earliest possible moment.

(*c*) A Federal State Party to this Convention shall, at the request of any other Contracting State transmitted through the Secretary-General of the United Nations, supply a statement of the law and practice of the Federation and its constituent units in regard to any particular provision of the Convention showing the extent to which effect has been given to that provision by legislative or other action.

*Reservations*

*Article* 42

1. At the time of signature, ratification or accession, any State may make reservations to Articles of the Convention other than to Articles 1, 3, 4, 16 (1), 33, 36–46 inclusive.

2. Any State making a reservation in accordance with paragraph 1 of this Article may at any time withdraw the reservation by a communication to that effect addressed to the Secretary-General of the United Nations.

*Entry into Force*

*Article* 43

1. This Convention shall come into force on the ninetieth day following the day of deposit of the sixth instrument of ratification or accession.

2. For each State ratifying or acceding to the Convention after the deposit of the sixth instrument of ratification or accession, the Convention shall enter into force on the ninetieth day following the date of deposit by such State of its instrument of ratification or accession.

## Denunciation

*Article* 44

1. Any Contracting State may denounce this Convention at any time by a notification addressed to the Secretary-General of the United Nations.

2. Such denunciation shall take effect for the Contracting State concerned one year from the date upon which it is received by the Secretary-General of the United Nations.

3. Any State which has made a declaration or notification under Article 40 may, at any time thereafter, by a notification to the Secretary-General of the United Nations, declare that the Convention shall cease to extend to such territory one year after the date of receipt of the notification by the Secretary-General.

## Revision

*Article* 45

1. Any Contracting State may request revision of this Convention at any time by a notification addressed to the Secretary-General of the United Nations.

2. The General Assembly of the United Nations shall recommend the steps, if any, to be taken in respect of such request.

## Notifications by the Secretary-General of the United Nations

*Article* 46

The Secretary-General of the United Nations shall inform all Members of the United Nations and non-member States referred to in Article 39:

(*a*) Of declarations and notifications in accordance with section B of Article 1;

(*b*) Of signatures, ratifications and accessions in accordance with Article 39;

(*c*) Of declarations and notifications in accordance with Article 40;

(*d*) Of reservations and withdrawals in accordance with Article 42;

(*e*) Of the date on which this Convention will come into force in accordance with Article 43;

(*f*) Of denunciations and notifications in accordance with Article 44;

(*g*) Of requests for revision in accordance with Article 45.

*In faith whereof* the undersigned, duly authorized, have signed this Convention on behalf of their respective Governments,

*Done* at Geneva, this twenty-eighth day of July, one thousand nine hundred and fifty-one, in a single copy, of which the English and French texts are equally authentic and which shall remain deposited in the archives of the United Nations, and certified true copies of which shall be delivered to all Members of the United Nations and to the non-member States referred to in Article 39.

# XI. CONVENTION RELATING TO THE STATUS OF STATELESS PERSONS, 1954

Statelessness has become a very serious problem, and measures to reduce its incidence have not readily found favour with States (see the Convention set out below). The persistence of statelessness has necessitated the creation of a regime which will give stateless persons a stable basis of life in host countries. The Convention concerning the status of stateless persons was adopted by a U.N. Conference, New York, 13–23 September 1954, and came into force on 6 June 1960. The text in several languages appears in *United Nations Treaty Series*, Vol. 360, p. 117; and *U.K. Treaty Series*, Misc. No. 41, 1960, Cmnd. 1098. Thirty-seven States remain parties.

For further reference see United Nations, Dept. of Social Affairs, *A Study of Statelessness*, 1949, Sales No. 1949, XIV. 2; Weis, *International and Comparative Law Quarterly*, 10 (1961), p. 255.

*TEXT*

## Preamble

*The High Contracting Parties,*

*Considering* that the Charter of the United Nations and the Universal Declaration of Human Rights approved on 10 December 1948 by the General Assembly of the United Nations have affirmed the principle that human beings shall enjoy fundamental rights and freedoms without discrimination,

*Considering* that the United Nations has, on various occasions, manifested its profound concern for stateless persons and endeavoured to assure stateless persons the widest possible exercise of these fundamental rights and freedoms,

*Considering* that only those stateless persons who are also refugees are covered by the Convention relating to the Status of Refugees of 28 July 1951, and that there are many stateless persons who are not covered by that Convention,

*Considering* that it is desirable to regulate and improve the status of stateless persons by an international agreement.

*Have agreed* as follows:

## CHAPTER I
### General Provisions

*Definition of the term 'Stateless Person'*

*Article* 1

1. For the purpose of this Convention, the term 'stateless person' means a

person who is not considered as a national by any State under the operation of its law.

2. This Convention shall not apply:

(i) To persons who are at present receiving from organs or agencies of the United Nations other than the United Nations High Commissioner for Refugees protection or assistance so long as they are receiving such protection or assistance;

(ii) To persons who are recognized by the competent authorities of the country in which they have taken residence as having the rights and obligations which are attached to the possession of the nationality of that country;

(iii) To persons with respect to whom there are serious reasons for considering that:

(a) They have committed a crime against peace, a war crime, or a crime against humanity, as defined in the international instruments drawn up to make provisions in respect of such crimes;

(b) They have committed a serious non-political crime outside the country of their residence prior to their admission to that country;

(c) They have been guilty of acts contrary to the purposes and principles of the United Nations.

*General obligations*

*Article* 2

Every stateless person has duties to the country in which he finds himself, which require in particular that he conform to its laws and regulations as well as to measures taken for the maintenance of public order.

*Non-discrimination*

*Article* 3

The Contracting States shall apply the provisions of this Convention to stateless persons without discrimination as to race, religion or country of origin.

*Religion*

*Article* 4

The Contracting States shall accord to stateless persons within their territories treatment at least as favourable as that accorded to their nationals with respect to freedom to practise their religion and freedom as regards the religious education of their children.

*Rights Granted Apart from this Convention*

*Article* 5

Nothing in this Convention shall be deemed to impair any rights and benefits granted by a Contracting State to stateless persons apart from this Convention.

*The Term 'In the same Circumstances'*

*Article* 6

For the purpose of this Convention, the term 'in the same circumstances' implies that any requirements (including requirements as to length and conditions of sojourn or residence) which the particular individual would have to fulfil for the enjoyment of the right in question, if he were not a stateless person, must be fulfilled by him, with the exception of requirements which by their nature a stateless person is incapable of fulfilling.

*Exemption from Reciprocity*

*Article* 7

1. Except where this Convention contains more favourable provisions, a Contracting State shall accord to stateless persons the same treatment as is accorded to aliens generally.

2. After a period of three years' residence, all stateless persons shall enjoy exemption from legislative reciprocity in the territory of the Contracting States.

3. Each Contracting State shall continue to accord to stateless persons the rights and benefits to which they were already entitled, in the absence of reciprocity, at the date of entry into force of this Convention for that State.

4. The Contracting States shall consider favourably the possibility of according to stateless persons, in the absence of reciprocity, rights and benefits beyond those to which they are entitled according to paragraphs 2 and 3, and to extending exemption from reciprocity to stateless persons who do not fulfil the conditions provided for in paragraphs 2 and 3.

5. The provisions of paragraphs 2 and 3 apply both to the rights and benefits referred to in Articles 13, 18, 19, 21 and 22 of this Convention and to rights and benefits for which this Convention does not provide.

*Exemption from Exceptional Measures*

*Article* 8

With regard to exceptional measures which may be taken against the person, property or interests of nationals or former nationals of a foreign

State, the Contracting States shall not apply such measures to a stateless person solely on account of his having previously possessed the nationality of the foreign State in question. Contracting States which, under their legislation, are prevented from applying the general principle expressed in this Article shall, in appropriate cases, grant exemptions in favour of such stateless persons.

### *Provisional Measures*

*Article* 9

Nothing in this Convention shall prevent a Contracting State, in time of war or other grave and exceptional circumstances, from taking provisionally measures which it considers to be essential to the national security in the case of a particular person, pending a determination by the Contracting State that that person is in fact a stateless person and that the continuance of such measures is necessary in his case in the interests of national security.

### *Continuity of Residence*

*Article* 10

1. Where a stateless person has been forcibly displaced during the Second World War and removed to the territory of a Contracting State, and is resident there, the period of such enforced sojourn shall be considered to have been lawful residence within that territory.

2. Where a stateless person has been forcibly displaced during the Second World War from the territory of a Contracting State and has, prior to the date of entry into force of this Convention, returned there for the purpose of taking up residence, the period of residence before and after such enforced displacement shall be regarded as one uninterrupted period for any purpose for which uninterrupted residence is required.

### *Stateless Seamen*

*Article* 11

In the case of stateless persons regularly serving as crew members on board a ship flying the flag of a Contracting State, that State shall give sympathetic consideration to their establishment on its territory and the issue of travel documents to them or their temporary admission to its territory particularly with a view to facilitating their establishment in another country.

## CHAPTER II
Juridical Status

*Personal Status*

*Article* 12

1. The personal status of a stateless person shall be governed by the law of the country of his domicile or, if he has no domicile, by the law of the country of his residence.

2. Rights previously acquired by a stateless person and dependent on personal status, more particularly rights attaching to marriage, shall be respected by a Contracting State, subject to compliance, if this be necessary, with the formalities required by the law of that State, provided that the right in question is one which would have been recognized by the law of that State had he not become stateless.

*Movable and Immovable Property*

*Article* 13

The Contracting States shall accord to a stateless person treatment as favourable as possible and, in any event, not less favourable than that accorded to aliens generally in the same circumstances, as regards the acquisition of movable and immovable property and other rights pertaining thereto, and to leases and other contracts relating to movable and immovable property.

*Artistic Rights and Industrial Property*

*Article* 14

In respect of the protection of industrial property, such as inventions, designs or models, trade marks, trade names, and of rights in literary, artistic and scientific works, a stateless person shall be accorded in the country in which he has his habitual residence the same protection as is accorded to nationals of that country. In the territory of any other Contracting State, he shall be accorded the same protection as is accorded in that territory to nationals of the country in which he has his habitual residence.

*Right of Association*

*Article* 15

As regards non-political and non-profit-making associations and trade unions the Contracting States shall accord to stateless persons lawfully staying in their territory treatment as favourable as possible, and in any event, not less favourable than that accorded to aliens generally in the same circumstances.

*Access to Courts*

*Article* 16

1. A stateless person shall have free access to the Courts of Law on the territory of all Contracting States.

2. A stateless person shall enjoy in the Contracting State in which he has his habitual residence the same treatment as a national in matters pertaining to access to the Courts, including legal assistance and exemption from *cautio judicatum solvi*.

3. A stateless person shall be accorded in the matters referred to in paragraph 2 in countries other than that in which he has his habitual residence the treatment granted to a national of the country of his habitual residence.

## CHAPTER III
### Gainful Employment

*Wage-earning Employment*

*Article* 17

1. The Contracting States shall accord to stateless persons lawfully staying in their territory treatment as favourable as possible and, in any event, not less favourable than that accorded to aliens generally in the same circumstances, as regards the right to engage in wage-earning employment.

2. The Contracting States shall give sympathetic consideration to assimilating the rights of all stateless persons with regard to wage-earning employment to those of nationals, and in particular of those stateless persons who have entered their territory pursuant to programmes of labour recruitment or under immigration schemes.

*Self-employment*

*Article* 18

The Contracting States shall accord to a stateless person lawfully in their territory treatment as favourable as possible and, in any event, not less favourable than that accorded to aliens generally in the same circumstances, as regards the right to engage on his own account in agriculture, industry, handicrafts and commerce and to establish commercial and industrial companies.

*Liberal Professions*

*Article* 19

Each Contracting State shall accord to stateless persons lawfully staying in their territory who hold diplomas recognized by the competent authorities of that State, and who are desirous of practising a liberal profession, treatment as favourable as possible and, in any event, not less favourable than that accorded to aliens generally in the same circumstances.

## CHAPTER IV
### Welfare

*Rationing*

*Article* 20

Where a rationing system exists, which applies to the population at large and regulates the general distribution of products in short supply, stateless persons shall be accorded the same treatment as nationals.

*Housing*

*Article* 21

As regards housing, the Contracting States, in so far as the matter is regulated by laws or regulations or is subject to the control of public authorities, shall accord to stateless persons lawfully staying in their territory treatment as favourable as possible and, in any event, not less favourable than that accorded to aliens generally in the same circumstances.

*Public Education*

*Article* 22

1. The Contracting States shall accord to stateless persons the same treatment as is accorded to nationals with respect to elementary education.
2. The Contracting States shall accord to stateless persons treatment as favourable as possible and, in any event, not less favourable than that accorded to aliens generally in the same circumstances, with respect to education other than elementary education and, in particular, as regards access to studies, the recognition of foreign school certificates, diplomas and degrees, the remission of fees and charges and the award of scholarships.

*Public Relief*

*Article* 23

The Contracting States shall accord to stateless persons lawfully staying in their territory the same treatment with respect to public relief and assistance as is accorded to their nationals.

### Labour Legislation and Social Security

*Article* 24

1. The Contracting States shall accord to stateless persons lawfully staying in their territory the same treatment as is accorded to nationals in respect of the following matters:

(*a*) In so far as such matters are governed by laws or regulations or are subject to the control of administrative authorities: remuneration, including family allowances where these form part of remuneration, hours of work, overtime arrangements, holidays with pay, restrictions on home work, minimum age of employment, apprenticeship and training, women's work and the work of young persons, and the enjoyment of the benefits of collective bargaining;

(*b*) Social security (legal provisions in respect of employment injury, occupational diseases, maternity, sickness, disability, old age, death, unemployment, family responsibilities and any other contingency which, according to national laws or regulations, is covered by a social security scheme), subject to the following limitations:

(i) There may be appropriate arrangements for the maintenance of acquired rights and rights in course of acquisition;

(ii) National laws or regulations of the country of residence may prescribe special arrangements concerning benefits or portions of benefits which are payable wholly out of public funds, and concerning allowances paid to persons who do not fulfil the contribution conditions prescribed for the award of a normal pension.

2. The right to compensation for the death of a stateless person resulting from employment injury or from occupational disease shall not be affected by the fact that the residence of the beneficiary is outside the territory of the Contracting State.

3. The Contracting States shall extend to stateless persons the benefits of agreements concluded between them, or which may be concluded between them in the future, concerning the maintenance of acquired rights and rights in the process of acquisition in regard to social security, subject only to the conditions which apply to nationals of the States signatory to the agreements in question.

4. The Contracting States will give sympathetic consideration to extending to stateless persons so far as possible the benefits of similar agreements which may at any time be in force between such Contracting States and non-contracting States.

# CHAPTER V
## Administrative Measures

*Administrative Assistance*

*Article* 25

1. When the exercise of a right by a stateless person would normally require the assistance of authorities of a foreign country to whom he cannot have recourse, the Contracting State in whose territory he is residing shall arrange that such assistance be afforded to him by their own authorities.

2. The authority or authorities mentioned in paragraph 1 shall deliver or cause to be delivered under their supervision to stateless persons such documents or certifications as would normally be delivered to aliens by or through their national authorities.

3. Documents or certifications so delivered shall stand in the stead of the official instruments delivered to aliens by or through their national authorities, and shall be given credence in the absence of proof to the contrary.

4. Subject to such exceptional treatment as may be granted to indigent persons, fees may be charged for the services mentioned herein, but such fees shall be moderate and commensurate with those charged to nationals for similar services.

5. The provisions of this article shall be without prejudice to Articles 27 and 28.

*Freedom of Movement*

*Article* 26

Each Contracting State shall accord to stateless persons lawfully in its territory the right to choose their place of residence and to move freely within its territory, subject to any regulations applicable to aliens generally in the same circumstances.

*Identity Papers*

*Article* 27

The Contracting States shall issue identity papers to any stateless person in their territory who does not possess a valid travel document.

*Travel Documents*

*Article* 28

The Contracting States shall issue to stateless persons lawfully staying in their territory travel documents for the purpose of travel outside their territory, unless compelling reasons of national security or public order otherwise require, and the provisions of the Schedule to this Convention shall apply with respect to such documents. The Contracting States may issue such a travel document to any other stateless person in their territory; they shall in particular give sympathetic consideration to the issue of such a travel document to stateless persons in their territory who are unable to obtain a travel document from the country of their lawful residence.

## Fiscal Charges

*Article* 29

1. The Contracting States shall not impose upon stateless persons duties, charges or taxes, of any description whatsoever, other or higher than those which are or may be levied on their nationals in similar situations.

2. Nothing in the above paragraph shall prevent the application to stateless persons of the laws and regulations concerning charges in respect of the issue to aliens of administrative documents including identity papers.

## Transfer of Assets

*Article* 30

1. A Contracting State shall, in conformity with its laws and regulations, permit stateless persons to transfer assets which they have brought into its territory, to another country where they have been admitted for the purpose of resettlement.

2. A Contracting State shall give sympathetic consideration to the application of stateless persons for permission to transfer assets wherever they may be and which are necessary for their resettlement in another country to which they have been admitted.

## Expulsion

*Article* 31

1. The Contracting States shall not expel a stateless person lawfully in their territory save on grounds of national security or public order.

2. The expulsion of such a stateless person shall be only in pursuance of a decision reached in accordance with due process of law. Except where compelling reasons of national security otherwise require, the stateless person shall be allowed to submit evidence to clear himself, and to appeal to and be represented for the purpose before the competent authority or a person or persons specially designated by the competent authority.

3. The Contracting States shall allow such a stateless person a reasonable period within which to seek legal admission into another country. The

Contracting States reserve the right to apply during that period such internal measures as they may deem necessary.

### Naturalization

*Article 32*

The Contracting States shall as far as possible facilitate the assimilation and naturalization of stateless persons. They shall in particular make every effort to expedite naturalization proceedings and to reduce as far as possible the charges and costs of such proceedings.

## CHAPTER VI
### Final Clauses

### Information on National Legislation

*Article 33*

The Contracting States shall communicate to the Secretary-General of the United Nations the laws and regulations which they may adopt to ensure the application of this Convention.

### Settlement of Disputes

*Article 34*

Any dispute between parties to this Convention relating to its interpretation or application, which cannot be settled by other means, shall be referred to the International Court of Justice at the request of any one of the parties to the dispute.

### Signature, Ratification and Accession

*Article 35*

1. This Convention shall be open for signature at the Headquarters of the United Nations until 31 December 1955.
2. It shall be open for signature on behalf of:

   (*a*) Any State Member of the United Nations;
   (*b*) Any other State invited to attend the United Nations Conference on the Status of Stateless Persons; and
   (*c*) Any State to which an invitation to sign or to accede may be addressed by the General Assembly of the United Nations.

3. It shall be ratified and the instruments of ratification shall be deposited with the Secretary-General of the United Nations.
4. It shall be open for accession by the States referred to in paragraph 2 of

this Article. Accession shall be effected by the deposit of an instrument of accession with the Secretary-General of the United Nations.

*Territorial Application Clause*

Article 36

1. Any State may, at the time of signature, ratification or accession, declare that this Convention shall extend to all or any of the territories for the international relations of which it is responsible. Such a declaration shall take effect when the Convention enters into force for the State concerned.

2. At any time thereafter any such extension shall be made by notification addressed to the Secretary-General of the United Nations and shall take effect as from the ninetieth day after the day of receipt by the Secretary-General of the United Nations of this notification, or as from the date of entry into force of the Convention for the State concerned, whichever is the later.

3. With respect to those territories to which this Convention is not extended at the time of signature, ratification or accession, each State concerned shall consider the possibility of taking the necessary steps in order to extend the application of this Convention to such territories, subject, where necessary for constitutional reasons, to the consent of the Governments of such territories.

*Federal Clause*

Article 37

In the case of a Federal or non-unitary State, the following provisions shall apply:

(a) With respect to those Articles of this Convention that come within the legislative jurisdiction of the federal legislative authority, the obligations of the Federal Government shall to this extent be the same as those of Parties which are not Federal States;

(b) With respect to those Articles of this Convention that come within the legislative jurisdiction of constituent States, provinces or cantons which are not, under the constitutional system of the Federation, bound to take legislative action, the Federal Government shall bring such articles with a favourable recommendation to the notice of the appropriate authorities of States, provinces or cantons at the earliest possible moment.

(c) A Federal State Party to this Convention shall, at the request of any other Contracting State transmitted through the Secretary-General of the United Nations, supply a statement of the law and practice of the Federation and its constituent units in regard to any particular provision of the Convention showing the extent to which effect has been given to that provision by legislative or other action.

*Reservations*

*Article* 38

1. At the time of signature, ratification or accession, any State may make reservations to articles of the Convention other than to Articles 1, 3, 4, 16 (1) and 33 to 42 inclusive.

2. Any State making a reservation in accordance with paragraph 1 of this article may at any time withdraw the reservation by a communication to that effect addressed to the Secretary-General of the United Nations.

*Entry into Force*

*Article* 39

1. This Convention shall come into force on the ninetieth day following the day of deposit of the sixth instrument of ratification or accession.

2. For each State ratifying or acceding to the Convention after the deposit of the sixth instrument of ratification or accession, the Convention shall enter into force on the ninetieth day following the date of deposit by such State of its instrument of ratification or accession.

*Denunciation*

*Article* 40

1. Any Contracting State may denounce this Convention at any time by a notification addressed to the Secretary-General of the United Nations.

2. Such denunciation shall take effect for the Contracting State concerned one year from the date upon which it is received by the Secretary-General of the United Nations.

3. Any State which has made a declaration or notification under Article 36 may, at any time thereafter, by a notification to the Secretary-General of the United Nations, declare that the Convention shall cease to extend to such territory one year after the date of receipt of the notification by the Secretary-General.

*Revision*

*Article* 41

1. Any Contracting State may request revision of this Convention at any time by a notification addressed to the Secretary-General of the United Nations.

2. The General Assembly of the United Nations shall recommend the steps, if any, to be taken in respect of such request.

*Notifications by the Secretary-General of the United Nations*

*Article* 42

The Secretary-General of the United Nations shall inform all Members of the United Nations and non-Member States referred to in Article 35:

(*a*)  Of signatures, ratifications and accessions in accordance with Article 35;

(*b*)  Of declarations and notifications in accordance with Article 36;

(*c*)  Of reservations and withdrawals in accordance with Article 38;

(*d*)  Of the date on which this Convention will come into force in accordance with Article 30;

(*e*)  Of denunciations and notifications in accordance with Article 40;

(*f*)  Of requests for revision in accordance with Article 41;

*In faith whereof* the undersigned, duly authorized, have signed this Convention on behalf of their respective Governments.

*Done* at New York, this twenty-eighth day of September, one thousand nine hundred and fifty-four, in a single copy, of which the English, French and Spanish texts are equally authentic and which shall remain deposited in the archives of the United Nations, and certified true copies of which shall be delivered to all Members of the United Nations and to the non-Member States referred to in Article 35.

## Schedule

### *Paragraph* 1

1. The travel document referred to in Article 28 of this Convention shall indicate that the holder is a stateless person under the terms of the Convention of 28 September 1954.

2. The document shall be made out in at least two languages, one of which shall be English or French.

3. The Contracting States will consider the desirability of adopting the model travel document attached hereto.

### *Paragraph* 2

Subject to the regulations obtaining in the country of issue, children may be included in the travel document of a parent or, in exceptional circumstances, of another adult.

### *Paragraph* 3

The fees charged for issue of the document shall not exceed the lowest scale of charges for national passports.

### Paragraph 4

Save in special or exceptional cases, the document shall be made valid for the largest possible number of countries.

### Paragraph 5

The document shall have a validity of not less than three months and not more than two years.

### Paragraph 6

1. The renewal or extension of the validity of the document is a matter for the authority which issued it, so long as the holder has not established lawful residence in another territory and resides lawfully in the territory of the said authority. The issue of a new document is, under the same conditions, a matter for the authority which issued the former document.

2. Diplomatic or consular authorities may be authorized to extend, for a period not exceeding six months, the validity of travel documents issued by their Governments.

3. The Contracting States shall give sympathetic consideration to renewing or extending the validity of travel documents or issuing new documents to stateless persons no longer lawfully resident in their territory who are unable to obtain a travel document from the country of their lawful residence.

### Paragraph 7

The Contracting States shall recognize the validity of the documents issued in accordance with the provisions of Article 28 of this Convention.

### Paragraph 8

The competent authorities of the country to which the stateless person desires to proceed shall, if they are prepared to admit him and if a visa is required, affix a visa on the document of which he is the holder.

### Paragraph 9

1. The Contracting States undertake to issue transit visas to stateless persons who have obtained visas for a territory of final destination.

2. The issue of such visas may be refused on grounds which would justify refusal of a visa to any alien.

### Paragraph 10

The fees for the issue of exit, entry or transit visas shall not exceed the lowest scale of charges for visas on foreign passports.

### Paragraph 11

When a stateless person has lawfully taken up residence in the territory of another Contracting State, the responsibility for the issue of a new document, under the terms and conditions of Article 28 shall be that of the competent authority of that territory, to which the stateless person shall be entitled to apply.

### Paragraph 12

The authority issuing a new document shall withdraw the old document and shall return it to the country of issue if it is stated in the document that it should be so returned; otherwise it shall withdraw and cancel the document.

### Paragraph 13

1. A travel document issued in accordance with Article 28 of this Convention shall, unless it contains a statement to the contrary, entitle the holder to re-enter the territory of the issuing State at any time during the period of its validity. In any case the period during which the holder may return to the country issuing the document shall not be less than three months, except when the country to which the stateless person proposes to travel does not insist on the travel document according the right of re-entry.

2. Subject to the provisions of the preceding sub-paragraph, a Contracting State may require the holder of the document to comply with such formalities as may be prescribed in regard to exit from or return to its territory.

### Paragraph 14

Subject only to the terms of paragraph 13, the provisions of this Schedule in no way affect the laws and regulations governing the conditions of admission to, transit through, residence and establishment in, and departure from, the territories of the Contracting States.

### Paragraph 15

Neither the issue of the document nor the entries made thereon determine or affect the status of the holder, particularly as regards nationality.

### Paragraph 16

The issue of the document does not in any way entitle the holder to the protection of the diplomatic or consular authorities of the country of issue, and does not *ipso facto* confer on these authorities a right of protection.

[Model Travel Document omitted.]

## XII. CONVENTION ON THE REDUCTION
## OF STATELESSNESS, 1961

The Convention was adopted by the U.N. Conference on the Elimination or Reduction of Future Statelessness, 24 March–18 April 1959 and 15–28 August 1961. The official source of the text is U.N. Document A/CONF. 9/15, 1961. The Convention entered into force on 13 December 1975. Fifteen States have become parties.

### TEXT

*The Contracting States,*

*Acting* in pursuance of resolution 896 (IX), adopted by the General Assembly of the United Nations on 4 December 1954,

*Considering* it desirable to reduce statelessness by international agreement,

*Have agreed* as follows:

*Article 1*

1. A Contracting State shall grant its nationality to a person born in its territory who would otherwise be stateless. Such nationality shall be granted:

(*a*) At birth, by operation of law, or

(*b*) Upon an application being lodged with the appropriate authority, by or on behalf of the person concerned, in the manner prescribed by the national law. Subject to the provisions of paragraph 2 of this Article, no such application may be rejected.

A Contracting State which provides for the grant of its nationality in accordance with sub-paragraph (*b*) of this paragraph may also provide for the grant of its nationality by operation of law at such age and subject to such conditions as may be prescribed by the national law.

2. A Contracting State may make the grant of its nationality in accordance with sub-paragraph (*b*) of paragraph 1 of this Article subject to one or more of the following conditions:

(*a*) That the application is lodged during a period, fixed by the Contracting State, beginning not later than at the age of eighteen years and ending not earlier than at the age of twenty-one years, so, however, that the person concerned shall be allowed at least one year during which he may himself make the application without having to obtain legal authorization to do so;

(*b*) That the person concerned has habitually resided in the territory of the Contracting State for such period as may be fixed by that State, not exceeding five years immediately preceding the lodging of the application nor ten years in all;

(c) That the person concerned has neither been convicted of an offence against national security nor has been sentenced to imprisonment for a term of five years or more on a criminal charge;

(d) That the person concerned has always been stateless.

3. Notwithstanding the provisions of paragraphs 1 (b) and 2 of this Article, a child born in wedlock in the territory of a Contracting State, whose mother has the nationality of that State, shall acquire at birth that nationality if it otherwise would be stateless.

4. A Contracting State shall grant its nationality to a person who would otherwise be stateless and who is unable to acquire the nationality of the Contracting State in whose territory he was born because he has passed the age for lodging his application or has not fulfilled the required residence conditions, if the nationality of one of his parents at the time of the person's birth was that of the Contracting State first above mentioned. If his parents did not possess the same nationality at the time of his birth, the question whether the nationality of the person concerned should follow that of the father or that of the mother shall be determined by the national law of such Contracting State. If application for such nationality is required, the application shall be made to the appropriate authority by or on behalf of the applicant in the manner prescribed by the national law. Subject to the provisions of paragraph 5 of this Article, such application shall not be refused.

5. The Contracting State may make the grant of its nationality in accordance with the provisions of paragraph 4 of this Article subject to one or more of the following conditions:

(a) That the application is lodged before the applicant reaches an age, being not less than twenty-three years, fixed by the Contracting State;

(b) That the person concerned has habitually resided in the territory of the Contracting State for such period immediately preceding the lodging of the application, not exceeding three years, as may be fixed by that State;

(c) That the person concerned has always been stateless.

*Article 2*

A foundling found in the territory of a Contracting State shall, in the absence of proof to the contrary, be considered to have been born within that territory of parents possessing the nationality of that State.

*Article 3*

For the purpose of determining the obligations of Contracting States under this convention, birth on a ship or in an aircraft shall be deemed to have taken place in the territory of the State whose flag the ship flies or in the territory of the State in which the aircraft is registered, as the case may be.

*Article* 4

1. A Contracting State shall grant its nationality to a person, not born in the territory of a Contracting State, who would otherwise be stateless, if the nationality of one of his parents at the time of the person's birth was that of that State. If his parents did not possess the same nationality at the time of his birth, the question whether the nationality of the person concerned should follow that of the father or that of the mother shall be determined by the national law of such Contracting State. Nationality granted in accordance with the provisions of this paragraph shall be granted:

(*a*) At birth, by operation of law, or

(*b*) Upon an application being lodged with the appropriate authority, by or on behalf of the person concerned, in the manner prescribed by the national law. Subject to the provisions of paragraph 2 of this Article, no such application may be rejected.

2. A Contracting State may make the grant of its nationality in accordance with the provisions of paragraph 1 of this Article subject to one or more of the following conditions:

(*a*) That the application is lodged before the applicant reaches an age, being not less than twenty-three years, fixed by the Contracting State;

(*b*) That the person concerned has habitually resided in the territory of the Contracting State for such period immediately preceding the lodging of the application, not exceeding three years, as may be fixed by the State;

(*c*) That the person concerned has not been convicted of an offence against national security;

(*d*) That the person concerned has always been stateless.

*Article* 5

1. If the law of a Contracting State entails loss of nationality as a consequence of any change in the personal status of a person such as marriage, termination of marriage, legitimation, recognition or adoption, such loss shall be conditional upon possession or acquisition of another nationality.

2. If, under the law of a Contracting State, a child born out of wedlock loses the nationality of that State in consequence of a recognition of affiliation, he shall be given an opportunity to recover that nationality by written application to the appropriate authority, and the conditions governing such application shall not be more rigorous than those laid down in paragraph 2 of Article 1 of this Convention.

*Article* 6

If the law of a Contracting State provides for loss of its nationality by a person's spouse or children as a consequence of that person losing or being deprived of that nationality, such loss shall be conditional upon their possession or acquisition of another nationality.

*Article* 7

1. (*a*) If the law of a Contracting State permits renunciation of nationality, such renunciation shall not result in loss of nationality unless the person concerned possesses or acquires another nationality.

(*b*) The provisions of sub-paragraph (*a*) of this paragraph shall not apply where their application would be inconsistent with the principles stated in Articles 13 and 14 of the Universal Declaration of Human Rights approved on 10 December 1948 by the General Assembly of the United Nations.

2. A national of a Contracting State who seeks naturalization in a foreign country shall not lose his nationality unless he acquires or has been accorded assurance of acquiring the nationality of that foreign country.

3. Subject to the provisions of paragraphs 4 and 5 of this Article, a national of a Contracting State shall not lose his nationality, so as to become stateless, on the ground of departure, residence abroad, failure to register or on any similar ground.

4. A naturalized person may lose his nationality on account of residence abroad for a period, not less than seven consecutive years, specified by the law of the Contracting State concerned if he fails to declare to the appropriate authority his intention to retain his nationality.

5. In that case of a national of a Contracting State, born outside its territory, the law of that State may make the retention of its nationality after the expiry of one year from his attaining his majority conditional upon residence at that time in the territory of the State or registration with the appropriate authority.

6. Except in the circumstances mentioned in this Article, a person shall not lose the nationality of a Contracting State, if such loss would render him stateless, notwithstanding that such loss is not expressly prohibited by any other provision of this convention.

*Article* 8

1. A Contracting State shall not deprive a person of its nationality if such deprivation would render him stateless.

2. Notwithstanding the provisions of paragraph 1 of this Article, a person may be deprived of the nationality of a Contracting State:

(*a*) In the circumstances in which, under paragraphs 4 and 5 of Article 7, it is permissible that a person should lose his nationality;

(*b*) Where the nationality has been obtained by misrepresentation or fraud.

3. Notwithstanding the provisions of paragraph 1 of this Article, a Contracting State may retain the right to deprive a person of his nationality, if at the time of signature, ratification or accession it specifies its retention of such right on one or more of the following grounds, being grounds existing in its national law at that time:

(a) That, inconsistently with his duty of loyalty to the Contracting State, the person
  (i) has, in disregard of an express prohibition by the Contracting State rendered or continued to render services to, or received or continued to receive emoluments from, another State, or
  (ii) has conducted himself in a manner seriously prejudicial to the vital interests of the State;

(b) That the person has taken an oath, or made a formal declaration, of allegiance to another State, or given definite evidence of his determination to repudiate his allegiance to the Contracting State.

4. A Contracting State shall not exercise a power of deprivation permitted by paragraphs 2 or 3 of this Article except in accordance with law, which shall provide for the person concerned the right to a fair hearing by a court or other independent body.

*Article* 9

A Contracting State may not deprive any person or group of persons of their nationality on racial, ethnic, religious or political grounds.

*Article* 10

1. Every treaty between Contracting States providing for the transfer of territory shall include provisions designed to secure that no person shall become stateless as a result of the transfer. A Contracting State shall use its best endeavours to secure that any such treaty made by it with a State which is not a party to this convention includes such provisions.

2. In the absence of such provisions a Contracting State to which territory is transferred or which otherwise acquires territory shall confer its nationality on such persons as would otherwise become stateless as a result of the transfer or acquisition.

*Article* 11

The Contracting States shall promote the establishment within the framework of the United Nations, as soon as may be after the deposit of the sixth instrument of ratification or accession, of a body to which a person claiming the benefit of this convention may apply for the examination of his claim and for assistance in presenting it to the appropriate authority.

*Article* 12

1. In relation to a Contracting State which does not, in accordance with the provisions of paragraph 1 of Article 1 or of Article 4 of this Convention, grant its nationality at birth by operation of law, the provisions of paragraph 1 of Article 4, as the case may be, shall apply to persons born before as well as to persons born after the entry into force of this convention.

2. The provisions of paragraph 4 of Article 1 of this convention shall apply to persons born before as well as to persons born after its entry into force.

3. The provisions of Article 2 of this convention shall apply only to foundlings found in the territory of a Contracting State after the entry into force of the convention for that State.

*Article* 13

This convention shall not be construed as affecting any provisions more conducive to the reduction of statelessness which may be contained in the law of any Contracting State now or hereafter in force, or may be contained in any other convention, treaty or agreement now or hereafter in force between two or more Contracting States.

*Article* 14

Any dispute between Contracting States concerning the interpretation or application of this convention which cannot be settled by other means shall be submitted to the International Court of Justice at the request of any one of the parties to the dispute.

*Article* 15

1. This convention shall apply to all non-self-governing, trust, colonial and other non-metropolitan territories for the international relations of which any Contracting State is responsible; the Contracting State concerned shall, subject to the provisions of paragraph 2 of this Article, at the time of signature, ratification or accession, declare the non-metropolitan territory or territories to which the convention shall apply *ipso facto* as a result of such signature, ratification or accession.

2. In any case in which, for the purpose of nationality, a non-metropolitan territory is not treated as one with the metropolitan territory, or in any case in which the previous consent of a non-metropolitan territory is required by the constitutional laws or practices of the Contracting State or of the non-metropolitan territory for the application of the convention to that territory, that Contracting State shall endeavour to secure the needed consent of the non-metropolitan territory within the period of twelve months from the date of signature of the convention by that Contracting State, and when such consent has been obtained the Contracting State shall notify the Secretary-General of the United Nations. This convention shall apply to the territory

or territories named in such notification from the date of its receipt by the Secretary-General.

3. After the expiry of the twelve-month period mentioned in paragraph 2 of this Article, the Contracting States concerned shall inform the Secretary-General of the results of the consultations with those non-metropolitan territories for whose international relations they are responsible and whose consent to the application of this convention may have been withheld.

*Article* 16

1. This convention shall be open for signature at the Headquarters of the United Nations from 30 August 1961 to 31 May 1962.

2. This convention shall be open for signature on behalf of:

> (*a*) Any State Member of the United Nations;
> (*b*) Any other State invited to attend the United Nations Conference on the Elimination or Reduction of Future Statelessness;
> (*c*) Any State to which an invitation to sign or to accede may be addressed by the General Assembly of the United Nations.

3. This convention shall be ratified and the instruments of ratification shall be deposited with the Secretary-General of the United Nations.

4. This convention shall be open for accession by the States referred to in paragraph 2 of this Article. Accession shall be effected by the deposit of an instrument of accession with the Secretary-General of the United Nations.

*Article* 17

1. At the time of signature, ratification or accession any State may make a reservation in respect of Articles 11, 14 or 15.

2. No other reservations to this convention shall be admissible.

*Article* 18

1. This convention shall enter into force two years after the date of the deposit of the sixth instrument of ratification or accession.

2. For each State ratifying or acceding to this convention after the deposit of the sixth instrument of ratification or accession, it shall enter into force on the ninetieth day after the deposit by such State of its instrument of ratification or accession or on the date on which this convention enters into force in accordance with the provisions of paragraph 1 of this Article, whichever is the later.

*Article* 19

1. Any Contracting State may denounce this convention at any time by a written notification addressed to the Secretary-General of the United Nations. Such denunciation shall take effect for the Contracting State

concerned one year after the date of its receipt by the Secretary-General.

2. In cases where, in accordance with the provisions of Article 15, this convention has become applicable to a non-metropolitan territory of a Contracting State, that State may at any time thereafter, with the consent of the territory concerned, give notice to the Secretary-General of the United Nations denouncing this convention separately in respect of that territory. The denunciation shall take effect one year after the date of the receipt of such notice by the Secretary-General, who shall notify all other Contracting States of such notice and the date of receipt thereof.

*Article* 20

1. The Secretary-General of the United Nations shall notify all Members of the United Nations and the non-member States referred to in Article 16 of the following particulars:

- (*a*) Signatures, ratifications and accessions under Article 16;
- (*b*) Reservations under Article 17;
- (*c*) The date upon which this convention enters into force in pursuance of Article 18;
- (*d*) Denunciations under Article 19.

2. The Secretary-General of the United Nations shall, after the deposit of the sixth instrument of ratification or accession at the latest, bring to the attention of the General Assembly the question of the establishment, in accordance with Article 11, of such a body as therein mentioned.

*Article* 21

This convention shall be registered by the Secretary-General of the United Nations on the date of its entry into force.

*In witness whereof* the undersigned Plenipotentiaries have signed this Convention.

*Done* at New York, this thirtieth day of August, one thousand nine hundred and sixty-one, in a single copy, of which the Chinese, English, French, Russian and Spanish texts are equally authentic and which shall be deposited in the archives of the United Nations, and certified copies of which shall be delivered by the Secretary-General of the United Nations to all Members of the United Nations and to the non-member States referred to in Article 16 of this Convention.

# XIII. CONVENTION ON THE POLITICAL RIGHTS OF WOMEN, 1953

The Convention was opened for signature on 31 March 1953 and entered into force on 7 July 1954. Ninety-seven States have become parties. For the text in various languages: *United Nations Treaty Series*, Vol. 193, p. 135; *U.K. Treaty Series*, No. 101 (1967), Cmnd. 3449.

See, further, *Convention on the Political Rights of Women: History and Commentary*, ST/SOA/27, U.N. Sales No. 1955, IV, 17; and *Yearbook on Human Rights*, 1948, p. 439 (Bogota Convention).

## TEXT

*The Contracting Parties,*

*Desiring* to implement the principle of equality of rights for men and women contained in the Charter of the United Nations,

*Recognizing* that everyone has the right to take part in the government of his country, directly or indirectly through freely chosen representatives, and has the right to equal access to public service in his country, and desiring to equalize the status of men and women in the enjoyment and exercise of political rights, in accordance with the provisions of the Charter of the United Nations and of the Universal Declaration of Human Rights,

*Having resolved* to conclude a Convention for this purpose,

*Hereby agree* as hereinafter provided:

*Article I*

Women shall be entitled to vote in all elections on equal terms with men, without any discrimination.

*Article II*

Women shall be eligible for election to all publicly elected bodies, established by national law, on equal terms with men, without any discrimination.

*Article III*

Women shall be entitled to hold public office and to exercise all public functions, established by national law, on equal terms with men, without any discrimination.

*Article IV*

1. This Convention shall be open for signature on behalf of any Member of the United Nations and also on behalf of any other State to which an invitation has been addressed by the General Assembly.

2. This Convention shall be ratified and the instruments of ratification shall be deposited with the Secretary-General of the United Nations.

*Article V*

1. This Convention shall be open for accession to all States referred to in paragraph I of Article IV.

2. Accession shall be effected by the deposit of an instrument of accession with the Secretary-General of the United Nations.

*Article VI*

1. This Convention shall come into force on the ninetieth day following the date of deposit of the sixth instrument of ratification or accession.

2. For each State ratifying or acceding to the Convention after the deposit of the sixth instrument of ratification or accession the Convention shall enter into force on the ninetieth day after deposit by such State of its instrument of ratification or accession.

*Article VII*

In the event that any State submits a reservation to any of the Articles of this Convention at the time of signature, ratification or accession, the Secretary-General shall communicate the text of the reservation to all States which are or may become parties to this Convention. Any State which objects to the reservation may, within a period of ninety days from the date of the said communication (or upon the date of its becoming a party to the Convention), notify the Secretary-General that it does not accept it. In such case, the Convention shall not enter into force as between such State and the State making the reservation.

*Article VIII*

1. Any State may denounce this Convention by written notification to the Secretary-General of the United Nations. Denunciation shall take effect one year after the date of receipt of the notification by the Secretary-General.

2. This Convention shall cease to be in force as from the date when the denunciation which reduces the number of parties to less than six becomes effective.

*Article IX*

Any dispute which may arise between any two or more Contracting States concerning the interpretation or application of this Convention which is not settled by negotiation, shall at the request of any one of the parties to the dispute be referred to the International Court of Justice for decision unless they agree to another mode of settlement.

*Article X*

The Secretary-General of the United Nations shall notify all Members of the United Nations and the non-member States contemplated in paragraph I of Article IV of this Convention of the following:

(*a*) Signatures and instruments of ratification received in accordance with Article IV;

(*b*) Instruments of accession received in accordance with Article V;

(*c*) The date upon which this Convention enters into force in accordance with Article VI;

(*d*) Communications and notifications received in accordance with Article VII;

(*e*) Notifications of denunciation received in accordance with paragraph 1 of Article VIII;

(*f*) Abrogation in accordance with paragraph 2 of Article VIII.

*Article XI*

1. This Convention, of which the Chinese, English, French, Russian and Spanish texts shall be equally authentic, shall be deposited in the archives of the United Nations.

2. The Secretary-General of the United Nations shall transmit a certified copy to all Members of the United Nations and to the non-member States contemplated in paragraph 1 of Article IV.

*In faith whereof* the undersigned, being duly authorized thereto by their respective Governments, have signed the present Convention, opened for signature at New York, on the thirty-first day of March, one thousand nine hundred and fifty-three.

## XIV. DECLARATION ON THE ELIMINATION OF ALL FORMS OF INTOLERANCE AND OF DISCRIMINATION BASED ON RELIGION OR BELIEF, 1981

This Declaration was adopted without vote by the General Assembly of the United Nations on 25 November 1981 (Resolution 36/55). For the background see *Yearbook of the United Nations*, 1981, pp. 879–83. The Declaration was prepared by the Human Rights Commission of the Economic and Social Council. For an earlier proposal of a Draft Convention on the subject see the second edition of this work, p. 111.

### TEXT

*The General Assembly*,

*Considering* that one of the basic principles of the Charter of the United Nations is that of the dignity and equality inherent in all human beings, and that all Member States have pledged themselves to take joint and separate action in co-operation with the Organization to promote and encourage universal respect for and observance of human rights and fundamental freedoms for all, without distinction as to race, sex, language or religion,

*Considering* that the Universal Declaration of Human Rights and the International Covenants on Human Rights proclaim the principles of non-discrimination and equality before the law and the right to freedom of thought, conscience, religion and belief,

*Considering* that the disregard and infringement of human rights and fundamental freedoms, in particular of the right to freedom of thought, conscience, religion or whatever belief, have brought, directly or indirectly, wars and great suffering to mankind, especially where they serve as a means of foreign interference in the internal affairs of other States and amount to kindling hatred between peoples and nations,

*Considering* that religion or belief, for anyone who professes either, is one of the fundamental elements in his conception of life and that freedom of religion or belief should be fully respected and guaranteed,

*Considering* that it is essential to promote understanding, tolerance and respect in matters relating to freedom of religion and belief and to ensure that the use of religion or belief for ends inconsistent with the Charter of the United Nations, other relevant instruments of the United Nations and the purposes and principles of the present Declaration is inadmissible,

*Convinced* that freedom of religion and belief should also contribute to the attainment of the goals of world peace, social justice and friendship among peoples and to the elimination of ideologies or practices of colonialism and racial discrimination,

*Noting with satisfaction* the adoption of several, and the coming into force of some, conventions, under the aegis of the United Nations and of the specialized agencies, for the elimination of various forms of discrimination,

*Concerned* by manifestations of intolerance and by the existence of discrimination in matters of religion or belief still in evidence in some areas of the world,

*Resolved* to adopt all necessary measures for the speedy elimination of such intolerance in all its forms and manifestations and to prevent and combat discrimination on the ground of religion or belief,

*Proclaims* this Declaration on the Elimination of All Forms of Intolerance and of Discrimination Based on Religion or Belief:

*Article* 1

1. Everyone shall have the right to freedom of thought, conscience and religion. This right shall include freedom to have a religion or whatever belief of his choice, and freedom, either individually or in community with others and in public or private, to manifest his religion or belief in worship, observance, practice and teaching.

2. No one shall be subject to coercion which would impair his freedom to have a religion or belief of his choice.

3. Freedom to manifest one's religion or beliefs may be subject only to such limitations as are prescribed by law and are necessary to protect public safety, order, health or morals or the fundamental rights and freedoms of others.

*Article* 2

1. No one shall be subject to discrimination by any State, institution, group of persons, or person on grounds of religion or other beliefs.

2. For the purposes of the present Declaration, the expression "intolerance and discrimination based on religion or belief" means any distinction, exclusion, restriction or preference based on religion or belief and having as its purpose or as its effect nullification or impairment of the recognition, enjoyment or exercise of human rights and fundamental freedoms on an equal basis.

*Article* 3

Discrimination between human beings on grounds of religion or belief constitutes an affront to human dignity and a disavowal of the principles of the Charter of the United Nations, and shall be condemned as a violation of the human rights and fundamental freedoms proclaimed in the Universal Declaration of Human Rights and enunciated in detail in the International Covenants on Human Rights, and as an obstacle to friendly and peaceful relations between nations.

*Article* 4

1. All States shall take effective measures to prevent and eliminate discrimination on the grounds of religion or belief in the recognition, exercise and enjoyment of human rights and fundamental freedoms in all fields of civil, economic, political, social and cultural life.

2. All States shall make all efforts to enact or rescind legislation where necessary to prohibit any such discrimination, and to take all appropriate measures to combat intolerance on the grounds of religion or other beliefs in this matter.

*Article* 5

1. The parents or, as the case may be, the legal guardians of the child have the right to organize the life within the family in accordance with their religion or belief and bearing in mind the moral education in which they believe the child should be brought up.

2. Every child shall enjoy the right to have access to education in the matter of religion or belief in accordance with the wishes of his parents or, as the case may be, legal guardians, and shall not be compelled to receive teaching on religion or belief against the wishes of his parents or legal guardians, the best interests of the child being the guiding principle.

3. The child shall be protected from any form of discrimination on the ground of religion or belief. He shall be brought up in a spirit of understanding, tolerance, friendship among peoples, peace and universal brotherhood, respect for freedom of religion or belief of others, and in full consciousness that his energy and talents should be devoted to the service of his fellow men.

4. In the case of a child who is not under the care either of his parents or of legal guardians, due account shall be taken of their expressed wishes or of any other proof of their wishes in the matter of religion or belief, the best interests of the child being the guiding principle.

5. Practices of a religion or beliefs in which a child is brought up must not be injurious to his physical or mental health or to his full development, taking into account Article 1, paragraph 3, of the present Declaration.

*Article* 6

In accordance with Article 1 of the present Declaration, and subject to the provisions of Article 1, paragraph 3, the right to freedom of thought, conscience, religion or belief shall include, *inter alia*, the following freedoms:

- (*a*) To worship or assemble in connection with a religion or belief, and to establish and maintain places for these purposes;
- (*b*) To establish and maintain appropriate charitable or humanitarian institutions;

(c) To make, acquire and use to an adequate extent the necessary articles and materials related to the rites or customs of a religion or belief;

(d) To write, issue and disseminate relevant publications in these areas;

(e) To teach a religion or belief in places suitable for these purposes;

(f) To solicit and receive voluntary financial and other contributions from individuals and institutions;

(g) To train, appoint, elect or designate by succession appropriate leaders called for by the requirements and standards of any religion or belief;

(h) To observe days of rest and to celebrate holidays and ceremonies in accordance with the precepts of one's religion or belief;

(i) To establish and maintain communications with individuals and communities in matters of religion and belief at the national and international levels.

*Article* 7

The rights and freedoms set forth in the present Declaration shall be accorded in national legislation in such a manner that everyone shall be able to avail himself of such rights and freedoms in practice.

*Article* 8

Nothing in the present Declaration shall be construed as restricting or derogating from any right defined in the Universal Declaration of Human Rights and the International Covenants on Human Rights.

## PART TWO

# IMPLEMENTATION AND STANDARD-SETTING IN CONVENTIONS SPONSORED BY THE UNITED NATIONS

## INTRODUCTION

THE documents that follow are concerned with standard-setting, and at the same time provide for measures of implementation apart from the ordinary working of the national legal systems of individual States parties to the conventions. The International Covenants are intended to supersede the Universal Declaration of Human Rights, since the Covenants have undoubted legal force as treaties for the parties to them. On the Covenants see Ganji, *International Protection of Human Rights*, 1962; Schwelb, *American Journal of International Law*, 62 (1968), p. 827; Schwelb, in Eide and Schou (eds.), *International Protection of Human Rights*, 1967, p. 103; Capotorti, in the same work, p. 131; Schreiber, *Recueil des cours* (Hague Academy of International Law), Vol. 45 (1975, II), p. 299.

## I. INTERNATIONAL COVENANT ON ECONOMIC, SOCIAL, AND CULTURAL RIGHTS, 1966

This appears in the annex to a resolution adopted by the United Nations General Assembly on 16 December 1966. The Covenant entered into force on 3 January 1976; and ninety-nine States have become parties.

*TEXT*

### Preamble

*The States Parties to the present Covenant,*

Considering that, in accordance with the principles proclaimed in the Charter of the United Nations, recognition of the inherent dignity and of the equal and inalienable rights of all members of the human family is the foundation of freedom, justice and peace in the world,

*Recognizing* that these rights derive from the inherent dignity of the human person,

*Recognizing* that, in accordance with the Universal Declaration of Human Rights, the ideal of free human beings enjoying freedom from fear and want can only be achieved if conditions are created whereby everyone may enjoy his economic, social and cultural rights, as well as his civil and political rights,

*Considering* the obligation of States under the Charter of the United Nations to promote universal respect for, and observance of, human rights and freedoms,

*Realizing* that the individual, having duties to other individuals and to the community to which he belongs, is under a responsibility to strive for the promotion and observance of the rights recognized in the present Covenant,

*Agree* upon the following articles:

## PART I

*Article* 1

1. All peoples have the right of self-determination. By virtue of that right they freely determine their political status and freely pursue their economic, social and cultural development.

2. All peoples may, for their own ends, freely dispose of their natural wealth and resources without prejudice to any obligations arising out of international economic co-operation, based upon the principle of mutual benefit, and international law. In no case may a people be deprived of its own means of subsistence.

3. The States Parties to the present Covenant, including those having responsibility for the administration of Non-Self-Governing and Trust Territories, shall promote the realization of the right of self-determination, and shall respect that right, in conformity with the provisions of the Charter of the United Nations.

## PART II

*Article* 2

1. Each State Party to the present Covenant undertakes to take steps, individually and through international assistance and co-operation, especially economic and technical, to the maximum of its available resources, with a view to achieving progressively the full realization of the rights recognized in the present Covenant by all appropriate means, including particularly the adoption of legislative measures.

2. The States Parties to the present Covenant undertake to guarantee that the rights enunciated in the present Covenant will be exercised without discrimination of any kind as to race, colour, sex, language, religion, political or other opinion, national or social origin, property, birth or other status.

3. Developing countries, with due regard to human rights and their national economy, may determine to what extent they would guarantee the economic rights recognized in the present Covenant to non-nationals.

*Article* 3

The States Parties to the present Covenant undertake to ensure the equal right of men and women to the enjoyment of all economic, social and cultural rights set forth in the present Covenant.

*Article* 4

The States Parties to the present Covenant recognize that, in the enjoyment of those rights provided by the State in conformity with the present Covenant, the State may subject such rights only to such limitations as are determined by law only in so far as this may be compatible with the nature of these rights and solely for the purpose of promoting the general welfare in a democratic society.

*Article* 5

1. Nothing in the present Covenant may be interpreted as implying for any State, group or person any right to engage in any activity or to perform any act aimed at the destruction of any of the rights or freedoms recognized herein, or at their limitation to a greater extent than is provided for in the present Covenant.

2. No restriction upon or derogation from any of the fundamental human rights recognized or existing in any country in virtue of law, conventions, regulations or custom shall be admitted on the pretext that the present Covenant does not recognize such rights or that it recognizes them to a lesser extent.

## PART III

*Article* 6

1. The States Parties to the present Covenant recognize the right to work, which includes the right of everyone to the opportunity to gain his living by work which he freely chooses or accepts, and will take appropriate steps to safeguard this right.

2. The steps to be taken by a State Party to the present Covenant to achieve the full realization of this right shall include technical and vocational guidance and training programmes, policies and techniques to achieve steady economic, social and cultural development and full and productive employment under conditions safeguarding fundamental political and economic freedoms to the individual.

*Article* 7

The States Parties to the present Covenant recognize the right of everyone to the enjoyment of just and favourable conditions of work, which ensure, in particular:

(*a*) Remuneration which provides all workers, as a minimum with:
  (i) Fair wages and equal remuneration for work of equal value without distinction of any kind, in particular women being guaranteed conditions of work not inferior to those enjoyed by men, with equal pay for equal work;
  (ii) A decent living for themselves and their families in accordance with the provisions of the present Covenant;
(*b*) Safe and healthy working conditions;
(*c*) Equal opportunity for everyone to be promoted in his employment to an appropriate higher level, subject to no considerations other than those of seniority and competence;
(*d*) Rest, leisure and reasonable limitation of working hours and periodic holidays with pay, as well as remuneration for public holidays.

*Article* 8

1. The States Parties to the present Covenant undertake to ensure:

(*a*) The right of everyone to form trade unions and join the trade union of his choice, subject only to the rules of the organization concerned, for the promotion and protection of his economic and social interests. No restrictions may be placed on the exercise of this right other than those prescribed by law and which are necessary in a democratic society in the interests of national security or public order or for the protection of the rights and freedoms of others;

(b) The right of trade unions to establish national federations or confederations and the right of the latter to form or join international trade union organizations;

(c) The right of trade unions to function freely subject to no limitations other than those prescribed by law and which are necessary in a democratic society in the interests of national security or public order or for the protection of the rights and freedoms of others;

(d) The right to strike, provided that it is exercised in conformity with the laws of the particular country.

2. This Article shall not prevent the imposition of lawful restrictions on the exercise of these rights by members of the armed forces or of the police or of the administration of the State.

3. Nothing in this Article shall authorize States Parties to the International Labour Organization Convention of 1948 concerning Freedom of Association and Protection of the Right to Organize to take legislative measures which would prejudice, or apply the law in such a manner as would prejudice, the guarantees provided for in that Convention.

*Article* 9

The States Parties to the present Covenant recognize the right of everyone to social security, including social insurance.

*Article* 10

The States Parties to the present Covenant recognize that:

1. The widest possible protection and assistance should be accorded to the family, which is the natural and fundamental group unit of society, particularly for its establishment and while it is responsible for the care and education of dependent children. Marriage must be entered into with the free consent of the intending spouses.

2. Special protection should be accorded to mothers during a reasonable period before and after childbirth. During such period working mothers should be accorded paid leave or leave with adequate social security benefits.

3. Special measures of protection and assistance should be taken on behalf of all children and young persons without any discrimination for reasons of parentage or other conditions. Children and young persons should be protected from economic and social exploitation. Their employment in work harmful to their morals or health or dangerous to life or likely to

hamper their normal development should be punishable by law. States should also set age limits below which the paid employment of child labour should be prohibited and punishable by law.

*Article* 11

1. The States Parties to the present Covenant recognize the right of everyone to an adequate standard of living for himself and his family, including adequate food, clothing and housing, and to the continuous improvement of living conditions. The States Parties will take appropriate steps to ensure the realization of this right, recognizing to this effect the essential importance of international co-operation based on free consent.

2. The States Parties to the present Covenant, recognizing the fundamental right of everyone to be free from hunger, shall take, individually and through international co-operation, the measures, including specific programmes, which are needed:

(*a*) To improve methods of production, conservation and distribution of food by making full use of technical and scientific knowledge, by disseminating knowledge of the principles of nutrition and by developing or reforming agrarian systems in such a way as to achieve the most efficient development and utilization of natural resources;

(*b*) Taking into account the problems of both food-importing and food-exporting countries, to ensure an equitable distribution of world food supplies in relation to need.

*Article* 12

1. The States Parties to the present Covenant recognize the right of everyone to the enjoyment of the highest attainable standard of physical and mental health.

2. The steps to be taken by the States Parties to the present Covenant to achieve the full realization of this right shall include those necessary for:

(*a*) The provision for the reduction of the stillbirth-rate and of infant mortality and for the healthy development of the child;

(*b*) The improvement of all aspects of environmental and industrial hygiene;

(*c*) The prevention, treatment and control of epidemic, endemic, occupational and other diseases;

(*d*) The creation of conditions which would assure to all medical service and medical attention in the event of sickness.

*Article* 13

1. The States Parties to the present Covenant recognize the right of everyone to education. They agree that education shall be directed to the full

development of the human personality and the sense of its dignity, and shall strengthen the respect for human rights and fundamental freedoms. They further agree that education shall enable all persons to participate effectively in a free society, promote understanding, tolerance and friendship among all nations and all racial, ethnic or religious groups, and further the activities of the United Nations for the maintenance of peace.

2. The States Parties to the present Covenant recognize that, with a view to achieving the full realization of this right:

(a) Primary education shall be compulsory and available free to all;
(b) Secondary education in its different forms, including technical and vocational secondary education, shall be made generally available and accessible to all by every appropriate means, and in particular by the progressive introduction of free education;
(c) Higher education shall be made equally accessible to all, on the basis of capacity, by every appropriate means, and in particular by the progressive introduction of free education;
(d) Fundamental education shall be encouraged or intensified as far as possible for those persons who have not received or completed the whole period of their primary education;
(e) The development of a system of schools at all levels shall be actively pursued, an adequate fellowship system shall be established, and the material conditions of teaching staff shall be continuously improved.

3. The States Parties to the present Covenant undertake to have respect for the liberty of parents and, when applicable, legal guardians, to choose for their children schools, other than those established by the public authorities, which conform to such minimum educational standards as may be laid down or approved by the State and to ensure the religious and moral education of their children in conformity with their own convictions.

4. No part of this Article shall be construed so as to interfere with the liberty of individuals and bodies to establish and direct educational institutions, subject always to the observance of the principles set forth in paragraph 1 of this Article and to the requirement that the education given in such institutions shall conform to such minimum standards as may be laid down by the State.

*Article* 14

Each State Party to the present Covenant which, at the time of becoming a Party, has not been able to secure in its metropolitan territory or other territories under its jurisdiction compulsory primary education, free of charge, undertakes, within two years, to work out and adopt a detailed plan of action for the progressive implementation, within a reasonable number of years, to be fixed in the plan, of the principle of compulsory education free of charge for all.

*Article* 15

1. The States Parties to the present Covenant recognize the right of everyone:

 (*a*) To take part in cultural life;
 (*b*) To enjoy the benefits of scientific progress and its applications;
 (*c*) To benefit from the protection of the moral and material interests resulting from any scientific, literary or artistic production of which he is the author.

2. The steps to be taken by the States Parties to the present Covenant to achieve the full realization of this right shall include those necessary for the conservation, the development and the diffusion of science and culture.

3. The States Parties to the present Covenant undertake to respect the freedom indispensable for scientific research and creative activity.

4. The States Parties to the present Covenant recognize the benefits to be derived from the encouragement and development of international contacts and co-operation in the scientific and cultural fields.

## PART IV

*Article* 16

1. The States Parties to the present Covenant undertake to submit in conformity with this part of the Covenant reports on the measures which they have adopted and the progress made in achieving the observance of the rights recognized herein.

2. (*a*) All reports shall be submitted to the Secretary-General of the United Nations, who shall transmit copies to the Economic and Social Council for consideration in accordance with the provisions of the present Covenant.

 (*b*) The Secretary-General of the United Nations shall also transmit to the specialized agencies copies of the reports, or any relevant parts therefrom, from States Parties to the present Covenant which are also members of these specialized agencies in so far as these reports, or parts therefrom, relate to any matters which fall within the responsibilities of the said agencies in accordance with their constitutional instruments.

*Article* 17

1. The States Parties to the present Covenant shall furnish their reports in stages, in accordance with a programme to be established by the Economic and Social Council within one year of the entry into force of the present Covenant after consultation with the States Parties and the specialized agencies concerned.

2. Reports may indicate factors and difficulties affecting the degree of fulfilment of obligations under the present Covenant.

3. Where relevant information has previously been furnished to the United Nations or to any specialized agency by any State Party to the present Covenant, it will not be necessary to reproduce that information, but a precise reference to the information so furnished will suffice.

*Article* 18

Pursuant to its responsibilities under the Charter of the United Nations in the field of human rights and fundamental freedoms, the Economic and Social Council may make arrangements with the specialized agencies in respect of their reporting to it on the progress made in achieving the observance of the provisions of the present Covenant falling within the scope of their activities. These reports may include particulars of decisions and recommendations on such implementation adopted by their competent organs.

*Article* 19

The Economic and Social Council may transmit to the Commission on Human Rights for study and general recommendation or as appropriate for information the reports concerning human rights submitted by States in accordance with Articles 16 and 17, and those concerning human rights submitted by the specialized agencies in accordance with Article 18.

*Article* 20

The States Parties to the present Covenant and the specialized agencies concerned may submit comments to the Economic and Social Council on any general recommendation under Article 19 or reference to such general recommendation in any report of the Commission on Human Rights or any documentation referred to therein.

*Article* 21

The Economic and Social Council may submit from time to time to the General Assembly reports with recommendations of a general nature and a summary of the information received from the States Parties to the present Covenant and the specialized agencies on the measures taken and the progress made in achieving general observance of the rights recognized in the present Covenant.

*Article* 22

The Economic and Social Council may bring to the attention of other organs of the United Nations, their subsidiary organs and specialized agencies concerned with furnishing technical assistance any matters arising out of the reports referred to in this part of the present Covenant which may assist such bodies in deciding, each within its field of competence, on the advisability of international measures likely to contribute to the effective progressive implementation of the present Covenant.

*Article* 23

The States Parties to the present Covenant agree that international action for the achievement of the rights recognized in the present Covenant includes such methods as the conclusion of conventions, the adoption of recommendations, the furnishing of technical assistance and the holding of regional meetings and technical meetings for the purpose of consultation and study organized in conjunction with the Governments concerned.

*Article* 24

Nothing in the present Covenant shall be interpreted as impairing the provisions of the Charter of the United Nations and of the constitutions of the specialized agencies which define the respective responsibilities of the various organs of the United Nations and of the specialized agencies in regard to the matters dealt with in the present Covenant.

*Article* 25

Nothing in the present Covenant shall be interpreted as impairing the inherent right of all peoples to enjoy and utilize fully and freely their natural wealth and resources.


# PART V

*Article* 26

1. The present Covenant is open for signature by any State Member of the United Nations or member of any of its specialized agencies, by any State Party to the Statute of the International Court of Justice, and by any other State which has been invited by the General Assembly of the United Nations to become a party to the present Covenant.

2. The present Covenant is subject to ratification. Instruments of ratification shall be deposited with the Secretary-General of the United Nations.

3. The present Covenant shall be open to accession by any State referred to in paragraph 1 of this Article.

4. Accession shall be effected by the deposit of an instrument of accession with the Secretary-General of the United Nations.

5. The Secretary-General of the United Nations shall inform all States which have signed the present Covenant or acceded to it of the deposit of each instrument of ratification or accession.

*Article* 27

1. The present Covenant shall enter into force three months after the date of the deposit with the Secretary-General of the United Nations of the thirty-fifth instrument of ratification or instrument of accession.

2. For each State ratifying the present Covenant or acceding to it after the deposit of the thirty-fifth instrument of ratification or instrument of accession, the present Covenant shall enter into force three months after the date of the deposit of its own instrument of ratification or instrument of accession.

*Article* 28

The provisions of the present Covenant shall extend to all parts of federal States without any limitations or exceptions.

*Article* 29

1. Any State Party to the present Covenant may propose an amendment and file it with the Secretary-General of the United Nations. The Secretary-General shall thereupon communicate any proposed amendments to the States Parties to the present Covenant with a request that they notify him whether they favour a conference of States Parties for the purpose of considering and voting upon the proposals. In the event that at least one third of the States Parties favours such a conference, the Secretary-General shall convene the conference under the auspices of the United Nations. Any amendment adopted by a majority of the States Parties present and voting at the conference shall be submitted to the General Assembly of the United Nations for approval.

2. Amendments shall come into force when they have been approved by the General Assembly of the United Nations and accepted by a two-thirds majority of the State Parties to the present Covenant in accordance with their respective constitutional processes.

3. When amendments come into force they shall be binding on those States Parties which have accepted them, other States Parties still being bound by the provisions of the present Covenant and any earlier amendment which they have accepted.

*Article* 30

Irrespective of the notifications made under Article 26, paragraph 5, the Secretary-General of the United Nations shall inform all States referred to in paragraph 1 of the same Article of the following particulars:

(*a*) Signatures, ratifications and accessions under Article 26;
(*b*) The date of the entry into force of the present Covenant under Article 27 and the date of the entry into force of any amendments under Article 29.

*Article* 31

1. The present Covenant, of which the Chinese, English, French, Russian and Spanish texts are equally authentic, shall be deposited in the archives of the United Nations.

2. The Secretary-General of the United Nations shall transmit certified copies of the present Covenant to all States referrred to in Article 26.

# II. INTERNATIONAL COVENANT ON CIVIL AND POLITICAL RIGHTS, 1966

This was adopted at the same time as the last Covenant. The Covenant entered into force on 23 March 1976; and ninety-five States have become parties.

With respect to inter-state complaints under the optional procedure provided for in Article 41 there is an overlap with the procedure under Article 24 of the European Convention on Human Rights, below. See further on this issue Resolution (70) 17 of the Committee of Ministers of the Council of Europe, adopted by the Ministers' Deputies on 15 May 1970.

Generally see Henkin, *The International Bill of Rights*, 1981.

## TEXT

### Preamble

*The States Parties to the present Covenant,*

*Considering* that, in accordance with the principles proclaimed in the Charter of the United Nations, recognition of the inherent dignity and of the equal and inalienable rights of all members of the human family is the foundation of freedom, justice and peace in the world,

*Recognizing* that these rights derive from the inherent dignity of the human person,

*Recognizing* that, in accordance with the Universal Declaration of Human Rights, the ideal of free human beings enjoying civil and political freedom and freedom from fear and want can only be achieved if conditions are created whereby everyone may enjoy his civil and political rights, as well as his economic, social and cultural rights,

*Considering* the obligation of States under the Charter of the United Nations to promote universal respect for, and observance of, human rights and freedoms,

*Realizing* that the individual, having duties to other individuals and to the community to which he belongs, is under a responsibility to strive for the promotion and observance of the rights recognized in the present Covenant,

*Agree* upon the following articles:

## PART I

*Article 1*

1. All peoples have the right of self-determination. By virtue of that right they freely determine their political status and freely pursue their economic, social and cultural development.

2. All peoples may, for their own ends, freely dispose of their natural

wealth and resources without prejudice to any obligations arising out of international economic co-operation, based upon the principle of mutual benefit, and international law. In no case may a people be deprived of its own means of subsistence.

3. The States Parties to the present Covenant, including those having responsibility for the administration of Non-Self-Governing and Trust Territories, shall promote the realization of the right of self-determination, and shall respect that right, in conformity with the provisions of the Charter of the United Nations.

## PART II

*Article* 2

1. Each State Party to the present Covenant undertakes to respect and to ensure to all individuals within its territory and subject to its jurisdiction the rights recognized in the present Covenant, without distinction of any kind, such as race, colour, sex, language, religion, political or other opinion, national or social origin, property, birth or other status.

2. Where not already provided for by existing legislative or other measures, each State Party to the present Covenant undertakes to take the necessary steps, in accordance with its constitutional processes and with the provisions of the present Covenant, to adopt such legislative or other measures as may be necessary to give effect to the rights recognized in the present Covenant.

3. Each State Party to the present Covenant undertakes:

   (*a*) To ensure that any person whose rights or freedoms as herein recognized are violated shall have an effective remedy, notwithstanding that the violation has been committed by persons acting in an official capacity;

   (*b*) To ensure that any person claiming such a remedy shall have his right thereto determined by competent judicial, administrative or legislative authorities, or by any other competent authority provided for by the legal system of the State, and to develop the possibilities of judicial remedy;

   (*c*) To ensure that the competent authorities shall enforce such remedies when granted.

*Article* 3

The States Parties to the present Covenant undertake to ensure the equal right of men and women to the enjoyment of all civil and political rights set forth in the present Covenant.

*Article* 4

1. In time of public emergency which threatens the life of the nation and the existence of which is officially proclaimed, the State Parties to the present Covenant may take measures derogating from their obligations under the present Covenant to the extent strictly required by the exigencies of the situation, provided that such measures are not inconsistent with their other obligations under international law and do not involve discrimination solely on the ground of race, colour, sex, language, religion or social origin.

2. No derogation from Articles 6, 7, 8 (paragraphs 1 and 2), 11, 15, 16 and 18 may be made under this provision.

3. Any State Party to the present Covenant availing itself of the right of derogation shall immediately inform the other States Parties to the present Covenant, through the intermediary of the Secretary-General of the United Nations of the provisions from which it has derogated and of the reasons by which it was actuated. A further communication shall be made, through the same intermediary on the date on which it terminates such derogation.

*Article* 5

1. Nothing in the present Covenant may be interpreted as implying for any State, group or person any right to engage in any activity or perform any act aimed at the destruction of any of the rights and freedoms recognized herein or at their limitation to a greater extent than is provided for in the present Covenant.

2. There shall be no restriction upon or derogation from any of the fundamental human rights recognized or existing in any State Party to the present Covenant pursuant to law, conventions, regulations or custom on the pretext that the present Covenant does not recognize such rights or that it recognizes them to a lesser extent.

# PART III

*Article* 6

1. Every human being has the inherent right to life. This right shall be protected by law. No one shall be arbitrarily deprived of his life.

2. In countries which have not abolished the death penalty, sentence of death may be imposed only for the most serious crimes in accordance with the law in force at the time of the commission of the crime and not contrary to the provisions of the present Covenant and to the Covention on the Prevention and Punishment of the Crime of Genocide. This penalty can only be carried out pursuant to a final judgment rendered by a competent court.

3. When deprivation of life constitutes the crime of genocide, it is understood that nothing in this Article shall authorize any State Party to the present Covenant to derogate in any way from any obligation assumed under the provisions of the Convention on the Prevention and Punishment of the Crime of Genocide.

4. Anyone sentenced to death shall have the right to seek pardon or commutation of the sentence. Amnesty, pardon or commutation of the sentence of death may be granted in all cases.

5. Sentence of death shall not be imposed for crimes committed by persons below eighteen years of age and shall not be carried out on pregnant women.

6. Nothing in this Article shall be invoked to delay or to prevent the abolition of capital punishment by any State Party to the present Covenant.

*Article* 7

No one shall be subjected to torture or to cruel, inhuman or degrading treatment or punishment. In particular, no one shall be subjected without his free consent to medical or scientific experimentation.

*Article* 8

1. No one shall be held in slavery; slavery and the slave-trade in all their forms shall be prohibited.

2. No one shall be held in servitude.

3. (*a*) No one shall be required to perform forced or compulsory labour;

   (*b*) Paragraph 3 (*a*) shall not be held to preclude, in countries where imprisonment with hard labour may be imposed as a punishment for a crime, the performance of hard labour in pursuance of a sentence to such punishment by a competent court;

   (*c*) For the purpose of this paragraph the term 'forced or compulsory labour' shall not include:

   (i) Any work or service, not referred to in sub-paragraph (*b*), normally required of a person who is under detention in consequence of a lawful order of a court, or of a person during conditional release from such detention;

   (ii) Any service of a military character and, in countries where conscientious objection is recognized, any national service required by law of conscientious objectors;

   (iii) Any service exacted in cases of emergency or calamity threatening the life or well-being of the community;

   (iv) Any work or service which forms part of normal civil obligations.

*Article* 9

1. Everyone has the right to liberty and security of person. No one shall be subjected to arbitrary arrest or detention. No one shall be deprived of his

liberty except on such grounds and in accordance with such procedures as are established by law.

2. Anyone who is arrested shall be informed, at the time of arrest, of the reasons for his arrest and shall be promptly informed of any charges against him.

3. Anyone arrested or detained on a criminal charge shall be brought promptly before a judge or other officer authorized by law to exercise judicial power and shall be entitled to trial within a reasonable time or to release. It shall not be the general rule that persons awaiting trial shall be detained in custody, but release may be subject to guarantees to appear for trial, at any other stage of the judicial proceedings, and, should occasion arise, for execution of the judgment.

4. Anyone who is deprived of his liberty by arrest or detention shall be entitled to take proceedings before a court, in order that that court may decide without delay on the lawfulness of his detention and order his release if the detention is not lawful.

5. Anyone who has been the victim of unlawful arrest or detention shall have an enforceable right to compensation.

*Article* 10

1. All persons deprived of their liberty shall be treated with humanity and with respect for the inherent dignity of the human person.

2. (*a*) Accused persons shall, save in exceptional circumstances, be segregated from convicted persons and shall be subject to separate treatment appropriate to their status as unconvicted persons;

(*b*) Accused juvenile persons shall be separated from adults and brought as speedily as possible for adjudication.

3. The penitentiary system shall comprise treatment of prisoners the essential aim of which shall be their reformation and social rehabilitation. Juvenile offenders shall be segregated from adults and be accorded treatment appropriate to their age and legal status.

*Article* 11

No one shall be imprisoned merely on the ground of inability to fulfil a contractual obligation.

*Article* 12

1. Everyone lawfully within the territory of a State shall, within that territory, have the right to liberty of movement and freedom to choose his residence.

2. Everyone shall be free to leave any country, including his own.

3. The above-mentioned rights shall not be subject to any restrictions except those which are provided by law, are necessary to protect national security, public order (*ordre public*), public health or morals or the rights and

freedoms of others, and are consistent with the other rights recognized in the present Covenant.

4. No one shall be arbitrarily deprived of the right to enter his own country.

*Article* 13

An alien lawfully in the territory of a State Party to the present Covenant may be expelled therefrom only in pursuance of a decision reached in accordance with law and shall, except where compelling reasons of national security otherwise require, be allowed to submit the reasons against his expulsion and to have his case reviewed by, and be represented for the purpose before, the competent authority or a person or persons especially designated by the competent authority.

*Article* 14

1. All persons shall be equal before the courts and tribunals. In the determination of any criminal charge against him, or of his rights and obligations in a suit at law, everyone shall be entitled to a fair and public hearing by a competent, independent and impartial tribunal established by law. The Press and the public may be excluded from all or part of a trial for reasons of morals, public order (*ordre public*) or national security in a democratic society, or when the interest of the private lives of the parties so requires, or to the extent strictly necessary in the opinion of the court in special circumstances where publicity would prejudice the interests of justice; but any judgement rendered in a criminal case or in a suit at law shall be made public except where the interest of juvenile persons otherwise requires or the proceedings concern matrimonial disputes or the guardianship of children.

2. Everyone charged with a criminal offence shall have the right to be presumed innocent until proved guilty according to law.

3. In the determination of any criminal charge against him, everyone shall be entitled to the following minimum guarantees, in full equality:

- (*a*) To be informed promptly and in detail in a language which he understands of the nature and cause of the charge against him;
- (*b*) To have adequate time and facilities for the preparation of his defence and to communicate with counsel of his own choosing;
- (*c*) To be tried without undue delay;
- (*d*) To be tried in his presence, and to defend himself in person or through legal assistance of his own choosing; to be informed, if he does not have legal assistance, of this right; and to have legal assistance assigned to him, in any case where the interests of justice so require, and without payment by him in any such case if he does not have sufficient means to pay for it;

(*e*) To examine, or have examined, the witnesses against him and to obtain the attendance and examination of witnesses on his behalf under the same conditions as witnesses against him;

(*f*) To have the free assistance of an interpreter if he cannot understand or speak the language used in court;

(*g*) Not to be compelled to testify against himself or to confess guilt.

4. In the case of juvenile persons, the procedure shall be such as will take account of their age and the desirability of promoting their rehabilitation.

5. Everyone convicted of a crime shall have the right to his conviction and sentence being reviewed by a higher tribunal according to law.

6. When a person has by a final decision been convicted of a criminal offence and when subsequently his conviction has been reversed or he has been pardoned on the ground that a new or newly discovered fact shows conclusively that there has been a miscarriage of justice, the person who has suffered punishment as a result of such conviction shall be compensated according to law, unless it is proved that the non-disclosure of the unknown fact in time is wholly or partly attributable to him.

7. No one shall be liable to be tried or punished again for an offence for which he has already been finally convicted or acquitted in accordance with the law and penal procedure of each country.

*Article* 15

1. No one shall be held guilty of any criminal offence on account of any act or omission which did not constitute a criminal offence, under national or international law, at the time when it was committed. Nor shall a heavier penalty be imposed than the one that was applicable at the time when the criminal offence was committed. If, subsequent to the commission of the offence, provision is made by law for the imposition of a lighter penalty, the offender shall benefit thereby.

2. Nothing in this article shall prejudice the trial and punishment of any person for any act or omission which, at the time when it was committed, was criminal according to the general principles of law recognized by the community of nations.

*Article* 16

Everyone shall have the right to recognition everywhere as a person before the law.

*Article* 17

1. No one shall be subjected to arbitrary or unlawful interference with his privacy, family, home or correspondence, nor to unlawful attacks on his honour and reputation.

2. Everyone has the right to the protection of the law against such interference or attacks.

*Article* 18

1. Everyone shall have the right to freedom of thought, conscience and religion. This right shall include freedom to have or to adopt a religion or belief of his choice, and freedom, either individually or in community with others and in public or private, to manifest his religion or belief in worship, observance, practice and teaching.

2. No one shall be subject to coercion which would impair his freedom to have or to adopt a religion or belief of his choice.

3. Freedom to manifest one's religion or beliefs may be subject only to such limitations as are prescribed by law and are necessary to protect public safety, order, health, or morals or the fundamental rights and freedoms of others.

4. The States Parties to the present Covenant undertake to have respect for the liberty of parents and, when applicable, legal guardians to ensure the religious and moral education of their children in conformity with their own convictions.

*Article* 19

1. Everyone shall have the right to hold opinions without interference.

2. Everyone shall have the right to freedom of expression; this right shall include freedom to seek, receive and impart information and ideas of all kinds, regardless of frontiers, either orally, in writing or in print, in the form of art, or through any other media of his choice.

3. The exercise of the rights provided for in paragraph 2 of this article carries with it special duties and responsibilities. It may therefore be subject to certain restrictions, but these shall only be such as are provided by law and are necessary:

    (*a*) For respect of the rights or reputations of others;
    (*b*) For the protection of national security or of public order (*ordre public*), or of public health or morals.

*Article* 20

1. Any propaganda for war shall be prohibited by law.

2. Any advocacy of national, racial or religious hatred that constitutes incitement to discrimination, hostility or violence shall be prohibited by law.

*Article* 21

The right of peaceful assembly shall be recognized. No restrictions may be placed on the exercise of this right other than those imposed in conformity with the law and which are necessary in a democratic society in the interests of national security or public safety, public order (*ordre public*), the protection of public health or morals or the protection of the rights and freedoms of others.

*Article* 22

1. Everyone shall have the right to freedom of association with others, including the right to form and join trade unions for the protection of his interests.

2. No restrictions may be placed on the exercise of this right other than those which are prescribed by law and which are necessary in a democratic society in the interests of national security or public safety, public order (*ordre public*), the protection of public health or morals or the protection of the rights and freedoms of others. This Article shall not prevent the imposition of lawful restrictions on members of the armed forces and of the police in their exercise of this right.

3. Nothing in this article shall authorize States Parties to the International Labour Organization Convention of 1948 concerning Freedom of Association and Protection of the Right to Organize to take legislative measures which would prejudice, or to apply the law in such a manner as to prejudice, the guarantees provided for in that Convention.

*Article* 23

1. The family is the natural and fundamental group unit of society and is entitled to protection by society and the State.

2. The right of men and women of marriageable age to marry and to found a family shall be recognized.

3. No marriage shall be entered into without the free and full consent of the intending spouses.

4. States Parties to the present Covenant shall take appropriate steps to ensure equality of rights and responsibilities of spouses as to marriage, during marriage and at its dissolution. In the case of dissolution, provision shall be made for the necessary protection of any children.

*Article* 24

1. Every child shall have, without any discrimination as to race, colour, sex, language, religion, national or social origin, property or birth, the right to such measures of protection as are required by his status as a minor, on the part of his family, society and the State.

2. Every child shall be registered immediately after birth and shall have a name.

3. Every child has the right to acquire a nationality.

*Article* 25

Every citizen shall have the right and the opportunity, without any of the distinctions mentioned in Article 2 and without unreasonable restrictions:

  (*a*)  To take part in the conduct of public affairs, directly or through freely chosen representatives;
  (*b*)  To vote and to be elected at genuine periodic elections which shall be by universal and equal suffrage and shall be held by secret ballot, guaranteeing the free expression of the will of the electors;
  (*c*)  To have access, on general terms of equality, to public service in his country.

*Article* 26

All persons are equal before the law and are entitled without any discrimination to the equal protection of the law. In this respect, the law shall prohibit any discrimination and guarantee to all persons equal and effective protection against discrimination on any ground such as race, colour, sex, language, religion, political or other opinion, national or social origin, property, birth or other status.

*Article* 27

In those States in which ethnic, religious or linguistic minorities exist, persons belonging to such minorities shall not be denied the right, in community with the other members of their group, to enjoy their own culture, to profess and practise their own religion, or to use their own language.


# PART IV

*Article* 28

1. There shall be established a Human Rights Committee (hereafter referred to in the present Covenant as the Committee). It shall consist of eighteen members and shall carry out the functions hereinafter provided.

2. The Committee shall be composed of nationals of the States Parties to the present Covenant who shall be persons of high moral character and recognized competence in the field of human rights, consideration being given to the usefulness of the participation of some persons having legal experience.

3. The members of the Committee shall be elected and shall serve in their personal capacity.

*Article* 29

1. The members of the Committee shall be elected by secret ballot from a list of persons possessing the qualifications prescribed in Article 28 and nominated for the purpose by the States Parties to the present Covenant.

2. Each State Party to the present Covenant may nominate not more than two persons. These persons shall be nationals of the nominating State.

3. A person shall be eligible for renomination.

*Article* 30

1. The initial election shall be held no later than six months after the date of the entry into force of the present Covenant.

2. At least four months before the date of each election to the Committee, other than an election to fill a vacancy declared in accordance with Article 34, the Secretary-General of the United Nations shall address a written invitation to the States Parties to the present Covenant to submit their nominations for membership of the Committee within three months.

3. The Secretary-General of the United Nations shall prepare a list in alphabetical order of all the persons thus nominated, with an indication of the States Parties which have nominated them, and shall submit it to the States Parties to the present Covenant no later than one month before the date of each election.

4. Elections of the members of the Committee shall be held at a meeting of the States Parties to the present Covenant convened by the Secretary-General of the United Nations at the Headquarters of the United Nations. At that meeting, for which two thirds of the States Parties to the present Covenant shall constitute a quorum, the persons elected to the Committee shall be those nominees who obtain the largest number of votes and an absolute majority of the votes of the representatives of States Parties present and voting.

*Article* 31

1. The Committee may not include more than one national of the same State.

2. In the election of the Committee, consideration shall be given to equitable geographical distribution of membership and to the representation of the different forms of civilization and of the principal legal systems.

*Article* 32

1. The members of the Committee shall be elected for a term of four years. They shall be eligible for re-election if renominated. However, the terms of nine of the members elected at the first election shall expire at the end of two years; immediately after the first election, the names of these nine

members shall be chosen by lot by the Chairman of the meeting referred to in Article 30, paragraph 4.

2. Elections at the expiry of office shall be held in accordance with the preceding Articles of this part of the present Covenant.

*Article 33*

1. If, in the unanimous opinion of the other members, a member of the Committee has ceased to carry out his functions for any cause other than absence of a temporary character, the Chairman of the Committee shall notify the Secretary-General of the United Nations, who shall then declare the seat of that member to be vacant.

2. In the event of the death or the resignation of a member of the Committee, the Chairman shall immediately notify the Secretary-General of the United Nations, who shall declare the seat vacant from the date of death or the date on which the resignation takes effect.

*Article 34*

1. When a vacancy is declared in accordance with Article 33 and if the term of office of the member to be replaced does not expire within six months of the declaration of the vacancy, the Secretary-General of the United Nations shall notify each of the States Parties to the present Covenant, which may within two months submit nominations in accordance with Article 29 for the purpose of fulfilling the vacancy.

2. The Secretary-General of the United Nations shall prepare a list in alphabetical order of the persons thus nominated and shall submit it to the States Parties to the present Covenant. The election to fill the vacancy shall then take place in accordance with the relevant provisions of this part of the present Covenant.

3. A member of the Committee elected to fill a vacancy declared in accordance with Article 33 shall hold office for the remainder of the term of the member who vacated the seat of the Committee under the provisions of that Article.

*Article 35*

The members of the Committee shall, with the approval of the General Assembly of the United Nations, receive emoluments from United Nations resources on such terms and conditions as the General Assembly may decide, having regard to the importance of the Committee's responsibilities.

*Article 36*

The Secretary-General of the United Nations shall provide the necessary staff and facilities for the effective performance of the functions of the Committee under the present Covenant.

*Article* 37

1. The Secretary-General of the United Nations shall convene the initial meeting of the Committee at the Headquarters of the United Nations.

2. After its initial meeting, the Committee shall meet at such times as shall be provided in its rules of procedure.

3. The Committee shall normally meet at the Headquarters of the United Nations or at the United Nations Office at Geneva.

*Article* 38

Every member of the Committee shall, before taking up his duties, make a solemn declaration in open committee that he will perform his functions impartially and conscientiously.

*Article* 39

1. The Committee shall elect its officers for a term of two years. They may be re-elected.

2. The Committee shall establish its own rules of procedure, but these rules shall provide, *inter alia*, that:

  (*a*) Twelve members shall constitute a quorum;
  (*b*) Decisions of the Committee shall be made by a majority vote of the members present.

*Article* 40

1. The States Parties to the present Covenant undertake to submit reports on the measures they have adopted which give effect to the rights recognized herein and on the progress made in the enjoyment of those rights:

  (*a*) Within one year of the entry into force of the present Covenant for the States Parties concerned;
  (*b*) Thereafter whenever the Committee so requests.

2. All reports shall be submitted to the Secretary-General of the United Nations, who shall transmit them to the Committee for consideration. Reports shall indicate the factors and difficulties, if any, affecting the implementation of the present Covenant.

3. The Secretary-General of the United Nations may, after consultation with the Committee, transmit to the specialized agencies concerned copies of such parts of the reports as may fall within their field of competence.

4. The Committee shall study the reports submitted by the States Parties to the present Covenant. It shall transmit its reports, and such general comments as it may consider appropriate, to the States Parties. The Committee may also transmit to the Economic and Social Council these comments along with the copies of the reports it has received from States Parties to the present Covenant.

5. The States Parties to the present Covenant may submit to the Committee observations on any comments that may be made in accordance with paragraph 4 of this Article.

*Article* 41

1. A State Party to the present Covenant may at any time declare under this article that it recognizes the competence of the Committee to receive and consider communications to the effect that a State Party claims that another State Party is not fulfilling its obligations under the present Covenant. Communications under this article may be received and considered only if submitted by a State Party which has made a declaration recognizing in regard to itself the competence of the Committee. No communication shall be received by the Committee if it concerns a State Party which has not made such a declaration. Communications received under this Article shall be dealt with in accordance with the following procedure:

(*a*) If a State Party to the present Covenant considers that another State Party is not giving effect to the provisions of the present Covenant, it may, by written communication, bring the matter to the attention of that State Party. Within three months after the receipt of the communication, the receiving State shall afford the State which sent the communication an explanation or any other statement in writing clarifying the matter, which should include, to the extent possible and pertinent, reference to domestic procedures and remedies taken, pending, or available in the matter.

(*b*) If the matter is not adjusted to the satisfaction of both States Parties concerned within six months after the receipt by the receiving State of the initial communication, either State shall have the right to refer the matter to the Committee, by notice given to the Committee and to the other State.

(*c*) The Committee shall deal with a matter referred to it only after it has ascertained that all available domestic remedies have been invoked and exhausted in the matter, in conformity with the generally recognized principles of international law. This shall not be the rule where the application of the remedies is unreasonably prolonged.

(*d*) The Committee shall hold closed meetings when examining communications under this article.

(*e*) Subject to the provisions of sub-paragraph (*c*), the Committee shall make available its good offices to the States Parties concerned with a view to a friendly solution of the matter on the basis of respect for human rights and fundamental freedoms as recognized in the present Covenant.

(*f*) In any matter referred to it, the Committee may call upon the States

Parties concerned, referred to in sub-paragraph (*b*), to supply any relevant information.

(*g*) The States Parties concerned, referred to in sub-paragraph (*b*), shall have the right to be represented when the matter is being considered in the Committee and to make submissions orally and/or in writing.

(*h*) The Committee shall, within twelve months after the date of receipt of notice under sub-paragraph (*b*), submit a report:

(i) If a solution within the terms of sub-paragraph (*e*) is reached, the Committee shall confine its report to a brief statement of the facts and of the solution reached;

(ii) If a solution within the terms of sub-paragraph (*e*) is not reached, the Committee shall confine its report to a brief statement of the facts; the written submissions and record of the oral submissions made by the States Parties concerned shall be attached to the report.

In every matter, the report shall be communicated to the States Parties concerned.

2. The provisions of this Article shall come into force when ten States Parties to the present Covenant have made declarations under paragraph 1 of this Article. Such declarations shall be deposited by the States Parties with the Secretary-General of the United Nations, who shall transmit copies thereof to the other States Parties. A declaration may be withdrawn at any time by notification to the Secretary-General. Such a withdrawal shall not prejudice the consideration of any matter which is the subject of a communication already transmitted under this Article; no further communication by any State Party shall be received after the notification of withdrawal of the declaration has been received by the Secretary-General, unless the State Party concerned has made a new declaration.

*Article* 42

1. (*a*) If a matter referred to the Committee in accordance with Article 41 is not resolved to the satisfaction of the States Parties concerned, the Committee may, with the prior consent of the States Parties concerned, appoint an *ad hoc* Conciliation Commission (hereinafter referred to as the Commission). The good offices of the Commission shall be made available to the States Parties concerned with a view to an amicable solution of the matter on the basis of respect for the present Covenant;

(*b*) The Commission shall consist of five persons acceptable to the States Parties concerned. If the States Parties concerned fail to reach agreement within three months on all or part of the composition of the Commission the members of the Commission concerning whom no agreement has been reached shall be elected by secret ballot by a two-thirds majority vote of the Committee from among its members.

2. The members of the Commission shall serve in their personal capacity. They shall not be nationals of the States Parties concerned, or of a State not party to the present Covenant, or of a State Party which has not made a declaration under Article 41.

3. The Commission shall elect its own Chairman and adopt its own rules of procedure.

4. The meetings of the Commission shall normally be held at the Headquarters of the United Nations or at the United Nations Office at Geneva. However, they may be held at such other convenient places as the Commission may determine in consultation with the Secretary-General of the United Nations and the States Parties concerned.

5. The secretariat provided in accordance with Article 36 shall also service the commissions appointed under this article.

6. The information received and collated by the Committee shall be made available to the Commission and the Commission may call upon the States Parties concerned to supply any other relevant information.

7. When the Commission has fully considered the matter, but in any event not later than twelve months after having been seized of the matter, it shall submit to the Chairman of the Committee a report for communication to the States Parties concerned.

- (a) If the Commission is unable to complete its consideration of the matter within twelve months, it shall confine its report to a brief statement of the status of its consideration of the matter.
- (b) If an amicable solution to the matter on the basis of respect for human rights as recognized in the present Covenant is reached, the Commission shall confine its report to a brief statement of the facts and of the solution reached.
- (c) If a solution within the terms of sub-paragraph (b) is not reached, the Commission's report shall embody its findings on all questions of fact relevant to the issues between the States Parties concerned, and its views on the possibilities of an amicable solution of the matter. This report shall also contain the written submissions and a record of the oral submissions made by the States Parties concerned.
- (d) If the Commission's report is submitted under sub-paragraph (c), the States Parties concerned shall, within three months of the receipt of the report, notify the Chairman of the Committee whether or not they accept the contents of the report of the Commission.

8. The provisions of this Article are without prejudice to the responsibilities of the Committee under Article 41.

9. The States Parties concerned shall share equally all the expenses of the members of the Commission in accordance with estimates to be provided by the Secretary-General of the United Nations.

10. The Secretary-General of the United Nations shall be empowered to pay the expenses of the members of the Commission, if necessary, before reimbursement by the States Parties concerned, in accordance with paragraph 9 of this Article.

*Article* 43

The members of the Committee, and of the *ad hoc* conciliation commissions which may be appointed under Article 42, shall be entitled to the facilities, privileges and immunities of experts on mission for the United Nations as laid down in the relevant sections of the Convention on the Privileges and Immunities of the United Nations.

*Article* 44

The provisions for the implementation of the present Covenant shall apply without prejudice to the procedures prescribed in the field of human rights by or under the constituent instruments and the conventions of the United Nations and of the specialized agencies and shall not prevent the States Parties to the present Covenant from having recourse to other procedures for settling a dispute in accordance with general or special international agreements in force between them.

*Article* 45

The Committee shall submit to the General Assembly of the United Nations through the Economic and Social Council, an annual report on its activities.

# PART V

*Article* 46

Nothing in the present Covenant shall be interpreted as impairing the provisions of the Charter of the United Nations and of the constitutions of the specialized agencies which define the respective responsibilities of the various organs of the United Nations and of the specialized agencies in regard to the matters dealt with in the present Covenant.

*Article* 47

Nothing in the present Covenant shall be interpreted as impairing the inherent right of all peoples to enjoy and utilize fully and freely their natural wealth and resources.

## PART VI

*Article* 48

1. The present Covenant is open for signature by any State Member of the United Nations or member of any of its specialized agencies, by any State Party to the Statute of the International Court of Justice, and by any other State which has been invited by the General Assembly of the United Nations to become a party to the present Covenant.

2. The present Covenant is subject to ratification. Instruments of ratification shall be deposited with the Secretary-General of the United Nations.

3. The present Covenant shall be open to accession by any State referred to in paragraph 1 of this article.

4. Accession shall be effected by the deposit of an instrument of accession with the Secretary-General of the United Nations.

5. The Secretary-General of the United Nations shall inform all States which have signed this Covenant or acceded to it of the deposit of each instrument of ratification or accession.

*Article* 49

1. The present Covenant shall enter into force three months after the date of the deposit with the Secretary-General of the United Nations of the thirty-fifth instrument of ratification or instrument of accession.

2. For each State ratifying the present Covenant or acceding to it after the deposit of the thirty-fifth instrument of ratification or instrument of accession, the present Covenant shall enter into force three months after the date of the deposit of its own instrument of ratification or instrument of accession.

*Article* 50

The provisions of the present Covenant shall extend to all parts of federal States without any limitations or exceptions.

*Article* 51

1. Any State Party to the present Covenant may propose an amendment and file it with the Secretary-General of the United Nations. The Secretary-General of the United Nations shall thereupon communicate any proposed amendments to the States Parties to the present Covenant with a request that they notify him whether they favour a conference of States Parties for the purpose of considering and voting upon the proposals. In the event that at least one third of the States Parties favours such a conference, the Secretary-General shall convene the conference under the auspices of the United Nations. Any amendment adopted by a majority of the States

Parties present and voting at the conference shall be submitted to the General Assembly of the United Nations for approval.

2. Amendments shall come into force when they have been approved by the General Assembly of the United Nations and accepted by a two-thirds majority of the States Parties to the present Covenant in accordance with their respective constitutional processes.

3. When amendments come into force, they shall be binding on those States Parties which have accepted them, other States Parties still being bound by the provisions of the present Covenant and any earlier amendment which they have accepted.

*Article* 52

Irrespective of the notifications made under Article 48, paragraph 5, the Secretary-General of the United Nations shall inform all States referred to in paragraph 1 of the same Article of the following particulars:

(*a*) Signatures, ratifications and accessions under Article 48;
(*b*) The date of the entry into force of the present Covenant under Article 49 and the date of the entry into force of any amendments under Article 51.

*Article* 53

1. The present Covenant, of which the Chinese, English, French, Russian and Spanish texts are equally authentic, shall be deposited in the archives of the United Nations.

2. The Secretary-General of the United Nations shall transmit certified copies of the present Covenant to all States referred to in Article 48.

# III. OPTIONAL PROTOCOL TO THE INTERNATIONAL COVENANT ON CIVIL AND POLITICAL RIGHTS, 1966

The Protocol entered into force on 23 March 1976; and fifty-five States have become parties. On the Human Rights Committee see McGoldrick, *The Human Rights Committee: Its Role in the Development of the International Covenant on Civil and Political Rights*, 1991.

## TEXT

*The States Parties to the present Protocol,*

*Considering* that in order further to achieve the purposes of the Covenant on Civil and Political Rights (hereinafter referred to as the Covenant) and the implementation of its provisions it would be appropriate to enable the Human Rights Committee set up in Part IV of the Covenant (hereinafter referred to as the Committee) to receive and consider, as provided in the present Protocol, communications from individuals claiming to be victims of violations of any of the rights set forth in the Covenant,

*Have agreed* as follows:

*Article* 1

A State Party to the Covenant that becomes a party to the present Protocol recognizes the competence of the Committee to receive and consider communications from individuals subject to its jurisdiction who claim to be victims of a violation by that State Party of any of the rights set forth in the Covenant. No communication shall be received by the Committee if it concerns a State Party to the Covenant which is not a party to the present Protocol.

*Article* 2

Subject to the provisions of Article 1, individuals who claim that any of their rights enumerated in the Covenant have been violated and who have exhausted all available domestic remedies may submit a written communication to the Committee for consideration.

*Article* 3

The Committee shall consider inadmissible any communication under the present Protocol which is anonymous, or which it considers to be an abuse of the right of submission of such communications or to be incompatible with the provisions of the Covenant.

*Article* 4

1. Subject to the provisions of Article 3, the Committee shall bring any communications submitted to it under the present Protocol to the attention

of the State Party to the present Protocol alleged to be violating any provision of the Covenant.

2. Within six months, the receiving State shall submit to the Committee written explanations or statements clarifying the matter and the remedy, if any, that may have been taken by that State.

*Article 5*

1. The Committee shall consider communications received under the present Protocol in the light of all written information made available to it by the individual and by the State Party concerned.

2. The Committee shall not consider any communication from an individual unless it has ascertained that:

  (*a*) The same matter is not examined under another procedure of international investigation or settlement;

  (*b*) The individual has exhausted all available domestic remedies. This shall not be the rule where the application of the remedies is unreasonably prolonged.

3. The Committee shall hold closed meetings when examining communications under the present Protocol.

4. The Committee shall forward its views to the State Party concerned and to the individual.

*Article 6*

The Committee shall include in its annual report under Article 45 of the Covenant a summary of its activities under the present Protocol.

*Article 7*

Pending the achievement of the objectives of resolution 1514 (XV) adopted by the General Assembly of the United Nations on 14 December 1960 concerning the Declaration on the Granting of Independence to Colonial Countries and Peoples, the provisions of the present Protocol shall in no way limit the right of petition granted to these peoples by the Charter of the United Nations and other international conventions and instruments under the United Nations and its specialized agencies.

*Article 8*

1. The present Protocol is open for signature by any State which has signed the Covenant.

2. The present Protocol is subject to ratification by any State which has ratified or acceded to the Covenant. Instruments of ratification shall be deposited with the Secretary-General of the United Nations.

3. The present Protocol shall be open to accession by any State which has ratified or acceded to the Covenant.

4. Accession shall be effected by the deposit of an instrument of accession with the Secretary-General of the United Nations.

5. The Secretary-General of the United Nations shall inform all States which have signed the present Protocol or acceded to it of the deposit of each instrument of ratification or accession.

*Article* 9

1. Subject to the entry into force of the Covenant, the present Protocol shall enter into force three months after the date of the deposit with the Secretary-General of the United Nations of the tenth instrument of ratification or instrument of accession.

2. For each State ratifying the present Protocol or acceding to it after the deposit of the tenth instrument of ratification or instrument of accession, the present Protocol shall enter into force three months after the date of the deposit of its own instrument of ratification or instrument of accession.

*Article* 10

The provisions of the present Protocol shall extend to all parts of federal States without any limitations or exceptions.

*Article* 11

1. Any State Party to the present Protocol may propose an amendment and file it with the Secretary-General of the United Nations. The Secretary-General shall thereupon communicate any proposed amendments to the States Parties to the present Protocol with a request that they notify him whether they favour a conference of States Parties for the purpose of considering and voting upon the proposal. In the event that at least one third of the States Parties favours such a conference, the Secretary-General shall convene the conference under the auspices of the United Nations. Any amendment adopted by a majority of the States Parties present and voting at the conference shall be submitted to the General Assembly of the United Nations for approval.

2. Amendments shall come into force when they have been approved by the General Assembly of the United Nations and accepted by a two-thirds majority of the States Parties to the present Protocol in accordance with their respective constitutional processes.

3. When amendments come into force, they shall be binding on those States Parties which have accepted them, other States Parties still being bound by the provisions of the present Protocol and any earlier amendment which they have accepted.

*Article* 12

1. Any State Party may denounce the present Protocol at any time by written notification addressed to the Secretary-General of the United Nations. Denunciation shall take effect three months after the date of receipt of the notification by the Secretary-General.

2. Denunciation shall be without prejudice to the continued application of the provisions of the present Protocol to any communication submitted under Article 2 before the effective date of denunciation.

*Article* 13

Irrespective of the notifications made under Article 8, paragraph 5, of the present Protocol, the Secretary-General of the United Nations shall inform all States referred to in Article 48, paragraph 1, of the Covenant of the following particulars:

(*a*) Signatures, ratifications and accessions under Article 8;
(*b*) The date of the entry into force of the present Protocol under Article 9 and the date of the entry into force of any amendments under Article 11;
(*c*) Denunciations under Article 12.

*Article* 14

1. The present Protocol, of which the Chinese, English, French, Russian and Spanish texts are equally authentic, shall be deposited in the archives of the United Nations.

2. The Secretary-General of the United Nations shall transmit certified copies of the present Protocol to all States referred to in Article 48 of the Covenant.

## IV. INTERNATIONAL CONVENTION ON THE ELIMINATION OF ALL FORMS OF RACIAL DISCRIMINATION, 1966

The great theme which pervades the provisions of the U.N. Charter and other instruments, both national and international, concerned with human rights and civil liberties, is that of equality. It has slowly come to be recognized that racial discrimination and resulting conflict are a major issue in world affairs. The Convention, opened for signature on 7 March 1966, was adopted by the General Assembly of the United Nations on 21 December 1965. It has been signed by seventy-one States and a hundred and twenty-eight States have become parties. For the text in various languages see *U.K. Treaty Series*, Misc. No. 77, 1969, Cmnd. 4108. The individual complaints procedure under Article 14 is not yet operative.

For further reference see Philip Mason, *Patterns of Dominance*, 1970; Schwelb, *International and Comparative Law Quarterly*, 15 (1966), p. 996; Brownlie, *Principles of Public International Law*, 4th ed., 1990, pp. 598–601; Meron, *American Journal of International Law*, vol. 79 (1985), p. 283.

The link between the issue of racial equality and decolonization is established in the resolution of the General Assembly of the United Nations (printed as an annex below) Resolution 2106 (XX), B, associated with the adoption by the General Assembly of the Convention itself. See further Resolution 2547 (XXIV) adopted by the General Assembly on 15 December 1969.

## TEXT

*The States Parties to this Convention,*

*Considering* that the Charter of the United Nations is based on the principles of the dignity and equality inherent in all human beings, and that all Member States have pledged themselves to take joint and separate action, in co-operation with the Organization, for the achievement of one of the purposes of the United Nations which is to promote and encourage universal respect for and observance of human rights and fundamental freedoms for all, without distinction as to race, sex, language or religion,

*Considering* that the Universal Declaration of Human Rights proclaims that all human beings are born free and equal in dignity and rights and that everyone is entitled to all the rights and freedoms set out therein, without distinction of any kind, in particular as to race, colour or national origin,

*Considering* that all human beings are equal before the law and are entitled to equal protection of the law against any discrimination and against any incitement to discrimination,

*Considering* that the United Nations has condemned colonialism and all practices of segregation and discrimination associated therewith, in whatever form and wherever they exist, and that the Declaration on the Granting of Independence to Colonial Countries and Peoples of 14

December 1960 (General Assembly resolution 1514 (XV)) has affirmed and solemnly proclaimed the necessity of bringing them to a speedy and unconditional end,

*Considering* that the United Nations Declaration on the Elimination of All Forms of Racial Discrimination of 20 November 1963 (General Assembly resolution 1940 (XVIII) solemnly affirms the necessity of speedily eliminating racial discrimination throughout the world in all its forms and manifestations and of securing understanding of and respect for the dignity of the human person,

*Convinced* that any doctrine of superiority based on racial differentiation is scientifically false, morally condemnable, socially unjust and dangerous, and that there is no justification for racial discrimination, in theory or in practice, anywhere,

*Reaffirming* that discrimination between human beings on the grounds of race, colour or ethnic origin is an obstacle to friendly and peaceful relations among nations and is capable of disturbing peace and security among peoples and the harmony of persons living side by side even within one and the same State,

*Convinced* that the existence of racial barriers is repugnant to the ideals of any human society,

*Alarmed* by manifestations of racial discrimination still in evidence in some areas of the world and by governmental policies based on racial superiority or hatred, such as policies of *apartheid*, segregation or separation,

*Resolved* to adopt all necessary measures for speedily eliminating racial discrimination in all its forms and manifestations, and to prevent and combat racist doctrines and practices in order to promote understanding between races and to build an international community free from all forms of racial segregation and racial discrimination,

*Bearing in mind* the Convention concerning Discrimination in respect of Employment and Occupation adopted by the International Labour Organization in 1958, and the Convention against Discrimination in Education adopted by the United Nations Educational, Scientific and Cultural Organization in 1960,

*Desiring* to implement the principles embodied in the United Nations Declaration on the Elimination of All Forms of Racial Discrimination and to secure the earliest adoption of practical measures to that end,

*Have agreed* as follows:

## PART I

*Article* 1

1. In this Convention, the term 'racial discrimination' shall mean any distinction, exclusion, restriction or preference based on race, colour,

descent, or national or ethnic origin which has the purpose or effect of nullifying or impairing the recognition, enjoyment or exercise, on an equal footing, of human rights and fundamental freedoms in the political, economic, social, cultural or any other field of public life.

2. This Convention shall not apply to distinctions, exclusions, restrictions or preferences made by a State Party to this Convention between citizens and non-citizens.

3. Nothing in this Convention may be interpreted as affecting in any way the legal provisions of States Parties concerning nationality, citizenship or naturalization, provided that such provisions do not discriminate against any particular nationality.

4. Special measures taken for the sole purpose of securing adequate advancement of certain racial or ethnic groups or individuals requiring such protection as may be necessary in order to ensure such groups or individuals equal enjoyment or exercise of human rights and fundamental freedoms shall not be deemed racial discrimination, provided, however, that such measures do not, as a consequence, lead to the maintenance of separate rights for different racial groups and that they shall not be continued after the objectives for which they were taken have been achieved.

*Article 2*

1. States Parties condemn racial discrimination and undertake to pursue by all appropriate means and without delay a policy of eliminating racial discrimination in all its forms and promoting understanding among all races, and, to this end:

> (*a*) Each State Party undertakes to engage in no act or practice of racial discrimination against persons, groups of persons or institutions and to ensure that all public authorities and public institutions, national and local, shall act in conformity with this obligation;
>
> (*b*) Each State Party undertakes not to sponsor, defend or support racial discrimination by any persons or organizations;
>
> (*c*) Each State Party shall take effective measures to review governmental, national and local policies, and to amend, rescind or nullify any laws and regulations which have the effect of creating or perpetuating racial discrimination wherever it exists;
>
> (*d*) Each State Party shall prohibit and bring to an end, by all appropriate means, including legislation as required by circumstances, racial discrimination by any persons, group or organization;
>
> (*e*) Each State Party undertakes to encourage, where appropriate, integrationist multi-racial organizations and movements and other means of eliminating barriers between races, and to discourage anything which tends to strengthen racial division.

2. States Parties shall, when the circumstances so warrant, take, in the social, economic, cultural and other fields, special and concrete measures to ensure the adequate development and protection of certain racial groups or individuals belonging to them, for the purpose of guaranteeing them the full and equal enjoyment of human rights and fundamental freedoms. These measures shall in no case entail as a consequence the maintenance of unequal or separate rights for different racial groups after the objectives for which they were taken have been achieved.

## Article 3

States Parties particularly condemn racial segregation and *apartheid* and undertake to prevent, prohibit and eradicate all practices of this nature in territories under their jurisdiction.

## Article 4

States Parties condemn all propaganda and all organizations which are based on ideas or theories of superiority of one race or group of persons of one colour or ethnic origin, or which attempt to justify or promote racial hatred and discrimination in any form, and undertake to adopt immediate and positive measures designed to eradicate all incitement to, or acts of, such discrimination and, to this end, with due regard to the principles embodied in the Universal Declaration of Human Rights and the rights expressly set forth in Article 5 of this Convention, *inter alia*:

(*a*) Shall declare an offence punishable by law all dissemination of ideas based on racial superiority or hatred, incitement to racial discrimination, as well as all acts of violence or incitement to such acts against any race or group of persons of another colour or ethnic origin, and also the provision of any assistance to racist activities, including the financing thereof;

(*b*) Shall declare illegal and prohibit organizations, and also organized and all other propaganda activities, which promote and incite racial discrimination, and shall recognize participation in such organizations or activities as an offence punishable by law;

(*c*) Shall not permit public authorities or public institutions, national or local, to promote or incite racial discrimination.

## Article 5

In compliance with the fundamental obligations laid down in Article 2 of this Convention, States Parties undertake to prohibit and to eliminate racial discrimination in all its forms and to guarantee the right of everyone, without distinction as to race, colour, or national or ethnic origin, to equality before the law, notably in the enjoyment of the following rights:

(*a*) The right to equal treatment before the tribunals and all other organs administering justice;

(*b*) The right to security of person and protection by the State against violence or bodily harm, whether inflicted by government officials or by any individual, group or institution;

(*c*) Political rights, in particular the rights to participate in elections—to vote and to stand for election—on the basis of universal and equal suffrage, to take part in the Government as well as in the conduct of public affairs at any level and to have equal access to public service;

(*d*) Other civil rights, in particular:

   (i) The right to freedom of movement and residence within the border of the State;

   (ii) The right to leave any country, including one's own, and to return to one's country;

   (iii) The right to nationality;

   (iv) The right to marriage and choice of spouse;

   (v) The right to own property alone as well as in association with others;

   (vi) The right to inherit;

   (vii) The right to freedom of thought, conscience and religion;

   (viii) The right to freedom of opinion and expression;

   (ix) The right to freedom of peaceful assembly and association;

(*e*) Economic, social and cultural rights, in particular:

   (i) The rights to work, to free choice of employment, to just and favourable conditions of work, to protection against unemployment, to equal pay for equal work, to just and favourable remuneration;

   (ii) The right to form and join trade unions;

   (iii) The right to housing;

   (iv) The right to public health, medical care, social security and social services;

   (v) The right to education and training;

   (vi) The right to equal participation in cultural activities;

(*f*) The right to access to any place or service intended for use by the general public, such as transport, hotels, restaurants, cafés, theatres and parks.

*Article* 6

States Parties shall assure to everyone within their jurisdiction effective protection and remedies, through the competent national tribunals and other State institutions, against any acts of racial discrimination which violate his human rights and fundamental freedoms contrary to this Convention, as well as the right to seek from such tribunals just and adequate reparation or satisfaction for any damage suffered as a result of such discrimination.

*Article* 7

States Parties undertake to adopt immediate and effective measures, particularly in the fields of teaching, education, culture and information, with a view to combating prejudices which lead to racial discrimination and to promoting understanding, tolerance and friendship among nations and racial or ethnical groups, as well as to propagating the purposes and principles of the Charter of the United Nations, the Universal Declaration of Human Rights, the United Nations Declaration on the Elimination of All Forms of Racial Discrimination, and this Convention.

## PART II

*Article* 8

1. There shall be established a Committee on the Elimination of Racial Discrimination (hereinafter referred to as the Committee) consisting of eighteen experts of high moral standing and acknowledged impartiality elected by States Parties from among their nationals, who shall serve in their personal capacity, consideration being given to equitable geographical distribution and to the representation of the different forms of civilization as well as of the principal legal systems.

2. The members of the Committee shall be elected by secret ballot from a list of persons nominated by the States Parties. Each State Party may nominate one person from among its own nationals.

3. The initial election shall be held six months after the date of the entry into force of this Convention. At least three months before the date of each election the Secretary-General of the United Nations shall address a letter to the States Parties inviting them to submit their nominations within two months. The Secretary-General shall prepare a list in alphabetical order of all persons thus nominated, indicating the States Parties which have nominated them, and shall submit it to the States Parties.

4. Elections of the members of the Committee shall be held at a meeting of States Parties convened by the Secretary-General at United Nations Headquarters. At that meeting, for which two-thirds of the States Parties shall constitute a quorum, the persons elected to the Committee shall be those nominees who obtain the largest number of votes and an absolute majority of the votes of the representatives of States Parties present and voting.

5. (*a*) The members of the Committee shall be elected for a term of four years. However, the terms of nine of the members elected at the first election shall expire at the end of two years; immediately after the first election the names of these nine members shall be chosen by lot by the Chairman of the Committee.

(*b*) For the filling of casual vacancies, the State Party whose expert has ceased to function as a member of the Committee shall appoint another expert from among its nationals, subject to the approval of the Committee.

6. States Parties shall be responsible for the expenses of the members of the Committee while they are in performance of Committee duties.

*Article* 9

1. States Parties undertake to submit to the Secretary-General of the United Nations, for consideration by the Committee, a report on the legislative, judicial, administrative or other measures which they have adopted and which give effect to the provisions of this Convention: (*a*) within one year after the entry into force of the Convention for the State concerned; and (*b*) thereafter every two years and whenever the Committee so requests. The Committee may request further information from the States Parties.

2. The Committee shall report annually, through the Secretary-General, to the General Assembly of the United Nations on its activities and may make suggestions and general recommendations based on the examination of the reports and information received from the States Parties. Such suggestions and general recommendations shall be reported to the General Assembly together with comments, if any, from States Parties.

*Article* 10

1. The Committee shall adopt its own rules of procedure.

2. The Committee shall elect its officers for a term of two years.

3. The secretariat of the Committee shall be provided by the Secretary-General of the United Nations.

4. The meetings of the Committee shall normally be held at United Nations Headquarters.

*Article* 11

1. If a State Party considers that another State Party is not giving effect to the provisions of this Convention, it may bring the matter to the attention of the Committee. The Committee shall then transmit the communication to the State Party concerned. Within three months, the receiving State shall submit to the Committee written explanations or statements clarifying the matter and the remedy, if any, that may have been taken by that State.

2. If the matter is not adjusted to the satisfaction of both parties, either by bilateral negotiations or by any other procedure open to them, within six months after the receipt by the receiving State of the initial communication, either State shall have the right to refer the matter again to the Committee by notifying the Committee and also the other State.

3. The Committee shall deal with a matter referred to it in accordance

with paragraph 2 of this Article after it has ascertained that all available domestic remedies have been invoked and exhausted in the case, in conformity with the generally recognized principles of international law. This shall not be the rule where the application of the remedies is unreasonably prolonged.

4. In any matter referred to it, the Committee may call upon the States Parties concerned to supply any other relevant information.

5. When any matter arising out of this Article is being considered by the Committee, the States Parties concerned shall be entitled to send a representative to take part in the proceedings of the Committee, without voting rights, while the matter is under consideration.

*Article* 12

1. (*a*) After the Committee has obtained and collated all the information it deems necessary, the Chairman shall appoint an *ad hoc* Conciliation Commission (hereinafter referred to as the Commission) comprising five persons who may or may not be members of the Committee. The members of the Commission shall be appointed with the unanimous consent of the parties to the dispute, and its good offices shall be made available to the States concerned with a view to an amicable solution of the matter on the basis of respect for this Convention.

(*b*) If the States Parties to the dispute fail to reach agreement within three months on all or part of the composition of the Commission, the members of the Commission not agreed upon by the States Parties to the dispute shall be elected by secret ballot by a two-thirds majority vote of the Committee from among its own members.

2. The members of the Commission shall serve in their personal capacity. They shall not be nationals of the States Parties to the dispute or of a State not Party to this Convention.

3. The Commission shall elect its own Chairman and adopt its own rules of procedure.

4. The meetings of the Commission shall normally be held at United Nations Headquarters or at any other convenient place as determined by the Commission.

5. The secretariat provided in accordance with Article 10, paragraph 3, of this Convention shall also service the Commission whenever a dispute among States Parties brings the Commission into being.

6. The States Parties to the dispute shall share equally all the expenses of the members of the Commission in accordance with estimates to be provided by the Secretary-General of the United Nations.

7. The Secretary-General shall be empowered to pay the expenses of the members of the Commission, if necessary, before reimbursement by the States Parties to the dispute in accordance with paragraph 6 of this Article.

8. The information obtained and collated by the Committee shall be made available to the Commission, and the Commission may call upon the States concerned to supply any other relevant information.

*Article* 13

1. When the Commission has fully considered the matter, it shall prepare and submit to the Chairman of the Committee a report embodying its findings on all questions of fact relevant to the issue between the parties and containing such recommendations as it may think proper for the amicable solution of the dispute.

2. The Chairman of the Committee shall communicate the report of the Commission to each of the States Parties to the dispute. These States shall, within three months, inform the Chairman of the Committee whether or not they accept the recommendations contained in the report of the Commission.

3. After the period provided for in paragraph 2 of this Article, the Chairman of the Committee shall communicate the report of the Commission and the declarations of the States Parties concerned to the other States Parties to this Convention.

*Article* 14

1. A State Party may at any time declare that it recognizes the competence of the Committee to receive and consider communications from individuals or groups of individuals within its jurisdiction claiming to be victims of a violation by that State Party of any of the rights set forth in this Convention. No communication shall be received by the Committee if it concerns a State Party which has not made such a declaration.

2. Any State Party which makes a declaration as provided for in paragraph 1 of this Article may establish or indicate a body within its national legal order which shall be competent to receive and consider petitions from individuals and groups of individuals within its jurisdiction who claim to be victims of a violation of any of the rights set forth in this Convention and who have exhausted other available local remedies.

3. A declaration made in accordance with paragraph 1 of this Article and the name of any body established or indicated in accordance with paragraph 2 of this Article shall be deposited by the State Party concerned with the Secretary-General of the United Nations, who shall transmit copies thereof to the other States Parties. A declaration may be withdrawn at any time by notification to the Secretary-General, but such a withdrawal shall not affect communications pending before the Committee.

4. A register of petitions shall be kept by the body established or indicated in accordance with paragraph 2 of this Article, and certified copies of the register shall be filed annually through appropriate channels with the

Secretary-General on the understanding that the contents shall not be publicly disclosed.

5. In the event of failure to obtain satisfaction from the body established or indicated in accordance with paragraph 2 of this Article, the petitioner shall have the right to communicate the matter to the Committee within six months.

6. (*a*) The Committee shall confidentially bring any communication referred to it to the attention of the State Party alleged to be violating any provision of this Convention, but the identity of the individual or groups of individuals concerned shall not be revealed without his or their express consent. The Committee shall not receive anonymous communications.

(*b*) Within three months, the receiving State shall submit to the Committee written explanations or statements clarifying the matter and the remedy, if any, that may have been taken by that State.

7. (*a*) The Committee shall consider communications in the light of all information made available to it by the State Party concerned and by the petitioner. The Committee shall not consider any communication from a petitioner unless it has ascertained that the petitioner has exhausted all available domestic remedies. However, this shall not be the rule where the application of the remedies is unreasonably prolonged.

(*b*) The Committee shall forward its suggestions and recommendations, if any, to the State Party concerned and to the petitioner.

8. The Committee shall include in its annual report a summary of such communications and, where appropriate, a summary of the explanations and statements of the States Parties concerned and of its own suggestions and recommendations.

9. The Committee shall be competent to exercise the functions provided for in this Article only when at least ten States Parties to this Convention are bound by declarations in accordance with paragraph 1 of this Article.

*Article* 15

1. Pending the achievement of the objectives of the Declaration on the Granting of Independence to Colonial Countries and Peoples, contained in General Assembly resolution 1514 (XV) of 14 December 1960, the provisions of this Convention shall in no way limit the right of petition granted to these peoples by other international instruments or by the United Nations and its specialized agencies.

2. (*a*) The Committee established under Article 8, paragraph 1, of this Convention shall receive copies of the petitions from, and submit expressions of opinion and recommendations on these petitions to, the bodies of the United Nations which deal with matters directly related to the principles and objectives of this Convention in their consideration of petitions from the inhabitants of Trust and Non-Self-Governing Territories and all

other territories to which General Assembly resolution 1514 (XV) applies, relating to matters covered by this Convention which are before these bodies.

(b) The Committee shall receive from the competent bodies of the United Nations copies of the reports concerning the legislative, judicial, administrative or other measures directly related to the principles and objectives of this Convention applied by the administering Powers within the Territories mentioned in sub-paragraph (a) of this paragraph, and shall express opinions and make recommendations to these bodies.

3. The Committee shall include in its report to the General Assembly a summary of the petitions and reports it has received from United Nations bodies, and the expressions of opinion and recommendations of the Committee relating to the said petitions and reports.

4. The Committee shall request from the Secretary-General of the United Nations all information relevant to the objectives of this Convention and available to him regarding the Territories mentioned in paragraph 2 (a) of this Article.

*Article* 16

The provisions of this Convention concerning the settlement of disputes or complaints shall be applied without prejudice to other procedures for settling disputes or complaints in the field of discrimination laid down in the constituent instruments of, or in conventions adopted by, the United Nations and its specialized agencies, and shall not prevent the States Parties from having recourse to other procedures for settling a dispute in accordance with general or special international agreements in force between them.

## PART III

*Article* 17

1. This Convention is open for signature by any State Member of the United Nations or member of any of its specialized agencies, by any State Party to the Statute of the International Court of Justice, and by any other State which has been invited by the General Assembly of the United Nations to become a Party to this Convention.

2. This Convention is subject to ratification. Instruments of ratification shall be deposited with the Secretary-General of the United Nations.

*Article* 18

1. This Convention shall be open to accession by any State referred to in Article 17, paragraph 1, of the Convention.

2. Accession shall be effected by the deposit of an instrument of accession with the Secretary-General of the United Nations.

*Article* 19

1. This Convention shall enter into force on the thirtieth day after the date of the deposit with the Secretary-General of the United Nations of the twenty-seventh instrument of ratification or instrument of accession.

2. For each State ratifying this Convention or acceding to it after the deposit of the twenty-seventh instrument of ratification or instrument of accession, the Convention shall enter force on the thirtieth day after the date of the deposit of its own instrument of ratification or instrument of accession.

*Article* 20

1. The Secretary-General of the United Nations shall receive and circulate to all States which are or may become Parties to this Convention reservations made by States at the time of ratification or accession. Any State which objects to the reservation shall, within a period of ninety days from the date of the said communication, notify the Secretary-General that it does not accept it.

2. A reservation incompatible with the object and purpose of this Convention shall not be permitted, nor shall a reservation the effect of which would inhibit the operation of any of the bodies established by this Convention be allowed. A reservation shall be considered incompatible or inhibitive if at least two-thirds of the States Parties to this Convention object to it.

3. Reservations may be withdrawn at any time by notification to this effect addressed to the Secretary-General. Such notification shall take effect on the date on which it is received.

*Article* 21

A State Party may denounce this Convention by written notification to the Secretary-General of the United Nations. Denunciation shall take effect one year after the date of receipt of the notification by the Secretary-General.

*Article* 22

Any dispute between two or more States Parties with respect to the interpretation or application of this Convention, which is not settled by negotiation or by the procedures expressly provided for in this Convention, shall, at the request of any of the parties to the dispute, be referred to the International Court of Justice for decision, unless the disputants agree to another mode of settlement.

*Article* 23

1. A request for the revision of this Convention may be made at any time by any State Party by means of a notification in writing addressed to the Secretary-General of the United Nations.

2. The General Assembly of the United Nations shall decide upon the steps, if any, to be taken in respect of such a request.

*Article* 24

The Secretary-General of the United Nations shall inform all States referred to in Article 17, paragraph 1, of this Convention of the following particulars:

    (*a*) Signatures, ratifications and accessions under Articles 17 and 18;
    (*b*) The date of entry into force of this Convention under Article 19;
    (*c*) Communications and declarations received under Articles 14, 20 and 23;
    (*d*) Denunciations under Article 21.

*Article* 25

1. This Convention, of which the Chinese, English, French, Russian and Spanish texts are equally authentic, shall be deposited in the archives of the United Nations.

2. The Secretary-General of the United Nations shall transmit certified copies of this Convention to all States belonging to any of the categories mentioned in Article 17, paragraph 1, of the Convention.

*In faith whereof* the undersigned, being duly authorized thereto by their respective Governments, have signed the present Convention, opened for signature at New York, on the seventh day of March, one thousand nine hundred and sixty-six.


## ANNEX

*The General Assembly,*

*Recalling* the Declaration on the Granting of Independence to Colonial Countries and Peoples contained in its resolution 1514 (XV) of 14 December 1960.

*Bearing in mind* its resolution 1654 (XVI) of 27 November 1961, which established the Special Committee on the Situation with regard to the Implementation of the Declaration on the Granting of Independence to Colonial Countries and Peoples to examine the application of the Declaration and to carry out its provisions by all means at its disposal,

*Bearing in mind also* the provisions of Article 15 of the International

Convention on the Elimination of All Forms of Racial Discrimination contained in the annex to resolution 2106 A (XX) above,

*Recalling* that the General Assembly has established other bodies to receive and examine petitions from the peoples of colonial countries,

*Convinced* that close co-operation between the Committee on the Elimination of Racial Discrimination, established by the International Convention on the Elimination of All Forms of Racial Discrimination, and the bodies of the United Nations charged with receiving and examining petitions from the peoples of colonial countries will facilitate the achievement of the objectives of both the Convention and the Declaration on the Granting of Independence to Colonial Countries and Peoples,

*Recognizing* that the elimination of racial discrimination in all its forms is vital to the achievement of fundamental human rights and to the assurance of the dignity and worth of the human person, and thus constitutes a pre-emptory obligation under the Charter of the United Nations,

1. *Calls upon* the Secretary-General to make available to the Committee on the Elimination of Racial Discrimination, periodically or at its request, all information in his possession relevant to Article 15 of the International Convention on the Elimination of All Forms of Racial Discrimination;

2. *Requests* the Special Committee on the Situation with regard to the Implementation of the Granting of Independence to Colonial Countries and Peoples, and all other bodies of the United Nations authorized to receive and examine petitions from the peoples of the colonial countries, to transmit to the Committee on the Elimination of Racial Discrimination, periodically or at its request, copies of petitions from those peoples relevant to the Convention, for the comments and recommendations of the said Committee;

3. *Requests* the bodies referred to in paragraph 2 above to include in their annual reports to the General Assembly a summary of the action taken by them under the terms of the present resolution.

*1406th plenary meeting*
*21 December 1965*

# V. INTERNATIONAL CONVENTION ON THE SUPPRESSION AND PUNISHMENT OF THE CRIME OF APARTHEID, 1973

This Convention was adopted by the United Nations General Assembly and opened for signature as a consequence of Resolution 3068 (XXVIII), adopted on 30 November 1973. The Resolution was adopted by 91 votes in favour, and with 26 abstentions. Portugal, South Africa, the United Kingdom and the United States voted against the Resolution. The basis of the opposition of the United States is set forth in *Digest of United States Practice in International Law*, 1973, pp. 130–2. In particular, it is pointed out that the new Convention was 'not necessary in view of the broad, all-inclusive provisions of the International Convention on the Elimination of All Forms of Racial Discrimination'.

Eighty-eight States have become parties to the Convention which entered into force on 18 July 1976. Western States have avoided signature, ratification or accession. The Convention originated in a Guinea-U.S.S.R. proposal submitted to the General Assembly in 1971.

## TEXT

*The States Parties to the present Convention,*

*Recalling* the provisions of the Charter of the United Nations, in which all Members pledged themselves to take joint and separate action in co-operation with the Organization for the achievement of universal respect for, and observance of, human rights and fundamental freedoms for all without distinction as to race, sex, language or religion,

*Considering* the Universal Declaration of Human Rights, which states that all human beings are born free and equal in dignity and rights and that everyone is entitled to all the rights and freedoms set forth in the Declaration, without distinction of any kind, such as race, colour or national origin.

*Considering* the Declaration on the Granting of Independence to Colonial Countries and Peoples, in which the General Assembly stated that the process of liberation is irresistible and irreversible and that, in the interests of human dignity, progress and justice, an end must be put to colonialism and all practices of segregation and discrimination associated therewith,

*Observing* that, in accordance with the International Convention on the Elimination of All Forms of Racial Discrimination, States particularly condemn racial segregation and *apartheid* and undertake to prevent, prohibit and eradicate all practices of this nature in territories under their jurisdiction,

*Observing* that, in the Convention on the Prevention and Punishment of the Crime of Genocide, certain acts which may also be qualified as acts of *apartheid* constitute a crime under international law,

*Observing* that, in the Convention of the Non-Applicability of Statutory

Limitations to War Crimes and Crimes Against Humanity, 'inhuman acts resulting from the policy of *apartheid*' are qualified as crimes against humanity,

*Observing* that the General Assembly of the United Nations has adopted a number of resolutions in which the policies and practices of *apartheid* are condemned as a crime against humanity,

*Observing* that the Security Council has emphasized that *apartheid*, its continued intensification and expansion, seriously disturbs and threatens international peace and security,

*Convinced* that an International Convention on the Suppression and Punishment of the Crime of *Apartheid* would make it possible to take more effective measures at the international and national levels with a view to the suppression and punishment of the crime of *apartheid*,

*Have agreed* as follows:

### Article I

1. The States Parties to the present Convention declare that *apartheid* is a crime against humanity and that inhuman acts resulting from the policies and practices of *apartheid* and similar policies and practices of racial segregation and discrimination, as defined in Article II of the Convention, are crimes violating the principles of international law, in particular the purposes and principles of the Charter of the United Nations, and constituting a serious threat to international peace and security.

2. The States Parties to the present Convention declare criminal those organizations, institutions and individuals committing the crime of *apartheid*.

### Article II

For the purpose of the present Convention, the term 'the crime of *apartheid*', which shall include similar policies and practices of racial segregation and discrimination as practised in southern Africa, shall apply to the following inhuman acts committed for the purpose of establishing and maintaining domination by one racial group of persons over any other racial group of persons and systematically oppressing them:

(a) Denial to a member or members of a racial group or groups of the right to life and liberty of person:
  (i) By murder of members of a racial group or groups;
  (ii) By the infliction upon the members of a racial group or groups of serious bodily or mental harm by the infringement of their freedom or dignity, or by subjecting them to torture or to cruel, inhuman or degrading treatment or punishment;
  (iii) By arbitrary arrest and illegal imprisonment of the members of a racial group or groups;
(b) Deliberate imposition on a racial group or groups of living conditions

calculated to cause its or their physical destruction in whole or in part;

(c) Any legislative measures and other measures calculated to prevent a racial group or groups from participation in the political, social, economic and cultural life of the country and the deliberate creation of conditions preventing the full development of such a group or groups, in particular by denying to members of a racial group or groups basic human rights and freedoms, including the right to work, the right to form recognized trade unions, the right to education, the right to leave and to return to their country, the right to a nationality, the right to freedom of movement and residence, the right to freedom of opinion and expression, and the right to freedom of peaceful assembly and association;

(d) Any measures, including legislative measures, designed to divide the population along racial lines by the creation of separate reserves and ghettos for the members of a racial group or groups, the prohibition of mixed marriages among members of various racial groups, the expropriation of landed property belonging to a racial group or groups or to members thereof;

(e) Exploitation of the labour of the members of a racial group or groups, in particular by submitting them to forced labour;

(f) Persecution of organizations and persons, by depriving them of fundamental rights and freedoms, because they oppose *apartheid*.

*Article III*

International criminal responsibility shall apply, irrespective of the motive involved, to individuals, members of organizations and institutions and representatives of the State, whether residing in the territory of the State in which the acts are perpetrated or in some other State, whenever they:

(a) Commit, participate in, directly incite or conspire in the commission of the acts mentioned in Article II of the present Convention;

(b) Directly abet, encourage or co-operate in the commission of the crime of *apartheid*.

*Article IV*

The States Parties to the present Convention undertake:

(a) To adopt any legislative or other measures necessary to suppress as well as to prevent any encouragement of the crime of *apartheid* and similar segregationist policies or their manifestations and to punish persons guilty of that crime;

(b) To adopt legislative, judicial and administrative measures to prosecute, bring to trial and punish in accordance with their jurisdiction persons responsible for, or accused of, the acts defined in Article II of the present Convention, whether or not such persons reside in the territory of the State in which the acts are committed or are nationals of that State or of some other State or are stateless persons.

*Article V*

Persons charged with the acts enumerated in Article II of the present Convention may be tried by a competent tribunal of any State Party to the Convention which may acquire jurisdiction over the person of the accused or by an international penal tribunal jurisdiction with respect to those States Parties which shall have accepted its jurisdiction.

*Article VI*

The States Parties to the present Convention undertake to accept and carry out in accordance with the Charter of the United Nations the decisions taken by the Security Council aimed at the prevention, suppression and punishment of the crime of *apartheid*, and to co-operate in the implementation of decisions adopted by other competent organs of the United Nations with a view to achieving the purposes of the Convention.

*Article VII*

1. The States Parties to the present Convention undertake to submit periodic reports to the group established under Article IX on the legislative, judicial, administrative or other measures that they have adopted and that give effect to the provisions of the Convention.

2. Copies of the reports shall be transmitted through the Secretary-General of the United Nations to the Special Committee on *Apartheid*.

*Article VIII*

Any State Party to the present Convention may call upon any competent organ of the United Nations to take such action under the Charter of the United Nations as it considers appropriate for the prevention and suppression of the crime of *apartheid*.

*Article IX*

1. The Chairman of the Commission on Human Rights shall appoint a group consisting of three members of the Commission on Human Rights, who are also representatives of States Parties to the present Convention, to consider reports submitted by States Parties in accordance with Article VII.

2. If, among the members of the Commission on Human Rights, there are no representatives of States Parties to the present Convention or if there are fewer than three such representatives, the Secretary-General of the United Nations shall, after consulting all States Parties to the Convention, designate a representative of the State Party or representatives of the States

Parties which are not members of the Commission on Human Rights to take part in the work of the group established in accordance with paragraph 1 of this Article, until such time as representatives of the States Parties to the Convention are elected to the Commission on Human Rights.

3. The group may meet for a period of not more than five days, either before the opening or after the closing of the session of the Commission on Human Rights, to consider the reports submitted in accordance with Article VII.

*Article X*

1. The States Parties to the present Convention empower the Commission on Human Rights;

> (*a*) To request United Nations organs, when transmitting copies of petitions under Article 15 of the International Convention on the Elimination of All Forms of Racial Discrimination, to draw its attention to complaints concerning acts which are enumerated in Article II of the present Convention;
>
> (*b*) To prepare, on the basis of reports from competent organs of the United Nations and periodic reports from States Parties to the present Convention, a list of individuals, organizations, institutions and representatives of States which are alleged to be responsible for the crimes enumerated in Article II of the Convention, as well as those against whom legal proceedings have been undertaken by States Parties to the Convention;
>
> (*c*) To request information from the competent United Nations organs concerning measures taken by the authorities responsible for the administration of Trust and Non-Self-Governing Territories, and all other Territories to which General Assembly resolution 1514 (XV) of 14 December 1960 applies, with regard to such individuals alleged to be responsible for crimes under Article II of the Convention who are believed to be under their territorial and administrative jurisdiction.

2. Pending the achievement of the objectives of the Declaration on the Granting of Independence to Colonial Countries and Peoples, contained in General Assembly resolution 1514 (XV), the provisions of the present Convention shall in no way limit the right of petition granted to those peoples by other international instruments or by the United Nations and its specialized agencies.

*Article XI*

1. Acts enumerated in Article II of the present Convention shall not be considered political crimes for the purpose of extradition.

2. The States Parties to the present Convention undertake in such cases to

grant extradition in accordance with their legislation and with the treaties in force.

## Article XII

Disputes between States Parties arising out of the interpretation, application or implementation of the present Convention which have not been settled by negotiation shall, at the request of the States Parties to the dispute, be brought before the International Court of Justice, save where the parties to the dispute have agreed on some other form of settlement.

## Article XIII

The present Convention is open for signature by all States. Any State which does not sign the Convention before its entry into force may accede to it.

## Article XIV

1. The present Convention is subject to ratification. Instruments of ratification shall be deposited with the Secretary-General of the United Nations.

2. Accession shall be effected by the deposit of an instrument of accession with the Secretary-General of the United Nations.

## Article XV

1. The present Convention shall enter force on the thirtieth day after the date of the deposit with the Secretary-General of the United Nations of the twentieth instrument of ratification or accession.

2. For each State ratifying the present Convention or acceding to it after the deposit of the twentieth instrument of ratification or instrument of accession, the Convention shall enter into force on the thirtieth day after the date of the deposit of its own instrument of ratification or instrument of accession.

## Article XVI

A State Party may denounce the present Convention by written notification to the Secretary-General of the United Nations. Denunciation shall take effect one year after the date of receipt of the notification by the Secretary-General.

## Article XVII

1. A request for the revision of this Convention may be made at any time by any State Party by means of a notification in writing addressed to the Secretary-General of the United Nations.

2. The General Assembly of the United Nations shall decide upon the steps, if any, to be taken in respect of such request.

*Article XVIII*

The Secretary-General of the United Nations shall inform all States of the following particulars:

(*a*) Signatures, ratifications and accessions under Articles XIII and XIV;

(*b*) The date of entry into force of the present Convention under Article XV;

(*c*) Denunciations under Article XVI;

(*d*) Notifications under Article XVII.

*Article XIX*

1. The present Convention, of which the Chinese, English, French, Russian and Spanish texts are equally authentic, shall be deposited in the archives of the United Nations.

2. The Secretary-General of the United Nations shall transmit certified copies of the present Convention to all States.

# VI. CONVENTION ON THE ELIMINATION OF ALL FORMS OF DISCRIMINATION AGAINST WOMEN, 1979

The text which follows was adopted by the United Nations General Assembly on 18 December 1979 (130 votes in favour, none against; ten abstentions). The Convention came into force on 3 September 1981. One hundred and three States have become parties. The precursor to the Convention was the Declaration on Elimination of Discrimination against Women adopted unanimously by the General Assembly on 7 November 1967: for the text see the first edition of the present work, p. 183.

Reference should also be made to the I.L.O. Convention Concerning Equal Remuneration for Men and Women Workers for Work of Equal Value, below.

On the standard of non-discrimination in general international law see Brownlie, *Principles of Public International Law*, 4th ed., 1990, pp. 598–601. On sexual equality see Daw, *Malaya Law Review*, Vol. 12 (1970), pp. 308–36; McDougal, Lasswell and Chen, *American Journal of International Law*, Vol. 69 (1975), pp. 497–533.

## TEXT

*The States Parties to the present Convention,*

*Noting* that the Charter of the United Nations reaffirms faith in fundamental human rights, in the dignity and worth of the human person and in the equal rights of men and women,

*Noting* that the Universal Declaration of Human Rights affirms the principle of the inadmissibility of discrimination and proclaims that all human beings are born free and equal in dignity and rights and that everyone is entitled to all the rights and freedoms set forth therein, without distinction of any kind, including distinction based on sex,

*Noting* that the States Parties to the International Covenants on Human Rights have the obligation to ensure the equal right of men and women to enjoy all economic, social, cultural, civil and political rights,

*Considering* the international conventions concluded under the auspices of the United Nations and the specialized agencies promoting equality of rights of men and women,

*Noting also* the resolutions, declarations and recommendations adopted by the United Nations and the specialized agencies promoting equality of rights of men and women,

*Concerned,* however, that despite these various instruments extensive discrimination against women continues to exist,

*Recalling* that discrimination against women violates the principles of equality of rights and respect for human dignity, is an obstacle to the participation of women, on equal terms with men, in the political, social, economic and cultural life of their countries, hampers the growth of the prosperity of society and the family and makes more difficult the full development of the potentialities of women in the service of their countries and of humanity,

*Concerned* that in situations of poverty women have the least access to food, health, education, training and opportunities for employment and other needs,

*Convinced* that the establishment of the new international economic order based on equity and justice will contribute significantly towards the promotion of equality between men and women,

*Emphasizing* that the eradication of *apartheid*, of all forms of racism, racial discrimination, colonialism, neo-colonialism, aggression, foreign occupation and domination and interference in the internal affairs of States is essential to the full enjoyment of the rights of men and women,

*Affirming* that the strengthening of international peace and security, relaxation of international tension, mutual co-operation among all States irrespective of their social and economic systems, general and complete disarmament, and in particular nuclear disarmament under strict and effective international control, the affirmation of the principles of justice, equality and mutual benefit in relations among countries and the realization of the right of peoples under alien and colonial domination and foreign occupation to self-determination and independence, as well as respect for national sovereignty and territorial integrity, will promote social progress and development and as a consequence will contribute to the attainment of full equality between men and women,

*Convinced* that the full and complete development of a country, the welfare of the world and the cause of peace require the maximum participation of women on equal terms with men in all fields,

*Bearing in mind* the great contribution of women to the welfare of the family and to the development of society, so far not fully recognized, the social significance of maternity and the role of both parents in the family and in the upbringing of children, and aware that the role of women in procreation should not be a basis for discrimination but that the upbringing of children requires a sharing of responsibility between men and women and society as a whole,

*Aware* that a change in the traditional role of men as well as the role of women in society and in the family is needed to achieve full equality between men and women,

*Determined* to implement the principles set forth in the Declaration on the Elimination of Discrimination against Women and, for that purpose, to adopt the measures required for the elimination of such discrimination in all its forms and manifestations,

*Have agreed* on the following:

# PART I

*Article* 1

For the purposes of the present Convention, the term 'discrimination against women' shall mean any distinction, exclusion or restriction made on the basis of sex which has the effect or purpose of impairing or nullifying the recognition, enjoyment or exercise by women, irrespective of their marital status, on a basis of equality of men and women, of human rights and fundamental freedoms in the political, economic, social, cultural, civil or any other field.

*Article* 2

States Parties condemn discrimination against women in all its forms, agree to pursue by all appropriate means and without delay a policy of eliminating discrimination against women and, to this end, undertake;

(*a*)  To embody the principle of the equality of men and women in their national constitutions or other appropriate legislation if not yet incorporated therein and to ensure, through law and other appropriate means, the practical realization of this principle;

(*b*)  To adopt appropriate legislative and other measures, including sanctions where appropriate, prohibiting all discrimination against women;

(*c*)  To establish legal protection of the rights of women on an equal basis with men and to ensure through competent national tribunals and other public institutions the effective protection of women against any act of discrimination;

(*d*)  To refrain from engaging in any act or practice of discrimination against women and to ensure that public authorities and institutions shall act in conformity with this obligation;

(*e*)  To take all appropriate measures to eliminate discrimination against women by any person, organization or enterprise;

(*f*)  To take all appropriate measures, including legislation, to modify or abolish existing laws, regulations, customs and practices which constitute discrimination against women;

(*g*)  To repeal all national penal provisions which constitute discrimination against women.

*Article* 3

States Parties shall take in all fields, in particular in the political, social, economic and cultural fields, all appropriate measures, including legislation, to ensure the full development and advancement of women, for the purpose of guaranteeing them the exercise and enjoyment of human rights and fundamental freedoms on a basis of equality with men.

*Article* 4

1. Adoption by States Parties of temporary special measures aimed at accelerating *de facto* equality between men and women shall not be considered discrimination as defined in the present Convention, but shall in no way entail as a consequence the maintenance of unequal or separate standards; these measures shall be discontinued when the objectives of equality of opportunity and treatment have been achieved.

2. Adoption by States Parties of special measures, including those measures contained in the present Convention, aimed at protecting maternity shall not be considered discriminatory.

*Article* 5

States Parties shall take all appropriate measures:

- (*a*) To modify the social and cultural patterns of conduct of men and women, with a view to achieving the elimination of prejudices and customary and all other practices which are based on the idea of the inferiority or the superiority of either of the sexes or on stereotyped roles for men and women;
- (*b*) To ensure that family education includes a proper understanding of maternity as a social function and the recognition of the common responsibility of men and women in the upbringing and development of their children, it being understood that the interest of the children is the primordial consideration in all cases.

*Article* 6

States Parties shall take all appropriate measures, including legislation, to suppress all forms of traffic in women and exploitation of prostitution of women.

# PART II

*Article* 7

States Parties shall take all appropriate measures to eliminate discrimination against women in the political and public life of the country and, in particular, shall ensure to women, on equal terms with men, the right:

- (*a*) To vote in all elections and public referenda and to be eligible for election to all publicly elected bodies;
- (*b*) To participate in the formulation of government policy and the implementation thereof and to hold public office and perform all public functions at all levels of government;

(c) To participate in non-governmental organizations and associations concerned with the public and political life of the country.

*Article 8*

States Parties shall take all appropriate measures to ensure to women, on equal terms with men and without any discrimination, the opportunity to represent their Governments at the international level and to participate in the work of international organizations.

*Article 9*

1. States Parties shall grant women equal rights with men to acquire, change or retain their nationality. They shall ensure in particular that neither marriage to an alien nor change of nationality by the husband during marriage shall automatically change the nationality of the wife, render her stateless or force upon her the nationality of the husband.

2. States Parties shall grant women equal rights with men with respect to the nationality of their children.

## PART III

*Article 10*

States Parties shall take all appropriate measures to eliminate discrimination against women in order to ensure to them equal rights with men in the field of education and in particular to ensure, on a basis of equality of men and women:

(a) The same conditions for career and vocational guidance, for access to studies and for the achievement of diplomas in educational establishments of all categories in rural as well as in urban areas; this equality shall be ensured in pre-school, general, technical, professional and higher technical education, as well as in all types of vocational training;

(b) Access to the same curricula, the same examinations, teaching staff with qualifications of the same standard and school premises and equipment of the same equality;

(c) The elimination of any stereotyped concept of the roles of men and women at all levels and in all forms of education by encouraging co-education and other types of education which will help to achieve this aim and, in particular, by the revision of textbooks and school programmes and the adaptation of teaching methods;

(d) The same opportunities to benefit from scholarships and other study grants;

(e) The same opportunities for access to programmes of continuing education, including adult and functional literacy programmes, particularly those aimed at reducing, at the earliest possible time, any gap in education existing between men and women;

(*f*) The reduction of female student drop-out rates and the organization of programmes for girls and women who have left school prematurely;

(*g*) The same opportunities to participate actively in sports and physical education;

(*h*) Access to specific educational information to help to ensure the health and well-being of families, including information and advice on family planning.

*Article* 11

1. States Parties shall take all appropriate measures to eliminate discrimination against women in the field of employment in order to ensure, on a basis of equality of men and women, the same rights, in particular:

(*a*) The right to work as an inalienable right of all human beings;

(*b*) The right to the same employment opportunities, including the application of the same criteria for selection in matters of employment;

(*c*) The right to free choice of profession and employment, the right to promotion, job security and all benefits and conditions of service and the right to receive vocational training and retraining, including apprenticeships, advanced vocational training and recurrent training;

(*d*) The right to equal remuneration, including benefits, and to equal treatment in respect of work of equal value, as well as equality of treatment in the evaluation of the quality of work;

(*e*) The right to social security, particularly in cases of retirement, unemployment, sickness, invalidity and old age and other incapacity to work, as well as the right to paid leave;

(*f*) The right to protection of health and to safety in working conditions, including the safeguarding of the function of reproduction.

2. In order to prevent discrimination against women on the grounds of marriage or maternity and to ensure their effective right to work, States Parties shall take appropriate measures:

(*a*) To prohibit, subject to the imposition of sanctions, dismissal on the grounds of pregnancy or of maternity leave and discrimination in dismissals on the basis of marital status;

(*b*) To introduce maternity leave with pay or with comparable social benefits without loss of former employment, seniority or social allowances;

(*c*) To encourage the provision of the necessary supporting social services to enable parents to combine family obligations with work responsibilities and participation in public life, in particular through promoting the establishment and development of a network of child-care facilities;

(d) To provide special protection to women during pregnancy in types of work proved to be harmful to them.

3. Protective legislation relating to matters covered in this article shall be reviewed periodically in the light of scientific and technological knowledge and shall be revised, repealed or extended as necessary.

*Article* 12

1. States Parties shall take all appropriate measures to eliminate discrimination against women in the field of health care in order to ensure, on a basis of equality of men and women, access to health care services, including those related to family planning.

2. Notwithstanding the provisions of paragraph 1 of this Article, States Parties shall ensure to women appropriate services in connexion with pregnancy, confinement and the post-natal period, granting free services where necessary, as well as adequate nutrition during pregnancy and lactation.

*Article* 13

States Parties shall take all appropriate measures to eliminate discrimination against women in other areas of economic and social life in order to ensure, on a basis of equality of men and women, the same rights, in particular:

(a) The right to family benefits;
(b) The right to bank loans, mortgages and other forms of financial credit;
(c) The right to participate in recreational activities, sports and all aspects of cultural life.

*Article* 14

1. States Parties shall take into account the particular problems faced by rural women and the significant roles which rural women play in the economic survival of their families, including their work in the non-monetized sectors of the economy, and shall take all appropriate measures to ensure the application of the provisions of this Convention to women in rural areas.

2. States Parties shall take all appropriate measures to eliminate discrimination against women in rural areas in order to ensure, on a basis of equality of men and women, that they participate in and benefit from rural development and, in particular, shall ensure to such women the right:

(a) To participate in the elaboration and implementation of development planning at all levels;

(b) To have access to adequate health care facilities, including information, counselling and services in family planning;

(c) To benefit directly from social security programmes;

(d) To obtain all types of training and education, formal and non-formal, including that relating to functional literacy, as well as, *inter alia*, the benefit of all community and extension services, in order to increase their technical proficiency;

(e) To organize self-help groups and co-operatives in order to obtain equal access to economic opportunities through employment or self-employment;

(f) To participate in all community activities;

(g) To have access to agricultural credit and loans, marketing facilities, appropriate technology and equal treatment in land and agrarian reform as well as in land resettlement schemes;

(h) To enjoy adequate living conditions, particularly in relation to housing, sanitation, electricity and water supply, transport and communications.


# PART IV

*Article* 15

1. States Parties shall accord to women equality with men before the law.

2. States Parties shall accord to women, in civil matters, a legal capacity identical to that of men and the same opportunities to exercise that capacity. In particular, they shall give women equal rights to conclude contracts and to administer property and shall treat them equally in all stages of procedure in courts and tribunals.

3. States Parties agree that all contracts and all other private instruments of any kind with a legal effect which is directed at restricting the legal capacity of women shall be deemed null and void.

4. States Parties shall accord to men and women the same rights with regard to the law relating to the movement of persons and the freedom to choose their residence and domicile.

*Article* 16

1. States Parties shall take all appropriate measures to eliminate discrimination against women in all matters relating to marriage and family relations and in particular shall ensure, on a basis of equality of men and women:

(*a*)  The same right to enter into marriage;

(*b*)  The same right freely to choose a spouse and to enter into marriage only with their free and full consent;

(*c*)  The same rights and responsibilities during marriage and at its dissolution;

(*d*)  The same rights and responsibilities as parents, irrespective of their marital status, in matters relating to their children; in all cases the interests of the children shall be paramount;

(*e*)  The same rights to decide freely and responsibly on the number and spacing of their children and to have access to the information, education and means to enable them to exercise these rights;

(*f*)  The same rights and responsibilities with regard to guardianship, wardship, trusteeship and adoption of children, or similar institutions where these concepts exist in national legislation; in all cases the interests of the children shall be paramount;

(*g*)  The same personal rights as husband and wife, including the right to choose a family name, a profession and an occupation;

(*h*)  The same rights for both spouses in respect of the ownership, acquisition, management, administration, enjoyment and disposition of property, whether free of charge or for a valuable consideration.

2. The betrothal and marriage of a child shall have no legal effect, and all necessary action, including legislation, shall be taken to specify a minimum age for marriage and to make the registration of marriages in an official registry compulsory.


## PART V

*Article* 17

1. For the purpose of considering the progress made in the implementation of the present Convention, there shall be established a Committee on the Elimination of Discrimination against Women (hereinafter referred to as the Committee) consisting, at the time of entry into force of the Convention, of eighteen and, after ratification of or accession to the Convention by the thirty-fifth State Party, of twenty-three experts of high moral standing and competence in the field covered by the Convention. The experts shall be elected by States Parties from among their nationals and shall serve in their personal capacity, consideration being given to equitable geographical distribution and to the representation of the different forms of civilization as well as the principal legal system.

2. The members of the Committee shall be elected by secret ballot from a list of persons nominated by States Parties. Each State Party may nominate one person from among its own nationals.

3. The initial election shall be held six months after the date of the entry into force of the present Convention. At least three months before the date of each election the Secretary-General of the United Nations shall address a letter to the States Parties inviting them to submit their nominations within two months. The Secretary-General shall prepare a list in alphabetical order of all persons thus nominated, indicating the States Parties which have nominated them, and shall submit it to the States Parties.

4. Elections of the members of the Committee shall be held at a meeting of States Parties convened by the Secretary-General at United Nations Headquarters. At that meeting, for which two thirds of the States Parties shall constitute a quorum, the persons elected to the Committee shall be those nominees who obtain the largest number of votes and an absolute majority of the votes of the representatives of States Parties present and voting.

5. The members of the Committee shall be elected for a term of four years. However, the terms of nine of the members elected at the first election shall expire at the end of two years; immediately after the first election the names of these nine members shall be chosen by lot by the Chairman of the Committee.

6. The election of the five additional members of the Committee shall be held in accordance with the provisions of paragraphs 2, 3 and 4 of this Article, following the thirty-fifth ratification or accession. The terms of two of the additional members elected on this occasion shall expire at the end of two years, the names of these two members having been chosen by lot by the Chairman of the Committee.

7. For the filling of casual vacancies, the State Party whose expert has ceased to function as a member of the Committee shall appoint another expert from among its nationals, subject to the approval of the Committee.

8. The members of the Committee shall, with the approval of the General Assembly, receive emoluments from United Nations resources on such terms and conditions as the Assembly may decide, having regard to the importance of the Committee's responsibilities.

9. The Secretary-General of the United Nations shall provide the necessary staff and facilities for the effective performance of the functions of the Committee under the present Convention.

*Article* 18

1. States Parties undertake to submit to the Secretary-General of the United Nations, for consideration by the Committee, a report of the legislative, judicial, administrative or other measures which they have adopted to give effect to the provisions of the present Convention and on the progress made in this respect:

(*a*) Within one year after the entry into force for the State concerned; and

(*b*) Thereafter at least every four years and further whenever the Committee so requests.

2. Reports may indicate factors and difficulties affecting the degree of fulfilment of obligations under the present Convention.

*Article* 19

1. The Committee shall adopt its own rules of procedure.

2. The Committee shall elect its officers for a term of two years.

*Article* 20

1. The Committee shall normally meet for a period of not more than two weeks annually in order to consider the reports submitted in accordance with Article 18 of the present Convention.

2. The meetings of the Committee shall normally be held at United Nations Headquarters or at any other convenient place as determined by the Committee.

*Article* 21

1. The Committee shall, through the Economic and Social Council, report annually to the General Assembly of the United Nations on its activities and may make suggestions and general recommendations based on the examination of reports and information received from the States Parties. Such suggestions and general recommendations shall be included in the report of the Committee together with comments, if any, from States Parties.

2. The Secretary-General shall transmit the reports of the Committee to the Commission on the Status of Women for its information.

*Article* 22

The specialized agencies shall be entitled to be represented at the consideration of the implementation of such provisions of the present Convention as fall within the scope of their activities. The Committee may invite the specialized agencies to submit reports on the implementation of the Convention in areas falling within the scope of their activities.

# PART VI

*Article* 23

Nothing in this Convention shall affect any provisions that are more conducive to the achievement of equality between men and women which may be contained:

(a) In the legislation of a State Party; or
(b) In any other international convention, treaty or agreement in force for that State.

## Article 24

States Parties undertake to adopt all necessary measures at the national level aimed at achieving the full realization of the rights recognized in the present Convention.

## Article 25

1. The present Convention shall be open for signature by all States.

2. The Secretary-General of the United Nations is designated as the depositary of the present Convention.

3. The present Convention is subject to ratification. Instruments of ratification shall be deposited with the Secretary-General of the United Nations.

4. The present Convention shall be open to accession by all States. Accession shall be effected by the deposit of an instrument of accession with the Secretary-General of the United Nations.

## Article 26

1. A request for the revision of the present Convention may be made at any time by any State Party by means of a notification in writing addressed to the Secretary-General of the United Nations.

2. The General Assembly of the United Nations shall decide upon the steps, if any, to be taken in respect of such a request.

## Article 27

1. The present Convention shall enter into force on the thirtieth day after the date of deposit with the Secretary-General of the United Nations of the twentieth instrument of ratification or accession.

2. For each State ratifying the present Convention or acceding to it after the deposit of the twentieth instrument of ratification or accession, the Convention shall enter into force on the thirtieth day after the date of the deposit of its own instrument of ratification or accession.

## Article 28

1. The Secretary-General of the United Nations shall receive and circulate to all States the text of reservations made by States at the time of ratification or accession.

2. A reservation incompatible with the object and purpose of the present Convention shall not be permitted.

3. Reservations may be withdrawn at any time by notification to this effect addressed to the Secretary-General of the United Nations, who shall then inform all States thereof. Such notification shall take effect on the date on which it is received.

*Article* 29

1. Any dispute between two or more States Parties concerning the interpretation or application of the present Convention which is not settled by negotiation shall, at the request of one of them, be submitted to arbitration. If within six months from the date of the request for arbitration the parties are unable to agree on the organization of the arbitration, any one of those parties may refer the dispute to the International Court of Justice by request in conformity with the Statute of the Court.

2. Each State Party may at the time of signature or ratification of this Convention or accession thereto declare that it does not consider itself bound by paragraph 1 of this article. The other States Parties shall not be bound by that paragraph with respect to any State Party which has made such a reservation.

3. Any State Party which has made a reservation in accordance with paragraph 2 of this article may at any time withdraw that reservation by notification to the Secretary-General of the United Nations.

*Article* 30

The present Convention, the Arabic, Chinese, English, French, Russian and Spanish texts of which are equally authentic, shall be deposited with the Secretary-General of the United Nations.

IN WITNESS WHEREOF the undersigned, duly authorized, have signed the present Convention.

# VII. CONVENTION ON THE RIGHTS OF THE CHILD, 1989

The Convention was adopted by the General Assembly of the United Nations without vote on 20 November 1989 (U.N. Doc. A/44/25). The text appears in the Annex to the Resolution. The Convention entered into force on 2 September 1990 one month after the twentieth State ratified it (in accordance with Article 49(1)). At least sixty-two States have become Parties.

The Convention is an elaboration of human rights standards in respect of the child. However, human rights standards were applicable to the child (as an individual) independently of the new instrument by virtue of the principles of general international law. The rights of the child are also the subject of Article 24 of the International Covenant on Civil and Political Rights (see above).

In 1979 the United Nations Human Rights Commission began consideration of a Polish proposal for a draft Convention on the Rights of the Child. The precursors of the Convention of 1989 include the Universal Declaration of Human Rights, Articles 2 and 25(2) (see above, pp. 21–7), and the Declaration of the Rights of the Child adopted by the General Assembly on 20 December 1959 (for the text see the second edition of this work, p. 108).

For comment on the Convention see Cohen, *International Legal Materials*, Vol. 28 (1989), p. 1448, and McGoldrick, *International Journal of Law and the Family*, Vol. 5 (1991), p. 132.

## TEXT

### Convention on the Rights of the Child

### Preamble

*The States Parties to the present Convention,*

*Considering* that, in accordance with the principles proclaimed in the Charter of the United Nations, recognition of the inherent dignity and of the equal and inalienable rights of all members of the human family is the foundation of freedom, justice and peace in the world,

*Bearing in mind* that the peoples of the United Nations have, in the Charter, reaffirmed their faith in fundamental human rights and in the dignity and worth of the human person, and have determined to promote social progress and better standards of life in larger freedom,

*Recognizing* that the United Nations has, in the Universal Declaration of Human Rights and in the International Covenants on Human Rights, proclaimed and agreed that everyone is entitled to all the rights and freedoms set forth therein, without distinction of any kind, such as race, colour, sex, language, religion, political or other opinion, national or social origin, property, birth or other status,

*Recalling* that, in the Universal Declaration of Human Rights, the United Nations has proclaimed that childhood is entitled to special care and assistance,

*Convinced* that the family, as the fundamental group of society and the natural environment for the growth and well-being of all its members and particularly children, should be afforded the necessary protection and assistance so that it can fully assume its responsibilities within the community,

*Recognizing* that the child, for the full and harmonious development of his or her personality, should grow up in a family environment, in an atmosphere of happiness, love and understanding,

*Considering* that the child should be fully prepared to live an individual life in society, and brought up in the spirit of the ideals proclaimed in the Charter of the United Nations, and in particular in the spirit of peace, dignity, tolerance, freedom, equality and solidarity,

*Bearing in mind* that the need to extend particular care to the child has been stated in the Geneva Declaration of the Rights of the Child of 1924 and in the Declaration of the Rights of the Child adopted by the General Assembly on 20 November 1959 and recognized in the Universal Declaration of Human Rights, in the International Covenant on Civil and Political Rights (in particular in Articles 23 and 24), in the International Covenant on Economic, Social and Cultural Rights (in particular in Article 10) and in the statutes and relevant instruments of specialized agencies and international organizations concerned with the welfare of children,

*Bearing in mind* that, as indicated in the Declaration of the Rights of the Child, 'the child, by reason of his physical and mental immaturity, needs special safeguards and care, including appropriate legal protection, before as well as after birth',

*Recalling* the provisions of the Declaration on Social and Legal Principles relating to the Protection and Welfare of Children, with Special Reference to Foster Placement and Adoption Nationally and Internationally; the United Nations Standard Minimum Rules for the Administration of Juvenile Justice (The Beijing Rules); and the Declaration on the Protection of Women and Children in Emergency and Armed Conflict,

*Recognizing* that, in all countries in the world, there are children living in exceptionally difficult conditions, and that such children need special consideration,

*Taking due account* of the importance of the traditions and cultural values of each people for the protection and harmonious development of the child,

*Recognizing* the importance of international co-operation for improving the living conditions of children in every country, in particular in the developing countries,

*Have agreed* as follows:

# PART I

*Article* 1

For the purposes of the present Convention, a child means every human being below the age of eighteen years unless, under the law applicable to the child, majority is attained earlier.

*Article* 2

1. States Parties shall respect and ensure the rights set forth in the present Convention to each child within their jurisdiction without discrimination of any kind, irrespective of the child's or his or her parent's or legal guardian's race, colour, sex, language, religion, political or other opinion, national, ethnic or social origin, property, disability, birth or other status.

2. States Parties shall take all appropriate measures to ensure that the child is protected against all forms of discrimination or punishment on the basis of the status, activities, expressed opinions, or beliefs of the child's parents, legal guardians, or family members.

*Article* 3

1. In all actions concerning children, whether undertaken by public or private social welfare institutions, courts of law, administrative authorities or legislative bodies, the best interests of the child shall be a primary consideration.

2. States Parties undertake to ensure the child such protection and care as is necessary for his or her well-being, taking into account the rights and duties of his or her parents, legal guardians, or other individuals legally responsible for him or her, and, to this end, shall take all appropriate legislative and administrative measures.

3. States Parties shall ensure that the institutions, services and facilities responsible for the care or protection of children shall conform with the standards established by competent authorities, particularly in the areas of safety, health, in the number and suitability of their staff, as well as competent supervision.

*Article* 4

States Parties shall undertake all appropriate legislative, administrative, and other measures for the implementation of the rights recognized in the present Convention. With regard to economic, social and cultural rights, States Parties shall undertake such measures to the maximum extent of their available resources and, where needed, within the framework of international co-operation.

*Article* 5

States Parties shall respect the responsibilities, rights and duties of parents or, where applicable, the members of the extended family or community as provided for by local custom, legal guardians or other persons legally responsible for the child, to provide, in a manner consistent with the evolving capacities of the child, appropriate direction and guidance in the exercise by the child of the rights recognized in the present Convention.

*Article* 6

1. States Parties recognize that every child has the inherent right to life.

2. States Parties shall ensure to the maximum extent possible the survival and development of the child.

*Article* 7

1. The child shall be registered immediately after birth and shall have the right from birth to a name, the right to acquire a nationality and, as far as possible, the right to know and be cared for by his or her parents.

2. States Parties shall ensure the implementation of these rights in accordance with their national law and their obligations under the relevant international instruments in this field, in particular where the child would otherwise be stateless.

*Article* 8

1. States Parties undertake to respect the right of the child to preserve his or her identity, including nationality, name and family relations as recognized by law without unlawful interference.

2. Where a child is illegally deprived of some or all of the elements of his or her identity, States Parties shall provide appropriate assistance and protection, with a view to speedily re-establishing his or her identity.

*Article* 9

1. States Parties shall ensure that a child shall not be separated from his or her parents against their will, except when competent authorities subject to judicial review determine, in accordance with applicable law and procedures, that such separation is necessary for the best interests of the child. Such determination may be necessary in a particular case such as one involving abuse or neglect of the child by the parents, or one where the parents are living separately and a decision must be made as to the child's place of residence.

2. In any proceedings pursuant to paragraph 1 of the present Article, all interested parties shall be given an opportunity to participate in the proceedings and make their views known.

3. States Parties shall respect the right of the child who is separated from one or both parents to maintain personal relations and direct contact with both parents on a regular basis, except if it is contrary to the child's best interests.

4. Where such separation results from any action initiated by a State Party, such as the detention, imprisonment, exile, deportation or death (including death arising from any cause while the person is in the custody of the State) of one or both parents or of the child, that State Party shall, upon request, provide the parents, the child or, if appropriate, another member of the family with the essential information concerning the whereabouts of the absent member(s) of the family unless the provision of the information would be detrimental to the well-being of the child. States Parties shall further ensure that the submission of such a request shall of itself entail no adverse consequences for the person(s) concerned.

*Article* 10

1. In accordance with the obligation of States Parties under Article 9, paragraph 1, applications by a child or his or her parents to enter or leave a State Party for the purpose of family reunification shall be dealt with by States Parties in a positive, humane and expeditious manner. States Parties shall further ensure that the submission of such a request shall entail no adverse consequences for the applicants and for the members of their family.

2. A child whose parents reside in different States shall have the right to maintain on a regular basis, save in exceptional circumstances personal relations and direct contacts with both parents. Towards that end and in accordance with the obligation of States Parties under Article 9, paragraph 2, States Parties shall respect the right of the child and his or her parents to leave any country, including their own, and to enter their own country. The right to leave any country shall be subject only to such restrictions as are prescribed by law and which are necessary to protect the national security, public order (*ordre public*), public health or morals or the rights and freedoms of others and are consistent with the other rights recognized in the present Convention.

*Article* 11

1. States Parties shall take measures to combat the illicit transfer and non-return of children abroad.

2. To this end, States Parties shall promote the conclusion of bilateral or multilateral agreements or accession to existing agreements.

*Article* 12

1. States Parties shall assure to the child who is capable of forming his or her own views the right to express those views freely in all matters affecting

the child, the views of the child being given due weight in accordance with the age and maturity of the child.

2. For this purpose, the child shall in particular be provided the opportunity to be heard in any judicial and administrative proceedings affecting the child, either directly, or through a representative or an appropriate body, in a manner consistent with the procedural rules of national law.

*Article* 13

1. The child shall have the right to freedom of expression; this right shall include freedom to seek, receive and impart information and ideas of all kinds, regardless of frontiers, either orally, in writing or in print, in the form of art, or through any other media of the child's choice.

2. The exercise of this right may be subject to certain restrictions, but these shall only be such as are provided by law and are necessary:

   (*a*) For respect of the rights or reputations of others; or

   (*b*) For the protection of national security or of public order (*ordre public*), or of public health or morals.

*Article* 14

1. States Parties shall respect the right of the child to freedom of thought, conscience and religion.

2. States Parties shall respect the rights and duties of the parents and, when applicable, legal guardians, to provide direction to the child in the exercise of his or her right in a manner consistent with the evolving capacities of the child.

3. Freedom to manifest one's religion or beliefs may be subject only to such limitations as are prescribed by law and are necessary to protect public safety, order, health or morals, or the fundamental rights and freedoms of others.

*Article* 15

1. States Parties recognize the rights of the child to freedom of association and to freedom of peaceful assembly.

2. No restrictions may be placed on the exercise of these rights other than those imposed in conformity with the law and which are necessary in a democratic society in the interests of national security or public safety, public order (*ordre public*), the protection of public health or morals or the protection of the rights and freedoms of others.

*Article* 16

1. No child shall be subjected to arbitrary or unlawful interference with his or her privacy, family, home or correspondence, nor to unlawful attacks on his or her honour and reputation.

2. The child has the right to the protection of the law against such interference or attacks.

*Article* 17

States Parties recognize the important function performed by the mass media and shall ensure that the child has access to information and material from a diversity of national and international sources, especially those aimed at the promotion of his or her social, spiritual and moral well-being and physical and mental health. To this end, States Parties shall:

(a) Encourage the mass media to disseminate information and material of social and cultural benefit to the child and in accordance with the spirit of Article 29;

(b) Encourage international co-operation in the production, exchange and dissemination of such information and material from a diversity of cultural, national and international sources;

(c) Encourage the production and dissemination of children's books;

(d) Encourage the mass media to have particular regard to the linguistic needs of the child who belongs to a minority group or who is indigenous;

(e) Encourage the development of appropriate guidelines for the protection of the child from information and material injurious to his or her well-being, bearing in mind the provisions of Articles 13 and 18.

*Article* 18

1. States Parties shall use their best efforts to ensure recognition of the principle that both parents have common responsibilities for the upbringing and development of the child. Parents or, as the case may be, legal guardians, have the primary responsibility for the upbringing and development of the child. The best interests of the child will be their basic concern.

2. For the purpose of guaranteeing and promoting the rights set forth in the present Convention, States Parties shall render appropriate assistance to parents and legal guardians in the performance of their child-rearing responsibilities and shall ensure the development of institutions, facilities and services for the care of children.

3. States Parties shall take all appropriate measures to ensure that children of working parents have the right to benefit from child-care services and facilities for which they are eligible.

*Article* 19

1. States Parties shall take all appropriate legislative, administrative, social and educational measures to protect the child from all forms of physical or mental violence, injury or abuse, neglect or negligent treatment, maltreat-

ment or exploitation, including sexual abuse, while in the care of parent(s), legal guardian(s) or any other person who has the care of the child.

2. Such protective measures should, as appropriate, include effective procedures for the establishment of social programmes to provide necessary support for the child and for those who have the care of the child, as well as for other forms of prevention and for identification, reporting, referral, investigation, treatment and follow-up of instances of child maltreatment described heretofore, and, as appropriate, for judicial involvement.

*Article* 20

1. A child temporarily or permanently deprived of his or her family environment, or in whose own best interests cannot be allowed to remain in that environment, shall be entitled to special protection and assistance provided by the State.

2. States Parties shall in accordance with their national laws ensure alternative care for such a child.

3. Such care could include, *inter alia*, foster placement, *kafalah* of Islamic law, adoption or if necessary placement in suitable institutions for the care of children. When considering solutions, due regard shall be paid to the desirability of continuity in a child's upbringing and to the child's ethnic, religious, cultural and linguistic background.

*Article* 21

States Parties that recognize and/or permit the system of adoption shall ensure that the best interests of the child shall be the paramount consideration and they shall:

(*a*) Ensure that the adoption of a child is authorized only by competent authorities who determine, in accordance with applicable law and procedures and on the basis of all pertinent and reliable information, that the adoption is permissible in view of the child's status concerning parents, relatives and legal guardians and that, if required, the persons concerned have given their informed consent to the adoption on the basis of such counselling as may be necessary;

(*b*) Recognize that inter-country adoption may be considered as an alternative means of child's care, if the child cannot be placed in a foster or an adoptive family or cannot in any suitable manner be cared for in the child's country of origin;

(*c*) Ensure that the child concerned by inter-country adoption enjoys safeguards and standards equivalent to those existing in the case of national adoption;

(*d*) Take all appropriate measures to ensure that, in inter-country adoption, the placement does not result in improper financial gain for those involved in it;

(*e*) Promote, where appropriate, the objectives of the present article by concluding bilateral or multilateral arrangements or agreements, and endeavour, within this framework, to ensure that the placement of the child in another country is carried out by competent authorities or organs.

*Article* 22

1. States Parties shall take appropriate measures to ensure that a child who is seeking refugee status or who is considered a refugee in accordance with applicable international or domestic law and procedures shall, whether unaccompanied or accompanied by his or her parents or by any other person, receive appropriate protection and humanitarian assistance in the enjoyment of applicable rights set forth in the present Convention and in other international human rights or humanitarian instruments to which the said States are Parties.

2. For this purpose, States Parties shall provide, as they consider appropriate, co-operation in any efforts by the United Nations and other competent inter-governmental organizations or non-governmental organizations co-operating with the United Nations to protect and assist such a child and to trace the parents or other members of the family of any refugee child in order to obtain information necessary for reunification with his or her family. In cases where no parents or other members of the family can be found the child shall be accorded the same protection as any other child permanently or temporarily deprived of his or her family environment for any reason, as set forth in the present Convention.

*Article* 23

1. States Parties recognize that a mentally or physically disabled child should enjoy a full and decent life, in conditions which ensure dignity, promote self-reliance and facilitate the child's active participation in the community.

2. States Parties recognize the right of the disabled child to special care and shall encourage and ensure the extension, subject to available resources, to the eligible child and those responsible for his or her care, of assistance for which application is made and which is appropriate to the child's condition and to the circumstances of the parents or others caring for the child.

3. Recognizing the special needs of a disabled child, assistance extended in accordance with paragraph 2 of the present article shall be provided free of charge, whenever possible, taking into account the financial resources of the parents or others caring for the child, and shall be designed to ensure that the disabled child has effective access to and receives education, training, health care services, rehabilitation services, preparation for employment and recreation opportunities in a manner conducive to the child's achieving

the fullest possible social integration and individual development, including his or her cultural and spiritual development.

4. States Parties shall promote, in the spirit of international co-operation, the exchange of appropriate information in the field of preventive health care and of medical, psychological and functional treatment of disabled children, including dissemination of and access to information concerning methods of rehabilitation, education and vocational services, with the aim of enabling States Parties to improve their capabilities and skills and to widen their experience in these areas. In this regard, particular account shall be taken of the needs of developing countries.

*Article* 24

1. States Parties recognize the right of the child to the enjoyment of the highest attainable standard of health and to facilities for the treatment of illness and rehabilitation of health. States Parties shall strive to ensure that no child is deprived of his or her right of access to such health care services.

2. States Parties shall pursue full implementation of this right and, in particular, shall take appropriate measures:

   (*a*) To diminish infant and child mortality;
   (*b*) To ensure the provision of necessary medical assistance and health care to all children with emphasis on the development of primary health care;
   (*c*) To combat disease and malnutrition, including within the framework of primary health care, through, *inter alia*, the application of readily available technology and through the provision of adequate nutritious foods and clean drinking-water, taking into consideration the dangers and risks of environmental pollution;
   (*d*) To ensure appropriate pre-natal and post-natal health care for mothers;
   (*e*) To ensure that all segments of society, in particular parents and children, are informed, have access to education and are supported in the use of basic knowledge of child health and nutrition, the advantages of breast-feeding, hygiene and environmental sanitation and the prevention of accidents;
   (*f*) To develop preventive health care, guidance for parents and family planning education and services.

3. States Parties shall take all effective and appropriate measures with a view to abolishing traditional practices prejudicial to the health of children.

4. States Parties undertake to promote and encourage international co-operation with a view to achieving progressively the full realization of the right recognized in the present article. In this regard, particular account shall be taken of the needs of developing countries.

*Article* 25

States Parties recognize the right of a child who has been placed by the competent authorities for the purposes of care, protection or treatment of his or her physical or mental health, to a periodic review of the treatment provided to the child and all other circumstances relevant to his or her placement.

*Article* 26

1. States Parties shall recognize for every child the right to benefit from social security, including social insurance, and shall take the necessary measures to achieve the full realization of this right in accordance with their national law.

2. The benefits should, where appropriate, be granted, taking into account the resources and the circumstances of the child and persons having responsibility for the maintenance of the child, as well as any other consideration relevant to an application for benefits made by or on behalf of the child.

*Article* 27

1. States Parties recognize the right of every child to a standard of living adequate for the child's physical, mental, spiritual, moral and social development.

2. The parent(s) or others responsible for the child have the primary responsibility to secure, within their abilities and financial capacities, the conditions of living necessary for the child's development.

3. States Parties, in accordance with national conditions and within their means, shall take appropriate measures to assist parents and others responsible for the child to implement this right and shall in case of need provide material assistance and support programmes, particularly with regard to nutrition, clothing and housing.

4. States Parties shall take all appropriate measures to secure the recovery of maintenance for the child from the parents or other persons having financial responsibility for the child, both within the State Party and from abroad. In particular, where the person having financial responsibility for the child lives in a State different from that of the child, States Parties shall promote the accession to international agreements or the conclusion of such agreements, as well as the making of other appropriate arrangements.

*Article* 28

1. States Parties recognize the right of the child to education, and with a view to achieving this right progressively and on the basis of equal opportunity, they shall, in particular:

(a) Make primary education compulsory and available free to all;

(b) Encourage the development of different forms of secondary education, including general and vocational education, make them available and accessible to every child, and take appropriate measures such as the introduction of free education and offering financial assistance in case of need;

(c) Make higher education accessible to all on the basis of capacity by every appropriate means;

(d) Make educational and vocational information and guidance available and accessible to all children;

(e) Take measures to encourage regular attendance at schools and the reduction of drop-out rates.

2. States Parties shall take all appropriate measures to ensure that school discipline is administered in a manner consistent with the child's human dignity and in conformity with the present Convention.

3. States Parties shall promote and encourage international co-operation in matters relating to education, in particular with a view to contributing to the elimination of ignorance and illiteracy throughout the world and facilitating access to scientific and technical knowledge and modern teaching methods. In this regard, particular account shall be taken of the needs of developing countries.

*Article* 29

1. States Parties agree that the education of the child shall be directed to:

(a) The development of the child's personality, talents and mental and physical abilities to their fullest potential;

(b) The development of respect for human rights and fundamental freedoms, and for the principles enshrined in the Charter of the United Nations;

(c) The development of respect for the child's parents, his or her own cultural identity, language and values, for the national values of the country in which the child is living, the country from which he or she may originate, and for civilizations different from his or her own;

(d) The preparation of the child for responsible life in a free society, in the spirit of understanding, peace, tolerance, equality of sexes, and friendship among all peoples, ethnic, national and religious groups and persons of indigenous origin;

(e) The development of respect for the natural environment.

2. No part of the present Article or Article 28 shall be construed so as to interfere with the liberty of individuals and bodies to establish and direct educational institutions, subject always to the observance of the principles

set forth in paragraph 1 of the present Article and to the requirements that the education given in such institutions shall conform to such minimum standards as may be laid down by the State.

*Article 30*

In those States in which ethnic, religious or linguistic minorities or persons of indigenous origin exist, a child belonging to such a minority or who is indigenous shall not be denied the right, in community with other members of his or her group, to enjoy his or her own culture, to profess and practise his or her own religion, or to use his or her own language.

*Article 31*

1. States Parties recognize the right of the child to rest and leisure, to engage in play and recreational activities appropriate to the age of the child and to participate freely in cultural life and the arts.

2. States Parties shall respect and promote the right of the child to participate fully in cultural and artistic life and shall encourage the provision of appropriate and equal opportunities for cultural, artistic, recreational and leisure activity.

*Article 32*

1. States Parties recognize the right of the child to be protected from economic exploitation and from performing any work that is likely to be hazardous or to interfere with the child's education, or to be harmful to the child's health or physical, mental, spiritual, moral or social development.

2. States Parties shall take legislative, administrative, social and educational measures to ensure the implementation of the present article. To this end, and having regard to the relevant provisions of other international instruments, States Parties shall in particular:

   (*a*) Provide for a minimum age or minimum ages for admission to employment;
   (*b*) Provide for appropriate regulation of the hours and conditions of employment;
   (*c*) Provide for appropriate penalties or other sanctions to ensure the effective enforcement of the present article.

*Article 33*

States Parties shall take all appropriate measures, including legislative, administrative, social and educational measures, to protect children from the illicit use of narcotic drugs and psychotropic substances as defined in the relevant international treaties, and to prevent the use of children in the illicit production and trafficking of such substances.

*Article* 34

States Parties undertake to protect the child from all forms of sexual exploitation and sexual abuse. For these purposes, States Parties shall in particular take all appropriate national, bilateral and multilateral measures to prevent:

(*a*) The inducement or coercion of a child to engage in any unlawful sexual activity;

(*b*) The exploitative use of children in prostitution or other unlawful sexual practices;

(*c*) The exploitative use of children in pornographic performances and materials.

*Article* 35

States Parties shall take all appropriate national, bilateral and multilateral measures to prevent the abduction of, the sale of or traffic in children for any purpose or in any form.

*Article* 36

States Parties shall protect the child against all other forms of exploitation prejudicial to any aspects of the child's welfare.

*Article* 37

States Parties shall ensure that:

(*a*) No child shall be subjected to torture or other cruel, inhuman or degrading treatment or punishment. Neither capital punishment nor life imprisonment without possibility of release shall be imposed for offences committed by persons below eighteen years of age;

(*b*) No child shall be deprived of his or her liberty unlawfully or arbitrarily. The arrest, detention or imprisonment of a child shall be in conformity with the law and shall be used only as a measure of last resort and for the shortest appropriate period of time;

(*c*) Every child deprived of liberty shall be treated with humanity and respect for the inherent dignity of the human person, and in a manner which takes into account the needs of persons of his or her age. In particular, every child deprived of liberty shall be separated from adults unless it is considered in the child's best interest not to do so and shall have the right to maintain contact with his or her family through correspondence and visits, save in exceptional circumstances;

(*d*) Every child deprived of his or her liberty shall have the right to prompt access to legal and other appropriate assistance, as well as the right to challenge the legality of the deprivation of his or her liberty before a court or other competent, independent and impartial authority, and to a prompt decision on any such action.

### Article 38

1. States Parties undertake to respect and to ensure respect for rules of international humanitarian law applicable to them in armed conflicts which are relevant to the child.

2. States Parties shall take all feasible measures to ensure that persons who have not attained the age of fifteen years do not take a direct part in hostilities.

3. States Parties shall refrain from recruiting any person who has not attained the age of fifteen years into their armed forces. In recruiting among those persons who have attained the age of fifteen years but who have not attained the age of eighteen years, States Parties shall endeavour to give priority to those who are oldest.

4. In accordance with their obligations under international humanitarian law to protect the civilian population in armed conflicts, States Parties shall take all feasible measures to ensure protection and care of children who are affected by an armed conflict.

### Article 39

States Parties shall take all appropriate measures to promote physical and psychological recovery and social reintegration of a child victim of: any form of neglect, exploitation, or abuse; torture or any other form of cruel, inhuman or degrading treatment or punishment; or armed conflicts. Such recovery and reintegration shall take place in an environment which fosters the health, self-respect and dignity of the child.

### Article 40

1. States Parties recognize the right of every child alleged as, accused of, or recognized as having infringed the penal law to be treated in a manner consistent with the promotion of the child's sense of dignity and worth, which reinforces the child's respect for the human rights and fundamental freedoms of others and which takes into account the child's age and the desirability of promoting the child's reintegration and the child's assuming a constructive role in society.

2. To this end, and having regard to the relevant provisions of international instruments, States Parties shall, in particular, ensure that:

   (a) No child shall be alleged as, be accused of, or recognized as having infringed the penal law by reason of acts or omissions that were not prohibited by national or international law at the time they were committed;

(b) Every child alleged as or accused of having infringed the penal law has at least the following guarantees:

   (i) To be presumed innocent until proven guilty according to law;

   (ii) To be informed promptly and directly of the charges against him or her, and, if appropriate, through his or her parents or legal guardians, and to have legal or other appropriate assistance in the preparation and presentation of his or her defence;

   (iii) To have the matter determined without delay by a competent, independent and impartial authority or judicial body in a fair hearing according to law, in the presence of legal or other appropriate assistance and, unless it is considered not to be in the best interest of the child, in particular, taking into account his or her age or situation, his or her parents or legal guardians;

   (iv) Not to be compelled to give testimony or to confess guilt; to examine or have examined adverse witnesses and to obtain the participation and examination of witnesses on his or her behalf under conditions of equality;

   (v) If considered to have infringed the penal law, to have this decision and any measures imposed in consequence thereof reviewed by a higher competent, independent and impartial authority or judicial body according to law;

   (vi) To have the free assistance of an interpreter if the child cannot understand or speak the language used;

   (vii) To have his or her privacy fully respected at all stages of the proceedings.

3. States Parties shall seek to promote the establishment of laws, procedures, authorities and institutions specifically applicable to children alleged as, accused of, or recognized as having infringed the penal law, and, in particular:

(a) The establishment of a minimum age below which children shall be presumed not to have the capacity to infringe the penal law;

(b) Whenever appropriate and desirable, measures for dealing with such children without resorting to judicial proceedings, providing that human rights and legal safeguards are fully respected.

4. A variety of dispositions, such as care, guidance and supervision orders; counselling; probation; foster care; education and vocational training programmes and other alternatives to institutional care shall be available to ensure that children are dealt with in a manner appropriate to their well-being and proportionate both to their circumstances and the offence.

*Article* 41

Nothing in the present Convention shall affect any provisions which are more conducive to the realization of the rights of the child and which may be contained in:

   (*a*) The law of a State Party; or
   (*b*) International law in force for that State.

## PART II

*Article* 42

States Parties undertake to make the principles and provisions of the Convention widely known, by appropriate and active means, to adults and children alike.

*Article* 43

1. For the purpose of examining the progress made by States Parties in achieving the realization of the obligations undertaken in the present Convention, there shall be established a Committee on the Rights of the Child, which shall carry out the functions hereinafter provided.

2. The Committee shall consist of ten experts of high moral standing and recognized competence in the field covered by this Convention. The members of the Committee shall be elected by States Parties from among their nationals and shall serve in their personal capacity, consideration being given to equitable geographical distribution, as well as to the principal legal systems.

3. The members of the Committee shall be elected by secret ballot from a list of persons nominated by States Parties. Each State Party may nominate one person from among its own nationals.

4. The initial election to the Committee shall be held no later than six months after the date of the entry into force of the present Convention and thereafter every second year. At least four months before the date of each election, the Secretary-General of the United Nations shall address a letter to States Parties inviting them to submit their nominations within two months. The Secretary-General shall subsequently prepare a list in alphabetical order of all persons thus nominated, indicating States Parties which have nominated them, and shall submit it to the States Parties to the present Convention.

5. The elections shall be held at meetings of States Parties convened by the Secretary-General at United Nations Headquarters. At those meetings, for which two thirds of States Parties shall constitute a quorum, the persons

elected to the Committee shall be those who obtain the largest number of votes and an absolute majority of the votes of the representatives of States Parties present and voting.

6. The members of the Committee shall be elected for a term of four years. They shall be eligible for re-election if renominated. The term of five of the members elected at the first election shall expire at the end of two years; immediately after the first election, the names of these five members shall be chosen by lot by the Chairman of the meeting.

7. If a member of the Committee dies or resigns or declares that for any other cause he or she can no longer perform the duties of the Committee, the State Party which nominated the member shall appoint another expert from among its nationals to serve for the remainder of the term, subject to the approval of the Committee.

8. The Committee shall establish its own rules of procedure.

9. The Committee shall elect its officers for a period of two years.

10. The meetings of the Committee shall normally be held at United Nations Headquarters or at any other convenient place as determined by the Committee. The Committee shall normally meet annually. The duration of the meetings of the Committee shall be determined, and reviewed, if necessary, by a meeting of the States Parties to the present Convention, subject to the approval of the General Assembly.

11. The Secretary-General of the United Nations shall provide the necessary staff and facilities for the effective performance of the functions of the Committee under the present Convention.

12. With the approval of the General Assembly, the members of the Committee established under the present Convention shall receive emoluments from United Nations resources on such terms and conditions as the Assembly may decide.

*Article* 44

1. States Parties undertake to submit to the Committee, through the Secretary-General of the United Nations, reports on the measures they have adopted which give effect to the rights recognized herein and on the progress made on the enjoyment of those rights:

(*a*) Within two years of the entry into force of the Convention for the State Party concerned;

(*b*) Thereafter every five years.

2. Reports made under the present Article shall indicate factors and difficulties, if any, affecting the degree of fulfilment of the obligations under the present Convention. Reports shall also contain sufficient information to

provide the Committee with a comprehensive understanding of the implementation of the Convention in the country concerned.

3. A State Party which has submitted a comprehensive initial report to the Committee need not, in its subsequent reports submitted in accordance with paragraph 1 (*b*) of the present Article, repeat basic information previously provided.

4. The Committee may request from States Parties further information relevant to the implementation of the Convention.

5. The Committee shall submit to the General Assembly, through the Economic and Social Council, every two years, reports on its activities.

6. States Parties shall make their reports widely available to the public in their own countries.

*Article* 45

In order to foster the effective implementation of the Convention and to encourage international co-operation in the field covered by the Convention:

(*a*) The specialized agencies, the United Nations Children's Fund, and other United Nations organs shall be entitled to be represented at the consideration of the implementation of such provisions of the present Convention as fall within the scope of their mandate. The Committee may invite the specialized agencies, the United Nations Children's Fund and other competent bodies as it may consider appropriate to provide expert advice on the implementation of the Convention in areas falling within the scope of their respective mandates. The Committee may invite the specialized agencies, the United Nations Children's Fund, and other United Nations organs to submit reports on the implementation of the Convention in areas falling within the scope of their activities;

(*b*) The Committee shall transmit, as it may consider appropriate, to the specialized agencies, the United Nations Children's Fund and other competent bodies, any reports from States Parties that contain a request, or indicate a need, for technical advice or assistance, along with the Committee's observations and suggestions, if any, on these requests or indications;

(*c*) The Committee may recommend to the General Assembly to request the Secretary-General to undertake on its behalf studies on specific issues relating to the rights of the child;

(*d*) The Committee may make suggestions and general recommendations based on information received pursuant to Articles 44 and 45 of the present Convention. Such suggestions and general recommendations shall be transmitted to any State Party concerned and reported to the General Assembly, together with comments, if any, from States Parties.

# PART III

*Article* 46

The present Convention shall be open for signature by all States.

*Article* 47

The present Convention is subject to ratification. Instruments of ratification shall be deposited with the Secretary-General of the United Nations.

*Article* 48

The present Convention shall remain open for accession by any State. The instruments of accession shall be deposited with the Secretary-General of the United Nations.

*Article* 49

1. The present Convention shall enter into force on the thirtieth day following the date of deposit with the Secretary-General of the United Nations of the twentieth instrument of ratification or accession.

2. For each State ratifying or acceding to the Convention after the deposit of the twentieth instrument of ratification or accession, the Convention shall enter into force on the thirtieth day after the deposit by such State of its instrument of ratification or accession.

*Article* 50

1. Any State Party may propose an amendment and file it with the Secretary-General of the United Nations. The Secretary-General shall thereupon communicate the proposed amendment to States Parties, with a request that they indicate whether they favour a conference of States Parties for the purpose of considering and voting upon the proposals. In the event that, within four months from the date of such communication, at least one third of the States Parties favour such a conference, the Secretary-General shall convene the conference under the auspices of the United Nations. Any amendment adopted by a majority of States Parties present and voting at the conference shall be submitted to the General Assembly for approval.

2. An amendment adopted in accordance with paragraph 1 of the present article shall enter into force when it has been approved by the General Assembly of the United Nations and accepted by a two-thirds majority of States Parties.

3. When an amendment enters into force, it shall be binding on those States Parties which have accepted it, other States Parties still being bound by the provisions of the present Convention and any earlier amendments which they have accepted.

*Article* 51

1. The Secretary-General of the United Nations shall receive and circulate to all States the text of reservations made by States at the time of ratification or accession.

2. A reservation incompatible with the object and purpose of the present Convention shall not be permitted.

3. Reservations may be withdrawn at any time by notification to that effect addressed to the Secretary-General of the United Nations, who shall then inform all States. Such notification shall take effect on the date on which it is received by the Secretary-General.

*Article* 52

A State Party may denounce the present Convention by written notification to the Secretary-General of the United Nations. Denunciation becomes effective one year after the date of receipt of the notification by the Secretary-General.

*Article* 53

The Secretary-General of the United Nations is designated as the depositary of the present Convention.

*Article* 54

The original of the present Convention, of which the Arabic, Chinese, English, French, Russian and Spanish texts are equally authentic, shall be deposited with the Secretary-General of the United Nations.

In witness thereof the undersigned plenipotentiaries, being duly authorized thereto by their respective Governments, have signed the present Convention.

# VIII. INTERNATIONAL CONVENTION ON THE PROTECTION OF THE RIGHTS OF ALL MIGRANT WORKERS AND THEIR FAMILIES, 1990

The Convention was adopted by the General Assembly of the United Nations during its forty-fifth session. The Convention constituted an elaboration of human rights standards and consequently migrant workers will remain protected by human rights standards even in States which do not become Parties to the Convention.

The Convention provides for the establishment of a Committee to monitor its implementation, together with optional procedures for the examination and determination of complaints on behalf of States Party to the Convention, and on behalf of individuals, concerning breaches of the obligations created by the Convention by a State Party.

## TEXT

### Convention on the Protection of the Rights of All Migrant Workers and Members of Their Families
#### Preamble

*The States Parties to the Present Convention,*

*Taking into account* the principles embodied in the basic instruments of the United Nations concerning human rights, in particular the Universal Declaration of Human Rights, the International Covenant on Economic, Social and Cultural Rights, the International Covenant on Civil and Political Rights, the International Convention on the Elimination of All Forms of Racial Discrimination, the Convention on the Elimination of All Forms of Discrimination against Women and the Convention on the Rights of the Child,

*Taking into account also* the principles and standards set forth in the relevant instruments elaborated within the framework of the International Labour Organization, especially the Conventions concerning Migration for Employment (No. 97) and Migrations in Abusive Conditions and the Promotion of Equality of Opportunity and Treatment of Migrant Workers (No. 143), the Recommendations concerning Migration for Employment (No. 86) and Migrant Workers (No. 151), and the Conventions concerning Forced Labour (No. 29) and the Abolition of Forced Labour (No. 105),

*Reaffirming* the importance of the principles contained in the Convention against Discrimination in Education of the United Nations Educational, Scientific and Cultural Organization,

*Recalling* the Convention against Torture and other Cruel, Inhuman or Degrading Treatment or Punishment, the Declaration of the Fourth United Nations Congress on the Prevention of Crime and the Treatment of Offenders, the Code of Conduct for Law Enforcement Officials, and the Slavery Conventions,

*Recalling also* that one of the objectives of the International Labour Organisation, as stated in its Constitution, is the protection of the interests of workers when employed in countries other than their own, as well as the expertise and experience of the said Organisation in matters related to migrant workers and members of their families,

*Recognizing* the importance of the work carried out in connection with migrant workers and members of their families in various organs of the United Nations system, in particular in the Commission on Human Rights and the Commission for Social Development, and in the Food and Agriculture Organization of the United Nations, the United Nations Educational, Scientific and Cultural Organization and the World Health Organization and in other international organizations,

*Recognizing also* the progress made by certain States on a regional or bilateral basis towards the protection of the rights of migrant workers and members of their families as well as the importance and usefulness of bilateral and multilateral agreements in this field,

*Realizing* the importance and extent of the migration phenomenon, which involves millions of people and affects a large number of States in the international community,

*Aware* of the impact of the flows of migrant workers on States and people concerned, and desiring to establish norms which may contribute to harmonize the attitudes of States through the acceptance of basic principles concerning the treatment of migrant workers and members of their families,

*Considering* the situation of vulnerability in which migrant workers and members of their families frequently find themselves owing, among other things, to their absence from the State of origin and to the difficulties they may encounter arising from their presence in the State of employment,

*Convinced* that the rights of migrant workers and members of their families have not been sufficiently recognized everywhere and therefore require appropriate international protection,

*Taking into account* the fact that migration is often the cause of serious problems for the members of the families of migrant workers as well as for the workers themselves, in particular because of the scattering of the family,

*Bearing in mind* that the human problems involved in migration are even more serious in the case of irregular migration and convinced therefore that appropriate action should be encouraged in order to prevent and eliminate clandestine movements and ,trafficking in migrant workers, while at the same time assuring the protection of their fundamental human rights,

*Considering* that workers who are non-documented or in an irregular situation are frequently employed under less favourable conditions of work than other workers and that certain employers find this an inducement to seek such labour in order to reap the benefits of unfair competition,

*Considering also* that recourse to the employment of migrant workers who are in an irregular situation will be discouraged if the fundamental human rights of all migrant workers are more widely recognized and, moreover, that granting certain additional rights to migrant workers and members of their families in a regular situation will encourage all migrants and employers to respect and comply with the laws and procedures established by the States concerned,

*Convinced therefore* of the need to bring about the international protection of the rights of all migrant workers and members of their families, reaffirming and establishing basic norms in a comprehensive convention which could be applied universally,

*Have agreed on the following articles*:

## PART I

### Scope and definitions

*Article* 1

1. The present Convention is applicable, except as otherwise provided hereafter, to all migrant workers and members of their families without distinction of any kind such as sex, race, colour, language, religion or conviction, political or other opinion, national, ethnic or social origin, nationality, age, economic position, property, marital status, birth or other status.

2. The present Convention shall apply during the entire migration process of migrant workers and members of their families, which comprises preparation for migration, departure, transit and the entire period of stay and remunerated activity in the State of employment as well as return to the State of origin or the State of habitual residence.

*Article* 2

For the purposes of the present Convention:

1. The term 'migrant worker' refers to a person who is to be engaged, is engaged or has been engaged in a remunerated activity in a State of which he or she is not a national.

2. (*a*) The term 'frontier worker' refers to a migrant worker who retains his or her habitual residence in a neighbouring State to which he or she normally returns every day or at least once a week;

(*b*) The term 'seasonal worker' refers to a migrant worker whose work by its character is dependent on seasonal conditions and is performed only during part of the year;

(*c*) The term 'seafarer', which includes a fisherman, refers to a migrant worker employed on board a vessel registered in a State of which he or she is not a national;

(*d*) The term 'worker on an offshore installation' refers to a migrant worker employed on an offshore installation that is under the jurisdiction of a State of which he or she is not a national;

(*e*) The term 'itinerant worker' refers to a migrant worker who, having his or her habitual residence in one State, has to travel to another State or States for short periods, owing to the nature of his or her occupation;

(*f*) The term 'project-tied worker' refers to a migrant worker admitted to a State of employment for a defined period to work solely on a specific project being carried out in that State by his or her employer;

(*g*) The term 'specified-employment worker' refers to a migrant worker:

(i) Who has been sent by his or her employer for a restricted and defined period of time to a State of employment to undertake a specific assignment or duty; or

(ii) Who engages for a restricted and defined period of time in work that requires professional, commercial, technical or other highly specialized skill; or

(iii) Who, upon the request of his or her employer in the State of employment, engages for a restricted and defined period of time in work whose nature is transitory or brief;

and who is required to depart from the State of employment either at the expiration of his or her authorized period of stay, or earlier if he or she no longer undertakes that specific assignment or duty or engages in that work;

(*h*) The term 'self-employed worker' refers to a migrant worker who is engaged in a remunerated activity otherwise than under a contract of employment and who earns his or her living through this activity normally working alone or together with members of his or her family, and to any other migrant worker recognized as self-employed by applicable legislation of the State of employment or bilateral or multilateral agreements.

*Article* 3

The present Convention shall not apply to:

(*a*) Persons sent or employed by international organizations and agencies or persons sent or employed by a State outside its territory to perform official functions, whose admission and status are regulated by general international law or by specific international agreements or conventions;

(*b*) Persons sent or employed by a State or on its behalf outside its territory who participate in development programmes and other co-operation programmes, whose admission and status are regulated by agreement with the State of employment and who, in accordance with that agreement, are not considered migrant workers;

(c) Persons taking up residence in a State different from their State of origin as investors;

(d) Refugees and stateless persons, unless such application is provided for in the relevant national legislation of, or international instruments in force for, the State Party concerned;

(e) Students and trainees;

(f) Seafarers and workers on an offshore installation who have not been admitted to take up residence and engage in a remunerated activity in the State of employment.

*Article* 4

For the purposes of the present Convention the term 'members of the family' refers to persons married to migrant workers or having with them a relationship that, according to applicable law, produces effects equivalent to marriage, as well as their dependent children and other dependent persons who are recognized as members of the family by applicable legislation or applicable bilateral or multilateral agreements between the States concerned.

*Article* 5

For the purposes of the present Convention, migrant workers and members of their families:

(a) Are considered as documented or in a regular situation if they are authorized to enter, to stay and to engage in a remunerated activity in the State of employment pursuant to the law of that State and to international agreements to which that State is a Party;

(b) Are considered as non-documented or in an irregular situation if they do not comply with the conditions provided for in subparagraph (a) of this article.

*Article* 6

For the purposes of the present Convention:

(a) The term 'State of origin' means the State of which the person concerned is a national;

(b) The term 'State of employment' means a State where the migrant worker is to be engaged, is engaged or has been engaged in a remunerated activity, as the case may be;

(c) The term 'State of transit' means any State through which the person concerned passes on any journey to the State of employment or from the State of employment to the State of origin or the State of habitual residence.

## PART II

### *Non-discrimination with respect to rights*

*Article 7*

States Parties undertake, in accordance with the international instruments concerning human rights, to respect and to ensure to all migrant workers and members of their families within their territory or subject to their jurisdiction the rights provided for in the present Convention without distinction of any kind such as sex, race, colour, language, religion or conviction, political or other opinion, national, ethnic or social origin, nationality, age, economic position, property, marital status, birth or other status.

## PART III

### *Human rights of all migrant workers and members of their families*

*Article 8*

1. Migrant workers and members of their families shall be free to leave any State, including their State of origin. This right shall not be subject to any restrictions except those that are provided by law, are necessary to protect national security, public order (*ordre public*), public health or morals or the rights and freedoms of others and are consistent with the other rights recognized in this Part of the Convention.

2. Migrant workers and members of their families shall have the right at any time to enter and remain in their State of origin.

*Article 9*

The right to life of migrant workers and members of their families shall be protected by law.

*Article 10*

No migrant worker or member of his or her family shall be subjected to torture or to cruel, inhuman or degrading treatment or punishment.

*Article 11*

1. No migrant worker or member of his or her family shall be held in slavery or servitude.

2. No migrant worker or member of his or her family shall be required to perform forced or compulsory labour.

3. Paragraph 2 of this Article shall not be held to preclude, in States where imprisonment with hard labour may be imposed as a punishment for a crime, the performance of hard labour in pursuance of a sentence to such punishment by a competent court.

4. For the purpose of this Article the term 'forced or compulsory labour' shall not include:

(*a*) Any work or service not referred to in paragraph 3 of this Article normally required of a person who is under detention in consequence of a lawful order of a court or of a person during conditional release from such detention;

(*b*) Any service exacted in cases of emergency or calamity threatening the life or well-being of the community;

(*c*) Any work or service that forms part of normal civil obligations so far as it is imposed also on citizens of the State concerned.

*Article* 12

1. Migrant workers and members of their families shall have the right to freedom of thought, conscience and religion. This right shall include freedom to have or to adopt a religion or belief of their choice and freedom either individually or in community with others and in public or private to manifest their religion or belief in worship, observance, practice and teaching.

2. Migrant workers and members of their families shall not be subject to coercion that would impair their freedom to have or to adopt a religion or belief of their choice.

3. Freedom to manifest one's religion or belief may be subject only to such limitations as are prescribed by law and are necessary to protect public safety, order, health or morals or the fundamental rights and freedoms of others.

4. States Parties to the present Convention undertake to have respect for the liberty of parents, at least one of whom is a migrant worker, and, when applicable, legal guardians to ensure the religious and moral education of their children in conformity with their own convictions.

*Article* 13

1. Migrant workers and members of their families shall have the right to hold opinions without interference.

2. Migrant workers and members of their families shall have the right to freedom of expression; this right shall include freedom to seek, receive and impart information and ideas of all kinds, regardless of frontiers, either orally, in writing or in print, in the form of art or through any other media of their choice.

3. The exercise of the rights provided for in paragraph 2 of this Article carries with it special duties and responsibilities. It may therefore be subject to certain restrictions, but these shall only be such as are provided by law and are necessary:

> (*a*) For respect of the rights or reputation of others;
> (*b*) For the protection of the national security of the States concerned or of public order (*ordre public*) or of public health or morals;
> (*c*) For the purpose of preventing any propaganda for war;
> (*d*) For the purpose of preventing any advocacy of national, racial or religious hatred that constitutes incitement to discrimination, hostility or violence.

*Article* 14

No migrant worker or member of his or her family shall be subjected to arbitrary or unlawful interference with his or her privacy, family, home, correspondence or other communications, or to unlawful attacks on his or her honour and reputation. Each migrant worker and member of his or her family shall have the right to the protection of the law against such interference or attacks.

*Article* 15

No migrant worker or member of his or her family shall be arbitrarily deprived of property, whether owned individually or in association with others. Where, under the legislation in force in the State of employment, the assets of a migrant worker or a member of his or her family are expropriated in whole or in part, the person concerned shall have the right to fair and adequate compensation.

*Article* 16

1. Migrant workers and members of their families shall have the right to liberty and security of person.

2. Migrant workers and members of their families shall be entitled to effective protection by the State against violence, physical injury, threats and intimidation, whether by public officials or by private individuals, groups or institutions.

3. Any verification by law enforcement officials of the identity of migrant workers or members of their families shall be carried out in accordance with procedures established by law.

4. Migrant workers and members of their families shall not be subjected individually or collectively to arbitrary arrest or detention; they shall not be deprived of their liberty except on such grounds and in accordance with such procedures as are established by law.

5. Migrant workers and members of their families who are arrested shall be

informed at the time of arrest as far as possible in a language they understand of the reasons for their arrest and they shall be promptly informed in
a language they understand of any charges against them.

6. Migrant workers and members of their families who are arrested or
detained on a criminal charge shall be brought promptly before a judge or
other officer authorized by law to exercise judicial power and shall be
entitled to trial within a reasonable time or to release. It shall not be the
general rule that while awaiting trial they shall be detained in custody, but
release may be subject to guarantees to appear for trial, at any other stage
of the judicial proceedings and, should the occasion arise, for the execution
of the judgment.

7. When a migrant worker or a member of his or her family is arrested or
committed to prison or custody pending trial or is detained in any other
manner:

    (a) The consular or diplomatic authorities of his or her State of origin or
        of a State representing the interests of that State shall, if he or she so
        requests, be informed without delay of his or her arrest or detention
        and of the reasons therefor;

    (b) The person concerned shall have the right to communicate with the
        said authorities. Any communication by the person concerned to the
        said authorities shall be forwarded without delay, and he or she shall
        also have the right to receive communications sent by the said
        authorities without delay;

    (c) The person concerned shall be informed without delay of this right
        and of rights deriving from relevant treaties, if any, applicable
        between the States concerned, to correspond and to meet with rep-
        resentatives of the said authorities and to make arrangements with
        them for his or her legal representation.

8. Migrant workers and members of their families who are deprived of their
liberty by arrest or detention shall be entitled to take proceedings before a
court, in order that that court may decide without delay on the lawfulness
of their detention and order their release if the detention is not lawful.
When they attend such proceedings, they shall have the assistance, if
necessary without cost to them, of an interpreter, if they cannot understand
or speak the language used.

9. Migrant workers and members of their families who have been victims of unlawful arrest or detention shall have an enforceable right to
compensation.

*Article* 17

1. Migrant workers and members of their families who are deprived of their
liberty shall be treated with humanity and with respect for the inherent
dignity of the human person and for their cultural identity.

2. Accused migrant workers and members of their families shall, save in exceptional circumstances, be separated from convicted persons and shall be subject to separate treatment appropriate to their status as unconvicted persons. Accused juvenile persons shall be separated from adults and brought as speedily as possible for adjudication.

3. Any migrant worker or a member of his or her family who is detained in a State of transit or in a State of employment for violation of provisions relating to migration, shall be held, in so far as practicable, separately from convicted persons or persons detained pending trial.

4. During any period of imprisonment in pursuance of a sentence imposed by a court of law, the essential aim of the treatment of a migrant worker or a member of his or her family shall be his or her reformation and social rehabilitation. Juvenile offenders shall be separated from adults and be accorded treatment appropriate to their age and legal status.

5. During detention or imprisonment, migrant workers and members of their families shall enjoy the same rights as nationals to visits by members of their families.

6. Whenever a migrant worker is deprived of his or her liberty, the competent authorities of the State concerned shall pay attention to the problems that may be posed for members of his or her family, in particular for spouses and minor children.

7. Migrant workers and members of their families who are subjected to any form of detention or imprisonment in accordance with the law in force in the State of employment or in the State of transit shall enjoy the same rights as nationals of those States who are in the same situation.

8. If a migrant worker or a member of his or her family is detained for the purpose of verifying any infraction of provisions related to migration, he or she shall not bear any costs arising therefrom.

*Article* 18

1. Migrant workers and members of their families shall have the right to equality with nationals of the State concerned before the courts and tribunals. In the determination of any criminal charge against them or of their rights and obligations in a suit of law, they shall be entitled to a fair and public hearing by a competent, independent and impartial tribunal established by law.

2. Migrant workers and members of their families who are charged with a criminal offence shall have the right to be presumed innocent until proven guilty according to law.

3. In the determination of any criminal charge against them, migrant workers and members of their families shall be entitled to the following minimum guarantees:

(*a*)  To be informed promptly and in detail in a language they understand of the nature and cause of the charge against them;

(*b*)  To have adequate time and facilities for the preparation of their defence and to communicate with counsel of their own choosing;

(*c*)  To be tried without undue delay;

(*d*)  To be tried in their presence and to defend themselves in person or through legal assistance of their own choosing; to be informed, if they do not have legal assistance, of this right; and to have legal assistance assigned to them, in any case where the interests of justice so require and without payment by them in any such case if they do not have sufficient means to pay for it;

(*e*)  To examine or have examined the witnesses against them and to obtain the attendance and examination of witnesses on their behalf under the same conditions as witnesses against them;

(*f*)  To have the free assistance of an interpreter if they cannot understand or speak the language used in court;

(*g*)  Not to be compelled to testify against themselves or to confess guilt.

4. In the case of juvenile persons, the procedure shall be such as will take account of their age and the desirability of promoting their rehabilitation.

5. Migrant workers and members of their families convicted of a crime shall have the right to their conviction and sentence being reviewed by a higher tribunal according to law.

6. When a migrant worker or member of his or her family has, by a final decision, been convicted of a criminal offence and when subsequently his or her conviction has been reversed or he or she has been pardoned on the ground that a new or newly discovered fact shows conclusively that there has been a miscarriage of justice, the person who has suffered punishment as a result of such conviction shall be compensated according to law, unless it is proved that the non-disclosure of the unknown fact in time is wholly or partly attributable to that person.

7. No migrant worker or member of his or her family shall be liable to be tried or punished again for an offence for which he or she has already been finally convicted or acquitted in accordance with the law and penal procedure of the State concerned.

*Article* 19

1. No migrant worker or member of his or her family shall be held guilty of any criminal offence on account of any act or omission that did not constitute a criminal offence under national or international law at the time when the criminal offence was committed, nor shall a heavier penalty be imposed than the one that was applicable at the time when it was committed. If, subsequent to the commission of the offence, provision is made by law for the imposition of a lighter penalty, he or she shall benefit thereby.

2. Humanitarian considerations related to the status of a migrant worker, in particular with respect to his or her right of residence or work, should be taken into account in imposing a sentence for a criminal offence committed by a migrant worker or a member of his or her family.

*Article* 20

1. No migrant worker or member of his or her family shall be imprisoned merely on the ground of failure to fulfil a contractual obligation.

2. No migrant worker or member of his or her family shall be deprived of his or her authorization of residence or work permit or expelled merely on the ground of failure to fulfil an obligation arising out of a work contract unless fulfilment of that obligation constitutes a condition for such authorization or permit.

*Article* 21

It shall be unlawful for anyone, other than a public official duly authorized by law, to confiscate, destroy or attempt to destroy identity documents, documents authorizing entry to or stay, residence or establishment in the national territory or work permits. No authorized confiscation of such documents shall take place without delivery of a detailed receipt. In no case shall it be permitted to destroy the passport or equivalent document of a migrant worker or a member of his or her family.

*Article* 22

1. Migrant workers and members of their families shall not be subject to measures of collective expulsion. Each case of expulsion shall be examined and decided individually.

2. Migrant workers and members of their families may be expelled from the territory of a State Party only in pursuance of a decision taken by the competent authority in accordance with law.

3. The decision shall be communicated to them in a language they understand. Upon their request where not otherwise mandatory, the decision shall be communicated to them in writing and, save in exceptional circumstances on account of national security, the reasons for the decision likewise stated. The persons concerned shall be informed of these rights before or at the latest at the time the decision is rendered.

4. Except where a final decision is pronounced by a judicial authority, the person concerned shall have the right to submit the reason against his or her expulsion and to have his or her case reviewed by the competent authority, unless compelling reasons of national security require otherwise. Pending such review, the person concerned shall have the right to seek a stay of the decision of expulsion.

5. If a decision of expulsion that has already been executed is subsequently

annulled, the person concerned shall have the right to seek compensation according to law and the earlier decision shall not be used to prevent him or her from re-entering the State concerned.

6. In case of expulsion, the person concerned shall have a reasonable opportunity before or after departure to settle any claims for wages and other entitlements due to him or her and any pending liabilities.

7. Without prejudice to the execution of a decision of expulsion, a migrant worker or a member of his or her family who is subject to such a decision may seek entry into a State other than his or her State of origin.

8. In case of expulsion of a migrant worker or a member of his or her family the costs of expulsion shall not be borne by him or her. The person concerned may be required to pay his or her own travel costs.

9. Expulsion from the State of employment shall not in itself prejudice any rights of a migrant worker or a member of his or her family acquired in accordance with the law of that State, including the right to receive wages and other entitlements due to him or her.

## Article 23

Migrant workers and members of their families shall have the right to have recourse to the protection and assistance of the consular or diplomatic authorities of their State of origin or of a State representing the interests of that State whenever the rights recognized in the present Convention are impaired. In particular, in case of expulsion, the person concerned shall be informed of this right without delay and the authorities of the expelling State shall facilitate the exercise of such right.

## Article 24

Every migrant worker and every member of his or her family shall have the right to recognition everywhere as a person before the law.

## Article 25

1. Migrant workers shall enjoy treatment not less favourable than that which applies to nationals of the State of employment in respect of remuneration and:

- (a) Other conditions of work, that is to say overtime, hours of work, weekly rest, holidays with pay, safety, health, termination of the employment relationship and any other conditions of work which, according to national law and practice, are covered by this term;
- (b) Other terms of employment, that is to say minimum age of employment, restriction on home work and any other matters which, according to national law and practice, are considered a term of employment.

2. It shall not be lawful to derogate in private contracts of employment from the principle of equality of treatment referred to in paragraph 1 of this article.

3. States Parties shall take all appropriate measures to ensure that migrant workers are not deprived of any rights derived from this principle by reason of any irregularity in their stay or employment. In particular, employers shall not be relieved of any legal or contractual obligations, nor shall their obligations be limited in any manner by reason of any such irregularity.

*Article* 26

1. States Parties recognize the right of migrant workers and members of their families:

> (*a*) To take part in meetings and activities of trade unions and of any other associations established in accordance with law, with a view to protecting their economic, social, cultural and other interests, subject only to the rules of the organization concerned;
>
> (*b*) To join freely any trade union and any such association as aforesaid, subject only to the rules of the organization concerned;
>
> (*c*) To seek the aid and assistance of any trade union and of any such association as aforesaid.

2. No restrictions may be placed on the exercise of these rights other than those that are prescribed by law and which are necessary in a democratic society in the interests of national security, public order (*ordre public*) or the protection of the rights and freedoms of others.

*Article* 27

1. With respect to social security, migrant workers and members of their families shall enjoy in the State of employment the same treatment granted to nationals in so far as they fulfil the requirements provided for by the applicable legislation of that State and the applicable bilateral and multilateral treaties. The competent authorities of the State of origin and the State of employment can at any time establish the necessary arrangements to determine the modalities of application of this norm.

2. Where the applicable legislation does not allow migrant workers and members of their families a benefit, the States concerned shall examine the possibility of reimbursing interested persons the amount of contributions made by them with respect to that benefit on the basis of the treatment granted to nationals who are in similar circumstances.

*Article* 28

Migrant workers and members of their families shall have the right to receive any medical care that is urgently required for the preservation of their life or the avoidance of irreparable harm to their health on the basis of equality of treatment with nationals of the State concerned. Such emergency medical care shall not be refused to them by reason of any irregularity with regard to stay or employment.

*Article* 29

Each child of a migrant worker shall have the right to a name, to registration of birth and to a nationality.

*Article* 30

Each child of a migrant worker shall have the basic right of access to education on the basis of equality of treatment with nationals of the State concerned. Access to public pre-school educational institutions or schools shall not be refused or limited by reason of the irregular situation with respect to stay or employment of either parent or by reason of the irregularity of the child's stay in the State of employment.

*Article* 31

1. States Parties shall ensure respect for the cultural identity of migrant workers and members of their families and shall not prevent them from maintaining their cultural links with their State of origin.

2. States Parties may take appropriate measures to assist and encourage efforts in this respect.

*Article* 32

Upon the termination of their stay in the State of employment, migrant workers and members of their families shall have the right to transfer their earnings and savings and, in accordance with the applicable legislation of the States concerned, their personal effects and belongings.

*Article* 33

1. Migrant workers and members of their families shall have the right to be informed by the State of origin, the State of employment or the State of transit as the case may be concerning:

    (*a*) Their rights arising out of the present Convention;
    (*b*) The conditions of admission, their rights and obligations under the law and practice of the State concerned and such other matters as will enable them to comply with administrative or other formalities in that State.

2. States Parties shall take all measures they deem appropriate to disseminate the said information or to ensure that it is provided by employers, trade unions or other appropriate bodies or institutions. As appropriate, they shall co-operate with other States concerned.

3. Such adequate information shall be provided upon request to migrant

workers and members of their families, free of charge, and, as far as possible, in a language they are able to understand.

*Article 34*

Nothing in this Part of the present Convention shall have the effect of relieving migrant workers and the members of their families from either the obligation to comply with the laws and regulations of any State of transit and the State of employment or the obligation to respect the cultural identity of the inhabitants of such States.

*Article 35*

Nothing in this Part of the present Convention shall be interpreted as implying the regularization of the situation of migrant workers or members of their families who are non-documented or in an irregular situation or any right to such regularization of their situation, nor shall it prejudice the measures intended to ensure sound and equitable conditions for international migration as provided in Part VI.


# PART IV

*Other rights of migrant workers and members of their families who are documented or in a regular situation*

*Article 36*

Migrant workers and members of their families who are documented or in a regular situation in the State of employment shall enjoy the rights set forth in this Part of the present Convention in addition to those set forth in Part III.

*Article 37*

Before their departure, or at the latest at the time of their admission to the State of employment, migrant workers and members of their families shall have the right to be fully informed by the State of origin or the State of employment, as appropriate, of all conditions applicable to their admission and particularly those concerning their stay and the remunerated activities in which they may engage as well as of the requirements they must satisfy in the State of employment and the authority to which they must address themselves for any modification of those conditions.

*Article 38*

1. States of employment shall make every effort to authorize migrant workers and members of their families to be temporarily absent without

effect upon their authorization to stay or to work, as the case may be. In doing so, States of employment shall take into account the special needs and obligations of migrant workers and members of their families, in particular in their States of origin.

2. Migrant workers and members of their families shall have the right to be fully informed of the terms on which such temporary absences are authorized.

*Article 39*

1. Migrant workers and members of their families shall have the right to liberty of movement in the territory of the State of employment and freedom to choose their residence there.

2. The rights mentioned in paragraph 1 of this article shall not be subject to any restrictions except those that are provided by law, are necessary to protect national security, public order (*ordre public*), public health or morals, or the rights and freedoms of others and are consistent with the other rights recognized in the present Convention.

*Article 40*

1. Migrant workers and members of their families shall have the right to form associations and trade unions in the State of employment for the promotion and protection of their economic, social, cultural and other interests.

2. No restrictions may be placed on the exercise of this right other than those that are prescribed by law and are necessary in a democratic society in the interests of national security, public order (*ordre public*) or the protection of the rights and freedoms of others.

*Article 41*

1. Migrant workers and members of their families shall have the right to participate in public affairs of their State of origin and to vote and to be elected at elections of that State, in accordance with its legislation.

2. The States concerned shall, as appropriate and in accordance with their legislation, facilitate the exercise of these rights.

*Article 42*

1. States Parties shall consider the establishment of procedures or institutions through which account may be taken, both in States of origin and in States of employment, of special needs, aspirations and obligations of migrant workers and members of their families and shall envisage, as appropriate, the possibility for migrant workers and members of their families to have their freely chosen representatives in those institutions.

2. States of employment shall facilitate, in accordance with their national

legislation, the consultation or participation of migrant workers and members of their families in decisions concerning the life and administration of local communities.

3. Migrant workers may enjoy political rights in the State of employment if that State, in the exercise of its sovereignty, grants them such rights.

*Article* 43

1. Migrant workers shall enjoy equality of treatment with nationals of the State of employment in relation to:

- (*a*) Access to educational institutions and services subject to the admission requirements and other regulations of the institutions and services concerned;
- (*b*) Access to vocational guidance and placement services;
- (*c*) Access to vocational training and retraining facilities and institutions;
- (*d*) Access to housing, including social housing schemes, and protection against exploitation in respect of rents;
- (*e*) Access to social and health services, provided that the requirements for participation in the respective schemes are met;
- (*f*) Access to co-operatives and self-managed enterprises without implying a change of their migration status and subject to the rules and regulations of the bodies concerned;
- (*g*) Access to and participation in cultural life.

2. States Parties shall promote conditions to ensure effective equality of treatment to enable migrant workers to enjoy the rights mentioned in paragraph 1 of this Article whenever the terms of their stay, as authorized by the State of employment, meet the appropriate requirements.

3. States of employment shall not prevent an employer of migrant workers from establishing housing or social or cultural facilities for them. Subject to Article 70 of the present Convention, a State of employment may make the establishment of such facilities subject to the requirements generally applied in that State concerning their installation.

*Article* 44

1. States Parties, recognizing that the family is the natural and fundamental group unit of society and is entitled to protection by society and the State, shall take appropriate measures to ensure the protection of the unity of the families of migrant workers.

2. States Parties shall take measures that they deem appropriate and that fall within their competence to facilitate the reunification of migrant workers with their spouses or persons who have with the migrant worker a relationship that, according to applicable law, produces effects equivalent to marriage, as well as with their minor dependent unmarried children.

3. States of employment, on humanitarian grounds, shall favourably con-

sider granting equal treatment, as set forth in paragraph 2 of this Article, to other family members of migrant workers.

*Article* 45

1. Members of the family of migrant workers shall, in the State of employment, enjoy equality of treatment with nationals of that State in relation to:

(a) Access to educational institutions and services, subject to the admission requirements and other regulations of the institutions and services concerned;

(b) Access to vocational guidance and training institutions and services, provided that requirements for participation are met;

(c) Access to social and health services, provided that requirements for participation in the respective schemes are met;

(d) Access to and participation in cultural life.

2. States of employment shall pursue a policy, where appropriate in collaboration with the States of origin, aimed at facilitating the integration of children of migrant workers in the local school system, particularly in respect of teaching them the local language.

3. States of employment shall endeavour to facilitate for the children of migrant workers the teaching of their mother tongue and culture and, in this regard, States of origin shall collaborate whenever appropriate.

4. States of employment may provide special schemes of education in the mother tongue of children of migrant workers, if necessary in collaboration with the States of origin.

*Article* 46

Migrant workers and members of their families shall, subject to the applicable legislation of the States concerned, as well as relevant international agreements and the obligations of the States concerned arising out of their participation in customs unions, enjoy exemption from import and export duties and taxes in respect of their personal and household effects as well as the equipment necessary to engage in the remunerated activity for which they were admitted to the State of employment:

(a) Upon departure from the State of origin or State of habitual residence;

(b) Upon initial admission to the State of employment;

(c) Upon final departure from the State of employment;

(d) Upon final return to the State of origin or State of habitual residence.

*Article* 47

1. Migrant workers shall have the right to transfer their earnings and savings, in particular those funds necessary for the support of their families, from the State of employment to their State of origin or any other State.

Such transfers shall be made in conformity with procedures established by applicable legislation of the State concerned and in conformity with applicable international agreements.

2. States concerned shall take appropriate measures to facilitate such transfers.

*Article* 48

1. Without prejudice to applicable double taxation agreements, migrant workers and members of their families shall, in the matter of earnings in the State of employment:

   (*a*) Not be liable to taxes, duties or charges of any description higher or more onerous than those imposed on nationals in similar circumstances;

   (*b*) Be entitled to deductions or exemptions from taxes of any description and to any tax allowances applicable to nationals in similar circumstances, including tax allowances for dependent members of their families.

2. States Parties shall endeavour to adopt appropriate measures to avoid double taxation of the earnings and savings of migrant workers and members of their families.

*Article* 49

1. Where separate authorizations to reside and to engage in employment are required by national legislation, the States of employment shall issue to migrant workers authorization of residence for at least the same period of time as their authorization to engage in remunerated activity.

2. Migrant workers who in the State of employment are allowed freely to choose their remunerated activity shall neither be regarded as in an irregular situation nor shall they lose their authorization of residence by the mere fact of the termination of their remunerated activity prior to the expiration of their work permits or similar authorizations.

3. In order to allow migrant workers referred to in paragraph 2 of this Article sufficient time to find alternative remunerated activities, the authorization of residence shall not be withdrawn at least for a period corresponding to that during which they may be entitled to unemployment benefits.

*Article* 50

1. In the case of death of a migrant worker or dissolution of marriage, the State of employment shall favourably consider granting family members of that migrant worker residing in that State on the basis of family reunion an

authorization to stay; the State of employment shall take into account the length of time they have already resided in that State.

2. Members of the family to whom such authorization is not granted shall be allowed before departure a reasonable period of time in order to enable them to settle their affairs in the State of employment.

3. The provisions of paragraphs 1 and 2 of this Article may not be interpreted as adversely affecting any right to stay and work otherwise granted to such family members by the legislation of the State of employment or by bilateral and multilateral treaties applicable to that State.

*Article 51*

Migrant workers who in the State of employment are not permitted freely to choose their remunerated activity shall neither be regarded as in an irregular situation nor shall they lose their authorization of residence by the mere fact of the termination of their remunerated activity prior to the expiration of their work permit, except where the authorization of residence is expressly dependent upon the specific remunerated activity for which they were admitted. Such migrant workers shall have the right to seek alternative employment, participation in public work schemes and retraining during the remaining period of their authorization to work, subject to such conditions and limitations as are specified in the authorization to work.

*Article 52*

1. Migrant workers in the State of employment shall have the right freely to choose their remunerated activity, subject to the following restrictions or conditions.

2. For any migrant worker a State of employment may:

(a) Restrict access to limited categories of employment, functions, services or activities where this is necessary in the interests of this State and provided for by national legislation;

(b) Restrict free choice of remunerated activity in accordance with its legislation concerning recognition of occupational qualifications acquired outside its territory. However, States Parties concerned shall endeavour to provide for recognition of such qualifications.

3. For migrant workers whose permission to work is limited in time, a State of employment may also:

(a) Make the right freely to choose their remunerated activities subject to the condition that the migrant worker has resided lawfully in its territory for the purpose of remunerated activity for a period of time prescribed in its national legislation that should not exceed two years;

(*b*) Limit access by a migrant worker to remunerated activities in pursuance of a policy of granting priority to its nationals or to persons who are assimilated to them for these purposes by virtue of legislation or bilateral or multilateral agreements. Any such limitation shall cease to apply to a migrant worker who has resided lawfully in its territory for the purpose of remunerated activity for a period of time prescribed in its national legislation that should not exceed five years.

4. States of employment shall prescribe the conditions under which a migrant worker who has been admitted to take up employment may be authorized to engage in work on his or her own account and vice versa. Account shall be taken of the period during which the worker has already been lawfully in the State of employment.

*Article* 53

1. Members of a migrant worker's family who have themselves an authorization of residence or admission that is without limit of time or is automatically renewable shall be permitted freely to choose their remunerated activity under the same conditions as are applicable to the said migrant worker in accordance with Article 52 of the present Convention.

2. With respect to members of a migrant worker's family who are not permitted freely to choose their remunerated activity, States Parties shall consider favourably granting them priority in obtaining permission to engage in a remunerated activity over other workers who seek admission to . the State of employment, subject to applicable bilateral and multilateral agreements.

*Article* 54

1. Without prejudice to the terms of their authorization of residence or their permission to work and the rights provided for in Articles 25 and 27 of the present Convention, migrant workers shall enjoy equality of treatment with nationals of the State of employment in respect of:

(*a*) Protection against dismissal;
(*b*) Unemployment benefits;
(*c*) Access to public work schemes intended to combat unemployment;
(*d*) Access to alternative employment in the event of loss of work or termination of other remunerated activity subject to article 52 of the present Convention.

2. If a migrant worker claims that the terms of his or her work contract have been violated by his or her employer, he or she shall have the right to address his or her case to the competent authorities of the State of employment, on terms provided for in Article 18, paragraph 1, of the present Convention.

*Article* 55

Migrant workers who have been granted permission to engage in a remunerated activity, subject to the conditions attached to such permission, shall be entitled to equality of treatment with nationals of the State of employment in the exercise of that remunerated activity.

*Article* 56

1. Migrant workers and members of their families referred to in this Part of the present Convention may not be expelled from a State of employment, except for reasons defined in the national legislation of that State, and subject to the safeguards established in Part III.

2. Expulsion shall not be resorted to for the purpose of depriving a migrant worker or a member of his or her family of the rights arising out of the authorization of residence and the work permit.

3. In considering whether to expel a migrant worker or a member of his or her family, account should be taken of humanitarian considerations and of the length of time that the person concerned has already resided in the State of employment.

# PART V

*Provisions applicable to particular categories of migrant workers and members of their families*

*Article* 57

The particular categories of migrant workers and members of their families specified in this Part of the present Convention who are documented or in a regular situation shall enjoy the rights set forth in Part III and, except as modified below, the rights set forth in Part IV.

*Article* 58

1. Frontier workers, as defined in Article 2, paragraph 2 (*a*), of the present Convention, shall be entitled to the rights provided for in Part IV that can be applied to them by reason of their presence and work in the territory of the State of employment, taking into account that they do not have their habitual residence in that State.

2. States of employment shall consider favourably granting frontier workers the right freely to choose their remunerated activity after a specified period of time. The granting of that right shall not affect their status as frontier workers.

*Article* 59

1. Seasonal workers, as defined in Article 2, paragraph 2 (*b*), of the present Convention, shall be entitled to the rights provided for in Part IV that can be applied to them by reason of their presence and work in the territory of the State of employment and that are compatible with their status in that State as seasonal workers, taking into account that they are present in that State for only part of the year.

2. The State of employment shall, subject to paragraph 1 of this Article, consider granting seasonal workers who have been employed in its territory for a significant period of time the possibility of taking up other remunerated activities and giving them priority over other workers who seek admission to that State, subject to applicable bilateral and multilateral agreements.

*Article* 60

Itinerant workers, as defined in Article 2, paragraph 2 (*e*), of the present Convention, shall be entitled to the rights provided for in Part IV that can be granted to them by reason of their presence and work in the territory of the State of employment and that are compatible with their status as itinerant workers in that State.

*Article* 61

1. Project-tied workers, as defined in Article 2, paragraph 2 (*f*), of the present Convention, and members of their families shall be entitled to the rights provided for in Part IV except the provisions of Article 43, paragraphs 1 (*b*) and (*c*) and Article 43, paragraph 1 (*d*), as it pertains to social housing schemes, Article 45 (*b*), and Articles 52 to 55.

2. If a project-tied worker claims that the terms of his or her work contract have been violated by his or her employer, he or she shall have the right to address his or her case to the competent authorities of the State which has jurisdiction over that employer, on terms provided for in Article 18, paragraph 1, of the present Convention.

3. Subject to bilateral or multilateral agreements in force for them, the States Parties concerned shall endeavour to enable project-tied workers to remain adequately protected by the social security systems of their States of origin or habitual residence during their engagement in the project. States Parties concerned shall take appropriate measures with the aim of avoiding any denial of rights or duplication of payments in this respect.

4. Without prejudice to the provisions of Article 47 of the present Convention and to relevant bilateral or multilateral agreements, States Parties concerned shall permit payment of the earnings of project-tied workers in their State of origin or habitual residence.

*Article* 62

1. Specified-employment workers as defined in Article 2, paragraph 2 (*g*), of the present Convention, shall be entitled to the rights provided for in Part IV, except the provisions of Article 43, paragraphs 1 (*b*) and (*c*); Article 43, paragraph 1 (*d*), as it pertains to social housing schemes; Article 52; and Article 54, paragraph 1 (*d*).

2. Members of the family of specified-employment workers shall be entitled to the rights relating to family members of migrant workers in Part IV of the present Convention, except the provisions of Article 53.

*Article* 63

1. Self-employed workers, as defined in Article 2, paragraph 2 (*h*), of the present Convention, shall be entitled to the rights provided for in Part IV with the exception of those rights which are exclusively applicable to workers having a contract of employment.

2. Without prejudice to Articles 52 and 79 of the present Convention, the termination of the economic activity of the self-employed workers shall not in itself imply the withdrawal of the authorization for them or for the members of their families to stay or to engage in a remunerated activity in the State of employment except where the authorization of residence is expressly dependent upon the specific remunerated activity for which they were admitted.

## PART VI

*Promotion of sound, equitable, humane and lawful conditions
in connection with international migration of workers and
members of their families*

*Article* 64

1. Without prejudice to Article 79 of the present Convention, the States Parties concerned shall as appropriate consult and co-operate with a view to promoting sound, equitable and humane conditions in connection with international migration of workers and members of their families.

2. In this respect due regard shall be paid not only to labour needs and resources, but also to the social, economic and cultural and other needs of migrant workers and members of their families involved, as well as to the consequences of such migration for the communities concerned.

*Article* 65

1. States Parties shall maintain appropriate services to deal with ques-

tions concerning international migration of workers and members of their families. Their functions shall include, *inter alia*:

(*a*) The formulation and implementation of policies regarding such migration;

(*b*) An exchange of information, consultation and co-operation with the competent authorities of other States Parties involved in such migration;

(*c*) The provision of appropriate information, particularly to employers, workers and their organizations on policies, laws and regulations relating to migration and employment, on agreements concluded with other States concerning migration and on other relevant matters;

(*d*) The provision of information and appropriate assistance to migrant workers and members of their families regarding requisite authorizations and formalities and arrangements for departure, travel, arrival, stay, remunerated activities, exit and return, as well as on conditions of work and life in the State of employment and on customs, currency, tax and other relevant laws and regulations.

2. States Parties shall facilitate as appropriate the provision of adequate consular and other services that are necessary to meet the social, cultural and other needs of migrant workers and members of their families.

*Article* 66

1. Subject to paragraph 2 of this Article, the right to undertake operations with a view to the recruitment of workers for employment in another State shall be restricted to:

(*a*) Public services or bodies of the State in which such operations take place;

(*b*) Public services or bodies of the State of employment on the basis of agreement between the States concerned;

(*c*) A body established by virtue of a bilateral or multilateral agreement.

2. Subject to any authorization, approval and supervision by the public authorities of the States Parties concerned as may be established pursuant to the legislation and practice of those States, agencies, prospective employers or persons acting on their behalf may also be permitted to undertake the said operations.

*Article* 67

1. States Parties concerned shall co-operate as appropriate in the adoption of measures regarding the orderly return of migrant workers and members of their families to the State of origin when they decide to return or their authorization of residence or employment expires or when they are in the State of employment in an irregular situation.

2. Concerning migrant workers and members of their families in a regular situation, States Parties concerned shall co-operate as appropriate, on terms agreed upon by those States, with a view to promoting adequate economic conditions for their resettlement and to facilitating their durable social and cultural reintegration in the State of origin.

*Article 68*

1. States Parties, including States of transit, shall collaborate with a view to preventing and eliminating illegal or clandestine movements and employment of migrant workers in an irregular situation. The measures to be taken to this end within the jurisdiction of each State concerned shall include:

(a) Appropriate measures against the dissemination of misleading information relating to emigration and immigration;

(b) Measures to detect and eradicate illegal or clandestine movements of migrant workers and members of their families and to impose effective sanctions on persons, groups or entities which organize, operate or assist in organizing or operating such movements;

(c) Measures to impose effective sanctions on persons, groups or entities which use violence, threats or intimidation against migrant workers or members of their family in an irregular situation.

2. States of employment shall take all adequate and effective measures to eliminate employment in their territory of migrant workers in an irregular situation, including, whenever appropriate, sanctions on employers of such workers. The rights of migrant workers *vis-à-vis* their employer arising from employment shall not be impaired by these measures.

*Article 69*

1. States Parties shall, when there are migrant workers and members of their families within their territory in an irregular situation, take appropriate measures to ensure that such a situation does not persist.

2. Whenever States Parties concerned consider the possibility of regularizing the situation of such persons in accordance with applicable national legislation and bilateral or multilateral agreements, appropriate account shall be taken of the circumstances of their entry, the duration of their stay in the States of employment and other relevant considerations, in particular those relating to their family situation.

*Article 70*

States Parties shall take measures not less favourable than those applied to nationals to ensure that working and living conditions of migrant workers and members of their families in a regular situation are in keeping with the standards of fitness, safety, health and principles of human dignity.

*Article* 71

1. States Parties shall facilitate, whenever necessary, the repatriation to the State of origin of the bodies of the deceased migrant workers or members of their families.

2. As regards compensation matters relating to the death of a migrant worker or a member of his or her family, States Parties shall, as appropriate, provide assistance to the persons concerned with a view to the prompt settlement of such matters. Settlement of these matters shall be carried out on the basis of applicable national law in accordance with the provisions of the present Convention and any relevant bilateral or multilateral agreements.

# PART VII

## *Application of the Convention*

*Article* 72

1. (*a*) For the purpose of reviewing the application of the present Convention, there shall be established a Committee on the Protection of the Rights of All Migrant Workers and Members of Their Families (hereinafter referred to as 'the Committee');

(*b*) The Committee shall consist, at the time of entry into force of the present Convention, of ten and, after the entry into force of the Convention for the forty-first State Party, of fourteen experts of high moral standing, impartiality and recognized competence in the field covered by the present Convention.

2. (*a*) Members of the Committee shall be elected by secret ballot by the States Parties from a list of persons nominated by the States Parties, due consideration being given to equitable geographical distribution, including both States of origin and States of employment, and to the representation of the principal legal systems. Each State Party may nominate one person from among its own nationals;

(*b*) Members shall be elected and serve in their personal capacity.

3. The initial election shall be held no later than six months after the date of the entry into force of the present Convention and subsequent elections every second year. At least four months before the date of each election, the Secretary-General of the United Nations shall address a letter to all States Parties inviting them to submit their nominations within two months. The Secretary-General shall prepare a list in alphabetical order of all persons thus nominated, indicating the States Parties that have nominated them, and shall submit it to the States Parties not later than one month before the

date of the corresponding election, together with the curricula vitae of the persons thus nominated.

4. Elections of members of the Committee shall be held at a meeting of States Parties convened by the Secretary-General at United Nations Headquarters. At that meeting, for which two thirds of the States Parties shall constitute a quorum, the persons elected to the Committee shall be those nominees who obtain the largest number of votes and an absolute majority of votes of the States Parties present and voting.

5. (a) The members of the Committee shall serve for a term of four years. However, the terms of five of the members elected in the first election shall expire at the end of two years; immediately after the first election, the names of these five members shall be chosen by lot by the Chairman of the meeting of States Parties;

(b) The election of the four additional members of the Committee shall be held in accordance with the provisions of paragraphs 2, 3 and 4 of this article, following the entry into force of the present Convention for the forty-first State Party. The term of two of the additional members elected on this occasion shall expire at the end of two years; the names of these members shall be chosen by lot by the Chairman of the meeting of States Parties;

(c) The members of the Committee shall be eligible for re-election if renominated.

6. If a member of the Committee dies or resigns or declares that for any other cause he or she can no longer perform the duties of the Committee, the State Party that nominated the expert shall appoint another expert from among its own nationals for the remaining part of the term. The new appointment is subject to the approval of the Committee.

7. The Secretary-General of the United Nations shall provide the necessary staff and facilities for the effective performance of the functions of the Committee.

8. The members of the Committee shall receive emoluments from United Nations resources on such terms and conditions as the General Assembly may decide.

9. The members of the Committee shall be entitled to the facilities, privileges and immunities of experts on mission for the United Nations as laid down in the relevant sections of the Convention on the Privileges and Immunities of the United Nations.

*Article 73*

1. States Parties undertake to submit to the Secretary-General of the United Nations for consideration by the Committee a report on the legislative, judicial, administrative and other measures they have taken to give effect to the provisions of the Convention:

(*a*) Within one year after the entry into force of the Convention for the State Party concerned;

(*b*) Thereafter every five years and whenever the Committee so requests.

2. Reports made under this article shall also indicate factors and difficulties, if any, affecting the implementation of the present Convention and shall include information on the characteristics of migration flows in which the State Party concerned is involved.

3. The Committee shall decide any further guidelines applicable to the content of the reports.

4. States Parties shall make their reports widely available to the public in their own countries.

*Article* 74

1. The Committee shall examine the reports submitted by each State Party and shall transmit such comments as it may consider appropriate to the State Party concerned. This State Party may submit to the Committee observations on any comment made by the Committee in accordance with this article. The Committee may request supplementary information from States Parties when considering these reports.

2. The Secretary-General of the United Nations shall, in due time before the opening of each regular session of the Committee, transmit to the Director-General of the International Labour Office copies of the reports submitted by States Parties concerned and information relevant to the consideration of these reports in order to enable the Office to assist the Committee with the expertise the Office may provide regarding those matters dealt with by the Convention that fall within the sphere of competence of the International Labour Organisation. The Committee shall consider in its deliberations such comments and materials as the Office may provide.

3. The Secretary-General of the United Nations may also, after consultation with the Committee, transmit to other specialized agencies as well as to intergovernmental organizations, copies of such parts of these reports as may fall within their competence.

4. The Committee may invite the specialized agencies and organs of the United Nations, as well as intergovernmental organizations and other concerned bodies to submit, for consideration by the Committee, written information on such matters dealt with in the Convention as fall within the scope of their activities.

5. The International Labour Office shall be invited by the Committee to appoint representatives to participate, in a consultative capacity, in the meetings of the Committee.

6. The Committee may invite representatives of other specialized agencies

and organs of the United Nations, as well as of intergovernmental organizations, to be present and heard in its meetings whenever matters falling within their field of competence are considered.

7. The Committee shall present an annual report to the General Assembly of the United Nations on the implementation of the present Convention, containing its own considerations and recommendations, based, in particular, on the examination of the reports and any observations presented by States Parties.

8. The Secretary-General of the United Nations shall transmit the annual reports of the Committee to the States Parties to the present Convention, the Economic and Social Council, the Commission on Human Rights of the United Nations, the Director-General of the International Labour Office and other relevant organizations.

*Article 75*

1. The Committee shall adopt its own rules of procedure.

2. The Committee shall elect its officers for a term of two years.

3. The Committee shall normally meet annually.

4. The meetings of the Committee shall normally be held at United Nations Headquarters.

*Article 76*

1. A State Party to the present Convention may at any time declare under this article that it recognizes the competence of the Committee to receive and consider communications to the effect that a State Party claims that another State Party is not fulfilling its obligations under the present Convention. Communications under this article may be received and considered only if submitted by a State Party that has made a declaration recognizing in regard to itself the competence of the Committee. No communication shall be received by the Committee if it concerns a State Party which has not made such a declaration. Communications received under this article shall be dealt with in accordance with the following procedure:

(*a*) If a State Party to the present Convention considers that another State Party is not fulfilling its obligations under the present Convention, it may, by written communication, bring the matter to the attention of that State Party. The State Party may also inform the Committee of the matter. Within three months after the receipt of the communication the receiving State shall afford the State that sent the communication an explanation, or any other statement in writing clarifying the matter which should include, to the extent possible and pertinent, reference to domestic procedures and remedies taken, pending or available in the matter;

(b) If the matter is not adjusted to the satisfaction of both States Parties concerned within six months after the receipt by the receiving State of the initial communication, either State shall have the right to refer the matter to the Committee, by notice given to the Committee and to the other State;

(c) The Committee shall deal with a matter referred to it only after it has ascertained that all available domestic remedies have been invoked and exhausted in the matter, in conformity with the generally recognized principles of international law. This shall not be the rule where, in the view of the Committee, the application of the remedies is unreasonably prolonged;

(d) Subject to the provisions of subparagraph (c) of this paragraph, the Committee shall make available its good offices to the States Parties concerned with a view to a friendly solution of the matter on the basis of the respect for the obligations set forth in the present Convention;

(e) The Committee shall hold closed meetings when examining communications under this article;

(f) In any matter referred to it in accordance with subparagraph (b) of this paragraph, the Committee may call upon the States Parties concerned, referred to in subparagraph (b), to supply any relevant information;

(g) The States Parties concerned, referred to in subparagraph (b) of this paragraph, shall have the right to be represented when the matter is being considered by the Committee and to make submissions orally and/or in writing;

(h) The Committee shall, within twelve months after the date of receipt of notice under subparagraph (b) of this paragraph, submit a report:

(i) If a solution within the terms of subparagraph (d) of this paragraph is reached, the Committee shall confine its report to a brief statement of the facts and of the solution reached;

(ii) If a solution within the terms of subparagraph (d) is not reached, the Committee shall, in its report, set forth the relevant facts concerning the issue between the States Parties concerned. The written submissions and record of the oral submissions made by the States Parties concerned shall be attached to the report. The Committee may also communicate only to the States Parties concerned any views that it may consider relevant to the issue between them.

In every matter, the report shall be communicated to the States Parties concerned.

2. The provisions of this Article shall come into force when ten States Parties to the present Convention have made a declaration under para-

graph 1 of this Article. Such declarations shall be deposited by the States Parties with the Secretary-General of the United Nations, who shall transmit copies thereof to the other States Parties. A declaration may be withdrawn at any time by notification to the Secretary-General. Such a withdrawal shall not prejudice the consideration of any matter that is the subject of a communication already transmitted under this Article; no further communication by any State Party shall be received under this Article after the notification of withdrawal of the declaration has been received by the Secretary-General, unless the State Party concerned has made a new declaration.

*Article 77*

1. A State Party to the present Convention may at any time declare under this Article that it recognizes the competence of the Committee to receive and consider communications from or on behalf of individuals subject to its jurisdiction who claim that their individual rights as established by the present Convention have been violated by that State Party. No communication shall be received by the Committee if it concerns a State Party that has not made such a declaration.

2. The Committee shall consider inadmissible any communication under this article which is anonymous or which it considers to be an abuse of the right of submission of such communications or to be incompatible with the provisions of the present Convention.

3. The Committee shall not consider any communications from an individual under this article unless it has ascertained that:

(*a*) The same matter has not been, and is not being, examined under another procedure of international investigation or settlement; and

(*b*) The individual has exhausted all available domestic remedies; this shall not be the rule where, in the view of the Committee, the application of the remedies is unreasonably prolonged or is unlikely to bring effective relief to that individual.

4. Subject to the provisions of paragraph 2 of this Article, the Committee shall bring any communications submitted to it under this Article to the attention of the State Party to the present Convention that has made a declaration under paragraph 1 and is alleged to be violating any provisions of the present Convention. Within six months, the receiving State shall submit to the Committee written explanations or statements clarifying the matter and the remedy, if any, that may have been taken by that State.

5. The Committee shall consider communications received under this Article in the light of all information made available to it by or on behalf of the individual and by the State Party concerned.

6. The Committee shall hold closed meetings when examining communications under this Article.

7. The Committee shall forward its views to the State Party concerned and to the individual.

8. The provisions of this Article shall come into force when ten States Parties to the present Convention have made declarations under paragraph 1 of this Article. Such declarations shall be deposited by the States Parties with the Secretary-General of the United Nations, who shall transmit copies thereof to the other States Parties. A declaration may be withdrawn at any time by notification to the Secretary-General. Such a withdrawal shall not prejudice the consideration of any matter that is the subject of a communication already transmitted under this Article; no further communication by or on behalf of an individual shall be received under this Article after the notification of withdrawal of the declaration has been received by the Secretary-General, unless the State Party has made a new declaration.

*Article* 78

The provisions of Article 76 of the present Convention shall be applied without prejudice to any procedures for settling disputes or complaints in the field covered by the present Convention laid down in the constituent instruments of, or in conventions adopted by, the United Nations and its specialized agencies and shall not prevent the States Parties from having recourse to any procedures for settling a dispute in accordance with international agreements in force between them.


## PART VIII

*General provisions*

*Article* 79

Nothing in the present Convention shall affect the right of each State Party to establish the criteria governing admission of migrant workers and members of their families. Concerning other matters related to their legal situation and treatment as migrant workers and members of their families, States Parties shall be subject to the limitations set forth in the present Convention.

*Article* 80

Nothing in the present Convention shall be interpreted as impairing the provisions of the Charter of the United Nations and of the constitutions of the specialized agencies which define the respective responsibilities of the various organs of the United Nations and of the specialized agencies in regard to the matters dealt with in the present Convention.

*Article* 81

1. Nothing in the present Convention shall affect more favourable rights or freedoms granted to migrant workers and members of their families by virtue of:

(*a*) The law or practice of a State Party; or
(*b*) Any bilateral or multilateral treaty in force for the State Party concerned.

2. Nothing in the present Convention may be interpreted as implying for any State, group or person any right to engage in any activity or perform any act that would impair any of the rights and freedoms as set forth in the present Convention.

*Article* 82

The rights of migrant workers and members of their families provided for in the present Convention may not be renounced. It shall not be permissible to exert any form of pressure upon migrant workers and members of their families with a view to their relinquishing or foregoing any of the said rights. It shall not be possible to derogate by contract from rights recognized in the present Convention. States Parties shall take appropriate measures to ensure that these principles are respected.

*Article* 83

Each State Party to the present Convention undertakes:

(*a*) To ensure that any person whose rights or freedoms as herein recognized are violated shall have an effective remedy, notwithstanding that the violation has been committed by persons acting in an official capacity;
(*b*) To ensure that any persons seeking such a remedy shall have his or her claim reviewed and decided by competent judicial, administrative or legislative authorities, or by any other competent authority provided for by the legal system of the State, and to develop the possibilities of judicial remedy;
(*c*) To ensure that the competent authorities shall enforce such remedies when granted.

*Article* 84

Each State Party undertakes to adopt the legislative and other measures that are necessary to implement the provisions of the present Convention.

## PART IX

### *Final provisions*

*Article* 85

The Secretary-General of the United Nations is designated as the depositary of the present Convention.

*Article* 86

1. The present Convention shall be open for signature by all States. It is subject to ratification.

2. The present Convention shall be open to accession by any State.

3. Instruments of ratification or accession shall be deposited with the Secretary-General of the United Nations.

*Article* 87

1. The present Convention shall enter into force on the first day of the month following a period of three months after the date of the deposit of the twentieth instrument of ratification or accession.

2. For each State ratifying or acceding to the present Convention after its entry into force, the Convention shall enter into force on the first day of the month following a period of three months after the date of the deposit of its own instrument of ratification or accession.

*Article* 88

A State ratifying or acceding to the present Convention may not exclude the application of any Part of it, or, without prejudice to Article 3, exclude any particular category of migrant workers from its application.

*Article* 89

1. Any State Party may denounce the present Convention, not earlier than five years after the Convention has entered into force for the State concerned, by means of a notification in writing addressed to the Secretary-General of the United Nations.

2. Such denunciation shall become effective on the first day of the month following the expiration of a period of twelve months after the date of the receipt of the notification by the Secretary-General of the United Nations.

3. Such a denunciation shall not have the effect of releasing the State Party from its obligations under the present Convention in regard to any act or omission which occurs prior to the date at which the denunciation becomes effective, nor shall denunciation prejudice in any way the continued consideration of any matter which is already under consideration by the Committee prior to the date at which the denunciation becomes effective.

4. Following the date at which the denunciation of a State Party becomes effective, the Committee shall not commence consideration of any new matter regarding that State.

*Article 90*

1. After five years from the entry into force of the Convention a request for the revision of the Convention may be made at any time by any State Party by means of a notification in writing addressed to the Secretary-General of the United Nations. The Secretary-General shall thereupon communicate any proposed amendments to the States Parties with a request that they notify him whether they favour a conference of States Parties for the purpose of considering and voting upon the proposals. In the event that within four months from the date of such communication at least one third of the States Parties favours such a conference, the Secretary-General shall convene the conference under the auspices of the United Nations. Any amendment adopted by a majority of the States Parties present and voting shall be submitted to the General Assembly for approval.

2. Amendments shall come into force when they have been approved by the General Assembly of the United Nations and accepted by a two-thirds majority of the States Parties in accordance with their respective constitutional processes.

3. When amendments come into force, they shall be binding on those States Parties that have accepted them, other States Parties still being bound by the provisions of the present Convention and any earlier amendment that they have accepted.

*Article 91*

1. The Secretary-General of the United Nations shall receive and circulate to all States the text of reservations made by States at the time of signature, ratification or accession.

2. A reservation incompatible with the object and purpose of the present Convention shall not be permitted.

3. Reservations may be withdrawn at any time by notification to this effect addressed to the Secretary-General of the United Nations, who shall then inform all States thereof. Such notification shall take effect on the date on which it is received.

*Article 92*

1. Any dispute between two or more States Parties concerning the interpretation or application of the present Convention that is not settled by negotiation shall, at the request of one of them, be submitted to arbitration. If within six months from the date of the request for arbitration the Parties are unable to agree on the organization of the arbitration, any one of those

Parties may refer the dispute to the International Court of Justice by request in conformity with the Statute of the Court.

2. Each State Party may at the time of signature or ratification of the present Convention or accession thereto declare that it does not consider itself bound by paragraph 1 of this Article. The other States Parties shall not be bound by that paragraph with respect to any State Party that has made such a declaration.

3. Any State Party that has made a declaration in accordance with paragraph 2 of this Article may at any time withdraw that declaration by notification to the Secretary-General of the United Nations.

*Article* 93

1. The present Convention, of which the Arabic, Chinese, English, French, Russian and Spanish texts are equally authentic, shall be deposited with the Secretary-General of the United Nations.

2. The Secretary-General of the United Nations shall transmit certified copies of the present Convention to all States.

## PART THREE

# CONTRIBUTION OF THE INTERNATIONAL LABOUR ORGANIZATION

## INTRODUCTION

THE International Labour Organization is one of twelve Specialized Agencies brought into relationship with the United Nations under Articles 57 and 63 of the United Nations Charter. The Organization started its life in 1919, and it has the distinction of being in advance of other international institutions in that its major concern is social justice. The preamble to the Constitution begins: 'Whereas universal and lasting peace can be established only if it is based upon social justice...'. In the era of the United Nations there was more emphasis on the attainment of social justice as an aim of international co-operation and action. The Constitution of the I.L.O., with various amendments of 1964 indicated (these are not yet in force), is contained in Brownlie, *Basic Documents in International Law*, 3rd ed., 1983, p. 49. The aims of the I.L.O. are set out in the Declaration adopted by the General Conference of the I.L.O. in 1944, printed below.

The I.L.O. has played a prominent and pioneer role in standard-setting in carefully drafted conventions dealing with specific subject matters. This Part includes a selection of the conventions concluded under I.L.O. auspices. The I.L.O., along with other Specialized Agencies, submits periodic reports to the Commission on Human Rights of the Economic and Social Council of the United Nations.

On the work of the I.L.O. see: *The I.L.O. and Human Rights* (Report of the Director-General (Part I) to the International Labour Conference, Fifty-Second Session, 1968; Report Presented by the International Labour Organization to the International Conference on Human Rights, 1968), International Labour Office, Geneva, 1968; C. Wilfred Jenks, *Social Justice in the Law of Nations*, 1970; the same, *The International Protection of Trade Union Freedom*, 1957; the same, *Human Rights and International Labour Standards*, 1960; McNair, *The Expansion of International Law*, 1962; pp. 29–52; Landy,

*The Effectiveness of International Supervision: Thirty Years of ILO Experience*, 1966. Further references: *The Impact of International Labour Conventions and Recommendations*, I.L.O., Geneva, 1976; Valticos, *International Labour Law*, 1979.

# I. DECLARATION CONCERNING THE AIMS AND PURPOSES OF THE INTERNATIONAL LABOUR ORGANIZATION, 1944

## TEXT

The General Conference of the International Labour Organization, meeting in its Twenty-sixth Session in Philadelphia, hereby adopts, this tenth day of May in the year nineteen hundred and forty-four, the present Declaration of the aims and purposes of the International Labour Organization and of the principles which should inspire the policy of its Members.

## I

The Conference reaffirms the fundamental principles on which the Organization is based and, in particular, that:

(*a*) labour is not a commodity;

(*b*) freedom of expression and of association are essential to sustained progress;

(*c*) poverty anywhere constitutes a danger to prosperity everywhere;

(*d*) the war against want requires to be carried on with unrelenting vigour within each nation, and by continuous and concerted international effort in which the representatives of workers and employers, enjoying equal status with those of Governments, join with them in free discussion and democratic decision with a view to the promotion of the common welfare.

## II

Believing that experience has fully demonstrated the truth of the statement in the Constitution of the International Labour Organization that lasting peace can be established only if it is based on social justice, the Conference affirms that:

(*a*) all human beings, irrespective of race, creed, or sex, have the right to pursue both their material well-being and their spiritual development in conditions of freedom and dignity, of economic security, and equal opportunity;

(*b*) the attainment of the conditions in which this shall be possible must constitute the central aim of national and international policy;

(*c*) all national and international policies and measures, in particular those of an economic and financial character, should be judged in this light and accepted only in so far as they be held to promote and not to hinder the achievement of this fundamental objective;

(d) it is a responsibility of the International Labour Organization to examine and consider all international economic and financial policies and measures in the light of this fundamental objective;

(e) in discharging the tasks entrusted to it the International Labour Organization, having considered all relevant economic and financial factors, may include in its decisions and recommendations any provisions which it considers appropriate.

## III

The Conference recognizes the solemn obligation of the International Labour Organization to further among the nations of the world programmes which will achieve:

(a) full employment and the raising of standards of living;

(b) the employment of workers in the occupations in which they can have the satisfaction of giving the fullest measure of their skill and attainments and make their greatest contribution to the common well-being;

(c) the provision, as a means to the attainment of this end and under adequate guarantees for all concerned, of facilities for training and the transfer to labour, including migration for employment and settlement;

(d) Policies in regard to wages and earnings, hours and other conditions of work calculated to ensure a just share of the fruits of progress to all, and a minimum living wage to all employed and in need of such protection;

(e) the effective recognition of the right of collective bargaining, the co-operation of management and labour in the continuous improvement of productive efficiency, and the collaboration of workers and employers in the preparation and application of social and economic measures;

(f) the extension of social security measures to provide a basic income to all in need of such protection and comprehensive medical care;

(g) adequate protection for the life and health of workers in all occupations;

(h) provision for child welfare and maternity protection;

(i) the provision of adequate nutrition, housing, and facilities for recreation and culture;

(j) the assurance of equality of educational and vocational opportunity.

## IV

Confident that the fuller and broader utilization of the world's productive resources necessary for the achievement of the objectives set forth in this Declaration can be secured by effective international and national action, including measures to expand production and consumption, to avoid severe economic fluctuations, to promote the economic and social advancement of the less developed regions of the world, to assure greater stability in world prices of primary products, and to promote a high and steady volume of international trade, the Conference pledges the full co-operation of the International Labour Organization with such international bodies as may be entrusted with a share of the responsibility for this great task and for the promotion of the health, education, and well-being of all peoples.

## V

The Conference affirms that the principles set forth in this Declaration are fully applicable to all peoples everywhere and that, while the manner of their application must be determined with due regard to the stage of social and economic development reached by each people, their progressive application to peoples who are still dependent, as well as to those who have already achieved self-government, is a matter of concern to the whole civilized world.

## II. CONVENTION CONCERNING FORCED OR COMPULSORY LABOUR, 1930

The Convention was adopted by the General Conference of the I.L.O. on 10 June 1930, entered into force on 1 May 1932, and has received not less than 136 ratifications. The Convention is aimed at practices in colonial countries and certain independent States at a certain stage of development. Its focus is thus on forced labour as a form of economic exploitation. For the text in English and French: *United Nations Treaty Series*, Vol. 39, p. 55.

The definition of forced labour is not an easy matter. The technical difficulties are discussed by Fawcett, *The Application of the European Convention on Human Rights*, 2nd ed., 1987, pp. 56–63. Fawcett comments (p. 48): 'the margin between the planned use of labour and the direction of labour, between free and compulsory employment, can become almost indiscernibly narrow.'

For further reference see Avins, *International and Comparative Law Quarterly*, 16 (1967), p. 29.

### TEXT

*The General Conference of the International Labour Organization,*

> *Having been convened* at Geneva by the Governing Body of the International Labour Office, and having met in its Fourteenth Session on 10 June 1930, and
>
> *Having decided* upon the adoption of certain proposals with regard to forced or compulsory labour, which is included in the first item on the agenda of the Session, and
>
> *Having determined* that these proposals shall take the form of an international Convention,

*adopts* this twenty-eighth day of June of the year one thousand nine hundred and thirty the following Convention, which may be cited as the Forced Labour Convention, 1930, for ratification by the Members of the International Labour Organization in accordance with the provisions of the Constitution of the International Labour Organization:

*Article 1*

1. Each Member of the International Labour Organization which ratifies this Convention undertakes to suppress the use of forced or compulsory labour in all its forms within the shortest possible period.

2. With a view to this complete suppression, recourse to forced or compulsory labour may be had, during the transitional period, for public purposes only and as an exceptional measure, subject to the conditions and guarantees hereinafter provided.

3. At the expiration of a period of five years after the coming into force of this Convention, and when the Governing Body of the International

Labour Office prepares the report provided for in Article 31 below, the said Governing Body shall consider the possibility of the suppression of forced or compulsory labour in all its forms without a further transitional period and the desirability of placing this question on the agenda of the Conference.

*Article 2*

1. For the purposes of this Convention the term 'forced or compulsory labour' shall mean all work or service which is exacted from any person under the menace of any penalty and for which the said person has not offered himself voluntarily.

2. Nevertheless, for the purposes of this Convention, the term 'forced or compulsory labour' shall not include—

  (*a*) any work or service exacted in virtue of compulsory military service laws for work of a purely military character;
  (*b*) any work or service which forms part of the normal civic obligations of the citizens of a fully self-governing country;
  (*c*) any work or service exacted from any person as a consequence of a conviction in a court of law, provided that the said work or service is carried out under the supervision and control of a public authority and that the said person is not hired to or placed at the disposal of private individuals, companies or associations;
  (*d*) any work or service exacted in cases of emergency, that is to say, in the event of war or of a calamity or threatened calamity, such as fire, flood, famine, earthquake, violent epidemic or epizootic diseases, invasion by animal, insect or vegetable pests, and in general any circumstance that would endanger the existence or the well-being of the whole or part of the population;
  (*e*) minor communal services of a kind which, being performed by the members of the community in the direct interest of the said community, can therefore be considered as normal civic obligations incumbent upon the members of the community, provided that the members of the community or their direct representatives shall have the right to be consulted in regard to the need for such services.

*Article 3*

For the purposes of this Convention the term 'competent authority' shall mean either an authority of the metropolitan country or the highest central authority in the territory concerned.

*Article 4*

1. The competent authority shall not impose or permit the imposition of forced or compulsory labour for the benefit of private individuals, companies or associations.

2. Where such forced or compulsory labour for the benefit of private individuals, companies or associations exists at the date on which a Member's ratification of this Convention is registered by the Director-General of the International Labour Office, the Member shall completely suppress such forced or compulsory labour from the date on which this Convention comes into force for that Member.

*Article 5*

1. No concession granted to private individuals, companies or associations shall involve any form of forced or compulsory labour for the production or the collection of products which such private individuals, companies or associations utilize or in which they trade.

2. Where concessions exist containing provisions involving such forced or compulsory labour, such provisions shall be rescinded as soon as possible, in order to comply with Article 1 of this Convention.

*Article 6*

Officials of the administration, even when they have the duty of encouraging the populations under their charge to engage in some form of labour, shall not put constraint upon the said populations or upon any individual members thereof to work for private individuals, companies or associations.

*Article 7*

1. Chiefs who do not exercise administrative functions shall not have recourse to forced or compulsory labour.

2. Chiefs who exercise administrative functions may, with the express permission of the competent authority, have recourse to forced or compulsory labour, subject to the provisions of Article 10 of this Convention.

3. Chiefs who are duly recognized and who do not receive adequate remuneration in other forms may have the enjoyment of personal services, subject to due regulation and provided that all necessary measures are taken to prevent abuses.

*Article 8*

1. The responsibility for every decision to have recourse to forced or compulsory labour shall rest with the highest civil authority in the territory concerned.

2. Nevertheless, that authority may delegate powers to the highest local authorities to exact forced or compulsory labour which does not involve the removal of the workers from their place of habitual residence. That authority may also delegate, for such periods and subject to such conditions as may be laid down in the regulations provided for in Article 23 of this Convention, powers to the highest local authorities to exact forced or compulsory labour which involves the removal of the workers from their

place of habitual residence for the purpose of facilitating the movement of officials of the administration, when on duty, and for the transport of Government stores.

*Article* 9

Except as otherwise provided for in Article 10 of this Convention, any authority competent to exact forced or compulsory labour shall, before deciding to have recourse to such labour, satisfy itself—

(*a*) that the work to be done or the service to be rendered is of important direct interest for the community called upon to do the work or render the service;

(*b*) that the work or service is of present or imminent necessity;

(*c*) that it has been impossible to obtain voluntary labour for carrying out the work or rendering the service by the offer of rates of wages and conditions of labour not less favourable than those prevailing in the area concerned for similar work or service; and

(*d*) that the work or service will not lay too heavy a burden upon the present population, having regard to the labour available and its capacity to undertake the work.

*Article* 10

1. Forced or compulsory labour exacted as a tax and forced or compulsory labour to which recourse is had for the execution of public works by chiefs who exercise administrative functions shall be progressively abolished.

2. Meanwhile, where forced or compulsory labour is exacted as a tax, and where recourse is had to forced or compulsory labour for the execution of public works by chiefs who exercise administrative functions, the authority concerned shall first satisfy itself:

(*a*) that the work to be done or the service to be rendered is of important direct interest for the community called upon to do the work or render the service;

(*b*) that the work or the service is of present or imminent necessity;

(*c*) that the work or service will not lay too heavy a burden upon the present population, having regard to the labour available and its capacity to undertake the work;

(*d*) that the work or service will not entail the removal of the workers from their place of habitual residence;

(*e*) that the execution of the work or the rendering of the service will be directed in accordance with the exigencies of religion, social life and agriculture.

*Article* 11

1. Only adult able-bodied males who are of an apparent age of not less than 18 and not more than 45 years may be called upon for forced or

compulsory labour. Except in respect of the kinds of labour provided for in Article 10 of this Convention, the following limitations and conditions shall apply:

    (*a*) whenever possible prior determination by a medical officer appointed by the administration that the persons concerned are not suffering from any infectious or contagious disease and that they are physically fit for the work required and for the conditions under which it is to be carried out;

    (*b*) exemption of school teachers and pupils and of officials of the administration in general;

    (*c*) the maintenance in each community of the number of adult able-bodied men indispensable for family and social life;

    (*d*) respect for conjugal and family ties.

2. For the purposes of sub-paragraph (*c*) of the preceding paragraph, the regulations provided for in Article 23 of this Convention shall fix the proportion of the resident adult able-bodied males who may be taken at any one time for forced or compulsory labour, provided always that this proportion shall in no case exceed 25 per cent. In fixing this proportion the competent authority shall take account of the density of the population, of its social and physical development, of the seasons, and of the work which must be done by the persons concerned on their own behalf in their locality, and, generally, shall have regard to the economic and social necessities of the normal life of the community concerned.

*Article* 12

1. The maximum period for which any person may be taken for forced or compulsory labour of all kinds in any one period of twelve months shall not exceed sixty days, including the time spent in going to and from the place of work.

2. Every person from whom forced or compulsory labour is exacted shall be furnished with a certificate indicating the periods of such labour which he has completed.

*Article* 13

1. The normal working hours of any person from whom forced or compulsory labour is exacted shall be the same as those prevailing in the case of voluntary labour, and the hours worked in excess of the normal working hours shall be remunerated at the rates prevailing in the case of overtime for voluntary labour.

2. A weekly day of rest shall be granted to all persons from whom forced or compulsory labour of any kind is exacted and this day shall coincide as far as possible with the day fixed by tradition or custom in the territories or regions concerned.

*Article* 14

1. With the exception of the forced or compulsory labour provided for in Article 10 of this Convention, forced or compulsory labour of all kinds shall be remunerated in cash at rates not less than those prevailing for similar kinds of work either in the district in which the labour is employed or in the district from which the labour is recruited, whichever may be the higher.

2. In the case of labour to which recourse is had by chiefs in the exercise of their administrative functions, payment of wages in accordance with the provisions of the preceding paragraph shall be introduced as soon as possible.

3. The wages shall be paid to each worker individually and not to his tribal chief or to any other authority.

4. For the purpose of payment of wages the days spent in travelling to and from the place of work shall be counted as working days.

5. Nothing in this Article shall prevent ordinary rations being given as a part of wages, such rations to be at least equivalent in value to the money payment they are taken to represent, but deductions from wages shall not be made either for the payment of taxes or for special food, clothing or accommodation supplied to a worker for the purpose of maintaining him in a fit condition to carry on his work under the special conditions of any employment, or for the supply of tools.

*Article* 15

1. Any laws or regulations relating to workmen's compensation for accidents or sickness arising out of the employment of the worker and any laws or regulations providing compensation for the dependants of deceased or incapacitated workers which are or shall be in force in the territory concerned shall be equally applicable to persons from whom forced or compulsory labour is exacted and to voluntary workers.

2. In any case it shall be an obligation on any authority employing any worker on forced or compulsory labour to ensure the subsistence of any such worker who, by accident or sickness arising out of his employment, is rendered wholly or partially incapable of providing for himself, and to take measures to ensure the maintenance of any persons actually dependent upon such a worker in the event of his incapacity or decease arising out of his employment.

*Article* 16

1. Except in cases of special necessity, persons from whom forced or compulsory labour is exacted shall not be transferred to districts where the food and climate differ so considerably from those to which they have been accustomed as to endanger their health.

2. In no case shall the transfer of such workers be permitted unless all

measures relating to hygiene and accommodation which are necessary to adapt such workers to the conditions and to safeguard their health can be strictly applied.

3. When such a transfer cannot be avoided, measures of gradual habituation to the new conditions of diet and of climate shall be adopted on competent medical advice.

4. In cases where such workers are required to perform regular work to which they are not accustomed, measures shall be taken to ensure their habituation to it, especially as regards progressive training, the hours of work and the provision of rest intervals, and any increase or amelioration of diet which may be necessary.

*Article* 17

Before permitting recourse to forced or compulsory labour for works of construction or maintenance which entail the workers remaining at the workplaces for considerable periods, the competent authority shall satisfy itself—

(1) that all necessary measures are taken to safeguard the health of the workers and to guarantee the necessary medical care, and, in particular, (*a*) that the workers are medically examined before commencing the work and at fixed intervals during the period of service, (*b*) that there is an adequate medical staff, provided with the dispensaries, infirmaries, hospitals and equipment necessary to meet all requirements, and (*c*) that the sanitary conditions of the workplaces, the supply of drinking water, food, fuel, and cooking utensils, and, where necessary, of housing and clothing, are satisfactory;

(2) that definite arrangements are made to ensure the subsistence of the families of the workers, in particular by facilitating the remittance, by a safe method, of part of the wages to the family, at the request or with the consent of the workers;

(3) that the journeys of the workers to and from the workplaces are made at the expense and under the responsibility to the administration, which shall facilitate such journeys by making the fullest use of all available means of transport;

(4) that, in case of illness or accident causing incapacity to work of a certain duration, the worker is repatriated at the expense of the administration;

(5) that any worker who may wish to remain as a voluntary worker at the end of his period of forced or compulsory labour is permitted to do so without, for a period of two years, losing his right to repatriation free of expense to himself.

*Article* 18

1. Forced or compulsory labour for the transport of persons or goods, such

as the labour of porters or boatmen, shall be abolished within the shortest possible period. Meanwhile the competent authority shall promulgate regulations determining, *inter alia*, (*a*) that such labour shall only be employed for the purpose of facilitating the movement of officials of the administration, when on duty, or for the transport of Government stores, or, in cases of very urgent necessity, the transport of persons other than officials, (*b*) that the workers so employed shall be medically certified to be physically fit, where medical examination is possible, and that where such medical examination is not practicable the person employing such workers shall be held responsible for ensuring that they are physically fit and not suffering from any infectious or contagious disease, (*c*) the maximum load which these workers may carry, (*d*) the maximum distance from their homes to which they may be taken, (*e*) the maximum number of days per month or other period for which they may be taken, including the days spent in returning to their homes, and (*f*) the persons entitled to demand this form of forced or compulsory labour and the extent to which they are entitled to demand it.

2. In fixing the maxima referred to under (*c*), (*d*) and (*e*) in the foregoing paragraph, the competent authority shall have regard to all relevant factors, including the physical development of the population from which the workers are recruited, the nature of the country through which they must travel and the climatic conditions.

3. The competent authority shall further provide that the normal daily journey of such workers shall not exceed a distance corresponding to an average working day of eight hours, it being understood that account shall be taken not only of the weight to be carried and the distance to be covered, but also of the nature of the road, the season and all other relevant factors, and that, where hours of journey in excess of the normal daily journey are exacted, they shall be remunerated at rates higher than the normal rates.

*Article* 19

1. The competent authority shall only authorize recourse to compulsory cultivation as a method of precaution against famine or a deficiency of food supplies and always under the condition that the food or produce shall remain the property of the individuals or the community producing it.

2. Nothing in this Article shall be construed as abrogating the obligation on members of a community, where production is organized on a communal basis by virtue of law or custom and where the produce or any profit accruing from the sale thereof remain the property of the community, to perform the work demanded by the community by virtue of law or custom.

*Article* 20

Collective punishment laws under which a community may be punished for crimes committed by any of its members shall not contain provisions for forced or compulsory labour by the community as one of the methods of punishment.

*Article 21*

Forced or compulsory labour shall not be used for work underground in mines.

*Article 22*

The annual reports that Members which ratify this Convention agree to make to the International Labour Office, pursuant to the provisions of Article 22 of the Constitution of the International Labour Organization, on the measures they have taken to give effect to the provisions of this Convention, shall contain as full information as possible, in respect of each territory concerned, regarding the extent to which recourse has been had to forced or compulsory labour in that territory, the purposes for which it has been employed, the sickness and death rates, hours of work, methods of payment of wages and rates of wages, and any other relevant information.

*Article 23*

1. To give effect to the provisions of this Convention the competent authority shall issue complete and precise regulations governing the use of forced or compulsory labour.

2. These regulations shall contain, *inter alia*, rules permitting any person from whom forced or compulsory labour is exacted to forward all complaints relative to the conditions of labour to the authorities and ensuring that such complaints will be examined and taken into consideration.

*Article 24*

Adequate measures shall in all cases be taken to ensure that the regulations governing the employment of forced or compulsory labour are strictly applied, either by extending the duties of any existing labour inspectorate which has been established for the inspection of voluntary labour to cover the inspection of forced or compulsory labour or in some other appropriate manner. Measures shall also be taken to ensure that the regulations are brought to the knowledge of persons from whom such labour is exacted.

*Article 25*

The illegal exaction of forced or compulsory labour shall be punishable as a penal offence and it shall be an obligation on any Member ratifying this Convention to ensure that the penalties imposed by law are really adequate and are strictly enforced.

*Article 26*

1. Each Member of the International Labour Organization which ratifies this Convention undertakes to apply it to the territories placed under its

sovereignty, jurisdiction, protection, suzerainty, tutelage or authority, so far as it has the right to accept obligations affecting matters of internal jurisdiction; provided that, if such Member may desire to take advantage of the provisions of Article 35 of the Constitution of the International Labour Organization, it shall append to its ratification a declaration stating—

(1) the territories to which it intends to apply the provisions of this Convention without modification;

(2) the territories to which it intends to apply the provisions of this Convention with modifications, together with details of the said modifications;

(3) the territories in respect of which it reserves its decision.

2. The aforesaid declaration shall be deemed to be an integral part of the ratification and shall have the force of ratification. It shall be open to any Member, by a subsequent declaration, to cancel in whole or in part the reservations made, in pursuance of the provisions of subparagraphs (2) and (3) of this Article, in the original declaration.

*Article 27*

The formal ratifications of this Convention under the conditions set forth in the Constitution of the International Labour Organization shall be communicated to the Director-General of the International Labour Office for registration.

*Article 28*

1. This Convention shall be binding only upon those Members whose ratifications have been registered with the International Labour Office.

2. It shall come into force twelve months after the date on which the ratifications of two Members of the International Labour Organization have been registered with the Director-General.

3. Thereafter, this Convention shall come into force for any Member twelve months after the date on which the ratification has been registered.

*Article 29*

As soon as the ratifications of two Members of the International Labour Organization have been registered with the International Labour Office, the Director-General of the International Labour Office shall so notify all the Members of the International Labour Organization. He shall likewise notify them of the registration of ratifications which may be communicated subsequently by other Members of the Organization.

*Article 30*

1. A Member which has ratified this Convention may denounce it after the expiration of ten years from the date on which the Convention first comes

into force, by an act communicated to the Director-General of the International Labour Office for registration. Such denunciation shall not take effect until one year after the date on which it is registered with the International Labour Office.

2. Each Member which has ratified this Convention and which does not, within the year following the expiration of the period of ten years mentioned in the preceding paragraph, exercise the right of denunciation provided for in this article, will be bound for another period of five years and, thereafter, may denounce this Convention at the expiration of each period of five years under the terms provided for in this Article.

*Article* 31

At the expiration of each period of five years after the coming into force of this Convention, the Governing Body of the International Labour Office shall present to the General Conference a report on the working of this Convention and shall consider the desirability of placing on the agenda of the Conference the question of its revision in whole or in part.

*Article* 32

1. Should the Conference adopt a new Convention revising this Convention in whole or in part, the ratification by a Member of the new revising Convention shall *ipso jure* involve denunciation of this Convention without any requirement of delay, notwithstanding the provisions of Article 30 above, if and when the new revising Convention shall have come into force.

2. As from the date of the coming into force of the new revising Convention, the present Convention shall cease to be open to ratification by the Members.

3. Nevertheless, this Convention shall remain in force in its actual form and content for those Members which have ratified it but have not ratified the revising Convention.

*Article* 33

The French and English texts of this Convention shall both be authentic.

## III. CONVENTION CONCERNING THE ABOLITION OF FORCED LABOUR, 1957

This complements other conventions, including the Slavery Convention, 1926 (above), the Supplementary Convention on Abolition on Slavery, etc., 1956 (above), and the Forced Labour Convention, 1930 (above). It was adopted by the General Conference of the I.L.O. on 25 June 1957, entered into force on 17 January 1959, and has received not less than 117 ratifications. For the text in various languages see: *United Nations Treaty Series*, Vol. 320, p. 291.

The present Convention is concerned especially with forced labour as a means of political coercion.

### TEXT

*The General Conference of the International Labour Organization,*

*Having been convened* at Geneva by the Governing Body of the International Labour Office, and having met in its Fortieth Session on 5 June 1957,

*Having considered* the question of forced labour, which is the fourth item on the agenda of the session, and

*Having noted* the provisions of the Forced Labour Convention, 1930, and

*Having noted* that the Slavery Convention 1926, provided that all necessary measures shall be taken to prevent compulsory or forced labour from developing into conditions analogous to slavery and that the Supplementary Convention on the Abolition of Slavery, the Slave Trade and Institutions and Practices Similar to Slavery, 1956, provided for the complete abolition of debt bondage and serfdom, and

*Having noted* that the Protection of Wages Convention, 1949, provided that wages shall be paid regularly and prohibits methods of payment which deprive the worker of a genuine possibility of terminating his employment, and

*Having decided* upon the adoption of further proposals with regard to the abolition of certain forms of forced or compulsory labour constituting a violation of the rights of man referred to in the Charter of the United Nations and enunciated by the Universal Declaration of Human Rights, and

*Having determined* that these proposals shall take the form of an international convention,

*Adopts* this twenty-fifth day of June of the year one thousand nine hundred and fifty-seven the following convention, which may be cited as the Abolition of Forced Labour Convention, 1957.

*Article* 1

Each member of the International Labour Organization which ratifies this

Convention undertakes to suppress and not to make use of any form of forced or compulsory labour—

(a) As a means of political coercion or education or as a punishment for holding or expressing political views or views ideologically opposed to the established political, social or economic system;

(b) As a method of mobilizing and using labour for purposes of economic development;

(c) As a means of labour discipline;

(d) As a punishment for having participated in strikes;

(e) As a means of racial, social, national or religious discrimination.

*Article* 2

Each member of the International Labour Organization which ratifies this Convention undertakes to take effective measures to secure the immediate and complete abolition of forced or compulsory labour as specified in Article 1 of this Convention.

*Article* 3

The formal ratifications of this Convention shall be communicated to the Director-General of the International Labour Office for registration.

*Article* 4

This Convention shall be binding only upon those members of the International Labour Organization whose ratifications have been registered with the Director-General.

2. It shall come into force twelve months after the date on which the ratifications of two members have been registered with the Director-General.

3. Thereafter, this Convention shall come into force for any member twelve months after the date on which its ratification has been registered.

*Article* 5

1. A member which has ratified this Convention may denounce it after the expiration of ten years from the date on which the Convention first comes into force, by an act communicated to the Director-General of the International Labour Office for registration. Such denunciation shall not take effect until one year after the date on which it is registered.

2. Each member which has ratified this Convention and which does not, within the year following the expiration of the period of ten years mentioned in the preceding paragraph, exercise the right of denunciation provided for in this article, will be bound for another period of ten years and, thereafter, may denounce this Convention at the expiration of each period of ten years under the terms provided for in this Article.

*Article* 6

1. The Director-General of the International Labour Office shall notify all Members of the International Labour Organization of the registration of all ratifications and denunciations communicated to him by the members of the Organization.

2. When notifying the members of the Organization of the registration of the second ratification communicated to him, the Director-General shall draw the attention of the members of the Organization to the date upon which the Convention will come into force.

*Article* 7

The Director-General of the International Labour Office shall communicate to the Secretary-General of the United Nations for registration in accordance with Article 102 of the Charter of the United Nations full particulars of all ratifications and acts of denunciation registered by him in accordance with the provisions of the preceding articles.

*Article* 8

At such times as it may consider necessary the Governing Body of the International Labour Office shall present to the General Conference a report on the working of this Convention and shall examine the desirability of placing on the agenda of the Conference the question of its revision in whole or in part.

*Article* 9

1. Should the Conference adopt a new Convention revising this Convention in whole or in part, then, unless the new Convention otherwise provides—

(*a*) The ratification by a member of the new revising convention shall *ipso jure* involve the immediate denunciation of this Convention, notwithstanding the provisions of Article 5 above, if and when the new revising convention shall have come into force;

(*b*) As from the date when the new revising convention comes into force this Convention shall cease to be open to ratification by the members.

2. This Convention shall in any case remain in force in its actual form and content for those members which have ratified it but have not ratified the revising convention.

*Article* 10

The English and French versions of the text of this Convention are equally authoritative.

# IV. FREEDOM OF ASSOCIATION AND PROTECTION OF THE RIGHT TO ORGANIZE CONVENTION, 1948

This was adopted by the General Conference of the I.L.O. on 9 July 1948, entered into force on 4 July 1950, and has been ratified by not less than 100 States. For the text in various languages see: *United Nations Treaty Series*, Vol. 68, p. 17.

This Convention and the one which follows (below) protect the major points of trade-union activity and power: freedom to organize and freedom to indulge in collective bargaining. Similar freedom is provided for employers. See also the Right of Association (Agriculture) Convention, 1921; and the Right of Association (Non-Metropolitan Territories) Convention, 1947; *United Nations Treaty Series*, Vol. 171, p. 329; *Yearbook on Human Rights*, 1948, p. 420. It has been pointed out that none of the Conventions recognizes in terms the right to strike.

For further reference see *The I.L.O. and Human Rights*, 1968, pp. 32–41; and the Collective Agreements Recommendation adopted by the I.L.O. General Conference on 29 June 1951, *Yearbook on Human Rights*, 1951, p. 472.

In 1950 the I.L.O. Governing Body decided to establish a Fact-finding and Conciliation Commission on Freedom of Association: see the *Yearbook on Human Rights*, 1949, p. 293. This needs the consent of governments before it can act. However, in the case of a ratified convention the complaints procedure under Article 26 of the Constitution of the I.L.O. applies. There is also a Committee on Freedom of Information established in 1951. On the various procedures, see Wolf, in Meron (ed.), *Human Rights in International Law*, 1984, II, pp. 290–3.

*TEXT*

*The General Conference of the International Labour Organization,*

*Having* been convened at San Francisco by the Governing Body of the International Labour Office, and having met in its thirty-first session on 17 June 1948;

*Having decided* to adopt, in the form of a Convention, certain proposals concerning freedom of association and protection of the right to organize, which is the seventh item on the agenda of the session;

*Considering* that the Preamble to the Constitution of the International Labour Organization declares 'recognition of the principle of freedom of association' to be a means of improving conditions of labour and of establishing peace;

*Considering* that the Declaration of Philadelphia reaffirms that 'freedom of expression and of association are essential to sustained progress';

*Considering* that the International Labour Conference, at its thirtieth session, unanimously adopted the principles which should form the basis for international regulation;

*Considering* that the General Assembly of the United Nations, at its second session, endorsed these principles and requested the International Labour Organization to continue every effort in order that it may be possible to adopt one or several international Conventions;

*Adopts* this ninth day of July of the year one thousand nine hundred and forty-eight the following Convention, which may be cited as the Freedom of Association and Protection of the Right to Organize Convention, 1948:

## PART I
### Freedom of Association

*Article* 1

Each Member of the International Labour Organization for which this Convention is in force undertakes to give effect to the following provisions.

*Article* 2

Workers and employers, without distinction whatsoever, shall have the right to establish and, subject only to the rules of the organization concerned, to join organizations of their own choosing without previous authorization.

*Article* 3

1. Workers' and employers' organizations shall have the right to draw up their constitutions and rules, to elect their representatives in full freedom, to organize their administration and activities and to formulate their programmes.

2. The public authorities shall refrain from any interference which would restrict this right or impede the lawful exercise thereof.

*Article* 4

Workers' and employers' organizations shall not be liable to be dissolved or suspended by administrative authority.

*Article* 5

Workers' and employers' organizations shall have the right to establish and join federations and confederations and any such organization, federation or confederation shall have the right to affiliate with international organizations of workers and employers.

*Article* 6

The provisions of Articles 2, 3 and 4 hereof apply to federations and confederations of workers' and employers' organizations.

*Article* 7

The acquisition of legal personality by workers' and employers' organizations, federations and confederations shall not be made subject to conditions of such a character as to restrict the application of the provisions of Articles 2, 3 and 4 hereof.

*Article* 8

1. In exercising the rights provided for in this Convention workers and employers and their respective organizations, like other persons or organized collectivities, shall respect the law of the land.

2. The law of the land shall not be such as to impair, nor shall it be so applied as to impair, the guarantees provided for in this Convention.

*Article* 9

1. The extent to which the guarantees provided for in this Convention shall apply to the armed forces and the police shall be determined by national laws or regulations.

2. In accordance with the principle set forth in paragraph 8 of Article 19 of the Constitution of the International Labour Organization the ratification of this Convention by any Member shall not be deemed to affect any existing law, award, custom or agreement in virtue of which members of the armed forces or the police enjoy any right guaranteed by this Convention.

*Article* 10

In this Convention the term 'organization' means any organization of workers or of employers for furthering and defending the interests of workers or of employers.

# PART II
## Protection of the Right to Organize

*Article* 11

Each Member of the International Labour Organization for which this Convention is in force undertakes to take all necessary and appropriate measures to ensure that workers and employers may exercise freely the right to organize.

# PART III
## Miscellaneous Provisions

*Article* 12

1. In respect of the territories referred to in Article 35 of the Constitution of the International Labour Organization as amended by the Constitution of

the International Labour Organization Instrument of Amendment, 1946, other than the territories referred to in paragraphs 4 and 5 of the said article as so amended, each Member of the Organization which ratifies this Convention shall communicate to the Director-General of the International Labour Office with or as soon as possible after its ratification a declaration stating:

(a) The territories in respect of which it undertakes that the provisions of the Convention shall be applied without modification;

(b) The territories in respect of which it undertakes that the provisions of the Convention shall be applied subject to modifications, together with details of the said modifications;

(c) The territories in respect of which the Convention is inapplicable and in such cases the grounds on which it is inapplicable;

(d) The territories in respect of which it reserves its decision.

2. The undertakings referred to in sub-paragraphs (a) and (b) of paragraph 1 of this Article shall be deemed to be an integral part of the ratification and shall have the force of ratification.

3. Any Member may at any time by a subsequent declaration cancel in whole or in part any reservations made in its original declaration in virtue of sub-paragraph (b), (c) or (d) of paragraph 1 of this Article.

4. Any Member may, at any time at which this Convention is subject to denunciation in accordance with the provisions of Article 16, communicate to the Director-General a declaration modifying in any other respect the terms of any former declaration and stating the present position in respect of such territories as it may specify.

*Article* 13

1. Where the subject matter of this Convention is within the self-governing powers of any non-metropolitan territory, the Member responsible for the international relations of that territory may, in agreement with the Government of the territory, communicate to the Director-General of the International Labour Office a declaration accepting on behalf of the territory the obligations of this Convention.

2. A declaration accepting the obligations of this Convention may be communicated to the Director-General of the International Labour Office:

(a) By two or more Members of the Organization in respect of any territory which is under their joint authority; or

(b) By any international authority responsible for the administration of any territory, in virtue of the Charter of the United Nations or otherwise, in respect of any such territory.

3. Declarations communicated to the Director-General of the International

Labour Office in accordance with the preceding paragraphs of this article shall indicate whether the provisions of the Convention will be applied in the territory concerned without modification or subject to modifications; when the declaration indicates that the provisions of the Convention will be applied subject to modifications it shall give details of the said modifications.

4. The Member, Members or international authority concerned may at any time by a subsequent declaration renounce in whole or in part the right to have recourse to any modification indicated in any former declaration.

5. The Member, Members or international authority concerned may, at any time at which this Convention is subject to denunciation in accordance with the provisions of Article 16, communicate to the Director-General of the International Labour Office a declaration modifying in any other respect the terms of any former declaration and stating the present position in respect of the application of the Convention.

PART IV
Final Provisions

*Article* 14

The formal ratifications of this Convention shall be communicated to the Director-General of the International Labour Office for registration.

*Article* 15

1. This Convention shall be binding only upon those Members of the International Labour Organization whose ratifications have been registered with the Director-General.

2. It shall come into force twelve months after the date on which the ratifications of two Members have been registered with the Director-General.

3. Thereafter, this Convention shall come into force for any Member twelve months after the date on which its ratification has been registered.

*Article* 16

1. A Member which has ratified this Convention may denounce it after the expiration of ten years from the date on which the Convention first comes into force, by an act communicated to the Director-General of the International Labour Office for registration. Such denunciation shall not take effect until one year after the date on which it is registered.

2. Each Member which has ratified this Convention and which does not, within the year following the expiration of the period of ten years mentioned in the preceding paragraph, exercise the right of denunciation provided for in this Article, will be bound for another period of ten years

and, thereafter, may denounce this Convention at the expiration of each period of ten years under the terms provided for in this Article.

*Article* 17

1. The Director-General of the International Labour Office shall notify all Members of the International Labour Organization of the registration of all ratifications, declarations and denunciations communicated to him by the Members of the Organization.

2. When notifying the Members of the Organization of the registration of the second ratification communicated to him, the Director-General shall draw the attention of the Members of the Organization to the date upon which the Convention will come into force.

*Article* 18

The Director-General of the International Labour Office shall communicate to the Secretary-General of the United Nations for registration in accordance with Article 102 of the Charter of the United Nations full particulars of all ratifications, declarations and acts of denunciation registered by him in accordance with the provisions of the preceding articles.

*Article* 19

At the expiration of each period of ten years after the coming into force of this Convention, the Governing Body of the International Labour Office shall present to the General Conference a report on the working of this Convention and shall consider the desirability of placing on the agenda of the Conference the question of its revision in whole or in part.

*Article* 20

1. Should the Conference adopt a new Convention revising this Convention in whole or in part, then, unless the new Convention otherwise provides,

> (*a*) The ratification by a Member of the new revising Convention shall *ipso jure* involve the immediate denunciation of this Convention, notwithstanding the provisions of Article 16 above, if and when the new revising Convention shall have come into force;
>
> (*b*) As from the date when the new revising Convention comes into force this Convention shall cease to be open to ratification by the Members.

2. This Convention shall in any case remain in force in its actual form and content for those Members which have ratified it but have not ratified the revising Convention.

*Article* 21

The English and French versions of the text of this Convention are equally authoritative.

## V. RIGHT TO ORGANIZE AND COLLECTIVE BARGAINING CONVENTION, 1949

This was adopted by the General Conference of the I.L.O. on 1 July 1949, entered into force on 18 July 1951, and has been ratified by not less than 121 States. For the text in various languages see *United Nations Treaty Series*, Vol. 96, p. 257. See, further, the note at p. 260 above.

*TEXT*

[Preamble omitted.]

*Article* 1

1. Workers shall enjoy adequate protection against acts of anti-union discrimination in respect of their employment.

2. Such protection shall apply more particularly in respect of acts calculated to:

   (*a*) Make the employment of a worker subject to the condition that he shall not join a union or shall relinquish trade union membership;
   (*b*) Cause the dismissal of or otherwise prejudice a worker by reason of union membership or because of participation in union activities outside working hours or, with the consent of the employer, within working hours.

*Article* 2

1. Workers' and employers' organizations shall enjoy adequate protection against any acts of interference by each other or each others' agents or members in their establishment, functioning or administration.

2. In particular, acts which are designed to promote the establishment of workers' organizations under the domination of employers or employers' organizations, or to support workers' organizations by financial or other means, with the object of placing such organizations under the control of employers or employers' organizations, shall be deemed to constitute acts of interference within the meaning of this Article.

*Article* 3

Machinery appropriate to national conditions shall be established, where necessary, for the purpose of ensuring respect for the right to organize as defined in the preceding Articles.

*Article* 4

Measures appropriate to national conditions shall be taken, where necessary, to encourage and promote the full development and utilization of machinery for voluntary negotiation between employers or employers' organizations and workers' organizations, with a view to the regulation of terms and conditions of employment by means of collective agreements.

*Article* 5

1. The extent to which the guarantees provided for in this Convention shall apply to the armed forces and the police shall be determined by national laws or regulations.

2. In accordance with the principle set forth in paragraph 8 of Article 19 of the Constitution of the International Labour Organization the ratification of this Convention by any Member shall not be deemed to affect any existing law, award, custom or agreement in virtue of which members of the armed forces or the police enjoy any right guaranteed by this Convention.

*Article* 6

This Convention does not deal with the position of public servants engaged in the administration of the State, nor shall it be construed as prejudicing their rights or status in any way.

*Article* 7

The formal ratifications of this Convention shall be communicated to the Director-General of the International Labour Office for registration.

*Article* 8

1. This Convention shall be binding only upon those Members of the International Labour Organization whose ratifications have been registered with the Director-General.

2. It shall come into force twelve months after the date on which the ratifications of two Members have been registered with the Director-General.

3. Thereafter, this Convention shall come into force for any Member twelve months after the date on which its ratification has been registered.

*Article* 9

1. Declarations communicated to the Director-General of the International Labour Office in accordance with paragraph 2 of Article 35 of the Constitution of the International Labour Organization shall indicate:

- (*a*) The territories in respect of which the Member concerned undertakes that the provisions of the Convention shall be applied without modification;
- (*b*) The territories in respect of which it undertakes that the provisions of the Convention shall be applied subject to modifications, together with details of the said modifications;

(c) The territories in respect of which the Convention is inapplicable and in such cases the grounds on which it is inapplicable;

(d) The territories in respect of which it reserves its decision pending further consideration of the position.

2. The undertakings referred to in sub-paragraphs (a) and (b) of paragraph 1 of this Article shall be deemed to be an integral part of the ratification and shall have the force of ratification.

3. Any Member may at any time by a subsequent declaration cancel in whole or in part any reservation made in its original declaration in virtue of sub-paragraphs (b), (c) or (d) of paragraph 1 of this Article.

4. Any Member may, at any time at which the Convention is subject to denunciation in accordance with the provisions of Article 11, communicate to the Director-General a declaration modifying in any other respect the terms of any former declaration and stating the present position in respect of such territories as it may specify.

*Article* 10

1. Declarations communicated to the Director-General of the International Labour Office in accordance with paragraphs 4 or 5 of Article 35 of the Constitution of the International Labour Organization shall indicate whether the provisions of the Convention will be applied in the territory concerned without modification or subject to modifications; when the declaration indicates that the provisions of the Convention will be applied subject to modifications, it shall give details of the said modifications.

2. The Member, Members or international authority concerned may at any time by a subsequent declaration renounce in whole or in part the right to have recourse to any modification indicated in any former declaration.

3. The Member, Members or international authority concerned may, at any time at which this Convention is subject to denunciation in accordance with the provisions of Article 11, communicate to the Director-General a declaration modifying in any other respect the terms of any former declaration and stating the present position in respect of the application of the Convention.

*Article* 11

1. A Member which has ratified this Convention may denounce it after the expiration of ten years from the date on which the Convention first comes into force, by an act communicated to the Director-General of the International Labour Office for registration. Such denunciation shall not take effect until one year after the date on which it is registered.

2. Each Member which has ratified this Convention and which does not, within the year following the expiration of the period of ten years

mentioned in the preceding paragraph, exercise the right of denunciation provided for in this article, will be bound for another period of ten years and, thereafter, may denounce this Convention at the expiration of each period of ten years under the terms provided for in this Article.

*Article* 12

1. The Director-General of the International Labour Office shall notify all Members of the International Labour Organization of the registration of all ratifications, declarations, and denunciations communicated to him by the Members of the Organization.

2. When notifying the Members of the Organization of the registration of the second ratification communicated to him, the Director-General shall draw the attention of the Members of the Organization to the date upon which the Convention will come into force.

*Article* 13

The Director-General of the International Labour Office shall communicate to the Secretary-General of the United Nations for registration in accordance with Article 102 of the Charter of the United Nations full particulars of all ratifications, declarations and acts of denunciation registered by him in accordance with the provisions of the preceding articles.

*Article* 14

At the expiration of each period of ten years after the coming into force of this Convention, the Governing Body of the International Labour Office shall present to the General Conference a report on the working of this Convention and shall consider the desirability of placing on the agenda of the Conference the question of its revision in whole or in part.

*Article* 15

1. Should the Conference adopt a new Convention revising this Convention in whole or in part, then, unless the new Convention otherwise provides,

(*a*) The ratification by a Member of the new revising Convention shall *ipso jure* involve the immediate denunciation of this Convention, notwithstanding the provisions of Article 11 above, if and when the new revising Convention shall have come into force;

(*b*) As from the date when the new revising Convention comes into force this Convention shall cease to be open to ratification by the Members.

2. This Convention shall in any case remain in force in its actual form and content for those Members which have ratified it but have not ratified the revising Convention.

*Article* 16

The English and French versions of the text of this Convention are equally authoritative.

# VI. EQUAL REMUNERATION CONVENTION, 1951

The full title is Convention Concerning Equal Remuneration for Men and Women Workers for Work of Equal Value. The Convention was adopted by the General Conference of the I.L.O. on 29 June 1951, entered into force on 23 May 1953, and has been ratified by not less than 111 States. For the text in various languages see *United Nations Treaty Series*, Vol. 165, p. 304. See also the Equal Remuneration Recommendation, 1951, adopted at the same time.

Equality as between the sexes in the matter of wages and salaries has achieved but slow and reluctant recognition, even in the more advanced societies.

## TEXT

[Preamble omitted.]

*Article* 1

For the purpose of this Convention:

(*a*) The term 'remuneration' includes the ordinary, basic or minimum wage or salary and any additional emoluments whatsoever payable directly or indirectly, whether in cash or in kind, by the employer to the worker and arising out of the worker's employment;

(*b*) The term 'equal remuneration for men and women workers for work of equal value' refers to rates of remuneration established without discrimination based on sex.

*Article* 2

1. Each Member shall, by means appropriate to the methods in operation for determining rates of remuneration, promote and, in so far as is consistent with such methods, ensure the application to all workers of the principle of equal remuneration for men and women workers for work of equal value.

2. This principle may be applied by means of:

(*a*) National laws or regulations;
(*b*) Legally established or recognized machinery for wage determination;
(*c*) Collective agreements between employers and workers; or
(*d*) A combination of these various means.

*Article* 3

1. Where such action will assist in giving effect to the provisions of this Convention measures shall be taken to promote appraisal of jobs on the basis of the work to be performed.

2. The methods to be followed in this appraisal may be decided upon by the authorities responsible for the determination of rates of remuneration, or, where such rates are determined by collective agreements, by the parties thereto.

3. Differential rates between workers which correspond, without regard to sex, to differences, as determined by such objective appraisal, in the work to be performed shall not be considered as being contrary to the principle of equal remuneration for men and women workers for work of equal value.

*Article* 4

Each Member shall co-operate as appropriate with the employers' and workers' organizations concerned for the purpose of giving effect to the provisions of this Convention.

*Article* 5

The formal ratifications of this Convention shall be communicated to the Director-General of the International Labour Office for registration.

*Article* 6

1. This Convention shall be binding only upon those Members of the International Labour Organization whose ratifications have been registered with the Director-General.

2. It shall come into force twelve months after the date on which the ratifications of two Members have been registered with the Director-General.

3. Thereafter, this Convention shall come into force for any Member twelve months after the date on which its ratification has been registered.

*Article* 7

1. Declarations communicated to the Director-General of the International Labour Office in accordance with paragraph 2 of Article 35 of the Constitution of the International Labour Organization shall indicate:

  (*a*)  The territories in respect of which the Member concerned undertakes that the provisions of the Convention shall be applied without modification;

  (*b*)  The territories in respect of which it undertakes that the provisions of the Convention shall be applied subject to modifications, together with details of the said modifications;

  (*c*)  The territories in respect of which the Convention is inapplicable and in such cases the grounds on which it is inapplicable;

  (*d*)  The territories in respect of which it reserves its decisions pending further consideration of the position.

2. The undertakings referred to in sub-paragraphs (*a*) and (*b*) of paragraph 1 of this Article shall be deemed to be an integral part of the ratification and shall have the force of ratification.

3. Any Member may at any time by a subsequent declaration cancel in whole or in part any reservation made in its original declaration by virtue of sub-paragraphs (*b*), (*c*) or (*d*) of paragraph 1 of this Article.

4. Any Member may, at any time at which the Convention is subject to denunciation in accordance with the provisions of Article 9, communicate to the Director-General a declaration modifying in any other respect the terms of any former declaration and stating the present position in respect of such territories as it may specify.

*Article* 8

1. Declarations communicated to the Director-General of the International Labour Office in accordance with paragraphs 4 or 5 of Article 35 of the Constitution of the International Labour Organization shall indicate whether the provisions of the Convention will be applied in the territory concerned without modification or subject to modifications; when the declaration indicates that the provisions of the Convention will be applied subject to modifications, it shall give details of the said modifications.

2. The Member, Members or international authority concerned may at any time by a subsequent declaration renounce in whole or in part the right to have recourse to any modification indicated in any former declaration.

3. The Member, Members or international authority concerned may, at any time at which this Convention is subject to denunciation in accordance with the provisions of Article 9, communicate to the Director-General a declaration modifying in any other respect the terms of any former declaration and stating the present position in respect of the application of the Convention.

*Article* 9

1. A Member which has ratified this Convention may denounce it after the expiration of ten years from the date on which the Convention first comes into force, by an act communicated to the Director-General of the International Labour Office for registration. Such denunciation shall not take effect until one year after the date on which it is registered.

2. Each Member which has ratified this Convention and which does not, within the year following the expiration of the period of ten years mentioned in the preceding paragraph, exercise the right of denunciation provided for in this Article, will be bound for another period of ten years and, thereafter, may denounce this Convention at the expiration of each period of ten years under the terms provided for in this Article.

*Article* 10

1. The Director-General of the International Labour Office shall notify all Members of the International Labour Organization of the registration of all ratifications, declarations and denunciations communicated to him by the Members of the Organization.

2. When notifying the Members of the Organization of the registration of the second ratification communicated to him, the Director-General shall draw the attention of the Members of the Organization to the date upon which the Convention will come into force.

*Article* 11

The Director-General of the International Labour Office shall communicate to the Secretary-General of the United Nations for registration in accordance with Article 102 of the Charter of the United Nations full particulars of all ratifications, declarations and acts of denunciation registered by him in accordance with the provisions of the preceding Articles.

*Article* 12

At such times as it may consider necessary the Governing Body of the International Labour Office shall present to the General Conference a report of the working of this Convention and shall examine the desirability of placing on the agenda of the Conference the question of its revision in whole or in part.

*Article* 13

1. Should the Conference adopt a new Convention revising this Convention in whole or in part, then, unless the new Convention otherwise provides:

(*a*) The ratification by a Member of the new revising Convention shall *ipso jure* involve the immediate denunciation of this Convention, notwithstanding the provisions of Article 9 above, if and when the new revising Convention shall have come into force;

(*b*) As from the date when the new revising Convention comes into force this Convention shall cease to be open to ratification by Members.

2. This Convention shall in any case remain in force in its actual form and content for those Members which have ratified it but have not ratified the revising Convention.

*Article* 14

The English and French versions of the text of this Convention are equally authoritative.

# VII. DISCRIMINATION (EMPLOYMENT AND OCCUPATION) CONVENTION, 1958

The most important aspect of this Convention is its application to racial matters, but it is aimed at other forms of discrimination as well. The Convention was adopted by the General Conference of the I.L.O. on 25 June 1958, entered into force on 15 June 1960, and has been ratified by not less than 112 States. For the text in various languages see *United Nations Treaty Series*, Vol. 362, p. 31. The relevant Recommendation of the International Labour Conference is also reproduced below.

## TEXT

*The General Conference of the International Labour Organization,*

*Having been convened* at Geneva by the Governing Body of the International Labour Office, and having met in its Forty-second Session on 4 June 1958, and

*Having decided* upon the adoption of certain proposals with regard to discrimination in the field of employment and occupation, which is the fourth item on the agenda of the session, and

*Having determined* that these proposals shall take the form of an international Convention, and

*Considering* that the Declaration of Philadelphia affirms that all human beings, irrespective of race, creed or sex, have the right to pursue both their material well-being and their spiritual development in conditions of freedom and dignity, of economic security and equal opportunity, and

*Considering further* that discrimination constitutes violation of rights enunciated by the Universal Declaration of Human Rights,

*Adopts* this twenty-fifth day of June of the year one thousand nine hundred and fifty-eight the following Convention, which may be cited as the Discrimination (Employment and Occupation) Convention, 1958:

*Article* 1

1. For the purpose of this Convention the term 'discrimination' includes:

(a) Any distinction, exclusion or preference made on the basis of race, colour, sex, religion, political opinion, national extraction or social origin, which has the effect of nullifying or impairing equality of opportunity or treatment in employment or occupation;

(b) Such other distinction, exclusion or preference which has the effect of nullifying or impairing equality of opportunity or treatment in employment or occupation as may be determined by the Member concerned after consultation with representative employers' and workers' organizations, where such exist, and with other appropriate bodies.

2. Any distinction, exclusion or preference in respect of a particular job based on the inherent requirements thereof shall not be deemed to be discrimination.

3. For the purpose of this Convention the terms 'employment' and 'occupation' include access to vocational training, access to employment and to particular occupations, and terms and conditions of employment.

*Article 2*

Each Member for which this Convention is in force undertakes to declare and pursue a national policy designed to promote, by methods appropriate to national conditions and practice, equality of opportunity and treatment in respect of employment and occupation, with a view to eliminating any discrimination thereof.

*Article 3*

Each Member for which this Convention is in force undertakes, by methods appropriate to national conditions and practice—

(*a*)   To seek the co-operation of employers' and workers' organizations and other appropriate bodies in promoting the acceptance and observance of this policy;

(*b*)   To enact such legislation and to promote such educational programmes as may be calculated to secure the acceptance and observance of the policy;

(*c*)   To repeal any statutory provisions and modify any administrative instructions or practices which are inconsistent with the policy;

(*d*)   To pursue the policy in respect of employment under the direct control of a national authority;

(*e*)   To ensure observance of the policy in activities of vocational guidance, vocational training and placement services under the direction of a national authority;

(*f*)   To indicate in its annual reports on the application of the Convention the action taken in pursuance of the policy and the results secured by such action.

*Article 4*

Any measures affecting an individual who is justifiably suspected of, or engaged in, activities prejudicial to the security of the State shall not be deemed to be discrimination, provided that the individual concerned shall have the right to appeal to a competent body established in accordance with national practice.

*Article 5*

1. Special measures of protection or assistance provided for in other

Conventions or Recommendations adopted by the International Labour Conference shall not be deemed to be discrimination.

2. Any Member may, after consultation with representative employers' and workers' organizations, where such exist, determine that other special measures designed to meet the particular requirements of persons who, for reasons such as sex, age, disablement, family responsibilities or social or cultural status, are generally recognized to require special protection or assistance, shall not be deemed to be discrimination.

*Article* 6

Each Member which ratifies this Convention undertakes to apply it to non-metropolitan territories in accordance with the provisions of the Constitution of the International Labour Organization.

*Article* 7

The formal ratifications of this Convention shall be communicated to the Director-General of the International Labour Office for registration.

*Article* 8

1. This Convention shall be binding only upon those Members of the International Labour Organization whose ratifications have been registered with the Director-General.

2. It shall come into force twelve months after the date on which the ratifications of two Members have been registered with the Director-General.

3. Thereafter, this Convention shall come into force for any Member twelve months after the date on which its ratification has been registered.

*Article* 9

1. A Member which has ratified this Convention may denounce it after the expiration of ten years from the date on which the Convention first comes into force, by an act communicated to the Director-General of the International Labour Office for registration. Such denunciation shall not take effect until one year after the date on which it is registered.

2. Each Member which has ratified this Convention and which does not, within the year following the expiration of the period of ten years mentioned in the preceding paragraph, exercise the right of denunciation provided for in this Article, will be bound for another period of ten years and, thereafter, may denounce this Convention at the expiration of each period of ten years under the terms provided for in this Article.

*Article* 10

1. The Director-General of the International Labour Office shall notify all Members of the International Labour Organization of the registration of all

ratifications and denunciations communicated to him by the Members of the Organization.

2. When notifying the Members of the Organization of the registration of the second ratification communicated to him, the Director-General shall draw the attention of the Members of the Organization to the date upon which the Convention will come into force.

## Article 11

The Director-General of the International Labour Office shall communicate to the Secretary-General of the United Nations for registration in accordance with Article 102 of the Charter of the United Nations full particulars of all ratifications and acts of denunciation registered by him in accordance with the provisions of the preceding articles.

## Article 12

At such times as it may consider necessary the Governing Body of the International Labour Office shall present to the General Conference a report on the working of this Convention and shall examine the desirability of placing on the agenda of the Conference the question of its revision in whole or in part.

## Article 13

1. Should the Conference adopt a new Convention revising this Convention in whole or in part, then, unless the new Convention otherwise provides—

   (a) The ratification by a Member of the new revising Convention shall *ipso jure* involve the immediate denunciation of this Convention, notwithstanding the provisions of Article 9 above, if and when the new revising Convention shall have come into force;
   (b) As from the date when the new revising Convention comes into force this Convention shall cease to be open to ratification by the Members.

2. This Convention shall in any case remain in force in its actual form and content for those Members which have ratified it but have not ratified the revising Convention.

## Article 14

The English and French versions of the text of this Convention are equally authoritative.

# DISCRIMINATION (EMPLOYMENT AND OCCUPATION) RECOMMENDATION, 1958

*The General Conference of the International Labour Organization,*

*Having been convened* at Geneva by the Governing Body of the International Labour Office, and having met in its Forty-second Session on 4 June 1958, and

*Having decided* upon the adoption of certain proposals with regard to discrimination in the field of employment and occupation, which is the fourth item on the agenda of the session, and

*Having determined* that these proposals shall take the form of a Recommendation supplementing the Discrimination (Employment and Occupation) Convention, 1958,

*Adopts* this twenty-fifth day of June of the Year one thousand nine hundred and fifty-eight the following Recommendation, which may be cited as the Discrimination (Employment and Occupation) Recommendation, 1958;

The Conference recommends that each Member should apply the following provisions:

## I. Definitions

1. (1) For the purpose of this Recommendation the term 'discrimination' includes—

(*a*) Any distinction, exclusion or preference made on the basis of race, colour, sex, religion, political opinion, national extraction or social origin, which has the effect of nullifying or impairing equality of opportunity or treatment in employment or occupation;

(*b*) Such other distinction, exclusion or preference which has the effect of nullifying or impairing equality of opportunity or treatment in employment or occupation as may be determined by the Member concerned after consultation with representative employers' and workers' organizations, where such exist, and with other appropriate bodies.

(2) Any distinction, exclusion or preference in respect of a particular job based on the inherent requirements thereof is not deemed to be discrimination.

(3) For the purpose of this Recommendation the terms 'employment' and 'occupation' include access to vocational training, access to employment and to particular occupations, and terms and conditions of employment.

## II. Formulation and Application of Policy

2. Each Member should formulate a national policy for the prevention of discrimination in employment and occupation. This policy should be applied by means of legislative measures, collective agreements between representative employers' and workers' organizations or in any other manner consistent with national conditions and practice, and should have regard to the following principles:

(a) The promotion of equality of opportunity and treatment in employment and occupation is a matter of public concern;

(b) All persons should, without discrimination, enjoy equality of opportunity and treatment in respect of—

   (i) Access to vocational guidance and placement services;

   (ii) Access to training and employment of their own choice on the basis of individual suitability for such training or employment;

   (iii) Advancement in accordance with their individual character, experience, ability and diligence;

   (iv) Security of tenure of employment;

   (v) Remuneration for work of equal value;

   (vi) Conditions of work including hours of work, rest periods, annual holidays with pay, occupational safety and occupational health measures, as well as social security measures and welfare facilities and benefits provided in connexion with employment;

(c) Government agencies should apply non-discriminatory employment policies in all their activities;

(d) Employers should not practise or countenance discrimination in engaging or training any person for employment, in advancing or retaining such person in employment, or in fixing terms and conditions of employment; nor should any person or organization obstruct or interfere, either directly or indirectly, with employers in pursuing this principle;

(e) In collective negotiations and industrial relations the parties should respect the principle of equality of opportunity and treatment in employment and occupation, and should ensure that collective agreements contain no provisions of a discriminatory character in respect of access to, training for, advancement in or retention of employment or in respect of the terms and conditions of employment;

(f) Employers' and workers' organizations should not practise or countenance discrimination in respect of admission, retention or membership or participation in their affairs.

3. Each Member should—

(a) Ensure application of the principles of non-discrimination—

   (i) In respect of employment under the direct control of a national authority;

      (ii) In the activities of vocational guidance, vocational training and placement services under the direction of a national authority;

(b) Promote their observance, where practicable and necessary, in respect of other employment and other vocational guidance, vocational training and placement services by such methods as—

      (i) Encouraging state, provincial or local government departments or agencies and industries and undertakings operated under public ownership or control to ensure the application of the principles;

     (ii) Making eligibility for contracts involving the expenditure of public funds dependent on observance of the principles;

   (iii) Making eligibility for grants to training establishments and for a licence to operate a private employment agency or a private vocational guidance office dependent on observance of the principles.

4. Appropriate agencies, to be assisted where practicable by advisory committees composed of representatives of employers' and workers' organizations, where such exist, and of other interested bodies, should be established for the purpose of promoting application of the policy in all fields of public and private employment, and in particular—

  (a) To take all practicable measures to foster public understanding and acceptance of the principles of non-discrimination;

  (b) To receive, examine and investigate complaints that the policy is not being observed and, if necessary by conciliation, to secure the correction of any practices regarded as in conflict with the policy; and

  (c) To consider further any complaints which cannot be effectively settled by conciliation and to render opinions or issue decisions concerning the manner in which discriminatory practices revealed should be corrected.

5. Each Member should repeal any statutory provisions and modify any administrative instruction or practices which are inconsistent with the policy.

6. Application of the policy should not adversely affect special measures designed to meet the particular requirements of persons who, for reasons such as sex, age, disablement, family responsibilities or social or cultural status are generally recognized to require special protection or assistance.

7. Any measures affecting an individual who is justifiably suspected of, or engaged in, activities prejudicial to the security of the State should not be deemed to be discrimination, provided that the individual concerned has the right to appeal to a competent body established in accordance with national practice.

8. With respect to immigrant workers of foreign nationality and the members of their families, regard should be had to the provisions of the

Migration for Employment Convention (Revised), 1949, relating to equality of treatment and the provisions of the Migration for Employment Recommendation (Revised), 1949, relating to the lifting of restrictions on access to employment.

9. There should be continuing co-operation between the competent authorities, representatives of employers and workers and appropriate bodies to consider what further positive measures may be necessary in the light of national conditions to put the principles of non-discrimination into effect.

## III. Co-ordination of Measures for the Prevention of Discrimination in all Fields

10. The authorities responsible for action against discrimination in employment and occupation should co-operate closely and continuously with the authorities responsible for action against discrimination in other fields in order that measures taken in all fields may be co-ordinated.

## VIII. EQUALITY OF TREATMENT
## (SOCIAL SECURITY) CONVENTION, 1962

The Convention concerns one aspect of a particularly sensitive aspect of the principle of equality, namely, equality of treatment for non-nationals. The Convention was adopted by the General Conference of the I.L.O. on 28 June 1962, entered into force on 25 April 1964, and has been ratified by not less than 38 States. For the text in various languages see *United Nations Treaty Series*, Vol. 494, p. 271.

See, further, the Social Security (Minimum Standards) Convention, 1952, *United Nations Treaty Series*, Vol. 210, p. 131; and *The I.L.O. and Human Rights*, 1968, pp. 54–5.

*TEXT*

[Preamble omitted.]

*Article* 1

In this Convention—

(a) the term 'legislation' includes any social security rules as well as laws and regulations;

(b) the term 'benefits' refers to all benefits, grants and pensions, including any supplements or increments;

(c) the term 'benefits granted under transitional schemes' means either benefits granted to persons who have exceeded a prescribed age at the date when the legislation applicable came into force, or benefits granted as a transitional measure in consideration of events occurring or periods completed outside the present boundaries of the territory of a Member;

(d) the term 'death grant' means any lump sum payable in the event of death;

(e) the term 'residence' means ordinary residence;

(f) the term 'prescribed' means determined by or in virtue of national legislation as defined in subparagraph (a) above;

(g) the term 'refugee' has the meaning assigned to it in Article 1 of the Convention relating to the Status of Refugees of 28 July 1951;

(h) the term 'stateless person' has the meaning assigned to it in Article 1 of the Convention relating to the Status of Stateless Persons of 28 September 1954.

*Article* 2

1. Each Member may accept the obligations of this Convention in respect of any one or more of the following branches of social security for which it

has in effective operation legislation covering its own nationals within its own territory:

(a)  medical care;
(b)  sickness benefit;
(c)  maternity benefit;
(d)  invalidity benefit;
(e)  old-age benefit;
(f)  survivors' benefit;
(g)  employment injury benefit;
(h)  unemployment benefit; and
(i)  family benefit.

2. Each Member for which this Convention is in force shall comply with its provisions in respect of the branch or branches of social security for which it has accepted the obligations of the Convention.

3. Each Member shall specify in its ratification in respect of which branch or branches of social security it accepts the obligations of this Convention.

4. Each Member which has ratified this Convention may subsequently notify the Director-General of the International Labour Office that it accepts the obligations of the Convention in respect of one or more branches of social security not already specified in its ratification.

5. The undertakings referred to in paragraph 4 of this Article shall be deemed to be an integral part of the ratification and to have the force of ratification as from the date of notification.

6. For the purpose of the application of this Convention, each Member accepting the obligations thereof in respect of any branch of social security which has legislation providing for benefits of the type indicated in clause (a) or (b) below shall communicate to the Director-General of the International Labour Office a statement indicating the benefits provided for by its legislation which it considers to be—

(a)  benefits other than those the grant of which depends either on direct financial participation by the persons protected or their employer, or on a qualifying period of occupational activity; or
(b)  benefits granted under transitional schemes.

7. The communication referred to in paragraph 6 of this Article shall be made at the time of ratification or at the time of notification in accordance with paragraph 4 of this Article; as regards any legislation adopted subsequently, the communication shall be made within three months of the date of the adoption of such legislation.

*Article* 3

1. Each Member for which this Convention is in force shall grant within its

territory to the nationals of any other Member for which the Convention is in force equality of treatment under its legislation with its own nationals, both as regards coverage and as regards the right to benefits, in respect of every branch of social security for which it has accepted the obligations of the Convention.

2. In the case of survivors' benefits, such equality of treatment shall also be granted to the survivors of the nationals of a Member for which the Convention is in force, irrespective of the nationality of such survivors.

3. Nothing in the preceding paragraphs of this Article shall require a Member to apply the provisions of these paragraphs, in respect of the benefits of a specified branch of social security, to the nationals of another Member which has legislation relating to that branch but does not grant equality of treatment in respect thereof to the nationals of the first Member.

*Article 4*

1. Equality of treatment as regards the grant of benefits shall be accorded without any condition of residence: Provided that equality of treatment in respect of the benefits of a specified branch of social security may be made conditional on residence in the case of nationals of any Member the legislation of which makes the grant of benefits under that branch conditional on residence on its territory.

2. Notwithstanding the provisions of paragraph 1 of this Article, the grant of the benefits referred to in paragraph 6 (*a*) of Article 2—other than medical care, sickness benefit, employment injury benefit and family benefit—may be made subject to the condition that the beneficiary has resided on the territory of the Member in virtue of the legislation of which the benefit is due, or, in the case of a survivor, that the deceased has resided there, for a period which shall not exceed—

(*a*) six months immediately preceding the filing of claim, for grant of maternity benefit and unemployment benefit;
(*b*) five consecutive years immediately preceding the filing of claim, for grant of invalidity benefit, or immediately preceding death, for grant of survivors' benefit;
(*c*) ten years after the age of 18, which may include five consecutive years immediately preceding the filing of claim, for grant of old-age benefit.

3. Special provisions may be prescribed in respect of benefits granted under transitional schemes.

4. The measures necessary to prevent the cumulation of benefits shall be determined, as necessary, by special arrangements between the Members concerned.

*Article* 5

1. In addition to the provisions of Article 4, each Member which has accepted the obligations of this Convention in respect of the branch or branches of social security concerned shall guarantee both to its own nationals and to the nationals of any other Member which has accepted the obligations of the Convention in respect of the branch or branches in question, when they are resident abroad, provision of invalidity benefits, old-age benefits, survivors' benefits and death grants, and employment injury pensions, subject to measures for this purpose being taken, where necessary, in accordance with Article 8.

2. In case of residence abroad, the provision of invalidity, old-age and survivors' benefits of the type referred to in paragraph 6 (*a*) of Article 2 may be made subject to the participation of the Members concerned in schemes for the maintenance of rights as provided for in Article 7.

3. The provisions of this Article do not apply to benefits granted under transitional schemes.

*Article* 6

In addition to the provisions of Article 4, each Member which has accepted the obligations of this Convention in respect of family benefits shall guarantee the grant of family allowances both to its own nationals and to the nationals of any other Member which has accepted the obligations of this Convention for that branch, in respect of children who reside on the territory of any such Member, under conditions and within limits to be agreed upon by the Members concerned.

*Article* 7

1. Members for which this Convention is in force shall, upon terms being agreed between the Members concerned in accordance with Article 8, endeavour to participate in schemes for the maintenance of the acquired rights and rights in course of acquisition under their legislation of the nationals of Members for which the Convention is in force, for all branches of social security in respect of which the Members concerned have accepted the obligations of the Convention.

2. Such schemes shall provide, in particular, for the totalization of periods of insurance, employment or residence and of assimilated periods for the purpose of the acquisition, maintenance or recovery of rights and for the calculation of benefits.

3. The cost of invalidity, old-age and survivors' benefits as so determined shall either be shared among the Members concerned, or be borne by the Member on whose territory the beneficiaries reside, as may be agreed upon by the Members concerned.

*Article* 8

The Members for which this Convention is in force may give effect to their obligations under the provisions of Articles 5 and 7 by ratification of the Maintenance of Migrants' Pension Rights Convention, 1935, by the application of the provisions of that Convention as between particular Members by mutual agreement, or by any multilateral or bilateral agreement giving effect to these obligations.

*Article* 9

The provisions of this Convention may be derogated from by agreements between Members which do not affect the rights and duties of other Members and which make provision for the maintenance of rights in course of acquisition and of acquired rights under conditions at least as favourable on the whole as those provided for in this Convention.

*Article* 10

1. The provisions of this Convention apply to refugees and stateless persons without any condition of reciprocity.
2. This Convention does not apply to special schemes for civil servants, special schemes for war victims, or public assistance.
3. This Convention does not require any Member to apply the provisions thereof to persons who, in accordance with the provisions of international instruments, are exempted from its national social security legislation.

*Article* 11

The Members for which this Convention is in force shall afford each other administrative assistance free of charge with a view to facilitating the application of the Convention and the execution of their respective social security legislation.

*Article* 12

1. This Convention does not apply to benefits payable prior to the coming into force of the Convention for the Member concerned in respect of the branch of social security under which the benefit is payable.
2. The extent to which the Convention applies to benefits attributable to contingencies occurring before its coming into force for the Member concerned in respect of the branch of social security under which the benefit is payable thereafter shall be determined by multilateral or bilateral agreement or in default thereof by the legislation of the Member concerned.

*Article* 13

This Convention shall not be regarded as revising any existing Convention.

*Article* 14

The formal ratifications of this Convention shall be communicated to the Director-General of the International Labour Office for registration.

*Article* 15

1. This Convention shall be binding only upon those Members of the International Labour Organization whose ratifications have been registered with the Director-General.

2. It shall come into force twelve months after the date on which the ratifications of two Members have been registered with the Director-General.

3. Thereafter, this Convention shall come into force for any Member twelve months after the date on which its ratification has been registered.

*Article* 16

1. A Member which has ratified this Convention may denounce it after the expiration of ten years from the date on which the Convention first comes into force, by an act communicated to the Director-General of the International Labour Office for registration. Such denunciation shall not take effect until one year after the date on which it is registered.

2. Each Member which has ratified this Convention and which does not, within the year following the expiration of the period of ten years mentioned in the preceding paragraph, exercise the right of denunciation provided for in this Article, will be bound for another period of ten years and, thereafter, may denounce this Convention at the expiration of each period of ten years under the terms provided for in this Article.

*Article* 17

1. The Director-General of the International Labour Office shall notify all Members of the International Labour Organization of the registration of all ratifications and denunciations communicated to him by the Members of the Organization.

2. When notifying the Members of the Organization of the registration of the second ratification communicated to him, the Director-General shall draw the attention of the Members of the Organization to the date upon which the Convention will come into force.

*Article* 18

The Director-General of the International Labour Office shall communicate to the Secretary-General of the United Nations for registration in accordance with Article 102 of the Charter of the United Nations full particulars of all ratifications and acts of denunciation registered by him in accordance with the provisions of the preceding Articles.

*Article* 19

At such times as it may consider necessary the Governing Body of the International Labour Office shall present to the General Conference a report on the working of this Convention and shall examine the desirability of placing on the agenda of the Conference the question of its revision in whole or in part.

*Article* 20

1. Should the Conference adopt a new Convention revising the Convention in whole or in part, then, unless the new Convention otherwise provides:

    (*a*) The ratification by a Member of the new revising Convention shall *ipso jure* involve the immediate denunciation of this Convention, notwithstanding the provisions of Article 16 above, if and when the new revising Convention shall have come into force;

    (*b*) As from the date when the new revising Convention comes into force this Convention shall cease to be open to ratification by the Members.

2. This Convention shall in any case remain in force in its actual form and content for those Members which have ratified it but have not ratified the revising Convention.

*Article* 21

The English and French versions of the text of this Convention are equally authoritative.

# IX. SOCIAL POLICY (BASIC AIMS AND STANDARDS) CONVENTION, 1962

The Convention was adopted by the General Conference of the I.L.O. on 22 June 1962, entered into force on 23 April 1964, and has been ratified by not less than 32 States. For the text in various languages: *United Nations Treaty Series*, Vol. 494, p. 249.

## TEXT

*The General Conference of the International Labour Organization,*

*Having been convened* at Geneva by the Governing Body of the International Labour Office, and having met in its Forty-sixth Session on 6 June 1962, and

*Having decided* upon the adoption of certain proposals concerning the revision of the Social Policy (Non-Metropolitan Territories) Convention, 1947, which is the tenth item on the agenda of the Session, primarily with a view to making its continued application and ratification possible for independent States, and

*Considering* that these proposals must take the form of an international Convention, and

*Considering* that economic development must serve as a basis for social progress, and

*Considering* that every effort should be made, on an international, regional or national basis, to secure financial and technical assistance safe-guarding the interests of the population, and

*Considering* that, in appropriate cases, international, regional or national action should be taken with a view to establishing conditions of trade which would encourage production at a high level of efficiency and make possible the maintenance of a reasonable standard of living, and

*Considering* that all possible steps should be taken by appropriate international, regional and national measures to promote improvement in such fields as public health, housing, nutrition, education, the welfare of children, the status of women, conditions of employment, the remuneration of wage earners and independent producers, the protection of migrant workers, social security, standards of public services and general production, and

*Considering* that all possible steps should be taken effectively to interest and associate the population in the framing and execution of measures of social progress,

*Adopts* this twenty-second day of June of the year one thousand nine hundred and sixty-two the following Convention, which may be cited as the Social Policy (Basic Aims and Standards) Convention, 1962:

# PART I
## General Principles

*Article* 1

1. All policies shall be primarily directed to the well-being and development of the population and to the promotion of its desire for social progress.

2. All policies of more general application shall be formulated with due regard to their effect upon the well-being of the population.

# PART II
## Improvement of Standards of Living

*Article* 2

The improvement of standards of living shall be regarded as the principal objective in the planning of economic development.

*Article* 3

1. All practicable measures shall be taken in the planning of economic development to harmonize such development with the healthy evolution of the communities concerned.

2. In particular, efforts shall be made to avoid the disruption of family life and traditional social units, especially by—

   (*a*) close study of the causes and effects of migratory movements and appropriate action where necessary;

   (*b*) the promotion of town and village planning in areas where economic needs result in the concentration of population;

   (*c*) the prevention and elimination of congestion in urban areas;

   (*d*) the improvement of living conditions in rural areas and the establishment of suitable industries in rural areas where adequate manpower is available.

*Article* 4

The measures to be considered by the competent authorities for the promotion of productive capacity and the improvement of standards of living of agricultural producers shall include—

   (*a*) the elimination to the fullest practicable extent of the causes of chronic indebtedness;

   (*b*) the control of the alienation of agricultural land to non-agriculturalists so as to ensure that such alienation takes place only when it is in the best interest of the country;

(c) the control, by the enforcement of adequate laws or regulations, of the ownership and use of land and resources to ensure that they are used, with due regard to customary rights, in the best interests of the inhabitants of the country;

(d) the supervision of tenancy arrangements and of working conditions with a view to securing for tenants and labourers the highest practicable standards of living and an equitable share in any advantages which may result from improvements in productivity or in price levels;

(e) the reduction of production and distribution costs by all practicable means and in particular by forming, encouraging and assisting producers' and consumers' co-operatives.

*Article* 5

1. Measures shall be taken to secure for independent producers and wage earners conditions which will give them scope to improve living standards by their own efforts and will ensure the maintenance of minimum standards of living as ascertained by means of official inquiries into living conditions, conducted after consultation with the representative organizations of employers and workers.

2. In ascertaining the minimum standards of living, account shall be taken of such essential family needs of the workers as food and its nutritive value, housing, clothing, medical care and education.

## PART III
### Provisions concerning Migrant Workers

*Article* 6

Where the circumstances under which workers are employed involve their living away from their homes, the terms and conditions of their employment shall take account of their normal family needs.

*Article* 7

Where the labour resources of one area are used on a temporary basis for the benefit of another area, measures shall be taken to encourage the transfer of part of the workers' wages and savings from the area of labour utilization to the area of labour supply.

*Article* 8

1. Where the labour resources of a country are used in an area under a different administration, the competent authorities of the countries concerned shall, whenever necessary or desirable, enter into agreements for the

purpose of regulating matters of common concern arising in connection with the application of the provisions of this Convention.

2. Such agreements shall provide that the worker shall enjoy protection and advantages not less than those enjoyed by workers resident in the area of labour utilization.

3. Such agreements shall provide for facilities for enabling the worker to transfer part of his wages and savings to his home.

*Article* 9

Where workers and their families move from low-cost to higher-cost areas, account shall be taken of the increased cost of living resulting from the change.

## PART IV
### Remuneration of Workers and Related Questions

*Article* 10

1. The fixing of minimum wages by collective agreements freely negotiated between trade unions which are representative of the workers concerned and employers or employers' organizations shall be encouraged.

2. Where no adequate arrangements exist for the fixing of minimum wages by collective agreement, the necessary arrangements shall be made whereby minimum rates of wages can be fixed in consultation with representatives of the employers and workers, including representatives of their respective organizations, where such exist.

3. The necessary measures shall be taken to ensure that the employers and workers concerned are informed of the minimum wage rates in force and that wages are not paid at less than these rates in cases where they are applicable.

4. A worker to whom minimum rates are applicable and who, since they became applicable, has been paid wages at less than these rates shall be entitled to recover, by judicial or other means authorized by law, the amount by which he has been underpaid, subject to such limitation of time as may be determined by law or regulation.

*Article* 11

1. The necessary measures shall be taken to ensure the proper payment of all wages earned and employers shall be required to keep registers of wage payments, to issue to workers statements of wage payments and to take other appropriate steps to facilitate the necessary supervision.

2. Wages shall normally be paid in legal tender only.

3. Wages shall normally be paid direct to the individual worker.

4. The substitution of alcohol or other spirituous beverages for all or any part of wages for services performed by the worker shall be prohibited.

5. Payment of wages shall not be made in taverns or stores, except in the case of workers employed therein.

6. Unless there is an established local custom to the contrary, and the competent authority is satisfied that the continuance of this custom is desired by the workers, wages shall be paid regularly at such intervals as will lessen the likelihood of indebtedness among the wage earners.

7. Where food, housing, clothing and other essential supplies and services form part of remuneration, all practicable steps shall be taken by the competent authority to ensure that they are adequate and their cash value properly assessed.

8. All practicable measures shall be taken—

> (*a*) to inform the workers of their wage rights;
>
> (*b*) to prevent any unauthorized deductions from wages; and
>
> (*c*) to restrict the amounts deductible from wages in respect of supplies and services forming part of remuneration to the proper cash value thereof.

*Article* 12

1. The maximum amounts and manner of repayment of advances on wages shall be regulated by the competent authority.

2. The competent authority shall limit the amount of advances which may be made to a worker in consideration of his taking up employment; the amount of advances permitted shall be clearly explained to the worker.

3. Any advance in excess of the amount laid down by the competent authority shall be legally irrecoverable and may not be recovered by the withholding of amounts of pay due to the worker at a later date.

*Article* 13

1. Voluntary forms of thrift shall be encouraged among wage earners and independent producers.

2. All practicable measures shall be taken for the protection of wage earners and independent producers against usury, in particular by action aiming at the reduction of rates of interest on loans, by the control of the operations of money lenders, and by the encouragement of facilities for borrowing money for appropriate purposes through co-operative credit organizations or through institutions which are under the control of the competent authority.

## PART V
### Non-Discrimination on Grounds of Race, Colour, Sex, Belief, Tribal Association or Trade Union Affiliation

*Article* 14

1. It shall be an aim of policy to abolish all discrimination among workers on grounds of race, colour, sex, belief, tribal association or trade union affiliation in respect of—

   (*a*) labour legislation and agreements which shall afford equitable economic treatment to all those lawfully resident or working in the country;
   (*b*) admission to public or private employment;
   (*c*) conditions of engagement and promotion;
   (*d*) opportunities for vocational training;
   (*e*) conditions of work;
   (*f*) health, safety and welfare measures;
   (*g*) discipline;
   (*h*) participation in the negotiation of collective agreements;
   (*i*) wage rates, which shall be fixed according to the principle of equal pay for work of equal value in the same operation and undertaking.

2. All practicable measures shall be taken to lessen, by raising the rates applicable to the lower-paid workers, any existing differences in wage rates due to discrimination by reason of race, colour, sex, belief, tribal association or trade union affiliation.

3. Workers from one country engaged for employment in another country may be granted in addition to their wages benefits in cash or in kind to meet any reasonable personal or family expenses resulting from employment away from their homes.

4. The foregoing provisions of this Article shall be without prejudice to such measures as the competent authority may think it necessary or desirable to take for the safeguarding of motherhood and for ensuring the health, safety and welfare of women workers.

## PART VI
### Education and Training

*Article* 15

1. Adequate provision shall be made to the maximum extent possible under local conditions, for the progressive development of broad systems of

education, vocational training and apprenticeship, with a view to the effective preparation of children and young persons of both sexes for a useful occupation.

2. National laws or regulations shall prescribe the school-leaving age and the minimum age for and conditions of employment.

3. In order that the child population may be able to profit by existing facilities for education and in order that the extension of such facilities may not be hindered by a demand for child labour, the employment of persons below the school-leaving age during the hours when the schools are in session shall be prohibited in areas where educational facilities are provided on a scale adequate for the majority of the children of school age.

*Article* 16

1. In order to secure high productivity through the development of skilled labour, training in new techniques of production shall be provided in suitable cases.

2. Such training shall be organized by or under the supervision of the competent authorities, in consultation with the employers' and workers' organizations of the country from which the trainees come and of the country of training.

## PART VII
### Final Provisions

*Article* 17

The formal ratifications of this Convention shall be communicated to the Director-General of the International Labour Office for registration.

*Article* 18

1. This Convention shall be binding only upon those Members of the International Labour Organization whose ratifications have been registered with the Director-General.

2. It shall come into force twelve months after the date on which the ratifications of two Members have been registered with the Director-General.

3. Thereafter, this Convention shall come into force for any Member twelve months after the date on which its ratification has been registered.

*Article* 19

The coming into force of this Convention shall not involve the *ipso jure* denunciation of the Social Policy (Non-Metropolitan Territories) Convention, 1947, by any Member for which that Convention continues to remain in force, nor shall it close that Convention to further ratification.

*Article* 20

1. A Member which has ratified this Convention may denounce it after the expiration of ten years from the date on which the Convention first comes into force, by an act communicated to the Director-General of the International Labour Office for registration. Such denunciation shall not take effect until one year after the date on which it is registered.

2. Each Member which has ratified this Convention and which does not, within the year following the expiration of the period of ten years mentioned in the preceding paragraph, exercise the right of denunciation provided for in this Article, will be bound for another period of ten years and, thereafter, may denounce this Convention at the expiration of each period of ten years under the terms provided for in this Article.

*Article* 21

1. The Director-General of the International Labour Office shall notify all Members of the International Labour Organization of the registration of all ratifications and denunciations communicated to him by the Members of the Organization.

2. When notifying the Members of the Organization of the registration of the second ratification communicated to him, the Director-General shall draw the attention of the Members of the Organization to the date upon which the Convention will come into force.

*Article* 22

The Director-General of the International Labour Office shall communicate to the Secretary-General of the United Nations for registration in accordance with Article 102 of the Charter of the United Nations full particulars of all ratifications and acts of denunciation registered by him in accordance with the provisions of the preceding Articles.

*Article* 23

At such times as it may consider necessary the Governing Body of the International Labour Office shall present to the General Conference a report on the working of this Convention and shall consider the desirability of placing on the agenda of the Conference the question of its revision in whole or in part.

*Article* 24

1. Should the Conference adopt a new Convention revising this Convention in whole or in part, then, unless the new Convention otherwise provides:

    (*a*) the ratification by a Member of the new revising Convention shall *ipso jure* involve the immediate denunciation of this Convention, notwithstanding the provisions of Article 20 above, if and when the new revising Convention shall have come into force;

(b) as from the date when the new revising Convention comes into force this Convention shall cease to be open to ratification by the Members.

2. This Convention shall in any case remain in force in its actual form and content for those Members which have ratified it but have not ratified the revising Convention.

*Article* 25

The English and French versions of the text of this Convention are equally authoritative.

# X. EMPLOYMENT POLICY CONVENTION, 1964

This is concerned with economic security and the right to work: see the Universal Declaration of Human Rights, Article 23. The Convention was adopted by the General Conference of the I.L.O. on 9 July 1964, entered into force on 15 July 1966, and has received not less than 74 ratifications. For the text in various languages see *United Nations Treaty Series*, Vol. 569, p. 65.

See, further, *The I.L.O. and Human Rights*, International Labour Office, 1968, pp. 76–84.

## TEXT

*The General Conference of the International Labour Organization,*

*Having been convened* at Geneva by the Governing Body of the International Labour Office, and having met in its Forty-eighth Session on 17 June 1964, and

*Considering* that the Declaration of Philadelphia recognizes the solemn obligation of the International Labour Organization to further among the nations of the world programmes which will achieve full employment and the raising of standards of living, and that the Preamble to the Constitution of the International Labour Organization provides for the prevention of unemployment and the provision of an adequate living wage, and

*Considering further* that under the terms of the Declaration of Philadelphia it is the responsibility of the International Labour Organization to examine and consider the bearing of economic and financial policies upon unemployment policy in the light of the fundamental objective that 'all human beings, irrespective of race, creed or sex, have the right to pursue both their material well-being and their spiritual development in conditions of freedom and dignity, of economic security and equal opportunity', and

*Considering* that the Universal Declaration of Human Rights provides that 'everyone has the right to work, to free choice of employment, to just and favourable conditions of work and to protection against unemployment', and

*Noting* the terms of existing international labour Conventions and Recommendations of direct relevance to employment policy, and in particular of the Employment Service Convention and Recommendation, 1948, the Vocational Guidance Recommendation, 1949, the Vocational Training Recommendation, 1962, and the Discrimination (Employment and Occupation) Convention and Recommendation, 1958, and

*Considering* that these instruments should be placed in the wider framework of an international programme for economic expansion on the basis of full, productive and freely chosen employment, and

*Having decided* upon the adoption of certain proposals with regard to employment policy, which are included in the eighth item on the agenda of the session, and

*Having determined* that these proposals shall take the form of an international Convention,

*Adopts* this ninth day of July of the year one thousand nine hundred and sixty-four the following Convention, which may be cited as the Employment Policy Convention, 1964:

*Article* 1

1. With a view to stimulating economic growth and development, raising levels of living, meeting manpower requirements and overcoming unemployment and underemployment, each Member shall declare and pursue, as a major goal, an active policy designed to promote full, productive and freely chosen employment.

2. The said policy shall aim at ensuring that—

   (*a*) there is work for all who are available for and seeking work;

   (*b*) such work is as productive as possible;

   (*c*) there is freedom of choice of employment and the fullest possible opportunity for each worker to qualify for, and to use his skills and endowments in, a job for which he is well suited, irrespective of race, colour, sex, religion, political opinion, national extraction or social origin.

3. The said policy shall take due account of the stage and level of economic development and the mutual relationships between employment objectives and other economic and social objectives, and shall be pursued by methods that are appropriate to national conditions and practices.

*Article* 2

Each Member shall, by such methods and to such extent as may be appropriate under national conditions—

   (*a*) decide on and keep under review, within the framework of a coordinated economic and social policy, the measures to be adopted for attaining the objectives specified in Article 1;

   (*b*) take such steps as may be needed, including when appropriate the establishment of programmes, for the application of these measures.

*Article* 3

In the application of this Convention, representatives of the persons affected by the measures to be taken, and in particular representatives of employers and workers, shall be consulted concerning employment policies, with a view to taking fully into account their experience and views and securing their full co-operation in formulating and enlisting support for such policies.

*Article* 4

The formal ratifications of this Convention shall be communicated to the Director-General of the International Labour Office for registration.

*Article* 5

1. This Convention shall be binding only upon those Members of the International Labour Organization whose ratifications have been registered with the Director-General.

2. It shall come into force twelve months after the date on which the ratifications of two Members have been registered with the Director-General.

3. Thereafter, this Convention shall come into force for any Member twelve months after the date on which its ratification has been registered.

*Article* 6

1. A Member which has ratified this Convention may denounce it after the expiration of ten years from the date on which the Convention first comes into force, by an act communicated to the Director-General of the International Labour Office for registration. Such denunciation shall not take effect until one year after the date on which it is registered.

2. Each Member which has ratified this Convention and which does not, within the year following the expiration of the period of ten years mentioned in the preceding paragraph, exercise the right of denunciation provided for in this Article, will be bound for another period of ten years and, thereafter, may denounce this Convention at the expiration of each period of ten years under the terms provided for in this Article.

*Article* 7

1. The Director-General of the International Labour Office shall notify all Members of the International Labour Organization of the registration of all ratifications and denunciations communicated to him by the Members of the Organization.

2. When notifying the Members of the Organization of the registration of the second ratification communicated to him, the Director-General shall draw the attention of the Members of the Organization to the date upon which the Convention will come into force.

*Article* 8

The Director-General of the International Labour Office shall communicate to the Secretary-General of the United Nations for registration in accordance with Article 102 of the Charter of the United Nations full particulars of all ratifications and acts of denunciation registered by him in accordance with the provisions of the preceding Articles.

*Article* 9

At such times as it may consider necessary the Governing Body of the International Labour Office shall present to the General Conference a report on the working of this Convention and shall examine the desirability of placing on the agenda of the Conference the question of its revision in whole or in part.

*Article* 10

1. Should the Conference adopt a new Convention revising this Convention in whole or in part, then, unless the new Convention otherwise provides—

    (*a*) the ratification by a Member of the new revising Convention shall *ipso jure* involve the immediate denunciation of this Convention, notwithstanding the provisions of Article 6 above, if and when the new revising Convention shall have come into force;

    (*b*) as from the date when the new revising Convention comes into force this Convention shall cease to be open to ratification by the Members.

2. This Convention shall in any case remain in force in its actual form and content for those Members which have ratified it but have not ratified the revising Convention.

*Article* 11

The English and French versions of the text of this Convention are equally authoritative.

# XI. CONVENTION CONCERNING INDIGENOUS AND TRIBAL PEOPLES IN INDEPENDENT COUNTRIES, 1989

The Convention (No. 169) was adopted during the 76th session of the I.L.O. in 1989. The new instrument revises the provisions of the Indigenous and Tribal Populations Convention, 1957 (No. 107). It has been ratified by three states.

## TEXT

*The General Conference of the International Labour Organisation,*

*Having been convened* at Geneva by the Governing Body of the International Labour Office, and having met in its 76th Session on 7 June 1989, and

*Noting* the international standards contained in the Indigenous and Tribal Populations Convention and Recommendation, 1957, and

*Recalling* the terms of the Universal Declaration of Human Rights, the International Covenant on Economic, Social and Cultural Rights, the International Covenant on Civil and Political Rights, and the many international instruments on the prevention of discrimination, and

*Considering* that the developments which have taken place in international law since 1957, as well as developments in the situation of indigenous and tribal peoples in all regions of the world, have made it appropriate to adopt new international standards on the subject with a view to removing the assimilationist orientation of the earlier standards, and

*Recognising* the aspirations of these peoples to exercise control over their own institutions, ways of life and economic development and to maintain and develop their identities, languages and religions, within the framework of the States in which they live, and

*Noting* that in many parts of the world these peoples are unable to enjoy their fundamental human rights to the same degree as the rest of the population of the States within which they live, and that their laws, values, customs and perspectives have often been eroded, and

*Calling attention* to the distinctive contributions of indigenous and tribal peoples to the cultural diversity and social and ecological harmony of humankind and to international co-operation and understanding, and

*Noting* that the following provisions have been framed with the co-operation of the United Nations, the Food and Agriculture Organisation of the United Nations, the United Nations Educational, Scientific and Cultural Organisation and the World Health Organisation, as well as of the Inter-American Indian Institute, at appropriate levels and in their respective fields, and that it is proposed to continue this co-operation in promoting and securing the application of these provisions, and

*Having decided* upon the adoption of certain proposals with regard to the partial revision of the Indigenous and Tribal Populations Convention, 1957 (No. 107), which is the fourth item on the agenda of the session, and

*Having determined* that these proposals shall take the form of an international Convention revising the Indigenous and Tribal Populations Convention, 1957;

*Adopts* this twenty-seventh day of June of the year one thousand nine hundred and eighty-nine the following Convention, which may be cited as the Indigenous and Tribal Peoples Convention, 1989:

## PART I
### General Policy

*Article* 1

1. This Convention applies to:

   (*a*) tribal peoples in independent countries whose social, cultural and economic conditions distinguish them from other sections of the national community, and whose status is regulated wholly or partially by their own customs or traditions or by special laws or regulations;

   (*b*) peoples in independent countries who are regarded as indigenous on account of their descent from the populations which inhabited the country, or a geographical region to which the country belongs, at the time of conquest or colonisation or the establishment of present state boundaries and who, irrespective of their legal status, retain some or all of their own social, economic, cultural and political institutions.

2. Self-identification as indigenous or tribal shall be regarded as a fundamental criterion for determining the groups to which the provisions of this Convention apply.

3. The use of the term 'peoples' in this Convention shall not be construed as having any implications as regards the rights which may attach to the term under international law.

*Article* 2

1. Governments shall have the responsibility for developing, with the participation of the peoples concerned, co-ordinated and systematic action to protect the rights of these peoples and to guarantee respect for their integrity.

2. Such action shall include measures for:

(a) ensuring that members of these peoples benefit on an equal footing from the rights and opportunities which national laws and regulations grant to other members of the population;

(b) promoting the full realisation of the social, economic and cultural rights of these peoples with respect for their social and cultural identity, their customs and traditions and their institutions;

(c) assisting the members of the peoples concerned to eliminate socio-economic gaps that may exist between indigenous and other members of the national community, in a manner compatible with their aspirations and ways of life.

*Article* 3

1. Indigenous and tribal peoples shall enjoy the full measure of human rights and fundamental freedoms without hindrance or discrimination. The provisions of the Convention shall be applied without discrimination to male and female members of these peoples.

2. No form of force or coercion shall be used in violation of the human rights and fundamental freedoms of the peoples concerned, including the rights contained in this Convention.

*Article* 4

1. Special measures shall be adopted as appropriate for safeguarding the persons, institutions, property, labour, cultures and environment of the peoples concerned.

2. Such special measures shall not be contrary to the freely-expressed wishes of the peoples concerned.

3. Enjoyment of the general rights of citizenship, without discrimination, shall not be prejudiced in any way by such special measures.

*Article* 5

In applying the provisions of this Convention:

(a) the social, cultural, religious and spiritual values and practices of these peoples shall be recognised and protected, and due account shall be taken of the nature of the problems which face them both as groups and as individuals;

(b) the integrity of the values, practices and institutions of these peoples shall be respected;

(c) policies aimed at mitigating the difficulties experienced by these peoples in facing new conditions of life and work shall be adopted, with the participation and co-operation of the peoples affected.

*Article* 6

1. In applying the provisions of this Convention, governments shall:

(a) consult the peoples concerned, through appropriate procedures and in particular through their representative institutions, whenever consideration is being given to legislative or administrative measures which may affect them directly;

(b) establish means by which these peoples can freely participate, to at least the same extent as other sectors of the population, at all levels of decision-making in elective institutions and administrative and other bodies responsible for policies and programmes which concern them;

(c) establish means for the full development of these peoples' own institutions and initiatives, and in appropriate cases provide the resources necessary for this purpose.

2. The consultations carried out in application of this Convention shall be undertaken, in good faith and in a form appropriate to the circumstances, with the objective of achieving agreement or consent to the proposed measures.

*Article 7*

1. The peoples concerned shall have the right to decide their own priorities for the process of development as it affects their lives, beliefs, institutions and spiritual well-being and the lands they occupy or otherwise use, and to exercise control, to the extent possible, over their own economic, social and cultural development. In addition, they shall participate in the formulation, implementation and evaluation of plans and programmes for national and regional development which may affect them directly.

2. The improvement of the conditions of life and work and levels of health and education of the peoples concerned, with their participation and co-operation, shall be a matter of priority in plans for the overall economic development of areas they inhabit. Special projects for development of the areas in question shall also be so designed as to promote such improvement.

3. Governments shall ensure that, whenever appropriate, studies are carried out, in co-operation with the peoples concerned, to assess the social, spiritual, cultural and environmental impact on them of planned development activities. The results of these studies shall be considered as fundamental criteria for the implementation of these activities.

4. Governments shall take measures, in co-operation with the peoples concerned, to protect and preserve the environment of the territories they inhabit.

*Article 8*

1. In applying national laws and regulations to the peoples concerned, due regard shall be had to their customs or customary laws.

2. These peoples shall have the right to retain their own customs and

institutions, where these are not incompatible with fundamental rights defined by the national legal system and with internationally recognised human rights. Procedures shall be established, whenever necessary, to resolve conflicts which may arise in the application of this principle.

3. The application of paragraphs 1 and 2 of this Article shall not prevent members of these peoples from exercising the rights granted to all citizens and from assuming the corresponding duties.

*Article* 9

1. To the extent compatible with the national legal system and internationally recognised human rights, the methods customarily practised by the peoples concerned for dealing with offences committed by their members shall be respected.

2. The customs of these peoples in regard to penal matters shall be taken into consideration by the authorities and courts dealing with such cases.

*Article* 10

1. In imposing penalties laid down by general law on members of these peoples account shall be taken of their economic, social and cultural characteristics.

2. Preference shall be given to methods of punishment other than confinement in prison.

*Article* 11

The exaction from members of the peoples concerned of compulsory personal services in any form, whether paid or unpaid, shall be prohibited and punishable by law, except in cases prescribed by law for all citizens.

*Article* 12

The peoples concerned shall be safeguarded against the abuse of their rights and shall be able to take legal proceedings, either individually or through their representative bodies, for the effective protection of these rights. Measures shall be taken to ensure that members of these peoples can understand and be understood in legal proceedings, where necessary through the provision of interpretation or by other effective means.

## PART II
### Land

*Article* 13

1. In applying the provisions of this Part of the Convention governments shall respect the special importance for the cultures and spiritual values of

the peoples concerned of their relationship with the lands or territories, or both as applicable, which they occupy or otherwise use, and in particular the collective aspects of this relationship.

2. The use of the term 'lands' in Articles 15 and 16 shall include the concept of territories, which covers the total environment of the areas which the peoples concerned occupy or otherwise use.

*Article* 14

1. The rights of ownership and possession of the peoples concerned over the lands which they traditionally occupy shall be recognised. In addition, measures shall be taken in appropriate cases to safeguard the right of the peoples concerned to use lands not exclusively occupied by them, but to which they have traditionally had access for their subsistence and traditional activities. Particular attention shall be paid to the situation of nomadic peoples and shifting cultivators in this respect.

2. Governments shall take steps as necessary to identify the lands which the peoples concerned traditionally occupy, and to guarantee effective protection of their rights of ownership and possession.

3. Adequate procedures shall be established within the national legal system to resolve land claims by the peoples concerned.

*Article* 15

1. The rights of the peoples concerned to the natural resources pertaining to their lands shall be specially safeguarded. These rights include the right of these peoples to participate in the use, management and conservation of these resources.

2. In cases in which the State retains the ownership of mineral or subsurface resources or rights to other resources pertaining to lands, governments shall establish or maintain procedures through which they shall consult these peoples, with a view to ascertaining whether and to what degree their interests would be prejudiced, before undertaking or permitting any programmes for the exploration or exploitation of such resources pertaining to their lands. The peoples concerned shall wherever possible participate in the benefits of such activities, and shall receive fair compensation for any damages which they may sustain as a result of such activities.

*Article* 16

1. Subject to the following paragraphs of this Article, the peoples concerned shall not be removed from the lands which they occupy.

2. Where the relocation of these peoples is considered necessary as an exceptional measure, such relocation shall take place only with their free and informed consent. Where their consent cannot be obtained, such

relocation shall take place only following appropriate procedures established by national laws and regulations, including public inquiries where appropriate, which provide the opportunity for effective representation of the peoples concerned.

3. Whenever possible, these peoples shall have the right to return to their traditional lands, as soon as the grounds for relocation cease to exist.

4. When such return is not possible, as determined by agreement or, in the absence of such agreement, through appropriate procedures, these peoples shall be provided in all possible cases with lands of quality and legal status at least equal to that of the lands previously occupied by them, suitable to provide for their present needs and future development. Where the peoples concerned express a preference for compensation in money or in kind, they shall be so compensated under appropriate guarantees.

5. Persons thus relocated shall be fully compensated for any resulting loss or injury.

*Article* 17

1. Procedures established by the peoples concerned for the transmission of land rights among members of these peoples shall be respected.

2. The peoples concerned shall be consulted whenever consideration is being given to their capacity to alienate their lands or otherwise transmit their rights outside their own community.

3. Persons not belonging to these peoples shall be prevented from taking advantage of their customs or of lack of understanding of the laws on the part of their members to secure the ownership, possession or use of land belonging to them.

*Article* 18

Adequate penalties shall be established by law for unauthorised intrusion upon, or use of, the lands of the peoples concerned, and governments shall take measures to prevent such offences.

*Article* 19

National agrarian programmes shall secure to the peoples concerned treatment equivalent to that accorded to other sectors of the population with regard to:

(*a*) the provision of more land for these peoples when they have not the area necessary for providing the essentials of a normal existence, or for any possible increase in their numbers;

(*b*) the provision of the means required to promote the development of the lands which these peoples already possess.

## PART III
### Recruitment and Conditions of Employment

*Article* 20

1. Governments shall, within the framework of national laws and regulations, and in co-operation with the peoples concerned, adopt special measures to ensure the effective protection with regard to recruitment and conditions of employment of workers belonging to these peoples, to the extent that they are not effectively protected by laws applicable to workers in general.

2. Governments shall do everything possible to prevent any discrimination between workers belonging to the peoples concerned and other workers, in particular as regards:

(a) admission to employment, including skilled employment, as well as measures for promotion and advancement;

(b) equal remuneration for work of equal value;

(c) medical and social assistance, occupational safety and health, all social security benefits and any other occupationally related benefits, and housing;

(d) the right of association and freedom for all lawful trade union activities, and the right to conclude collective agreements with employers or employers' organisations.

3. The measures taken shall include measures to ensure:

(a) that workers belonging to the peoples concerned, including seasonal, casual and migrant workers in agricultural and other employment, as well as those employed by labour contractors, enjoy the protection afforded by national law and practice to other such workers in the same sectors, and that they are fully informed of their rights under labour legislation and of means of redress available to them;

(b) that workers belonging to these peoples are not subjected to working conditions hazardous to their health, in particular through exposure to pesticides or other toxic substances;

(c) that workers belonging to these peoples are not subjected to coercive recruitment systems, including bonded labour and other forms of debt servitude;

(d) that workers belonging to these peoples enjoy equal opportunities and equal treatment in employment for men and women, and protection from sexual harassment.

4. Particular attention shall be paid to the establishment of adequate labour inspection services in areas where workers belonging to the peoples

concerned undertake wage employment, in order to ensure compliance with the provisions of this Part of this Convention.

## PART IV
### Vocational Training, Handicrafts and Rural Industries

*Article* 21

Members of the peoples concerned shall enjoy opportunities at least equal to those of other citizens in respect of vocational training measures.

*Article* 22

1. Measures shall be taken to promote the voluntary participation of members of the peoples concerned in vocational training programmes of general application.

2. Whenever existing programmes of vocational training of general application do not meet the special needs of the peoples concerned, governments shall, with the participation of these peoples, ensure the provision of special training programmes and facilities.

3. Any special training programmes shall be based on the economic environment, social and cultural conditions and practical needs of the peoples concerned. Any studies made in this connection shall be carried out in co-operation with these peoples, who shall be consulted on the organisation and operation of such programmes. Where feasible, these peoples shall progressively assume responsibility for the organisation and operation of such special training programmes, if they so decide.

*Article* 23

1. Handicrafts, rural and community-based industries, and subsistence economy and traditional activities of the peoples concerned, such as hunting, fishing, trapping and gathering, shall be recognised as important factors in the maintenance of their cultures and in their economic self-reliance and development. Governments shall, with the participation of these people and whenever appropriate, ensure that these activities are strengthened and promoted.

2. Upon the request of the peoples concerned, appropriate technical and financial assistance shall be provided wherever possible, taking into account the traditional technologies and cultural characteristics of these peoples, as well as the importance of sustainable and equitable development.

## PART V
### Social Security and Health

*Article* 24

Social security schemes shall be extended progressively to cover the peoples concerned, and applied without discrimination against them.

*Article* 25

1. Governments shall ensure that adequate health services are made available to the peoples concerned, or shall provide them with resources to allow them to design and deliver such services under their own responsibility and control, so that they may enjoy the highest attainable standard of physical and mental health.

2. Health services shall, to the extent possible, be community-based. These services shall be planned and administered in co-operation with the peoples concerned and take into account their economic, geographic, social and cultural conditions as well as their traditional preventive care, healing practices and medicines.

3. The health care system shall give preference to the training and employment of local community health workers, and focus on primary health care while maintaining strong links with other levels of health care services.

4. The provision of such health services shall be co-ordinated with other social, economic and cultural measures in the country.

## PART VI
### Education and Means of Communication

*Article* 26

Measures shall be taken to ensure that members of the peoples concerned have the opportunity to acquire education at all levels on at least an equal footing with the rest of the national community.

*Article* 27

1. Education programmes and services for the peoples concerned shall be developed and implemented in co-operation with them to address their special needs, and shall incorporate their histories, their knowledge and technologies, their value systems and their further social, economic and cultural aspirations.

2. The competent authority shall ensure the training of members of these peoples and their involvement in the formulation and implementation of education programmes, with a view to the progressive transfer of responsibility for the conduct of these programmes to these peoples as appropriate.

3. In addition, governments shall recognise the right of these peoples to establish their own educational institutions and facilities, provided that such institutions meet minimum standards established by the competent authority in consultation with these peoples. Appropriate resources shall be provided for this purpose.

*Article* 28

1. Children belonging to the peoples concerned shall, wherever practicable, be taught to read and write in their own indigenous language or in the language most commonly used by the group to which they belong. When this is not practicable, the competent authorities shall undertake consultations with these peoples with a view to the adoption of measures to achieve this objective.

2. Adequate measures shall be taken to ensure that these peoples have the opportunity to attain fluency in the national language or in one of the official languages of the country.

3. Measures shall be taken to preserve and promote the development and practice of the indigenous languages of the peoples concerned.

*Article* 29

The imparting of general knowledge and skills that will help children belonging to the peoples concerned to participate fully and on an equal footing in their own community and in the national community shall be an aim of education for these peoples.

*Article* 30

1. Governments shall adopt measures appropriate to the traditions and cultures of the peoples concerned, to make known to them their rights and duties, especially in regard to labour, economic opportunities, education and health matters, social welfare and their rights deriving from this Convention.

2. If necessary, this shall be done by means of written translations and through the use of mass communications in the languages of these peoples.

*Article* 31

Educational measures shall be taken among all sections of the national community, and particularly among those that are in most direct contact with the peoples concerned, with the object of eliminating prejudices that they may harbour in respect of these peoples. To this end, efforts shall be made to ensure that history textbooks and other educational materials provide a fair, accurate and informative portrayal of the societies and cultures of these peoples.

## PART VII
### Contacts and Co-operation Across Borders

*Article* 32

Governments shall take appropriate measures, including by means of international agreements, to facilitate contacts and co-operation between indigenous and tribal peoples across borders, including activities in the economic, social, cultural, spiritual and environmental fields.

## PART VIII
### Administration

*Article* 33

1. The governmental authority responsible for the matters covered in this Convention shall ensure that agencies or other appropriate mechanisms exist to administer the programmes affecting the peoples concerned, and shall ensure that they have the means necessary for the proper fulfilment of the functions assigned to them.

2. These programmes shall include:

(a) the planning, co-ordination, execution and evaluation, in co-operation with the peoples concerned, of the measures provided for in this Convention;

(b) the proposing of legislative and other measures to the competent authorities and supervision of the application of the measures taken, in co-operation with the peoples concerned.

## PART IX
### General Provisions

*Article* 34

The nature and scope of the measures to be taken to give effect to this Convention shall be determined in a flexible manner, having regard to the conditions characteristic of each country.

*Article* 35

The application of the provisions of this Convention shall not adversely affect rights and benefits of the peoples concerned pursuant to other Conventions and Recommendations, international instruments, treaties, or national laws, awards, custom or agreements.

## PART X
### Final Provisions

*Article* 36

This Convention revises the Indigenous and Tribal Populations Convention, 1957.

*Article* 37

The formal ratifications of this Convention shall be communicated to the Director-General of the International Labour Office for registration.

*Article* 38

1. This Convention shall be binding only upon those Members of the International Labour Organisation whose ratifications have been registered with the Director-General.

2. It shall come into force twelve months after the date on which the ratifications of two Members have been registered with the Director-General.

3. Thereafter, this Convention shall come into force for any Member twelve months after the date on which its ratification has been registered.

*Article* 39

1. A Member which has ratified this Convention may denounce it after the expiration of ten years from the date on which the Convention first comes into force, by an act communicated to the Director-General of the International Labour Office for registration. Such denunciation shall not take effect until one year after the date on which it is registered.

2. Each Member which has ratified this Convention and which does not, within the year following the expiration of the period of ten years mentioned in the preceding paragraph, exercise the right of denunciation provided for in this Article, will be bound for another period of ten years and, thereafter, may denounce this Convention at the expiration of each period of ten years under the terms provided for in this Article.

*Article* 40

1. The Director-General of the International Labour Office shall notify all Members of the International Labour Organisation of the registration of all ratifications and denunciations communicated to him by the Members of the Organisation.

2. When notifying the Members of the Organisation of the registration of the second ratification communicated to him, the Director-General shall draw the attention of the Members of the Organisation to the date upon which the Convention will come into force.

*Article* 41

The Director-General of the International Labour Office shall communicate to the Secretary-General of the United Nations for registration in accordance with Article 102 of the Charter of the United Nations full particulars of all ratifications and acts of denunciation registered by him in accordance with the provisions of the preceding Articles.

*Article* 42

At such times as it may consider necessary the Governing Body of the International Labour Office shall present to the General Conference a report on the working of this Convention and shall examine the desirability of placing on the agenda of the Conference the question of its revision in whole or in part.

*Article* 43

1. Should the Conference adopt a new Convention revising this Convention in whole or in part, then, unless the new Convention otherwise provides—

   (*a*) the ratification by a Member of the new revising Convention shall *ipso jure* involve the immediate denunciation of this Convention, notwithstanding the provisions of Article 39 above, if and when the new revising Convention shall have come into force;
   (*b*) as from the date when the new revising Convention comes into force this Convention shall cease to be open to ratification by the Members.

2. This Convention shall in any case remain in force in its actual form and content for those Members which have ratified it but have not ratified the revising Convention.

*Article* 44

The English and French versions of the text of this Convention are equally authoritative.

# CONTRIBUTION OF THE UNITED NATIONS EDUCATIONAL, SCIENTIFIC, AND CULTURAL ORGANIZATION

UNESCO is a Specialized Agency associated with the United Nations. Several aspects of its work concern human rights; in particular, problems of illiteracy in many countries, and the production and dissemination of studies which combat racial prejudice.

See further *What is UNESCO?*, Unesco Information Manuals—1; *Bulletin of Human Rights*, Division of Human Rights, U.N. Office at Geneva.

In 1978 the Director-General of UNESCO convened an International Congress on the Teaching of Human Rights: see the Final Document, 55–78/CONF. 401/33; *Bulletin of Human Rights*, No. 21 (July–Sept. 1978), pp. 83–6.

In 1978 the Executive Board of UNESCO adopted the procedure for examining communications concerning violations of human rights in relation to education, science, culture and information: see further Robertson and Merrills, *Human Rights in the World*, 3rd ed., 1989, pp. 244–5; and Marks, in Hannum (ed.), *Guide to International Human Rights Practice*, 1984, pp. 94–107.

# CONVENTION AGAINST DISCRIMINATION IN EDUCATION, 1960

The Convention can be compared with the I.L.O. Convention concerning discrimination in respect of employment and occupation, above. The United Nations Sub-Commission on Prevention of Discrimination and Protection of Minorities initiated study of discrimination in education, and in due course it was decided to ask UNESCO to consider the possibility of drafting and adopting a convention on the subject. The General Conference of UNESCO adopted a Convention on 14 December 1960. The Convention entered into force on 22 May 1962 and sixty-eight States, including the United Kingdom, have become parties.

For the text in various languages: *United Nations Treaty Series*, Vol. 429, p. 93; *U.K. Treaty Series*, No. 44 (1962), Cmnd. 1760. See also the Protocol instituting a Conciliation and Good Offices Commission to be responsible for seeking the Settlement of any Disputes which may arise between States Parties to the Convention against Discrimination in Education, adopted at Paris, 10 December 1962, *U.K. Treaty Series* No. 23 (1969), Cmnd. 3894. The Protocol entered into force on 24 October 1968 and has twenty-three parties, including the United Kingdom.

## TEXT

*The General Conference of the United Nations Educational, Scientific and Cultural Organization, meeting in Paris from 14 November to 15 December 1960, at its eleventh session,*

*Recalling* that the Universal Declaration of Human Rights asserts the principle of non-discrimination and proclaims that every person has the right to education,

*Considering* that discrimination in education is a violation of rights enunciated in that declaration,

*Considering* that, under the terms of its constitution, the United Nations Educational, Scientific and Cultural Organization has the purpose of instituting collaboration among the nations with a view to furthering for all universal respect for human rights and equality of educational opportunity.

*Recognizing* that, consequently, the United Nations Educational, Scientific and Cultural Organization, while respecting the diversity of national educational systems, has the duty not only to proscribe any form of discrimination in education but also to promote equality of opportunity and treatment for all in education,

*Having* before it proposals concerning the different aspects of discrimination in education, constituting item 17.1.4 of the agenda of the session,

*Having decided* at its tenth session that this question should be made the subject of an international convention as well as of recommendations to Member States,

*Adopts* this Convention on the fourteenth day of December 1960.

*Article* 1

1. For the purposes of this Convention, the term 'discrimination' includes any distinction, exclusion, limitation or preference which, being based on race, colour, sex, language, religion, political or other opinion, national or social origin, economic condition or birth, has the purpose or effect of nullifying or impairing equality of treatment in education and in particular:

(a) Of depriving any person or group of persons of access to education of any type or at any level;

(b) Of limiting any person or group of persons to education of an inferior standard;

(c) Subject to the provisions of Article 2 of this convention, of establishing or maintaining separate educational systems or institutions for persons or groups of persons; or

(d) Of inflicting on any person or group of persons conditions which are incompatible with the dignity of man.

2. For the purposes of this convention, the term 'education' refers to all types and levels of education, and includes access to education, the standard and quality of education, and the conditions under which it is given.

*Article* 2

When permitted in a State, the following situations shall not be deemed to constitute discrimination, within the meaning of Article 1 of this convention:

(a) The establishment or maintenance of separate educational systems or institutions for pupils of the two sexes, if these systems or institutions offer equivalent access to education, provide a teaching staff with qualifications of the same standard as well as school premises and equipment of the same quality, and afford the opportunity to take the same or equivalent courses of study;

(b) The establishment or maintenance, for religious or linguistic reasons, of separate educational systems or institutions offering an education which is in keeping with the wishes of the pupil's parents or legal guardians, if participation in such systems or attendance at such institutions is optional and if the education provided conforms to such standards as may be laid down or approved by the competent authorities, in particular for education of the same level;

(c) The establishment or maintenance of private educational institutions, if the object of the institutions is not to secure the exclusion of any group but to provide educational facilities in addition to those provided by the public authorities, if the institutions are conducted in accordance with that object, and if the education provided conforms with such standards as may be laid down or approved by the competent authorities, in particular for education of the same level.

*Article* 3

In order to eliminate and prevent discrimination within the meaning of this Convention, the States parties thereto undertake:

(*a*) To abrogate any statutory provisions and any administrative instructions and to discontinue any administrative practices which involve discrimination in education:

(*b*) To ensure, by legislation where necessary, that there is no discrimination in the admission of pupils to educational institutions;

(*c*) Not to allow any differences of treatment by the public authorities between nationals, except on the basis of merit or need, in the matter of school fees and the grant of scholarships or other forms of assistance to pupils and necessary permits and facilities for the pursuit of studies in foreign countries;

(*d*) Not to allow, in any form of assistance granted by the public authorities to educational institutions, any restrictions or preference based solely on the ground that pupils belong to a particular group;

(*e*) To give foreign nationals resident within their territory the same access to education as that given to their own nationals.

*Article* 4

The States parties to this Convention undertake furthermore to formulate, develop and apply a national policy which, by methods appropriate to the circumstances and to national usage, will tend to promote equality of opportunity and of treatment in the matter of education and in particular:

(*a*) To make primary education free and compulsory; make secondary education in its different forms generally available and accessible to all; make higher education equally accessible to all on the basis of individual capacity; assure compliance by all with the obligation to attend school prescribed by law;

(*b*) To ensure that the standards of education are equivalent in all public educational institutions of the same level, and that the conditions relating to the quality of the education provided are also equivalent;

(*c*) To encourage and intensify by appropriate methods the education of persons who have not yet received any primary education or who have not completed the entire primary education course and the continuation of their education on the basis of individual capacity;

(*d*) To provide training for the teaching profession without discrimination.

*Article* 5

1. The States parties to this Convention agree that:

(a) Education shall be directed to the full development of the human personality and to the strengthening of respect for human rights and fundamental freedoms; it shall promote understanding, tolerance and friendship among all nations, racial or religious groups, and shall further the activities of the United Nations for the maintenance of peace;

(b) It is essential to respect the liberty of parents and, where applicable, of legal guardians, firstly to choose for their children institutions other than those maintained by the public authorities but conforming to such minimum educational standards as may be laid down or approved by the competent authorities and, secondly, to ensure in a manner consistent with the procedures followed in the State for the application of its legislation, the religious and moral education of the children in conformity with their own convictions; and no person or group of persons should be compelled to receive religious instruction inconsistent with his or their convictions;

(c) It is essential to recognize the right of members of national minorities to carry on their own educational activities, including the maintenance of schools and, depending on the educational policy of each State, the use or the teaching of their own language, provided however:

   (i) That this right is not exercised in a manner which prevents the members of these minorities from understanding the culture and language of the community as a whole and from participating in its activities, or which prejudices national sovereignty;

   (ii) That the standard of education is not lower than the general standard laid down or approved by the competent authorities; and

   (iii) That attendance at such schools is optional.

2. The States parties to this Convention undertake to take all necessary measures to ensure the application of the principles enunciated in paragraph 1 of this Article.

*Article 6*

In the application of this Convention, the States parties to it undertake to pay the greatest attention to any recommendations hereafter adopted by the General Conference of the United Nations Educational, Scientific and Cultural Organization defining the measures to be taken against the different forms of discrimination in education and for the purpose of ensuring equality of opportunity and treatment in education.

*Article 7*

The States parties to this Convention shall in their periodic reports submitted to the General Conference of the United Nations Educational,

Scientific and Cultural Organization on dates and in a manner to be determined by it, give information on the legislative and administrative provisions which they have adopted and other action which they have taken for the application of this convention, including that taken for the formulation and the development of the national policy defined in Article 4 as well as the results achieved and the obstacles encountered in the application of that policy.

*Article* 8

Any dispute which may arise between any two or more States parties to this convention concerning the interpretation or application of this Convention, which is not settled by negotiation shall at the request of the parties to the dispute be referred, failing other means of settling the dispute, to the International Court of Justice for decision.

*Article* 9

Reservations to this Convention shall not be permitted.

*Article* 10

This Convention shall not have the effect of diminishing the rights which individuals or groups may enjoy by virtue of agreements concluded between two or more States, where such rights are not contrary to the letter or spirit of this Convention.

*Article* 11

This Convention is drawn up in English, French, Russian and Spanish, the four texts being equally authoritative.

*Article* 12

1. This Convention shall be subject to ratification or acceptance by States members of the United Nations Educational, Scientific and Cultural Organization in accordance with their respective constitutional procedures.
2. The instruments of ratification or acceptance shall be deposited with the Director-General of the United Nations Educational, Scientific and Cultural Organization.

*Article* 13

1. This Convention shall be open to accession by all States not members of the United Nations Educational, Scientific and Cultural Organization which are invited to do so by the Executive Board of the Organization.
2. Accession shall be effected by the deposit of an instrument of accession with the Director-General of the United Nations Educational, Scientific and Cultural Organization.

*Article* 14

This Convention shall enter into force three months after the date of the deposit of the third instrument of ratification, acceptance or accession, but only with respect to those States which have deposited their respective instruments on or before that date. It shall enter into force with respect to any other State three months after the deposit of its instrument of ratification, acceptance or accession.

*Article* 15

The States parties to this Convention recognize that the convention is applicable not only to their metropolitan territory but also to all non-self-governing, trust, colonial and other territories for the international relations of which they are responsible; they undertake to consult, if necessary, the governments or other competent authorities of these territories on or before ratification, acceptance or accession with a view to securing the application of the Convention to those territories, and to notify the Director-General of the United Nations Educational, Scientific and Cultural Organization of the territories to which it is accordingly applied, the notification to take effect three months after the date of its receipt.

*Article* 16

1. Each State party to this convention may denounce the Convention on its own behalf or on behalf of any territory for whose international relations it is responsible.

2. The denunciation shall be notified by an instrument in writing, deposited with the Director-General of the United Nations Educational, Scientific and Cultural Organization.

3. The denunciation shall take effect twelve months after the receipt of the instrument of denunciation.

*Article* 17

The Director-General of the United Nations Educational, Scientific and Cultural Organization shall inform the States Members of the Organization, the States not members of the Organization which are referred to in Article 13, as well as the United Nations, of the deposit of all the instruments of ratification, acceptance and accession provided for in Articles 12 and 13, and of the notifications and denunciations provided for in Articles 15 and 16 respectively.

*Article* 18

1. This Convention may be revised by the General Conference of the United Nations Educational, Scientific and Cultural Organization. Any

such revision shall, however, bind only the States which shall become parties to the revising Convention.

2. If the General Conference should adopt a new convention revising this Convention in whole or in part, then, unless the new convention otherwise provides, this Convention shall cease to be open to ratification, acceptance or accession as from the date on which the new revising convention enters into force.

*Article* 19

In conformity with Article 102 of the Charter of the United Nations, this Convention shall be registered with the Secretariat of the United Nations Educational, Scientific and Cultural Organization.

## PART FIVE

# EUROPEAN INSTITUTIONS AND CONVENTIONS

## INTRODUCTION

THE instruments in this Part generally derive from the work of the Council of Europe, an organization created in 1949 as a sort of social and ideological counterpart to the military aspects of European co-operation represented in the North Atlantic Treaty Organization. The Council of Europe was inspired partly by interest in promotion of European unity, and partly by the political desire for solidarity in the face of the ideology of Communism. The existing membership of the Council of Europe is as follows: (*a*) the original ten signatories of the Statute of the Council of Europe, viz. Belgium, Denmark, France, Ireland, Italy, Luxembourg, The Netherlands, Norway, Sweden, and the United Kingdom; (*b*) thirteen other States, viz. Greece, Turkey, Iceland, the Federal Republic of Germany, Austria, Cyprus, Switzerland, Malta, Portugal, Spain, Liechtenstein, San Marino, and Finland.

# I. THE EUROPEAN CONVENTION ON HUMAN RIGHTS AND ITS FIVE PROTOCOLS

The European Convention was the first essay in giving specific legal content to human rights in an international agreement, and combining this with the establishment of machinery for supervision and enforcement. However, it is important to understand that the role of the Commission and its associated bodies (the European Court of Human Rights and the Committee of Ministers) is that of review, and not that of an appeal court from the decisions of national tribunals. Their task is to ensure that the standards of the Convention and its Protocols are observed by the administrations of the States concerned. The work of the European Commission and Court has had certain important consequences: valuable material has been provided for the elaboration of the provisions on civil liberties; and anomalies have been exposed in national systems of law, with the result in some cases that the relevant national legislation has been changed for the better. Several individual cases have in fact had the function of providing test cases, and/or have raised issues affecting a whole class of persons; for example, a linguistic minority.

The European Convention was signed in Rome on 4 November 1950 and entered into force on 3 September 1953. Twenty-two States have ratified the Convention: Austria, Belgium, Cyprus, Denmark, Finland, France, Greece, Germany, Iceland, Ireland, Italy, Luxembourg, Malta, The Netherlands, Norway, Portugal, San Marino, Spain, Sweden, Switzerland, Turkey and the United Kingdom.

Twenty-two States have recognized the right of individual petition to the European Commission, and also the compulsory jurisdiction of the European Court of Human Rights.

The first Protocol to the Convention entered into force on 18 May 1954; the second and third Protocols on 21 September 1970; the fourth Protocol on 2 May 1968; the fifth Protocol on 20 December 1971; the sixth Protocol on 1 March 1985; the seventh Protocol on 1 November 1988; and the eighth Protocol on 1 January 1990. The ninth Protocol is not yet in force, and the tenth Protocol has not yet been opened for signature. The texts of the Protocols follow that of the principal Convention below.

See generally Fawcett, *The Application of the European Convention on Human Rights*, 2nd ed., 1987; Jacobs, *The European Convention on Human Rights*, 1975; Higgins, in Meron (ed.), *Human Rights in International Law*, 1984, II, pp. 495–549; Janis and Kay, *European Human Rights Law*, 1990.

Current information may be obtained from the following publications (annual editions appear): Council of Europe, *European Convention on Human Rights: Collected Texts*; European Commission on Human Rights, *Stock-Taking on the European Convention on Human Rights*. The Council of Europe also publishes a *Bibliography to the European Convention on Human Rights*; and an annual paper, *Activities of the Council of Europe in the Field of Human Rights*.

## TEXT

The Governments signatory hereto, being Members of the Council of Europe,

*Considering* the Universal Declaration of Human Rights proclaimed by the General Assembly of the United Nations on 10 December 1948;

*Considering* that this Declaration aims at securing the universal and effective recognition and observance of the Rights therein declared;

*Considering* that the aim of the Council of Europe is the achievement of greater unity between its Members and that one of the methods by which the aim is to be pursued is the maintenance and further realization of Human Rights and Fundamental Freedoms;

*Reaffirming* their profound belief in those Fundamental Freedoms which are the foundation of justice and peace in the world and are best maintained on the one hand by an effective political democracy and on the other by a common understanding and observance of the Human Rights upon which they depend;

*Being resolved*, as the Governments of European countries which are likeminded and have a common heritage of political traditions, ideals, freedom and the rule of law to take the first steps for the collective enforcement of certain of the Rights stated in the Universal Declaration;

*Have agreed as follows:*

*Article* 1

The High Contracting Parties shall secure to everyone within their jurisdiction the rights and freedoms defined in Section 1 of this Convention.

## Section I

*Article* 2

1. Everyone's right to life shall be protected by law. No one shall be deprived of his life intentionally save in the execution of a sentence of a court following his conviction of a crime for which this penalty is provided by law.

2. Deprivation of life shall not be regarded as inflicted in contravention of this Article when it results from the use of force which is no more than absolutely necessary:

- (*a*) in defence of any person from unlawful violence;
- (*b*) in order to effect a lawful arrest or to prevent the escape of a person lawfully detained;
- (*c*) in action lawfully taken for the purpose of quelling a riot or insurrection.

*Article* 3

No one shall be subjected to torture or to inhuman or degrading treatment or punishment.

*Article* 4

1. No one shall be held in slavery or servitude.

2. No one shall be required to perform forced or compulsory labour.

3. For the purpose of this Article the term 'forced or compulsory labour' shall not include:

> (*a*) any work required to be done in the ordinary course of detention imposed according to the provisions of Article 5 of this Convention or during conditional release from such detention;
>
> (*b*) any service of a military character or, in case of conscientious objectors in countries where they are recognized, service exacted instead of compulsory military service;
>
> (*c*) any service exacted in case of an emergency or calamity threatening the life or well-being of the community;
>
> (*d*) any work or service which forms part of normal civic obligations.

*Article* 5

1. Everyone has the right to liberty and security of person. No one shall be deprived of his liberty save in the following cases and in accordance with a procedure prescribed by law;

> (*a*) the lawful detention of a person after conviction by a competent court;
>
> (*b*) the lawful arrest or detention of a person for non-compliance with the lawful order of a court or in order to secure the fulfilment of any obligation prescribed by law;
>
> (*c*) the lawful arrest or detention of a person effected for the purpose of bringing him before the competent legal authority on reasonable suspicion of having committed an offence or when it is reasonably considered necessary to prevent his committing an offence or fleeing after having done so;
>
> (*d*) the detention of a minor by lawful order for the purpose of educational supervision or his lawful detention for the purpose of bringing him before the competent legal authority;
>
> (*e*) the lawful detention of persons for the prevention of the spreading of infectious diseases, of persons of unsound mind, alcoholics or drug addicts, or vagrants;
>
> (*f*) the lawful arrest or detention of a person to prevent his effecting an unauthorized entry into the country or of a person against whom action is being taken with a view to deportation or extradition.

2. Everyone who is arrested shall be informed promptly, in a language which he understands, of the reasons for his arrest and of any charge against him.

3. Everyone arrested or detained in accordance with the provisions of paragraph 1 (c) of this Article shall be brought promptly before a judge or other officer authorized by law to exercise judicial power and shall be entitled to trial within a reasonable time or to release pending trial. Release may be conditioned by guarantees to appear for trial.

4. Everyone who is deprived of his liberty by arrest or detention shall be entitled to take proceedings by which the lawfulness of his detention shall be decided speedily by a court and his release ordered if the detention is not lawful.

5. Everyone who has been the victim of arrest or detention in contravention of the provisions of this article shall have an enforceable right to compensation.

*Article* 6

1. In the determination of his civil rights and obligations or of any criminal charge against him, everyone is entitled to a fair and public hearing within a reasonable time by an independent and impartial tribunal established by law. Judgment shall be pronounced publicly but the press and public may be excluded from all or part of the trial in the interest of morals, public order or national security in a democratic society, where the interests of juveniles or the protection of the private life of the parties so require, or to the extent strictly necessary in the opinion of the court in special circumstances where publicity would prejudice the interests of justice.

2. Everyone charged with a criminal offence shall be presumed innocent until proved guilty according to law.

3. Everyone charged with a criminal offence has the following minimum rights:

  (a) to be informed promptly, in a language which he understands and in detail, of the nature and cause of the accusation against him;
  (b) to have adequate time and facilities for the preparation of his defence;
  (c) to defend himself in person or through legal assistance of his own choosing or, if he has not sufficient means to pay for legal assistance, to be given it free when the interests of justice so require;
  (d) to examine or have examined witnesses against him and to obtain the attendance and examination of witnesses on his behalf under the same conditions as witnesses against him;
  (e) to have the free assistance of an interpreter if he cannot understand or speak the language used in court.

*Article* 7

1. No one shall be held guilty of any criminal offence on account of any act or omission which did not constitute a criminal offence under national or

international law at the time when it was committed. Nor shall a heavier penalty be imposed than the one that was applicable at the time the criminal offence was committed.

2. This article shall not prejudice the trial and punishment of any person for any act or omission which, at the time when it was committed, was criminal according to the general principles of law recognized by civilized nations.

### Article 8

1. Everyone has the right to respect for his private and family life, his home and his correspondence.

2. There shall be no interference by a public authority with the exercise of this right except such as is in accordance with the law and is necessary in a democratic society in the interests of national security, public safety or the economic well-being of the country, for the prevention of disorder or crime, for the protection of health or morals, or for the protection of the rights and freedoms of others.

### Article 9

1. Everyone has the right to freedom of thought, conscience and religion; this right includes freedom to change his religion or belief, and freedom, either alone or in community with others and in public or private, to manifest his religion or belief, in worship, teaching, practice and observance.

2. Freedom to manifest one's religion or beliefs shall be subject only to such limitations as are prescribed by law and are necessary in a democratic society in the interests of public safety, for the protection of public order, health or morals, or for the protection of the rights and freedoms of others.

### Article 10

1. Everyone has the right to freedom of expression. This right shall include freedom to hold opinions and to receive and impart information and ideas without interference by public authority and regardless of frontiers. This article shall not prevent States from requiring the licensing of broadcasting, television or cinema enterprises.

2. The exercise of these freedoms, since it carries with it duties and responsibilities, may be subject to such formalities, conditions, restrictions or penalties as are prescribed by law and are necessary in a democratic society, in the interests of national security, territorial integrity or public safety, for the prevention of disorder or crime, for the protection of health or morals, for the protection of the reputation or rights of others, for preventing the disclosure of information received in confidence, or for maintaining the authority and impartiality of the judiciary.

*Article* 11

1. Everyone has the right to freedom of peaceful assembly and to freedom of association with others, including the right to form and to join trade unions for the protection of his interests.

2. No restrictions shall be placed on the exercise of these rights other than such as are prescribed by law and are necessary in a democratic society in the interests of national security or public safety, for the prevention of disorder or crime, for the protection of health or morals or for the protection of the rights and freedoms of others. This Article shall not prevent the imposition of lawful restrictions on the exercise of these rights by members of the armed forces, of the police or of the administration of the State.

*Article* 12

Men and women of marriageable age have the right to marry and to found a family, according to the national laws governing the exercise of this right.

*Article* 13

Everyone whose rights and freedoms as set forth in this Convention are violated shall have an effective remedy before a national authority notwithstanding that the violation has been committed by persons acting in an official capacity.

*Article* 14

The enjoyment of the rights and freedoms set forth in this Convention shall be secured without discrimination on any ground such as sex, race, colour, language, religion, political or other opinion, national or social origin, association with a national minority, property, birth or other status.

*Article* 15

1. In time of war or other public emergency threatening the life of the nation any High Contracting Party may take measures derogating from its obligations under this Convention to the extent strictly required by the exigencies of the situation, provided that such measures are not inconsistent with its other obligations under international law.

2. No derogation from Article 2, except in respect of deaths resulting from lawful acts of war, or from Articles 3, 4 (paragraph 1) and 7 shall be made under this provision.

3. Any High Contracting Party availing itself of this right of derogation shall keep the Secretary-General of the Council of Europe fully informed of the measures which it has taken and the reasons therefor. It shall also inform the Secretary-General of the Council of Europe when such measures

have ceased to operate and the provisions of the Convention are again being fully executed.

*Article* 16

Nothing in Articles 10, 11 and 14 shall be regarded as preventing the High Contracting Parties from imposing restrictions on the political activity of aliens.

*Article* 17

Nothing in this Convention may be interpreted as implying for any State, group or person any right to engage in any activity or perform any act aimed at the destruction of any of the rights and freedoms set forth herein or at their limitation to a greater extent than is provided for in the Convention.

*Article* 18

The restrictions permitted under this Convention to the said rights and freedoms shall not be applied for any purpose other than those for which they have been prescribed.

## Section II

*Article* 19

To ensure the observance of the engagements undertaken by the High Contracting Parties in the present Convention, there shall be set up:

1. A European Commission of Human Rights hereinafter referred to as 'the Commission';

2. A European Court of Human Rights, hereinafter referred to as 'the Court'.

## Section III

*Article* 20

The Commission shall consist of a number of members equal to that of the High Contracting Parties. No two members of the Commission may be nationals of the same State.

*Article* 21

1. The members of the Commission shall be elected by the Committee of Ministers by an absolute majority of votes, from a list of names drawn up by the Bureau of the Consultative Assembly; each group of the Represen-

tatives of the High Contracting Parties in the Consultative Assembly shall put forward three candidates, of whom two at least shall be its nationals.

2. As far as applicable, the same procedure shall be followed to complete the Commission in the event of other States subsequently becoming Parties to this Convention, and in filling casual vacancies.

*Article* 22

1. The members of the Commission shall be elected for a period of six years. They may be re-elected. However, of the members elected at the first election, the terms of seven members shall expire at the end of three years.

2. The members whose terms are to expire at the end of the initial period of three years shall be chosen by lot by the Secretary-General of the Council of Europe immediately after the first election has been completed.

3. A member of the Commission elected to replace a member whose term of office has not expired shall hold office for the remainder of his predecessor's term.

4. The members of the Commission shall hold office until replaced. After having been replaced, they shall continue to deal with such cases as they already have under consideration.

*Article* 23

The members of the Commission shall sit on the Commission in their individual capacity.

*Article* 24

Any High Contracting Party may refer to the Commission, through the Secretary-General of the Council of Europe, any alleged breach of the provisions of the Convention by another High Contracting Party.

*Article* 25

1. The Commission may receive petitions addressed to the Secretary-General of the Council of Europe from any person, non-governmental organization or group of individuals claiming to be the victim of a violation by one of the High Contracting Parties of the rights set forth in this Convention, provided that the High Contracting Party against which the complaint has been lodged has declared that it recognizes the competence of the Commission to receive such petitions. Those of the High Contracting Parties who have made such a declaration undertake not to hinder in any way the effective exercise of this right.

2. Such declarations may be made for a specific period.

3. The declarations shall be deposited with the Secretary-General of the Council of Europe who shall transmit copies thereof to the High Contracting Parties and publish them.

4. The Commission shall only exercise the powers provided for in this Article when at least six High Contracting Parties are bound by declarations made in accordance with the preceding paragraphs.

*Article* 26

The Commission may only deal with the matter after all domestic remedies have been exhausted, according to the generally recognized rules of international law, and within a period of six months from the date on which the final decision was taken.

*Article* 27

1. The Commission shall not deal with any petition submitted under Article 25 which

    (*a*) is anonymous, or
    (*b*) is substantially the same as a matter which has already been examined by the Commission or has already been submitted to another procedure or international investigation or settlement and if it contains no relevant new information.

2. The Commission shall consider inadmissible any petition submitted under Article 25 which it considers incompatible with the provisions of the present Convention, manifestly ill-founded, or an abuse of the right of petition.

3. The Commission shall reject any petition referred to it which it considers inadmissible under Article 26.

*Article* 28

In the event of the Commission accepting a petition referred to it:

    (*a*) it shall, with a view to ascertaining the facts undertake together with the representatives of the parties an examination of the petition and, if need be, an investigation, for the effective conduct of which the States concerned shall furnish all necessary facilities, after an exchange of views with the Commission:
    (*b*) it shall place itself at the disposal of the parties concerned with a view to securing a friendly settlement of the matter on the basis of respect for Human Rights as defined in this Convention.

*Article* 29

1. The Commission shall perform the functions set out in Article 28 by means of a Sub-Commission consisting of seven members of the Commission.

2. Each of the parties concerned may appoint as members of this Sub-Commission a person of its choice.

3. The remaining members shall be chosen by lot in accordance with arrangements prescribed in the Rules of Procedure of the Commission.

*Article 30*

If the Sub-Commission succeeds in effecting a friendly settlement in accordance with Article 28, it shall draw up a Report which shall be sent to the States concerned, to the Committee of Ministers and to the Secretary-General of the Council of Europe for publication. This Report shall be confined to a brief statement of the facts and of the solution reached.

*Article 31*

1. If a solution is not reached, the Commission shall draw up a Report on the facts and state its opinion as to whether the facts found disclose a breach by the State concerned of its obligations under the Convention. The opinions of all the members of the Commission on this point may be stated in the Report.

2. The Report shall be transmitted to the Committee of Ministers. It shall also be transmitted to the States concerned, who shall not be at liberty to publish it.

3. In transmitting the Report to the Committee of Ministers the Commission may make such proposals as it thinks fit.

*Article 32*

1. If the question is not referred to the Court in accordance with Article 48 of this Convention within a period of three months from the date of the transmission of the Report to the Committee of Ministers, the Committee of Ministers shall decide by a majority of two-thirds of the members entitled to sit on the Committee whether there has been a violation of the Convention.

2. In the affirmative case the Committee of Ministers shall prescribe a period during which the Contracting Party concerned must take the measures required by the decision of the Committee of Ministers.

3. If the High Contracting Party concerned has not taken satisfactory measures within the prescribed period, the Committee of Ministers shall decide by the majority provided for in paragraph 1 above what effect shall be given to its original decision and shall publish the Report.

4. The High Contracting Parties undertake to regard as binding on them any decision which the Committee of Ministers may take in application of the preceding paragraphs.

*Article 33*

The Commission shall meet *in camera*.

*Article* 34

The Commission shall take its decision by a majority of the Members present and voting; the Sub-Commission shall take its decisions by a majority of its members.

*Article* 35

The Commission shall meet as the circumstances require. The meetings shall be convened by the Secretary-General of the Council of Europe.

*Article* 36

The Commission shall draw up its own rules of procedure.

*Article* 37

The secretariat of the Commission shall be provided by the Secretary-General of the Council of Europe.


Section IV

*Article* 38

The European Court of Human Rights shall consist of a number of judges equal to that of the Members of the Council of Europe. No two judges may be nationals of the same State.

*Article* 39

1. The members of the Court shall be elected by the Consultative Assembly by a majority of the votes cast from a list of persons nominated by the Members of the Council of Europe; each Member shall nominate three candidates, of whom two at least shall be its nationals.

2. As far as applicable, the same procedure shall be followed to complete the Court in the event of the admission of new members of the Council of Europe, and in filling casual vacancies.

3. The candidates shall be of high moral character and must either possess the qualifications required for appointment to high judicial office or be jurisconsults of recognized competence.

*Article* 40

1. The members of the Court shall be elected for a period of nine years. They may be re-elected. However, of the members elected at the first election the terms of four members shall expire at the end of three years, and the terms of four more members shall expire at the end of six years.

2. The members whose terms are to expire at the end of the initial periods

of three and six years shall be chosen by lot by the Secretary-General immediately after the first election has been completed.

3. A member of the Court elected to replace a member whose term of office has not expired shall hold office for the remainder of his predecessor's term.

4. The members of the Court shall hold office until replaced. After having been replaced, they shall continue to deal with such cases as they already have under consideration.

*Article* 41

The Court shall elect its President and Vice-President for a period of three years. They may be re-elected.

*Article* 42

The members of the Court shall receive for each day of duty a compensation to be determined by the Committee of Ministers.

*Article* 43

For the consideration of each case brought before it the Court shall consist of a Chamber composed of seven judges. There shall sit as an *ex officio* member of the Chamber the judge who is a national of any State party concerned, or, if there is none, a person of its choice who shall sit in the capacity of judge; the names of the other judges shall be chosen by lot by the President before the opening of the case.

*Article* 44

Only the High Contracting Parties and the Commission shall have the right to bring a case before the Court.

*Article* 45

The jurisdiction of the Court shall extend to all cases concerning the interpretation and application of the present Convention which the High Contracting Parties or the Commission shall refer to it in accordance with Article 48.

*Article* 46

1. Any of the High Contracting Parties may at any time declare that it recognizes as compulsory *ipso facto* and without special agreement the jurisdiction of the Court in all matters concerning the interpretation and application of the present Convention.

2. The declarations referred to above may be made unconditionally or on condition of reciprocity on the part of several or certain other High Contracting Parties or for a specified period.

3. These declarations shall be deposited with the Secretary-General of the

Council of Europe who shall transmit copies thereof to the High Contracting Parties.

*Article* 47

The Court may only deal with a case after the Commission has acknowledged the failure of efforts for a friendly settlement and within the period of three months provided for in Article 32.

*Article* 48

The following may bring a case before the Court, provided that the High Contracting Party concerned, if there is only one, or the High Contracting Parties concerned, if there is more than one, are subject to the compulsory jurisdiction of the Court or, failing that, with the consent of the High Contracting Party concerned, if there is only one, or of the High Contracting Parties concerned if there is more than one:

(*a*) the Commission;
(*b*) a High Contracting Party whose national is alleged to be a victim;
(*c*) a High Contracting Party which referred the case to the Commission;
(*d*) a High Contracting Party against which the complaint has been lodged.

*Article* 49

In the event of dispute as to whether the Court has jurisdiction, the matter shall be settled by the decision of the Court.

*Article* 50

If the Court finds that a decision or a measure taken by a legal authority or any other authority of a High Contracting Party, is completely or partially in conflict with the obligations arising from the present Convention, and if the internal law of the said Party allows only partial reparation to be made for the consequences of this decision or measure, the decision of the Court shall, if necessary, afford just satisfaction to the injured party.

*Article* 51

1. Reasons shall be given for the judgment of the Court.

2. If the judgment does not represent in whole or in part the unanimous opinion of the judges, any judge shall be entitled to deliver a separate opinion.

*Article* 52

The judgment of the Court shall be final.

*Article* 53

The High Contracting Parties undertake to abide by the decision of the Court in any case to which they are parties.

*Article* 54

The judgment of the Court shall be transmitted to the Committee of Ministers which shall supervise its execution.

*Article* 55

The Court shall draw up its own rules and shall determine its own procedure.

*Article* 56

1. The first election of the members of the Court shall take place after the declarations by the High Contracting Parties mentioned in Article 46 have reached a total of eight.

2. No case can be brought before the Court before this election.


Section V

*Article* 57

On receipt of a request from the Secretary-General of the Council of Europe any High Contracting Party shall furnish an explanation of the manner in which its internal law ensures the effective implementation of any of the provisions of this Convention.

*Article* 58

The expenses of the Commission and the Court shall be borne by the Council of Europe.

*Article* 59

The members of the Commission and of the Court shall be entitled, during the discharge of their functions, to the privileges and immunities provided for in Article 40 of the Statute of the Council of Europe and in the agreements made thereunder.

*Article* 60

Nothing in this Convention shall be construed as limiting or derogating from any of the human rights and fundamental freedoms which may be ensured under the laws of any High Contracting Party or under any other agreement to which it is a Party.

*Article* 61

Nothing in this Convention shall prejudice the powers conferred on the Committee of Ministers by the Statute of the Council of Europe.

*Article* 62

The High Contracting Parties agree that, except by special agreement, they will not avail themselves of treaties, conventions or declarations in force between them for the purpose of submitting, by way of petition, a dispute arising out of the interpretation or application of this Convention to a means of settlement other than those provided for in this Convention.

*Article* 63

1. Any State may at the time of its ratification or at any time thereafter declare by notification addressed to the Secretary-General of the Council of Europe that the present Convention shall extend to all or any of the territories for whose international relations it is responsible.

2. The Convention shall extend to the territory or territories named in the notification as from the thirtieth day after the receipt of this notification by the Secretary-General of the Council of Europe.

3. The provisions of this Convention shall be applied in such territories with due regard, however, to local requirements.

4. Any State which has made a declaration in accordance with paragraph 1 of this article may at any time thereafter declare on behalf of one or more of the territories to which the declaration relates that it accepts the competence of the Commission to receive petitions from individuals, non-governmental organizations or groups of individuals in accordance with Article 25 of the present Convention.

*Article* 64

1. Any State may, when signing this Convention or when depositing its instrument of ratification, make a reservation in respect of any particular provision of the Convention to the extent that any law then in force in its territory is not in conformity with the provision. Reservations of a general character shall not be permitted under this article.

2. Any reservation made under this article shall contain a brief statement of the law concerned.

*Article* 65

1. A High Contracting Party may denounce the present Convention only after the expiry of five years from the date of which it became a Party to it and after six months' notice contained in a notification addressed to the Secretary-General of the Council of Europe, who shall inform the other High Contracting Parties.

2. Such a denunciation shall not have the effect of releasing the High Contracting Party concerned from its obligations under this Convention in respect of any act which, being capable of constituting a violation of such obligations, may have been performed by it before the date at which the denunciation became effective.

3. Any High Contracting Party which shall cease to be a Member of the Council of Europe shall cease to be a Party to this Convention under the same conditions.

4. The Convention may be denounced in accordance with the provisions of the preceding paragraphs in respect of any territory to which it has been declared to extend under the terms of Article 63.

*Article* 66

1. This Convention shall be open to the signature of the Members of the Council of Europe. It shall be ratified. Ratifications shall be deposited with the Secretary-General of the Council of Europe.

2. The present Convention shall come into force after the deposit of ten instruments of ratification.

3. As regards any signatory ratifying subsequently, the Convention shall come into force at the date of the deposit of its instrument of ratification.

4. The Secretary-General of the Council of Europe shall notify all the Members of the Council of Europe of the entry into force of the Convention, the names of the High Contracting Parties who have ratified it, and the deposit of all instruments of ratification which may be effected subsequently.

*Done* at Rome this 4th day of November, 1950, in English and French, both texts being equally authentic, in a single copy which shall remain deposited in the archives of the Council of Europe. The Secretary-General shall transmit certified copies to each of the signatories.

### Protocols

1. *Enforcement of certain Rights and Freedoms not included in Section I of the Convention*

The Governments signatory hereto, being Members of the Council of Europe,

Being resolved to take steps to ensure the collective enforcement of certain rights and freedoms other than those already included in Section I of the Convention for the Protection of Human Rights and Fundamental Freedoms signed at Rome on 4th November, 1950 (hereinafter referred to as 'the Convention'),

Have agreed as follows:

*Article* 1

Every natural or legal person is entitled to the peaceful enjoyment of his possessions. No one shall be deprived of his possessions except in the public interest and subject to the conditions provided for by law and by the general principles of international law.

The preceding provisions shall not, however, in any way impair the right of a State to enforce such laws as it deems necessary to control the use of property in accordance with the general interest or to secure the payment of taxes or other contributions or penalties.

*Article* 2

No person shall be denied the right to education. In the exercise of any functions which it assumes in relation to education and to teaching, the State shall respect the right of parents to ensure such education and teaching in conformity with their own religious and philosophical convictions.

*Article* 3

The High Contracting Parties undertake to hold free elections at reasonable intervals by secret ballot, under conditions which will ensure the free expression of the opinion of the people in the choice of the legislature.

*Article* 4

Any High Contracting Party may at the time of signature or ratification or at any time thereafter communicate to the Secretary-General of the Council of Europe a declaration stating the extent to which it undertakes that the provisions of the present Protocol shall apply to such of the territories for the international relations of which it is responsible as are named therein.

Any High Contracting Party which has communicated a declaration in virtue of the preceding paragraph may from time to time communicate a further declaration modifying the terms of any former declaration or terminating the application of the provisions of this Protocol in respect of any territory.

A declaration made in accordance with this article shall be deemed to have been made in accordance with paragraph 1 of Article 63 of the Convention.

*Article* 5

As between the High Contracting Parties the provisions of Articles 1, 2, 3 and 4 of this Protocol shall be regarded as additional articles to the Convention and all the provisions of the Convention shall apply accordingly.

*Article* 6

This Protocol shall be open for signature by the Members of the Council of Europe, who are the signatories of the Convention; it shall be ratified at the same time as or after the ratification of the Convention. It shall enter into force after the deposit of ten instruments of ratification. As regards any signatory ratifying subsequently, the Protocol shall enter into force at the date of the deposit of its instrument of ratification.

The instruments of ratification shall be deposited with the Secretary-General of the Council of Europe, who will notify all Members of the names of those who have ratified.

*Done* at Paris on the 20th day of March 1952, in English and French, both texts being equally authentic, in a single copy which shall remain deposited in the archives of the Council of Europe. The Secretary-General shall transmit certified copies to each of the signatory Governments.

## 2. *Conferring upon the European Court of Human Rights competence to give Advisory Opinions*

The member States of the Council of Europe signatory hereto:

Having regard to the provisions of the Convention for the Protection of Human Rights and Fundamental Freedoms signed at Rome on 4 November 1950 (hereinafter referred to as 'the Convention'), and in particular Article 19 instituting, among other bodies, a European Court of Human Rights (hereinafter referred to as 'the Court');

Considering that it is expedient to confer upon the Court competence to give advisory opinions subject to certain conditions;

Have agreed as follows:

### Article 1

1. The Court may, at the request of the Committee of Ministers, give advisory opinions on legal questions concerning the interpretation of the Convention and the Protocols thereto.

2. Such opinions shall not deal with any question relating to the content or scope of the rights or freedoms defined in Section I of the Convention and in the Protocols thereto, or with any other question which the Commission, the Court, or the Committee of Ministers might have to consider in consequence of any such proceedings as could be instituted in accordance with the Convention.

3. Decisions of the Committee of Ministers to request an advisory opinion of the Court shall require a two-thirds majority vote of the representatives entitled to sit on the Committee.

### Article 2

The Court shall decide whether a request for an advisory opinion submitted by the Committee of Ministers is within its consultative competence as defined in Article 1 of this Protocol.

*Article* 3

1. For the consideration of requests for an advisory opinion, the Court shall sit in plenary session.

2. Reasons shall be given for advisory opinions of the Court.

3. If the advisory opinion does not represent in whole or in part the unanimous opinion of the judges, any judge shall be entitled to deliver a separate opinion.

4. Advisory opinions of the Court shall be communicated to the Committee of Ministers.

*Article* 4

The powers of the Court under Article 55 of the Convention shall extend to the drawing up of such rules and the determination of such procedure as the Court may think necessary for the purposes of this Protocol.

*Article* 5

1. This Protocol shall be open to signature by Member States of the Council of Europe, signatories to the Convention, who may become Parties to it by:

   (*a*) signature without reservation in respect of ratification or acceptance;
   (*b*) signature with reservation in respect of ratification or acceptance, followed by ratification or acceptance. Instruments of ratification or acceptance shall be deposited with the Secretary-General of the Council of Europe.

2. This Protocol shall enter into force as soon as all the States Parties to the Convention shall have become Parties to the Protocol in accordance with the provisions of paragraph 1 of this Article.

3. From the date of the entry into force of this Protocol, Articles 1 to 4 shall be considered an integral part of the Convention.

4. The Secretary-General of the Council of Europe shall notify the Member States of the Council of:

   (*a*) any signature without reservation in respect of ratification or acceptance;
   (*b*) any signature with reservation in respect of ratification or acceptance;
   (*c*) the deposit of any instrument of ratification or acceptance;
   (*d*) the date of entry into force of this Protocol in accordance with paragraph 2 of this Article.

In witness whereof the undersigned, being duly authorized thereto, have signed this Protocol.

*Done* at Strasbourg, this 6th day of May 1963, in English and in French, both texts being equally authoritative, in a single copy which shall remain deposited in the archives of the Council of Europe. The Secretary-General shall transmit certified copies to each of the signatory States.

### 3. *Amending Articles 29, 30, and 94 of the Convention*

The member States of the Council of Europe, signatories to this Protocol,

Considering that it is advisable to amend certain provisions of the Convention for the Protection of Human Rights and Fundamental Freedoms signed at Rome on 4 November 1960 (hereinafter referred to as 'the Convention') concerning the procedure of the European Commission of Human Rights,

Have agreed as follows:

*Article* 1

1. Article 29 of the Convention is deleted.

2. The following provision shall be inserted in the Convention:

'*Article* 29

After it has accepted a petition submitted under Article 25, the Commission may nevertheless decide unanimously to reject the petition if, in the course of its examination, it finds that the existence of one of the grounds for non-acceptance provided for in Article 27 has been established.

In such a case, the decision shall be communicated to the parties.'

*Article* 2

In Article 30 of the Convention, the word 'Sub-Commission' shall be replaced by the word 'Commission'.

*Article* 3

1. At the beginning of Article 34 of the Convention, the following shall be inserted:

'Subject to the provisions of Article 29. . . .'

2. At the end of the same article, the sentence 'the Sub-Commission shall take its decisions by a majority of its members' shall be deleted.

*Article* 4

1. The Protocol shall be open to signature by the member States of the Council of Europe, who may become Parties to it either by:

(*a*) signature without reservation in respect of ratification or acceptance, or

(*b*) signature with reservation in respect of ratification or acceptance, followed by ratification or acceptance. Instruments of ratification or acceptance shall be deposited with the Secretary-General of the Council of Europe.

2. This Protocol shall enter into force as soon as all States Parties to the Convention shall have become Parties to the Protocol, in accordance with the provisions of paragraph 1 of this Article.

3. The Secretary-General of the Council of Europe shall notify the Member States of the Council of:

(a) any signature without reservation in respect of ratification or acceptance;

(b) any signature with reservation in respect of ratification or acceptance;

(c) the deposit of any instrument of ratification or acceptance;

(d) the date of entry into force of this Protocol in accordance with paragraph 2 of this Article.

In witness whereof the undersigned, being duly authorised thereto, have signed this Protocol.

*Done* at Strasbourg, this 6th day of May 1963, in English and in French, both texts being equally authoritative, in a single copy which shall remain deposited in the archives of the Council of Europe. The Secretary-General shall transmit certified copies to each of the signatory States.

### 4. *Securing certain Rights and Freedoms other than those included in the Convention and in Protocol No. 1*

The Governments signatory hereto, being Members of the Council of Europe.

Being resolved to take steps to ensure the collective enforcement of certain rights and freedoms other than those already included in Section I of the Convention for the Protection of Human Rights and Fundamental Freedoms signed at Rome on 4 November 1950 (hereinafter referred to as 'the Convention') and in Articles 1 to 3 of the First Protocol to the Convention, signed at Paris on 20 March 1952,

Have agreed as follows:

*Article* 1

No one shall be deprived of his liberty merely on the ground of inability to fulfil a contractual obligation.

*Article* 2

1. Everyone lawfully within the territory of a State shall, within that territory, have the right to liberty of movement and freedom to choose his residence.

2. Everyone shall be free to leave any country, including his own.

3. No restrictions shall be placed on the exercise of these rights other than such as are in accordance with law and are necessary in a democratic society in the interests of national security or public safety, for the main-

tenance of 'ordre public', for the prevention of crime, for the protection of health and morals, or for the protection of the rights and freedoms of others.

4. The rights set forth in paragraph 1 may also be subject, in particular areas, to restrictions imposed in accordance with law and justified by the public interest in a democratic society.

*Article* 3

1. No one shall be expelled, by means either of an individual or of a collective measure, from the territory of the State of which he is a national.

2. No one shall be deprived of the right to enter the territory of the State of which he is a national.

*Article* 4

Collective expulsion of aliens is prohibited.

*Article* 5

1. Any High Contracting Party may, at the time of signature or ratification of this Protocol, or at any time thereafter, communicate to the Secretary-General of the Council of Europe a declaration stating the extent to which it undertakes that the provisions of this Protocol shall apply to such of the territories for the international relations of which it is responsible as are named therein.

2. Any High Contracting Party which has communicated a declaration in virtue of the preceding paragraph may, from time to time, communicate a further declaration modifying the terms of any former declaration or terminating the application of the provisions of this Protocol in respect of any territory.

3. A declaration made in accordance with this article shall be deemed to have been made in accordance with paragraph 1 of Article 63 of the Convention.

4. The territory of any State to which this Protocol applies by virtue of ratification or acceptance by that State, and each territory to which this Protocol is applied by virtue of a declaration by that State under this article, shall be treated as separate territories for the purpose of the references in Articles 2 and 3 to the territory of a State.

*Article* 6

1. As between the High Contracting Parties the provisions of Articles 1 to 5 of this Protocol shall be regarded as additional articles to the Convention, and all the provisions of the Convention shall apply accordingly.

2. Nevertheless, the right of individual recourse recognized by a declaration made under Article 25 of the Convention, or the acceptance of the compulsory jurisdiction of the Court by a declaration made under Article 46 of

the Convention, shall not be effective in relation to this Protocol unless the High Contracting Party concerned has made a statement recognizing such right, or accepting such jurisdiction, in respect of all or any of Articles 1 to 4 of the Protocol.

*Article* 7

1. This Protocol shall be open for signature by the members of the Council of Europe who are the signatories of the Convention; it shall be ratified at the same time as or after the ratification of the Convention. It shall enter into force after the deposit of five instruments of ratification. As regards any signatory ratifying subsequently, the Protocol shall enter into force at the date of the deposit of its instrument of ratification.

2. The instruments of ratification shall be deposited with the Secretary-General of the Council of Europe, who will notify all members of the names of those who have ratified.

In witness thereof, the undersigned, being duly authorized thereto, have signed this Protocol.

*Done* at Strasbourg, this 16th day of September 1963, in English and in French, both texts being equally authoritative, in a single copy which shall remain deposited in the archives of the Council of Europe. The Secretary-General shall transmit certified copies to each of the signatory States.

### 5. *Amending Articles 22 and 40 of the Convention*

The Governments signatory hereto, being Members of the Council of Europe.

Considering that certain inconveniences have arisen in the application of the provisions of Articles 22 and 40 of the Convention for the Protection of Human Rights and Fundamental Freedoms signed at Rome on 4th November 1950 (hereinafter referred to as 'the Convention') relating to the length of the terms of office of the members of the European Commission of Human Rights (hereinafter referred to as 'the Commission') and of the European Court of Human Rights (hereinafter referred to as the Court');

Considering that it is desirable to ensure as far as possible an election every three years of one half of the members of the Commission and of one third of the members of the Court;

Considering therefore that it is desirable to amend certain provisions of the Convention,

Have agreed as follows:

*Article* 1

In Article 22 of the Convention, the following two paragraphs shall be inserted after paragraph (2):

'(3) In order to ensure that, as far as possible, one half of the membership of the Commission shall be renewed every three years, the Committee of Ministers may decide, before proceeding to any subsequent election, that the term or terms of office of one or more members to be elected shall be for a period other than six years but not more than nine and not less than three years.

(4) In cases where more than one term of office is involved and the Committee of Ministers applies the preceding paragraph, the allocation of the terms of office shall be effected by the drawing of lots by the Secretary-General, immediately after the election.'

### Article 2

In Article 22 of the Convention, the former paragraphs (3) and (4) shall become respectively paragraphs (5) and (6).

### Article 3

In Article 40 of the Convention, the following two paragraphs shall be inserted after paragraph (2):

'(3) In order to ensure that, as far as possible, one third of the membership of the Court shall be renewed every three years, the Consultative Assembly may decide, before proceeding to any subsequent election, that the term or terms of office of one or more members to be elected shall be for a period other than nine years but not more than twelve and not less than six years.

(4) In cases where more than one term of office is involved and the Consultative Assembly applies the preceding paragraph, the allocation of the terms of office shall be effected by the drawing of lots by the Secretary-General immediately after the election.'

### Article 4

In Article 40 of the Convention, the former paragraphs (3) and (4) shall become respectively paragraphs (5) and (6).

### Article 5

1. This Protocol shall be open to signature by Members of the Council of Europe, signatories to the Convention, who may become Parties to it by:

(a) signature without reservation in respect of ratification or acceptance;
(b) signature with reservation in respect of ratification or acceptance, followed by ratification or acceptance.

Instruments of ratification or acceptance shall be deposited with the Secretary-General of the Council of Europe.

2. This Protocol shall enter into force as soon as all Contracting Parties to

the Convention shall have become Parties to the Protocol, in accordance with the provisions of paragraph 1 of this Article.

3. The Secretary-General of the Council of Europe shall notify the Members of the Council of:

(a) any signature without reservation in respect of ratification or acceptance;

(b) any signature with reservation in respect of ratification or acceptance;

(c) the deposit of any instrument of ratification or acceptance;

(d) the date of entry into force of this Protocol in accordance with paragraph 2 of this Article.

In witness whereof the undersigned, being duly authorized thereto, have signed this Protocol.

*Done* at Strasbourg, this 20th day of January 1966, in English and in French, both texts being equally authoritative, in a single copy which shall remain deposited in the archives of the Council of Europe. The Secretary-General shall transmit certified copies to each of the signatory Governments.

### 6. *Concerning the Abolition of the Death Penalty*

The member States of the Council of Europe, signatory to this Protocol to the Convention for the Protection of Human Rights and Fundamental Freedoms, signed at Rome on 4 November 1950 (hereinafter referred to as 'the Convention'),

Considering that the evolution that has occurred in several member States of the Council of Europe expresses a general tendency in favour of abolition of the death penalty;

Have agreed as follows:

*Article* 1

The death penalty shall be abolished. No one shall be condemned to such penalty or executed.

*Article* 2

A State may make provision in its law for the death penalty in respect of acts committed in time of war or of imminent threat of war; such penalty shall be applied only in the instances laid down in the law and in accordance with its provisions. The State shall communicate to the Secretary General of the Council of Europe the relevant provisions of that law.

*Article* 3

No derogation from the provisions of this Protocol shall be made under Article 15 of the Convention.

*Article* 4

No reservation may be made under Article 64 of the Convention in respect of the provisions of this Protocol.

*Article* 5

1. Any State may at the time of signature or when depositing its instrument of ratification, acceptance or approval, specify the territory or territories to which this Protocol shall apply.

2. Any State may at any later date, by a declaration addressed to the Secretary General of the Council of Europe, extend the application of this Protocol to any other territory specified in the declaration. In respect of such territory the Protocol shall enter into force on the first day of the month following the date of receipt of such declaration by the Secretary General.

3. Any declaration made under the two preceding paragraphs may, in respect of any territory specified in such declaration, be withdrawn by a notification addressed to the Secretary General. The withdrawal shall become effective on the first day of the month following the date of receipt of such notification by the Secretary General.

*Article* 6

As between the States Parties the provisions of Articles 1 to 5 of this Protocol shall be regarded as additional articles to the Convention and all the provisions of the Convention shall apply accordingly.

*Article* 7

This Protocol shall be open for signature by the member States of the Council of Europe, signatories to the Convention. It shall be subject to ratification, acceptance or approval. A member State of the Council of Europe may not ratify, accept or approve this Protocol unless it has, simultaneously or previously, ratified the Convention. Instruments of ratification, acceptance or approval shall be deposited with the Secretary General of the Council of Europe.

*Article* 8

1. This Protocol shall enter into force on the first day of the month following the date on which five member States of the Council of Europe have expressed their consent to be bound by the Protocol in accordance with the provisions of Article 7.

2. In respect of any member State which subsequently expresses its consent to be bound by it, the Protocol shall enter into force on the first day of the month following the date of the deposit of the instrument of ratification, acceptance or approval.

*Article* 9

The Secretary General of the Council of Europe shall notify the member States of the Council of:

(*a*) any signature;
(*b*) the deposit of any instrument of ratification, acceptance or approval;
(*c*) any date of entry into force of this Protocol in accordance with Articles 5 and 8;
(*d*) any other act, notification or communication relating to this Protocol.

In witness whereof the undersigned, being duly authorised thereto, have signed this Protocol.

Done at Strasbourg, this 28th day of April 1983, in English and French, both texts being equally authentic, in a single copy which shall be deposited in the archives of the Council of Europe. The Secretary General of the Council of Europe shall transmit certified copies to each member State of the Council of Europe.

### 7. *Concerning Various Matters*

The member States of the Council of Europe signatory hereto,

Being resolved to take further steps to ensure the collective enforcement of certain rights and freedoms by means of the Convention for the Protection of Human Rights and Fundamental Freedoms signed at Rome on 4 November 1950 (hereinafter referred to as 'the Convention'),

Have agreed as follows:

*Article* 1

1. An alien lawfully resident in the territory of a State shall not be expelled therefrom except in pursuance of a decision reached in accordance with law and shall be allowed:

(*a*) to submit reasons against his expulsion,
(*b*) to have his case reviewed, and
(*c*) to be represented for these purposes before the competent authority or a person or persons designated by that authority.

2. An alien may be expelled before the exercise of his rights under paragraph 1.a, b and c of this Article, when such expulsion is necessary in the interests of public order or is grounded on reasons of national security.

*Article* 2

1. Everyone convicted of a criminal offence by a tribunal shall have the right to have his conviction or sentence reviewed by a higher tribunal. The exercise of this right, including the grounds on which it may be exercised, shall be governed by law.

2. This right may be subject to exceptions in regard to offences of a minor character, as prescribed by law, or in cases in which the person concerned was tried in the first instance by the highest tribunal or was convicted following an appeal against acquittal.

*Article* 3

When a person has by a final decision been convicted of a criminal offence and when subsequently his conviction has been reversed, or he has been pardoned, on the ground that a new or newly discovered fact shows conclusively that there has been a miscarriage of justice, the person who has suffered punishment as a result of such conviction shall be compensated according to the law or the practice of the State concerned, unless it is proved that the nondisclosure of the unknown fact in time is wholly or partly attributable to him.

*Article* 4

1. No one shall be liable to be tried or punished again in criminal proceedings under the jurisdiction of the same State for an offence for which he has already been finally acquitted or convicted in accordance with the law and penal procedure of that State.

2. The provisions of the preceding paragraph shall not prevent the reopening of the case in accordance with the law and penal procedure of the State concerned, if there is evidence of new or newly discovered facts, or if there has been a fundamental defect in the previous proceedings, which could affect the outcome of the case.

3. No derogation from this Article shall be made under Article 15 of the Convention.

*Article* 5

Spouses shall enjoy equality of rights and responsibilities of a private law character between them, and in their relations with their children, as to marriage, during marriage and in the event of its dissolution. This Article shall not prevent States from taking such measures as are necessary in the interests of the children.

*Article* 6

1. Any State may at the time of signature or when depositing its instrument of ratification, acceptance or approval, specify the territory or territories to which this Protocol shall apply and state the extent to which it undertakes that the provisions of this Protocol shall apply to such territory or territories.

2. Any State may at any later day, by a declaration addressed to the Secretary General of the Council of Europe, extend the application of this Protocol to any other territory specified in the declaration. In respect of such territory the Protocol shall enter into force on the first day of the

month following the expiration of a period of two months after the date of receipt by the Secretary General of such declaration.

3. Any declaration made under the two preceding paragraphs may, in respect of any territory specified in such declaration, be withdrawn or modified by a notification addressed to the Secretary General. The withdrawal or modification shall become effective on the first day of the month following the expiration of a period of two months after the date of receipt of such notification by the Secretary General.

4. A declaration made in accordance with this Article shall be deemed to have been made in accordance with paragraph 1 of Article 63 of the Convention.

5. The territory of any State to which this Protocol applies by virtue of ratification, acceptance or approval by that State, and each territory to which this Protocol is applied by virtue of a declaration by that State under this Article, may be treated as separate territories for the purpose of the reference in Article 1 to the territory of a State.

*Article* 7

1. As between the States Parties, the provisions of Articles 1 to 6 of this Protocol shall be regarded as additional Articles to the Convention, and all the provisions of the Convention shall apply accordingly.

2. Nevertheless, the right of individual recourse recognised by a declaration made under Article 25 of the Convention, or the acceptance of the compulsory jurisdiction of the Court by a declaration made under Article 46 of the Convention, shall not be effective in relation to this Protocol unless the State concerned has made a statement recognising such right, or accepting such jurisdiction in respect of Articles 1 to 5 of this Protocol.

*Article* 8

This Protocol shall be open for signature by member States of the Council of Europe which have signed the Convention. It is subject to ratification, acceptance or approval. A member State of the Council of Europe may not ratify, accept or approve this Protocol without previously or simultaneously ratifying the Convention. Instruments of ratification, acceptance or approval shall be deposited with the Secretary General of the Council of Europe.

*Article* 9

1. This Protocol shall enter into force on the first day of the month following the expiration of a period of two months after the date on which seven member States of the Council of Europe have expressed their consent to be bound by the Protocol in accordance with the provisions of Article 8.

2. In respect of any member State which subsequently expresses its consent to be bound by it, the Protocol shall enter into force on the first day of the

month following the expiration of a period of two months after the date of the deposit of the instrument of ratification, acceptance or approval.

*Article* 10

The Secretary General of the Council of Europe shall notify all the member States of the Council of Europe of:

(*a*) any signature;

(*b*) the deposit of any instrument of ratification, acceptance or approval;

(*c*) any date of entry into force of this Protocol in accordance with Articles 6 and 9;

(*d*) any other act, notification or declaration relating to this Protocol.

In witness whereof the undersigned, being duly authorised thereto, have signed this Protocol.

Done at Strasbourg, this 22nd day of November 1984, in English and French, both texts being equally authentic, in a single copy which shall be deposited in the archives of the Council of Europe. The Secretary General of the Council of Europe shall transmit certified copies to each member State of the Council of Europe.

## 8. *Concerning Various Matters*

The member States of the Council of Europe, signatories to this Protocol to the Convention for the Protection of Human Rights and Fundamental Freedoms, signed at Rome on 4 November 1950 (hereinafter referred to as 'the Convention'),

Considering that it is desirable to amend certain provisions of the Convention with a view to improving and in particular to expediting the procedure of the European Commission of Human Rights,

Considering that it is also advisable to amend certain provisions of the Convention concerning the procedure of the European Court of Human Rights,

Have agreed as follows:

*Article* 1

1. The existing text of Article 20 of the Convention shall become paragraph 1 of that Article and shall be supplemented by the following four paragraphs:

'2. The Commission shall sit in plenary session. It may, however, set up Chambers, each composed of at least seven members. The Chambers may examine petitions submitted under Article 25 of this Convention which can be dealt with on the basis of established case law or which raise no serious question affecting the interpretation or application of the Convention. Subject to this restriction and to the provisions of paragraph

5 of this Article, the Chambers shall exercise all the powers conferred on the Commission by the Convention.

The member of the Commission elected in respect of a High Contracting Party against which a petition has been lodged shall have the right to sit on a Chamber to which that petition has been referred.

3. The Commission may set up committees, each composed of at least three members, with the power, exercisable by a unanimous vote, to declare inadmissible or strike from its list of cases a petition submitted under Article 25, when such a decision can be taken without further examination.

4. A Chamber or committee may at any time relinquish jurisdiction in favour of the plenary Commission, which may also order the transfer to it of any petition referred to a Chamber or committee.

5. Only the plenary Commission can exercise the following powers:

(a) the examination of applications submitted under Article 24;

(b) the bringing of a case before the Court in accordance with Article 48a;

(c) the drawing up of rules of procedure in accordance with Article 36.'

*Article 2*

Article 21 of the Convention shall be supplemented by the following third paragraph:

'3. The candidates shall be of high moral character and must either possess the qualifications required for appointment to high judicial office or be persons of recognised competence in national or international law.'

*Article 3*

Article 23 of the Convention shall be supplemented by the following sentence:

'During their term of office they shall not hold any position which is incompatible with their independence and impartiality as members of the Commission or the demands of this office.'

*Article 4*

The text, with modifications, of Article 28 of the Convention shall become paragraph 1 of that Article and the text, with modifications, of Article 30 shall become paragraph 2. The new text of Article 28 shall read as follows:

'*Article 28*

1. In the event of the Commission accepting a petition referred to it:

(a) it shall, with a view to ascertaining the facts, undertake together with the representatives of the parties an examination of the petition and, if need be, an investigation, for the effective conduct of which the States concerned shall furnish all necessary facilities, after an exchange of views with the Commission;

(b) it shall at the same time place itself at the disposal of the parties concerned with a view to securing a friendly settlement of the matter on the basis of respect for Human Rights as defined in this Convention.

2. If the Commission succeeds in effecting a friendly settlement, it shall draw up a Report which shall be sent to the States concerned, to the Committee of Ministers and to the Secretary General of the Council of Europe for publication. This Report shall be confined to a brief statement of the facts and of the solution reached.'

*Article* 5

In the first paragraph of Article 29 of the Convention, the word 'unanimously' shall be replaced by the words 'by a majority of two-thirds of its members'.

*Article* 6

The following provision shall be inserted in the Convention:

'*Article* 30

1. The Commission may at any stage of the proceedings decide to strike a petition out of its list of cases where the circumstances lead to the conclusion that:

(a) the applicant does not intend to pursue his petition, or
(b) the matter has been resolved, or
(c) for any other reason established by the Commission, it is no longer justified to continue the examination of the petition.

However, the Commission shall continue the examination of a petition if respect for Human Rights as defined in this Convention so requires.

2. If the Commission decides to strike a petition out of its list after having accepted it, it shall draw up a Report which shall contain a statement of the facts and the decision striking out the petition together with the reasons therefor. The Report shall be transmitted to the parties, as well as to the Committee of Ministers for information. The Commission may publish it.

3. The Commission may decide to restore a petition to its list of cases if it considers that the circumstances justify such a course.'

*Article* 7

In Article 31 of the Convention, paragraph 1 shall read as follows:

'1. If the examination of a petition has not been completed in accordance with Article 28 (paragraph 2), 29 or 30, the Commission shall draw up a

Report on the facts and state its opinion as to whether the facts found disclose a breach by the State concerned of its obligations under the Convention. The individual opinions of members of the Commission on this point may be stated in the Report.'

*Article* 8

Article 34 of the Convention shall read as follows:

'Subject to the provisions of Articles 20 (paragraph 3) and 29, the Commission shall take its decisions by a majority of the members present and voting.'

*Article* 9

Article 40 of the Convention shall be supplemented by the following seventh paragraph:

'7. The members of the Court shall sit on the Court in their individual capacity. During their term of office they shall not hold any position which is incompatible with their independence and impartiality as members of the Court or the demands of this office.'

*Article* 10

Article 41 of the Convention shall read as follows:

'The Court shall elect its President and one or two Vice-Presidents for a period of three years. They may be re-elected.'

*Article* 11

In the first sentence of Article 43 of the Convention, the word 'seven' shall be replaced by the word 'nine'.

*Article* 12

1. This Protocol shall be open for signature by member States of the Council of Europe signatories to the Convention, which may express their consent to be bound by:

(*a*) signature without reservation as to ratification, acceptance or approval, or
(*b*) signature subject to ratification, acceptance or approval, followed by ratification, acceptance or approval.

2. Instruments of ratification, acceptance or approval shall be deposited with the Secretary General of the Council of Europe.

*Article* 13

This Protocol shall enter into force on the first day of the month following the expiration of a period of three months after the date on which all Parties to the Convention have expressed their consent to be bound by the Protocol in accordance with the provisions of Article 12.

*Article* 14

The Secretary General of the Council of Europe shall notify the member States of the Council of:

(*a*) any signature:
(*b*) the deposit of any instrument of ratification, acceptance or approval;
(*c*) the date of entry into force of this Protocol in accordance with Article 13;
(*d*) any other act, notification or communication relating to this Protocol.

In witness whereof the undersigned, being duly authorised thereto, have signed this Protocol.

Done at Vienna, this 19th day of March 1985, in English and French, both texts being equally authentic, in a single copy which shall be deposited in the archives of the Council of Europe. The Secretary General of the Council of Europe shall transmit certified copies to each member State of the Council of Europe.

### 9. *Concerning access to the Court by Individuals*

The member States of the Council of Europe, signatories to this Protocol to the Convention for the Protection of Human Rights and Fundamental Freedoms, signed at Rome on 4 November 1950 (hereinafter referred to as 'the Convention'),

Being resolved to make further improvements to the procedure under the Convention,

Have agreed as follows:

*Article* 1

For Parties to the Convention which are bound by this Protocol, the Convention shall be amended as provided in Articles 2 to 5.

*Article* 2

Article 31, paragraph 2, of the Convention, shall read as follows:

'2. The Report shall be transmitted to the Committee of Ministers. The Report shall also be transmitted to the States concerned, and, if it deals with a petition submitted under Article 25, the applicant. The States concerned and the applicant shall not be at liberty to publish it.'

*Article* 3

Article 44 of the Convention shall read as follows:

'Only the High Contracting Parties, the Commission, and persons, non-governmental organisations or groups of individuals having submitted a petition under Article 25 shall have the right to bring a case before the Court.'

*Article* 4

Article 45 of the Convention shall read as follows:

'The jurisdiction of the Court shall extend to all cases concerning the interpretation and application of the present Convention which are referred to it in accordance with Article 48.'

*Article* 5

Article 48 of the Convention shall read as follows:

'1. The following may refer a case to the Court, provided that the High Contracting Party concerned, if there is only one, or the High Contracting Parties concerned, if there is more than one, are subject to the compulsory jurisdiction of the Court or, failing that, with the consent of the High Contracting Party concerned, if there is only one, or of the High Contracting Parties concerned if there is more than one:

    (*a*) the Commission;
    (*b*) a High Contracting Party whose national is alleged to be a victim;
    (*c*) a High Contracting Party which referred the case to the Commission;
    (*d*) a High Contracting Party against which the complaint has been lodged;
    (*e*) the person, non-governmental organisation or group of individuals having lodged the complaint with the Commission.'

2. If a case is referred to the Court only in accordance with paragraph 1.*e*, it shall first be submitted to a panel composed of three members of the Court. There shall sit as an *ex-officio* member of the panel the judge who is elected in respect of the High Contracting Party against which the complaint has been lodged, or, it there is none, a person of its choice who shall sit in the capacity of judge. If the complaint has been lodged against more than one High Contracting Party, the size of the panel shall be increased accordingly.

If the case does not raise a serious question affecting the interpretation or application of the Convention and does not for any other reason warrant consideration by the Court, the panel may, by a unanimous vote, decide that it shall not be considered by the Court. In that event, the Committee of Ministers shall decide, in accordance with the provisions of Article 32, whether there has been a violation of the Convention.'

*Article* 6

1. This Protocol shall be open for signature by member States of the Council of Europe signatories to the Convention, which may express their consent to be bound by:

(*a*) signature without reservation as to ratification, acceptance or approval; or

(*b*) signature subject to ratification, acceptance or approval, followed by ratification, acceptance or approval.

2. The instruments of ratification, acceptance or approval shall be deposited with the Secretary General of the Council of Europe.

*Article* 7

1. This Protocol shall enter into force on the first day of the month following the expiration of a period of three months after the date on which ten member States of the Council of Europe have expressed their consent to be bound by the Protocol in accordance with the provisions of Article 6.

2. In respect of any member State which subsequently expresses its consent to be bound by it, the Protocol shall enter into force on the first day of the month following the expiration of a period of three months after the date of signature or of the deposit of the instrument of ratification, acceptance or approval.

*Article* 8

The Secretary General of the Council of Europe shall notify all the member States of the Council of Europe of:

(*a*) any signature;

(*b*) the deposit of any instrument of ratification, acceptance or approval;

(*c*) any date of entry into force of this Protocol in accordance with Article 7;

(*d*) any other act, notification or declaration relating to this Protocol.

In witness whereof the undersigned, being duly authorised thereto, have signed this Protocol.

Done at Rome, this 6th day of November 1990, in English and French, both texts being equally authentic, in a single copy which shall be deposited in the archives of the Council of Europe. The Secretary General of the Council of Europe shall transmit certified copies to each member State of the Council of Europe.

### 10. *Concerning Various Matters (Provisional text)*

The member States of the Council of Europe, signatories to this Protocol to the Convention for the Protection of Human Rights and Fundamental

Freedoms, signed at Rome on 4 November 1950 (hereinafter referred to as 'the Convention'),

Considering that it is advisable to amend Article 32 of the Convention with a view to the reduction of the two-thirds majority provided therein,

Have agreed as follows:

*Article* 1

The words 'of two-thirds' shall be deleted from paragraph 1 of Article 32 of the Convention.

*Article* 2

1. This Protocol shall be open for signature by member States of the Council of Europe signatories to the Convention, which may express their consent to be bound by:

> (*a*) signature without reservation as to ratification, acceptance or approval, or
>
> (*b*) signature subject to ratification, acceptance or approval, followed by ratification, acceptance or approval.

2. Instruments of ratification, acceptance or approval shall be deposited with the Secretary General of the Council of Europe.

*Article* 3

This Protocol shall enter into force on the first day of the month following the expiration of a period of three months after the date on which all Parties to the Convention have expressed their consent to be bound by the Protocol in accordance with the provisions of Article 2.

*Article* 4

The Secretary General of the Council of Europe shall notify the member States of the Council of:

> (*a*) any signature;
>
> (*b*) the deposit of any instrument of ratification, acceptance or approval;
>
> (*c*) the date of entry into force of this Protocol in accordance with Article 3;
>
> (*b*) any other act, notification or communication relating to this Protocol.

In witness whereof the undersigned, being duly authorised thereto, have signed this Protocol.

Done at ... this ... day of ..., in English and French, both texts being equally authentic, in a single copy which shall be deposited in the archives of the Council of Europe. The Secretary General of the Council of Europe shall transmit certified copies to each member State of the Council of Europe.

## II. EUROPEAN SOCIAL CHARTER, 1961

This was intended to be complementary to the European Convention on Human Rights. The Charter is concerned to develop and protect social and economic rights, whilst the Convention is concerned with political and civil rights: but this division is by no means exact.

The Charter was signed at Turin on 18 October 1961, and came into force on 26 February 1965: see *Treaty Series*, No. 38 (1965), Cmnd. 2643 (English and French texts, declarations made on ratification). See, further, the European Code of Social Security signed at Strasbourg on 16 April 1964, in force in 1968: *Treaty Series*, No. 10 (1969), Cmnd. 3871 (does not include the Protocol); *European Treaty Series*, No. 48; *European Yearbook*, vol. xii, p. 397.

For extended commentary see Harris, *The European Social Charter*, Charlottesville, 1984; and Robertson and Harris, *Human Rights in the World*, 3rd ed., 1989, pp. 245–55. Twenty states have ratified the Charter.

## TEXT

*The Governments signatory hereto, being Members of the Council of Europe,*

*Considering* that the aim of the Council of Europe is the achievement of greater unity between its Members for the purpose of safeguarding and realizing the ideals and principles which are their common heritage and of facilitating their economic and social progress, in particular by the maintenance and further realization of human rights and fundamental freedoms;

*Considering* that in the European Convention for the Protection of Human Rights and Fundamental Freedoms signed at Rome on 4th November 1950, and the Protocol thereto signed at Paris on 20th March 1952, the member States of the Council of Europe agreed to secure to their populations the civil and political rights and freedoms therein specified;

*Considering* that the enjoyment of social rights should be secured without discrimination on grounds of race, colour, sex, religion, political opinion, national extraction or social origin;

*Being resolved* to make every effort in common to improve the standard of living and to promote the social well-being of both their urban and rural populations by means of appropriate institutions and action,

*Have agreed as follows*:

## PART I

The Contracting Parties accept as the aim of their policy, to be pursued by all appropriate means, both national and international in character, the attainment of conditions in which the following rights and principles may be effectively realized:

(1) Everyone shall have the opportunity to earn his living in an occupation freely entered upon.

(2) All workers have the right to just conditions of work.

(3) All workers have the right to safe and healthy working conditions.

(4) All workers have the right to a fair remuneration sufficient for a decent standard of living for themselves and their families.

(5) All workers and employers have the right to freedom of association in national or international organizations for the protection of their economic and social interests.

(6) All workers and employers have the right to bargain collectively.

(7) Children and young persons have the right to a special protection against the physical and moral hazards to which they are exposed.

(8) Employed women, in case of maternity, and other employed women as appropriate, have the right to a special protection in their work.

(9) Everyone has the right to appropriate facilities for vocational guidance with a view to helping him choose an occupation suited to his personal aptitude and interests.

(10) Everyone has the right to appropriate facilities for vocational training.

(11) Everyone has the right to benefit from any measures enabling him to enjoy the highest possible standard of health attainable.

(12) All workers and their dependents have the right to social security.

(13) Anyone without adequate resources has the right to social and medical assistance.

(14) Everyone has the right to benefit from social welfare services.

(15) Disabled persons have the right to vocational training, rehabilitation and resettlement, whatever the origin and nature of their disability.

(16) The family as a fundamental unit of society has the right to appropriate social, legal and economic protection to ensure its full development.

(17) Mothers and children, irrespective of marital status and family relations, have the right to appropriate social and economic protection.

(18) The nationals of any one of the Contracting Parties have the right to engage in any gainful occupation in the territory of any one of the others on a footing of equality with the nationals of the latter, subject to restrictions based on cogent economic or social reasons.

(19) Migrant workers who are nationals of a Contracting Party and their families have the right to protection and assistance in the territory of any other Contracting Party.

# PART II

The Contracting Parties undertake, as provided for in Part III, to consider themselves bound by the obligations laid down in the following articles and paragraphs.

### The Right to Work

*Article* 1

With a view to ensuring the effective exercise of the right to work, the Contracting Parties undertake:

(1) to accept as one of their primary aims and responsibilities the achievement and maintenance of as high and stable a level of employment as possible, with a view to the attainment of full employment;
(2) to protect effectively the right of the worker to earn his living in an occupation freely entered upon;
(3) to establish or maintain free employment services for all workers;
(4) to provide or promote appropriate vocational guidance, training and rehabilitation.

### The Right to Just Conditions of Work

*Article* 2

With a view to ensuring the effective exercise of the right to just conditions of work, the Contracting Parties undertake:

(1) to provide for reasonable daily and weekly working hours, the working week to be progressively reduced to the extent that the increase of productivity and other relevant factors permit;
(2) to provide for public holidays with pay;
(3) to provide for a minimum of two weeks annual holiday with pay;
(4) to provide for additional paid holidays or reduced working hours for workers engaged in dangerous or unhealthy occupations as prescribed;
(5) to ensure a weekly rest period which shall, as far as possible, coincide with the day recognized by tradition or custom in the country or region concerned as a day of rest.

### The Right to Safe and Healthy Working Conditions

*Article* 3

With a view to ensuring the effective exercise of the right to safe and healthy working conditions, the Contracting Parties undertake:

(1) to issue safety and health regulations;
(2) to provide for the enforcement of such regulations by measures of supervision;
(3) to consult, as appropriate, employers' and workers' organizations on measures intended to improve industrial safety and health.

### The Right to a Fair Remuneration

*Article* 4

With a view to ensuring the effective exercise of the right to a fair remuneration, the Contracting Parties undertake:

(1) to recognize the right of workers to a remuneration such as will give them and their families a decent standard of living;
(2) to recognize the right of workers to an increased rate of remuneration for overtime work subject to exceptions in particular cases;
(3) to recognize the right of men and women workers to equal pay for work of equal value;
(4) to recognize the right of all workers to a reasonable period of notice for termination of employment;
(5) to permit deductions from wages only under conditions and to the extent prescribed by national laws or regulations or fixed by collective agreements or arbitration awards.

The exercise of these rights shall be achieved by freely concluded collective agreements, by statutory wage-fixing machinery, or by other means appropriate to national conditions.

### The Right to Organize

*Article* 5

With a view to ensuring or promoting the freedom of workers and employers to form local, national or international organizations for the protection of their economic and social interests and to join those organizations, the Contracting Parties undertake that national law shall not be such as to impair, nor shall it be so applied as to impair, this freedom. The extent to which the guarantees provided for in this article shall apply to the police shall be determined by national laws or regulations. The principle governing the application to the members of the armed forces of these guarantees and the extent to which they shall apply to persons in this category shall equally be determined by national laws or regulations.

## The Right to Bargain Collectively

*Article* 6

With a view to ensuring the effective exercise of the right to bargain collectively, the Contracting Parties undertake:

(1) to promote joint consultation between workers and employers;
(2) to promote, where necessary and appropriate, machinery for voluntary negotiations between employers or employers' organizations and worker's organizations, with a view to the regulation of terms and conditions of employment by means of collective agreements;
(3) to promote the establishment and use of appropriate machinery for conciliation and voluntary arbitration for the settlement of labour disputes;

and recognize:

(4) the right to workers and employers to collective action in cases of conflicts of interest, including the right to strike, subject to obligations that might arise out of collective agreements previously entered into.

## The Right of Children and Young Persons to Protection

*Article* 7

With a view to ensuring the effective exercise of the right of children and young persons to protection, the Contracting Parties undertake:

(1) to provide that the minimum age of admission to employment shall be 15 years, subject to exceptions for children employed in prescribed light work without harm to their health, morals or education;
(2) to provide that a higher minimum age of admission to employment shall be fixed with respect to prescribed occupations regarded as dangerous or unhealthy;
(3) to provide that persons who are still subject to compulsory education shall not be employed in such work as would deprive them of the full benefit of their education;
(4) to provide that the working hours of persons under 16 years of age shall be limited in accordance with the needs of their development, and particularly with their need for vocational training;
(5) to recognize the right of young workers and apprentices to a fair wage or other appropriate allowances;
(6) to provide that the time spent by young persons in vocational training during the normal working hours with the consent of the employer shall be treated as forming part of the working day;

(7) to provide that employed persons of under 18 years of age shall be entitled to not less than three weeks' annual holiday with pay;

(8) to provide that persons under 18 years of age shall not be employed in night work with the exception of certain occupations provided for by national laws or regulations;

(9) to provide that persons under 18 years of age employed in occupations prescribed by national laws or regulations shall be subject to regular medical control;

(10) to ensure special protection against physical and moral dangers to which children and young persons are exposed, and particularly against those resulting directly or indirectly from their work.

### The Right of Employed Women to Protection

*Article* 8

With a view to ensuring the effective exercise of the right of employed women to protection, the Contracting Parties undertake:

(1) to provide either by paid leave, by adequate social security benefits or by benefits from public funds for women to take leave before and after childbirth up to a total of at least 12 weeks;

(2) to consider it as unlawful for an employer to give a woman notice of dismissal during her absence on maternity leave or to give her notice of dismissal at such a time that the notice would expire during such absence;

(3) to provide that mothers who are nursing their infants shall be entitled to sufficient time off for this purpose;

(4) (*a*) to regulate the employment of women workers on night work in industrial employment;

(*b*) to prohibit the employment of women workers in underground mining, and, as appropriate, on all other work which is unsuitable for them by reason of its dangerous, unhealthy, or arduous nature.

### The Right to Vocational Guidance

*Article* 9

With a view to ensuring the effective exercise of the right to vocational guidance, the Contracting Parties undertake to provide or promote, as necessary, a service which will assist all persons, including the handicapped, to solve problems related to occupational choice and progress, with due regard to the individual's characteristics and their relation to occupational opportunity: this assistance should be available free of charge, both to young persons, including school children, and to adults.

### The Right to Vocational Training

*Article* 10

With a view to ensuring the effective exercise of the right to vocational training, the Contracting Parties undertake:

(1) to provide or promote, as necessary, the technical and vocational training of all persons, including the handicapped, in consultation with employers' and workers' organizations, and to grant facilities for access to higher technical and university education, based solely on individual aptitude;

(2) to provide or promote a system of apprenticeship and other systematic arrangements for training young boys and girls in their various employments;

(3) to provide or promote, as necessary:
    (*a*) adequate and readily available training facilities for adult workers;
    (*b*) special facilities for the re-training of adult workers needed as a result of technological development or new trends in employment;

(4) to encourage the full utilization of the facilities provided by appropriate measures such as:
    (*a*) reducing or abolishing any fees or charges;
    (*b*) granting financial assistance in appropriate cases;
    (*c*) including in the normal working hours time spent on supplementary training taken by the worker, at the request of his employer, during employment;
    (*d*) ensuring, through adequate supervision, in consultation with the employers' and workers' organizations, the efficiency of apprenticeship and other training arrangements for young workers, and the adequate protection of young workers generally.

### The Right to Protection of Health

*Article* 11

With a view to ensuring the effective exercise of the right to protection of health, the Contracting Parties undertake, either directly or in co-operation with public or private organizations, to take appropriate measures designed *inter alia*:

(1) to remove as far as possible the causes of ill-health;

(2) to provide advisory and educational facilities for the promotion of health and the encouragement of individual responsibility in matters of health;

(3) to prevent as far as possible epidemic, endemic and other diseases.

*The Right to Social Security*

*Article* 12

With a view to ensuring the effective exercise of the right to social security, the Contracting Parties undertake:

(1) to establish or maintain a system of social security;

(2) to maintain the social security system at a satisfactory level at least equal to that required for ratification of International Labour Convention (No. 102) Concerning Minimum Standards of Social Security;

(3) to endeavour to raise progressively the system of social security to a higher level;

(4) to take steps, by the conclusion of appropriate bilateral and multilateral agreements, or by other means, and subject to the conditions laid down in such agreements, in order to ensure:

(*a*) equal treatment with their own nationals of the nationals of other Contracting Parties in respect of social security rights, including the retention of benefits arising out of social security legislation, whatever movements the persons protected may undertake between the territories of the Contracting Parties.

(*b*) the granting, maintenance and resumption of social security rights by such means as the accumulation of insurance or employment periods completed under the legislation of each of the Contracting Parties.

*The Right to Social and Medical Assistance*

*Article* 13

With a view to ensuring the effective exercise of the right to social and medical assistance, the Contracting Parties undertake:

(1) to ensure that any person who is without adequate resources and who is unable to secure such resources either by his own efforts or from other sources, in particular by benefits under a social security scheme, be granted adequate assistance, and, in case of sickness, the care necessitated by his condition;

(2) to ensure that persons receiving such assistance shall not, for that reason, suffer from a diminution of their political or social rights;

(3) to provide that everyone may receive by appropriate public or private services such advice and personal help as may be required to prevent, to remove, or to alleviate personal or family want;

(4) to apply the provisions referred to in paragraphs 1, 2 and 3 of this article on an equal footing with their nationals to nationals of other Contracting Parties lawfully within their territories, in accordance

with their obligations under the European Convention on Social and Medical Assistance, signed at Paris on 11th December 1953.[1]

### The Right to Benefit from Social Welfare Services

*Article* 14

With a view to ensuring the effective exercise of the right to benefit from social welfare services, the Contracting Parties undertake:

(1) to promote or provide services which, by using methods of social work, would contribute to the welfare and development of both individuals and groups in the community, and to their adjustment to the social environment;

(2) to encourage the participation of individuals and voluntary or other organizations in the establishment and maintenance of such services.

### The Right of Physically or Mentally Disabled Persons to Vocational Training, Rehabilitation and Social Resettlement

*Article* 15

With a view to ensuring the effective exercise of the right of the physically or mentally disabled to vocational training, rehabilitation and resettlement, the Contracting Parties undertake:

(1) to take adequate measures for the provision of training facilities, including, where necessary, specialized institutions, public or private;

(2) to take adequate measures for the placing of disabled persons in employment, such as specialized placing services, facilities for sheltered employment and measures to encourage employers to admit disabled persons to employment.

### The Right of the Family to Social, Legal and Economic Protection

*Article* 16

With a view to ensuring the necessary conditions for the full development of the family, which is a fundamental unit of society, the Contracting Parties undertake to promote the economic, legal and social protection of family life by such means as social and family benefits, fiscal arrangements, provision of family housing, benefits for the newly married, and other appropriate means.

---

[1] 'Treaty Series No. 42 (1955)', Cmnd. 9512.

*The Right of Mothers and Children to Social and Economic Protection*

*Article* 17

With a view to ensuring the effective exercise of the right of mothers and children to social and economic protection, the Contracting Parties will take all appropriate and necessary measures to that end, including the establishment or maintenance of appropriate institutions or services.

*The Right to Engage in a Gainful Occupation in the Territory of Other Contracting Parties*

*Article* 18

With a view to ensuring the effective exercise of the right to engage in a gainful occupation in the territory of any other Contracting Party, the Contracting Parties undertake:

(1) to apply existing regulations in a spirit of liberality;

(2) to simplify existing formalities and to reduce or abolish chancery dues and other charges payable by foreign workers or their employers;

(3) to liberalize, individually or collectively, regulations governing the employment of foreign workers;

and recognize:

(4) the right of their nationals to leave the country to engage in a gainful occupation in the territories of the other Contracting Parties.

*The Right of Migrant Workers and their Families to Protection and Assistance*

*Article* 19

With a view to ensuring the effective exercise of the right of migrant workers and their families to protection and assistance in the territory of any other Contracting Party, the Contracting Parties undertake:

(1) to maintain or to satisfy themselves that there are maintained adequate and free services to assist such workers, particularly in obtaining accurate infomation, and to take all appropriate steps, so far as national laws and regulations permit, against misleading propaganda relating to emigration and immigration;

(2) to adopt appropriate measures within their own jurisdiction to facilitate the departure, journey and reception of such workers and their families, and to provide, within their own jurisdiction, appropriate services for health, medical attention and good hygienic conditions during the journey;

(3) to promote co-operation, as appropriate, between social services, public and private, in emigration and immigration countries;

(4) to secure for such workers lawfully within their territories, in so far as such matters are regulated by law or regulations or are subject to the control of administrative authorities, treatment not less favourable than that of their own nationals in respect of the following matters:

(*a*) remuneration and other employment and working conditions;

(*b*) membership of trade unions and enjoyment of the benefits of collective bargaining;

(*c*) accommodation;

(5) to secure for such workers lawfully within their territories treatment not less favourable than that of their own nationals with regard to employment taxes, dues or contributions payable in respect of employed persons;

(6) to facilitate as far as possible the reunion of the family of a foreign worker permitted to establish himself in the territory;

(7) to secure for such workers lawfully within their territories treatment not less favourable than that of their own nationals in respect of legal proceedings relating to matters referred to in this article;

(8) to secure that such workers lawfully residing within their territories are not expelled unless they endanger national security or offend against public interest or morality;

(9) to permit, within legal limits, the transfer of such parts of the earnings and savings of such workers as they may desire;

(10) to extend the protection and assistance provided for in this article to self-employed migrants in so far as such measures apply.


# PART III

## *Undertakings*

*Article* 20

1. Each of the Contracting Parties undertakes:

(*a*) to consider Part I of this Charter as a declaration of the aims which it will pursue by all appropriate means, as stated in the introductory paragraph of that Part;

(*b*) to consider itself bound by at least five of the following articles of Part II of this Charter: Articles 1, 5, 6, 12, 13, 16 and 19;

(*c*) in addition to the articles selected by it in accordance with the preceeding sub-paragraphs, to consider itself bound by such a number of articles or numbered paragraphs of Part II of the

Charter as it may select, provided that the total number of articles or numbered paragraphs by which it is bound is not less than 10 articles or 45 numbered paragraphs.

2. The articles or paragraphs selected in accordance with sub-paragraphs (*b*) and (*c*) of paragraph 1 of this Article shall be notified to the Secretary-General of the Council of Europe at the time when the instrument of ratification or approval of the Contracting Party concerned is deposited.

3. Any Contracting Party may, at a later date, declare by notification to the Secretary-General that it considers itself bound by any Articles or any numbered paragraphs of Part II of the Charter which it has not already accepted under the terms of paragraph 1 of this Article. Such undertakings subsequently given shall be deemed to be an integral part of the ratification or approval, and shall have the same effect as from the thirtieth day after the date of the notification.

4. The Secretary-General shall communicate to all the signatory Governments and to the Director-General of the International Labour Office any notification which he shall have received pursuant to this Part of the Charter.

5. Each Contracting Party shall maintain a system of labour inspection appropriate to national conditions.


## PART IV

### Reports concerning Accepted Provisions

*Article* 21

The Contracting Parties shall send to the Secretary-General of the Council of Europe a report at two-yearly intervals, in a form to be determined by the Committee of Ministers, concerning the application of such provisions of Part II of the Charter as they have accepted.


### Reports concerning Provisions which are not accepted

*Article* 22

The Contracting Parties shall send to the Secretary-General, at appropriate intervals as requested by the Committee of Ministers, reports relating to the provisions of Part II of the Charter which they did not accept at the time of their ratification or approval or in a subsequent notification. The Committee of Ministers shall determine from time to time in respect of which provisions such reports shall be requested and the form of the reports to be provided.

## Communication of Copies

*Article* 23

1. Each Contracting Party shall communicate copies of its reports referred to in Articles 21 and 22 to such of its national organizations as are members of the international organizations of employers and trade unions to be invited under Article 27, paragraph 2, to be represented at meetings of the Sub-committee of the Governmental Social Committee.

2. The Contracting Parties shall forward to the Secretary-General any comments on the said reports received from these national organizations, if so requested by them.

## Examination of the Reports

*Article* 24

The reports sent to the Secretary-General in accordance with Articles 21 and 22 shall be examined by a Committee of Experts, who shall have also before them any comments forwarded to the Secretary-General in accordance with paragraph 2 of Article 23.

## Committee of Experts

*Article* 25

1. The Committee of Experts shall consist of not more than seven members appointed by the Committee of Ministers from a list of independent experts of the highest integrity and of recognized competence in international social questions, nominated by the Contracting Parties.

2. The members of the Committee shall be appointed for a period for six years. They may be reappointed. However, of the members first appointed, the terms of office of two members shall expire at the end of four years.

3. The members whose terms of office are to expire at the end of the initial period of four years shall be chosen by lot by the Committee of Ministers immediately after the first appointment has been made.

4. A member of the Committee of Experts appointed to replace a member whose term of office has not expired shall hold office for the remainder of his predecessor's term.

## Participation of the International Labour Organization

*Article* 26

The International Labour Organization shall be invited to nominate a representative to participate in a consultative capacity in the deliberations of the Committee of Experts.

*Sub-Committee of the Governmental Social Committee*

*Article* 27

1. The reports of the Contracting Parties and the conclusions of the Committee of Experts shall be submitted for examination to a Sub-committee of the Governmental Social Committee of the Council of Europe.

2. The Sub-committee shall be composed of one representative of each of the Contracting Parties. It shall invite no more than two international organizations of employers and no more than two international trade union organizations as it may designate to be represented as observers in a consultative capacity at its meetings. Moreover, it may consult no more than two representatives of international non-governmental organizations having consultative status with the Council of Europe, in respect of questions with which the organizations are particularly qualified to deal, such as social welfare, and the economic and social protection of the family.

3. The Sub-committee shall present to the Committee of Ministers a report containing its conclusions and append the report of the Committee of Experts.

*Consultative Assembly*

*Article* 28

The Secretary-General of the Council of Europe shall transmit to the Consultative Assembly the conclusions of the Committee of Experts. The Consultative Assembly shall communicate its views on these Conclusions to the Committee of Ministers.

*Committee of Ministers*

*Article* 29

By a majority of two-thirds of the members entitled to sit on the Committee, the Committee of Ministers may, on the basis of the report of the Sub-committee, and after consultation with the Consultative Assembly, make to each Contracting Party any necessary recommendations.


# PART V

*Derogations in time of War or Public Emergency*

*Article* 30

1. In time of war or other public emergency threatening the life of the nation any Contracting Party may take measures derogating from its obli-

gations under this Charter to the extent strictly required by the exigencies of the situation, provided that such measures are not inconsistent with its other obligations under international law.

2. Any Contracting Party which has availed itself of this right of derogation shall, within a reasonable lapse of time, keep the Secretary-General of the Council of Europe fully informed of the measures taken and of the reasons therefor. It shall likewise inform the Secretary-General when such measures have ceased to operate and the provisions of the Charter which it has accepted are again being fully executed.

3. The Secretary-General shall in turn inform other Contracting Parties and the Director-General of the International Labour Office of all communications received in accordance with paragraph 2 of this Article.

## Restrictions

*Article* 31

1. The rights and principles set forth in Part I when effectively realized, and their effective exercise as provided for in Part II, shall not be subject to any restrictions or limitations not specified in those Parts, except such as are prescribed by law and are necessary in a democratic society for the protection of the rights and freedoms of others or for the protection of public interest, national security, public health, or morals.

2. The restrictions permitted under this Charter to the rights and obligations set forth herein shall not be applied for any purpose other than that for which they have been prescribed.

## Relations between the Charter and Domestic Law or International Agreements

*Article* 32

The provisions of this Charter shall not prejudice the provisions of domestic law or of any bilateral or multilateral treaties, conventions or agreements which are already in force, or may come into force, under which more favourable treatment would be accorded to the persons protected.

## Implementation by Collective Agreements

*Article* 33

1. In member States where the provisions of paragraphs 1, 2, 3, 4 and 5 of Article 2, paragraphs 4, 6 and 7 of Article 7 and paragraphs 1, 2, 3, and 4 of Article 10 of Part II of this Charter are matters normally left to agreements between employers or employers' organizations and workers' organizations, or are normally carried out otherwise than by law, the

undertakings of those paragraphs may be given and compliance with them shall be treated as effective if their provisions are applied through such agreements or other means to the great majority of the workers concerned.

2. In member States where these provisions are normally the subject of legislation, the undertakings concerned may likewise be given, and compliance with them shall be regarded as effective if the provisions are applied by law to the great majority of the workers concerned.

### *Territorial Application*

*Article 34*

1. This Charter shall apply to the metropolitan territory of each Contracting Party. Each signatory Government may, at the time of signature or of the deposit of its instrument of ratification or approval, specify, by declaration addressed to the Secretary-General of the Council of Europe, the territory which shall be considered to be its metropolitan territory for this purpose.

2. Any Contracting Party may, at the time of ratification or approval of this Charter or at any time thereafter, declare by notification addressed to the Secretary-General of the Council of Europe, that the Charter shall extend in whole or in part to a non-metropolitan territory or territories specified in the said declaration for whose international relations it is responsible or for which it assumes international responsibility. It shall specify in the declaration the Articles or paragraphs of Part II of the Charter which it accepts as binding in respect of the territories named in the declaration.

3. The Charter shall extend to the territory or territories named in the aforesaid declarations as from the thirtieth day after the date on which the Secretary-General shall have received notification of such declaration.

4. Any Contracting Party may declare at a later date by notification addressed to the Secretary-General of the Council of Europe, that, in respect of one or more of the territories to which the Charter has been extended in accordance with paragraph 2 of this Article, it accepts as binding any Articles or any numbered paragraphs which it has not already accepted in respect of that territory or territories. Such undertakings subsequently given shall be deemed to be an integral part of the original declaration in respect of the territory concerned, and shall have the same effect as from the thirtieth day after the date of the notification.

5. The Secretary-General shall communicate to the other signatory Governments and to the Director-General of the International Labour Office any notification transmitted to him in accordance with this Article.

*Signature, Ratification and Entry into Force*

*Article* 35

1. This Charter shall be open for signature by the Members of the Council of Europe. It shall be ratified or approved. Instruments of ratification or approval shall be deposited with the Secretary-General of the Council of Europe.

2. This Charter shall come into force as from the thirtieth day after the date of deposit of the fifth instrument of ratification or approval.

3. In respect of any signatory Government ratifying subsequently, the Charter shall come into force as from the thirtieth day after the date of deposit of its instrument of ratification or approval.

4. The Secretary-General shall notify all the Members of the Council of Europe and the Director-General of the International Labour Office, of the entry into force of the Charter, the names of the Contracting Parties which have ratified or approved it and the subsequent deposit of any instruments of ratification or approval.

*Amendments*

*Article* 36

Any Member of the Council of Europe may propose amendments to this Charter in a communication addressed to the Secretary-General of the Council of Europe. The Secretary-General shall transmit to the other Members of the Council of Europe any amendments so proposed, which shall then be considered by the Committee of Ministers and submitted to the Consultative Assembly for opinion. Any amendments approved by the Committee of Ministers shall enter into force as from the thirtieth day after all the Contracting Parties have informed the Secretary-General of their acceptance. The Secretary-General shall notify all the Members of the Council of Europe and the Director-General of the International Labour Office of the entry into force of such amendments.

*Denunciation*

*Article* 37

1. Any Contracting Party may denounce this Charter only at the end of a period of five years from the date on which the Charter entered into force for it, or at the end of any successive period of two years, and, in each case, after giving six months notice to the Secretary-General of the Council of Europe, who shall inform the other Parties and the Director-General of the International Labour Office accordingly. Such denunciation shall not affect

the validity of the Charter in respect of the other Contracting Parties provided that at all times there are not less than five such Contracting Parties.

2. Any Contracting Party may, in accordance with the provisions set out in the preceding paragraph, denounce any Article or paragraph of Part II of the Charter accepted by it provided that the number of Articles or paragraphs by which this Contracting Party is bound shall never be less than 10 in the former case and 45 in the latter and that this number of Articles or paragraphs shall continue to include the Articles selected by the Contracting Party among those to which special reference is made in Article 20, paragraph 1, sub-paragraph (*b*).

3. Any Contracting Party may denounce the present Charter or any of the Articles or paragraphs of Part II of the Charter, under the conditions specified in paragraph 1 of this Article in respect of any territory to which the said Charter is applicable by virtue of a declaration made in accordance with paragraph 2 of Article 34.

*Appendix*

*Article* 38

The Appendix to this Charter shall form an integral part of it.

In witness whereof, the undersigned, being duly authorized thereto, have signed this Charter.

Done at Turin, this 18th day of October 1961, in English and French, both texts being equally authoritative, in a single copy which shall be deposited within the archives of the Council of Europe. The Secretary-General shall transmit certified copies to each of the Signatories.


## APPENDIX TO THE SOCIAL CHARTER
Scope of the Social Charter in Terms of Persons Protected:


1. Without prejudice to Article 12, paragraph 4 and Article 13, paragraph 4, the persons covered by Articles 1 to 17 include foreigners only in so far as they are nationals of other Contracting Parties lawfully resident or working regularly within the territory of the Contracting Party concerned, subject to the understanding that these articles are to be interpreted in the light of the provisions of Articles 18 and 19.

This interpretation would not prejudice the extension of similar facilities to other persons by any of the Contracting Parties.

2. Each Contracting Party will grant to refugees as defined in the Convention relating to the Status of Refugees, signed at Geneva on 28th July,

1951,[1] and lawfully staying in its territory, treatment as favourable as possible, and in any case not less favourable than under the obligations accepted by the Contracting Party under the said Convention and under any other existing international instruments applicable to those refugees.

<table>
<tr><td align="center">PART I</td><td></td><td align="center">PART II</td></tr>
<tr><td align="center">Paragraph 18</td><td align="center">and</td><td align="center">Article 18, paragraph 1</td></tr>
</table>

It is understood that these provisions are not concerned with the question of entry into the territories of the Contracting Parties and do not prejudice the provisions of the European Convention on Establishment, signed at Paris on 13th December, 1955.[2]

## PART II

*Article 1, paragraph 2*

This provision shall not be interpreted as prohibiting or authorizing any union security clause or practice.

*Article 4, paragraph 4*

This provision shall be so understood as not to prohibit immediate dismissal for any serious offence.

*Article 4, paragraph 5*

It is understood that a Contracting Party may give the undertaking required in this paragraph if the great majority of workers are not permitted to suffer deductions from wages either by law or through collective agreements or arbitration awards, the exceptions being those persons not so covered.

*Article 6, paragraph 4*

It is understood that each Contracting Party may, in so far as it is concerned, regulate the exercise of the right to strike by law, provided that any further restriction that this might place on the right can be justified under the terms of Article 31.

*Article 7, paragraph 8*

It is understood that a Contracting Party may give the undertaking required in this paragraph if it fulfils the spirit of the undertaking by providing by law that the great majority of persons under 18 years of age shall not be employed in night work.

---

[1] Above, p. 50.
[2] 'Miscellaneous No. 1 (1957)', Cmnd. 41.

*Article* 12, *paragraph* 4

The words 'and subject to the conditions laid down in such agreements' in the introduction to this paragraph are taken to imply *inter alia* that with regard to benefits which are available independently of any insurance contribution a Contracting Party may require the completion of a prescribed period of residence before granting such benefits to nationals of other Contracting Parties.

*Article* 13, *paragraph* 4

Governments not Parties to the European Convention on Social and Medical Assistance may ratify the Social Charter in respect of this paragraph provided that they grant to nationals of other Contracting Parties a treatment which is in conformity with the provisions of the said Convention.

*Article* 19, *paragraph* 6

For the purpose of this provision, the term 'family of a foreign worker' is understood to mean at least his wife and dependent children under the age of 21 years.

## *PART III*

It is understood that the Charter contains legal obligations of an international character, the application of which is submitted solely to the supervision provided for in Part IV thereof.

*Article* 20, *paragraph* 1

It is understood that the 'numbered paragraphs' may include articles consisting of only one paragraph.

## *PART V*

*Article* 30

The term 'in time of war or other public emergency' shall be so understood as to cover also the *threat* of war.

# III. THE EUROPEAN CONVENTION FOR THE PREVENTION OF TORTURE AND INHUMAN OR DEGRADING TREATMENT OR PUNISHMENT, 1987

The Convention entered into force on 1 February 1989. Fifteen States have become Parties to the Convention.

The Convention originated in the Legal Affairs Committee of the Council of Europe and parallels the Convention on the same subject adopted by the General Assembly of the United Nations in 1984 (see above, p. 38). However, the regional Convention has a distinctive feature, the constitution of the European Committee for the Prevention of Torture and Inhuman or Degrading Treatment or Punishment. Each Party to the Convention is obliged to permit visits by the Committee 'to any place within its jurisdiction where persons are deprived of their liberty by a public authority' (Article 2). For an example of a report under Article 10, see the Report to the United Kingdom Government on the Visit to the United Kingdom, doc.CPT/Inf.(91)15. For the Government's response, see doc.CPT/Inf.(91)16.

## TEXT

The member States of the Council of Europe, signatory hereto,

Having regard to the provisions of the Convention for the Protection of Human Rights and Fundamental Freedoms;

Recalling that, under Article 3 of the same Convention, 'no one shall be subjected to torture or to inhuman or degrading treatment or punishment';

Noting that the machinery provided for in that Convention operates in relation to persons who allege that they are victims of violations of Article 3;

Convinced that the protection of persons deprived of their liberty against torture and inhuman or degrading treatment or punishment could be strengthened by non-judicial means of a preventive character based on visits,

Have agreed as follows:

## CHAPTER I

*Article 1*

There shall be established a European Committee for the Prevention of Torture and Inhuman or Degrading Treatment or Punishment (hereinafter referred to as 'the Committee'). The Committee shall, by means of visits, examine the treatment of persons deprived of their liberty with a view to strengthening, if necessary, the protection of such persons from torture and from inhuman or degrading treatment or punishment.

*Article* 2

Each Party shall permit visits, in accordance with this Convention, to any place within its jurisdiction where persons are deprived of their liberty by a public authority.

*Article* 3

In the application of this Convention, the Committee and the competent national authorities of the Party concerned shall co-operate with each other.

## CHAPTER II

*Article* 4

1. The Committee shall consist of a number of members equal to that of the Parties.

2. The members of the Committee shall be chosen from among persons of high moral character, known for their competence in the field of human rights or having professional experience in the areas covered by this Convention.

3. No two members of the Committee may be nationals of the same State.

4. The members shall serve in their individual capacity, shall be independent and impartial, and shall be available to serve the Committee effectively.

*Article* 5

1. The members of the Committee shall be elected by the Committee of Ministers of the Council of Europe by an absolute majority of votes, from a list of names drawn up by the Bureau of the Consultative Assembly of the Council of Europe; each national delegation of the Parties in the Consultative Assembly shall put forward three candidates, of whom two at least shall be its nationals.

2. The same procedure shall be followed in filling casual vacancies.

3. The members of the Committee shall be elected for a period of four years. They may only be re-elected once. However, among the members elected at the first election, the terms of three members shall expire at the end of two years. The members whose terms are to expire at the end of the initial period of two years shall be chosen by lot by the Secretary General of the Council of Europe immediately after the first election has been completed.

*Article* 6

1. The Committee shall meet in camera. A quorum shall be equal to the majority of its members. The decisions of the Committee shall be taken by

a majority of the members present, subject to the provisions of Article 10, paragraph 2.

2. The Committee shall draw up its own rules of procedure.

3. The Secretariat of the Committee shall be provided by the Secretary General of the Council of Europe.

## CHAPTER III

*Article* 7

1. The Committee shall organise visits to places referred to in Article 2. Apart from periodic visits, the Committee may organise such other visits as appear to it to be required in the circumstances.

2. As a general rule, the visits shall be carried out by at least two members of the Committee. The Committee may, if it considers it necessary, be assisted by experts and interpreters.

*Article* 8

1. The Committee shall notify the Government of the Party concerned of its intention to carry out a visit. After such notification, it may at any time visit any place referred to in Article 2.

2. A Party shall provide the Committee with the following facilities to carry out its task:

  (*a*) access to its territory and the right to travel without restriction;
  (*b*) full information on the places where persons deprived of their liberty are being held;
  (*c*) unlimited access to any place where persons are deprived of their liberty, including the right to move inside such places without restriction;
  (*d*) other information available to the Party which is necessary for the Committee to carry out its task. In seeking such information, the Committee shall have regard to applicable rules of national law and professional ethics.

3. The Committee may interview in private persons deprived of their liberty.

4. The Committee may communicate freely with any person whom it believes can supply relevant information.

5. If necessary, the Committee may immediately communicate observations to the competent authorities of the Party concerned.

*Article* 9

1. In exceptional circumstances, the competent authorities of the Party concerned may make representations to the Committee against a visit at the

time or to the particular place proposed by the Committee. Such representations may only be made on grounds of national defence, public safety, serious disorder in places where persons are deprived of their liberty, the medical condition of a person or that an urgent interrogation relating to a serious crime is in progress.

2. Following such representations, the Committee and the Party shall immediately enter into consultations in order to clarify the situation and seek agreement on arrangements to enable the Committee to exercise its functions expeditiously. Such arrangements may include the transfer to another place of any person whom the Committee proposed to visit. Until the visit takes place, the Party shall provide information to the Committee about any person concerned.

*Article* 10

1. After each visit, the Committee shall draw up a report on the facts found during the visit, taking account of any observations which may have been submitted by the Party concerned. It shall transmit to the latter its report containing any recommendations it considers necessary. The Committee may consult with the Party with a view to suggesting, if necessary, improvements in the protection of persons deprived of their liberty.

2. If the Party fails to co-operate or refuses to improve the situation in the light of the Committee's recommendations, the Committee may decide, after the Party has had an opportunity to make known its views, by a majority of two-thirds of its members to make a public statement on the matter.

*Article* 11

1. The information gathered by the Committee in relation to a visit, its report and its consultations with the Party concerned shall be confidential.

2. The Committee shall publish its report, together with any comments of the Party concerned, whenever requested to do so by that Party.

3. However, no personal data shall be published without the express consent of the person concerned.

*Article* 12

Subject to the rules of confidentiality in Article 11, the Committee shall every year submit to the Committee of Ministers a general report on its activities which shall be transmitted to the Consultative Assembly and made public.

*Article* 13

The members of the Committee, experts and other persons assisting the Committee are required, during and after their terms of office, to maintain the confidentiality of the facts or information of which they have become aware during the discharge of their functions.

*Article* 14

1. The names of persons assisting the Committee shall be specified in the notification under Article 8, paragraph 1.

2. Experts shall act on the instructions and under the authority of the Committee. They shall have particular knowledge and experience in the areas covered by this Convention and shall be bound by the same duties of independence, impartiality and availability as the members of the Committee.

3. A Party may exceptionally declare that an expert or other person assisting the Committee may not be allowed to take part in a visit to a place within its jurisdiction.

## CHAPTER IV

*Article* 15

Each Party shall inform the Committee of the name and address of the authority competent to receive notifications to its Government, and of any liaison officer it may appoint.

*Article* 16

The Committee, its members and experts referred to in Article 7, paragraph 2, shall enjoy the privileges and immunities set out in the annex to this Convention.

*Article* 17

1. This Convention shall not prejudice the provisions of domestic law or any international agreement which provide greater protection for persons deprived of their liberty.

2. Nothing in this Convention shall be construed as limiting or derogating from the competence of the organs of the European Convention on Human Rights or from the obligations assumed by the Parties under that Convention.

3. The Committee shall not visit places which representatives or delegates of protecting powers or the International Committee of the Red Cross effectively visit on a regular basis by virtue of the Geneva Conventions of 12 August 1949 and the Additional Protocols of 18 June 1977 thereto.

## CHAPTER V

*Article* 18

This Convention shall be open for signature by the member States of the Council of Europe. It is subject to ratification, acceptance or approval.

Instruments of ratification, acceptance or approval shall be deposited with the Secretary General of the Council of Europe.

*Article* 19

1. This Convention shall enter into force on the first day of the month following the expiration of a period of three months after the date on which seven member States of the Council of Europe have expressed their consent to be bound by the Convention in accordance with the provisions of Article 18.

2. In respect of any member State which subsequently expresses its consent to be bound by it, the Convention shall enter into force on the first day of the month following the expiration of a period of three months after the date of the deposit of the instrument of ratification, acceptance or approval.

*Article* 20

1. Any State may at the time of signature or when depositing its instrument of ratification, acceptance or approval, specify the territory or territories to which this Convention shall apply.

2. Any State may at any later date, by a declaration addressed to the Secretary General of the Council of Europe, extend the application of this Convention to any other territory specified in the declaration. In respect of such territory the Convention shall enter into force on the first day of the month following the expiration of a period of three months after the date of receipt of such declaration by the Secretary General.

3. Any declaration made under the two preceding paragraphs may, in respect of any territory specified in such declaration, be withdrawn by a notification addressed to the Secretary General. The withdrawal shall become effective on the first day of the month following the expiration of a period of three months after the date of receipt of such notification by the Secretary General.

*Article* 21

No reservation may be made in respect of the provisions of this Convention.

*Article* 22

1. Any Party may, at any time, denounce this Convention by means of a notification addressed to the Secretary General of the Council of Europe.

2. Such denunciation shall become effective on the first day of the month following the expiration of a period of twelve months after the date of receipt of the notification by the Secretary General.

*Article* 23

The Secretary General of the Council of Europe shall notify the member States of the Council of Europe of:

(a) any signature;

(b) the deposit of any instrument of ratification, acceptance or approval;

(c) any date of entry into force of this Convention in accordance with Articles 19 and 20;

(d) any other act, notification or communication relating to this Convention, except for action taken in pursuance of Articles 8 and 10.

In witness whereof, the undersigned, being duly authorised thereto, have signed this Convention.

Done at Strasbourg, this 26th day of November 1987, in English and French, both texts being equally authentic, in a single copy which shall be deposited in the archives of the Council of Europe. The Secretary General of the Council of Europe shall transmit certified copies to each member State of the Council of Europe.

## ANNEX

### Privileges and Immunities

(Article 16)

1. For the purpose of this annex, references to members of the Committee shall be deemed to include references to experts mentioned in Article 7, paragraph 2.

2. The members of the Committee shall, while exercising their functions and during journeys made in the exercise of their functions, enjoy the following privileges and immunities:

(a) immunity from personal arrest or detention and from seizure of their personal baggage and, in respect of words spoken or written and all acts done by them in their official capacity, immunity from legal process of every kind;

(b) exemption from any restrictions on their freedom of movement: on exit from and return to their country of residence, and entry into and exit from the country in which they exercise their functions, and from alien registration in the country which they are visiting or through which they are passing in the exercise of their functions.

3. In the course of journeys undertaken in the exercise of their functions, the members of the Committee shall, in the matter of customs and exchange control, be accorded:

(a) by their own government, the same facilities as those accorded to senior officials travelling abroad on temporary official duty;

(b) by the governments of other Parties, the same facilities as those accorded to representatives of foreign governments on temporary official duty.

4. Documents and papers of the Committee, insofar as they relate to the business of the Committee, shall be inviolable.

The official correspondence and other official communications of the Committee may not be held up or subjected to censorship.

5. In order to secure for the members of the Committee complete freedom of speech and complete independence in the discharge of their duties, the immunity from legal process in respect of words spoken or written and all acts done by them in discharging their duties shall continue to be accorded, notwithstanding that the persons concerned are no longer engaged in the discharge of such duties.

6. Privileges and immunities are accorded to the members of the Committee, not for the personal benefit of the individuals themselves but in order to safeguard the independent exercise of their functions. The Committee alone shall be competent to waive the immunity of its members; it has not only the right, but is under a duty, to waive the immunity of one of its members in any case where, in its opinion, the immunity would impede the course of justice, and where it can be waived without prejudice to the purpose for which the immunity is accorded.

# IV. FINAL ACT OF THE HELSINKI CONFERENCE, 1975

On 1 August 1975 there was adopted the Final Act of the Conference on Security and Co-operation in Europe in Helsinki. This contains a declaration of principles under the heading 'Questions relating to Security in Europe'. The Final Act was signed by representatives of thirty-five states, including the United States and the U.S.S.R. The Final Act constitutes an important statement of intent but the instrument is not a treaty and the understanding of the signatories was that it was not legally binding. See further *Digest of United States Practice in International Law*, 1975, pp. 7–12, 190–3, 236–8, 271, 325–7, 529–32, 591–4, 679–81, 688–91, 783–8; the same, 1976, pp. 141–6, 178–81; Russell, *American Journal of International Law*, Vol. 70 (1976), pp. 242–72; Schachter, *ibid.*, Vol. 71 (1977), pp. 296–304.

The declaration of principles includes a section entitled 'Respect for human rights and fundamental freedoms, including the freedom of thought, conscience, religion or belief'. The text contains a commitment to act in conformity with existing obligations in the field of human rights. In a technical and formal sense the Final Act is not at all innovative in respect of human rights and, indeed, the subject-matter is as much related to security and disarmament as it is to human rights, although this fact has not been conveyed to the public in many countries.

On 30 January 1992 ten former Soviet republics joined the Conference, raising the number of members to forty-eight.

## TEXT

The Conference on Security and Co-operation in Europe, which opened at Helsinki on 3 July 1973 and continued at Geneva from 18 September 1973 to 21 July 1975 and continued at Helsinki on 1 August 1975 by the High Representatives of Austria, Belgium, Bulgaria, Canada, Cyprus, Czechoslovakia, Denmark, Finland, France, the German Democratic Republic, the Federal Republic of Germany, Greece, the Holy See, Hungary, Iceland, Ireland, Italy, Liechtenstein, Luxembourg, Malta, Monaco, The Netherlands, Norway, Poland, Portugal, Romania, San Marino, Spain, Sweden, Switzerland, Turkey, the Union of Soviet Socialist Republics, the United Kingdom, the United States of America and Yugoslavia.

During the opening and closing stages of the Conference the participants were addressed by the Secretary-General of the United Nations as their guest of honour. The Director-General of UNESCO and the Executive Secretary of the United Nations Economic Commission for Europe addressed the Conference during its second stage.

During the meetings of the second stage of the Conference, contributions were received, and statements heard, from the following non-participating Mediterranean States on various agenda items: the Democratic and Popular Republic of Algeria, the Arab Republic of Egypt, Israel, the Kingdom of Morocco, the Syrian Arab Republic, Tunisia.

Motivated by the political will, in the interest of peoples, to improve and intensify their relations and to contribute in Europe to peace, security, justice and co-operation as well as to rapprochement among themselves and with the other States of the world.

Determined, in consequence, to give full effect to the results of the Conference and to assume, among their States and throughout Europe, the benefits deriving from those results and thus to broaden, deepen and make continuing and lasting the process of détente.

The High Representatives of the participating States have solemnly adopted the following:

## QUESTIONS RELATING TO SECURITY IN EUROPE

*The States participating in the Conference on Security and Co-operation in Europe,*

*Reaffirming* their objective of promoting better relations among themselves and ensuring conditions in which their people can live in true and lasting peace free from any threat to or attempt against their security;

*Convinced* of the need to exert efforts to make détente both a continuing and an increasingly viable and comprehensive process, universal in scope, and that the implementation of the results of the Conference on Security and Co-operation in Europe will be a major contribution to this process;

*Considering* that solidarity among peoples, as well as the common purpose of the participating States in achieving the aims as set forth by the Conference on Security and Co-operation in Europe, should lead to the development of better and closer relations among them in all fields and thus to overcoming the confrontation stemming from the character of their past relations, and to better mutual understanding;

*Mindful* of their common history and recognizing that the existence of elements common to their traditions and values can assist them in developing their relations, and desiring to search, fully taking into account the individuality and diversity of their positions and views, for possibilities of joining their efforts with a view to overcoming distrust and increasing confidence, solving the problems that separate them and co-operating in the interest of mankind;

*Recognizing* the indivisibility of security in Europe as well as their common interest in the development of co-operation throughout Europe and among themselves and expressing their intention to pursue efforts accordingly;

*Recognizing* the close link between peace and security in Europe and in the world as a whole and conscious of the need for each of them to make its contribution to the strengthening of world peace and security and to the promotion of fundamental rights, economic and social progress and well-being for all peoples;

*Have adopted the following:*

## (*a*) Declaration on Principles Guiding Relations between Participating States

*The participating States,*

*Reaffirming* their commitment to peace, security and justice and the continuing development of friendly relations and co-operation;

*Recognizing* that this commitment, which reflects the interest and aspirations of peoples, constitutes for each participating State a present and future responsibility, heightened by experience of the past;

*Reaffirming,* in conformity with their membership in the United Nations and in accordance with the purposes and principles of the United Nations, their full and active support for the United Nations and for the enhancement of its role and effectiveness in strengthening international peace, security and justice, and in promoting the solution of international problems, as well as the development of friendly relations and co-operation among States;

*Expressing* their common adherence to the principles which are set forth below and are in conformity with the Charter of the United Nations, as well as their common will to act, in the application of these principles, in conformity with the purpose and principles of the Charter of the United Nations;

*Declare* their determination to respect and put into practice, each of them in its relations with all other participating States, irrespective of their political, economic or social systems as well as of their size, geographical location or level of economic development, the following principles, which all are of primary significance, guiding their mutual relations;

### I. *Sovereign Equality, Respect for the Rights Inherent in Sovereignty*

The participating States shall respect each other's sovereign equality and individuality as well as all the rights inherent in and encompassed by its sovereignty, including in particular the right of every State to juridical equality, to territorial integrity and to freedom and political independence. They will also respect each other's right freely to choose and develop its political, social, economic and cultural systems as well as its right to determine its laws and regulations.

Within the framework of international law, all the participating States have equal rights and duties. They will respect each other's right to define and conduct as it wishes its relations with other States in accordance with international law and in the spirit of the present Declaration. They consider that their frontiers can be changed, in accordance with international law, by peaceful means and by agreement. They also have the right to belong or not to belong to international organizations, to be or not to be a party to bilateral or multilateral treaties including the right to be or not to be a party to treaties of alliance; they also have the right to neutrality.

## II. *Refraining from the Threat or Use of Force*

The participating States will refrain in their mutual relations, as well as in their international relations in general, from the threat or use of force against the territorial integrity or political independence of any State, or in any other manner inconsistent with the purposes of the United Nations and with the present Declaration. No consideration may be invoked to serve to warrant resort to the threat or use of force in contravention of this principle.

Accordingly, the participating States will refrain from any acts constituting a threat of force or direct or indirect use of force against another participating State. Likewise they will refrain from any manifestation of force for the purpose of inducing another participating State to renounce the full exercise of its sovereign rights. Likewise they will also refrain in their mutual relations from any act of reprisal by force.

No such threat or use of force will be employed as a means of settling disputes, or questions likely to give rise to disputes, between them.

## III. *Inviolability of Frontiers*

The participating States regard as inviolable all one another's frontiers as well as the frontiers of all States in Europe and therefore they will refrain now and in the future from assaulting these frontiers.

Accordingly, they will also refrain from any demand for, or act of, seizure and usurpation of part or all of the territory of any participating State.

## IV. *Territorial Integrity of States*

The participating States will respect the territorial integrity of each of the participating States.

Accordingly, they will refrain from any action inconsistent with the purposes and principles of the Charter of the United Nations against the territorial integrity, political independence or the unity of any participating State, and in particular from any such action constituting a threat or use of force.

The participating States will likewise refrain from making each other's territory the object of military occupation or other direct or indirect measures of force in contravention of international law, or the object of acquisition by means of such measures or the threat of them. No such occupation or acquisition will be recognized as legal.

## V. *Peaceful Settlement of Disputes*

The participating States will settle disputes among them by peaceful means in such a manner as not to endanger international peace and security, and justice.

They will endeavour in good faith and a spirit of co-operation to reach a rapid and equitable solution on the basis of international law.

For this purpose they will use such means as negotiation, enquiry, mediation, conciliation, arbitration, judicial settlement or other peaceful means of their own choice including any settlement procedure agreed to in advance of disputes to which they are parties.

In the event of failure to reach a solution by any of the above peaceful means, the parties to a dispute will continue to seek a mutually agreed way to settle the dispute peacefully.

Participating States, parties to a dispute among them, as well as other participating States, will refrain from any action which might aggravate the situation to such a degree as to endanger the maintenance of international peace and security and thereby make a peaceful settlement of the dispute more difficult.

## VI. *Non-intervention in Internal Affairs*

The participating States will refrain from any intervention, direct or indirect, individual or collective, in the internal or external affairs falling within the domestic jurisdiction of another participating State, regardless of their mutual relations.

They will accordingly refrain from any form of armed intervention or threat of such intervention against another participating State.

They will likewise in all circumstances refrain from any other act of military, or of political, economic or other coercion designed to subordinate to their own interest the exercise by another participating State of the rights inherent in its sovereignty and thus to secure advantages of any kind.

Accordingly, they will, inter alia, refrain from direct or indirect assistance to terrorist activities, or to subversive or other activities directed towards the violent overthrow of the regime of another participating State.

## VII. *Respect for Human Rights and Fundamental Freedoms, including the Freedom of Thought, Conscience, Religion or Belief*

The participating States will respect human rights and fundamental freedoms, including the freedom of thought, conscience, religion or belief, for all without distinction as to race, sex, language or religion.

They will promote and encourage the effective exercise of civil, political, economic, social, cultural and other rights and freedoms all of which derive from the inherent dignity of the human person and are essential for his free and full development.

Within this framework the participating States will recognize and respect the freedom of the individual to profess and practise, alone or in community with others, religion or belief acting in accordance with the dictates of his own conscience.

The participating States on whose territory national minorities exist will respect the right of persons belonging to such minorities to equality before the law, will afford them the full opportunity for the actual enjoyment of human rights and fundamental freedoms and will, in this manner, protect their legitimate interests in this sphere.

The participating States recognize the universal significance of human rights and fundamental freedoms, respect for which is an essential factor for the peace, justice and well-being necessary to ensure the development of friendly relations and co-operation among themselves as among all States.

They will constantly respect these rights and freedoms in their mutual relations and will endeavour jointly and separately, including in co-operation with the United Nations, to promote universal and effective respect for them.

They confirm the right of the individual to know and act upon his rights and duties in this field.

In the field of human rights and fundamental freedoms, the participating States will act in conformity with the purposes and principles of the Charter of the United Nations and with the Universal Declaration of Human Rights. They will also fulfil their obligations as set forth in the international declarations and agreements in this field, including inter alia the International Covenants on Human Rights, by which they may be bound.

## VIII. *Equal Rights and Self-determination of Peoples*

The participating States will respect the equal rights of peoples and their right to self-determination, acting at all times in conformity with the purposes and principles of the Charter of the United Nations and with the relevant norms of international law, including those relating to territorial integrity of States.

By virtue of the principle of equal rights and self-determination of peoples, all peoples always have the right, in full freedom, to determine, when and as they wish, their internal and external political status, without external interference, and to pursue as they wish their political, economic, social and cultural development.

The participating States reaffirm the universal significance of respect for and effective exercise of equal rights and self-determination of peoples for the development of friendly relations among themselves as among all States; they also recall the importance of the elimination of any form of violation of this principle.

## IX. *Co-operation among States*

The participating States will develop their co-operation with one another and with all States in all fields in accordance with the purposes and principles of the Charter of the United Nations. In developing their co-operation the participating States will place special emphasis on the fields as set forth within the framework of the Conference on Security and Co-operation in Europe, with each of them making its contribution in conditions of full equality.

They will endeavour, in developing their co-operation as equals, to promote mutual understanding and confidence, friendly and good-neighbourly relations among themselves, international peace, security and justice. They will equally endeavour, in developing their co-operation, to improve the well-being of peoples and contribute to the fulfilment of their aspirations through, inter alia, the benefits resulting from increased mutual knowledge and from progress and achievement in the economic, scientific, technological, social, cultural and humanitarian fields. They will take steps to promote conditions favourable to making these benefits available to all; they will take into account the interest of all in the narrowing of differences in the levels of economic development, and in particular the interest of developing countries throughout the world.

They confirm that governments, institutions, organizations and persons have a relevant and positive role to play in contributing toward the achievement of these aims of their co-operation.

They will strive, in increasing their co-operation as set forth above, to develop closer relations among themselves on an improved and more enduring basis for the benefit of peoples.

## X. *Fulfilment in Good Faith of Obligations under International Law*

The participating States will fulfil in good faith their obligations under international law, both those obligations arising from the generally recognized principles and rules of international law and those obligations arising from treaties or other agreements, in conformity with international law, to which they are parties.

In exercising their sovereign rights, including the right to determine their laws and regulations, they will conform with their legal obligations under international law; they will furthermore pay due regard to and implement the provisions in the Final Act of the Conference on Security and Co-operation in Europe.

The participating States confirm that in the event of a conflict between the obligations of the members of the United Nations under the Charter of the United Nations and their obligations under any treaty or other international agreement, their obligations under the Charter will prevail, in accordance with Article 103 of the Charter of the United Nations.

All the principles set forth above are of primary significance and, accordingly, they will be equally and unreservedly applied, each of them being interpreted taking into account the others.

The participating States express their determination fully to respect and apply these principles, as set forth in the present Declaration, in all aspects, to their mutual relations and co-operation in order to ensure to each participating State the benefits resulting from the respect and application of these principles by all.

The participating States, paying due regard to the principles above and, in particular, to the first sentence of the tenth principle, 'Fulfilment in good faith of obligations under international law', note that the present Declaration does not affect their rights and obligations, nor the corresponding treaties and other agreements and arrangements.

The participating States express the conviction that respect for these principles will encourage the development of normal and friendly relations and the progress of co-operation among them in all fields. They also express the conviction that respect for these principles will encourage the development of political contacts among them which in turn would contribute to better mutual understanding of their positions and views.

The participating States declare their intention to conduct their relations with all other States in the spirit of the principle contained in the present Declaration.

### (b) Matters Related to Giving Effect to Certain of the Above Principles

(i) *The participating States*

*Reaffirming* that they will respect and give effect to refraining from the threat or use of force and convinced of the necessity to make it an effective norm of international life,

*Declare* that they are resolved to respect and carry out, in their relations with one another, inter alia, the following provisions which are in conformity with the Declaration on Principles Guiding Relations between Participating States:

—To give effect and expression, by all the ways and forms which they consider appropriate, to the duty to refrain from the threat or use of force in their relations with one another.

—To refrain from any use of armed forces inconsistent with the purposes and principles of the Charter of the United Nations and the provisions of the Declaration on Principles Guiding Relations between Participating States, against another participating State, in particular from invasion of or attack on its territory.

—To refrain from any manifestation of force for the purpose of inducing another participating State to renounce the full exercise of its sovereign rights.

—To refrain from any act of economic coercion designed to subordinate to their own interest the exercise by another participating State of the rights inherent in its sovereignty and thus to secure advantages of any kind.

—To take effective measures which by their scope and by their nature constitute steps towards the ultimate achievement of general and complete disarmament under strict and effective international control.

—To promote, by all means which each of them considers appropriate, a climate of confidence and respect among peoples consonant with their duty to refrain from propaganda for wars of aggression or for any threat or use of force inconsistent with the purposes of the United Nations and with the Declaration on Principles Guiding Relations between Participating States, against another participating State.

—To make every effort to settle exclusively by peaceful means any dispute between them, the continuance of which is likely to endanger the maintenance of international peace and security in Europe, and to seek, first of all, a solution through the peaceful means set forth in Article 33 of the United Nations Charter.

—To refrain from any action which could hinder the peaceful settlement of disputes between the participating States.

(ii) *The participating States*

*Reaffirming* their determination to settle their disputes as set forth in the Principle of Peaceful Settlement of Disputes;

*Convinced* that the peaceful settlement of disputes is a complement to refraining from the threat or use of force, both being essential though not exclusive factors for the maintenance and consolidation of peace and security;

*Desiring* to reinforce and to improve the methods at their disposal for the peaceful settlement of disputes;

1. Are resolved to pursue the examination and elaboration of a generally acceptable method for the peaceful settlement of disputes aimed at complementing existing methods, and to continue to this end to work upon the 'Draft Convention on a European System for the Peaceful Settlement of Disputes' submitted by Switzerland during the second stage of the Conference on Security and Co-operation in Europe, as well as other proposals relating to it and directed towards the elaboration of such a method.

2. Decide that, on the invitation of Switzerland, a meeting of experts of all the participating States will be convoked in order to fulfil the mandate described in paragraph 1 above within the framework and under the procedures of the follow-up to the Conference laid down in the chapter 'Follow-up to the Conference'.

3. This meeting of experts will take place after the meeting of the representatives appointed by the Ministers of Foreign Affairs of the participating States, scheduled according to the chapter 'Follow-up to the Conference' for 1977; the results of the work of this meeting of experts will be submitted to Governments.

## 2. Document on Confidence-Building Measures and Certain Aspects of Security and Disarmament

*The participating States,*

*Desirous* of eliminating the causes of tension that may exist among them and thus of contributing to the strengthening of peace and security in the world;

*Determined* to strengthen confidence among them and thus to contribute to increasing stability and security in Europe;

*Determined* further to refrain in their mutual relations, as well as in their international relations in general, from the threat or use of force against the territorial integrity or political independence of any State, or in any other manner inconsistent with the purposes of the United Nations and with the Declaration on Principles Guiding Relations between Participating States as adopted in this Final Act;

*Recognizing* the need to contribute to reducing the dangers of armed conflict and of misunderstanding or miscalculation of military activities which could give rise to apprehension, particularly in a situation where the participating States lack clear and timely information about the nature of such activities;

*Taking into account* considerations relevant to efforts aimed at lessening tension and promoting disarmament;

*Recognizing* that the exchange of observers by invitation at military manoeuvres will help to promote contacts and mutual understanding;

*Having studied* the question of prior notification of major military movements in the context of confidence-building;

*Recognizing* that there are other ways in which individual States can contribute further to their common objectives;

*Convinced* of the political importance of prior notification of major military manoeuvres for the promotion of mutual understanding and the strengthening of confidence, stability and security;

*Accepting* the responsibility of each of them to promote these objectives and to implement this measure, in accordance with the accepted criteria and modalities, as essentials for the realization of these objectives;

*Recognizing* that this measure deriving from political decision rests upon a voluntary basis;

*Have adopted the following:*

### I. *Prior Notification of Major Military Manoeuvres*

They will notify their major military manoeuvres to all other participating States through usual diplomatic channels in accordance with the following provisions;

Notification will be given of major military manoeuvres exceeding a total of 25,000 troops, independently or combined with any possible air or naval components (in this context the word 'troops' includes amphibious and airborne troops). In the case of independent manoeuvres of amphibious or airborne troops, or of combined manoeuvres involving them, these troops will be included in this total. Furthermore, in the case of combined manoeuvres which do not reach the above total but which involve land forces together with significant numbers of either amphibious or airborne troops, or both, notification can also be given.

Notification will be given of major military manoeuvres which take place on the territory, in Europe, of any participating State as well as, if applicable, in the adjoining sea area and air space.

In the case of a participating State whose territory extends beyond Europe, prior notification need be given only of manoeuvres which take place in an area within 250 kilometres from its frontier facing or shared with any other European participating State. The participating State need not, however, give notification in cases in which that area is also contiguous to the participating States' frontier facing or shared with a non-European non-participating State.

Notification will be given 21 days or more in advance of the start of the manoeuvre or in the case of a manoeuvre arranged at shorter notice at the earliest possible opportunity prior to its starting date.

Notification will contain information of the designation, if any, the general purpose of and the States involved in the manoeuvre, the type or types and numerical strength of the forces engaged, the area and estimated time-frame of its conduct. The participating States will also, if possible, provide additional relevant information, particularly that related to the components of the forces engaged and the period of involvement of these forces.

### *Prior Notification of Other Military Manoeuvres*

The participating States recognize that they can contribute further to strengthening confidence and increasing security and stability, and to this end may also notify smaller-scale military manoeuvres to other participating States, with special regard for those near the area of such manoeuvres.

To the same end, the participating States also recognize that they may notify other military manoeuvres conducted by them.

## Exchange of Observers

The participating States will invite other participating States, voluntarily and on a bilateral basis, in a spirit of reciprocity and goodwill towards all participating States, to send observers to attend military manoeuvres.

The inviting State will determine in each case the number of observers, the procedures and conditions of their participation, and give other information which it may consider useful. It will provide appropriate facilities and hospitality.

The invitation will be given as far ahead as is conveniently possible through usual diplomatic channels.

## Prior Notification of Major Military Movements

In accordance with the Final Recommendations of the Helsinki Consultations the participating States studied the question of prior notification of major military movements as a measure to strengthen confidence.

Accordingly, the participating States recognize that they may, at their own discretion and with a view to contributing to confidence-building, notify their major military movements.

In the same spirit, further consideration will be given by the States participating in the Conference on Security and Co-operation in Europe to the question of prior notification of major military movements, bearing in mind, in particular, the experience gained by the implementation of the measures which are set forth in this document.

## Other Confidence-building Measures

The participating States recognize that there are other means by which their common objectives can be promoted.

In particular, they will, with due regard to reciprocity and with a view to better mutual understanding, promote exchanges by invitation among their military personnel, including visits by military delegations.

\* \* \*

In order to make a fuller contribution to their common objective of confidence-building, the participating States, when conducting their military activities in the area covered by the provisions for the prior notification of major military manoeuvres, will duly take into account and respect this objective.

They also recognize that the experience gained by the implementation of the provisions set forth above, together with further efforts, could lead to developing and enlarging measures aimed at strengthening confidence.

## II. *Questions Relating to Disarmament*

The participating States recognize the interest of all of them in efforts aimed at lessening military confrontation and promoting disarmament which are designed to complement political détente in Europe and to strengthen their security. They are convinced of the necessity to take effective measures in these fields which by their scope and by their nature constitute steps towards the ultimate achievement of general and complete disarmament under strict and effective international control, and which should result in strengthening peace and security throughout the world.

## III. *General Considerations*

Having considered the views expressed on various subjects related to the strengthening of security in Europe through joint efforts aimed at promoting détente and disarmament, the participating States, when engaged in such efforts, will, in this context, proceed, in particular, from the following essential considerations:

—The complementary nature of the political and military aspects of security;
—The interrelation between the security of each participating State and security in Europe as a whole and the relationship which exists, in the broader context of world security, between security in Europe and security in the Mediterranean area;
—Respect for the security interests of all States participating in the Conference on Security and Co-operation in Europe inherent in their sovereign equality;
—The importance that participants in negotiating fora see to it that information about relevant developments, progress and results is provided on an appropriate basis to other States participating in the Conference on Security and Co-operation in Europe and, in return, the justified interest of any of those States in having their views considered.

## CO-OPERATION IN THE FIELD OF ECONOMICS, OF SCIENCE AND TECHNOLOGY AND OF THE ENVIRONMENT

*The participating States,*

*Convinced* that their efforts to develop co-operation in the fields of trade, industry, science and technology, the environment and other areas of economic activity contribute to the reinforcement of peace and security in Europe and in the world as a whole,

*Recognizing* that co-operation in these fields would promote economic and social progress and the improvement of the conditions of life,

*Aware of* the diversity of their economic and social systems,

*Reaffirming* their will to intensify such co-operation between one another, irrespective of their systems,

*Recognizing* that such co-operation, with due regard for the different levels of economic development, can be developed, on the basis of equality and mutual satisfaction of the partners, and of reciprocity permitting, as a whole, an equitable distribution of advantages and obligations of comparable scale, with respect for bilateral and multilateral agreements,

*Taking into account* the interests of the developing countries throughout the world, including those among the participating countries as long as they are developing from the economic point of view; reaffirming their will to co-operate for the achievement of the aims and objectives established by the appropriate bodies of the United Nations in the pertinent documents concerning development, it being understood that each participating State maintains the positions it has taken on them; giving special attention to the least developed countries,

*Convinced* that the growing world-wide economic interdependence calls for increasing common and effective efforts towards the solution of major world economic problems such as food, energy, commodities, monetary and financial problems, and therefore emphasizes the need for promoting stable and equitable international economic relations, thus contributing to the continuous and diversified economic development of all countries,

*Having taken into account* the work already undertaken by relevant international organizations and wishing to take advantage of the possibilities offered by these organizations, in particular by the United Nations Economic Commission for Europe, for giving effect to the provisions of the final documents of the Conference,

*Considering* that the guidelines and concrete recommendations contained in the following texts are aimed at promoting further development of their mutual economic relations, and convinced that their co-operation in this field should take place in full respect for the principles guiding relations among participating States as set forth in the relevant document,

*Having adopted the following:*

## 1. Commercial Exchanges

### *General Provisions*

*The participating States,*

*Conscious* of the growing role of international trade as one of the most important factors in economic growth and social progress,

*Recognizing* that trade represents an essential sector of their co-operation, and bearing in mind that the provisions contained in the above preamble apply in particular to this sector,

*Considering* that the volume and structure of trade among the participating States do not in all cases correspond to the possibilities created by the current level of their economic, scientific and technological development,

are resolved to promote, on the basis of the modalities of their economic co-operation, the expansion of their mutual trade in goods and services, and to ensure conditions favourable to such development;

recognize the beneficial effects which can result for the development of trade from the application of most favoured nation treatment;

will encourage the expansion of trade on as broad a multilateral basis as possible, thereby endeavouring to utilize the various economic and commercial possibilities;

recognize the importance of bilateral and multilateral intergovernmental and other agreements for the long-term development of trade;

note the importance of monetary and financial questions for the development of international trade, and will endeavour to deal with them with a view to contributing to the continuous expansion of trade;

will endeavour to reduce or progressively eliminate all kinds of obstacles to the development of trade;

will foster a steady growth of trade while avoiding as far as possible abrupt fluctuations in their trade;

consider that their trade in various products should be conducted in such a way as not to cause or threaten to cause serious injury—and should the situation arise, market disruption—in domestic markets for these products and in particular to the detriment of domestic producers of like or directly competitive products; as regards the concept of market disruption, it is understood that it should not be invoked in a way inconsistent with the relevant provisions of their international agreements: if they resort to safeguard measures, they will do so in conformity with their commitments in this field arising from international agreements to which they are parties and will take account of the interests of the parties directly concerned;

will give due attention to measures for the promotion of trade and the diversification of its structure;

note that the growth and diversification of trade would contribute to widening the possibilities of choice of products;

consider it appropriate to create favourable conditions for the participation of firms, organizations and enterprises in the development of trade.

### Business Contacts and Facilities

*The participating States,*

*Conscious* of the importance of the contribution which an improvement of business contacts, and the accompanying growth of confidence in business relationships, could make to the development of commercial and economic relations,

will take measures further to improve conditions for the expansion of contacts between representatives of official bodies, of the different organizations, enterprises, firms and banks concerned with foreign trade, in particular, where useful, between sellers and users of products and services, for the purpose of studying commercial possibilities, concluding contracts, ensuring their implementation and providing after-sales services;

will encourage organizations, enterprises and firms concerned with foreign trade to take measures to accelerate the conduct of business negotiations;

will further take measures aimed at improving working conditions of representatives of foreign organizations, enterprises, firms and banks concerned with external trade, particularly as follows:

—by providing the necessary information, including information on legislation and procedures relating to the establishment and operation of permanent representation by the above mentioned bodies;

—by examining as favourably as possible requests for the establishment of permanent representation and of offices for this purpose, including, where appropriate, the opening of joint offices by two or more firms;

—by encouraging the provision, on conditions as favourable as possible and equal for all representatives of the above-mentioned bodies, of hotel accommodation, means of communication, and of other facilities normally required by them, as well as of suitable business and residential premises for purposes of permanent representation;

recognize the importance of such measures to encourage greater participation by small and medium sized firms in trade between participating States.

### Economic and Commercial Information

*The participating States,*

*Conscious* of the growing role of economic and commercial information in the development of international trade,

*Considering* that economic information should be of such a nature as to allow adequate market analysis and to permit the preparation of medium and long term forecasts, thus contributing to the establishment of a continuing flow of trade and a better utilization of commercial possibilities,

*Expressing their readiness* to improve the quality and increase the quantity and supply of economic and relevant administrative information,

*Considering* that the value of statistical information on the international level depends to a considerable extent on the possibility of its comparability,

will promote the publication and dissemination of economic and commercial information at regular intervals and as quickly as possible, in particular:

—statistics concerning production, national income, budget, consumption and productivity;
—foreign trade statistics drawn up on the basis of comparable classification including breakdown by product with indication of volume and value, as well as country of origin or destination;
—laws and regulations concerning foreign trade;
—information allowing forecasts of development of the economy to assist in trade promotion, for example, information on the general orientation of national economic plans and programmes;
—other information to help businessmen in commercial contacts, for example, periodic directories, lists, and where possible, organizational charts of firms and organizations concerned with foreign trade;

will in addition to the above encourage the development of the exchange of economic and commercial information through, where appropriate, joint commissions for economic, scientific and technical co-operation, national and joint chambers of commerce, and other suitable bodies;

will support a study, in the framework of the United Nations Economic Commission for Europe, of the possibilities of creating a multilateral system of notification of laws and regulations concerning foreign trade and changes therein;

will encourage international work on the harmonization of statistical nomenclatures, notably in the United Nations Economic Commission for Europe.

### Marketing

*The participating States,*

*Recognizing* the importance of adapting production to the requirements of foreign markets in order to ensure the expansion of international trade.

*Conscious* of the need of exporters to be as fully familiar as possible with and take account of the requirements of potential users,

will encourage organizations, enterprises and firms concerned with foreign trade to develop further the knowledge and techniques required for effective marketing;

will encourage the improvement of conditions for the implementation of measures to promote trade and to satisfy the needs of users in respect of imported products, in particular through market research and advertising measures as well as, where useful, the establishment of supply facilities, the furnishing of spare parts, the functioning of after sales services, and the training of the necessary local technical personnel;

will encourage international co-operation in the field of trade promotion, including marketing, and the work undertaken on these subjects within the international bodies, in particular the United Nations Economic Commission for Europe.

## 2. Industrial Co-operation and Projects of Common Interest

### *Industrial Co-operation*

*The participating States,*

*Considering* that industrial co-operation, being motivated by economic considerations, can

—create lasting ties thus strengthening long-term overall economic co-operation,
—contribute to economic growth as well as to the expansion and diversification of international trade and to a wider utilization of modern technology,
—lead to the mutually advantageous utilization of economic complementarities through better use of all factors of production, and
—accelerate the industrial development of all those who take part in such co-operation.

propose to encourage the development of industrial co-operation between the competent organizations, enterprises and firms of their countries;

consider that industrial co-operation may be facilitated by means of intergovernmental and other bilateral and multilateral agreements between the interested parties;

note that in promoting industrial co-operation they should bear in mind the economic structures and the development levels of their countries;

note that industrial co-operation is implemented by means of contracts concluded between competent organizations, enterprises and firms on the basis of economic considerations;

express their willingness to promote measures designed to create favourable conditions for industrial co-operation;

recognize that industrial co-operation covers a number of forms of economic relations going beyond the framework of conventional trade, and that in concluding contracts on industrial co-operation the partners will determine jointly the appropriate forms and conditions of co-operation, taking into account their mutual interest and capabilities;

recognize further that, if it is in their mutual interest, concrete forms such as the following may be useful for the development of industrial co-operation: joint production and sale, specialization in production and sale, construction, adaptation and modernization of industrial plants, co-operation for the setting up of complete industrial installations with a view to thus obtaining part of the resultant products, mixed companies, exchanges of 'know-how', of technical information, of patents and of licences, and joint industrial research within the framework of specific co-operation projects;

recognize that new forms of industrial co-operation can be applied with a view to meeting specific needs;

note the importance of economic, commercial, technical and administrative information such as to ensure the development of industrial co-operation;

consider it desirable:

—to improve the quality and the quantity of information relevant to industrial co-operation, in particular the laws and regulations, including those relating to foreign exchange, general orientation of national economic plans and programmes as well as programme priorities and economic conditions of the market; and
—to disseminate as quickly as possible published documentation thereon;

will encourage all forms of exchange of information and communication of experience relevant to industrial co-operation, including through contacts between potential partners and, where appropriate, through joint commissions for economic, industrial, scientific and technical co-operation, national and joint chambers of commerce, and other suitable bodies;

consider it desirable, with a view to expanding industrial co-operation, to encourage the exploration of co-operation possibilities and the implementation of co-operation projects and will take measures to this end, *inter alia*, by facilitating and increasing all forms of business contacts between competent organizations, enterprises and firms and between their respective qualified personnel;

note that the provisions adopted by the Conference relating to business contacts in the economic and commercial fields also apply to foreign organizations, enterprises and firms engaged in industrial co-operation, taking into account the specific conditions of this co-operation, and will endeavour to ensure, in particular, the existence of appropriate working conditions for personnel engaged in the implementation of co-operation projects;

consider it desirable that proposals for industrial co-operation projects should be sufficiently specific and should contain the necessary economic and technical data, in particular preliminary estimates of the cost of the project, information on the form of co-operation envisaged, and market possibilities, to enable potential partners to proceed with initial studies and to arrive at decisions in the shortest possible time;

will encourage the parties concerned with industrial co-operation to take measures to accelerate the conduct of negotiations for the conclusion of co-operation contracts;

recommend further the continued examination—for example within the framework of the United Nations Economic Commission for Europe—of means of improving the provision of information to those concerned or general conditions of industrial co-operation and guidance on the preparation of contracts in this field;

consider it desirable to further improve conditions for the implementation of industrial co-operation projects, in particular with respect to:

—the protection of the interests of the partners in industrial co-operation projects, including the legal protection of the various kinds of property involved;

—the consideration, in ways that are compatible with their economic systems, of the needs and possibilities of industrial co-operation within the framework of economic policy and particularly in national economic plans and programmes;

consider it desirable that the partners, when concluding industrial co-operation contracts, should devote due attention to provisions concerning the extension of the necessary mutual assistance and the provision of the necessary information during the implementation of these contracts, in particular with a view to attaining the required technical level and quality of the products resulting from such co-operation;

recognize the usefulness of an increased participation of small and medium sized firms in industrial co-operation projects.

### Projects of Common Interest

*The participating States,*

*Considering* that their economic potential and their natural resources permit, through common efforts, long-term co-operation in the implementation, including at the regional or sub-regional level, of major projects of common interest, and that these may contribute to the speeding-up of the economic development of the countries participating therein.

*Considering* it desirable that the competent organizations, enterprises and firms of all countries should be given the possibility of indicating their interest in participating in such projects, and, in case of agreement, of taking part in their implementation.

*Noting* that the provisions adopted by the Conference relating to industrial co-operation are also applicable to projects of common interest.

regard it as necessary to encourage, where appropriate, the investigation by competent and interested organizations, enterprises and firms of the possibilities for the carrying out of projects of common interest in the fields of energy resources and of the exploitation of raw materials, as well as of transport and communications;

regard it as desirable that organizations, enterprises and firms exploring the possibilities of taking part in projects of common interest exchange with their potential partners, through the appropriate channels, the requisite economic, legal, financial and technical information pertaining to these projects;

consider that the fields of energy resources, in particular, petroleum, natural gas and coal, and the extraction and processing of mineral raw materials, in particular, iron ore and bauxite, are suitable ones for strengthening long-term economic co-operation and for the development of trade which could result;

consider that possibilities for projects of common interest with a view to long-term economic co-operation also exist in the following fields:

—exchanges of electrical energy within Europe with a view to utilizing the capacity of the electrical power stations as rationally as possible;

—co-operation in research for new sources of energy and, in particular, in the field of nuclear energy;

—development of road networks and co-operation aimed at establishing a coherent navigable network in Europe;

—co-operation in research and the perfecting of equipment for multimodal transport operations and for the handling of containers;

recommend that the States interested in projects of common interest should consider under what conditions it would be possible to establish them, and if they so desire, create the necessary conditions for their actual implementation.

### 3. Provisions Concerning Trade and Industrial Co-operation

#### Harmonization of Standards

*The participating States,*

*Recognizing* the development of international harmonization of standards and technical regulations and of international co-operation in the field of certification as an important means of eliminating technical obstacles to international trade and industrial co-operation, thereby facilitating their development and increasing productivity.

reaffirm their interest to achieve the widest possible international harmonization of standards and technical regulations;

express their readiness to promote international agreements and other appropriate arrangements on acceptance of certificates of conformity with standards and technical regulations;

consider it desirable to increase international co-operation on standardization, in particular by supporting the activities of intergovernmental and other appropriate organizations in this field.

### Arbitration

*The participating States,*

*Considering* that the prompt and equitable settlement of disputes which may arise from commercial transactions relating to goods and services and contracts for industrial co-operation would contribute to expanding and facilitating trade and co-operation,

*Considering* that arbitration is an appropriate means of settling such disputes,

recommend, where appropriate, to organizations, enterprises and firms in their countries, to include arbitration clauses in commercial contracts and industrial co-operation contracts, or in special agreements;

recommend that the provisions on arbitration should provide for arbitration under a mutually acceptable set of arbitration rules, and permit arbitration in a third country, taking into account existing intergovernmental and other agreements in this field.

### Specific Bilateral Arrangements

*The participating States,*

*Conscious* of the need to facilitate trade and to promote the application of new forms of industrial co-operation,

will consider favourably the conclusion, in appropriate cases, of specific bilateral agreements concerning various problems of mutual interest in the fields of commercial exchanges and industrial co-operation, in particular with a view to avoiding double taxation and to facilitating the transfer of profits and the return of the value of the assets invested.

### 4. Science and Technology

*The participating States,*

*Convinced* that scientific and technological co-operation constitutes an important contribution to the strengthening of security and co-operation among them, in that it assists the effective solution of problems of common interest and the improvement of the conditions of human life,

*Considering* that in developing such co-operation, it is important to promote the sharing of information and experience, facilitating the study and transfer of scientific and technological achievements, as well as the access to such achievements on a mutually advantageous basis and in fields of co-operation agreed between interested parties,

*Considering* that it is for the potential partners, i.e. the competent organizations, institutions, enterprises, scientists and technologists of the participating States to determine the opportunities for mutually beneficial co-operation and to develop its details,

*Affirming* that such co-operation can be developed and implemented bilaterally and multilaterally at the governmental and non-governmental levels, for example, through intergovernmental and other agreements, international programmes, co-operative projects and commercial channels, while utilizing also various forms of contacts, including direct and individual contacts,

*Aware* of the need to take measures further to improve scientific and technological co-operation between them,

### *Possibilities for Improving Co-operation*

Recognize that possibilities exist for further improving scientific and technological co-operation, and to this end, express their intention to remove obstacles to such co-operation, in particular through:

—the improvement of opportunities for the exchange and dissemination of scientific and technological information among the parties interested in scientific and technological research and co-operation including information related to the organization and implementation of such co-operation;
—the expeditious implementation and improvement in organization, including programmes, of international visits of scientists and specialists in connexion with exchanges, conferences and co-operation;
—the wider use of commercial channels and activities for applied scientific and technological research and for the transfer of achievements obtained in this field while providing information on and protection of intellectual and industrial property rights;

### *Fields of Co-operation*

Consider that possibilities to expand co-operation exist within the areas given below as examples, noting that it is for potential partners in the participating countries to identify and develop projects and arrangements of mutual interest and benefit;

### *Agriculture*

Research into new methods and technologies for increasing the productivity of crop cultivation and animal husbandry; the application of chemistry to agriculture; the design, construction and utilization of agricultural machinery; technologies of irrigation and other agricultural land improvement works;

*Energy*

New technologies of production, transport and distribution of energy aimed at improving the use of existing fuels and sources of hydroenergy, as well as research in the field of new energy sources, including nuclear, solar and geothermal energy;

*New technologies, rational use of resources*

Research on new technologies and equipment designed in particular to reduce energy consumption and to minimize or eliminate waste;

*Transport technology*

Research on the means of transport and the technology applied to the development and operation of international, national and urban transport networks including container transport as well as transport safety;

*Physics*

Study of problems in high energy physics and plasma physics; research in the field of theoretical and experimental nuclear physics;

*Chemistry*

Research on problems in electrochemistry and the chemistry of polymers, of natural products, and metals and alloys, as well as the development of improved chemical technology, especially materials processing; practical application of the latest achievements of chemistry to industry, construction and other sectors of the economy;

*Meteorology and hydrology*

Meteorological and hydrological research, including methods of collection, evaluation and transmission of data and their utilization for weather forecasting and hydrology forecasting;

*Oceanography*

Oceanographic research, including the study of air/sea interactions;

*Seismological research*

Study and forecasting of earthquakes and associated geological changes; development and research of technology of seism-resisting constructions;

*Research on glaciology, permafrost and problems of life under conditions of cold*

Research on glaciology and permafrost; transportation and construction technologies; human adaptation to climatic extremes and changes in the living conditions of indigenous populations;

*Computer, communication and information technologies*

Development of computers as well as of telecommunications and information systems; technology associated with computers and telecommunications, including their use for management systems, for production processes, for automation, for the study of economic problems, in scientific research and for the collection, processing and dissemination of information;

*Space research*

Space exploration and the study of the earth's natural resources and the natural environment by remote sensing in particular with the assistance of satellites and rocket-probes;

*Medicine and public health*

Research on cardiovascular, tumour and virus diseases, molecular biology, neurophysiology; development and testing of new drugs; study of contemporary problems of pediatrics, gerontology and the organization and techniques of medical services;

*Environmental research*

Research on specific scientific and technological problems related to human environment.

## Forms and Methods of Co-operation

Express their view that scientific and technological co-operation should, in particular, employ the following forms and methods:

—exchange and circulation of books, periodicals and other scientific and technological publications and papers among interested organizations, scientific and technological institutions, enterprises and scientists and technologists, as well as participation in international programmes for the abstracting and indexing of publications;

—exchanges and visits as well as other direct contacts and communications among scientists and technologists, on the basis of mutual agreement and other arrangements, for such purposes as consultations, lecturing and conducting research, including the use of laboratories, scientific libraries, and other documentation centres in connexion therewith;

—holding of international and national conferences, symposia, seminars, courses and other meetings of a scientific and technological character, which would include the participation of foreign scientists and technologists;

—joint preparation and implementation of programmes and projects of mutual interest on the basis of consultation and agreement among all parties concerned, including, where possible and appropriate, exchanges of experience and research results, and correlation of research programmes, between scientific and technological research institutions and organizations;

—use of commercial channels and methods for identifying and transferring technological and scientific developments, including the conclusion of mutually benefical co-operation arrangements between firms and enterprises in fields agreed upon between them and for carrying out, where appropriate, joint research and development programmes and projects;

consider it desirable that periodic exchanges of views and information take place on scientific policy, in particular on general problems of orientation and administration of research and the question of a better use of large-scale scientific and experimental equipment on a co-operative basis;

recommend that, in developing co-operation in the field of science and technology, full use be made of existing practices of bilateral and multilateral co-operation, including that of a regional or sub-regional character, together with the forms and methods of co-operation described in this document;

recommend further that more effective utilization be made of the possibilities and capabilities of existing international organizations, intergovernmental and non-governmental, concerned with science and technology, for improving exchanges of information and experience, as well as for developing other forms of co-operation in fields of common interest, for example:

—in the United Nations Economic Commission for Europe, study of possibilities for expanding multilateral co-operation, taking into account models for projects and research used in various international organizations; and for sponsoring conferences, symposia, and study and working groups such as those which would bring together younger scientists and technologists with eminent specialists in their field;

—through their participation in particular international scientific and technological co-operation programmes, including those of UNESCO and other international organizations, pursuit of continuing progress towards the objectives of such programmes, notably those of UNISIST with particular respect to information policy guidance, technical advice, information contributions and data processing.

## 5. Environment

*The participating States,*

*Affirming* that the protection and improvement of the environment, as well as the protection of nature and the rational utilization of its resources in the interests of present and future generations, is one of the tasks of major importance to the well-being of peoples and the economic development of all countries and that many environmental problems, particularly in Europe, can be solved effectively only through close international co-operation,

*Acknowledging* that each of the participating States, in accordance with the principles of international law, ought to ensure, in a spirit of co-operation, that activities carried out on its territory do not cause degradation of the environment in another State or in areas lying beyond the limits of national jurisdiction,

*Considering* that the success of any environmental policy presupposes that all population groups and social forces, aware of their responsibilities, help to protect and improve the environment, which necessitates continued and thorough educative action, particularly with regard to youth,

*Affirming* that experience has shown that economic development and technological progress must be compatible with the protection of the environment and the preservation of historical and cultural values; that damage to the environment is best avoided by preventive measures; and that the ecological balance must be preserved in the exploitation and management of natural resources.

### Aims of Co-operation

Agree to the following aims of co-operation, in particular:

—to study, with a view to their solution, those environmental problems which, by their nature, are of a multilateral, bilateral, regional or sub-regional dimension; as well as to encourage the development of an interdisciplinary approach to environmental problems;
—to increase the effectiveness of national and international measures for the protection of the environment, by the comparison and, if appropriate, the harmonization of methods of gathering and analysing facts, by improving the knowledge of pollution phenomena and rational utilization of natural resources, by the exchange of information, by the harmonization of definitions and the adoption, as far as possible, of a common terminology in the field of the environment;
—to take the necessary measures to bring environmental policies closer together and, where appropriate and possible, to harmonize them;
—to encourage, where possible and appropriate, national and international efforts by their interested organizations, enterprises and firms in the development, production and improvement of equipment designed for monitoring, protecting and enhancing the environment.

### Fields of Co-operation

To attain these aims, the participating States will make use of every suitable opportunity to co-operate in the field of environment and, in particular, within the areas described below as examples:

*Control of air pollution*

Desulphurization of fossil fuels and exhaust gases; pollution control of heavy metals, particles, aerosols, nitrogen oxides, in particular those emitted by transport, power stations, and other industrial plants; systems and methods of observation and control of air pollution and its effects, including long-range transport of air pollutants;

*Water pollution control and fresh water utilization*

Prevention and control of water pollution, in particular of transboundary rivers and international lakes; techniques for the improvement of the quality of water and further development of ways and means for industrial and municipal sewage effluent purification; methods of assessment of fresh water resources and the improvement of their utilization, in particular by developing methods of production which are less polluting and lead to less consumption of fresh water;

*Protection of the marine environment*

Protection of the marine environment of participating States, and especially the Mediterranean Sea, from pollutants emanating from land-based sources and those from ships and other vessels, notably the harmful substances listed in Annexes I and II to the London Convention on the Prevention of Marine Pollution by the Dumping of Wastes and Other Matters; problems of maintaining marine ecological balances and food chains, in particular such problems as may arise from the exploration and exploitation of biological and mineral resources of the seas and the sea-bed;

*Land utilization and soils*

Problems associated with more effective use of lands, including land amelioration, reclamation and recultivation; control of soil pollution, water and air erosion, as well as other forms of soil degradation; maintaining and increasing the productivity of soils with due regard for the possible negative effects of the application of chemical fertilizers and pesticides;

*Nature conservation and nature reserves*

Protection of nature and nature reserves; conservation and maintenance of existing genetic resources, especially rare animal and plant species; conservation of natural ecological systems; establishment of nature reserves and other protected landscapes and areas, including their use for research, tourism, recreation and other purposes;

*Improvement of environmental conditions in areas of human settlement*

Environmental conditions associated with transport, housing, working areas, urban development and planning, water supply and sewage disposal systems; assessment of harmful effects of noise, and noise control methods; collection, treatment and utilization of wastes, including the recovery and recycling of materials; research on substitutes for non-biodegradable substances;

*Fundamental research, monitoring, forecasting and assessment of environmental changes*

Study of changes in climate, landscapes and ecological balances under the impact of both natural factors and human activities; forecasting of possible genetic changes in flora and fauna as a result of environmental pollution; harmonization of statistical data, development of scientific concepts and systems of monitoring networks, standardized methods of observation, measurement and assessment of changes in the biosphere; assessment of the effects of environmental pollution levels and degradation of the environment upon human health; study and development of criteria and standards for various environmental pollutants and regulation regarding production and use of various products;

*Legal and administrative measures*

Legal and administrative measures for the protection of the environment including procedures for establishing environmental impact assessments.

### Forms and Methods of Co-operation

The participating States declare that problems relating to the protection and improvement of the environment will be solved on both a bilateral and a multilateral, including regional and sub-regional, basis, making full use of existing patterns and forms of co-operation. They will develop co-operation in the field of the environment in particular by taking into consideration the Stockholm Declaration on the Human Environment, relevant resolutions of the United Nations General Assembly and the United Nations Economic Commission for Europe Prague symposium on environmental problems.

The participating States are resolved that co-operation in the field of the environment will be implemented in particular through:

—exchanges of scientific and technical information, documentation and research results, including information on the means of determining the possible effects on the environment of technical and economic activities;
—organization of conferences, symposia and meetings of experts;
—exchanges of scientists, specialists and trainees;
—joint preparation and implementation of programmes and projects for the study and solution of various problems of environmental protection;
—harmonization, where appropriate and necessary, of environmental protection standards and norms, in particular with the object of avoiding possible difficulties in trade which may arise from efforts to resolve ecological problems of production processes and which relate to the

achievement of certain environmental qualities in manufactured products;
—consultations on various aspects of environmental protection, as agreed upon among countries concerned, especially in connexion with problems which could have international consequences.

The participating States will further develop such co-operation by:

—promoting the progressive development, codification and implementation of international law as one means of preserving and enhancing the human environment, including principles and practices, as accepted by them, relating to pollution and other environmental damage caused by activities within the jurisdiction or control of their States affecting other countries and regions;
—supporting and promoting the implementation of relevant international Conventions to which they are parties, in particular those designed to prevent and combat marine and fresh water pollution, recommending States to ratify Conventions which have already been signed, as well as considering possibilities of accepting other appropriate Conventions to which they are not parties at present;
—advocating the inclusion, where appropriate and possible, of the various areas of co-operation into the programmes of work of the United Nations Economic Commission for Europe, supporting such co-operation within the framework of the Commission and of the United Nations Environment Programme, and taking into account the work of other component international organizations of which they are members;
—making wider use, in all types of co-operation, of information already available from national and international sources, including internationally agreed criteria, and utilizing the possibilities and capabilities of various competent international organizations.

The participating States agree on the following recommendations on specific measures:

—to develop through international co-operation an extensive programme for the monitoring and evaluation of the long-range transport of air pollutants, starting with sulphur dioxide and with possible extension to other pollutants, and to this end to take into account basic elements of a co-operation programme which were identified by the experts who met in Oslo in December 1974 at the invitation of the Norwegian Institute of Air Research;
—to advocate that within the framework of the United Nations Economic Commission for Europe a study be carried out of procedures and relevant experience relating to the activities of Governments in developing the capabilities of their countries to predict adequately environmental consequences of economic activities and technological development.

## 6. Co-operation in Other Areas

### *Development of Transport*

*The participating States,*

*Considering* that the improvement of the conditions of transport constitutes one of the factors essential to the development of co-operation among them,

*Considering* that it is necessary to encourage the development of transport and the solution of existing problems by employing appropriate national and international means,

*Taking into account* the work being carried out on these subjects by existing international organizations, especially by the Inland Transport Committee of the United Nations Economic Commission for Europe,

note that the speed of technical progress in the various fields of transport makes desirable a development of co-operation and an increase in exchanges of information among them;

declare themselves in favour of a simplification and a harmonization of administrative formalities in the field of international transport, in particular at frontiers;

consider it desirable to promote, while allowing for their particular national circumstances in this sector, the harmonization of administrative and technical provisions concerning safety in road, rail, river, air and sea transport;

express their intention to encourage the development of international inland transport of passengers and goods as well as the possibilities of adequate participation in such transport on the basis of reciprocal advantage;

declare themselves in favour, with due respect for their rights and international commitments, of the elimination of disparities arising from the legal provisions applied to traffic on inland waterways which are subject to international conventions and, in particular, of the disparity in the application of those provisions; and to this end invite the member States of the Central Commission for the Navigation of the Rhine, of the Danube Commission and of other bodies to develop the work and studies now being carried out, in particular within the United Nations Economic Commission for Europe;

express their willingness, with a view to improving international rail transport and with due respect for their rights and international commitments, to work towards the elimination of difficulties arising from disparities in existing international legal provisions governing the reciprocal railway transport of passengers and goods between their territories;

express the desire for intensification of the work being carried out by existing international organizations in the field of transport, especially that of the Inland Transport Committee of the United Nations Economic

Commission for Europe, and express their intention to contribute thereto by their efforts;

consider that examination by the participating States of the possibility of their accession to the different conventions or to membership of international organizations specializing in transport matters, as well as their efforts to implement conventions when ratified, could contribute to the strengthening of their co-operation in this field.

### Promotion of Tourism

*The participating States,*

*Aware* of the contribution made by international tourism to the development of mutual understanding among peoples to increased knowledge of other countries' achievements in various fields, as well as to economic, social and cultural progress,

*Recognizing* the interrelationship between the development of tourism and measures taken in other areas of economic activity,

express their intention to encourage increased tourism on both an individual and group basis in particular by:

—encouraging the improvement of the tourist infrastructure and co-operation in this field;

—encouraging the carrying out of joint tourist projects including technical co-operation, particularly where this is suggested by territorial proximity and the convergence of tourist interests;

—encouraging the exchange of information, including relevant laws and regulations, studies, data and documentation relating to tourism, and by improving statistics with a view to facilitating their comparability;

—dealing in a positive spirit with questions connected with the allocation of financial means for tourist travel abroad, having regard to their economic possibilities, as well as with those connected with the formalities required for such travel, taking into account other provisions on tourism adopted by the Conference;

—facilitating the activities of foreign travel agencies and passenger transport companies in the promotion of international tourism;

—encouraging tourism outside the high season;

—examining the possibilities of exchanging specialists and students in the field of tourism, with a view to improving their qualifications;

—promoting conferences and symposia on the planning and development of tourism;

consider it desirable to carry out in the appropriate international framework, and with the co-operation of the relevant national bodies, detailed studies on tourism, in particular:

—a comparative study on the status and activities of travel agencies as well as on ways and means of achieving better co-operation among them;

—a study of the problems raised by the seasonal concentration of vacations, with the ultimate objective of encouraging tourism outside peak periods;

—studies of the problems arising in areas where tourism has injured the environment;

consider also that interested parties might wish to study the following questions:

—uniformity of hotel classification; and

—tourist routes comprising two or more countries;

will endeavour, where possible, to ensure that the development of tourism does not injure the environment and artistic, historic and cultural heritage in their respective countries;

will pursue their co-operation in the field of tourism bilaterally and multilaterally with a view to attaining the above objectives.

### Economic and Social Aspects of Migrant Labour

*The participating States,*

*Considering* that the movements of migrant workers in Europe have reached substantial proportions, and that they constitute an important economic, social and human factor for host countries as well as for countries of origin,

*Recognizing* that workers' migrations have also given rise to a number of economic, social, human and other problems in both the receiving countries and the countries of origin,

*Taking due account* of the activities of the competent international organizations, more particularly the International Labour Organization, in this area,

are of the opinion that the problems arising bilaterally from the migration of workers in Europe as well as between the participating States should be dealt with by the parties directly concerned, in order to resolve these problems in their mutual interest, in the light of the concern of each State involved to take due account of the requirements resulting from its socio-economic situation, having regard to the obligation of each State to comply with the bilateral and multilateral agreements to which it is party, and with the following aims in view:

to encourage the efforts of the countries of origin directed towards increasing the possibilities of employment for their nationals in their own territories, in particular by developing economic co-operation appropriate for this purpose and suitable for the host countries and the countries of origin concerned;

to ensure, through collaboration between the host country and the country of origin, the conditions under which the orderly movement of workers might take place, while at the same time protecting their personal and social welfare and, if appropriate, to organize the recruitment of migrant workers and the provisions of elementary language and vocational training;

to ensure equality of rights between migrant workers and nationals of the host countries with regard to conditions of employment and work and to social security, and to endeavour to ensure that migrant workers may enjoy satisfactory living conditions, especially housing conditions;

to endeavour to ensure, as far as possible, that migrant workers may enjoy the same opportunities as nationals of the host countries of finding other suitable employment in the event of unemployment;

to regard with favour the provision of vocational training to migrant workers and, as far as possible, free instruction in the language of the host country, in the framework of their employment;

to confirm the right of migrant workers to receive, as far as possible, regular information in their own language, covering both their country of origin and the host country;

to ensure that the children of migrant workers established in the host country have access to the education usually given there, under the same conditions as the children of that country and, furthermore, to permit them to receive supplementary education in their own language, national culture, history and geography;

to bear in mind that migrant workers, particularly those who have acquired qualifications, can by returning to their countries after a certain period of time help to remedy the deficiency of skilled labour in their country of origin;

to facilitate, as far as possible, the reuniting of migrant workers with their families;

to regard with favour the efforts of the countries of origin to attract the savings of migrant workers, with a view to increasing, within the framework of their economic development, appropriate opportunities for employment, thereby facilitating the reintegration of these workers on their return home.

### Training of Personnel

*The participating States,*

*Conscious* of the importance of the training and advanced training of professional staff and technicians for the economic development of every country,

declare themselves willing to encourage co-operation in this field notably by promoting exchange of information on the subject of institutions, programmes and methods of training and advanced training open to professional staff and technicians in the various sectors of economic activity and especially in those of management, public planning, agriculture and commercial and banking techniques;

consider that it is desirable to develop, under mutually acceptable conditions, exchanges of professional staff and technicians, particularly through training activities, of which it would be left to the competent and interested bodies in the participating States to discuss the modalities—duration, financing, education and qualification levels of potential participants;

declare themselves in favour of examining, through appropriate channels, the possibilities of co-operating on the organization and carrying out of vocational training on the job, more particularly in professions involving modern techniques.

# QUESTIONS RELATING TO SECURITY AND CO-OPERATION IN THE MEDITERRANEAN

*The participating States,*

*Conscious* of the geographical, historical, cultural, economic and political aspects of their relationship with the non-participating Mediterranean States,

*Convinced* that security in Europe is to be considered in the broader context of world security and is closely linked with security in the Mediterranean area as a whole, and that accordingly the process of improving security should not be confined to Europe but should extend to other parts of the world, and in particular to the Mediterranean area,

*Believing* that the strengthening of security and the intensification of co-operation in Europe would stimulate positive processes in the Mediterranean region, and expressing their intention to contribute towards peace, security and justice in the region, in which ends the participating States and the non-participating Mediterranean States have a common interest,

*Recognizing* the importance of their mutual economic relations with the non-participating Mediterranean States, and conscious of their common interest in the further development of co-operation,

*Noting* with appreciation the interest expressed by the non-participating Mediterranean States in the Conference since its inception, and having duly taken their contributions into account,

*Declare their intention:*

—to promote the development of good-neighbourly relations with the non-participating Mediterranean States in conformity with the purposes and principles of the Charter of the United Nations, on which their relations are based, and with the United Nations Declaration on Principles of International Law concerning Friendly Relations and Co-operation among States and accordingly, in this context, to conduct their relations with the non-participating Mediterranean States in the spirit of the principles set forth in the Declaration on Principles Guiding Relations between Participating States;

—to seek, by further improving their relations with the non-participating Mediterranean States, to increase mutual confidence, so as to promote security and stability in the Mediterranean area as a whole;

—to encourage with the non-participating Mediterranean States the development of mutually beneficial co-operation in the various fields of economic activity, especially by expanding commercial exchanges, on the basis of a common awareness of the necessity for stability and progress in trade relations, of their mutual economic interests, and of differences in

the levels of economic development, thereby promoting their economic advancement and well-being;
—to contribute to a diversified development of the economies of the non-participating Mediterranean countries, whilst taking due account of their national development objectives, and to co-operate with them, especially in the sectors of industry, science and technology, in their efforts to achieve a better utilization of their resources, thus promoting a more harmonious development of economic relations;
—to intensify their efforts and their co-operation on a bilateral and multi-lateral basis with the non-participating Mediterranean States directed towards the improvement of the environment of the Mediterranean, especially the safeguarding of the biological resources and ecological balance of the sea, by appropriate measures including the prevention and control of pollution; to this end, and in view of the present situation, to co-operate through competent international organizations and in particular within the United Nations Environment Programme (UNEP);
—to promote further contacts and co-operation with the non-participating Mediterranean States in other relevant fields.

In order to advance the objectives set forth above, the participating States also declare their intention of maintaining and amplifying the contacts and dialogue as initiated by the CSCE with the non-participating Mediterranean States to include all the States of the Mediterranean, with the purpose of contributing to peace, reducing armed forces in the region, strengthening security, lessening tensions in the region, and widening the scope of co-operation, ends in which all share a common interest, as well as with the purpose of defining further common objectives.

The participating States would seek, in the framework of their multi-lateral efforts, to encourage progress and appropriate initiatives and to proceed to an exchange of views on the attainment of the above purposes.

# CO-OPERATION IN HUMANITARIAN AND OTHER FIELDS

*The participating States,*

*Desiring* to contribute to the strengthening of peace and understanding among peoples and to the spiritual enrichment of the human personality without distinction as to race, sex, language or religion,

*Conscious* that increased cultural and educational exchanges, broader dissemination of information, contacts between people, and the solution of humanitarian problems will contribute to the attainment of these aims,

*Determined* therefore to co-operate among themselves, irrespective of their political, economic and social systems, in order to create better conditions in the above fields, to develop and strengthen existing forms of co-operation and to work out new ways and means appropriate to these aims,

*Convinced* that this co-operation should take place in full respect for the principles guiding relations among participating States as set forth in the relevant document.

## 1. Human Contacts

*The participating States,*

*Considering* the development of contacts to be an important element in the strengthening of friendly relations and trust among peoples,

*Affirming*, in relation to their present effort to improve conditions in this area, the importance they attach to humanitarian considerations,

*Desiring* in this spirit to develop, with the continuance of détente, further efforts to achieve continuing progress in this field,

*And conscious* that the questions relevant hereto must be settled by the States concerned under mutually acceptable conditions,

*Make it their aim* to facilitate freer movement and contacts, individually and collectively, whether privately or officially, among persons, institutions and organizations of the participating States, and to contribute to the solution of the humanitarian problems that arise in that connexion,

*Declare their readiness* to these ends to take measures which they consider appropriate and to conclude agreements or arrangements among themselves, as may be needed, and

*Express their intention* now to proceed to the implementation of the following:

### (a) *Contacts and Regular Meetings on the Basis of Family Ties*

In order to promote further development of contacts on the basis of family ties the participating States will favourably consider applications for travel with the purpose of allowing persons to enter or leave their territory temporarily, and on a regular basis if desired, in order to visit members of their families.

Applications for temporary visits to meet members of their families will be dealt with without distinction as to the country of origin or destination: existing requirements for travel documents and visas will be applied in this spirit. The preparation and issue of such documents and visas will be effected within reasonable time limits; cases of urgent necessity—such as serious illness or death—will be given priority treatment. They will take such steps as may be necessary to ensure that the fees for official travel documents and visas are acceptable.

They confirm that the presentation of an application concerning contacts on the basis of family ties will not modify the rights and obligations of the applicant or of members of his family.

### (b) *Reunification of Families*

The participating States will deal in a positive and humanitarian spirit with the applications of persons who wish to be reunited with members of their family, with special attention being given to requests of an urgent character—such as requests submitted by persons who are ill or old.

They will deal with applications in this field as expeditiously as possible.

They will lower where necessary the fees charged in connexion with these applications to ensure that they are at a moderate level.

Applications for the purpose of family reunification which are not granted may be renewed at the appropriate level and will be reconsidered at reasonably short intervals by the authorities of the country of residence or destination, whichever is concerned; under such circumstances fees will be charged only when applications are granted.

Persons whose applications for family reunification are granted may bring with them or ship their household and personal effects; to this end the participating States will use all possibilities provided by existing regulations.

Until members of the same family are reunited meetings and contacts between them may take place in accordance with the modalities for contacts on the basis of family ties.

The participating States will support the effects of Red Cross and Red Crescent Societies concerned with the problems of family reunification.

They confirm that the presentation of an application concerning family reunification will not modify the rights and obligations of the applicant or of members of his family.

The receiving participating State will take appropriate care with regard to employment for persons from other participating States who take up permanent residence in that State in connexion with family reunification with its citizens and see that they are afforded opportunities equal to those enjoyed by its own citizens for education, medical assistance and social security.

### (c) *Marriage Between Citizens of Different States*

The participating States will examine favourably and on the basis of humanitarian considerations requests for exit or entry permits from persons who have decided to marry a citizen from another participating State.

The processing and issuing of the documents required for the above purposes and for the marriage will be in accordance with the provisions accepted for family reunification.

In dealing with requests from couples from different participating States, once married, to enable them and the minor children of their marriage to transfer their permanent residence to a State in which either one is normally a resident, the participating States will also apply the provisions accepted for family reunification.

### (d) *Travel for Personal or Professional Reasons*

The participating States intend to facilitate wider travel by their citizens for personal or professional reasons and to this end they intend in particular:

—gradually to simplify and to administer flexibly the procedures for exit and entry;

—to ease regulations concerning movement of citizens from the other participating States in their territory, with due regard to security requirements.

They will endeavour gradually to lower, where necessary, the fees for visas and official travel documents.

They intend to consider, as necessary, means—including, in so far as appropriate, the conclusion of multilateral or bilateral consular conventions or other relevant agreements or understandings—for the improvement of arrangements to provide consular services, including legal and consular assistance.

\* \* \*

They confirm that religious faiths, institutions and organizations, practising within the constitutional framework of the participating States, and their representatives can, in the field of their activities, have contacts and meetings among themselves and exchange information.

### (e) *Improvement of Conditions for Tourism on an Individual or Collective Basis*

The participating States consider that tourism contributes to a fuller knowledge of the life, culture and history of other countries, to the growth of understanding among peoples, to the improvement of contacts and to the broader use of leisure. They intend to promote the development of tourism, on an individual or collective basis, and, in particular, they intend:

—to promote visits to their respective countries by encouraging the provision of appropriate facilities and the simplification and expediting of necessary formalities relating to such visits;

—to increase, on the basis of appropriate agreements or arrangements where necessary, co-operation in the development of tourism, in particular by considering bilaterally possible ways to increase information relating to travel to other countries and to the reception and service of tourists, and other related questions of mutual interest.

### (f) *Meetings Among Young People*

The participating States intend to further the development of contacts and exchanges among young people by encouraging:

—increased exchanges and contacts on a short or long term basis among young people working, training or undergoing education through bilateral or multilateral agreements or regular programmes in all cases where it is possible;

—study by their youth organizations of the question of possible agreements relating to frameworks of multilateral youth co-operation;

—agreements or regular programmes relating to the organization of exchanges of students, of international youth seminars, of courses of professional training and foreign language study;

—the further development of youth tourism and the provision to this end of appropriate facilities;

—the development, where possible, of exchanges, contacts and co-operation on a bilateral or multilateral basis between their organizations which represent wide circles of young people working, training or undergoing education;

—awareness among youth of the importance of developing mutual understanding and of strengthening friendly relations and confidence among peoples.

### (g) *Sport*

In order to expand existing links and co-operation in the field of sport the participating States will encourage contacts and exchanges of this kind, including sports meetings and competitions of all sorts, on the basis of the established international rules, regulations and practice.

### (h) *Expansion of Contacts*

By way of further developing contacts among governmental institutions and non-governmental organizations and associations, including women's organizations, the participating States will facilitate the convening of meetings as well as travel by delegations, groups and individuals.

## 2. Information

*The participating States,*

*Conscious* of the need for an ever wider knowledge and understanding of the various aspects of life in other participating States,

*Acknowledging* the contribution of this process to the growth of confidence between peoples,

*Desiring*, with the development of mutual understanding between the participating States and with the further improvement of their relations, to continue further efforts towards progress in this field,

*Recognizing* the importance of the dissemination of information from the other participating States and of a better acquaintance with such information,

*Emphasizing* therefore the essential and influential role of the press, radio, television, cinema and news agencies and of the journalists working in these fields,

*Make it their aim* to facilitate the freer and wider dissemination of information of all kinds, to encourage co-operation in the field of information and the exchange of information with other countries, and to improve the conditions under which journalists from one participating State exercise their profession in another participating State, and

*Express their intention* in particular:

### (a) *Improvement of the Circulation of, Access to, and Exchange of Information*

(i) *Oral Information*

—To facilitate the dissemination of oral information through the encouragement of lectures and lecture tours by personalities and specialists from the other participating States, as well as exchanges of opinions at round table meetings, seminars, symposia, summer schools, congresses and other bilateral and multilateral meetings.

(ii) *Printed Information*

—To facilitate the improvement of the dissemination, on their territory, of newspapers and printed publications, periodical and non-periodical, from the other participating States. For this purpose:

they will encourage their competent firms and organizations to conclude agreements and contracts designed gradually to increase the quantities and the number of titles of newspapers and publications imported from the other participating States. These agreements and contracts should in particular mention the speediest conditions of delivery and the use of the normal channels existing in each country for the distribution of its own publications and newspapers, as well as forms and means of payment agreed between the parties making it possible to achieve the objectives aimed at by these agreements and contracts;

where necessary, they will take appropriate measures to achieve the above objectives and to implement the provisions contained in the agreements and contracts.

—To contribute to the improvement of access by the public to periodical and non-periodical printed publications imported on the bases indicated above. In particular:

they will encourage an increase in the number of places where these publications are on sale;

they will facilitate the availability of these periodical publications during congresses, conferences, official visits and other international events and to tourists during the season;

they will develop the possibilities for taking out subscriptions according to the modalities particular to each country;

they will improve the opportunities for reading and borrowing these publications in large public libraries and their reading rooms as well as in university libraries.

They intend to improve the possibilities for acquaintance with bulletins of official information issued by diplomatic missions and distributed by those missions on the basis of arrangements acceptable to the interested parties.

(iii) *Filmed and Broadcast Information*

—To promote the improvement of the dissemination of filmed and broadcast information. To this end:

they will encourage the wider showing and broadcasting of a greater variety of recorded and filmed information from the other participating States, illustrating the various aspects of life in their countries and received on the basis of such agreements or arrangements as may be necessary between the organizations and firms directly concerned;

they will facilitate the import by competent organizations and firms of recorded audio-visual material from the other participating States.

The participating States note the expansion in the dissemination of information broadcast by radio, and express the hope for the continuation of this process, so as to meet the interest of mutual understanding among peoples and the aims set forth by this Conference.

### (b) *Co-operation in the Field of Information*

—To encourage co-operation in the field of information on the basis of short or long term agreements or arrangements. In particular:

they will favour increased co-operation among mass media organizations, including press agencies, as well as among publishing houses and organizations;

they will favour co-operation among public or private, national or international radio and television organizations, in particular through the exchange of both live and recorded radio and television programmes, and through the joint production and the broadcasting and distribution of such programmes;

they will encourage meetings and contacts both between journalists' organizations and between journalists from the participating States;

they will view favourably the possibilities of arrangements between periodical publications as well as between newspapers from the participating States, for the purpose of exchanging and publishing articles;

they will encourage the exchange of technical information as well as the organization of joint research and meetings devoted to the exchange of experience and views between experts in the field of the press, radio and television.

### (c) *Improvement of Working Conditions for Journalists*

The participating States, desiring to improve the conditions under which journalists from one participating State exercise their profession in another participating State, intend in particular to:

—examine in a favourable spirit and within a suitable and reasonable time scale requests from journalists for visas;

—grant to permanently accredited journalists of the participating States, on the basis of arrangements, multiple entry and exit visas for specified periods;

—facilitate the issue to accredited journalists of the participating States of permits for stay in their country of temporary residence and, if and when these are necessary, of other official papers which it is appropriate for them to have;

—ease, on a basis of reciprocity, procedures for arranging travel by journalists of the participating States in the country where they are exercising their profession, and to provide progressively greater opportunities for such travel, subject to the observance of regulations relating to the existence of areas closed for security reasons;

—ensure that requests by such journalists for such travel receive, in so far as possible, an expeditious response, taking into account the time scale of the request;

—increase the opportunities for journalists of the participating States to communicate personally with their sources, including organizations and official institutions;

—grant to journalists of the participating States the right to import, subject only to its being taken out again, the technical equipment (photographic, cinematographic, tape recorder, radio and television) necessary for the exercise of their profession;[1]

—enable journalists of the other participating States, whether permanently or temporarily accredited, to transmit completely, normally and rapidly by means recognized by the participating States to the information organs which they represent, the results of their professional activity, including tape recordings and undeveloped film, for the purpose of publication or of broadcasting on the radio or television.

The participating States reaffirm that the legitimate pursuit of their professional activity will neither render journalists liable to expulsion nor otherwise penalize them. If an accredited journalist is expelled, he will be informed of the reasons for this act and may submit an application for re-examination of his case.


3. Co-operation and Exchanges in the Field of Culture

*The participating States,*

*Considering* that cultural exchanges and co-operation contribute to a better comprehension among people and among peoples, and thus promote a lasting understanding among States,

*Confirming* the conclusions already formulated in this field at the multi-lateral level, particularly at the Intergovernmental Conference on Cultural Policies in Europe, organized by UNESCO in Helsinki in June 1972, where interest was manifested in the active participation of the broadest possible social groups in an increasingly diversified cultural life,

*Desiring*, with the development of mutual confidence and the further improvement of relations between the participating States, to continue further efforts toward progress in this field,

*Disposed* in this spirit to increase substantially their cultural exchanges, with regard both to persons and to cultural works, and to develop among them an active co-operation, both at the bilateral and the multilateral level, in all the fields of culture,

---

[1] While recognizing that appropriate local personnel are employed by foreign journalists in many instances, the participating States note that the above provisions would be applied, subject to the observance of the appropriate rules, to persons from the other participating States, who are regularly and professionally engaged as technicians, photographers or camera-men of the press, radio, television or cinema.

*Convinced* that such a development of their mutual relations will contribute to the enrichment of the respective cultures, while respecting the originality of each, as well as to the reinforcement among them of a consciousness of common values, while continuing to develop cultural co-operation with other countries of the world,

*Declare* that they jointly set themselves the following objectives:

(*a*) to develop the mutual exchange of information with a view to a better knowledge of respective cultural achievements,

(*b*) to improve the facilities for the exchange and for the dissemination of cultural property,

(*c*) to promote access by all to respective cultural achievements,

(*d*) to develop contacts and co-operation among persons active in the field of culture,

(*e*) to seek new fields and forms of cultural co-operation,

Thus *give expression to* their common will to take progressive, coherent and long-term action in order to achieve the objectives of the present declaration; and

*Express their intention* now to proceed to the implementation of the following:

### Extension of Relations

To expand, and improve at the various levels co-operation and links in the field of culture, in particular by:

—concluding, where appropriate, agreements on a bilateral or multilateral basis, providing for the extension of relations among competent State institutions and non-governmental organization in the field of culture, as well as among people engaged in cultural activities, taking into account the need both for flexibility and the fullest possible use of existing agreements, and bearing in mind that agreements and also other arrangements constitute important means of developing cultural co-operation and exchanges;

—contributing to the development of direct communication and co-operation among relevant State institutions and non-governmental organizations, including, where necessary, such communication and co-operation carried out on the basis of special agreements and arrangements;

—encouraging direct contacts and communications among persons engaged in cultural activities, including, where necessary, such contacts and communications carried out on the basis of special agreements and arrangements.

### Mutual Knowledge

Within their competence to adopt on a bilateral and multilateral level, appropriate measures which would give their peoples a more comprehensive and complete mutual knowledge of their achievements in the various fields of culture, and among them:

—to examine jointly, if necessary with the assistance of appropriate international organizations, the possible creation in Europe and the structure of a bank of cultural data, which would collect information from the participating countries and make it available to its correspondents on their request, and to convene for this purpose a meeting of experts from interested States;

—to consider, if necessary in conjunction with appropriate international organizations, ways of compiling in Europe an inventory of documentary films of a cultural or scientific nature from the participating States;

—to encourage more frequent book exhibitions and to examine the possibility of organizing periodically in Europe a large-scale exhibition of books from the participating States;

—to promote the systematic exchange, between the institutions concerned and publishing houses, of catalogues of available books as well as of prepublication material which will include, as far as possible, all forthcoming publications; and also to promote the exchange of material between firms publishing encyclopaedias, with a view to improving the presentation of each country;

—to examine jointly questions of expanding and improving exchanges of information in the various fields of culture, such as theatre, music, library work as well as the conservation and restoration of cultural property.

### Exchanges and Dissemination

To contribute to the improvement of facilities for exchanges and the dissemination of cultural property, by appropriate means, in particular by:

—studying the possibilities for harmonizing and reducing the charges relating to international commercial exchanges of books and other cultural materials, and also for new means of insuring works of art in foreign exhibitions and for reducing the risks of damage or loss to which these works are exposed by their movement;

—facilitating the formalities of customs clearance, in good time for programmes of artistic events, of the works of art, materials and accessories appearing on lists agreed upon by the organizers of these events;

—encouraging meetings among representatives of competent organizations and relevant firms to examine measures within their field of activity—such as the simplification of orders, time limits for sending supplies and modalities of payment—which might facilitate international commercial exchanges of books;

—promoting the loan and exchange of films among their film institutes and film libraries;

—encouraging the exchange of information among interested parties concerning events of a cultural character foreseen in the participating States, in fields where this is most appropriate, such as music, theatre and the plastic and graphic arts, with a view to contributing to the compilation and publication of a calendar of such events, with the assistance, where necessary, of the appropriate international organizations;

—encouraging a study of the impact which the foreseeable development, and a possible harmonization among interested parties, of the technical means used for the dissemination of culture might have on the development of cultural co-operation and exchanges, while keeping in view the preservation of the diversity and originality of their respective cultures;

—encouraging, in the way they deem appropriate, within their cultural policies, the further development of interest in the cultural heritage of the other participating States, conscious of the merits and the value of each culture;

—endeavouring to ensure the full and effective application of the international agreements and conventions on copyrights and on circulation of cultural property to which they are party or to which they may decide in the future to become party.

### Access

To promote fuller mutual access by all to the achievements—works, experiences and performing arts—in the various fields of culture of their countries, and to that end to make the best possible efforts, in accordance with their competence, more particularly:

—to promote wider dissemination of books and artistic works, in particular by such means as:

facilitating, while taking full account of the international copyright conventions to which they are party, international contacts and communications between authors and publishing houses as well as other cultural institutions, with a view to a more complete mutual access to cultural achievements;

recommending that, in determining the size of editions, publishing houses take into account also the demand from the other participating States, and that rights of sale in other participating States be granted where possible to several sales organizations of the importing countries, by agreement between interested partners;

encouraging competent organizations and relevant firms to conclude agreements and contracts and contributing, by this means, to a gradual increase in the number and diversity of works by authors from the other participating States available in the original and in translation in their libraries and bookshops;

promoting, where deemed appropriate, an increase in the number of sales outlets where books by authors from the other participating States, imported in the original on the basis of agreements and contracts, and in translation, are for sale;

promoting, on a wider scale, the translation of works in the sphere of literature and other fields of cultural activity, produced in the languages of the other participating States, especially from the less widely-spoken languages, and the publication and dissemination of the translated works by such measures as:

encouraging more regular contacts between interested publishing houses; developing their efforts in the basic and advanced training of translators; encouraging, by appropriate means, the publishing houses of their countries to publish translations;

facilitating the exchange between publishers and interested institutions of lists of books which might be translated;

promoting between their countries the professional activity and co-operation of translators;

carrying out joint studies on ways of further promoting translations and their dissemination;

improving and expanding exchanges of books, bibliographies and catalogue cards between libraries;

—to envisage other appropriate measures which would permit, where necessary by mutual agreement among interested parties, the facilitation of access to their respective cultural achievements, in particular in the field of books;

—to contribute by appropriate means to the wider use of the mass media in order to improve mutual acquaintance with the cultural life of each;

—to seek to develop the necessary conditions for migrant workers and their families to preserve their links with their national culture, and also to adapt themselves to their new cultural environment;

—to encourage the competent bodies and enterprises to make a wider choice and effect wider distribution of full-length and documentary films from the other participating States, and to promote more frequent non-commercial showings, such as premières, film weeks and festivals, giving due consideration to films from countries whose cinematographic works are less well known;

—to promote, by appropriate means, the extension of opportunities for specialists from the other participating States to work with materials of a cultural character from film and audio-visual archives, within the framework of the existing rules for work on such archival materials;

—to encourage a joint study by interested bodies, where appropriate with the assistance of the competent international organizations, of the expediency and the conditions for the establishment of a repertory of their recorded television programmes of a cultural nature, as well as of the means of viewing them rapidly in order to facilitate their selection and possible acquisition.

### Contacts and Co-operation

To contribute, by appropriate means, to the development of contacts and co-operation in the various fields of culture, especially among creative artists and people engaged in cultural activities, in particular by making efforts to:

—promote for persons active in the field of culture, travel and meetings including, where necessary, those carried out on the basis of agreements, contracts or other special arrangements and which are relevant to their cultural co-operation;

—encourage in this way contacts among creative and performing artists and artistic groups with a view to their working together, making known their works in other participating States or exchanging views on topics relevant to their common activity;

—encourage, where necessary through appropriate arrangements, exchanges of trainees and specialists and the granting of scholarships for basic and advanced training in various fields of culture such as the arts and architecture, museums and libraries, literary studies and translation, and contribute to the creation of favourable conditions of reception in their respective institutions;

—encourage the exchange of experience in the training of organizers of cultural activities as well as of teachers and specialists in fields such as theatre, opera, ballet, music and fine arts;

—continue to encourage the organization of international meetings among creative artists, especially young creative artists, on current questions of artistic and literary creation which are of interest for joint study;

—study other possibilities for developing exchanges and co-operation among persons active in the field of culture, with a view to a better mutual knowledge of the cultural life of the participating States.

### Fields and Forms of Co-operation

To encourage the search for new fields and forms of cultural co-operation, to these ends contributing to the conclusion among interested parties, where necessary, of appropriate agreements and arrangements, and in this context to promote:

—joint studies regarding cultural policies, in particular in their social aspects, and as they relate to planning, town-planning, educational and environmental policies, and the cultural aspects of tourism;

—the exchange of knowledge in the realm of cultural diversity, with a view to contributing thus to a better understanding by interested parties of such diversity where it occurs;

—the exchange of information, and as may be appropriate, meetings of experts, the elaboration and the execution of research programmes and projects, as well as their joint evaluation, and the dissemination of the results, on the subjects indicated above;

—such forms of cultural co-operation and the development of such joint projects as:

international events in the fields of the plastic and graphic arts, cinema, theatre, ballet, music, folklore, etc.; book fairs and exhibitions, joint performances of operatic and dramatic works, as well as performances given by soloists, instrumental ensembles, orchestras, choirs and other artistic groups, including those composed of amateurs, paying due attention to the organization of international cultural youth events and the exchange of young artists;

the inclusion of works by writers and composers from the other participating States in the repertoires of soloists and artistic ensembles;

the preparation, translation and publication of articles, studies and monographs, as well of low-cost books and of artistic and literary collections, suited to making better known respective cultural achievements, envisaging for this purpose meetings among experts and representatives of publishing houses;

the co-production and the exchange of films and of radio and television programmes, by promoting, in particular, meetings among producers, technicians and representatives of the public authorities with a view to working out favourable conditions for the execution of specific joint projects and by encouraging, in the field of co-production, the establishment of international filming teams;

the organization of competitions for architects and town-planners, bearing in mind the possible implementation of the best projects and the formation, where possible, of international teams;

the implementation of joint projects of conserving, restoring and showing to advantage works of art, historical and archaeological monuments and sites of cultural interest, with the help, in appropriate cases, of international organizations of a governmental or non-governmental character as well as of private institutions—competent and active in these fields— envisaging for this purpose:

periodic meetings of experts of the interested parties to elaborate the necessary proposals, while bearing in mind the need to consider these questions in a wider social and economic context;

the publication in appropriate periodicals of articles designed to make

known and to compare, among the participating States, the most
significant achievements and innovations;

a joint study with a view to the improvement and possible harmonization of the different systems used to inventory and catalogue the
historical monuments and places of cultural interest in their countries;
the study of the possibilities for organizing international courses for
the training of specialists in different disciplines relating to restoration.

\*    \*    \*

*National minorities or regional cultures*

The participating States, recognizing the contribution that national
minorities or regional cultures can make to co-operation among them in
various fields of culture, intend, when such minorities or cultures exist
within their territory, to facilitate this contribution, taking into account the
legitimate interests of their members.

### 4. Co-operation and Exchanges in the Field of Education

*The participating States,*

*Conscious* that the development of relations of an international character
in the fields of education and science contributes to a better mutual understanding and is to the advantage of all peoples as well as to the benefit of
future generations,

*Prepared* to facilitate, between organizations, institutions and persons
engaged in education and science, the further development of exchanges of
knowledge and experience as well as of contacts, on the basis of special
arrangements where these are necessary,

*Desiring* to strengthen the links among educational and scientific establishments and also to encourage their co-operation in sectors of common
interest, particularly where the levels of knowledge and resources require
efforts to be concerted internationally, and

*Convinced* that progress in these fields should be accompanied and supported by a wider knowledge of foreign languages,

*Express* to these ends their intention in particular:

#### (a) *Extension of Relations*

To expand and improve at the various levels co-operation and links in the
fields of education and science, in particular by:

—concluding where appropriate, bilateral or multilateral agreements
providing for co-operation and exchanges among State institutions, non-
governmental bodies and persons engaged in activities in education and

science, bearing in mind the need both for flexibility and the fuller use of existing agreements and arrangements;

—promoting the conclusion of direct arrangements between universities and other institutions of higher education and research, in the framework of agreements between governments where appropriate;

—encouraging among persons engaged in education and science direct contacts and communications, including those based on special agreements or arrangements where these are appropriate.

### (b) *Access and Exchanges*

To improve access, under mutually acceptable conditions, for students, teachers and scholars of the participating States to each other's educational, cultural and scientific institutions, and to intensify exchanges among these institutions in all areas of common interest, in particular by:

—increasing the exchange of information on facilities for study and courses open to foreign participants, as well as on the conditions under which they will be admitted and received;

—facilitating travel between the participating States by scholars, teachers and students for purposes of study, teaching and research as well as for improving knowledge of each other's educational, cultural and scientific achievements;

—encouraging the award of scholarships for study, teaching and research in their countries to scholars, teachers and students of other participating States;

—establishing, developing or encouraging programmes providing for the broader exchange of scholars, teachers and students, including the organization of symposia, seminars and collaborative projects, and the exchanges of educational and scholarly information such as university publications and materials from libraries;

—promoting the efficient implementation of such arrangements and programmes by providing scholars, teachers and students in good time with more detailed information about their placing in universities and institutes and the programmes envisaged for them; by granting them the opportunity to use relevant scholarly, scientific and open archival materials; and by facilitating their travel within the receiving State for the purpose of study or research as well as in the form of vacation tours on the basis of the usual procedures;

—promoting a more exact assessment of the problems of comparison and equivalence of academic degrees and diplomas by fostering the exchange of information on the organization, duration and content of studies, the comparison of methods of assessing levels of knowledge and academic qualifications, and, where feasible, arriving at the mutual recognition of academic degrees and diplomas either through governmental agreements, where necessary, or direct arrangements between universities and other institutions of higher learning and research;

—recommending, moreover, to the appropriate international organizations that they should intensify their efforts to reach a generally acceptable solution to the problems of comparison and equivalence between academic degrees and diplomas.

### (c) *Science*

Within their competence to broaden and improve co-operation and exchanges in the field of science, in particular:

To increase, on a bilateral or multilateral basis, the exchange and dissemination of scientific information and documentation by such means as:

—making this information more widely available to scientists and research workers of the other participating States through, for instance, participation in international information-sharing programmes or through other appropriate arrangements;

—broadening and facilitating the exchange of samples and other scientific materials used particularly for fundamental research in the fields of natural sciences and medicine;

—inviting scientific institutions and universities to keep each other more fully and regularly informed about their current and contemplated research work in fields of common interest.

To facilitate the extension of communications and direct contacts between universities, scientific institutions and associations as well as among scientists and research workers, including those based where necessary on special agreements or arrangements, by such means as:

—further developing exchanges of scientists and research workers and encouraging the organization of preparatory meetings or working groups on research topics of common interest;

—encouraging the creation of joint teams of scientists to pursue research projects under arrangements made by the scientific institutions of several countries;

—assisting the organization and successful functioning of international conferences and seminars and participation in them by their scientists and research workers;

—furthermore envisaging, in the near future, a 'Scientific Forum' in the form of a meeting of leading personalities in science from the participating States to discuss interrelated problems of common interest concerning current and future developments in science, and to promote the expansion of contacts, communications and the exchange of information between scientific institutions and among scientists;

—foreseeing, at an early date, a meeting of experts representing the participating States and their national scientific institutions, in order to prepare such a 'Scientific Forum' in consultation with appropriate international organizations, such as UNESCO and the ECE;

—considering in due course what further steps might be taken with respect to the 'Scientific Forum'.

To develop in the field of scientific research, on a bilateral or multilateral basis, the co-ordination of programmes carried out in the participating States and the organization of joint programmes, especially in the areas mentioned below, which may involve the combined efforts of scientists and in certain cases the use of costly or unique equipment. The list of subjects in these areas is illustrative; and specific projects would have to be determined subsequently by the potential partners in the participating States, taking account of the contribution which could be made by appropriate international organizations and scientific institutions:

—*exact and natural sciences*, in particular fundamental research in such fields as mathematics, physics, theoretical physics, geophysics, chemistry, biology, ecology and astronomy;

—*medicine*, in particular basic research into cancer and cardiovascular diseases, studies on the diseases endemic in the developing countries, as well as medico-social research with special emphasis on occupational diseases, the rehabilitation of the handicapped and the care of mothers, children and the elderly;

—*the humanities and social sciences*, such as history, geography, philosophy, psychology, pedagogical research, linguistics, sociology, the legal, political and economic sciences; comparative studies on social, socio-economic and cultural phenomena which are of common interest to the participating States, especially the problems of human environment and urban development: and scientific studies on the methods of conserving and restoring monuments and works of art.

### (d) *Foreign Languages and Civilizations*

To encourage the study of foreign languages and civilizations as an important means of expanding communication among peoples for their better acquaintance with the culture of each country, as well as for the strengthening of international co-operation; to this end to stimulate, within their competence, the further development and improvement of foreign language teaching and the diversification of choice of languages taught at various levels, paying due attention to less widely-spread or studied languages, and in particular:

—to intensify co-operation aimed at improving the teaching of foreign languages through exchanges of information and experience concerning the development and application of effective modern teaching methods and technical aids, adapted to the needs of different categories of students, including methods of accelerated teaching; and to consider the possibility of conducting, on a bilateral or multilateral basis, studies of new methods of foreign language teaching;

—to encourage co-operation between institutions concerned, on a bilateral or multilateral basis, aimed at exploiting more fully the resources of modern educational technology in language teaching, for example through comparative studies by their specialists and, where agreed, through exchanges or transfers of audio-visual materials, of materials used for preparing textbooks, as well as of information about new types of technical equipment used for teaching languages;

—to promote the exchange of information on the experience acquired in the training of language teachers and to intensify exchanges on a bilateral basis of language teachers and students as well as to facilitate their participation in summer courses in languages and civilizations, wherever these are organized;

—to encourage co-operation among experts in the field of lexicography with the aim of defining the necessary terminological equivalents, particularly in the scientific and technical disciplines, in order to facilitate relations among scientific institutions and specialists;

—to promote the wider spread of foreign language study among the different types of secondary education establishments and greater possibilities of choice between an increased number of European languages; and in this context to consider, wherever appropriate, the possibilities for developing the recruitment and training of teachers as well as the organization of the student groups required;

—to favour, in higher education, a wider choice in the languages offered to language students and greater opportunities for other students to study various foreign languages; also to facilitate, where desirable, the organization of courses in languages and civilizations, on the basis of special arrangements as necessary, to be given by foreign lecturers, particularly from European countries having less widely-spread or studied languages;

—to promote, within the framework of adult education, the further development of specialized programmes, adapted to various needs and interests, for teaching foreign languages to their own inhabitants and the languages of host countries to interested adults from other countries; in this context to encourage interested institutions to co-operate, for example, in the elaboration of programmes for teaching by radio and television and by accelerated methods, and also, where desirable, in the definition of study objectives for such programmes, with a view to arriving at comparable levels of language proficiency;

—to encourage the association, where appropriate, of the teaching of foreign languages with the study of the corresponding civilizations and also to make further efforts to stimulate interest in the study of foreign languages, including relevant out-of-class activities.

(e) *Teaching Methods*

To promote the exchange of experience, on a bilateral or multilateral basis, in teaching methods at all levels of education, including those used in permanent and adult education, as well as the exchange of teaching materials, in particular by:

—further developing various forms of contacts and co-operation in the different fields of pedagogical science, for example through comparative or joint studies carried out by interested institutions or through exchanges of information on the results of teaching experiments;

—intensifying exchanges of information on teaching methods used in various educational systems and on results of research into the processes by which pupils and students acquire knowledge, taking account of relevant experience in different types of specialized education;

—facilitating exchanges of experience concerning the organization and functioning of education intended for adults and recurrent education, the relationships between these and other forms and levels of education, as well as concerning the means of adapting education, including vocational and technical training, to the needs of economic and social development in their countries;

—encouraging exchanges of experience in the education of youth and adults in international understanding, with particular reference to those major problems of mankind whose solution calls for a common approach and wider international co-operation;

—encouraging exchanges of teaching materials—including school textbooks, having in mind the possibility of promoting mutual knowledge and facilitating the presentation of each country in such books—as well as exchanges of information on technical innovations in the field of education.

\* \* \*

*National minorities or regional cultures*

The participating States, recognizing the contribution that national minorities or regional cultures can make to co-operation among them in various fields of education, intend, when such minorities or cultures exist within their territory, to facilitate this contribution, taking into account the legitimate interests of their members.

## FOLLOW-UP TO THE CONFERENCE

*The participating States,*

*Having considered and evaluated* the progress made at the Conference on Security and Co-operation in Europe,

*Considering further* that, within the broader context of the world, the Conference is an important part of the process of improving security and developing co-operation in Europe and that its results will contribute significantly to this process,

*Intending* to implement the provisions of the Final Act of the Conference in order to give full effect to its results and thus to further the process of improving security and developing co-operation in Europe,

*Convinced* that, in order to achieve the aims sought by the Conference, they should make further unilateral, bilateral and multilateral efforts and continue, in the appropriate forms set forth below, the multilateral process initiated by the Conference,

1. *Declare their resolve*, in the period following the Conference, to pay due regard to and implement the provisions of the Final Act of the Conference:

   (*a*) unilaterally in all cases which lend themselves to such action;
   (*b*) bilaterally, by negotiations with other participating States;
   (*c*) multilaterally, by meetings of experts of the participating States, and also within the framework of existing international organizations, such as the United Nations Economic Commission for Europe and UNESCO, with regard to educational, scientific and cultural co-operation;

2. *Declare furthermore their resolve* to continue the multilateral process initiated by the Conference:

   (*a*) by proceeding to a thorough exchange of views both on the implementation of the provisions of the Final Act and of the tasks defined by the Conference, as well as, in the context of the questions dealt with by the latter, on the deepening of their mutual relations, the improvement of security and the development of co-operation in Europe, and the development of the process of détente in the future;
   (*b*) by organizing to these ends meetings among their representatives, beginning with a meeting at the level of representatives appointed by the Ministers of Foreign Affairs. This meeting will define the appropriate modalities for the holding of other meetings which could include further similar meetings and the possibility of a new Conference;

3. The first of the meetings indicated above will be held at Belgrade in 1977. A preparatory meeting to organize this meeting will be held at

Belgrade on 15 June 1977. The preparatory meeting will decide on the date, duration, agenda and other modalities of the meeting of representatives appointed by the Ministers of Foreign Affairs;

4. The rules of procedure, the working methods and the scale of distribution for the expenses of the Conference will, *mutatis mutandis*, be applied to the meetings envisaged in paragraphs 1 (*c*), 2 and 3 above. All the above-mentioned meetings will be held in the participating States in rotation. The services of a technical secretariat will be provided by the host country.

The original of this Final Act, drawn up in English, French, German, Italian, Russian and Spanish, will be transmitted to the Government of the Republic of Finland, which will retain it in its archives. Each of the participating States will receive from the Government of the Republic of Finland a true copy of this Final Act.

The text of this Final Act will be published in each participating State, which will disseminate it and make it known as widely as possible.

The Government of the Republic of Finland is requested to transmit to the Secretary-General of the United Nations the text of this Final Act, which is not eligible for registration under Article 102 of the Charter of the United Nations, with a view to its circulation to all the members of the Organization as an official document of the United Nations.

The Government of the Republic of Finland is also requested to transmit the text of this Final Act to the Director-General of UNESCO and to the Executive Secretary of the United Nations Economic Commission for Europe.

Wherefore, the undersigned High Representatives of the participating States, mindful of the high political significance which they attach to the results of the Conference, and declaring their determination to act in accordance with the provisions contained in the above texts, have subscribed their signatures below:

Done at Helsinki,
on 1st August
1975
in the name of

## V. CONCLUDING DOCUMENT OF THE VIENNA
## MEETING OF THE CSCE CONFERENCE, 1989

This document includes a significant set of principles relating to the procedure for the examination of complaints of breaches of the human rights standards set by the Helsinki Final Act (above, p. 391). The relevant meetings took place in Vienna in the period 4 November 1986 to 17 January 1989, and were convened on the basis of the provisions of the Helsinki Final Act concerning the 'follow-up' to the Conference on Security and Co-operation in Europe.

The official title of the document is the 'Concluding Document of the Vienna Meeting (1986) of the Representatives of the Participating States of the Conference on Security and Co-operation in Europe'. The text appears in the publication, *CSCE: A Framework for Europe's Future*, U.S. Information Agency (no date). The two most pertinent sections of the Vienna Concluding Document are set forth below.

The procedure adopted in the Document was invoked by the United Kingdom in the case of Mrs. Doina Cornea, a citizen of Romania (*The Times*, 22 February 1989).

*TEXT*

### HUMAN DIMENSION OF THE CSCE

The participating States,

Recalling the undertakings entered into in the Final Act and in other CSCE documents concerning respect for all human rights and fundamental freedoms, human contacts and other issues of a related humanitarian character,

Recognizing the need to improve the implementation of their CSCE commitments and their co-operation in these areas which are hereafter referred to as the human dimension of the CSCE,

Have, on the basis of the principles and provisions of the Final Act and of other relevant CSCE documents, decided:

1. to exchange information and respond to requests for information and to representations made to them by other participating States on questions relating to the human dimension of the CSCE. Such communications may be forwarded through diplomatic channels or be addressed to any agency designated for these purposes;

2. to hold bilateral meetings with other participating States that so request, in order to examine questions relating to the human dimension of the CSCE, including situations and specific cases with a view to resolving

them. The date and place of such meetings will be arranged by mutual agreement through diplomatic channels;

3. that any participating State which deems it necessary may bring situations and cases in the human dimensions of the CSCE, including those which have been raised at the bilateral meetings described in paragraph 2, to the attention of other participating States through diplomatic channels;

4. that any participating State which deems it necessary may provide information on the exchange of information and the responses to its requests for information and to representations (paragraph 1) and on the results of the bilateral meetings (paragraph 2), including information concerning situations and specific cases, at the meetings of the Conference of the Human Dimension as well as at the main CSCE Follow-up Meetings.

The participating States decide further to convene a Conference on the Human Dimension of the CSCE in order to achieve further progress concerning respect for all human rights and fundamental freedoms, human contacts and other issues of a related humanitarian character. The Conference will hold three meetings before the next CSCE Follow-up Meeting.

The Conference will:

● review developments in the human dimension of the CSCE including the implementation of the relevant CSCE commitments;
● evaluate the functioning of the procedure described in paragraphs 1 to 4 and discuss the information provided according to paragraph 4;
● consider practical proposals for new measures aimed at improving the implementation of the commitments relating to the human dimension of the CSCE and enhancing the effectiveness of the procedures described in paragraphs 1 to 4.

On the basis of these proposals, the Conference will consider adopting new measures.

The first Meeting of the Conference will be held in Paris from 30 May to 23 June 1989.

The second Meeting of the Conference will be held in Copenhagen from 5 June to 29 June 1990.

The third Meeting of the Conference will be held in Moscow from 10 September to 4 October 1991.

The agenda, timetable and other organizational modalities are set out in Annex X.

The next main CSCE Follow-up Meeting, to held in Helsinki, commencing on 24 March 1992, will assess the functioning of the procedures set out in paragraphs 1 to 4 above and the progress made at the Meetings of the Conference on the Human Dimension of the CSCE. It will consider ways of further strengthening and improving these procedures and will take appropriate decisions.

## FOLLOW-UP TO THE CONFERENCE

In conformity with the relevant provisions of the Final Act and with their resolve and commitment to continue the multilateral process initiated by the CSCE, the participating States will hold further meetings regularly among their representatives.

The fourth main Follow-up meeting will be held in Helsinki, commencing on 24 March 1992.

The agenda, work programme and modalities of the main Vienna Meeting will be applied *mutatis mutandis* to the main Helsinki Meeting, unless other decisions on these questions are taken by the preparatory meeting mentioned below.

For the purpose of making the adjustments to the agenda, work programme and modalities applied at the main Vienna Meeting, a preparatory meeting will be held in Helsinki, commencing on 10 March 1992. It is understood that in this context adjustments concern those items requiring change as a result of the change in date and place, the drawing of lots, and the mention of the other meetings held in conformity with the decisions of the Vienna Meeting 1986. The duration of the preparatory meeting shall not exceed two weeks.

The agenda, work programme and modalities for CSCE follow-up meetings mentioned in this document have been prepared by the main Vienna Meeting. The results of these meetings will be taken into account, as appropriate, at the main Helsinki Meeting.

All the meetings referred to in this chapter will be held in conformity with paragraph 4 of the chapter on 'Follow-up to the Conference' of the Final Act.

The participating States examined the scope for rationalising the modalities for future CSCE follow-up meetings, for enhancing their effectiveness and for ensuring the best possible use of resources. In the light of their examination and in connection with the steps taken at the main Vienna Meeting, including the drawing up of mandates annexed to this document, they decided:

- to dispense with preparatory meetings unless otherwise agreed;
- bearing in mind the purpose of the meeting, to limit the number of subsidiary working bodies meeting simultaneously to the lowest possible;
- to limit the duration of meetings, unless otherwise agreed, to a period not exceeding four weeks;
- in the case of meetings to which non-governmental participants are invited to contribute, to make maximum use of the possibility of having informal meetings in order to allow for a more spontaneous discussion;
- to observe to the same extent as the host country its national day.

The main Helsinki Meeting will review these arrangements and other modalities in the light of experience, with a view to making any improvements which may be necessary.

The Government of Austria is requested to transmit the present document to the Secretary-General of the United Nations, to the Director-General of UNESCO and to the Executive Secretary of the United Nations Economic Commission for Europe and to other international organizations mentioned in this document. The Government of Austria is also requested to transmit the present document to the Governments of the non-participating Mediterranean States.

The text of this document will be published in each participating State, which will disseminate it and make it known as widely as possible.

The representatives of the participating States express their profound gratitude to the people and Government of Austria for the excellent organization of the Vienna Meeting and warm hospitality extended to the delegations which participated in the Meeting.

# VI. DOCUMENT OF THE COPENHAGEN MEETING OF THE CONFERENCE ON THE HUMAN DIMENSION OF THE CSCE, 1990

This document was adopted on 29 June 1990 by the thirty-five participating States of the Conference on Security and Co-operation in Europe (CSCE). The Copenhagen meeting was the second meeting convoked in accordance with the provisions relating to the Conference on the Human Dimension of the CSCE contained in the Vienna Concluding Document (above, p. 450).

*TEXT*

## DOCUMENT OF THE COPENHAGEN MEETING OF THE CONFERENCE ON THE HUMAN DIMENSION OF THE CSCE

The representatives of the participating States of the Conference on Security and Co-operation in Europe (CSCE), Austria, Belgium, Bulgaria, Canada, Cyprus, Czechoslovakia, Denmark, Finland, France, the German Democratic Republic, the Federal Republic of Germany, Greece, the Holy See, Hungary, Iceland, Ireland, Italy, Liechtenstein, Luxembourg, Malta, Monaco, The Netherlands, Norway, Poland, Portugal, Romania, San Marino, Spain, Sweden, Switzerland, Turkey, the Union of Soviet Socialist Republics, the United Kingdom, the United States of America and Yugoslavia, met in Copenhagen from 5 to 29 June 1990, in accordance with the provisions relating to the Conference on the Human Dimension of the CSCE contained in the Concluding Document of the Vienna Follow-up Meeting of the CSCE.

The representative of Albania attended the Copenhagen Meeting as observer.

The first Meeting of the Conference was held in Paris from 30 May to 23 June 1989.

The Copenhagen Meeting was opened and closed by the Minister for Foreign Affairs of Denmark.

The formal opening of the Copenhagen Meeting was attended by Her Majesty the Queen of Denmark and His Royal Highness the Prince Consort.

Opening statements were made by Ministers and Deputy Ministers of the participating States.

At a special meeting of the Ministers for Foreign Affairs of the participating States of the CSCE on 5 June 1990, convened on the invitation of the Minister for Foreign Affairs of Denmark, it was agreed to convene a Preparatory Committee in Vienna on 10 July 1990 to prepare a Summit Meeting in Paris of their Heads of State or Government.

The participating States welcome with great satisfaction the fundamental political changes that have occurred in Europe since the first Meeting of the Conference on the Human Dimension of the CSCE in Paris in 1989. They note that the CSCE process has contributed significantly to bringing about these changes and that these developments in turn have greatly advanced the implementation of the provisions of the Final Act and of the other CSCE documents.

They recognize that pluralistic democracy and the rule of law are essential for ensuring respect for all human rights and fundamental freedoms, the development of human contacts and the resolution of other issues of a related humanitarian character. They therefore welcome the commitment expressed by all participating States to the ideals of democracy and political pluralism as well as their common determination to build democratic societies based on free elections and the rule of law.

At the Copenhagen Meeting the participating States held a review of the implementation of their commitments in the field of the human dimension. They considered that the degree of compliance with the commitments contained in the relevant provisions of the CSCE documents had shown a fundamental improvement since the Paris Meeting. They also expressed the view, however, that further steps are required for the full realization of their commitments relating to the human dimension.

The participating States express their conviction that full respect for human rights and fundamental freedoms and the development of societies based on pluralistic democracy and the rule of law are prerequisites for progress in setting up the lasting order of peace, security, justice and co-operation that they seek to establish in Europe. They therefore reaffirm their commitment to implement fully all provisions of the Final Act and of the other CSCE documents relating to the human dimension and undertake to build on the progress they have made.

They recognize that co-operation among themselves, as well as the active involvement of persons, groups, organizations and institutions, will be essential to ensure continuing progress towards their shared objectives.

In order to strengthen respect for, and enjoyment of, human rights and fundamental freedoms, to develop human contacts and to resolve issues of a related humanitarian character, the participating States agree on the following:

# I

(1)    The participating States express their conviction that the protection and promotion of human rights and fundamental freedoms is one of the basic purposes of government, and reaffirm that the recognition of these rights and freedoms constitutes the foundation of freedom, justice and peace.

(2)    They are determined to support and advance those principles of justice which form the basis of the rule of law. They consider that the rule of law does not mean merely a formal legality which assures regularity and consistency in the achievement and enforcement of democratic order, but justice based on the recognition and full acceptance of the supreme value of the human personality and guaranteed by institutions providing a framework for its fullest expression.

(3)    They reaffirm that democracy is an inherent element of the rule of law. They recognize the importance of pluralism with regard to political organizations.

(4)    They confirm that they will respect each other's right freely to choose and develop, in accordance with international human rights standards, their political, social, economic and cultural systems. In exercising this right, they will ensure that their laws, regulations, practices and policies conform with their obligations under international law and are brought into harmony with the provisions of the Declaration on Principles and other CSCE commitments.

(5)    They solemnly declare that among those elements of justice which are essential to the full expression of the inherent dignity and of the equal and inalienable rights of all human beings are the following:

(5.1)    —free elections that will be held at reasonable intervals by secret ballot or by equivalent free voting procedure, under conditions which ensure in practice the free expression of the opinion of the electors in the choice of their representatives;

(5.2)    —a form of government that is representative in character, in which the executive is accountable to the elected legislature or the electorate;

(5.3)    —the duty of the government and public authorities to comply with the constitution and to act in a manner consistent with law;

(5.4)    —a clear separation between the State and political parties; in particular, political parties will not be merged with the State;

(5.5)    —the activity of the government and the administration as well as that of the judiciary will be exercised in accordance with the system established by law. Respect for that system must be ensured;

(5.6) —military forces and the police will be under the control of, and accountable to, the civil authorities;

(5.7) —human rights and fundamental freedoms will be guaranteed by law and in accordance with their obligations under international law;

(5.8) —legislation, adopted at the end of a public procedure, and regulations will be published, that being the condition for their applicability. Those texts will be accessible to everyone;

(5.9) —all persons are equal before the law and are entitled without any discrimination to the equal protection of the law. In this respect, the law will prohibit any discrimination and guarantee to all persons equal and effective protection against discrimination on any ground;

(5.10) —everyone will have an effective means of redress against administrative decisions, so as to guarantee respect for fundamental rights and ensure legal integrity;

(5.11) —administrative decisions against a person must be fully justifiable and must as a rule indicate the usual remedies available;

(5.12) —the independence of judges and the impartial operation of the public judicial service will be ensured;

(5.13) —the independence of legal practitioners will be recognized and protected, in particular as regards conditions for recruitment and practice;

(5.14) —the rules relating to criminal procedure will contain a clear definition of powers in relation to prosecution and the measures preceding and accompanying prosecution;

(5.15) —any person arrested or detained on a criminal charge will have the right, so that the lawfulness of his arrest or detention can be decided, to be brought promptly before a judge or other officer authorized by law to exercise this function;

(5.16) —in the determination of any criminal charge against him, or of his rights and obligations in a suit at law, everyone will be entitled to a fair and public hearing by a competent, independent and impartial tribunal established by law;

(5.17) —any person prosecuted will have the right to defend himself in person or through prompt legal assistance of his own choosing or, if he does not have sufficient means to pay for legal assistance, to be given it free when the interests of justice so require;

(5.18) —no one will be charged with, tried for or convicted of any criminal offence unless the offence is provided for by a law which defines the elements of the offence with clarity and precision;

(5.19) —everyone will be presumed innocent until proved guilty according to law;

(5.20) —considering the important contribution of international instruments in the field of human rights to the rule of law at a national level, the participating States reaffirm that they will consider acceding to the International Covenant on Civil and Political Rights, the International Covenant on Economic, Social and Cultural Rights and other relevant international instruments, if they have not yet done so;

(5.21)  —in order to supplement domestic remedies and better to ensure that the participating States respect the international obligations they have undertaken, the participating States will consider acceding to a regional or global international convention concerning the protection of human rights, such as the European Convention on Human Rights or the Optional Protocol to the International Covenant on Civil and Political Rights, which provide for procedures of individual recourse to international bodies.

(6)     The participating States declare that the will of the people, freely and fairly expressed through periodic and genuine elections, is the basis of the authority and legitimacy of all government. The participating States will accordingly respect the right of their citizens to take part in the governing of their country, either directly or through representatives freely chosen by them through fair electoral processes. They recognize their responsibility to defend and protect, in accordance with their laws, their international human rights obligations and their international commitments, the democratic order freely established through the will of the people against the activities of persons, groups or organizations that engage in or refuse to renounce terrorism or violence aimed at the overthrow of that order or of that of another participating State.

(7)     To ensure that the will of the people serves as the basis of the authority of government, the participating States will

(7.1)   —hold free elections at reasonable intervals, as established by law;

(7.2)   —permit all seats in at least one chamber of the national legislature to be freely contested in a popular vote;

(7.3)   —guarantee universal and equal suffrage to adult citizens;

(7.4)   —ensure that votes are cast by secret ballot or by equivalent free voting procedure, and that they are counted and reported honestly with the official results made public;

(7.5)   —respect the right of citizens to seek political or public office, individually or as representatives of political parties or organizations, without discrimination;

(7.6)   —respect the right of individuals and groups to establish, in full freedom, their own political parties or other political organizations and provide such political parties and organizations with the necessary legal guarantees to enable them to compete with each other on a basis of equal treatment before the law and by the authorities;

(7.7) —ensure that law and public policy work to permit political campaigning to be conducted in a fair and free atmosphere in which neither administrative action, violence nor intimidation bars the parties and the candidates from freely presenting their views and qualifications, or prevents the voters from learning and discussing them or from casting their vote free of fear of retribution;

(7.8) —provide that no legal or administrative obstacle stands in the way of unimpeded access to the media on a non-discriminatory basis for all political groupings and individuals wishing to participate in the electoral process;

(7.9) —ensure that candidates who obtain the necessary number of votes required by law are duly installed in office and are permitted to remain in office until their term expires or is otherwise brought to an end in a manner that is regulated by law in conformity with democratic parliamentary and constitutional procedures.

(8) The participating States consider that the presence of observers, both foreign and domestic, can enhance the electoral process for States in which elections are taking place. They therefore invite observers from any other CSCE participating States and any appropriate private institutions and organizations who may wish to do so to observe the course of their national election proceedings, to the extent permitted by law. They will also endeavour to facilitate similar access for election proceedings held below the national level. Such observers will undertake not to interfere in the electoral proceedings.

## II

(9) The participating States reaffirm that

(9.1) —everyone will have the right to freedom of expression including the right to communication. This right will include freedom to hold opinions and to receive and impart information and ideas without interference by public authority and regardless of frontiers. The exercise of this right may be subject only to such restrictions as are prescribed by law and are consistent with international standards. In particular, no limitation will be imposed on access to, and use of, means of reproducing documents of any kind, while respecting, however, rights relating to intellectual property, including copyright;

(9.2)   —everyone will have the right of peaceful assembly and demonstration. Any restrictions which may be placed on the exercise of these rights will be prescribed by law and consistent with international standards;

(9.3)   —the right of association will be guaranteed. The right to form and—subject to the general right of a trade union to determine its own membership—freely to join a trade union will be guaranteed. These rights will exclude any prior control. Freedom of association for workers, including the freedom to strike, will be guaranteed, subject to limitations prescribed by law and consistent with international standards;

(9.4)   —everyone will have the right to freedom of thought, conscience and religion. This right includes freedom to change one's religion or belief and freedom to manifest one's religion or belief, either alone or in community with others, in public or in private, through worship, teaching, practice and observance. The exercise of these rights may be subject only to such restrictions as are prescribed by law and are consistent with international standards;

(9.5)   —they will respect the right of everyone to leave any country, including his own, and to return to his country, consistent with a State's international obligations and CSCE commitments. Restrictions on this right will have the character of very rare exceptions, will be considered necessary only if they respond to a specific public need, pursue a legitimate aim and are proportionate to that aim, and will not be abused or applied in an arbitrary manner;

(9.6)   —everyone has the right peacefully to enjoy his property either on his own or in common with others. No one may be deprived of his property except in the public interest and subject to the conditions provided for by law and consistent with international commitments and obligations.

(10)    In reaffirming their commitment to ensure effectively the rights of the individual to know and act upon human rights and fundamental freedoms, and to contribute actively, individually or in association with others, to their promotion and protection, the participating States express their commitment to

(10.1)  —respect the right of everyone, individually or in association with others, to seek, receive and impart freely views and information on human rights and fundamental freedoms, including the rights to disseminate and publish such views and information;

(10.2)  —respect the rights of everyone, individually or in association with others, to study and discuss the observance of human rights and fundamental freedoms and to develop and discuss ideas for improved protection of human rights and better means for ensuring compliance with international human rights standards;

(10.3) —ensure that individuals are permitted to exercise the right to association, including the right to form, join and participate effectively in non-governmental organizations which seek the promotion and protection of human rights and fundamental freedoms, including trade unions and human rights monitoring groups;

(10.4) —allow members of such groups and organizations to have unhindered access to and communication with similar bodies within and outside their countries and with international organizations, to engage in exchanges, contacts and co-operation with such groups and organizations and to solicit, receive and utilize for the purpose of promoting and protecting human rights and fundamental freedoms voluntary financial contributions from national and international sources as provided for by law.

(11) The participating States further affirm that, where violations of human rights and fundamental freedoms are alleged to have occurred, the effective remedies available include

(11.1) —the right of the individual to seek and receive adequate legal assistance;

(11.2) —the right of the individual to seek and receive assistance from others in defending human rights and fundamental freedoms, and to assist others in defending human rights and fundamental freedoms;

(11.3) —the right of individuals or groups acting on their behalf to communicate with international bodies with competence to receive and consider information concerning allegations of human rights abuses.

(12) The participating States, wishing to ensure greater transparency in the implementation of the commitments undertaken in the Vienna Concluding Document under the heading of the human dimension of the CSCE, decide to accept as a confidence-building measure the presence of observers sent by participating States and representatives of non-governmental organizations and other interested persons at proceedings before courts as provided for in national legislation and international law; it is understood that proceedings may only be held *in camera* in the circumstances prescribed by law and consistent with obligations under international law and international commitments.

(13) The participating States decide to accord particular attention to the recognition of the rights of the child, his civil rights and his

individual freedoms, his economic, social and cultural rights, and his right to special protection against all forms of violence and exploitation. They will consider acceding to the Convention on the Rights of the Child, if they have not yet done so, which was opened for signature by States on 26 January 1990. They will recognize in their domestic legislation the rights of the child as affirmed in the international agreements to which they are Parties.

(14)     The participating States agree to encourage the creation, within their countries, of conditions for the training of students and trainees from other participating States, including persons taking vocational and technical courses. They also agree to promote travel by young people from their countries for the purpose of obtaining education in other participating States and to that end to encourage the conclusion, where appropriate, of bilateral and multilateral agreements between their relevant governmental institutions, organizations and educational establishments.

(15)     The participating States will act in such a way as to facilitate the transfer of sentenced persons and encourage those participating States which are not Parties to the Convention on the Transfer of Sentenced Persons, signed at Strasbourg on 21 November 1983, to consider acceding to the Convention.

(16)     The participating States

(16.1)   —reaffirm their commitment to prohibit torture and other cruel, inhuman or degrading treatment or punishment, to take effective legislative, administrative, judicial and other measures to prevent and punish such practices, to protect individuals from any psychiatric or other medical practices that violate human rights and fundamental freedoms and to take effective measures to prevent and punish such practices;

(16.2)   —intend, as a matter of urgency, to consider acceding to the Convention against Torture and Other Cruel, Inhuman or Degrading Treatment or Punishment, if they have not yet done so, and recognizing the competences of the Committee against Torture under Articles 21 and 22 of the Convention and withdrawing reservations regarding the competence of the Committee under Article 20;

(16.3)   —stress that no exceptional circumstances whatsoever, whether a state of war or a threat of war, internal political instability or any other public emergency, may be invoked as a justification of torture;

(16.4)   —will ensure that education and information regarding the prohibition against torture are fully included in the training of law enforcement personnel, civil or military, medical personnel, public officials and other persons who may be involved in the custody, interrogation or treatment of any individual subjected to any form of arrest, detention or imprisonment;

(16.5) —will keep under systematic review interrogation rules, instructions, methods and practices as well as arrangements for the custody and treatment of persons subjected to any form of arrest, detention or imprisonment in any territory under their jurisdiction, with a view to preventing any cases of torture;

(16.6) —will take up with priority for consideration and for appropriate action, in accordance with the agreed measures and procedures for the effective implementation of the commitments relating to the human dimension of the CSCE, any cases of torture and other inhuman or degrading treatment or punishment made known to them through official channels or coming from any other reliable source of information;

(16.7) —will act upon the understanding that preserving and guaranteeing the life and security of any individual subjected to any form of torture and other inhuman or degrading treatment or punishment will be the sole criterion in determining the urgency and priorities to be accorded in taking appropriate remedial action; and, therefore, the consideration of any cases of torture and other inhuman or degrading treatment or punishment within the framework of any other international body or mechanism may not be invoked as a reason for refraining from consideration and appropriate action in accordance with the agreed measures and procedures for the effective implementation of the commitments relating to the human dimension of the CSCE.

(17) The participating States

(17.1) —recall the commitment undertaken in the Vienna Concluding Document to keep the question of capital punishment under consideration and to co-operate within relevant international organizations;

(17.2) —recall, in this context, the adoption by the General Assembly of the United Nations, on 15 December 1989, of the Second Optional Protocol to the International Covenant on Civil and Political Rights, aiming at the abolition of the death penalty;

(17.3) —note the restrictions and safeguards regarding the use of the death penalty which have been adopted by the international community, in particular Article 6 of the International Covenant on Civil and Political Rights;

(17.4) —note the provisions of the Sixth Protocol to the European Convention for the Protection of Human Rights and Fundamental Freedoms, concerning the abolition of the death penalty;

(17.5)   —note recent measures taken by a number of participating States towards the abolition of capital punishment;

(17.6)   —note the activities of several non-governmental organizations on the question of the death penalty;

(17.7)   —will exchange information within the framework of the Conference on the Human Dimension on the question of the abolition of the death penalty and keep that question under consideration;

(17.8)   —will make available to the public information regarding the use of the death penalty.

(18)     The participating States

(18.1)   —note that the United Nations Commission on Human Rights has recognized the right of everyone to have conscientious objections to military service;

(18.2)   —note recent measures taken by a number of participating States to permit exemption from compulsory military service on the basis of conscientious objections;

(18.3)   —note the activities of several non-governmental organizations on the question of conscientious objections to compulsory military service;

(18.4)   —agree to consider introducing, where this has not yet been done, various forms of alternative service, which are compatible with the reasons for conscientious objection, such forms of alternative service being in principle of a non-combatant or civilian nature, in the public interest and of a non-punitive nature;

(18.5)   —will make available to the public information on this issue;

(18.6)   —will keep under consideration, within the framework of the Conference on the Human Dimension, the relevant questions related to the exemption from compulsory military service, where it exists, of individuals on the basis of conscientious objections to armed service, and will exchange information on these questions.

(19)     The participating States affirm that freer movement and contacts among their citizens are important in the context of the protection and promotion of human rights and fundamental freedoms. They will ensure that their policies concerning entry into their territories are fully consistent with the aims set out in the relevant provisions of the Final Act, the Madrid Concluding Document and the Vienna Concluding Document. While reaffirming their determination not to recede from the commitments contained in CSCE documents, they undertake to implement fully and improve pre-

sent commitments in the field of human contacts, including on a bilateral and multilateral basis. In this context they will

(19.1) —strive to implement the procedures for entry into their territories, including the issuing of visas and passport and customs control, in good faith and without unjustified delay. Where necessary, they will shorten the waiting time for visa decisions, as well as simplify practices and reduce administrative requirements for visa applications;

(19.2) —ensure, in dealing with visa applications, that these are processed as expeditiously as possible in order, *inter alia*, to take due account of important family, personal or professional considerations, especially in cases of an urgent, humanitarian nature;

(19.3) —endeavour, where necessary, to reduce fees charged in connection with visa applications to the lowest possible level.

(20) The participating States concerned will consult and, where appropriate, co-operate in dealing with problems that might emerge as a result of the increased movement of persons.

(21) The participating States recommend the consideration, at the next CSCE Follow-up Meeting in Helsinki, of the advisability of holding a meeting of experts on consular matters.

(22) The participating States reaffirm that the protection and promotion of the rights of migrant workers have their human dimension. In this context, they

(22.1) —agree that the protection and promotion of the rights of migrant workers are the concern of all participating States and that as such they should be addressed within the CSCE process;

(22.2) —reaffirm their commitment to implement fully in their domestic legislation the rights of migrant workers provided for in international agreements to which they are parties;

(22.3) —consider that, in future international instruments concerning the rights of migrant workers, they should take into account the fact that this issue is of importance for all of them;

(22.4) —express their readiness to examine, at future CSCE meetings, the relevant aspects of the further promotion of the rights of migrant workers and their families.

(23) The participating States reaffirm their conviction expressed in the Vienna Concluding Document that the promotion of economic, social and cultural rights as well as of civil and political rights is of paramount importance for human dignity and for the attainment of the legitimate aspirations of every individual. They also reaffirm their commitment taken in the Document of the Bonn Conference on Economic Co-operation in Europe to the promotion of social

justice and the improvement of living and working conditions. In the context of continuing their efforts with a view to achieving progressively the full realization of economic, social and cultural rights by all appropriate means, they will pay special attention to problems in the areas of employment, housing, social security, health, education and culture.

(24) The participating States will ensure that the exercise of all the human rights and fundamental freedoms set out above will not be subject to any restrictions except those which are provided by law and are consistent with their obligations under international law, in particular the International Covenant on Civil and Political Rights, and with their international commitments, in particular the Universal Declaration of Human Rights. These restrictions have the character of exceptions. The participating States will ensure that these restrictions are not abused and are not applied in an arbitrary manner, but in such a way that the effective exercise of these rights is ensured.

Any restriction on rights and freedoms must, in a democratic society, relate to one of the objectives of the applicable law and be strictly proportionate to the aim of that law.

(25) The participating States confirm that any derogations from obligations relating to human rights and fundamental freedoms during a state of public emergency must remain strictly within the limits provided for by international law, in particular the relevant international instruments by which they are bound, especially with respect to rights from which there can be no derogation. They also reaffirm that

(25.1) —measures derogating from such obligations must be taken in strict conformity with the procedural requirements laid down in those instruments;

(25.2) —the imposition of a state of public emergency must be proclaimed officially, publicly, and in accordance with the provisions laid down by law;

(25.3) —measures derogating from obligations will be limited to the extent strictly required by the exigencies of the situation;

(25.4) —such measures will not discriminate solely on the grounds of race, colour, sex, language, religion, social origin or of belonging to a minority.

# III

(26) The participating States recognize that vigorous democracy depends on the existence as an integral part of national life of

democratic values and practices as well as an extensive range of democratic institutions. They will therefore encourage, facilitate and, where appropriate, support practical co-operative endeavours and the sharing of information, ideas and expertise among themselves and by direct contacts and co-operation between individuals, groups and organizations in areas including the following:

—constitutional law, reform and development,
—electoral legislation, administration and observation,
—establishment and management of courts and legal systems,
—the development of an impartial and effective public service where recruitment and advancement are based on a merit system,
—law enforcement,
—local government and decentralization,
—access to information and protection of privacy,
—developing political parties and their role in pluralistic societies,
—free and independent trade unions,
—co-operative movements,
—developing other forms of free associations and public interest groups,
—journalism, independent media, and intellectual and cultural life,
—the teaching of democratic values, institutions and practices in educational institutions and the fostering of an atmosphere of free enquiry.

Such endeavours may cover the range of co-operation encompassed in the human dimension of the CSCE, including training, exchange of information, books and instructional materials, co-operative programmes and projects, academic and professional exchanges and conferences, scholarships, research grants, provision of expertise and advice, business and scientific contacts and programmes.

(27) The participating States will also facilitate the establishment and strengthening of independent national institutions in the area of human rights and the rule of law, which may also serve as focal points for co-ordination and collaboration between such institutions in the participating States. They propose that co-operation be encouraged between parliamentarians from participating States, including through existing inter-parliamentary associations and, *inter alia*, through joint commissions, television debates involving parliamentarians, meetings and round-table discussions. They will also encourage existing institutions, such as organizations within the United Nations system and the Council of Europe, to continue and expand the work they have begun in this area.

(28)    The participating States recognize the important expertise of the Council of Europe in the field of human rights and fundamental freedoms and agree to consider further ways and means to enable the Council of Europe to make a contribution to the human dimension of the CSCE. They agree that the nature of this contribution could be examined further in a future CSCE forum.

(29)    The participating States will consider the idea of convening a meeting or seminar of experts to review and discuss co-operative measures designed to promote and sustain viable democratic institutions in participating States, including comparative studies of legislation in participating States in the area of human rights and fundamental freedoms, *inter alia* drawing upon the experience acquired in this area by the Council of Europe and the activities of the Commission 'Democracy through Law'.

(30)    The participating States recognize that the questions relating to national minorities can only be satisfactorily resolved in a democratic political framework based on the rule of law, with a functioning independent judiciary. This framework guarantees full respect for human rights and fundamental freedoms, equal rights and status for all citizens, the free expression of all their legitimate interests and aspirations, political pluralism, social tolerance and the implementation of legal rules that place effective restraints on the abuse of governmental power.

They also recognize the important role of non-governmental organizations, including political parties, trade unions, human rights organizations and religious groups, in the promotion of tolerance, cultural diversity and the resolution of questions relating to national minorities.

They further reaffirm that respect for the rights of persons belonging to national minorities as part of universally recognized human rights is an essential factor for peace, justice, stability and democracy in the participating States.

(31)    Persons belonging to national minorities have the right to exercise fully and effectively their human rights and fundamental freedoms without any discrimination and in full equality before the law.

The participating States will adopt, where necessary, special measures for the purpose of ensuring to persons belonging to national minorities full equality with the other citizens in the exercise and enjoyment of human rights and fundamental freedoms.

(32)    To belong to a national minority is a matter of a person's individual choice and no disadvantage may arise from the exercise of such choice.

Persons belonging to national minorities have the right freely to express, preserve and develop their ethnic, cultural, linguistic or religious identity and to maintain and develop their culture in all its aspects, free of any attempts at assimilation against their will. In particular, they have the right

(32.1) —to use freely their mother tongue in private as well as in public;

(32.2) —to establish and maintain their own educational, cultural and religious institutions, organizations or associations, which can seek voluntary financial and other contributions as well as public assistance, in conformity with national legislation;

(32.3) —to profess and practise their religion, including the acquisition, possession and use of religious materials, and to conduct religious educational activities in their mother tongue;

(32.4) —to establish and maintain unimpeded contacts among themselves within their country as well as contacts across frontiers with citizens of other States with whom they share a common ethnic or national origin, cultural heritage or religious beliefs;

(32.5) —to disseminate, have access to and exchange information in their mother tongue;

(32.6) —to establish and maintain organizations or associations within their country and to participate in international non-governmental organizations.

Persons belonging to national minorities can exercise and enjoy their rights individually as well as in community with other members of their group. No disadvantage may arise for a person belonging to a national minority on account of the exercise or non-exercise of any such rights.

(33) The participating States will protect the ethnic, cultural, linguistic and religious identity of national minorities on their territory and create conditions for the promotion of that identity. They will take the necessary measures to that effect after due consultations, including contacts with organizations or associations of such minorities, in accordance with the decision-making procedures of each State.

Any such measures will be in conformity with the principles of equality and non-discrimination with respect to the other citizens of the participating State concerned.

(34) The participating States will endeavour to ensure that persons belonging to national minorities, notwithstanding the need to learn the official language or languages of the State concerned, have adequate opportunities for instruction of their mother tongue or in their mother tongue, as well as, wherever possible and necessary, for its use before public authorities, in conformity with applicable national legislation.

In the context of the teaching of history and culture in educational establishments, they will also take account of the history and culture of national minorities.

(35)   The participating States will respect the right of persons belonging to national minorities to effective participation in public affairs, including participation in the affairs relating to the protection and promotion of the identity of such minorities.

The participating States note the efforts undertaken to protect and create conditions for the promotion of the ethnic, cultural, linguistic and religious identity of certain national minorities by establishing, as one of the possible means to achieve these aims, appropriate local or autonomous administrations corresponding to the specific historical and territorial circumstances of such minorities and in accordance with the policies of the State concerned.

(36)   The participating States recognize the particular importance of increasing constructive co-operation among themselves on questions relating to national minorities. Such co-operation seeks to promote mutual understanding and confidence, friendly and good-neighbourly relations, international peace, security and justice.

Every participating State will promote a climate of mutual respect, understanding, co-operation and solidarity among all persons living on its territory, without distinction as to ethnic or national origin or religion, and will encourage the solution of problems through dialogue based on the principles of the rule of law.

(37)   None of these commitments may be interpreted as implying any right to engage in any activity or perform any action in contravention of the purposes and principles of the Charter of the United Nations, other obligations under international law or the provisions of the Final Act, including the principle of territorial integrity of States.

(38)   The participating States, in their efforts to protect and promote the rights of persons belonging to national minorities, will fully respect their undertakings under existing human rights conventions and other relevant international instruments and consider adhering to the relevant conventions, if they have not yet done so, including those providing for a right of complaint by individuals.

(39)   The participating States will co-operate closely in the competent international organizations to which they belong; including the United Nations and, as appropriate, the Council of Europe, bearing in mind their on-going work with respect to questions relating to national minorities.

They will consider convening a meeting of experts for a thorough discussion of the issue of national minorities.

(40)   The participating States clearly and unequivocally condemn totalitarianism, racial and ethnic hatred, anti-semitism, xenophobia and

discrimination against anyone as well as persecution on religious and ideological grounds. In this context, they also recognize the particular problems of Roma (gypsies).

They declare their firm intention to intensify the efforts to combat these phenomena in all their forms and therefore will

(40.1) —take effective measures, including the adoption, in conformity with their constitutional systems and their international obligations, of such laws as may be necessary, to provide protection against any acts that constitute incitement to violence against persons or groups based on national, racial, ethnic or religious discrimination, hostility or hatred, including anti-semitism;

(40.2) —commit themselves to take appropriate and proportionate measures to protect persons or groups who may be subject to threats or acts of discrimination, hostility or violence as a result of their racial, ethnic, cultural, linguistic or religious identity, and to protect their property;

(40.3) —take effective measures, in conformity with their constitutional systems, at the national, regional and local levels to promote understanding and tolerance, particularly in the fields of education, culture and information;

(40.4) —endeavour to ensure that the objectives of education include special attention to the problem of racial prejudice and hatred and to the development of respect for different civilizations and cultures;

(40.5) —recognize the right of the individual to effective remedies and endeavour to recognize, in conformity with national legislation, the right of interested persons and groups to initiate and support complaints against acts of discrimination, including racist and xenophobic acts;

(40.6) —consider adhering, if they have not yet done so, to the international instruments which address the problem of discrimination and ensure full compliance with the obligations therein, including those relating to the submission of periodic reports;

(40.7) —consider, also, accepting those international mechanisms which allow States and individuals to bring communications relating to discrimination before international bodies.

## V

(41) The participating States reaffirm their commitment to the human dimension of the CSCE and emphasize its importance as an integral part of a balanced approach to security and co-operation in Europe. They agree that the Conference on the Human Dimension

of the CSCE and the human dimension mechanism described in the section on the human dimension of the CSCE of the Vienna Concluding Document have demonstrated their value as methods of furthering their dialogue and co-operation and assisting in the resolution of relevant specific questions. They express their conviction that these should be continued and developed as part of an expanding CSCE process.

(42)      The participating States recognize the need to enhance further the effectiveness of the procedures described in paragraphs 1 to 4 of the section on the human dimension of the CSCE of the Vienna Concluding Document and with this aim decide

(42.1)      —to provide in as short a time as possible, but no later than four weeks, a written response to requests for information and to representations made to them in writing by other participating States under paragraph 1;

(42.2)      —that the bilateral meetings, as contained in paragraph 2, will take place as soon as possible, as a rule within three weeks of the date of the request;

(42.3)      —to refrain, in the course of a bilateral meeting held under paragraph 2, from raising situations and cases not connected with the subject of the meeting, unless both sides have agreed to do so.

(43)      The participating States examined practical proposals for new measures aimed at improving the implementation of the commitments relating to the human dimension of the CSCE. In this regard, they considered proposals related to the sending of observers to examine situations and specific cases, the appointment of rapporteurs to investigate and suggest appropriate solutions, the setting up of a Committee on the Human Dimension of the CSCE, greater involvement of persons, organizations and institutions in the human dimension mechanism and further bilateral and multilateral efforts to promote the resolution of relevant issues.

They decide to continue to discuss thoroughly in subsequent relevant CSCE fora these and other proposals designed to strengthen the human dimension mechanism, and to consider adopting, in the context of the further development of the CSCE process, appropriate new measures. They agree that these measures should contribute to achieving further effective progress, enhance conflict prevention and confidence in the field of the human dimension of the CSCE.

* * *

(44)      The representatives of the participating States express their profound gratitude to the people and Government of Denmark for the excellent organization of the Copenhagen Meeting and the warm

hospitality extended to the delegations which participated in the Meeting.

(45) In accordance with the provisions relating to the Conference on the Human Dimension of the CSCE contained in the Concluding Document of the Vienna Follow-up Meeting of the CSCE, the third Meeting of the Conference will take place in Moscow from 10 September to 4 October 1991.

# VII. THE CHARTER OF PARIS FOR A NEW EUROPE, 1990

In this declaration, adopted on 21 November 1990, the participating States of the Conference on Security and Co-operation in Europe (thirty-four in number since the unification of Germany) reaffirm their commitment to the principles of the Helsinki Final Act (above, p. 391). In particular, the opening section on 'Human rights, Democracy and the Rule of Law' relates to the protection of national minorities.

*TEXT*

## CHARTER OF PARIS
## FOR
## A NEW EUROPE

### A NEW ERA OF DEMOCRACY, PEACE AND UNITY

We, the Heads of State or Government of the States participating in the Conference on Security and Co-operation in Europe, have assembled in Paris at a time of profound change and historic expectations. The era of confrontation and division of Europe has ended. We declare that henceforth our relations will be founded on respect and co-operation.

Europe is liberating itself from the legacy of the past. The courage of men and women, the strength of the will of the peoples and the power of the ideas of the Helsinki Final Act have opened a new era of democracy, peace and unity in Europe.

Ours is a time for fulfilling the hopes and expectations our peoples have cherished for decades: steadfast commitment to democracy based on human rights and fundamental freedoms; prosperity through economic liberty and social justice; and equal security for all our countries.

The Ten Principles of the Final Act will guide us towards this ambitious future, just as they have lighted our way towards better relations for the past fifteen years. Full implementation of all CSCE commitments must form the basis for the initiatives we are now taking to enable our nations to live in accordance with their aspirations.

### *Human Rights, Democracy and Rule of Law*

We undertake to build, consolidate and strengthen democracy as the only system of goverment of our nations. In this endeavour, we will abide by the following:

Human rights and fundamental freedoms are the birthright of all human beings, are inalienable and are guaranteed by law. Their protection and promotion is the first responsibility of government. Respect for them is an essential safeguard against an over-mighty State. Their observance and full exercise are the foundation of freedom, justice and peace.

Democratic government is based on the will of the people, expressed regularly through free and fair elections. Democracy has as its foundation respect for the human person and the rule of law. Democracy is the best safeguard of freedom of expression, tolerance of all groups of society, and equality of opportunity for each person.

Democracy, with its representative and pluralist character, entails accountability to the electorate, the obligation of public authorities to comply with the law and justice administered impartially. No one will be above the law.

We affirm that, without discrimination,
every individual has the right to:

freedom of thought, conscience and religion or belief,
freedom of expression,
freedom of association and peaceful assembly,
freedom of movement;

no one will be:

subject to arbitrary arrest or detention,
subject to torture or other cruel, inhuman or degrading treatment or punishment;

everyone also has the right;

to know and act upon his rights,
to participate in free and fair elections,
to fair and public trial if charged with an offence,
to own property alone or in association and to exercise individual enterprise,
to enjoy his economic, social and cultural rights.

We affirm that the ethnic, cultural, linguistic and religious identity of national minorities will be protected and that persons belonging to national minorities have the right freely to express, preserve and develop that identity without any discrimination and in full equality before the law.

We will ensure that everyone will enjoy recourse to effective remedies, national or international, against any violation of his rights.

Full respect for these precepts is the bedrock on which we will seek to construct the new Europe.

Our States will co-operate and support each other with the aim of making democratic gains irreversible.

*Economic Liberty and Responsibility*

Economic liberty, social justice and environmental responsibility are indispensable for prosperity.

The free will of the individual, exercised in democracy and protected by the rule of law, forms the necessary basis for successful economic and social development. We will promote economic activity which respects and upholds human dignity.

Freedom and political pluralism are necessary elements in our common objective of developing market economies towards sustainable economic growth, prosperity, social justice, expanding employment and efficient use of economic resources. The success of the transition to market economy by countries making efforts to this effect is important and in the interest of us all. It will enable us to share a higher level of prosperity which is our common objective. We will co-operate to this end.

Preservation of the environment is a shared responsibility of all our nations. While supporting national and regional efforts in this field, we must also look to the pressing need for joint action on a wider scale.

*Friendly Relations among Participating States*

Now that a new era is dawning in Europe, we are determined to expand and strengthen friendly relations and co-operation among the States of Europe, the United States of America and Canada, and to promote friendship among our peoples.

To uphold and promote democracy, peace and unity in Europe, we solemnly pledge our full commitment to the Ten Principles of the Helsinki Final Act. We affirm the continuing validity of the Ten Principles and our determination to put them into practice. All the Principles apply equally and unreservedly, each of them being interpreted taking into account the others. They form the basis for our relations.

In accordance with our obligations under the Charter of the United Nations and commitments under the Helsinki Final Act, we renew our pledge to refrain from the threat or use of force against the territorial integrity or political independence of any State, or from acting in any other manner inconsistent with the principles or purposes of those documents. We recall that non-compliance with obligations under the Charter of the United Nations constitutes a violation of international law.

We reaffirm our commitment to settle disputes by peaceful means. We decide to develop mechanisms for the prevention and resolution of conflicts among the participating States.

With the ending of the division of Europe, we will strive for a new quality in our security relations while fully respecting each other's freedom of choice in that respect. Security is indivisible and the security of every participating State is inseparably linked to that of all the others. We therefore pledge to co-operate in strengthening confidence and security among us and in promoting arms control and disarmament.

We welcome the Joint Declaration of Twenty-Two States on the improvement of their relations.

Our relations will rest on our common adherence to democratic values and to human rights and fundamental freedoms. We are convinced that in order to strengthen peace and security among our States, the advancement of democracy, and respect for and effective exercise of human rights, are indispensable. We reaffirm the equal rights of peoples and their right to self-determination in conformity with the Charter of the United Nations and with the relevant norms of international law, including those relating to territorial integrity of States.

We are determined to enhance political consultation and to widen co-operation to solve economic, social, environmental, cultural and humanitarian problems. This common resolve and our growing interdependence will help to overcome the mistrust of decades, to increase stability and to build a united Europe.

We want Europe to be a source of peace, open to dialogue and to co-operation with other countries, welcoming exchanges and involved in the search for common responses to the challenges of the future.

### Security

Friendly relations among us will benefit from the consolidation of democracy and improved security.

We welcome the signature of the Treaty on Conventional Armed Forces in Europe by twenty-two participating States, which will lead to lower levels of armed forces. We endorse the adoption of a substantial new set of Confidence- and Security-building Measures which will lead to increased transparency and confidence among all participating States. These are important steps towards enhanced stability and security in Europe.

The unprecedented reduction in armed forces resulting from the Treaty on Conventional Armed Forces in Europe, together with new approaches to security and co-operation within the CSCE process, will lead to a new perception of security in Europe and a new dimension in our relations. In this context we fully recognize the freedom of States to choose their own security arrangements.

### Unity

Europe whole and free is calling for a new beginning. We invite our peoples to join in this great endeavour.

We note with great satisfaction the Treaty on the Final Settlement with respect to Germany signed in Moscow on 12 September 1990 and sincerely welcome the fact that the German people have united to become one State in accordance with the principles of the Final Act of the Conference on Security and Co-operation in Europe and in full accord with their neighbours. The establishment of the national unity of Germany is an important contribution to a just and lasting order of peace for a united, democratic Europe aware of its responsibility for stability, peace and co-operation.

The participation of both North American and European States is a fundamental characteristic of the CSCE; it underlies its past achievements and is essential to the future of the CSCE process. An abiding adherence to shared values and our common heritage are the ties which bind us together. With all the rich diversity of our nations, we are united in our commitment to expand our co-operation in all fields. The challenges confronting us can only be met by common action, co-operation and solidarity.

### The CSCE and the World

The destiny of our nations is linked to that of all other nations. We support fully the United Nations and the enhancement of its role in promoting international peace, security and justice. We reaffirm our commitment to the principles and purposes of the United Nations as enshrined in the Charter and condemn all violations of these principles. We recognize with satisfaction the growing role of the United Nations in world affairs and its increasing effectiveness, fostered by the improvement in relations among our States.

Aware of the dire needs of a great part of the world, we commit ourselves to solidarity with all other countries. Therefore, we issue a call from Paris today to all the nations of the world. We stand ready to join with any and all States in common efforts to protect and advance the community of fundamental human values.

## GUIDELINES FOR THE FUTURE

Proceeding from our firm commitment to the full implementation of all CSCE principles and provisions, we now resolve to give a new impetus to a balanced and comprehensive development of our co-operation in order to address the needs and aspirations of our peoples.

### Human Dimension

We declare our respect for human rights and fundamental freedoms to be irrevocable. We will fully implement and build upon the provisions relating to the human dimension of the CSCE.

Proceeding from the Document of the Copenhagen Meeting of the Conference on the Human Dimension, we will co-operate to strengthen democratic institutions and to promote the application of the rule of law. To that end, we decide to convene a seminar of experts in Oslo from 4 to 15 November 1991.

Determined to foster the rich contribution of national minorities to the life of our societies, we undertake further to improve their situation. We reaffirm our deep conviction that friendly relations among our peoples, as well as peace, justice, stability and democracy, require that the ethnic, cultural, linguistic and religious identity of national minorities be protected and conditions for the promotion of that identity be created. We declare that questions related to national minorities can only be satisfactorily resolved in a democratic political framework. We further acknowledge that the rights of persons belonging to national minorities must be fully respected as part of universal human rights. Being aware of the urgent need for increased co-operation on, as well as better protection of, national minorities, we decide to convene a meeting of experts on national minorities to be held in Geneva from 1 to 19 July 1991.

We express our determination to combat all forms of racial and ethnic hatred, anti-semitism, xenophobia and discrimination against anyone as well as persecution on religious and ideological grounds.

In accordance with our CSCE commitments, we stress that free movement and contacts among our citizens as well as the free flow of information and ideas are crucial for the maintenance and development of free societies and flourishing cultures. We welcome increased tourism and visits among our countries.

The human dimension mechanism has proved its usefulness, and we are consequently determined to expand it to include new procedures involving, *inter alia*, the services of experts or a roster of eminent persons experienced in human rights issues which could be raised under the mechanism. We shall provide, in the context of the mechanism, for individuals to be involved in the protection of their rights. Therefore, we undertake to develop further our commitments in this respect, in particular at the Moscow Meeting of the Conference on the Human Dimension, without prejudice to obligations under existing international instruments to which our States may be parties.

We recognize the important contribution of the Council of Europe to the promotion of human rights and the principles of democracy and the rule of law as well as to the development of cultural co-operation. We welcome moves by several participating States to join the Council of Europe and adhere to its European Convention on Human Rights. We welcome as well the readiness of the Council of Europe to make its experience available to the CSCE.

### Security

The changing political and military environment in Europe opens new possibilities for common efforts in the field of military security. We will build on the important achievements attained in the Treaty on Conventional Armed Forces in Europe and in the Negotiations on Confidence- and Security-building Measures. We undertake to continue the CSBM negotiations under the same mandate, and to seek to conclude them no later than the Follow-up Meeting of the CSCE to be held in Helsinki in 1992. We also welcome the decision of the participating States concerned to continue the CFE negotiation under the same mandate and to seek to conclude it no later than the Helsinki Follow-up Meeting. Following a period for national preparations, we look forward to a more structured co-operation among all participating States on security matters, and to discussions and consultations among the thirty-four participating States aimed at establishing by 1992, from the conclusion of the Helsinki Follow-up Meeting, new negotiations on disarmament and confidence and security building open to all participating States.

We call for the earliest possible conclusion of the Convention on an effectively verifiable, global and comprehensive ban on chemical weapons, and we intend to be original signatories to it.

We reaffirm the importance of the Open Skies initiative and call for the successful conclusion of the negotiations as soon as possible.

Although the threat of conflict in Europe has diminished, other dangers threaten the stability of our societies. We are determined to co-operate in defending democratic institutions against activities which violate the independence, sovereign equality or territorial integrity of the participating States. These include illegal activities involving outside pressure, coercion and subversion.

We unreservedly condemn, as criminal, all acts, methods and practices of terrorism and express our determination to work for its eradication both bilaterally and through multilateral co-operation. We will also join together in combating illicit trafficking in drugs.

Being aware that an essential complement to the duty of States to refrain from the threat or use of force is the peaceful settlement of disputes, both being essential factors for the maintenance and consolidation of international peace and security, we will not only seek effective ways of preventing, through political means, conflicts which may yet emerge, but also define, in conformity with international law, appropriate mechanisms for the peaceful resolution of any disputes which may arise. Accordingly, we undertake to seek new forms of co-operation in this area, in particular a range of methods for the peaceful settlement of disputes, including mandatory third-party involvement. We stress that full use should be made in this context of the opportunity of the Meeting on the Peaceful Settlement of Disputes which will be convened in Valletta at the beginning of 1991. The Council of Ministers for Foreign Affairs will take into account the Report of the Valletta Meeting.

## *Economic Co-operation*

We stress that economic co-operation based on market economy constitutes an essential element of our relations and will be instrumental in the construction of a prosperous and united Europe. Democratic institutions and economic liberty foster economic and social progress, as recognized in the Document of the Bonn Conference on Economic Co-operation, the results of which we strongly support.

We underline that co-operation in the economic field, science and technology is now an important pillar of the CSCE. The participating States should periodically review progress and give new impulses in these fields.

We are convinced that our overall economic co-operation should be expanded, free enterprise encouraged and trade increased and diversified according to GATT rules. We will promote social justice and progress and further the welfare of our peoples. We recognize in this context the importance of effective policies to address the problem of unemployment.

We reaffirm the need to continue to support democratic countries in transition towards the establishment of market economy and the creation of the basis for self-sustained economic and social growth, as already undertaken by the Group of twenty-four countries. We further underline the necessity of their increased integration, involving the acceptance of disciplines as well as benefits, into the international economic and financial system.

We consider that increased emphasis on economic co-operation within the CSCE process should take into account the interests of developing participating States.

We recall the link between respect for and promotion of human rights and fundamental freedoms and scientific progress. Co-operation in the field of science and technology will play an essential role in economic and social development. Therefore, it must evolve towards a greater sharing of appropriate scientific and technological information and knowledge with a view to overcoming the technological gap which exists among the participating States. We further encourage the participating States to work together in order to develop human potential and the spirit of free enterprise.

We are determined to give the necessary impetus to co-operation among our States in the fields of energy, transport and tourism for economic and social development. We welcome, in particular, practical steps to create optimal conditions for the economic and rational development of energy resources, with due regard for environmental considerations.

We recognize the important role of the European Community in the political and economic development of Europe. International economic organizations such as the United Nations Economic Commission for Europe (ECE), the Bretton Woods Institutions, the Organisation for

Economic Co-operation and Development (OECD), the European Free Trade Association (EFTA) and the International Chamber of Commerce (ICC) also have a significant task in promoting economic co-operation, which will be further enhanced by the establishment of the European Bank for Reconstruction and Development (EBRD). In order to pursue our objectives, we stress the necessity for effective co-ordination of the activities of these organizations and emphasize the need to find methods for all our States to take part in these activities.

## Environment

We recognize the urgent need to tackle the problems of the environment and the importance of individual and co-operative efforts in this area. We pledge to intensify our endeavours to protect and improve our environment in order to restore and maintain a sound ecological balance in air, water and soil. Therefore, we are determined to make full use of the CSCE as a framework for the formulation of common environmental commitments and objectives, and thus to pursue the work reflected in the Report of the Sofia Meeting on the Protection of the Environment.

We emphasize the significant role of a well-informed society in enabling the public and individuals to take initiatives to improve the environment. To this end, we commit ourselves to promoting public awareness and education on the environment as well as the public reporting of the environmental impact of policies, projects and programmes.

We attach priority to the introduction of clean and low-waste technology, being aware of the need to support countries which do not yet have their own means for appropriate measures.

We underline that environmental policies should be supported by appropriate legislative measures and administrative structures to ensure their effective implementation.

We stress the need for new measures providing for the systematic evaluation of compliance with the existing commitments and, moreover, for the development of more ambitious commitments with regard to notification and exchange of information about the state of the environment and potential environmental hazards. We also welcome the creation of the European Environment Agency (EEA).

We welcome the operational activities, problem-oriented studies and policy reviews in various existing international organizations engaged in the protection of the environment, such as the United Nations Environment Programme (UNEP), the United Nations Economic Commission for Europe (ECE) and the Organisation for Economic Co-operation and Development (OECD). We emphasize the need for strengthening their co-operation and for their efficient co-ordination.

## Culture

We recognize the essential contribution of our common European culture and our shared values in overcoming the division of the continent. Therefore, we underline our attachment to creative freedom and to the protection and promotion of our cultural and spiritual heritage, in all its richness and diversity.

In view of the recent changes in Europe, we stress the increased importance of the Cracow Symposium and we look forward to its consideration of guidelines for intensified co-operation in the field of culture. We invite the Council of Europe to contribute to this Symposium.

In order to promote greater familiarity amongst our peoples, we favour the establishment of cultural centres in cities of other participating States as well as increased co-operation in the audio-visual field and wider exchange in music, theatre, literature and the arts.

We resolve to make special efforts in our national policies to promote better understanding, in particular among young people, through cultural exchanges, co-operation in all fields of education and, more specifically, through teaching and training in the languages of other participating States. We intend to consider first results of this action at the Helsinki Follow-up Meeting in 1992.

## Migrant Workers

We recognize that the issues of migrant workers and their families legally residing in host countries have economic, cultural and social aspects as well as their human dimension. We reaffirm that the protection and promotion of their rights, as well as the implementation of relevant international obligations, is our common concern.

## Mediterranean

We consider that the fundamental political changes that have occurred in Europe have a positive relevance to the Mediterranean region. Thus, we will continue efforts to strengthen security and co-operation in the Mediterranean as an important factor for stability in Europe. We welcome the Report of the Palma de Mallorca Meeting on the Mediterranean, the results of which we all support.

We are concerned with the continuing tensions in the region, and renew our determination to intensify efforts towards finding just, viable and lasting solutions, through peaceful means, to outstanding crucial problems, based on respect for the principles of the Final Act.

We wish to promote favourable conditions for a harmonious development and diversification of relations with the non-participating Mediterranean

States. Enhanced co-operation with these States will be pursued with the aim of promoting economic and social development and thereby enhancing stability in the region. To this end, we will strive together with these countries towards a substantial narrowing of the prosperity gap between Europe and its Mediterranean neighbours.

### Non-governmental Organizations

We recall the major role that non-governmental organizations, religious and other groups and individuals have played in the achievement of the objectives of the CSCE and will further facilitate their activities for the implementation of the CSCE commitments by the participating States. These organizations, groups and individuals must be involved in an appropriate way in the activities and new structures of the CSCE in order to fulfil their important tasks.

## NEW STRUCTURES AND INSTITUTIONS OF THE CSCE PROCESS

Our common efforts to consolidate respect for human rights, democracy and the rule of law, to strengthen peace and to promote unity in Europe require a new quality of political dialogue and co-operation and thus development of the structures of the CSCE.

The intensification of our consultations at all levels is of prime importance in shaping our future relations. To this end, we decide on the following:

We, the Heads of State or Government, shall meet next time in Helsinki on the occasion of the CSCE Follow-up Meeting 1992. Thereafter, we will meet on the occasion of subsequent follow-up meetings.

Our Ministers for Foreign Affairs will meet, as a Council, regularly and at least once a year. These meetings will provide the central forum for political consultations within the CSCE process. The Council will consider issues relevant to the Conference on Security and Co-operation in Europe and take appropriate decisions.

The first meeting of the Council will take place in Berlin.

A Committee of Senior Officials will prepare the meetings of the Council and carry out its decisions. The Committee will review current issues and may take appropriate decisions, including in the form of recommendations to the Council.

Additional meetings of the representatives of the participating States may be agreed upon to discuss questions of urgent concern.

The Council will examine the development of provisions for convening meetings of the Committee of Senior Officials in emergency situations.

Meetings of other Ministers may also be agreed by the participating States.

In order to provide administrative support for these consultations we establish a Secretariat in Prague.

Follow-up meetings of the participating States will be held, as a rule, every two years to allow the participating States to take stock of developments, review the implementation of their commitments and consider further steps in the CSCE process.

We decide to create a Conflict Prevention Centre in Vienna to assist the Council in reducing the risk of conflict.

We decide to establish an Office for Free Elections in Warsaw to facilitate contacts and the exchange of information on elections within participating States.

Recognizing the important role parliamentarians can play in the CSCE process, we call for greater parliamentary involvement in the CSCE, in particular through the creation of a CSCE parliamentary assembly, involving members of parliaments from all participating States. To this end, we urge that contacts be pursued at parliamentary level to discuss the field of activities, working methods and rules of procedure of such a CSCE parliamentary structure, drawing on existing experience and work already undertaken in this field.

We ask our Ministers for Foreign Affairs to review this matter on the occasion of their first meeting as a Council.

\* \* \*

Procedural and organizational modalities relating to certain provisions contained in the Charter of Paris for a New Europe are set out in the Supplementary Document which is adopted together with the Charter of Paris.

We entrust to the Council the further steps which may be required to ensure the implementation of decisions contained in the present document, as well as in the Supplementary Document, and to consider further efforts for the strengthening of security and co-operation in Europe. The Council may adopt any amendment to the supplementary document which it may deem appropriate.

\* \* \*

The original of the Charter of Paris for a New Europe, drawn up in English, French, German, Italian, Russian and Spanish, will be transmitted to the Government of the French Republic, which will retain it in its archives. Each of the participating States will receive from the Government of the French Republic a true copy of the Charter of Paris.

The text of the Charter of Paris will be published in each participating State, which will disseminate it and make it known as widely as possible.

The Government of the French Republic is requested to transmit to the Secretary-General of the United Nations the text of the Charter of Paris for a New Europe which is not eligible for registration under Article 102 of the Charter of the United Nations, with a view to its circulation to all the members of the Organization as an official document of the United Nations.

The Government of the French Republic is also requested to transmit the text of the Charter of Paris to all the other international organizations mentioned in the text.

Wherefore, we, the undersigned High Representatives of the participating States, mindful of the high political significance we attach to the results of the Summit Meeting, and declaring our determination to act in accordance with the provisions we have adopted, have subscribed our signatures below:

Done
at Paris,
on 21
November
1990,
in the name of

# PART SIX

# LATIN AMERICAN DEVELOPMENTS

## INTRODUCTION

LATIN AMERICA provides a store of contradictions in the field of human rights. Legal and political sophistication belongs to some of the Latin American socially élite groups, and the outcome of this sophistication is a desire to adopt legal instruments such as the American Convention on Human Rights (below, p. 495), which is broadly similar to the European Convention (above, pp. 326–41). At the same time social conditions in nearly all of Latin America entail inequalities and deprivation on such a scale that recourse to guarantees of the classical Western political and civil rights is manifestly inadequate. Moreover, in the absence of general social and economic development, the position relating to civil and political rights is itself precarious. The successful use of international machinery to improve standards of government must normally depend upon the existence of a certain, reasonably uniform, level of development in the States concerned.

The position in Latin America has special features. The whole question of human rights is bound up with the status of aliens and their property: powerful foreign corporations will wish to rely on human rights standards to preserve an economic *status quo* favourable to their interests. More significant is the relation of human rights to the regional security system represented by the Organization of American States. There is abundant evidence that the concept of human rights in Latin America has been employed as a weapon against revolutionary regimes, particularly Cuba. Even so, formal adherence by governments to agreements containing guarantees of human rights will help politicians striving to improve social conditions, and will improve the possibility of reporting abuses.

For general reference see Gros Espiell, *Recueil des cours* (Hague Academy of International Law), Vol. 145 (1975, II), pp. 1–55; Buergenthal, *American Journal of International Law*, Vol. 69 (1975), pp. 828–36; Medina Quiroga, *The Battle of Human Rights*, 1988; Robertson and Merrills, *Human Rights in the World*, 3rd ed., 1989, pp. 161–93; Buergenthal, *American Journal of International Law*, Vol. 76 (1982), pp. 231–45.

# I. AMERICAN DECLARATION OF THE RIGHTS AND DUTIES OF MAN, 1948

The Declaration is to be found in the Final Act of the Ninth International Conference of American States, Bogotá, Colombia, held in 1948. It was based on a revision of a draft first prepared in 1946 by the Inter-American Juridical Committee. The Declaration was not intended to be binding, and its status was that of a recommendation of the Conference. However, in their practice the organs created in accordance with the American Convention on Human Rights (below, p. 495) have given a certain normative value to the Declaration: see the decision of the Commission in the *Case of Roach and Pinkerton* (27 March 1987) (General Secretariat of the O.A.S.); and the Advisory Opinion of the Inter-American Court of Human Rights of 14 July 1989 (OC-10/89); *Inter-American Court of Human Rights*, Series A, *Judgments and Opinions*, No. 10.

## TEXT

*Whereas:*

The American peoples have acknowledged the dignity of the individual, and their national constitutions recognize that juridical and political institutions, which regulate life in human society, have as their principal aim the protection of the essential rights of man and the creation of circumstances that will permit him to achieve spiritual and material progress and attain happiness;

The American States have on repeated occasions recognized that the essential rights of man are not derived from the fact that he is a national of a certain state, but are based upon attributes of his human personality;

The international protection of the rights of man should be the principal guide of an evolving American law;

The affirmation of essential human rights by the American States together with the guarantees given by the internal régimes of the states establish the initial system of protection considered by the American States as being suited to the present social and juridical conditions, not without a recognition on their part that they should increasingly strengthen that system in the international field as conditions become more favourable,

The Ninth International Conference of American States

*Agrees*

To adopt the following

# AMERICAN DECLARATION OF THE RIGHTS AND DUTIES OF MAN

## Preamble

All men are born free and equal, in dignity and in rights, and, being endowed by nature with reason and conscience, they should conduct themselves as brothers one to another.

The fulfillment of duty by each individual is a prerequisite to the rights of all. Rights and duties are interrelated in every social and political activity of man. While rights exalt individual liberty, duties express the dignity of that liberty.

Duties of a juridical nature presuppose others of a moral nature which support them in principle and constitute their basis.

Inasmuch as spiritual development is the supreme end of human existence and the highest expression thereof, it is the duty of man to serve that end with all his strength and resources.

Since culture is the highest social and historical expression of that spiritual development, it is the duty of man to preserve, practise and foster culture by every means within his power.

And, since moral conduct constitutes the noblest flowering of culture, it is the duty of every man always to hold it in high respect.

## Chapter One. Rights

*Article I*

Every human being has the right to life, liberty and the security of his person.

*Article II*

All persons are equal before the law and have the rights and duties established in this Declaration, without distinction as to race, sex, language, creed or any other factor.

*Article III*

Every person has the right freely to profess a religious faith, and to manifest and practice it both in public and in private.

*Article IV*

Every person has the right to freedom of investigation, of opinion, and of the expression and dissemination of ideas, by any medium whatsoever.

*Article V*

Every person has the right to the protection of the law against abusive attacks upon his honor, his reputation, and his private and family life.

*Article VI*

Every person has the right to establish a family, the basic element of society, and to receive protection therefor.

*Article VII*

All women, during pregnancy and the nursing period, and all children have the right to special protection, care and aid.

*Article VIII*

Every person has the right to fix his residence within the territory of the state of which he is a national, to move about freely within such territory, and not to leave it except by his own will.

*Article IX*

Every person has the right to the inviolability of his home.

*Article X*

Every person has the right to the inviolability and transmission of his correspondence.

*Article XI*

Every person has the right to the preservation of his health through sanitary and social measures relating to food, clothing, housing and medical care, to the extent permitted by public and community resources.

*Article XII*

Every person has the right to an education, which should be based on the principles of liberty, morality and human solidarity.

Likewise every person has the right to an education that will prepare him to attain a decent life, to raise his standard of living, and to be a useful member of society.

The right to an education includes the right to equality of opportunity in every case, in accordance with natural talents, merit and the desire to utilize the resources that the state or the community is in a position to provide.

Every person has the right to receive, free, at least a primary education.

*Article XIII*

Every person has the right to take part in the cultural life of the community, to enjoy the arts, and to participate in the benefits that result from intellectual progress, especially scientific discoveries.

He likewise has the right to the protection of his moral and material interests as regards his inventions or any literary, scientific or artistic works of which he is the author.

*Article XIV*

Every person has the right to work, under proper conditions, and to follow his vocation freely, in so far as existing conditions of employment permit.

Every person who works has the right to receive such remuneration as will, in proportion to his capacity and skill, assure him a standard of living suitable for himself and for his family.

*Article XV*

Every person has the right to leisure time, to wholesome recreation, and to the opportunity for advantageous use of his free time to his spiritual, cultural and physical benefit.

*Article XVI*

Every person has the right to social security which will protect him from the consequences of unemployment, old age, and any disabilities arising from causes beyond his control that make it physically or mentally impossible for him to earn a living.

*Article XVII*

Every person has the right to be recognized everywhere as a person having rights and obligations, and to enjoy the basic civil rights.

*Article XVIII*

Every person may resort to the courts to ensure respect for his legal rights. There should likewise be available to him a simple, brief procedure whereby the courts will protect him from acts of authority that, to his prejudice, violate any fundamental constitutional rights.

*Article XIX*

Every person has the right to the nationality to which he is entitled by law and to change it, if he so wishes, for the nationality of any other country that is willing to grant it to him.

*Article XX*

Every person having legal capacity is entitled to participate in the government of his country, directly or through his representatives, and to take part in popular elections, which shall be by secret ballot, and shall be honest, periodic and free.

*Article XXI*

Every person has the right to assemble peaceably with others in a formal public meeting or an informal gathering, in connection with matters of common interest of any nature.

## Article XXII

Every person has the right to associate with others to promote, exercise and protect his legitimate interests of a political, economic, religious, social, cultural, professional, labor union or other nature.

## Article XXIII

Every person has a right to own such private property as meets the essential needs of decent living and helps to maintain the dignity of the individual and of the home.

## Article XXIV

Every person has the right to submit respectful petitions to any competent authority, for reasons of either general or private interest, and the right to obtain a prompt decision thereon.

## Article XXV

No person may be deprived of his liberty except in the cases and according to the procedures established by pre-existing law.

No person may be deprived of liberty for nonfulfillment of obligations of a purely civil character.

Every individual who has been deprived of his liberty has the right to have the legality of his detention ascertained without delay by a court, and the right to be tried without undue delay, or otherwise, to be released. He also has the right to humane treatment during the time he is in custody.

## Article XXVI

Every accused person is presumed to be innocent until proved guilty.

Every person accused of an offense has the right to be given an impartial and public hearing, and to be tried by courts previously established in accordance with pre-existing laws, and not to receive cruel, infamous or unusual punishment.

## Article XXVII

Every person has the right, in case of pursuit not resulting from ordinary crimes, to seek and receive asylum in foreign territory, in accordance with the laws of each country and with international agreements.

## Article XXVIII

The rights of man are limited by the rights of others, by the security of all, and by the just demands of the general welfare and the advancement of democracy.

## Chapter Two. Duties

*Article XXIX*

It is the duty of the individual so to conduct himself in relation to others that each and every one may fully form and develop his personality.

*Article XXX*

It is the duty of every person to aid, support, educate and protect his minor children, and it is the duty of children to honor their parents always and to aid, support and protect them when they need it.

*Article XXXI*

It is the duty of every person to acquire at least an elementary education.

*Article XXXII*

It is the duty of every person to vote in the popular elections of the country of which he is a national, when he is legally capable of doing so.

*Article XXXIII*

It is the duty of every person to obey the law and other legitimate commands of the authorities of his country and those of the country in which he may be.

*Article XXXIV*

It is the duty of every able-bodied person to render whatever civil and military service his country may require for its defense and preservation, and, in case of public disaster, to render such services as may be in his power.

It is likewise his duty to hold any public office to which he may be elected by popular vote in the state of which he is a national.

*Article XXXV*

It is the duty of every person to co-operate with the state and the community with respect to social security and welfare, in accordance with his ability and with existing circumstances.

*Article XXXVI*

It is the duty of every person to pay the taxes established by law for the support of public services.

*Article XXXVII*

It is the duty of every person to work, as far as his capacity and possibilities permit, in order to obtain the means of livelihood or to benefit his community.

*Article XXXVIII*

It is the duty of every person to refrain from taking part in political activities that, according to law, are reserved exclusively to the citizens of the state in which he is an alien.

## II. AMERICAN CONVENTION ON HUMAN RIGHTS, 1969

The Bogotá Conference of 1948 had expressed a tentative interest in a proposal that an Inter-American Court be created to guarantee the basic rights of man, but no further development occurred until the Fifth Meeting of Consultation of Ministers of Foreign Affairs at Santiago, Chile, in 1959. The meeting resolved that the Inter-American Council of Jurists should prepare a draft Convention on Human Rights and that a convention should also be prepared on the creation of an Inter-American Court for the Protection of Human Rights.

The same meeting decided that an Inter-American Commission on Human Rights should be organized. The Commission came into being in 1960 as 'an autonomous entity of the Organization of American States, the function of which is to promote respect for human rights'. For the text of the statute see *The Inter-American System*, Inter-American Institute of International Legal Studies, 1966, p. 372. On the performance of the Commission see the same work, pp. 43–56; Schreiber, *The Inter-American Commission on Human Rights*, 1970; Cabranes, *Michigan Law Review*, 65 (1967), p. 1147 and pp. 1164–73; Buergenthal, *American Journal of International Law*, Vol. 69 (1975), pp. 828–36; Tardu, *ibid.*, Vol. 70 (1976), pp. 778–800. The Inter-American Commission has an enhanced status since the entry into force of the revised O.A.S. Charter in 1970.

The culmination of Latin American interest in human rights was the Inter-American Specialized Conference on Human Rights held at San José, Costa Rica, 7–22 November 1969. The American Convention on Human Rights was signed on 22 November 1969 by the following States: Chile, Colombia, Costa Rica, El Salvador, Ecuador, Guatemala, Honduras, Nicaragua, Panama, Paraguay, Uruguay, and Venezuela. The Convention has been ratified by twenty-three States. The Convention provides for a Commission and a Court, and bears a general resemblance to the European Convention, above. However, there are significant differences; for example, in the powers of the Commission, which are both broad and vague in the American Convention. The Commission created by the provisions of the Convention coincides with the pre-existing Inter-American Commission except that the Commission retains its previous powers in respect of states which did not ratify the new Convention: see Robertson and Merrills, *Human Rights in the World*, 3rd ed., 1989, pp. 168–77. A number of Reports on the situation in individual countries have been published.

The American Convention entered into force on 18 July 1978. Consequently the Inter-American Court of Human Rights was inaugurated on 3 September 1979. The seat of the Court is at San José, Costa Rica. By 1991 twelve States had recognised the jurisdiction of the Court: see the *Annual Report of the Inter-American Court of Human Rights*, General Secretariat, OAS.

*TEXT*

## Preamble

*The American States signatory to the present Convention,*

*Reaffirming* their intention to consolidate in this hemisphere, within the framework of democratic institutions, a system of personal liberty and social justice based on respect for the essential rights of man;

*Recognizing* that the essential rights of man are not derived from one's being a national of a certain state, but are based upon attributes of the human personality, and that they therefore justify international protection in the form of a convention reinforcing or complementing the protection provided by the domestic law of the American states;

*Considering* that these principles have been set forth in the Charter of the Organization of American States, in the American Declaration of the Rights and Duties of Man, and in the Universal Declaration of Human Rights, and that they have been reaffirmed and refined in other international instruments, worldwide as well as regional in scope;

*Reiterating* that, in accordance with the Universal Declaration of Human Rights, the ideal of free men enjoying freedom from fear and want can be achieved only if conditions are created whereby everyone may enjoy his economic, social, and cultural rights, as well as his civil and political rights; and

*Considering* that the Third Special Inter-American Conference (Buenos Aires, 1967) approved the incorporation into the Charter of the Organization itself of broader standards with respect to economic, social, and educational rights and resolved that an inter-American convention on human rights should determine the structure, competence, and procedure of the organs responsible for these matters,

Have agreed upon the following:

## PART I
### *STATE OBLIGATIONS AND RIGHTS PROTECTED*

### Chapter I. General Obligations

*Obligation to Respect Rights*

*Article* 1

1. The States Parties to this Convention undertake to respect the rights and freedoms recognized herein and to ensure to all persons subject to their jurisdiction the free and full exercise of those rights and freedoms, without any discrimination for reasons of race, color, sex, language, religion, polit-

ical or other opinion, national or social origin, economic status, birth, or any other social condition.

2. For the purposes of this Convention, 'person' means every human being.

*Domestic Legal Effects*

*Article 2*

Where the exercise of any of the rights or freedoms referred to in Article 1 is not already ensured by legislative or other provisions, the States Parties undertake to adopt, in accordance with their constitutional processes and the provisions of this Convention, such legislative or other measures as may be necessary to give effect to those rights or freedoms.

## Chapter II. Civil and Political Rights

*Right to Juridical Personality*

*Article 3*

Every person has the right to recognition as a person before the law.

*Right to Life*

*Article 4*

1. Every person has the right to have his life respected. This right shall be protected by law, and, in general, from the moment of conception. No one shall be arbitrarily deprived of his life.

2. In countries that have not abolished the death penalty, it may be imposed only for the most serious crimes and pursuant to a final judgment rendered by a competent court and in accordance with a law establishing such punishment, enacted prior to the commission of the crime. The application of such punishment shall not be extended to crimes to which it does not presently apply.

3. The death penalty shall not be reestablished in states that have abolished it.

4. In no case shall capital punishment be inflicted for political offenses or related common crimes.

5. Capital punishment shall not be imposed upon persons who, at the time the crime was committed, were under 18 years of age or over 70 years of age; nor shall it be applied to pregnant women.

6. Every person condemned to death shall have the right to apply for amnesty, pardon, or commutation of sentence, which may be granted in all

cases. Capital punishment shall not be imposed while such a petition is pending decision by the competent authority.

### Right to Humane Treatment

*Article* 5

1. Every person has the right to have his physical, mental, and moral integrity respected.

2. No one shall be subjected to torture or to cruel, inhuman, or degrading punishment or treatment. All persons deprived of their liberty shall be treated with respect for the inherent dignity of the human person.

3. Punishment shall not be extended to any person other than the criminal.

4. Accused persons shall, save in exceptional circumstances, be segregated from convicted persons, and shall be subject to separate treatment appropriate to their status as unconvicted persons.

5. Minors while subject to criminal proceedings shall be separated from adults and brought before specialized tribunals, as speedily as possible, so that they may be treated in accordance with their status as minors.

6. Punishments consisting of deprivation of liberty shall have as an essential aim the reform and social readaptation of the prisoners.

### Freedom from Slavery

*Article* 6

1. No one shall be subject to slavery or to involuntary servitude, which are prohibited in all their forms, as are the slave trade and traffic in women.

2. No one shall be required to perform forced or compulsory labor. This provision shall not be interpreted to mean that, in those countries in which the penalty established for certain crimes is deprivation of liberty at forced labor, the carrying out of such a sentence imposed by a competent court is prohibited. Forced labor shall not adversely affect the dignity or the physical or intellectual capacity of the prisoner.

3. For the purposes of this article the following do not constitute forced or compulsory labor:

    (*a*) work or service normally required of a person imprisoned in execution of a sentence or formal decision passed by the competent judicial authority. Such work or service shall be carried out under the supervision and control of public authorities, and any persons performing such work or service shall not be placed at the disposal of any private party, company, or juridical person;

    (*b*) military service and, in countries in which conscientious objectors are recognized, national service that the law may provide for in lieu of military service;

(*c*) service exacted in time of danger or calamity that threatens the existence or the well-being of the community; or

(*d*) work or service that forms part of normal civic obligations.

### Right to Personal Liberty

*Article* 7

1. Every person has the right to personal liberty and security.

2. No one shall be deprived of his physical liberty except for the reasons and under the conditions established beforehand by the constitution of the State Party concerned or by a law established pursuant thereto.

3. No one shall be subject to arbitrary arrest or imprisonment.

4. Anyone who is detained shall be informed of the reasons for his detention and shall be promptly notified of the charge or charges against him.

5. Any person detained shall be brought promptly before a judge or other officer authorized by law to exercise judicial power and shall be entitled to trial within a reasonable time or to be released without prejudice to the continuation of the proceedings. His release may be subject to guarantees to assure his appearance for trial.

6. Anyone who is deprived of his liberty shall be entitled to recourse to a competent court, in order that the court may decide without delay on the lawfulness of his arrest or detention and order his release if the arrest or detention is unlawful. In States Parties whose laws provide that anyone who believes himself to be threatened with deprivation of his liberty is entitled to recourse to a competent court in order that it may decide on the lawfulness of such threat, this remedy may not be restricted or abolished. The interested party or another person in his behalf is entitled to seek these remedies.

7. No one shall be detained for debt. This principle shall not limit the orders of a competent judicial authority issued for nonfulfillment of duties of support.

### Right to a Fair Trial

*Article* 8

1. Every person has the right to a hearing, with due guarantees and within a reasonable time, by a competent, independent, and impartial tribunal, previously established by law, in the substantiation of any accusation of a criminal nature made against him or for the determination of his rights and obligations of a civil, labor, fiscal, or any other nature.

2. Every person accused of a criminal offense has the right to be presumed innocent so long as his guilt has not been proven according to law. During

the proceedings, every person is entitled, with full equality, to the following minimum guarantees:

   (*a*)  the right of the accused to be assisted without charge by a translator or interpreter, if he does not understand or does not speak the language of the tribunal or court;

   (*b*)  prior notification in detail to the accused of the charges against him;

   (*c*)  adequate time and means for the preparation of his defense;

   (*d*)  the right of the accused to defend himself personally or to be assisted by legal counsel of his own choosing, and to communicate freely and privately with his counsel;

   (*e*)  the inalienable right to be assisted by counsel provided by the state, paid or not as the domestic law provides, if the accused does not defend himself personally or engage his own counsel within the time period established by law;

   (*f*)  the right of the defense to examine witnesses present in the court and to obtain the appearance, as witnesses, of experts or other persons who may throw light on the facts;

   (*g*)  the right not to be compelled to be a witness against himself or to plead guilty; and

   (*h*)  the right to appeal the judgment to a higher court.

3. A confession of guilt by the accused shall be valid only if it is made without coercion of any kind.

4. An accused person acquitted by a nonappealable judgment shall not be subjected to a new trial for the same cause.

5. Criminal proceedings shall be public, except insofar as may be necessary to protect the interests of justice.

### Freedom from Ex Post Facto Laws

*Article* 9

No one shall be convicted of any act or omission that did not constitute a criminal offense, under the applicable law, at the time it was committed. A heavier penalty shall not be imposed than the one that was applicable at the time the criminal offense was committed. If subsequent to the commission of the offense the law provides for the imposition of a lighter punishment, the guilty person shall benefit therefrom.

### Right to Compensation

*Article* 10

Every person has the right to be compensated in accordance with the law in the event he has been sentenced by a final judgment through a miscarriage of justice.

## Right to Privacy

*Article* 11

1. Everyone has the right to have his honor respected and his dignity recognized.

2. No one may be the object of arbitrary or abusive interference with his private life, his family, his home, or his correspondence, or of unlawful attacks on his honor or reputation.

3. Everyone has the right to the protection of the law against such interference or attacks.

## Freedom of Conscience and Religion

*Article* 12

1. Everyone has the right to freedom of conscience and of religion. This includes freedom to maintain or to change one's religion or beliefs, and freedom to profess or disseminate one's religion or beliefs either individually or together with others, in public or in private.

2. No one shall be subject to restrictions that might impair his freedom to maintain or to change his religion or beliefs.

3. Freedom to manifest one's religion and beliefs may be subject only to the limitations prescribed by law that are necessary to protect public safety, order, health, or morals, or the rights or freedoms of others.

4. Parents or guardians, as the case may be, have the right to provide for the religious and moral education of their children or wards that is in accord with their own convictions.

## Freedom of Thought and Expression

*Article* 13

1. Everyone shall have the right to freedom of thought and expression. This right shall include freedom to seek, receive, and impart information and ideas of all kinds, regardless of frontiers, either orally, in writing, in print, in the form of art, or through any other medium of one's choice.

2. The exercise of the right provided for in the foregoing paragraph shall not be subject to prior censorship but shall be subject to subsequent imposition of liability, which shall be expressly established by law to the extent necessary in order to ensure:

(*a*) respect for the rights or reputations of others; or
(*b*) the protection of national security, public order, or public health or morals.

3. The right of expression may not be restricted by indirect methods or means, such as the abuse of government or private controls over newsprint,

radio broadcasting frequencies, or equipment used in the dissemination of information, or by any other means tending to impede the communication and circulation of ideas and opinions.

4. Notwithstanding the provisions of paragraph 2 above, public entertainments may be subject by law to prior censorship for the sole purpose of regulating access to them for the moral protection of childhood and adolescence.

5. Any propaganda for war and any advocacy of national, racial, or religious hatred that constitute incitements to lawless violence or to any other similar illegal action against any person or group of persons on any grounds including those of race, color, religion, language, or national origin shall be considered as offenses punishable by law.

### Right of Reply

*Article* 14

1. Anyone injured by inaccurate or offensive statements or ideas disseminated to the public in general by a legally regulated medium of communication has the right to reply or make a correction using the same communications outlet, under such conditions as the law may establish.

2. The correction or reply shall not in any case remit other legal liabilities that may have been incurred.

3. For the effective protection of honor and reputation, every publisher, and every newspaper, motion picture, radio, and television company, shall have a person responsible, who is not protected by immunities or special privileges.

### Right of Assembly

*Article* 15

The right of peaceful assembly, without arms, is recognized. No restrictions may be placed on the exercise of this right other than those imposed in conformity with the law and necessary in a democratic society in the interest of national security, public safety or public order, or to protect public health or morals or the rights or freedoms of others.

### Freedom of Association

*Article* 16

1. Everyone has the right to associate freely for ideological, religious, political, economic, labor, social, cultural, sports, or other purposes.

2. The exercise of this right shall be subject only to such restrictions established by law as may be necessary in a democratic society, in the

interest of national security, public safety or public order, or to protect public health or morals or the rights and freedoms of others.

3. The provisions of this article do not bar the imposition of legal restrictions, including even deprivation of the exercise of the right of association, on members of the armed forces and the police.

## Right of the Family

*Article* 17

1. The family is the natural and fundamental group unit of society and is entitled to protection by society and the state.

2. The right of men and women of marriageable age to marry and to raise a family shall be recognized, if they meet the conditions required by domestic laws, insofar as such conditions do not affect the principle of nondiscrimination established in this Convention.

3. No marriage shall be entered into without the free and full consent of the intending spouses.

4. The States Parties shall take appropriate steps to ensure the equality of rights and the adequate balancing of responsibilities of the spouses as to marriage, during marriage, and in the event of its dissolution. In case of dissolution, provision shall be made for the necessary protection of any children solely on the basis of their own best interests.

5. The law shall recognize equal rights for children born out of wedlock and those born in wedlock.

## Right to a Name

*Article* 18

Every person has the right to a given name and to the surnames of his parents or that of one of them. The law shall regulate the manner in which this right shall be ensured for all, by the use of assumed names if necessary.

## Rights of the Child

*Article* 19

Every minor child has the right to the measures of protection required by his condition as a minor on the part of his family, society, and the state.

## Right to Nationality

*Article* 20

1. Every person has the right to a nationality.

2. Every person has the right to the nationality of the state in whose

territory he was born if he does not have the right to any other nationality.

3. No one shall be arbitrarily deprived of his nationality or of the right to change it.

### Right to Property

*Article* 21

1. Everyone has the right to the use and enjoyment of his property. The law may subordinate such use and enjoyment to the interest of society.

2. No one shall be deprived of his property except upon payment of just compensation, for reasons of public utility or social interest, and in the cases and according to the forms established by law.

3. Usury and any other form of exploitation of man by man shall be prohibited by law.

### Freedom of Movement and Residence

*Article* 22

1. Every person lawfully in the territory of a State Party has the right to move about in it and to reside in it subject to the provisions of the law.

2. Every person has the right to leave any country freely, including his own.

3. The exercise of the foregoing rights may be restricted only pursuant to a law to the extent necessary in a democratic society to prevent crime or to protect national security, public safety, public order, public morals, public health, or the rights or freedoms of others.

4. The exercise of the rights recognized in paragraph 1 may also be restricted by law in designated zones for reasons of public interest.

5. No one can be expelled from the territory of the state of which he is a national or be deprived of the right to enter it.

6. An alien lawfully in the territory of a State Party to this Convention may be expelled from it only pursuant to a decision reached in accordance with law.

7. Every person has the right to seek and be granted asylum in a foreign territory, in accordance with the legislation of the state and international conventions, in the event he is being pursued for political offenses or related common crimes.

8. In no case may an alien be deported or returned to a country, regardless of whether or not it is his country of origin, if in that country his right to life or personal freedom is in danger of being violated because of his race, nationality, religion, social status, or political opinions.

9. The collective expulsion of aliens is prohibited.

*Right to Participate in Government*

*Article* 23

1. Every citizen shall enjoy the following rights and opportunities:

   (*a*) to take part in the conduct of public affairs, directly or through freely chosen representatives;

   (*b*) to vote and to be elected in genuine periodic elections, which shall be by universal and equal suffrage and by secret ballot that guarantees the free expression of the will of the voters; and

   (*c*) to have access, under general conditions of equality, to the public service of his country.

2. The law may regulate the exercise of the rights and opportunities referred to in the preceding paragraph only on the basis of age, nationality, residence, language, education, civil and mental capacity, or sentencing by a competent court in criminal proceedings.

*Right to Equal Protection*

*Article* 24

All persons are equal before the law. Consequently, they are entitled, without discrimination, to equal protection of the law.

*Right to Judicial Protection*

*Article* 25

1. Everyone has the right to simple and prompt recourse, or any other effective recourse, to a competent court or tribunal for protection against acts that violate his fundamental rights recognized by the constitution or laws of the state concerned or by this Convention, even though such violation may have been committed by persons acting in the course of their official duties.

2. The States Parties undertake:

   (*a*) to ensure that any person claiming such remedy shall have his rights determined by the competent authority provided for by the legal system of the state;

   (*b*) to develop the possibilities of judicial remedy; and

   (*c*) to ensure that the competent authorities shall enforce such remedies when granted.

## Chapter III. Economic, Social, and Cultural Rights

### *Progressive Development*

*Article* 26

The States Parties undertake to adopt measures, both internally and through international co-operation, especially those of an economic and technical nature, with a view to achieving progressively, by legislation or other appropriate means, the full realization of the rights implicit in the economic, social, educational, scientific, and cultural standards set forth in the Charter of the Organization of American States as amended by the Protocol of Buenos Aires.

## Chapter IV. Suspension of Guarantees, Interpretation, and Application

### *Suspension of Guarantees*

*Article* 27

1. In time of war, public danger, or other emergency that threatens the independence or security of a State Party, it may take measures derogating from its obligations under the present Convention to the extent and for the period of time strictly required by the exigencies of the situation, provided that such measures are not inconsistent with its other obligations under international law and do not involve discrimination on the ground of race, color, sex, language, religion, or social origin.

2. The foregoing provision does not authorize any suspension of the following articles: Article 3 (Right to Juridical Personality), Article 4 (Right to Life), Article 5 (Right to Humane Treatment), Article 6 (Freedom from Slavery), Article 9 (Freedom from Ex Post Facto Laws), Article 12 (Freedom of Conscience and Religion), Article 17 (Rights of the Family), Article 18 (Right to a Name), Article 19 (Rights of the Child), Article 20 (Right to Nationality), and Article 23 (Right to Participate in Government) or of the judicial guarantees essential for the protection of such rights.

3. Any State Party availing itself of the right of suspension shall immediately inform the other States Parties, through the Secretary General of the Organization of American States, of the provisions the application of which it has suspended, the reasons that gave rise to the suspension, and the date set for the termination of such suspension.

### *Federal Clause*

*Article* 28

1. Where a State Party is constituted as a federal state, the national government of such State Party shall implement all the provisions of the

Convention over whose subject matter it exercises legislative and judicial jurisdiction.

2. With respect to the provisions over whose subject matter the constituent units of the federal state have jurisdiction, the national government shall immediately take suitable measures, in accordance with its constitution and its laws, to the end that the competent authorities of the constituent units may adopt appropriate provisions for the fulfillment of this Convention.

3. Whenever two or more States Parties agree to form a federation or other type of association they shall take care that the resulting federal or other compact contains the provisions necessary for continuing and rendering effective the standards of this Convention in the new state that is organized.

### Restrictions Regarding Interpretation

*Article* 29

No provision of this Convention shall be interpreted as:

(a) permitting any State Party, group, or person to suppress the enjoyment or exercise of the rights and freedoms recognized in this Convention or to restrict them to a greater extent than is provided for herein;

(b) restricting the enjoyment or exercise of any right or freedom recognized by virtue of the laws of any State Party or by virtue of another convention to which one of the said states is a party;

(c) precluding other rights or guarantees that are inherent in the human personality or derived from representative democracy as a form of government; or

(d) excluding or limiting the effect that the American Declaration of the Rights and Duties of Man and other international acts of the same nature may have.

### Scope of Restrictions

*Article* 30

The restrictions that, pursuant to this Convention, may be placed on the enjoyment or exercise of the rights or freedoms recognized herein may not be applied except in accordance with the laws enacted for reasons of general interest and in accordance with the purpose for which such restrictions have been established.

### Recognition of Other Rights

*Article* 31

Other rights and freedoms recognized in accordance with the procedures established in Articles 76 and 77 may be included in the system of protection of this Convention.

## Chapter V. Personal Responsibilities

*Relationship between Duties and Rights*

*Article* 32

1. Every person has responsibilities to his family, his community, and mankind.

2. The rights of each person are limited by the rights of others, by the security of all, and by the just demands of the general welfare, in a democratic society.

# PART II
## *MEANS OF PROTECTION*

### Chapter VI. Competent Organs

*Article* 33

The following organs shall have competence with respect to matters relating to the fulfillment of the commitments made by the States Parties to this Convention:

  (*a*) the Inter-American Commission on Human Rights, referred to as 'The Commission'; and

  (*b*) the Inter-American Court of Human Rights, referred to as 'The Court.'

### Chapter VII. Inter-American Commission on Human Rights

SECTION I. ORGANIZATION

*Article* 34

The Inter-American Commission on Human Rights shall be composed of seven members, who shall be persons of high moral character and recognized competence in the field of human rights.

*Article* 35

The Commission shall represent all the member countries of the Organization of American States.

*Article* 36

1. The members of the Commission shall be elected in a personal capacity

by the General Assembly of the Organization from a list of candidates proposed by the governments of the member states.

2. Each of those governments may propose up to three candidates, who may be nationals of the states proposing them or of any other member state of the Organization of American States. When a slate of three is proposed, at least one of the candidates shall be a national of a state other than the one proposing the slate.

*Article* 37

1. The members of the Commission shall be elected for a term of four years and may be reelected only once, but the terms of three of the members chosen in the first election shall expire at the end of two years. Immediately following that election the General Assembly shall determine the names of those three members by lot.

2. No two nationals of the same state may be members of the Commission.

*Article* 38

Vacancies that may occur on the Commission for reasons other than the normal expiration of a term shall be filled by the Permanent Council of the Organization in accordance with the provisions of the Statute of the Commission.

*Article* 39

The Commission shall prepare its Statute, which it shall submit to the General Assembly for approval. It shall establish its own Regulations.

*Article* 40

Secretariat services for the Commission shall be furnished by the appropriate specialized unit of the General Secretariat of the Organization. This unit shall be provided with the resources required to accomplish the tasks assigned to it by the Commission.

SECTION 2. FUNCTIONS

*Article* 41

The main functions of the Commission shall be to promote respect for and defense of human rights. In the exercise of its mandate, it shall have the following functions and powers:

(*a*)  to develop an awareness of human rights among the peoples of America;

(*b*)  to make recommendations to the governments of the member states, when it considers such action advisable, for the adoption of progressive measures in favour of human rights within the framework of

their domestic law and constitutional provisions as well as appropriate measures to further the observance of those rights;

(*c*) to prepare such studies or reports as it considers advisable in the
performance of its duties;

(*d*) to request the governments of the member states to supply it with
information on the measures adopted by them in matters of human
rights;

(*e*) to respond, through the General Secretariat of the Organization of
American States, to inquiries made by the member states on matters
related to human rights and, within the limits of its possibilities, to
provide those states with the advisory services they request;

(*f*) to take action on petitions and other communications pursuant to its
authority, under the provisions of Articles 44 through 51 of this
Convention; and

(*g*) to submit an annual report to the General Assembly of the Organization of American States.

*Article* 42

The States Parties shall transmit to the Commission a copy of each of the
reports and studies that they submit annually to the Executive Committees
of the Inter-American Economic and Social Council and the Inter-
American Council for Education, Science, and Culture, in their respective
fields, so that the Commission may watch over the promotion of the rights
implicit in the economic, social, educational, scientific, and cultural
standards set forth in the Charter of the Organization of American States as
amended by the Protocol of Buenos Aires.

*Article* 43

The States Parties undertake to provide the Commission with such information as it may request of them as to the manner in which their domestic
law ensures the effective application of any provisions of this Convention.

SECTION 3. COMPETENCE

*Article* 44

Any person or group of persons, or any nongovernmental entity legally
recognized in one or more member states of the Organization, may lodge
petitions with the Commission containing denunciations or complaints of
violation of this Convention by a State Party.

*Article* 45

1. Any State Party may, when it deposits its instrument of ratification of or
adherence to this Convention, or at any later time, declare that it recognizes the competence of the Commission to receive and examine com-

munications in which a State Party alleges that another State Party has committed a violation of a human right set forth in this Convention.

2. Communications presented by virtue of this article may be admitted and examined only if they are presented by a State Party that has made a declaration recognizing the aforementioned competence of the Commission. The Commission shall not admit any communication against a State Party that has not made such a declaration.

3. A declaration concerning recognition of competence may be made to be valid for an indefinite time, for a specified period, or for a specific case.

4. Declarations shall be deposited with the General Secretariat of the Organization of American States, which shall transmit copies thereof to the member states of that Organization.

*Article* 46

1. Admission by the Commission of a petition or communication lodged in accordance with Articles 44 or 45 shall be subject to the following requirements:

(a) that the remedies under domestic law have been pursued and exhausted in accordance with generally recognized principles of international law;

(b) that the petition or communication is lodged within a period of six months from the date on which the party alleging violation of his rights was notified of the final judgment;

(c) that the subject of the petition or communication is not pending before another international procedure for settlement; and

(d) that, in the case of Article 44, the petition contains the name, nationality, profession, domicile, and signature of the person or persons or of the legal representative of the entity lodging the petition.

2. The provisions of paragraphs 1 (a) and 1 (b) of this article shall not be applicable when:

(a) the domestic legislation of the state concerned does not afford due process of law for the protection of the right or rights that have allegedly been violated;

(b) the party alleging violation of his rights has been denied access to the remedies under domestic law or has been prevented from exhausting them; or

(c) there has been unwarranted delay in rendering a final judgment under the aforementioned remedies.

*Article* 47

The Commission shall consider inadmissible any petition or communication submitted under Articles 44 or 45 if:

(a) any of the requirements indicated in Article 46 has not been met;

(b) the petition or communication does not state facts that tend to establish a violation of the rights guaranteed by this Convention;

(c) the statements of the petitioner or of the state indicate that the petition or communication is manifestly groundless or obviously out of order; or

(d) the petition or communication is substantially the same as one previously studied by the Commission or by another international organization.

## SECTION 4. PROCEDURE

*Article* 48

1. When the Commission receives a petition or communication alleging violation of any of the rights protected by this Convention, it shall proceed as follows:

(a) If it considers the petition or communication admissible, it shall request information from the government of the state indicated as being responsible for the alleged violations and shall furnish that government a transcript of the pertinent portions of the petition or communication. This information shall be submitted within a reasonable period to be determined by the Commission in accordance with the circumstances of each case.

(b) After the information has been received, or after the period established has elapsed and the information has not been received, the Commission shall ascertain whether the grounds for the petition or communication still exist. If they do not, the Commission shall order the record to be closed.

(c) The Commission may also declare the petition or communication inadmissible or out of order on the basis of information or evidence subsequently received.

(d) If the record has not been closed, the Commission shall, with the knowledge of the parties, examine the matter set forth in the petition or communication in order to verify the facts. If necessary and advisable, the Commission shall carry out an investigation, for the effective conduct of which it shall request, and the states concerned shall furnish to it, all necessary facilities.

(e) The Commission may request the states concerned to furnish any pertinent information and, if so requested, shall hear oral statements or receive written statements from the parties concerned.

(f) The Commission shall place itself at the disposal of the parties concerned with a view to reaching a friendly settlement of the matter on the basis of respect for the human rights recognized in this Convention.

2. However, in serious and urgent cases, only the presentation of a petition or communication that fulfills all the formal requirements of admissibility shall be necessary in order for the Commission to conduct an investigation with the prior consent of the state in whose territory a violation has allegedly been committed.

*Article* 49

If a friendly settlement has been reached in accordance with paragraph 1 (*f*) of Article 48, the Commission shall draw up a report, which shall be transmitted to the petitioner and to the States Parties to this Convention, and shall then be communicated to the Secretary General of the Organization of American States for publication. This report shall contain a brief statement of the facts and of the solution reached. If any party in the case so requests, the fullest possible information shall be provided to it.

*Article* 50

1. If a settlement is not reached, the Commission shall, within the time limit established by its Statute, draw up a report setting forth the facts and stating its conclusions. If the report, in whole or in part, does not represent the unanimous agreement of the members of the Commission, any member may attach it to a separate opinion. The written and oral statements made by the parties in accordance with paragraph 1 (*e*) of Article 48 shall also be attached to the report.

2. The report shall be transmitted to the states concerned, which shall not be at liberty to publish it.

3. In transmitting the report, the Committee may make such proposals and recommendations as it sees fit.

*Article* 51

1. If, within a period of three months from the date of the transmittal of the report of the Commission to the states concerned, the matter has not either been settled or submitted by the Commission or by the state concerned to the Court and its jurisdiction accepted, the Commission may, by the vote of an absolute majority of its members, set forth its opinion and conclusions concerning the questions submitted for its consideration.

2. Where appropriate, the Commission shall make pertinent recommendations and shall prescribe a period within which the state is to take the measures that are incumbent upon it to remedy the situation examined.

3. When the prescribed period has expired, the Commission shall decide by the vote of an absolute majority of its members whether the state has taken adequate measures and whether to publish its report.

## Chapter VIII. Inter-American Court of Human Rights

*Article* 52

1. The Court shall consist of seven judges, nationals of the member states of the Organization, elected in an individual capacity from among jurists of the highest moral authority and of recognized competence in the field of human rights, who possess the qualifications required for the exercise of the highest judicial functions in conformity with the law of the state of which they are nationals or of the state that proposes them as candidates.

2. No two judges may be nationals of the same state.

*Article* 53

1. The judges of the Court shall be elected by secret ballot by an absolute majority vote of the States Parties to the Convention in the General Assembly of the Organization, from a panel of candidates proposed by those states.

2. Each of the States Parties may propose up to three candidates, nationals of the state that proposes them or of any other member state of the Organization of American States. When a slate of three is proposed, at least one of the candidates shall be a national of a state other than the one proposing the slate.

*Article* 54

1. The judges of the Court shall be elected for a term of six years and may be reelected only once. The term of three of the judges chosen in the first election shall expire at the end of three years. Immediately after the election, the names of the three judges shall be determined by lot in the General Assembly.

2. A judge elected to replace a judge whose term has not expired shall complete the term of the latter.

3. The judges shall continue in office until the expiration of their term. However, they shall continue to serve with regard to cases that they have begun to hear and that are still pending, for which purposes they shall not be replaced by the newly elected judges.

*Article* 55

1. If a judge is a national of any of the States Parties to a case submitted to the Court, he shall retain his right to hear that case.

2. If one of the judges called upon to hear a case should be a national of one of the States Parties to the case, any other State Party in the case may appoint a person of its choice to serve on the Court as an *ad hoc* judge.

3. If among the judges called upon to hear a case none is a national of any of the States Parties to the case, each of the latter may appoint an *ad hoc* judge.

4. An *ad hoc* judge shall possess the qualifications indicated in Article 52.

5. If several States Parties to the Convention should have the same interest in a case, they shall be considered as a single party for purposes of the above provisions. In case of doubt, the Court shall decide.

*Article* 56

Five judges shall constitute a quorum for the transaction of business by the Court.

*Article* 57

The Commission shall appear in all cases before the Court.

*Article* 58

1. The Court shall have its seat at the place determined by the States Parties to the Convention in the General Assembly of the Organization; however, it may convene in the territory of any member state of the Organization of American States when a majority of the Court consider it desirable, and with the prior consent of the state concerned.

The seat of the Court may be changed by the States Parties to the Convention in the General Assembly by a two thirds vote.

2. The Court shall appoint its own Secretary.

3. The Secretary shall have his office at the place where the Court has its seat and shall attend the meetings that the Court may hold away from its seat.

*Article* 59

The Court shall establish its Secretariat, which shall function under the direction of the Secretary of the Court, in accordance with the administrative standards of the General Secretariat of the Organization in all respects not incompatible with the independence of the Court. The staff of the Court's Secretariat shall be appointed by the Secretary General of the Organization, in consultation with the Secretary of the Court.

*Article* 60

The Court shall draw up its Statute, which it shall submit to the General Assembly for approval. It shall adopt its own Rules of Procedure.

SECTION 2. JURISDICTION AND FUNCTIONS

*Article* 61

1. Only the States Parties and the Commission shall have the right to submit a case to the Court.

2. In order for the Court to hear a case, it is necessary that the procedures set forth in Articles 48 to 50 shall have been completed.

*Article* 62

1. A State Party may, upon depositing its instrument of ratification or adherence to this Convention, or at any subsequent time, declare that it recognizes as binding, *ipso facto*, and not requiring special agreement, the jurisdiction of the Court on all matters relating to the interpretation or application of this Convention.

2. Such declaration may be made unconditionally, on the condition of reciprocity, for a specified period, or for specific cases. It shall be presented to the Secretary General of the Organization, who shall transmit copies thereof to the other member states of the Organization and to the Secretary of the Court.

3. The jurisdiction of the Court shall comprise all cases concerning the interpretation and application of the provisions of this Convention that are submitted to it, provided that the States Parties to the case recognize or have recognized such jurisdiction, whether by special declaration pursuant to the preceding paragraphs, or by a special agreement.

*Article* 63

1. If the Court finds that there has been a violation of a right or freedom protected by this Convention, the Court shall rule that the injured party be ensured the enjoyment of his right or freedom that was violated. It shall also rule, if appropriate, that the consequences of the measure or situation that constituted the breach of such right or freedom be remedied and that fair compensation be paid to the injured party.

2. In cases of extreme gravity and urgency, and when necessary to avoid irreparable damage to persons, the Court shall adopt such provisional measures as it deems pertinent in matters it has under consideration. With respect to a case not yet submitted to the Court, it may act at the request of the Commission.

*Article* 64

1. The member states of the Organization may consult the Court regarding the interpretation of this Convention or of other treaties concerning the protection of human rights in the American states. Within their spheres of competence, the organs listed in Chapter X of the Charter of the Organiza-

tion of American States, as amended by the Protocol of Buenos Aires, may in like manner consult the Court.

2. The Court, at the request of a member state of the Organization, may provide that state with opinions regarding the compatibility of any of its domestic laws with the aforesaid international instruments.

*Article 65*

To each regular session of the General Assembly of the Organization of American States the Court shall submit, for the Assembly's consideration, a report on its work during the previous year. It shall specify, in particular, the cases in which a state has not complied with its judgments, making any pertinent recommendations.

SECTION 3. PROCEDURE

*Article 66*

1. Reasons shall be given for the judgment of the Court.

2. If the judgment does not represent in whole or in part the unanimous opinion of the judges, any judge shall be entitled to have his dissenting or separate opinion attached to the judgment.

*Article 67*

The judgment of the Court shall be final and not subject to appeal. In case of disagreement as to the meaning or scope of the judgment, the Court shall interpret it at the request of any of the parties, provided the request is made within ninety days from the date of notification of the judgment.

*Article 68*

1. The States Parties to the Convention undertake to comply with the judgment of the Court in any case to which they are parties.

2. That part of a judgment that stipulates compensatory damages may be executed in the country concerned in accordance with domestic procedure governing the execution of judgments against the state.

*Article 69*

The parties to the case shall be notified of the judgment of the Court and it shall be transmitted to the States Parties to the Convention.

Chapter IX. Common Provisions

*Article 70*

1. The judges of the Court and the members of the Commission shall enjoy, from the moment of their election and throughout their term of

office, the immunities extended to diplomatic agents in accordance with international law. During the exercise of their official function they shall, in addition, enjoy the diplomatic privileges necessary for the performance of their duties.

2. At no time shall the judges of the Court or the members of the Commission be held liable for any decisions or opinions issued in the exercise of their functions.

*Article* 71

The position of judge of the Court or member of the Commission is incompatible with any other activity that might affect the independence or impartiality of such judge or member, as determined in the respective statues.

*Article* 72

The judges of the Court and the members of the Commission shall receive emoluments and travel allowances in the form and under the conditions set forth in their statutes, with due regard for the importance and independence of their office. Such emoluments and travel allowances shall be determined in the budget of the Organization of American States, which shall also include the expenses of the Court and its Secretariat. To this end, the Court shall draw up its own budget and submit it for approval to the General Assembly through the General Secretariat. The latter may not introduce any changes in it.

*Article* 73

The General Assembly may, only at the request of the Commission or the Court, as the case may be, determine sanctions to be applied against members of the Commission or judges of the Court when there are justifiable grounds for such action as set forth in the respective statutes. A vote of a two-thirds majority of the member states of the Organization shall be required for a decision in the case of members of the Commission and, in the case of judges of the Court, a two-thirds majority vote of the States Parties to the Convention shall also be required.

## PART III
### *GENERAL AND TRANSITORY PROVISIONS*

Chapter X. Signature, Ratification, Reservations, Amendments, Protocols, and Denunciation

*Article* 74

1. This Convention shall be open for signature and ratification by or adherence of any member state of the Organization of American States.

2. Ratification of or adherence to this Convention shall be made by the deposit of an instrument of ratification or adherence with the General Secretariat of the Organization of American States. As soon as eleven states have deposited their instruments of ratification or adherence, the Convention shall enter the force. With respect to any state that ratifies or adheres thereafter, the Convention shall enter into force on the date of the deposit of its instrument of ratification or adherence.

3. The Secretary General shall inform all member states of the Organization of the entry into force of the Convention.

*Article 75*

This Convention shall be subject to reservations only in conformity with the provisions of the Vienna Convention on the Law of Treaties signed on May 23, 1969.

*Article 76*

1. Proposals to amend this Convention may be submitted to the General Assembly for the action it deems appropriate by any State Party directly, and by the Commission or the Court through the Secretary General.

2. Amendments shall enter into force for the states ratifying them on the date when two thirds of the States Parties to this Convention have deposited their respective instruments of ratification. With respect to the other States Parties, amendments shall enter into force on the dates on which they deposit their respective instruments of ratification.

*Article 77*

1. In accordance with Article 31, any State Party and the Commission may submit proposed protocols to this Convention for consideration by the States Parties at the General Assembly with a view to gradually including other rights and freedoms within its system of protection.

2. Each Protocol shall determine the manner of its entry into force and shall be applied only among the States Parties to it.

*Article 78*

1. The States Parties may denounce this Convention at the expiration of a five-year period starting from the date of its entry into force and by means of notice given one year in advance. Notice of the denunciation shall be addressed to the Secretary General of the Organization, who shall inform the other States Parties.

2. Such a denunciation shall not have the effect of releasing the State Party concerned from the obligations contained in this Convention with respect to any act that may constitute a violation of those obligations and that has been taken by that state prior to the effective date of denunciation.

## Chapter XI. Transitory Provisions

### SECTION 1. INTER-AMERICAN COMMISSION ON HUMAN RIGHTS

*Article* 79

Upon the entry into force of this Convention, the Secretary General shall, in writing, request each member state of the Organization to present, within ninety days, its candidates for membership on the Inter-American Commission on Human Rights. The Secretary General shall prepare a list in alphabetical order of the candidates presented, and transmit it to the member states of the Organization at least thirty days prior to the next session of the General Assembly.

*Article* 80

The members of the Commission shall be elected by secret ballot of the General Assembly from the list of candidates referred to in Article 79. The candidates who obtain the largest number of votes and an absolute majority of the votes of the representatives of the member states shall be declared elected. Should it become necessary to have several ballots in order to elect all the members of the Commission, the candidates who receive the smallest number of votes shall be eliminated successively, in the manner determined by the General Assembly.

### SECTION 2. INTER-AMERICAN COURT OF HUMAN RIGHTS

*Article* 81

Upon the entry into force of this Convention, the Secretary General shall, in writing, request each State Party to present, within ninety days, its candidates for membership on the Inter-American Court of Human Rights. The Secretary-General shall prepare a list in alphabetical order of the candidates presented and transmit it to the States Parties at least thirty days prior to the next session of the General Assembly.

*Article* 82

The judges of the Court shall be elected from the list of candidates referred to in Article 81, by secret ballot of the States Parties to the Convention in the General Assembly. The candidates who obtain the largest number of votes and an absolute majority of the votes of the representatives of the States Parties shall be declared elected. Should it become necessary to have several ballots in order to elect all the judges of the Court, the candidates who receive the smallest number of votes shall be eliminated successively, in the manner determined by the States Parties.

[Statements and reservations, etc., omitted.]

# III. ADDITIONAL PROTOCOL TO THE AMERICAN CONVENTION ON HUMAN RIGHTS IN THE AREA OF ECONOMIC, SOCIAL AND CULTURAL RIGHTS, 1988

The States Parties to the American Convention on Human Rights adopted this Additional Protocol (the Protocol of San Salvador) on 14 November 1988.
The Protocol will come into force when eleven states have become parties.

*TEXT*

## Preamble

The States Parties to the American Convention on Human Rights 'Pact of San José, Costa Rica',

Reaffirming their intention to consolidate in this hemisphere, within the framework of democratic institutions, a system of personal liberty and social justice based on respect for the essential rights of man;

Recognizing that the essential rights of man are not derived from one's being a national of a certain State, but are based upon attributes of the human person, for which reason they merit international protection in the form of a convention reinforcing or complementing the protection provided by the domestic law of the American States;

Considering the close relationship that exists between economic, social and cultural rights, and civil and political rights, in that the different categories of rights constitute an indivisible whole based on the recognition of the dignity of the human person, for which reason both require permanent protection and promotion if they are to be fully realized, and the violation of some rights in favor of the realization of others can never be justified;

Recognizing the benefits that stem from the promotion and development of cooperation among states and international relations;

Recalling that, in accordance with the Universal Declaration of Human Rights and the American Convention on Human Rights, the ideal of free human beings enjoying freedom from fear and want can only be achieved if conditions are created whereby everyone may enjoy his economic, social and cultural rights as well as his civil and political rights;

Bearing in mind that, although fundamental economic, social and cultural rights have been recognized in earlier international instruments of both world and regional scope, it is essential that those rights be reaffirmed, developed, perfected and protected in order to consolidate in America, on the basis of full respect for the rights of the individual, the democratic representative form of government as well as the right of its peoples to development, self-determination, and the free disposal of their wealth and natural resources, and

Considering that the American Convention on Human Rights provides that draft additional protocols to that Convention may be submitted for consideration to the States Parties, meeting together on the occasion of the General Assembly of the Organization of American States, for the purpose of gradually incorporating other rights and freedoms into the protective system thereof,

Have agreed upon the following Additional Protocol to the American Convention on Human Rights 'Protocol of San Salvador':

*Article* 1

## Obligation to adopt measures

The States Parties to this Additional Protocol to the American Convention on Human Rights undertake to adopt the necessary measures, both domestically and through cooperation among the States, especially economic and technical, to the extent allowed by their available resources, and taking into account their degree of development, for the purpose of achieving progressively and pursuant to their internal legislations, the full observance of the rights recognized in this Protocol.

*Article* 2

## Obligation to enact domestic legislation

If the exercise of the rights set forth in this Protocol is not already guaranteed by legislative or other provisions, the States Parties undertake to adopt, in accordance with their constitutional processes and the provisions of this Protocol, such legislative or other measures as may be necessary for making those rights a reality.

*Article* 3

## Obligation of nondiscrimination

The States Parties to this Protocol undertake to guarantee the exercise of the rights set forth herein without discrimination of any kind for reasons related to race, color, sex, language, religion, political or other opinions, national or social origin, economic status, birth or any other social condition.

*Article* 4

## Inadmissibility of restrictions

A right which is recognized or in effect in a State by virtue of its internal legislation or international conventions may not be restricted or curtailed on the pretext that this Protocol does not recognize the right or recognizes it to a lesser degree.

*Article* 5

## Scope of restrictions and limitations

The States Parties may establish restrictions and limitations on the enjoyment and exercise of the rights established herein by means of laws promulgated for the purpose of preserving the general welfare in a democratic society only to the extent that they are not incompatible with the purpose and reason underlying those rights.

*Article* 6

## Right to work

1. Everyone has the right to work, which includes the opportunity to secure the means for living a dignified and decent existence by performing a freely elected or accepted lawful activity.

2. The States Parties undertake to adopt measures that will make the right to work fully effective, especially with regard to the achievement of full employment, vocational guidance, and the development of technical and vocational training projects, in particular those directed to the disabled. The States Parties also undertake to implement and strengthen programs that help to ensure suitable family care, so that women may enjoy a real opportunity to exercise the right to work.

*Article* 7

## Just, equitable and satisfactory conditions of work

The States Parties to this Protocol recognize that the right to work to which the foregoing article refers presupposes that everyone shall enjoy that right under just, equitable and satisfactory conditions, which the States Parties undertake to guarantee in their internal legislation, particularly with respect to:

(a) Remuneration which guarantees, as a minimum, to all workers dignified and decent living conditions for them and their families and fair and equal wages for equal work, without distinction;

(b) The right of every worker to follow his vocation and to devote himself to the activity that best fulfills his expectations and to change employment in accordance with the pertinent national regulations;

(c) The right of every worker to promotion or upward mobility in his employment, for which purpose account shall be taken of his qualifications, competence, integrity and seniority;

(d) Stability of employment, subject to the nature of each industry and occupation and the causes for just separation. In cases of unjustified dismissal, the worker shall have the right to indemnity or to reinstatement on the job or any other benefits provided by domestic legislation;

(*e*) Safety and hygiene at work;

(*f*) The prohibition of night work or unhealthy or dangerous working conditions and, in general, of all work which jeopardizes health, safety or morals, for persons under 18 years of age. As regards minors under the age of 16, the work day shall be subordinated to the provisions regarding compulsory education and in no case shall work constitute an impediment to school attendance or a limitation on benefiting from education received;

(*g*) A reasonable limitation of working hours, both daily and weekly. The days shall be shorter in the case of dangerous or unhealthy work or of night work;

(*h*) Rest, leisure and paid vacations as well as remuneration for national holidays.

*Article* 8

Trade union rights

1. The States Parties shall ensure:

(*a*) The right of workers to organize trade unions and to join the union of their choice for the purpose of protecting and promoting their interests. As an extension of that right, the States Parties shall permit trade unions to establish national federations or confederations, or to affiliate with those that already exist, as well as to form international trade union organizations and to affiliate with that of their choice. The States Parties shall also permit trade unions, federations and confederations to function freely;

(*b*) The right to strike.

2. The exercise of the rights set forth above may be subject only to restrictions established by law, provided that such restrictions are characteristic of a democratic society and necessary for safeguarding public order or for protecting public health or morals or the rights and freedoms of others. Members of the armed forces and the police and of other essential public services shall be subject to limitations and restrictions established by law.

3. No one may be compelled to belong to a trade union.

*Article* 9

Right to social security

1. Everyone shall have the right to social security protecting him from the consequences of old age and of disability which prevents him, physically or mentally, from securing the means for a dignified and decent existence. In the event of the death of a beneficiary, social security benefits shall be applied to his dependents.

2. In the case of persons who are employed, the right to social security shall cover at least medical care and an allowance or retirement benefit in the case of work accidents or occupational disease and, in the case of women, paid maternity leave before and after childbirth.

*Article* 10

## Right to health

1. Everyone shall have the right to health, understood to mean the enjoyment of the highest level of physical, mental and social well-being.

2. In order to ensure the exercise of the right to health, the States Parties agree to recognize health as a public good and, particularly, to adopt the following measures to ensure that right:

(*a*) Primary health care, that is, essential health care made available to all individuals and families in the community;

(*b*) Extension of the benefits of health services to all individuals subject to the State's jurisdiction;

(*c*) Universal immunization against the principal infectious diseases;

(*d*) Prevention and treatment of endemic, occupational and other diseases;

(*e*) Education of the population on the prevention and treatment of health problems, and

(*f*) Satisfaction of the health needs of the highest risk groups and of those whose poverty makes them the most vulnerable.

*Article* 11

## Right to a healthy environment

1. Everyone shall have the right to live in a healthy environment and to have access to basic public services.

2. The States Parties shall promote the protection, preservation and improvement of the environment.

*Article* 12

## Right to food

1. Everyone has the right to adequate nutrition which guarantees the possibility of enjoying the highest level of physical, emotional and intellectual development.

2. In order to promote the exercise of this right and eradicate malnutrition, the States Parties undertake to improve methods of production, supply and distribution of food, and to this end, agree to promote greater international cooperation in support of the relevant national policies.

*Article* 13

## Right to education

1. Everyone has the right to education.

2. The States Parties to this Protocol agree that education should be directed towards the full development of the human personality and human dignity and should strengthen respect for human rights, ideological pluralism, fundamental freedoms, justice and peace. They further agree that education ought to enable everyone to participate effectively in a democratic and pluralistic society and achieve a decent existence and should foster understanding, tolerance and friendship among all nations and all racial, ethnic or religious groups and promote activities for the maintenance of peace.

3. The States Parties to this Protocol recognize that in order to achieve the full exercise of the right to education:

   (*a*) Primary education should be compulsory and accessible to all without cost;

   (*b*) Secondary education in its different forms, including technical and vocational secondary education, should be made generally available and accessible to all by every appropriate means, and in particular, by the progressive introduction of free education;

   (*c*) Higher education should be made equally accessible to all on the basis of individual capacity, by every appropriate means, and in particular, by the progressive introduction of free education;

   (*d*) Basic education should be encouraged or intensified as far as possible for those persons who have not received or completed the whole cycle of primary instruction;

   (*e*) Programs of special education should be established for the handicapped, so as to provide special instruction and training to persons with physical disabilities or mental deficiencies.

4. In conformity with the domestic legislation of the States Parties, parents should have the right to select the type of education to be given to their children, provided that it conforms to the principles set forth above.

5. Nothing in this Protocol shall be interpreted as a restriction of the freedom of individuals and entities to establish and direct educational institutions in accordance with the domestic legislation of the States Parties.

*Article* 14

## Right to the benefits of culture

1. The States Parties to this Protocol recognize the right of everyone:

   (*a*) To take part in the cultural and artistic life of the community;

   (*b*) To enjoy the benefits of scientific and technological progress;

(c) To benefit from the protection of moral and material interests deriving from any scientific, literary or artistic production of which he is the author.

2. The steps to be taken by the States Parties to this Protocol to ensure the full exercise of this right shall include those necessary for the conservation, development and dissemination of science, culture and art.

3. The States Parties to this Protocol undertake to respect the freedom indispensable for scientific research and creative activity.

4. The States Parties to this Protocol recognize the benefits to be derived from the encouragement and development of international cooperation and relations in the fields of science, arts and culture, and accordingly agree to foster greater international cooperation in these fields.

*Article* 15

Right to the formation and the protection of families

1. The family is the natural and fundamental element of society and ought to be protected by the State, which should see to the improvement of its spiritual and material conditions.

2. Everyone has the right to form a family, which shall be exercised in accordance with the provisions of the pertinent domestic legislation.

3. The States Parties hereby undertake to accord adequate protection to the family unit and in particular:

  (a) To provide special care and assistance to mothers during a reasonable period before and after childbirth;
  (b) To guarantee adequate nutrition for children at the nursing stage and during school attendance years;
  (c) To adopt special measures for the protection of adolescents in order to ensure the full development of their physical, intellectual and moral capacities;
  (d) To undertake special programs of family training so as to help create a stable and positive environment in which children will receive and develop the values of understanding, solidarity, respect and responsibility.

*Article* 16

Rights of children

Every child, whatever his parentage, has the right to the protection that his status as a minor requires from his family, society and the State. Every child has the right to grow under the protection and responsibility of his parents; save in exceptional, judicially-recognized circumstances, a child of young age ought not to be separated from his mother. Every child has the right to free and compulsory education, at least in the elementary phase, and to continue his training at higher levels of the educational system.

## *Article* 17

### Protection of the elderly

Everyone has the right to special protection in old age. With this in view the States Parties agree to take progressively the necessary steps to make this right a reality and, particularly, to:

- (*a*) Provide suitable facilities, as well as food and specialized medical care, for elderly individuals who lack them and are unable to provide them for themselves;
- (*b*) Undertake work programs specifically designed to give the elderly the opportunity to engage in a productive activity suited to their abilities and consistent with their vocations or desires;
- (*c*) Foster the establishment of social organizations aimed at improving the quality of life for the elderly.

## *Article* 18

### Protection of the handicapped

Everyone affected by a diminution of his physical or mental capacities is entitled to receive special attention designed to help him achieve the greatest possible development of his personality. The States Parties agree to adopt such measures as may be necessary for this purpose and, especially, to:

- (*a*) Undertake programs specifically aimed at providing the handicapped with the resources and environment needed for attaining this goal, including work programs consistent with their possibilities and freely accepted by them or their legal representatives, as the case may be;
- (*b*) Provide special training to the families of the handicapped in order to help them solve the problems of coexistence and convert them into active agents in the physical, mental and emotional development of the latter;
- (*c*) Include the consideration of solutions to specific requirements arising from needs of this group as a priority component of their urban development plans;
- (*d*) Encourage the establishment of social groups in which the handicapped can be helped to enjoy a fuller life.

*Article* 19

## Means of protection

1. Pursuant to the provisions of this article and the corresponding rules to be formulated for this purpose by the General Assembly of the Organization of American States, the States Parties to this Protocol undertake to submit periodic reports on the progressive measures they have taken to ensure due respect for the rights set forth in this Protocol.

2. All reports shall be submitted to the Secretary General of the OAS, who shall transmit them to the Inter-American Economic and Social Council and the Inter-American Council for Education, Science and Culture so that they may examine them in accordance with the provisions of this article. The Secretary General shall send a copy of such reports to the Inter-American Commission on Human Rights.

3. The Secretary General of the Organization of American States shall also transmit to the specialized organizations of the inter-American system of which the States Parties to the present Protocol are members, copies or pertinent portions of the reports submitted, insofar as they relate to matters within the purview of those organizations, as established by their constituent instruments.

4. The specialized organizations of the inter-American system may submit reports to the Inter-American Economic and Social Council and the Inter-American Council for Education, Science and Culture relative to compliance with the provisions of the present Protocol in their fields of activity.

5. The annual reports submitted to the General Assembly by the Inter-American Economic and Social Council and the Inter-American Council for Education, Science and Culture shall contain a summary of the information received from the States Parties to the present Protocol and the specialized organizations concerning the progressive measures adopted in order to ensure respect for the rights acknowledged in the Protocol itself and the general recommendations they consider to be appropriate in this respect.

6. Any instance in which the rights established in paragraph a) of Article 8 and in Article 13 are violated by action directly attributable to a State Party to this Protocol may give rise, through participation of the Inter-American Commission on Human Rights and, when applicable, of the Inter-American Court of Human Rights, to application of the system of individual petitions governed by Article 44 through 51 and 61 through 69 of the American Convention on Human Rights.

7. Without prejudice to the provisions of the preceding paragraph, the Inter-American Commission on Human Rights may formulate such obser-

vations and recommendations as it deems pertinent concerning the status of the economic, social and cultural rights established in the present Protocol in all or some of the States Parties, which it may include in its Annual Report to the General Assembly or in a special report, whichever it considers more appropriate.

8. The Councils and the Inter-American Commission on Human Rights, in discharging the functions conferred upon them in this article, shall take into account the progressive nature of the observance of the rights subject to protection by this Protocol.

*Article* 20

## Reservations

The States Parties may, at the time of approval, signature, ratification or accession, make reservations to one or more specific provisions of this Protocol, provided that such reservations are not incompatible with the object and purpose of the Protocol.

*Article* 21

## Signature, ratification or accession.
## Entry into effect

1. This Protocol shall remain open to signature and ratification or accession by any State Party to the American Convention on Human Rights.

2. Ratification of or accession to this Protocol shall be effected by depositing an instrument of ratification or accession with the General Secretariat of the Organization of American States.

3. The Protocol shall enter into effect when eleven States have deposited their respective instruments of ratification or accession.

4. The Secretary General shall notify all the member States of the Organization of American States of the entry of the Protocol into effect.

*Article* 22

## Inclusion of other rights and expansion of those recognized

1. Any State Party and the Inter-American Commission on Human Rights may submit for the consideration of the States Parties meeting on the occasion of the General Assembly proposed amendments to include the recognition of other rights or freedoms or to extend or expand rights or freedoms recognized in this Protocol.

2. Such Amendments shall enter into effect for the States that ratify them on the date of deposit of the instrument of ratification corresponding to the number representing two thirds of the States Parties to this Protocol. For all other States Parties they shall enter into effect on the date on which they deposit their respective instrument of ratification.

# IV. THE INTER-AMERICAN CONVENTION TO PREVENT AND PUNISH TORTURE, 1985

The Convention was adopted as part of a resolution adopted at the third plenary session of the Organization of American States held at Cartagena de Indias on 9 December 1985.

Ten States have become parties and the Convention came into force on 28 February 1987. The text appears in the OAS Treaty Series, No. 67.

## TEXT

## THE GENERAL ASSEMBLY,
## CONSIDERING:

That at its eighth regular session the General Assembly requested the Inter-American Juridical Committee to prepare, in cooperation with the Inter-American Commission on Human Rights, a draft convention defining torture as an international crime [AG/RES. 368 (VIII-0/78];

That in pursuance of that mandate, the Inter-American Juridical Committee, in coordination with the Inter-American Commission on Human Rights, prepared a draft convention on the matter in 1980 and transmitted it to the Permanent Council;

That the Permanent Council forwarded the draft to the General Assembly, which, at its tenth regular session, adopted resolution AG/RES. 509 (X-0/80), by whose operative paragraph 2 provides as follows:

To forward that draft with its statement of reasons and the explanation of votes given by the members of the Committee to the governments of the member states for their consideration, so that they may formulate their observations and comments and send them to the Permanent Council before April 30, 1981, so that the Council may introduce the appropriate amendments in the draft Convention and submit it to the next regular session of the General Assembly.

That after receiving the observations and comments of the governments of several member states, the Permanent Council, through its Committee on Juridical and Political Affairs, undertook the study of the draft convention prepared by the Inter-American Juridical Committee and reported periodically to the General Assembly on the progress of the work related to the matter;

That the General Assembly repeatedly extended the mandate of the Permanent Council for the continued study of the draft convention [AG/

RES. 547 (XI-o/81), AG/RES. 624 (XII-o/82) and AG/RES. 664 (XIII-o/83)];

That at its fourteenth regular session the Permanent Council submitted a revised draft convention on the subject, contained in the document entitled 'Report of the Permanent Council on the Draft Convention Defining Torture as an International Crime' (AG/doc. 1812/84);

That at its fourteenth regular session the General Assembly expressed the need for considering the draft convention on the subject that had been prepared by the Inter-American Juridical Committee and revised by the Permanent Council and adopting an inter-American convention on the subject [AG/RES. 736 (XIV-o/84)];

That the Permanent Council submitted a further report on the study of this important topic (AG/doc. 1962/85) to the General Assembly at its fifteenth regular session; and

That during this regular session the draft contained in the report of the Permanent Council referred to in the preceding paragraph was considered and it was agreed to adopt a convention designed to prevent and punish torture,

RESOLVES:

1. To adopt the following Inter-American Convention to Prevent and Punish Torture:


## INTER-AMERICAN CONVENTION TO PREVENT AND PUNISH TORTURE

The American States signatory to the present Convention,

Aware of the provision of the American Convention on Human Rights that no one shall be subjected to torture or to cruel, inhuman, or degrading punishment or treatment;

Reaffirming that all acts of torture or any other cruel, inhuman, or degrading treatment or punishment constitute an offense against human dignity and a denial of the principles set forth in the Charter of the Organization of American States and in the Charter of the United Nations and are violations of the fundamental human rights and freedoms proclaimed in the American Declaration of the Rights and Duties of Man and the Universal Declaration of Human Rights;

Noting that, in order for the pertinent rules contained in the aforementioned global and regional instruments to take effect, it is necessary to draft an Inter-American Convention that prevents and punishes torture;

Reaffirming their purpose of consolidating in this hemisphere the conditions that allow for recognition of and respect for the inherent dignity of man, and ensure the full exercise of his fundamental rights and freedoms,

Have agreed upon the following:

*Article* 1

The States Parties shall prevent and punish torture in accordance with the terms of this Convention.

*Article* 2

For the purposes of this Convention, torture shall be understood to be any act intentionally performed whereby physical or mental pain or suffering is inflicted on a person for purposes of criminal investigation, as a means of intimidation, as personal punishment, as a preventive measure, as a penalty, or for any other purpose. Torture shall also be understood to be the use of methods upon a person intended to obliterate the personality of the victim or to diminish his physical or mental capacities, even if they do not cause physical pain or mental anguish.

The concept of torture shall not include physical or mental pain or suffering that is inherent in or solely the consequence of lawful measures, provided that they do not include the performance of the acts or use of the methods referred to in this article.

*Article* 3

The following shall be held guilty of the crime of torture:

(*a*) A public servant or employee who acting in that capacity orders, instigates or induces the use of torture, or who directly commits it or who, being able to prevent it, fails to do so.
(*b*) A person who at the instigation of a public servant or employee mentioned in subparagraph (*a*) orders, instigates or induces the use of torture, directly commits it or is an accomplice thereto.

*Article* 4

The fact of having acted under orders of a superior shall not provide exemption from the corresponding criminal liability.

*Article* 5

The existence of circumstances such as a state of war, threat of war, state of siege or of emergency, domestic disturbance or strife, suspension of constitutional guarantees, domestic political instability, or other public emergencies or disasters shall not be invoked or admitted as justification for the crime of torture.

Neither the dangerous character of the detainee or prisoner, nor the lack of security of the prison establishment or penitentiary shall justify torture.

*Article* 6

In accordance with the terms of Article 1, the States Parties shall take effective measures to prevent and punish torture within their jurisdiction.

The States Parties shall ensure that all acts of torture and attempts to commit torture are offenses under their criminal law and shall make such acts punishable by severe penalties that take into account their serious nature.

The States Parties likewise shall take effective measures to prevent and punish other cruel, inhuman, or degrading treatment or punishment within their jurisdiction.

*Article* 7

The States Parties shall take measures so that, in the training of police officers and other public officials responsible for the custody of persons temporarily or definitively deprived of their freedom, special emphasis shall be put on the prohibition of the use of torture in interrogation, detention, or arrest.

The States Parties likewise shall take similar measures to prevent other cruel, inhuman, or degrading treatment or punishment.

*Article* 8

The States Parties shall guarantee that any person making an accusation of having been subjected to torture within their jurisdiction shall have the right to an impartial examination of his case.

Likewise, if there is an accusation or well-grounded reason to believe that an act of torture has been committed within their jurisdiction, the States Parties shall guarantee that their respective authorities will proceed ex officio and immediately to conduct an investigation into the case and to initiate, whenever appropriate, the corresponding criminal process.

After all the domestic legal procedures of the respective State and the corresponding appeals have been exhausted, the case may be submitted to the international fora whose competence have been recognized by that State.

*Article* 9

The States Parties undertake to incorporate into their national laws regulations guaranteeing adequate compensation for victims of torture.

None of the provisions of this article shall affect the right to receive compensation that the victim or other persons may have by virtue of existing national legislation.

*Article* 10

No statement that is verified as having been obtained through torture shall be admissible as evidence in a legal proceeding, except in a legal action taken against a person or persons accused of having elicited it through acts of torture, and only as evidence that the accused obtained such statement by such means.

*Article* 11

The States Parties shall take the necessary steps to extradite anyone accused of having committed the crime of torture or sentenced for commission of that crime, in accordance with their respective national laws on extradition and their international commitments on this matter.

*Article* 12

Every State Party shall take the necessary measures to establish its jurisdiction over the crime described in this Convention in the following cases:

(*a*) When torture has been committed within its jurisdiction;
(*b*) When the alleged criminal is a national of that State; or
(*c*) When the victim is a national of that State and it so deems appropriate.

Every State Party shall also take the necessary measures to establish its jurisdiction over the crime described in this Convention when the alleged criminal is within the area under its jurisdiction and it does not proceed to extradite him in accordance with Article 11.

This Convention does not exclude criminal jurisdiction exercised in accordance with domestic law.

*Article* 13

The crime referred to in Article 2 shall be deemed to be included among the extraditable crimes in every extradition treaty entered into between States Parties. The States Parties undertake to include the crime of torture as an extraditable offence in every extradition treaty to be concluded between them.

Every State Party that makes extradition conditional on the existence of a treaty may, if it receives a request for extradition from another State Party with which it has no extradition treaty, consider this Convention as the legal basis for extradition in respect of the crime of torture. Extradition shall be subject to the other conditions that may be required by the law of the requested State.

States Parties which do not make extradition conditional on the existence of a treaty shall recognize such crimes as extraditable offences between themselves, subject to the conditions required by the law of the requested State.

Extradition shall not be granted nor shall the person sought be returned when there are grounds to believe that his life is in danger, that he will be subjected to torture or to cruel, inhuman or degrading treatment, or that he will be tried by special or ad hoc courts in the requesting State.

### Article 14

When a State Party does not grant the extradition, the case shall be submitted to its competent authorities as if the crime had been committed within its jurisdiction, for the purposes of investigation, and when appropriate, for criminal action, in accordance with its national law. Any decision adopted by these authorities shall be communicated to the State that has requested the extradition.

### Article 15

No provision of this Convention may be interpreted as limiting the right of asylum, when appropriate, nor as altering the obligations of the States Parties in the matter of extradition.

### Article 16

This Convention shall not affect the provisions of the American Convention on Human Rights, other conventions on the subject, or the Statutes of the Inter-American Commission on Human Rights, with respect to the crime of torture.

### Article 17

The States Parties shall inform the Inter-American Commission on Human Rights of any legislative, judicial, administrative, or other measures they adopt in application of this Convention.

In keeping with its duties and responsibilities, the Inter-American Commission on Human Rights will endeavor in its annual report to analyze the existing situation in the member states of the Organization of American States in regard to the prevention and elimination of torture.

### Article 18

This Convention is open to signature by the member states of the Organization of American States.

*Article* 19

This Convention is subject to ratification. The instruments of ratification shall be deposited with the General Secretariat of the Organization of American States.

*Article* 20

This Convention is open to accession by any other American state. The instruments of accession shall be deposited with the General Secretariat of the Organization of American States.

*Article* 21

The States Parties may, at the time of approval, signature, ratification, or accession, make reservations to this Convention, provided that such reservations are not incompatible with the object and purpose of the Convention and concern one or more specific provisions.

*Article* 22

This Convention shall enter into force on the thirtieth day following the date on which the second instrument of ratification is deposited. For each State ratifying or acceding to the Convention after the second instrument of ratification has been deposited, the Convention shall enter into force on the thirtieth day following the date on which that State deposits its instrument of ratification or accession.

*Article* 23

This Convention shall remain in force indefinitely, but may be denounced by any State Party. The instrument of denunciation shall be deposited with the General Secretariat of the Organization of American States. After one year from the date of deposit of the instrument of denunciation, this Convention shall cease to be in effect for the denouncing State but shall remain in force for the remaining States Parties.

*Article* 24

The original instrument of this Convention, the English, French, Portuguese, and Spanish texts of which are equally authentic, shall be deposited with the General Secretariat of the Organization of American States, which shall send a certified copy to the Secretariat of the United Nations for registration and publication, in accordance with the provisions of Article 102 of the United Nations Charter. The General Secretariat of the

Organization of American States shall notify the member states of the Organization and the states that have acceded to the Convention of signatures and of deposits of instruments of ratification, accession, and denunciation, as well as reservations, if any.

2. To remind the member states that, under the terms of Article 18 of the above Convention, it is open to signature by the member states of the Organization of American States.

3. To invite the governments of the member states to sign the Inter-American Convention to Prevent and Punish Torture during this fifteenth regular session of the General Assembly.

## PART SEVEN

# DEVELOPMENTS IN AFRICA

IN a general way African states have taken, or reacted to, initiatives involving human rights within the framework of the United Nations. The principle of racial equality and the principle of self-determination have been primary but not exclusive concerns.

Within the Organization of African Unity the trend of policy has been against forms of intervention by the organization and the principle of non-intervention has been maintained in the face of the notoriously disastrous situations in recent years in Equatorial Guinea, Uganda, and elsewhere. The focus of overt concern has, quite naturally, been the powerful white minority regimes in southern Africa. On the Organization of African Unity policy concerning non-interference in internal affairs see Akinyemi, *British Year Book of International Law*, Vol. 46 (1972–3), pp. 393–400; Elias, *Africa and the Development of International Law*, 1972.

# I. FIRST CONFERENCE OF INDEPENDENT
# AFRICAN STATES, 1958

This Conference was held at Accra, 15–22 April 1958. The Declaration and certain of the resolutions of the Conference are reproduced below.


## TEXT

## DECLARATION

We, the African States assembled here in Accra, in this our first Conference, conscious of our responsibilities to humanity and especially to the peoples of Africa, and desiring to assert our African personality on the side of peace, hereby proclaim and solemnly reaffirm our unswerving loyalty to the Charter of the United Nations, the Universal Declaration of Human Rights and the Declaration of the Asian-African Conference held at Bandung.

*We further assert* and proclaim the unity among ourselves and our solidarity with the dependent peoples of Africa as well as our friendship with all nations. We resolve to preserve the unity of purpose and action in international affairs which we have forged among ourselves in this historic Conference; to safeguard our hard-won independence, sovereignity and territorial integrity; and to preserve among ourselves the fundamental unity of outlook in foreign policy so that a distinctive African Personality will play its part in co-operation with other peace-loving nations to further the cause of peace.

*We pledge* ourselves to apply all our endeavours to avoid being committed to any action which might entangle our countries to the detriment of our interests and freedom; to recognize the right of the African peoples to independence and self-determination and to take appropriate steps to hasten the realization of this right; to affirm the right of the Algerian people to independence and self-determination and to exert all possible effort to hasten the realization of their independence; to uproot forever the evil of racial discrimination in all its forms wherever it may be found to persuade the Great Powers to discontinue the production and testing of nuclear and thermo-nuclear weapons; and to reduce conventional weapons.

*Furthermore*, mindful of the urgent need to raise the living standards of our peoples by developing to the fullest possible advantage the great and varied resources of our lands, We hereby pledge ourselves to co-ordinate our economic planning through a joint economic effort and study the economic potentialities, the technical possibilities and related problems existing in our respective States; to promote co-ordinated industrial planning either through our own individual efforts and/or through co-operation with Specialized Agencies of the United Nations; to take measures to increase trade among our countries by improving communications between our respective countries; and to encourage the investment of foreign capital and skills provided they do not compromise the independence, sovereignty and territorial integrity of our States.

*Desirous* of mobilizing the human resources of our respective countries in furtherance of our social and cultural aspirations, We will endeavour to promote and facilitate the exchange of teachers, professors, students, exhibitions, educational, cultural and scientific material which will improve cultural relations between the African States and inculcate greater knowledge amongst us through such efforts as joint youth festivals, sporting events, etc.; We will encourage and strengthen studies of African culture, history and geography in the institutions of learning in the African States; and We will take all measures in our respective countries to ensure that such studies are correctly orientated.

*We have charged* our Permanent Representatives at the United Nations to be the permanent machinery for co-ordinating all matters of common concern to our States; for examining and making recommendations on concrete practical steps for implementing our decisions; and for preparing the grounds for future Conferences.

*Faithful* to the obligations and responsibilities which history has thrown upon us as the vanguard of the complete emancipation of Africa, we do hereby affirm our dedication to the causes which we have proclaimed.

## RESOLUTIONS

### 1. Exchange of Views on Foreign Policy

*The Conference of Independent African States,*

*Having made* the widest exchange of views on all aspects of foreign policy,

*Having achieved* a unanimity on fundamental aims and principles,

*Desiring* to pursue a common foreign policy with a view to safeguarding the hard-won independence, sovereignty and territorial integrity of the Participating States,

*Deploring* the division of the greater part of the world into two antagonistic blocs,

1. Affirms the following fundamental principles:

A. Unswerving loyalty to and support of the Charter of the United Nations and respect for decisions of the United Nations;

B. Adherence to the principles enunciated at the Bandung Conference, namely:

   (i) Respect for the fundamental human rights and for the purposes and principles of the Charter of the United Nations.

  (ii) Respect for the sovereignty and territorial integrity of all nations.

 (iii) Recognition of the equality of all races and of the equality of all nations, large and small. . . .

## 2. The Future of the Dependent Territories in Africa

*The Conference of Independent African States,*

*Recognizing* that the existence of colonialism in any shape or form is a threat to the security and independence of the African States and to world peace,

*Considering* that the problems and the future of dependent territories in Africa are not the exclusive concern of the Colonial Powers but the responsibility of all members of the United Nations and in particular of the Independent African States,

*Condemning* categorically all colonial systems still enforced in our Continent and which impose arbitrary rule and repression on the people of Africa,

*Convinced* that a definite date should be set for the attainment of independence by each of the Colonial Territories in accordance with the will of the people of the territories and the provisions of the Charter of the United Nations,

1. Calls upon the Administering Powers to respect the Charter of the United Nations in this regard, and to take rapid steps to implement the provisions of the Charter and the political aspirations of the people, namely self-determination and independence, according to the will of the people;

2. Calls upon the Administering Powers to refrain from repression and arbitrary rule in these territories and to respect all human rights as provided for in the Charter of the United Nations and the Universal Declaration of Human Rights;

3. Calls upon the Administering Powers to bring to an end immediately every form of discrimination in these territories;

4. Recommends that all Participating Governments should give all possible assistance to the dependent peoples in their struggle to achieve self-determination and independence;

5. Recommends that the Independent African States assembled here should offer facilities for training and educating peoples of the dependent territories;

6. Decides that 15 April of every year be celebrated as Africa Freedom Day.

## 4. Racialism

*The Conference of Independent African States,*

*Considering* that the practice of racial discrimination and segregation is evil and inhuman,

*Deeply convinced* that racialism is a negation of the basic principles of human rights and dignity to the extent where it is becoming an element of such explosiveness which is spreading its poisonous influence more and more widely in some parts of Africa that it may well engulf our Continent in violence and bloodshed,

*Noting with abhorrence* the recent statement made by the head of the South African Government on his re-election to the effect that he will pursue a more relentless policy of discrimination and persecution of the coloured people in South Africa,

1. Condemns the practice of racial discrimination and segregation in all its aspects all over the world, especially in the Union of South Africa, in the Central African Federation, Kenya and in other parts of Africa;

2. Appeals to the religious bodies and spiritual leaders of the world to support all efforts directed towards the eradication of racialism and segregation;

3. Calls upon all members of the United Nations and all peoples of the world to associate themselves with the Resolutions passed by the United Nations and the Bandung Conference condemning this inhuman practice;

4. Calls upon all members of the United Nations to intensify their efforts to combat and eradicate this degrading form of injustice;

5. Recommends that all Participating Governments should take vigorous measures to eradicate where they arise vestiges of racial discrimination in their respective countries.

## II. SECOND CONFERENCE OF INDEPENDENT AFRICAN STATES, 1960

The Conference was held at Addis Ababa, 15–24 June 1960. Certain of its resolutions are reproduced below.

*TEXT*

### 9. Eradication of Colonial Rule from Africa

*The Conference of the Independent African States meeting in Addis Ababa,*

*Recalling* the declaration of Bandung and the resolutions of Accra and Monrovia proclaiming that colonialism in all its manifestations constitutes an evil which should speedily be brought to an end;

*Reaffirming* that the subjugation of peoples to alien domination and exploitation constitutes a denial of fundamental rights which is contrary to the Charter of the United Nations and the Universal Declaration of Human Rights, and is an impediment to the promotion of World Peace and Cooperation;

*Considering* that Africa is the only Continent where a large proportion of the inhabitants still live under colonial domination with all its privations and indignities;

*Considering* further that the present awakening of the people of Africa and the independence movements can no longer be contained, without the risk of seriously compromising relations between the diverse nations;

*Believing* that the restoration of natural rights and human dignity to the Africans, in those parts of Africa, at present under foreign subjugation, as well as the peaceful enjoyment of the hard-won freedom by the peoples of the Independent African States, could only be achieved through the complete eradication of colonial rule from our Continent;

*Recalling* the courageous stand taken by the freedom fighters in Africa, and saluting the memory of those who sacrificed their lives in defending the liberty of their respective countries;

*Conscious* of the responsibility of the Independent African States towards those peoples fighting for independence and also of the active solidarity which should be shown towards all African freedom fighters;

*Taking into consideration* the petitions presented by the representatives of the nationalist movements in the non-independent countries of Africa (Angola, Kenya, Uganda, Northern and Southern Rhodesia, Ruanda-Urundi, the Union of South Africa and South-West Africa);

1. Urges the Colonial Powers to fix dates in conformity with the will of the people for the immediate attainment of Independence by all non-independent countries and to communicate those dates to the people concerned;

2. Resolves that the Independent African States continue to exert concerted action to achieve through all possible peaceful means the complete eradication of colonial rule from Africa;

3. Condemns the practice of colonial Powers of enlisting Africans, against their own will, in foreign armed forces to suppress the liberation movements in Africa;

4. Appeals to the conscience of all Africans to resist enlistment in such foreign armed forces;

5. Appeals further to leaders, political parties and other organizations of non-independent countries, at this historical phase of their struggle, to unite in a national front to achieve speedy liberation of their countries;

6. Decides to establish a special fund to aid Freedom Fighters in Africa (Africa Freedom Fund);

7. Decides that such a fund be administered by an organ to be established by the Conference in accordance with rules and regulations to be adopted by the Conference;

8. Agrees that the Independent African States contribute to the Africa Freedom Fund on the basis of equitable shares to be agreed upon by the Conference;

9. Recommends to extend assistance and to accord facilities to genuine African political refugees;

10. Decides to offer, if so desired, its good offices to assist in settling differences among leaders and political parties of non-independent countries through its permanent machinery;

11. Appeals to the colonial Powers to refrain from suppressing national liberation movements, to release immediately all political prisoners, detainees and persons under restrictive orders.

### 10. Eradication of Colonial Rule from Africa: Means to Prevent New Forms of Colonialism in Africa

*The Conference of the Independent African States meeting in Addis Ababa,*

*Welcoming* the recent attainment of independence by several countries of Africa;

*Reaffirming* its faith in the total liberation and emancipation of Africa in the shortest possible time;

*Considering* the difficulties with which the emerging nations of Africa may be confronted in the political, economic and social fields;

*Noting* that new forms of colonialism could be introduced into these territories, under the guise of economic, financial and technical assistance;

*Considering* that some of the non-independent countries may, out of necessity and under pressure, enter into agreements and pacts with foreign Powers which would restrict in advance their total independence and hinder their future freedom of action;

1. Calls upon all colonial Powers to refrain from any action which might compromise the sovereignty and independence of the emerging States;

2. Declares that assistance to the emerging States should be without political conditions;

3. Urges the leaders of the emerging States to consider seriously this question before committing themselves to action which might prejudice the future of their countries;

4. Recommends that independent African States should consider the possibility of introducing a system whereby economic and technical aid can be provided by them collectively;

5. Urges the leaders of non-independent countries to resist any attempt at Balkanization which is detrimental to the ultimate goal of African unity;

6. Recommends that the Independent African States be wary of colonial penetration through economic means and that they institute effective control over the working machineries of foreign companies operating in their territories.

### 12. Policy of Apartheid and Racial Discrimination in Africa

*The Conference of Independent African States meeting in Addis Ababa,*

*Having learned* with indignation of the death of many African political leaders in the prisons of the Union of South Africa, thus adding to the already long list of victims of the shameful policy of racial discrimination;

*Recalling* resolution No. 1375 (XIV), adopted by the United Nations General Assembly, condemning the policy of apartheid and racial discrimination practised by the Government of the Union of South Africa;

*Recalling further* the Security Council's Resolution of April 1, 1960, recognizing the existence of a situation in South Africa which, if continued, might endanger international peace and security;

*Reaffirming* the declaration of Bandung and the resolutions adopted at Accra and Monrovia regarding this shameful policy;

*Noting* that, despite world opinion and the resolutions adopted by the United Nations, the Government of the Union of South Africa still persists in its evil policy of apartheid and racial discrimination;

1. Desires to pay homage to all victims of the shameful policy of apartheid and racial discrimination.

2. Decides to assist the victims of racial discrimination and furnish them

with all the means necessary to attain their political objectives of liberty and democracy;

3. Calls upon Member States to sever diplomatic relations or refrain from establishing diplomatic relations, as the case may be, to close African ports to all vessels flying the South African flag, to enact legislation prohibiting their ships from entering South African ports, to boycott all South African goods, to refuse landing and passage facilities to all aircraft belonging to the Government and companies registered under the laws of the Union of South Africa and to prohibit all South African aircraft from flying over the air-space of the Independent African States;

4. Invites the Arab States to approach all petroleum companies with a view to preventing Arab oil from being sold to the Union of South Africa and recommends that the African States refuse any concession to any company which continues to sell petroleum to the Union of South Africa;

5. Invites the Independent African States which are members of the British Commonwealth to take all possible steps to secure the exclusion of the Union of South Africa from the British Commonwealth;

6. Recommends that appropriate measures be taken by the United Nations in accordance with Article 41 of the Charter;

7. Appeals to world public opinion to persevere in the effort to put an end to the terrible situation caused by apartheid and racial discrimination;

8. Decides to instruct the Informal Permanent Machinery to take all steps necessary to secure that effect shall be given to the above recommendations and to furnish full information on cases of racial discrimination in the Union of South Africa, so that the outside world may be correctly informed about such practices.

## III. RESOLUTIONS OF THE FIRST ASSEMBLY OF THE·HEADS OF STATE AND GOVERNMENT OF THE ORGANIZATION OF AFRICAN UNITY, 1964

The text of the Charter of the Organization of African Unity may be found in Brownlie, *Basic Documents in International Law*, 3rd ed., 1983, p. 75. The First Assembly of the Heads of State and Government of the O.A.U. met in Cairo in July 1964. Certain of the resolutions adopted are set out below.

*TEXT*

### Racial Discrimination in the USA

*Recalling* United Nations General Assembly Resolution 1904 (XVIII) of 20 November 1963 containing a Declaration on the elimination of all forms of racial discrimination;

*Recalling* other resolutions of the General Assembly of the United Nations and of its Specialized Agencies on the elimination of all forms of racial discrimination;

*Taking into account* resolution CIAS/PLEN. 2 Res. 26–5 of the Summit Conference of Independent African States held at Addis Ababa in May 1963 condemning racial discrimination in all its forms in Africa and in all parts of the world;

*Considering* that a hundred years have passed since the Emancipation Proclamation was signed in the United States of America;

*Noting* with satisfaction the recent enactment of the Civil Rights Act designed to secure for American Negroes their basic human rights;

*Deeply disturbed*, however, by continuing manifestations of racial bigotry and racial oppression against Negro citizens of the United States of America;

*Reaffirms* that the existence of discriminatory practices is a matter of deep concern to Member States of the Organization of African Unity;

*Urges* the Government authorities in the United States of America to intensify their efforts to ensure the total elimination of all forms of discrimination based on race, colour, or ethnic origin.

### Report of the Committee of Liberation

*Recalling* Resolution No. CIAS/Plen/Rev/2(A) adopted by the Assembly of Heads of State and Government in Addis Ababa on 25 May 1963 and Resolution 15 (II) of the Second Session of the Council of Ministers held in Lagos, Nigeria;

*Having examined* the report of the Committee for the Liberation Movement of Africa;

*Noting with* satisfaction the work so far accomplished by the Co-ordination Committee;

*Noting* that some progress has been made by some nationalist liberation movements with the assistance of the Co-ordination Committee to establish common action fronts with a view to strengthening the effectiveness of their actions;

*Regretting* the continued existence of multiple rival movements in the territories under foreign domination in spite of efforts of the Committee;

*Considering* that certain Member States have not yet paid their voluntary contribution for 1963 to the Special Fund;

*Reaffirming* the will of Member States to continue by all means the intensification of the struggle for the independence of the territories under foreign domination;

1. Maintains the Liberation Committee as presently composed;

2. Decides the budget of the Special Fund to be £800,000 for the budget year 1964 which shall be collected from Member States in accordance with Article XXIII of the Charter of the Organization of African Unity;

3. Requests each Member State to pay its obligatory contribution in accordance with operative paragraph 2 above to the Special Liberation Fund in Dar-es-Salaam;

4. Requests the Administrative Secretary-General to exercise supervisory powers over the Committee Secretariat.

## Apartheid and Racial Discrimination

*Recalling* the previous resolutions of the Council of Ministers on apartheid and racial discrimination and in particular the resolution adopted by the Summit Conference held in Addis Ababa in May 1963;

*Reaffirming* resolution CM/Res. 13 (II);

*Having examined* the reports of the Administrative Provisional Secretary-General of the Organization of African Unity, the Resolutions of the International Conference on Economic Sanctions against South Africa which was held in London, in April 1964, the report of the Delegation of Foreign Ministers of Liberia, Tunisia, Madagascar and Sierra Leone appointed by the Conference of Heads of State and Government at Addis Ababa in May 1963, and the report of the African Group at the United Nations;

*Noting* with grave concern the consistent refusal of the South African Government to give consideration to appeals made by every sector of world opinion and their non-compliance with the resolutions of the United Nations Security Council and the General Assembly;

*Noting further* that the attitude of certain states towards the Government of South Africa and their continued close relations with that Government only encourages it to persist in its policies of apartheid and its contempt for the United Nations;

*Convinced* of the desirability of stepping up as a matter of urgency the action of the African States in regard to the application of sanctions against the South African Government;

*Expressing* its deep concern for the trials conducted according to the arbitrary and inhuman laws of the Government of South Africa against the opponents of policies of apartheid and for the recent convictions and sentences passed on African nationalists, particularly Nelson Mandela and Walter Sisulu;

1. Calls for the release of Nelson Mandela, Walter Sisulu, Mangalisso Sobukue and all other Nationalists imprisoned or detained under the arbitrary laws of South Africa;

2. Extends the mandate of the four Foreign Ministers of Liberia, Madagascar, Sierra Leone and Tunisia to continue their action before the Security Council;

3. Appeals to all oil producing countries to cease, as a matter of urgency, their supply of oil and petroleum products to South Africa;

4. Calls on all African States to implement forthwith the decision taken in Addis Ababa in May 1963 to boycott South African goods and to cease the supply of mineral and other raw materials and the importation of South African goods;

5. Requests the co-operation of all countries and in particular that of the Major Trading Partners in the boycott of South Africa;

6. Establishes a body within the OAU General Secretariat, entrusted, among others, with the following functions;

  (*a*) to plan co-ordination among the Member States and to ensure the strictest implementation of the resolutions of the Organization of African Unity;

  (*b*) to harmonize co-operation with friendly States with a view to implementing an effective boycott of South Africa;

  (*c*) to collect and disseminate information about States, foreign financial, economic and commercial institutions which trade with the Government of South Africa;

  (*d*) to promote, in co-operation with other international bodies, the campaign for international economic sanctions against South Africa by all appropriate means, in particular countering the propaganda and pressures of the South African Government.

# IV. THE AFRICAN CHARTER ON HUMAN AND PEOPLES' RIGHTS, 1981

The Charter was adopted on 17 June 1981 by the Eighteenth Assembly of the Heads of State and Government of the Organisation of African Unity. The treaty entered into force on 21 October 1986 and has been ratified by not less than thirty-five States. For comment see Umozurike, *American Journal of International Law*, Vol. 77 (1983), pp. 902–12; Bello, *Recueil des Cours*, Hague Academy of International Law, Vol. 194 (1985, V), pp. 13–268; D'Sa, *Australian Yearbook of International Law*, Vol. 10 (1987), pp. 101–30; Mbaye, Max Planck Institute, *Encyclopaedia of Public International Law*, Vol. 8, pp. 1–4; Robertson and Merrills, *Human Rights in the World*, 3rd ed., 1989, pp. 200–21. On the African Commission on Human and Peoples' Rights, see *The Review*, Int. Comm. of Jurists, No. 47, pp. 51–60.

*TEXT*

## AFRICAN CHARTER ON HUMAN AND PEOPLES' RIGHTS

### Preamble

The African States members of the Organization of African Unity, parties to the present convention entitled 'African Charter on Human and Peoples' Rights',

*Recalling* Decision 115 (XVI) of the Assembly of Heads of State and Government at its Sixteenth Ordinary Session held in Monrovia, Liberia, from 17 to 20 July 1979 on the preparation of a 'preliminary draft on an African Charter on Human and Peoples' Rights providing *inter alia* for the establishment of bodies to promote and protect human and peoples' rights';

*Considering* the Charter of the Organization of African Unity, which stipulates that 'freedom, equality, justice and dignity are essential objectives for the achievement of the legitimate aspirations of the African peoples';

*Reaffirming* the pledge they solemnly made in Article 2 of the said Charter to eradicate all forms of colonialism from Africa, to coordinate and intensify their cooperation and efforts to achieve a better life for the peoples of Africa and to promote international cooperation having due regard to the Charter of the United Nations and the Universal Declaration of Human Rights;

*Taking into consideration* the virtues of their historical tradition and the values of African civilization which should inspire and characterize their reflection on the concept of human and peoples' rights;

*Recognizing* on the one hand, that fundamental human rights stem from the attributes of human beings, which justifies their national and international protection and on the other hand that the reality and respect of peoples rights should necessarily guarantee human rights;

*Considering* that the enjoyment of rights and freedoms also implies the performance of duties on the part of everyone;

*Convinced* that it is henceforth essential to pay a particular attention to the right to development and that civil and political rights cannot be dissociated from economic, social and cultural rights in their conception as well as universality and that the satisfaction of economic, social and cultural rights is a guarantee for the enjoyment of civil and political rights;

*Conscious* of their duty to achieve the total liberation of Africa, the peoples of which are still struggling for their dignity and genuine independence, and undertaking to eliminate colonialism, neo-colonialism, apartheid, zionism and to dismantle aggressive foreign military bases and all forms of discrimination, particularly those based on race, ethnic group, color, sex, language, religion or political opinions;

*Reaffirming* their adherence to the principles of human and peoples' rights and freedoms contained in the declarations, conventions and other instruments adopted by the Organization of African Unity, the Movement of Non-Aligned Countries and the United Nations;

*Firmly convinced* of their duty to promote and protect human and peoples' rights and freedoms taking into account the importance traditionally attached to these rights and freedoms in Africa;

*Have agreed as follows:*

# PART I: RIGHTS AND DUTIES

## CHAPTER I
### Human and Peoples' Rights

*Article* 1

The Member States of the Organization of African Unity parties to the present Charter shall recognize the rights, duties and freedoms enshrined in this Charter and shall undertake to adopt legislative or other measures to give effect to them.

*Article* 2

Every individual shall be entitled to the enjoyment of the rights and freedoms recognized and guaranteed in the present Charter without distinction of any kind such as race, ethnic group, colour, sex, language, religion, political or any other opinion, national and social origin, fortune, birth or other status.

*Article* 3

1. Every individual shall be equal before the law.
2. Every individual shall be entitled to equal protection of the law.

*Article* 4

Human beings are inviolable. Every human being shall be entitled to respect for his life and the integrity of his person. No one may be arbitrarily deprived of this right.

*Article* 5

Every individual shall have the right to the respect of the dignity inherent in a human being and to the recognition of his legal status. All forms of exploitation and degradation of man particularly slavery, slave trade, torture, cruel, inhuman or degrading punishment and treatment shall be prohibited.

*Article* 6

Every individual shall have the right to liberty and to the security of his person. No one may be deprived of his freedom except for reasons and conditions previously laid down by law. In particular, no one may be arbitrarily arrested or detained.

*Article* 7

1. Every individual shall have the right to have his cause heard. This comprises:

   (*a*) the right to an appeal to competent national organs against acts of violating his fundamental rights as recognized and guaranteed by conventions, laws, regulations and customs in force;
   (*b*) the right to be presumed innocent until proved guilty by a competent court or tribunal;

(c) the right to defence, including the right to be defended by counsel of his choice;

(d) the right to be tried within a reasonable time by an impartial court or tribunal.

2. No one may be condemned for an act or omission which did not constitute a legally punishable offence at the time it was committed. No penalty may be inflicted for an offence for which no provision was made at the time it was committed. Punishment is personal and can be imposed only on the offender.

*Article* 8

Freedom of conscience, the profession and free practice of religion shall be guaranteed. No one may, subject to law and order, be submitted to measures restricting the exercise of these freedoms.

*Article* 9

1. Every individual shall have the right to receive information.

2. Every individual shall have the right to express and disseminate his opinions within the law.

*Article* 10

1. Every individual shall have the right to free association provided that he abides by the law.

2. Subject to the obligation of solidarity provided for in Article 29 no one may be compelled to join an association.

*Article* 11

Every individual shall have the right to assemble freely with others. The exercise of this right shall be subject only to necessary restrictions provided for by law in particular those enacted in the interest of national security, the safety, health, ethics and rights and freedoms of others.

*Article* 12

1. Every individual shall have the right to freedom of movement and residence within the borders of a State provided he abides by the law.

2. Every individual shall have the right to leave any country including his own, and to return to his country. This right may only be subject to restrictions provided for by law for the protection of national security, law and order, public health or morality.

3. Every individual shall have the right, when persecuted, to seek and obtain asylum in other countries in accordance with laws of those countries and international conventions.

4. A non-national legally admitted in a territory of a State Party to the present Charter, may only be expelled from it by virtue of a decision taken in accordance with the law.

5. The mass expulsion of non-nationals shall be prohibited. Mass expulsion shall be that which is aimed at national, racial, ethnic or religious groups.

*Article* 13

1. Every citizen shall have the right to participate freely in the government of his country, either directly or through freely chosen representatives in accordance with the provisions of the law.

2. Every citizen shall have the right of equal access to the public service of his country.

3. Every individual shall have the right of access to public property and services in strict equality of all persons before the law.

*Article* 14

The right to property shall be guaranteed. It may only be encroached upon in the interest of public need or in the general interest of the community and in accordance with the provisions of appropriate laws.

*Article* 15

Every individual shall have the right to work under equitable and satisfactory conditions, and shall receive equal pay for equal work.

*Article* 16

1. Every individual shall have the right to enjoy the best attainable state of physical and mental health.

2. States parties to the present Charter shall take the necessary measures to protect the health of their people and to ensure that they receive medical attention when they are sick.

*Article* 17

1. Every individual shall have the right to education.

2. Every individual may freely, take part in the cultural life of his community.

3. The promotion and protection of morals and traditional values recognized by the community shall be the duty of the State.

*Article* 18

1. The family shall be the natural unit and basis of society. It shall be protected by the State which shall take care of its physical health and morals.

2. The State shall have the duty to assist the family which is the custodian of morals and traditional values recognized by the community.

3. The State shall ensure the elimination of every discrimination against women and also censure the protection of the rights of the woman and the child as stipulated in international declarations and conventions.

4. The aged and the disabled shall also have the right to special measures of protection in keeping with their physical or moral needs.

*Article* 19

All peoples shall be equal; they shall enjoy the same respect and shall have the same rights. Nothing shall justify the domination of a people by another.

*Article* 20

1. All peoples shall have the right to existence. They shall have the unquestionable and inalienable right to self-determination. They shall freely determine their political status and shall pursue their economic and social development according to the policy they have freely chosen.

2. Colonized or oppressed peoples shall have the right to free themselves from the bonds of domination by resorting to any means recognized by the international community.

3. All peoples shall have the right to the assistance of the States parties to the present Charter in their liberation struggle against foreign domination, be it political, economic or cultural.

*Article* 21

1. All peoples shall freely dispose of their wealth and natural resources. This right shall be exercised in the exclusive interest of the people. In no case shall a people be deprived of it.

2. In case of spoliation the dispossessed people shall have the right to the lawful recovery of its property as well as to an adequate compensation.

3. The free disposal of wealth and natural resources shall be exercised without prejudice to the obligation of promoting international economic cooperation based on mutual respect, equitable exchange and the principles of international law.

4. States parties to the present Charter shall individually and collectively exercise the right to free disposal of their wealth and natural resources with a view to strengthening African unity and solidarity.

5. States parties to the present Charter shall undertake to eliminate all forms of foreign economic exploitation particularly that practised by international monopolies so as to enable their peoples to fully benefit from the advantages derived from their national resources.

*Article* 22

1. All peoples shall have the right to their economic, social and cultural development with due regard to their freedom and identity and in the equal enjoyment of the common heritage of mankind.

2. States shall have the duty, individually or collectively, to ensure the exercise of the right to development.

*Article* 23

1. All peoples shall have the right to national and international peace and security. The principles of solidarity and friendly relations implicitly affirmed by the Charter of the United Nations and reaffirmed by that of the Organization of African Unity shall govern relations between States.

2. For the purpose of strengthening peace, solidarity and friendly relations, States parties to the present Charter shall ensure that:

(*a*) any individual enjoying the right of asylum under Article 12 of the present Charter shall not engage in subversive activities against his country of origin or any other State party to the present Charter;

(*b*) their territories shall not be used as bases for subversive or terrorist activities against the people of any other State party to the present Charter.

*Article* 24

All peoples shall have the right to a general satisfactory environment favorable to their development.

*Article* 25

States parties to the present Charter shall have the duty to promote and ensure through teaching, education and publication, the respect of the rights and freedoms contained in the present Charter and to see to it that these freedoms and rights as well as corresponding obligations and duties are understood.

*Article* 26

States parties to the present Charter shall have the duty to guarantee the independence of the Courts and shall allow the establishment and improvement of appropriate national institutions entrusted with the promotion and protection of the rights and freedoms guaranteed by the present Charter.

## CHAPTER II
### Duties

*Article* 27

1. Every individual shall have duties towards his family and society, the State and other legally recognized communities and the international community.

2. The rights and freedoms of each individual shall be exercised with due regard to the rights of others, collective security, morality and common interest.

*Article* 28

Every individual shall have the duty to respect and consider his fellow beings without discrimination, and to maintain relations aimed at promoting, safeguarding and reinforcing mutual respect and tolerance.

*Article* 29

The individual shall also have the duty:

1. To preserve the harmonious development of the family and to work for the cohesion and respect of the family; to respect his parents at all times, to maintain them in case of need;

2. To serve his national community by placing his physical and intellectual abilities at its service;

3. Not to compromise the security of the State whose national or resident he is;

4. To preserve and strengthen social and national solidarity, particularly when the latter is threatened;

5. To preserve and strengthen the national independence and the territorial integrity of his country and to contribute to its defence in accordance with the law;

6. To work to the best of his abilities and competence, and to pay taxes imposed by law in the interest of the society;

7. To preserve and strengthen positive African cultural values in his relations with other members of the society, in the spirit of tolerance, dialogue and consultation and, in general, to contribute to the promotion of the moral well being of society;

8. To contribute to the best of his abilities, at all times and at all levels, to the promotion and achievement of African unity.

## PART II: MEASURES OF SAFEGUARD

### CHAPTER I
Establishment and Organization of the African
Commission on Human and Peoples' Rights

*Article 30*

An African Commission on Human and Peoples' Rights, hereinafter called 'the Commission', shall be established within the Organization of African Unity to promote human and peoples' rights and ensure their protection in Africa.

*Article 31*

1. The Commission shall consist of eleven members chosen from amongst African personalities of the highest reputation, known for their high morality, integrity, impartiality and competence in matters of human and peoples' rights; particular consideration being given to persons having legal experience.

2. The members of the Commission shall serve in their personal capacity.

*Article 32*

The Commission shall not include more than one national of the same State.

*Article 33*

The members of the Commission shall be elected by secret ballot by the Assembly of Heads of State and Government, from a list of persons nominated by the States parties to the present Charter.

*Article 34*

Each State party to the present Charter may not nominate more than two candidates. The candidates must have the nationality of one of the States parties to the present Charter. When two candidates are nominated by a State, one of them may not be a national of that State.

*Article 35*

1. The Secretary General of the Organization of African Unity shall invite States parties to the present Charter at least four months before the elections to nominate candidates;

2. The Secretary General of the Organization of African Unity shall make an alphabetical list of the persons thus nominated and communicate it to the Heads of State and Government at least one month before the elections.

*Article* 36

The members of the Commission shall be elected for a six year period and shall be eligible for re-election. However, the term of office of four of the members elected at the first election shall terminate after two years and the term of office of the three others, at the end of four years.

*Article* 37

Immediately after the first election, the Chairman of the Assembly of Heads of State and Government of the Organization of African Unity shall draw lots to decide the names of those members referred to in Article 36.

*Article* 38

After their election, the members of the Commission shall make a solemn declaration to discharge their duties impartially and faithfully.

*Article* 39

1. In case of death or resignation of a member of the Commission, the Chairman of the Commission shall immediately inform the Secretary General of the Organization of African Unity, who shall declare the seat vacant from the date of death or from the date on which the resignation takes effect.

2. If, in the unanimous opinion of other members of the Commission, a member has stopped discharging his duties for any reason other than a temporary absence, the Chairman of the Commission shall inform the Secretary General of the Organization of African Unity, who shall then declare the seat vacant.

3. In each of the cases anticipated above, the Assembly of Heads of State and Government shall replace the member whose seat became vacant for the remaining period of his term unless the period is less that six months.

*Article* 40

Every member of the Commission shall be in office until the date his successor assumes office.

*Article* 41

The Secretary General of the Organization of African Unity shall appoint the Secretary of the Commission. He shall also provide the staff and services necessary for the effective discharge of the duties of the Commission. The Organization of African Unity shall bear the costs of the staff and services.

*Article* 42

1. The Commission shall elect its Chairman and Vice Chairman for a two year period. They shall be eligible for re-election.

2. The Commission shall lay down its rules of procedure.

3. Seven members shall form a quorum.

4. In case of an equality of votes, the Chairman shall have a casting vote.

5. The Secretary General may attend the meetings of the Commission. He shall neither participate in deliberations nor shall he be entitled to vote. The Chairman of the Commission may, however, invite him to speak.

*Article* 43

In discharging their duties, members of the Commission shall enjoy diplomatic privileges and immunities provided for in the General Convention on the Privileges and Immunities of the Organization of African Unity.

*Article* 44

Provision shall be made for the emoluments and allowances of the members of the Commission in the Regular Budget of the Organization of African Unity.

## CHAPTER II
### Mandate of the Commission

*Article* 45

The functions of the Commission shall be:

1. To promote Human and Peoples' Rights and in particular:

   (*a*) to collect documents, undertake studies and researches on African problems in the field of human and peoples' rights, organize seminars, symposia and conferences, disseminate information, encourage national and local institutions concerned with human and peoples' rights, and should the case arise, give its views or make recommendations to Governments.

   (*b*) to formulate and lay down, principles and rules aimed at solving legal problems relating to human and peoples' rights and fundamental freedoms upon which African Governments may base their legislations.

   (*c*) co-operate with other African and international institutions concerned with the promotion and protection of human and peoples' rights.

2. Ensure the protection of human and peoples' rights under conditions laid down by the present Charter.

3. Interpret all the provisions of the present Charter at the request of a State party, an institution of the OAU or an African Organization recognized by the OAU.

4. Perform any other tasks which may be entrusted to it by the Assembly of Heads of State and Government.

## CHAPTER III
### Procedure of the Commission

*Article* 46

The Commission may resort to any appropriate method of investigation; it may hear from the Secretary General of the Organization of African Unity or any other person capable of enlightening it.

*Communication From States*

*Article* 47

If a State party to the present Charter has good reasons to believe that another State party to this Charter has violated the provisions of the Charter, it may draw, by written communication, the attention of that State to the matter. This communication shall also be addressed to the Secretary General of the OAU and to the Chairman of the Commission. Within three months of the receipt of the communication, the State to which the communication is addressed shall give the enquiring State, written explanation or statement elucidating the matter. This should include as much as possible relevant information relating to the laws and rules of procedure applied and applicable, and the redress already given or course of action available.

*Article* 48

If within three months from the date on which the original communication is received by the State to which it is addressed, the issue is not settled to the satisfaction of the two States involved through bilateral negotiation or by any other peaceful procedure, either State shall have the right to submit the matter to the Commission through the Chairman and shall notify the other States involved.

*Article* 49

Notwithstanding the provisions of Article 47, if a State party to the present Charter considers that another State party has violated the provisions of the Charter, it may refer the matter directly to the Commission by addressing a communication to the Chairman, to the Secretary General of the Organization of African Unity and the State concerned.

*Article* 50

The Commission can only deal with a matter submitted to it after making sure that all local remedies, if they exist, have been exhausted, unless it is obvious to the Commission that the procedure of achieving these remedies would be unduly prolonged.

*Article* 51

1. The Commission may ask the States concerned to provide it with all relevant information.

2. When the Commission is considering the matter, States concerned may be represented before it and submit written or oral representation.

*Article* 52

After having obtained from the States concerned and from other sources all the information it deems necessary and after having tried all appropriate means to reach an amicable solution based on the respect of Human and Peoples' Rights, the Commission shall prepare, within a reasonable period of time from the notification referred to in Article 48, a report stating the facts and its findings. This report shall be sent to the States concerned and communicated to the Assembly of Heads of State and Government.

*Article* 53

While transmitting its report, the Commission may make to the Assembly of Heads of State and Government such recommendations as it deems useful.

*Article* 54

The Commission shall submit to each ordinary Session of the Assembly of Heads of State and Government a report on its activities.

*Other Communications*

*Article* 55

1. Before each Session, the Secretary of the Commission shall make a list of the communications other than those of States parties to the present Charter and transmit them to the members of the Commission, who shall indicate which communications should be considered by the Commission.

2. A communication shall be considered by the Commission if a simple majority of its members so decide.

*Article* 56

Communications relating to human and peoples' rights referred to in Article 55 received by the Commission, shall be considered if they:

1. Indicate their authors even if the latter request anonymity,

2. Are compatible with the Charter of the Organization of African Unity or with the present Charter,

3. Are not written in disparaging or insulting language directed against the State concerned and its institutions or to the Organization of African Unity,

4. Are not based exclusively on news disseminated through the mass media,

5. Are sent after exhausting local remedies, if any, unless it is obvious that this procedure is unduly prolonged,

6. Are submitted within a reasonable period from the time local remedies are exhausted or from the date the Commission is seized of the matter, and

7. Do not deal with cases which have been settled by these States involved in accordance with the principles of the Charter of the United Nations, or the Charter of the Organization of African Unity or the provisions of the present Charter.

*Article 57*

Prior to any substantive consideration, all communications shall be brought to the knowledge of the State concerned by the Chairman of the Commission.

*Article 58*

1. When it appears after deliberations of the Commission that one or more communications apparently relate to special cases which reveal the existence of a series of serious or massive violations of human and peoples' rights, the Commission shall draw the attention of the Assembly of Heads of State and Government to these special cases.

2. The Assembly of Heads of State and Government may then request the Commission to undertake an in-depth study of these cases and make a factual report, accompanied by its findings and recommendations.

3. A case of emergency duly noticed by the Commission shall be submitted by the latter to the Chairman of the Assembly of Heads of State and Government who may request an in-depth study.

*Article 59*

1. All measures taken within the provisions of the present Chapter shall remain confidential until such a time as the Assembly of Heads of State and Government shall otherwise decide.

2. However, the report shall be published by the Chairman of the Commission upon the decision of the Assembly of Heads of State and Government.

3. The report on the activities of the Commission shall be published by its Chairman after it has been considered by the Assembly of Heads of State and Government.

# CHAPTER IV
## Applicable Principles

*Article* 60

The Commission shall draw inspiration from international law on human and peoples' rights, particularly from the provisions of various African instruments on human and peoples' rights, the Charter of the United Nations, the Charter of the Organization of African Unity, the Universal Declaration of Human Rights, other instruments adopted by the United Nations and by African countries in the field of human and peoples' rights as well as from the provisions of various instruments adopted within the Specialized Agencies of the United Nations of which the parties to the present Charter are members.

*Article* 61

The Commission shall also take into consideration, as subsidiary measures to determine the principles of law, other general or special international conventions, laying down rules expressly recognized by member states of the Organization of African Unity, African practices consistent with international norms on human and peoples' rights, customs generally accepted as law, general principles of law recognized by African states as well as legal precedents and doctrine.

*Article* 62

Each state party shall undertake to submit every two years, from the date the present Charter comes into force, a report on the legislative or other measures taken with a view to giving effect to the rights and freedoms recognized and guaranteed by the present Charter.

*Article* 63

1. The present Charter shall be open to signature, ratification or adherence of the member states of the Organization of African Unity.

2. The instruments of ratification or adherence to the present Charter shall be deposited with the Secretary General of the Organization of African Unity.

3. The present Charter shall come into force three months after the reception by the Secretary General of the instruments of ratification or adherence of a simple majority of the member states of the Organization of African Unity.

## PART III: GENERAL PROVISIONS

*Article* 64

1. After the coming into force of the present Charter, members of the Commission shall be elected in accordance with the relevant Articles of the present Charter.

2. The Secretary General of the Organization of African Unity shall convene the first meeting of the Commission at the Headquarters of the Organization within three months of the constitution of the Commission. Thereafter, the Commission shall be convened by its Chairman whenever necessary but at least once a year.

*Article* 65

For each of the States that will ratify or adhere to the present Charter after its coming into force, the Charter shall take effect three months after the date of the deposit by that State of its instrument of ratification or adherence.

*Article* 66

Special protocols or agreements may, if necessary, supplement the provisions of the present Charter.

*Article* 67

The Secretary General of the Organization of African Unity shall inform member states of the Organization of the deposit of each instrument of ratification or adherence.

*Article* 68

The present Charter may be amended if a State party makes a written request to that effect to the Secretary General of the Organization of African Unity. The Assembly of Heads of State and Government may only consider the draft amendment after all the States parties have been duly informed of it and the Commission has given its opinion on it at the request of the sponsoring State. The amendment shall be approved by a simple majority of the States parties. It shall come into force for each State which has accepted it in accordance with its constitutional procedure three months after the Secretary General has received notice of the acceptance.

## PART EIGHT

# THE CONCEPT OF EQUALITY

## INTRODUCTION

THE substance of this Part consists of a passage from the Dissenting Opinion of Judge Tanaka, the Japanese member of the International Court of Justice, in the *South-West Africa Cases* (Second Phase), 1966. In that case the Court (by the casting vote of the President) failed to deal with the merits of the submissions of the applicant States (Ethiopia and Liberia) that South Africa had violated her international obligations. However, half of the members of the Court, including Judge Tanaka, were prepared to deal with the issues of substance raised by the applications. In the circumstances and given the quality of the exposition the status of the Opinion as a Dissenting Opinion is of little relevance.

The passage reproduced is from the *Reports of Judgments, Advisory Opinions and Orders* of the International Court of Justice, 1966, at pp. 284–316. It contains what is probably the best exposition of the concept of equality in existing literature. Its importance derives from two sources: first, the lack of sound analysis of the concept in the literature at large; and second, the prominence of the principle of equality, or the standard of non-discrimination, in legislation and other instruments concerning human rights.

For further reference see the *Advisory Opinion on Minority Schools in Albania*, 1935; *Judgments, Orders and Advisory Opinions of the Permanent Court of International Justice*, Series A/B, No. 64; the U.S. Supreme Court in *Brown* v. *Board of Education*, 347 U.S. 483 (1954); the European Court of Human Rights in the *Case relating to certain aspects of the laws on the use of languages in education in Belgium* (the *Belgian Linguistics* case), Judgment of 23 July 1968, Publications of the European Court of Human Rights, Series A, 1968; *Ealing L.B.C.* v. *Race Relations Board* [1972], A.C. 342; *Ahmad* v. *Inner London Education Authority* [1978] 1 Q.B. 36; Brownlie, *Principles of Public International law*, 4th ed., 1990, pp. 598–601.

## DISSENTING OPINION OF JUDGE TANAKA,
## SOUTH WEST AFRICA CASES (SECOND PHASE),
## 1966

*TEXT*

Now we shall examine Nos. 3 and 4 of the Applicants' final submissions. Submission No. 3 reads as follows:

> 'Respondent, by laws and regulations, and official methods and measures, which are set out in the pleadings herein, has practised apartheid, i.e., has distinguished as to race, colour, national or tribal origin in establishing the rights and duties of the inhabitants of the Territory; that such practice is in violation of its obligations as stated in Article 2 of the Mandate and Article 22 of the Covenant of the League of Nations; and that Respondent has the duty forthwith to cease the practice of apartheid in the Territory;' (Applicants' final submissions, C.R. 65/35, p. 69).

At the same time, Applicants have presented another submission (Submission No. 4) which states as follows:

> 'Respondent, by virtue of economic, political, social and educational policies applied within the Territory, by means of laws and regulations, and official methods and measures, which are set out in the pleadings herein, has, in the light of applicable international standards or international legal norm, or both, failed to promote to the utmost the material and moral well-being and social progress of the inhabitants of the Territory; that its failure to do so is in violation of its obligations as stated in Article 2 of the Mandate and Article 22 of the Covenant; and that Respondent has the duty forthwith to cease its violations as aforesaid and to take all practicable action to fulfil its duties under such Articles;' (Applicants' final submissions, 19 May 1965, C.R. 65/35, pp. 69–70).

The President, Sir Percy Spender, for the purpose of clarification, addressed a question to the Applicants in relation to Submissions 3 and 4 in the Memorials at page 197, which are not fundamentally different from the above-mentioned Final Submissions Nos. 3 and 4. He asked what was the distinction between one (i.e., Submission No. 3) and the other (i.e., Submission No. 4). (C.R. 65/23, 28 April 1965, p. 31).

The response of the Applicants on this point was that the distinction between the two Submissions 3 and 4 was verbal only (19 May 1965, C.R. 65/35, p. 71). This response, being made after the amendment of the Applicants' submissions, may be considered as applicable to the amended Submissions Nos. 3 and 4.

It should be pointed out that the main difference between the original and the Final Submissions Nos. 3 and 4 is that a phrase, namely: 'in the light of applicable international standards or international legal norm, or both' is inserted between 'has' and 'failed to promote to the utmost...' which seems to make clear the substantive identity existing between these two submissions.

Now we shall analyse each of these submissions, which occupy the central issue of the whole of the Applicants' submissions and upon which the greater part of the arguments of the Parties has been focused. This issue is without doubt the question concerning the policy of apartheid which the Respondent as Mandatory is alleged to have practised.

First, we shall deal with the concept of apartheid. The Applicants, in defining apartheid, said: 'Respondent...has distinguished as to race, colour, national or tribal origin in establishing the rights and duties of the inhabitants of the Territory.'

It may be said that, as between the Parties, no divergence of opinion on the concept of apartheid itself exists, notwithstanding that the Respondent prefers to use other terminology, such as 'separate development', instead of 'apartheid'. Anyhow, it seems that there has been no argument concerning the concept of apartheid itself. Furthermore, we can also recognize that the Respondent has never denied its practice of apartheid; but it wants to establish the legality and reasonableness of this policy under the mandates system and its compatibility with the obligations of the Respondent as Mandatory, as well as its necessity to perform these obligations.

Submission No. 3 contends that such practice (i.e., the practice of apartheid) is in violation of its obligations as stated in Article 2 of the Mandate and Article 22 of the Covenant. However, the Applicants' contention is not clear as to whether the violation, by the practice of apartheid, of the Respondent's obligation is conceived from the viewpoint of politics or law. If we consider Submission No. 3, only on the basis of its literal interpretation, it may be considered to be from the viewpoint of politics; this means that the policy of apartheid is not in conformity with the objectives of the Mandate, namely the promotion of well-being and social progress of the inhabitants without regard to any conceivable legal norm or standards. If the Applicants maintain this position, the issue would be a matter of discretion and the case, so far as this point is concerned, would not be justiciable, as the Respondent has contended.

Now the Applicants do not allege the violation of obligations by the Respondent independently of any legal norm or standards. Since the Applicants amended Submission No. 4 in the Memorials and inserted a phrase 'in the light of applicable international standards or international legal norm', the violation of the obligations as stated in Article 2 of the Mandate and Article 22 of the Covenant (Submission No. 3) which is identical with the failure to promote to the utmost the material and moral well-being and social progress of the inhabitants of the Territory (Submission No. 4) has come to possess a special meaning; namely of a juridical character. Applicants' cause is no longer based directly on a violation of the well-being and progress by the practice of apartheid, but on the alleged violation of certain international standards or international legal norm and not directly on the obligation to promote the well-being and social progress of the inhabitants. There is no doubt that, if such standards and norm exist, their observance in itself may constitute a part of Respondent's general obligations to promote the well-being and social progress.

From what is said above, the relationship between the Applicants' Submissions Nos. 3 and 4 may be understood as follows. The two submissions deal with the same subject-matter, namely the illegal character of the policy and practice of apartheid. However, the contents of each submission are not quite the same, consequently the distinction between the two submissions is not verbal only, as Applicants stated in answer to the question of the President; each seems to be supplementary to the other.

Briefly, the Applicants' Submissions Nos. 3 and 4, as newly formulated, rest upon a norm and/or standard. This norm or standard has been added by the Applicants to Submission No. 4. The existence of this norm or standard to be applied to the Mandate relationships, according to the Applicants' allegation, constitutes a legal limitation of the Respondent's discretionary power and makes the practice of apartheid illegal, and accordingly a violation of the obligations incumbent on the Mandatory. What the Applicants mean by apartheid is as follows:

> 'Under apartheid, the status, rights, duties, opportunities and burdens of the population are determined and allotted arbitrarily on the basis of race, color and tribe, in a pattern which ignores the needs and capacities of the groups and individuals affected, and subordinates the interests and rights of the great majority of the people to the preferences of a minority. . . . It deals with apartheid in practice, as it actually is and as it actually has been in the life of the people of the Territory. . . .' (Memorials, p. 108.)

The Applicants contend the existence of a norm or standards which prohibit the practice of apartheid. These norm or standards are nothing other than those of non-discrimination or non-separation.

The Respondent denies the existence of a norm or standard to prohibit the practice of apartheid and tries to justify this practice from the discretionary nature of the Mandatory's power. The Respondent emphasizes that the practice of apartheid is only impermissible when it is carried out in bad faith.

From the viewpoint of the Applicants, the existence, and objective validity, of a norm of non-discrimination make the question of the intention or motivation irrelevant for the purposes of determining whether there has been a violation of this norm. The principle that a legal precept, as opposed to a moral one, in so far as it is not specifically provided otherwise, shall be applied objectively, independently of motivation on the part of those concerned and independently of other individual circumstances, may be applicable to the Respondent's defence of *bona fides*.

Here we are concerned with the existence of a legal norm or standards regarding non-discrimination. It is a question which is concerned with the sources of international law, and, at the same time, with the mandate law. Furthermore, the question is intimately related to the essence and nature of fundamental human rights, the promotion and encouragement of respect for which constitute one of the purposes of the United Nations (Article 1, paragraph 3, Charter of the United Nations), in which the principle of equality before the law occupies the most important part—a principle, from the Applicants' view, antithetical to the policy of apartheid.

What is meant by 'international norm or standards' can be understood as being related to the principle of equality before the law.

The question is whether a legal norm on equality before the law exists in the international sphere and whether it has a binding power upon the Respondent's conduct in carrying out its obligations as Mandatory. The question is whether the principle of equality before the law can find its place among the sources of international law which are referred to in Article 38, paragraph 1.

Now we shall examine one by one the sources of international law enumerated by the above-mentioned provision.

First we consider the international conventions (or treaties). Here we are not concerned with 'special' or 'particular' law-making bilateral treaties, but only with law-making multilateral treaties such as the Charter of the United Nations, the Constitution of the International Labour Organization, the Genocide Convention, which have special significance as legislative methods. However, even such law-making treaties bind only signatory States and they do not bind States which are not parties to them.

The question is whether the Charter of the United Nations contains a legal norm of equality before the law and the principle of non-discrimination on account of religion, race, colour, sex, language, political creed, etc. The achievement of international co-operation in 'promoting and encouraging respect for human rights and for fundamental freedoms for all without distinction as to race, sex, language, or religion' constitutes one of the purposes of the United Nations (Article 1, paragraph 3). Next, the General Assembly shall initiate studies and made recommendations for the purpose of: '... (*b*) ... and assisting in the realization of human rights and fundamental freedoms without distinction as to race, sex, language, or religion' (Article 13, paragraph 1 (*b*)). 'Universal respect for, and observance of, human rights and fundamental freedoms for all without distinction as to race, sex, language, or religion' is one of the items which shall be promoted by the United Nations in the field of international economic and social co-operation (Articles 55 (c), 56). In this field the Economic and Social Council may make recommendations for the purpose of promoting respect for, and observance of, human rights and fundamental freedoms for all (Article 62, paragraph 2, Charter). Finally, 'to encourage respect for human rights and for fundamental freedoms for all without distinction as to race, sex, language or religion' is indicated as one of the basic objectives of the trusteeship system (Article 76 (c)).

The repeated references in the Charter to the fundamental rights and freedoms—at least four times—presents itself as one of its differences from the Covenant of the League of Nations, in which the existence of intimate relationships between peace and respect for human rights were not so keenly felt as in the Charter of the United Nations. However, the Charter did not go so far as to give the definition to the fundamental rights and freedoms, nor to provide any machinery of implementation for the protection and guarantee of these rights and freedoms. The 'Universal Declaration of Human Rights and Fundamental Freedoms' of 1948 which wanted to formulate each right and freedom and give them concrete content, is no more than a declaration adopted by the General Assembly and not a treaty binding on the member States. The goal of the codification on the matter of human rights and freedoms has until now not been reached save in very limited degree, namely with the European Convention for the Protection of Human Rights and Fundamental Freedoms of 1953, the validity of which is only regional and not universal and with a few special conventions, such as 'genocide' and political rights of women, the application of which is limited to their respective matters.

In view of these situations, can the Applicants contend, as an interpretation of the Charter, that the existence of a legal norm on equality before the law, which prescribes non-discrimination on account of religion, race, colour, etc., accordingly forbids the practice of apartheid? Is what the Charter requires limited only 'to achieve international co-operation . . . in promoting and encouraging respect for human rights and for fundamental freedoms . . .' and other matters referred to above?

Under these circumstances it seems difficult to recognize that the Charter expressly imposes on member States any legal obligation with respect to the fundamental human rights and freedoms. On the other hand, we cannot ignore the enormous importance which the Charter attaches to the realization of fundamental human rights and freedoms. Article 56 states: 'All Members pledge themselves to take joint and separate action in co-operation with the Organization for the achievement of the purposes set forth in Article 55.' (Article 55 enumerates the purposes of international economic and social co-operation, in which 'universal respect for, and observance of, human rights and fundamental freedoms' is included.) Well, those who pledge themselves to take action in co-operation with the United Nations in respect of the promotion of universal respect for, and observance of, human rights and fundamental freedoms, cannot violate, without contradiction, these rights and freedoms. How can one, on the one hand, preach respect for human rights to others and, on the other hand, disclaim for oneself the obligation to respect them? From the provisions of the Charter referring to the human rights and fundamental freedoms it can be inferred that the legal obligation to respect human rights and fundamental freedoms is imposed on member States.

Judge Spiropoulos confirmed the binding character of the human rights provisions of the Charter:

'As the obligation to respect human rights was placed upon Member States by the Charter, it followed that any violation of human rights was a violation of the provision of the Charter.' (*G.A., O.R., 3rd Session, 6th Committee*, 138th Meeting, 7 December 1948, p. 765.)

Judge Jessup also attributed the same character to the human rights provisions:

'Since this book is written *de lege ferenda*, the attempt is made throughout to distinguish between the existing law and the future goals of the law. It is already the law, at least for Members of the United Nations, that respect for human dignity and fundamental human rights is obligatory. The duty is imposed by the Charter.' (Philip C. Jessup, *Modern Law of Nations*, 1948, p. 91.)

Without doubt, under the present circumstances, the international protection of human rights and fundamental freedoms is very imperfect. The work of codification in this field of law has advanced little from the viewpoint of defining each human right and freedom, as well as the machinery for their realization. But there is little doubt of the existence of human rights and freedoms; if not, respect for these is logically inconceivable; the Charter presupposes the existence of human rights and freedoms which shall be respected; the existence of such rights and freedoms is unthinkable without corresponding obligations of persons concerned and a legal norm underlying them. Furthermore, there is no doubt that these obligations are not only moral ones, and that they also have a legal character by the very nature of the subject-matter.

Therefore, the legislative imperfections in the definition of human rights and freedoms and the lack of mechanism for implementation, do not constitute a reason for denying their existence and the need for their legal protection.

Furthermore, it must be pointed out that the Charter provisions, as indicated above, repeatedly emphasize the principle of equality before the law by saying, 'without distinction as to race, sex, language or religion'.

Under the hypothesis that in the United Nations Charter there exists a legal norm or standards of non-discrimination, are the Applicants, referring to this norm, entitled to have recourse to the International Court of Justice according to Article 7, paragraph 2, of the Mandate? The Respondent contends that such an alleged norm does not constitute a part of the mandate agreement, and therefore the question on this norm falls outside the dispute, which, by the compromissory clause, is placed under the jurisdiction of the International Court of Justice. The Applicants' contention would amount to the introduction of a new element into the mandate agreement which is alien to this instrument.

It is evident that, as the Respondent contends, the mandate agreement does not stipulate equality before the law clause, and that this clause does not formally constitute a part of the mandate instrument. Nevertheless, the equality principle, as an integral part of the Charter of the United Nations or as an independent source of general international law, can be directly applied to the matter of the Mandate either as constituting a kind of law of the Mandate *in sensu lato* or, at least in respect of standards, as a principle of interpretation of the mandate agreement. Accordingly, the dispute concerning the legality of apartheid comes within the field of the interpretation and application of the provisions of the Mandate stipulated in Article 7, paragraph 2, of the Mandate.

This conclusion is justified only on the presupposition that the Respondent is bound by the Charter of the United Nations not only as a member State but also as a Mandatory. The Charter, being of the nature of special international law, or the law of the organized international community, must be applied to all matters which come within the purposes and competence of the United Nations and with which member States are concerned, including the matter of the Mandate. Logic requires that, so long as we recognize the unity of personality, the same principle must govern both the conduct of a member State in the United Nations itself and also its conduct as a mandatory, particularly in the matter of the protection and guarantee of human rights and freedoms.

Concerning the Applicants' contention attributing to the norm of non-discrimination or non-separation the character of customary international law, the following points must be noted.

The Applicants enumerate resolutions and declarations of international organs which condemn racial discrimination, segregation, separation and apartheid, and contend that the said resolutions and declarations were adopted by an overwhelming majority, and therefore have binding power in regard to an opposing State, namely the Respondent. Concerning the question whether the consent of all States is required for the creation of a customary international law or not, we consider that the answer must be in the negative for the reason that Article 38, paragraph 1 (*b*), of the Statute does not exclude the possibility of a few dissidents for the purpose of the creation of a customary international law and that the contrary view of a particular State or States would result in the permission of obstruction by veto, which could not have been expected by the legislator who drafted the said Article.

An important question involved in the Applicants' contention is whether resolutions and declarations of international organs can be recognized as a factor in the custom-generating process in the interpretation of Article 38, paragraph 1 (*b*), that is to say, as 'evidence of a general practice'.

According to traditional international law, a general practice is the result of the repetition of individual acts of States constituting consensus in regard to a certain content of a rule of law. Such repetition of acts is a historical process extending over a long period of time. The process of the formation of a customary law in this case may be described as individualistic. On the contrary, this process is going to change in adapting itself to changes in the way of international life. The appearance of organizations such as the League of Nations and the United Nations, with their agencies and affiliated institutions, replacing an important part of the traditional individualistic method of international negotiation by the method of 'parliamentary diplomacy' (Judgment on the *South West Africa* cases, *I.C.J. Reports 1962*, p. 346), is bound to influence the mode of generation of customary international law. A State, instead of pronouncing its view to a few States directly concerned, has the opportunity, through the medium of an organization, to declare its position to all members of the organization and to know immediately their reaction on the same matter. In former days, practice, repetition and *opinio juris sive necessitatis*, which are the ingredients of customary law might be combined together in a very long and slow process extending over centuries. In the contemporary age of highly developed techniques of communication and information, the formation of a custom through the medium of international organizations is greatly facilitated and accelerated; the establishment of such a custom would require no more than one generation or even far less than that. This is one of the examples of the transformation of law inevitably produced by change in the social substratum.

Of course, we cannot admit that individual resolutions, declarations, judgments, decisions, etc., have binding force upon the members of the organization. What is required for customary international law is the repetition of the same practice; accordingly, in this case resolutions, declarations, etc., on the same matter in the same, or diverse, organizations must take place repeatedly.

Parallel with such repetition, each resolution, declaration, etc., being considered as the manifestation of the collective will of individual participant States, the will of the international community can certainly be formulated more quickly and more accurately as compared with the traditional method of the normative process. This collective, cumulative and organic process of custom-generation can be characterized as the middle way between legislation by convention and the traditional process of custom making, and can be seen to have an important role from the viewpoint of the development of international law.

In short, the accumulation of authoritative pronouncements such as resolutions, declarations, decisions, etc., concerning the interpretation of the Charter by the competent organs of the international community can be characterized as evidence of the international custom referred to in Article 38, paragraph 1 (*b*).

In the present case the Applicants assert the existence of the international norm and standards of non-discrimination and non-separation and refer to this source of international law. They enumerate resolutions of the General Assembly which repeatedly and strongly deny the apartheid policy of racial discrimination as an interpretation of the Charter (General Assembly resolution 1178 (XII) of 26 November 1957; resolution 1248 (XIII) of 30 October 1958; resolution 1375 (XIV) of 17 November 1959; resolution 1598 (XV) of 13 April 1961; and resolutions of the Security Council (with regard to apartheid as practised in the Republic of South Africa); resolution of 7 August 1953 which declares the inconsistency of the policy of the South African Government with the principles contained in the Charter of the United Nations and with its obligations as a member State of the United Nations; resolution of 4 December 1963 which declares '. . . the policies of apartheid and racial discrimination . . . are abhorrent to the conscience of mankind . . .'. The Applicants cite also the report of the Committee on South West Africa for 1956).

Moreover, the 11 trust territories agreements, each of them containing a provision concerning the norm of official non-discrimination or non-separation on the basis of membership in a group or race, may be considered as contributions to the development of the universal acceptance of the norm of non-discrimination, in addition to the meaning which each provision possesses in each trusteeship agreement, by virtue of Article 38, paragraph 1 (*a*), of the Statute.

Furthermore, the Universal Declaration of Human Rights adopted by the General Assembly in 1948, although not binding in itself, constitutes evidence of the interpretation and application of the relevant Charter provisions. The same may be said of the Draft Declaration on Rights and Duties of States adopted by the International Law Commission in 1949, the Draft Covenant on civil and political rights, the Draft Covenant on Economic, Social and Cultural rights, the Declaration on the Elimination of all Forms of Racial Discrimination adopted by the General Assembly of the United Nations on 20 November 1963 and of regional treaties and declarations, particularly the European Convention for the Protection of Human Rights and Fundamental Freedoms signed on 3 September 1953, the Charter of the Organization of American States signed on 30 April 1948, the American Declaration of the Rights and Duties of Man, 1948, the Draft Declaration of International Rights and Duties, 1945.

From what has been said above, we consider that the norm of non-discrimination or non-separation on the basis of race has become a rule of customary international law as is contended by the Applicants, and as a result, the Respondent's obligations as Mandatory are governed by this legal norm in its capacity as a member of the United Nations either directly or at least by way of interpretation of Article 2, paragraph 2.

One of the contentions concerning the application of the said legal norm is that, if such a legal norm exists for judging the Respondent's obligations under Article 2, paragraph 2, of the Mandate, it would be the one in existence at the time the Mandate was entrusted to the Respondent. This is evidently a question of inter-temporal law.

The Respondent's position is that of denying the application of a new law to a matter which arose under an old law, namely the negation of retro-activity of a new customary law. The Applicant's argument is based on 'the relevance of the evolving practice and views of States, growth of experience and increasing knowledge in political and social science to the determination of obligations bearing on the nature and purpose of the Mandate in general, and Article 2 paragraph 2'; briefly, it rests on the assertion of the concept of the 'continuous, dynamic and ascending growth' of the obligation of the Mandatory.

Our view on this question is substantially not very different from that of the Applicants. The reason why we recognize the retroactive application of a new customary law to a matter which started more than 40 years ago is as follows.

The matter in question is in reality not that of an old law and a new law, that is to say, it is not a question which arises out of an amendment of a law and which should be decided on the basis of the principle of the protection of *droit acquis* and therefore of non-retroactivity. In the present case, the protection of the acquired rights of the Respondent is not the issue, but its obligations, because the main purposes of the mandate system are ethical and humanitarian. The Respondent has no right to behave in an inhuman way today as well as during these 40 years. Therefore, the recognition of the generation of a new customary international law on the matter of non-discrimination is not to be regarded as detrimental to the Mandatory, but as an authentic interpretation of the already existing provisions of Article 2, paragraph 2, of the Mandate and the Covenant. It is nothing other than a simple clarification of what was not so clear 40 years ago. What ought to have been clear 40 years ago has been revealed by the creation of a new customary law which plays the role of authentic interpretation the effect of which is retroactive.

Briefly, the method of the generation of customary international law is in the stage of transformation from being an individualistic process to being a collectivistic process. This phenomenon can be said to be the adaptation of the traditional creative process of international law to the reality of the growth of the organized international community. It can be characterized, considered from the sociological viewpoint, as a transition from traditional custom-making to international legislation by treaty.

Following the reference to Article 38, paragraph 1 (*b*), of the Statute, the Applicants base their contention on the legal norm alternatively on Article 38, paragraph 1 (*c*), of the Statute, namely 'the general principles of law recognized by civilized nations'.

Applicants refer to this source of international law both as an independent ground for the justification of the norm of non-discrimination and as a supplement and reinforcement of the other arguments advanced by them to demonstrate their theory.

The question is whether the legal norm of non-discrimination or non-separation denying the practice of apartheid can be recognized as a principle enunciated in the said provision.

The wording of this provision is very broad and vague; the meaning is not clear. Multiple interpretations ranging from the most strict to the most liberal are possible.

To decide this question we must clarify the meaning of 'general principles of law'. To restrict the meaning to private law principles or principles of procedural law seems from the viewpoint of literal interpretation untenable. So far as the 'general principles of law' are not qualified, the 'law' must be understood to embrace all branches of law, including municipal law, public law, constitutional and administrative law, private law, commercial law, substantive and procedural law, etc. Nevertheless, analogies drawn from these laws should not be made mechanically, that is to say, to borrow the expression of Lord McNair, 'by means of importing private law institutions "lock, stock and barrel" ready-made and fully equipped with a set of rules'. (*I.C.J. Reports 1950*, p. 148.)

What international law can with advantage borrow from these sources must be from the viewpoint of underlying or guiding 'principles'. These principles, therefore, must not be limited to statutory provisions and institutions of national laws: they must be extended to the fundamental concepts of each branch of law as well as to law in genèral so far as these can be considered as 'recognized by civilized nations.'

Accordingly, the general principles of law in the sense of Article 38, paragraph 1 (*c*), are not limited to certain basic principles of law such as the limitation of State sovereignty, third-party judgment, limitation of the right of self-defence, *pacta sunt servanda*, respect for acquired rights, liability for unlawful harm to one's neighbour, the principle of good faith, etc. The word 'general' may be understood to possess the same meaning as in the case of the '*general* theory of law', 'théorie *générale* de droit', 'die *Allgemeine* Rechtslehre', namely common to all branches of law. But the principles themselves are very extensive and can be interpreted to include not only the general theory of law, but the general theories of each branch of municipal law, so far as recognized by civilized nations. They may be conceived, furthermore, as including not only legal principles but the fundamental legal concepts of which the legal norms are composed such as person, right, duty, property, juristic act, contract, tort, succession, etc.

In short, they may include what can be considered as 'juridical truth' (Bin Cheng, *General Principles of Law as Applied by International Courts and Tribunals*, 1953, p. 24).

The question is whether a legal norm of non-discrimination and non-separation has come into existence in international society, as the Applicants contend. It is beyond all doubt that the presence of laws against racial discrimination and segregation in the municipal systems of virtually every State can be established by comparative law studies. The recognition of this norm by civilized nations can be ascertained. If the condition of 'general principles' is fulfilled, namely if we can say that the general principles include the norm concerning the protection of human rights by adopting the wide interpretation of the provision of Article 38, paragraph 1 (*c*), the norm will find its place among the sources of international law.

In this context we have to consider the relationship between a norm of a human rights nature and international law. Originally, general principles are considered to be certain private law principles found by the comparative law method and applicable by way of analogy to matters of an international character. These principles are of a nature common to all nations, that is of the character of *jus gentium*. These principles, which originally belong to private law and have the character of *jus gentium*, can be incorporated in international law so as to be applied to matters of an international nature by way of analogy, as we see in the case of the application of some rules of contract law to the interpretation of treaties. In the case of the international protection of human rights, on the contrary, what is involved is not the application by analogy of a principle or a norm of private law to a matter of international character, but the recognition of the juridical validity of a similar legal fact without any distinction as between the municipal and the international legal sphere.

In short, human rights which require protection are the same; they are not the product of a particular juridical system in the hierarchy of the legal order, but the same human rights must be recognized, respected and protected everywhere man goes. The uniformity of national laws on the protection of human rights is not derived, as in the cases of the law of contracts and commercial and maritime transactions, from considerations of expediency by the legislative organs or from the creative power of the custom of a community, but it already exists in spite of its more-or-less vague form. This is of nature *jus naturale* in roman law.

The unified national laws of the character of *jus gentium* and of the law of human rights, which is of the character of *jus naturale* in roman law, both constituting a part of the law of the world community which may be designated as World Law, Common Law of Mankind (Jenks), Trans-national Law (Jessup), etc., at the same time constitute a part of international law through the medium of Article 38, paragraph 1 (c). But there is a difference between these two cases. In the former, the general principles are presented as common elements among diverse national laws; in the latter, only one and the same law exists and this is valid through all kinds of human societies in relationships of hierarchy and co-ordination.

This distinction between the two categories of law of an international character is important in deciding the scope and extent of Article 38, paragraph 1 (c). The Respondent contends that the suggested application by the Applicants of a principle recognized by civilized nations is not a correct analogy and application as contemplated by Article 38, paragraph 1 (c). The Respondent contends that the alleged norm of non-differentiation as between individuals within a State on the basis of membership of a race, class or group could not be transferred by way of analogy to the international relationship, otherwise it would mean that all nations are to be treated equally despite the difference of race, colour, etc.—a conclusion which is absurd. (C.R. 65/47, p. 7.) If we limit the application of Article 38, paragraph 1 (c), to a strict analogical extension of certain principles of municipal law, we must recognize that the contention of the Respondent is well-founded. The said provision, however, does not limit its application to cases of analogy with municipal, or private law which has certainly been a most important instance of the application of this provision. We must include the international protection of human rights in the application of this provision. It must not be regarded as a case of analogy. In reality, there is only one human right which is valid in the international sphere as well as in the domestic sphere.

The question here is not of an 'international', that is to say, inter-State nature, but it is concerned with the question of the international validity of human rights, that is to say, the question whether a State is obliged to protect human rights in the international sphere as it is obliged in the domestic sphere.

The principle of the protection of human rights is derived from the concept of man as a *person* and his relationship with society which cannot be separated from universal human nature. Then existence of human rights does not depend on the will of a State; neither internally on its law or any other legislative measure, nor internationally on treaty or custom, in which the express or tacit will of a State constitutes the essential element.

A State or States are not capable of creating human rights by law or by convention; they can only confirm their existence and give them protection. The role of the State is no more than declaratory. It is exactly the same as the International Court of Justice ruling concerning the *Reservations to the Genocide Convention* case (*I.C.J. Reports 1951*, p. 23):

'The solution of these problems must be found in the special characteristics of the Genocide Convention.... The origins of the Convention show that it was the intention of the United Nations to condemn and punish genocide as "a crime under international law" involving a denial of the right of existence of entire human groups, a denial which shocks the conscience of mankind and results in great losses to humanity, and which is contrary to moral law and to the spirit and aims of the United Nations (resolution 96 (1) of the General Assembly, December 11th, 1946). The first consequence arising from this conception is that the principles underlying the Convention are principles which are recognized by civilized nations as binding on States, *even without any conventional obligation*. A second consequence is the universal character both of the condemnation of genocide and of the co-operation required "in order to liberate mankind from such an odious scourge" (Preamble to the Convention).' (Italics added.)

Human rights have always existed with the human being. They existed independently of, and before, the State. Alien and even stateless persons must not be deprived of them. Belonging to diverse kinds of communities and societies—ranging from family, club, corporation, to State and international community, the human rights of man must be protected everywhere in this social hierarchy, just as copyright is protected domestically and internationally. There must be no legal vacuum in the protection of human rights. Who can believe, as a reasonable man, that the existence of human rights depends upon the internal or international legislative measures, etc., of the State and that accordingly they can be validly abolished or modified by the will of the State?

If a law exists independently of the will of the State and, accordingly, cannot be abolished or modified even by its constitution, because it is deeply rooted in the conscience of mankind and of any reasonable man, it may be called 'natural law' in contrast to 'positive law'.

Provisions of the constitutions of some countries characterize fundamental human rights and freedoms as 'inalienable', 'sacred', 'eternal', 'inviolate', etc. Therefore, the guarantee of fundamental human rights and freedoms possesses a super-constitutional significance.

If we can introduce in the international field a category of law, namely *jus cogens*, recently examined by the International Law Commission, a kind of imperative law which constitutes the contrast to the *jus dispositivum*, capable of being changed by way of agreement between States, surely the law concerning the protection of human rights may be considered to belong to the *jus cogens*.

As an interpretation of Article 38, paragraph 1 (*c*), we consider that the concept of human rights and of their protection is included in the general principles mentioned in that article.

Such an interpretation would necessarily be open to the criticism of falling into the error of natural law dogma. But it is undeniable that in

Article 38, paragraph 1 (c), some natural law elements are inherent. It extends the concept of the source of international law beyond the limit of legal positivism according to which, the States being bound only by their own will, international law is nothing but the law of the consent and auto-limitation of the State. But this viewpoint, we believe, was clearly overruled by Article 38, paragraph 1 (c), by the fact that this provision does not require the consent of States as a condition of the recognition of the general principles. States which do not recognize this principle or even deny its validity are nevertheless subject to its rule. From this kind of source inter-national law could have the foundation of its validity extended beyond the will of States, that is to say, into the sphere of natural law and assume an aspect of its supra-national and supra-positive character.

The above-mentioned character of Article 38, paragraph 1 (c), of the Statute is proved by the process of the drafting of this article by the Committee of Jurists. The original proposal made by Baron Descamps referred to '*la conscience juridique des peuples civilisés*', a concept which clearly indicated an idea originating in natural law. This proposal met with the opposition of the positivist members of the Committee, represented by Mr. Root. The final draft, namely Article 38, paragraph 1 (c), is the product of a compromise between two schools, naturalist and positivist, and therefore the fact that the natural law idea became incorporated therein is not difficult to discover (see particularly Jean Spiropoulos, *Die Allgemeine Rechtsgrundsätze im Völkerrecht*, 1928, pp. 60 ff.; Bin Cheng, *op. cit.*, pp. 24–26).

Furthermore, an important role which can be played by Article 38, paragraph 1 (c), in filling in gaps in the positive sources in order to avoid *nonliquet* decisions, can only be derived from the natural law character of this provision. Professor Brierly puts it, 'its inclusion is important as a rejection of the positivistic doctrine, according to which international law consists solely of rules to which States have given their consent' (J. L. Brierly, *The Law of Nations*, 6th ed., p. 63). Mr. Rosenne comments on the general principles of law as follows:

> 'Having independent existence, their validity as legal norms does not derive from the consent of the parties as such. . . . The Statute places this element on a footing of formal equality with the two positivist elements of custom and treaty, and thus is positivist recognition of the Grotian concept of the co-existence implying no subordination of positive law and the so-called natural law of nations (in the Grotian sense).' (Shabtai Rosenne, *The International Court of Justice*, 1965, Vol. II, p. 610.)

Now the question is whether the alleged norm of non-discrimination and non-separation as a kind of protection of human rights can be considered as recognized by civilized nations and included in the general principles of law.

First the recognition of a principle by civilized nations, as indicated above, does not mean recognition by *all* civilized nations, nor does it mean recognition by an official act such as a legislative act; therefore the recognition is of a very elastic nature. The principle of equality before the law, however, is stipulated in the list of human rights recognized by the municipal system of virtually every State no matter whether the form of government be republican or monarchical and in spite of any differences in the degree of precision of the relevant provisions. This principle has become an integral part of the constitutions of most of the civilized countries in the world. Common-law countries must be included. (According to *Constitutions of Nations*, 2nd edn., by Amos J. Peaslee, 1956, Vol. I, p. 7, about 73 per cent of the national constitutions contain clauses respecting equality.)

The manifestation of the recognition of this principle does not need to be limited to the act of legislation as indicated above; it may include the attitude of delegations of member States in cases of participation in resolutions, declarations, etc., against racial discrimination adopted by the organs of the League of Nations, the United Nations and other organizations which, as we have seen above, constitute an important element in the generation of customary international law.

From what we have seen above, the alleged norm of non-discrimination and non-separation, being based on the United Nations Charter, particularly Articles 55 (*c*), 56, and on numerous resolutions and declarations of the General Assembly and other organs of the United Nations, and owing to its nature as a general principle, can be regarded as a source of international law according to the provisions of Article 38, paragraph 1 (*a*)−(*c*). In this case three kinds of sources are cumulatively functioning to defend the above-mentioned norm: (1) international convention, (2) international custom and (3) the general principles of law.

Practically the justification of any one of these is enough, but theoretically there may be a difference in the degree of importance among the three. From a positivistic, voluntaristic viewpoint, first the convention, and next the custom, is considered important, and general principles occupy merely a supplementary position. On the contrary, if we take the supra-national objective viewpoint, the general principles would come first and the two others would follow them. If we accept the fact that convention and custom are generally the manifestation and concretization of already existing general principles, we are inclined to attribute to this third source of international law the primary position vis-á-vis the other two.

To sum up, the principle of the protection of human rights has received recognition as a legal norm under three main sources of international law, namely (1) international conventions, (2) international custom and (3) the general principles of law. Now, the principle of equality before the law or equal protection by the law presents itself as a kind of human rights norm. Therefore, what has been said on human rights in general can be applied to the principle of equality. (Cf. Wilfred Jenks, *The Common Law of Mankind*,

1958, p. 121. The author recognizes the principle of respect for human rights including equality before the law as a general principle of law.)

Here we must consider the principle of equality in relationship to the Mandate. The contention of the Applicants is based on this principle as condemning the practice of apartheid. The Applicants contend not only that this practice is in violation of the obligations of the Respondent imposed upon it by Article 2 of the Mandate and Article 22 of the Covenant (Submission No. 3), but that the Respondent, by virtue of economic, political, social and educational policies has, in the light of applicable international standards or international legal norms, or both, failed to promote to the utmost the material and moral well-being and social progress of the inhabitants of the Territory. What the Applicants seek to establish seems to be that the Respondent's practice of apartheid constitutes a violation of international standards and/or an international legal norm, namely the principle of equality and, as a result, a violation of the obligations to promote to the utmost, etc. If the violation of this principle exists, this will be necessarily followed by failure to promote the well-being, etc. The question is whether the principle of equality is applicable to the relationships of the Mandate or not. The Respondent denies that the Mandate includes in its content the principle of equality as to race, colour, etc.

Regarding this point, we would refer to our above-mentioned view concerning the Respondent's contention that the alleged norm of non-discrimination of the Charter does not constitute a part of the mandate agreement, and therefore the question of this norm falls outside the dispute under Article 7, paragraph 2, of the Mandate.

We consider that the principle of equality, although it is not expressly mentioned in the mandate instrument constitutes, by its nature, an integral part of the mandates system and therefore is embodied in the Mandate. From the natural-law character of this principle its inclusion in the Mandate must be justified.

It appears to be a paradox that the inhabitants of the mandated territories are internationally more protected than citizens of States by the application of Article 7, paragraph 2, but this interpretation falls outside the scope of the present proceedings.

Next, we shall consider the content of the principle of equality which must be applied to the question of apartheid.


IV


As we have seen above, the objectives of the mandates system, being the material and moral well-being and social progress of the inhabitants of the territory, are in themselves of a political nature. Their achievement must be measured by the criteria of politics and the method of their realization belongs to the matter of the discretion conferred upon the Mandatory by Article 2, paragraph 1, of the Mandate, and Article 22 of the Covenant of the League.

The discretionary power of the Mandatory, however, is not unlimited. Besides the general rules which prohibit the Mandatory from abusing its power and *mala fides* in performing its obligations, and besides the individual provisions of the Mandate and the Covenant, the Mandatory is subject to the Charter of the United Nations as a member State, the customary international law, general principles of law, and other sources of international law enunciated in Article 38, paragraph 1. According to the contention of the Applicants, the norm and/or standards which prohibit the practice of apartheid, are either immediately or by way of interpretation of the Mandate binding upon the discretionary power of the Mandatory. The Respondent denies the existence of such norm and/or standards.

The divergence of views between the Parties is summarized in the following formula: whether or not the policy of racial discrimination or separate development is *per se* incompatible with the well-being and social progress of the inhabitants, or in other terms, whether the policy of apartheid is illegal (*bona fides* or *mala fides*), the result or effect. From the Respondent's standpoint apartheid is not *per se* prohibited but only a special kind of discrimination which leads to oppression is prohibited.

This divergence of fundamental standpoints between the Parties is reflected in their attitudes as to what extent their contentions depend on the evidence. Contrary to the Applicants' attitude in denying the necessity of calling witnesses and experts and of an inspection *in loco*, the Respondent abundantly utilized numerous witnesses and experts and requested the Court to visit South West Africa, South Africa and other parts of Africa to make an inspection *in loco*.

First, we shall examine the content of the norm and standards of which violation by the Respondents is alleged by the Applicants.

The Applicants contend, as set forth in the Memorials (p. 108) that the Respondent's violation of its obligations under the said paragraph 2 of Article 2 of the Mandate consists in a 'systematic course of positive action which inhibits the well-being, prevents the social progress and thwarts the development of the overwhelming majority' of the inhabitants of the Territory. In pursuit of such course of action, and as a pervasive feature thereof, the Respondent has, by governmental action, installed and maintained the policy of apartheid, or separate development. What is meant by apartheid is as follows:

'Under *apartheid*, the status, rights, duties, opportunities and burdens of the population are determined and allotted arbitrarily on the basis of race, color and tribe, in a pattern which ignores the needs and capacities of the groups and individuals affected, and subordinates the interests and rights of the great majority of the people to the preferences of a minority.' (Memorials, p. 108.)

Such policy, the Applicants contend, 'runs counter to modern conceptions of human rights, dignities and freedom, irrespective of race, colour or creed', which conclusion is denied by the Respondent.

The alleged legal norms of non-discrimination or non-separation by which, by way of interpretation of Article 2, paragraph 2, of the Mandate, apartheid becomes illegal, are defined by the Applicants as follows:

'In the following analysis of the relevant legal norms, the terms "non-discrimination" or "non-separation" are used in their prevalent and customary sense: stated negatively, the terms refer to the absence of governmental policies or actions which allot status, rights, duties, privileges or burdens on the basis of membership in a group, class or race rather than on the basis of individual merit, capacity or potential: stated affirmatively, the terms refer to governmental policies and actions the objective of which is to protect equality of opportunity and equal protection of the laws to individual persons as such.' (Reply, p. 274.)

What the Applicants want to establish, are the legal norms of 'non-discrimination' or 'non-separation' which are of a *per se*, non-qualified absolute nature, namely that the decision of observance or otherwise of the norm does not depend upon the motive, result, effect, etc. Therefore from the standpoint of the Applicants, the violation of the norm of non-discrimination is established if there exists a simple fact of discrimination without regard to the intent of oppression on the part of the Mandatory.

On the other hand, the Respondent does not recognize the existence of the norm of non-discrimination of an absolute character and seeks to prove the necessity of group differentiation in the administration of a multi-racial, multi-national, or multi-lingual community. The pleadings and verbatim records are extremely rich in examples of different treatment of diverse population groups in multi-cultural societies in the world. Many examples of different treatment quoted by the Respondent and testified to by the witnesses and experts appear to belong to the system of protection of minority groups in multi-cultural communities and cover not only the field of public law but also of private law.

The doctrine of different treatment of diverse population groups constitutes a fundamental political principle by which the Respondent administers not only the Republic of South Africa, but the neighbouring Territory of South West Africa. The geographical, historical, ethnological, economic and cultural differences and varieties between several population groups, according to the contention of the Respondent, have necessitated the adoption of the policy of apartheid or 'separate development'. This policy is said to be required for the purpose of the promotion of the well-being and social progress of the inhabitants of the Territory. The Respondent insists that each population group developing its own characteristics and individuality, to attain self-determination, separate development should be the best way to realize the well-being and social progress of the inhabitants. The other alternative, namely the mixed integral society in the sense of Western democracy would necessarily lead to competition, friction, struggle, chaos, bloodshed, and dictatorship as examples may be found in some other African countries. Therefore, the most appropriate method of administration of the Territory is the principle of indirect rule maintaining and utilizing the merits of tribalism.

Briefly, it seems that the idea underlying the policy of apartheid or separate development is the racial philosophy which is not entirely identical with ideological Nazism but attributes great importance to the racial or ethnological factors in the fields of politics, law, economy and culture. Next, the method of apartheid is of sociological and, therefore, strong deterministic tendency, as we can guess from the fact that at the oral proceedings the standpoint of the Respondent was energetically sustained by many witnesses—experts who were sociologists and ethnologists.

Contrary to the standpoint of the Applicants who condemn the policy of apartheid or separate development of the Respondent as illegal, the latter conceives this policy as something neutral. The Respondent says that it can be utilized as a tool to attain a particular end, good or bad, as a knife can serve a surgeon as well as a murderer.

Before we decide this question, general consideration of the content of the principle of equality before the law is required. Although the existence of this principle is universally recognized as we have seen above, its precise content is not very clear.

This principle has been recognized as one of the fundamental principles of modern democracy and government based on the rule of law. Judge Lauterpacht puts it:

> 'The claim to equality before the law is in a substantial sense the most fundamental of the rights of man. It occupies the first place in most written constitutions. It is the starting point of all other liberties. (Sir Hersch Lauterpacht, *An International Bill of the Rights of Man*, 1945, p. 115.)

Historically, this principle was derived from the Christian idea of the equality of all men before God. All mankind are children of God, and consequently, brothers and sisters, notwithstanding their natural and social differences, namely man and woman, husband and wife, master and slave, etc. The idea of equality of man is derived from the fact that human beings 'by the common possession of reason' distinguish themselves 'from other living beings'. (Lauterpacht, *op. cit.*, p. 116.) This idea existed already in the Stoic philosophy, and was developed by the scholastic philosophers and treated by natural law scholars and encyclopedists of the seventeenth and eighteenth centuries. It received legislative formulation, however, at the end of the eighteenth century first by the Bills of Rights of some American states, next by the Declaration of the French Revolution, and then in the course of the nineteenth century the equality clause, as we have seen above, became one of the common elements of the constitutions of modern European and other countries.

Examining the principle of equality before the law, we consider that it is philosophically related to the concepts of freedom and justice. The freedom of individual persons, being one of the fundamental ideas of law, is not unlimited and must be restricted by the principle of equality allotting to each individual a sphere of freedom which is due to him. In other words the freedom can exist only under the premise of the equality principle.

In what way is each individual allotted his sphere of freedom by the principle of equality? What is the content of this principle? The principle is that what is equal is to be treated equally and what is different is to be treated differently, namely proportionately to the factual difference. This is what was indicated by Aristotle as *justitia commutativa* and *justitia distributiva*.

The most fundamental point in the equality principle is that all human beings as persons have an equal value in themselves, that they are the aim itself and not means for others, and that, therefore, slavery is denied. The idea of equality of men as persons and equal treatment as such is of a metaphysical nature. It underlies all modern, democratic and humanitarian law systems as a principle of natural law. This idea, however, does not exclude the different treatment of persons from the consideration of the differences of factual circumstances such as sex, age, language, religion, economic condition, education, etc. To treat different matters equally in a mechanical way would be as unjust as to treat equal matters differently.

We know that law serves the concrete requirements of individual human beings and societies. If individuals differ one from another and societies also, their needs will be different, and accordingly, the content of law may not be identical. Hence is derived the relativity of law to individual circumstances.

This historical development of law tells us that, parallel to the trend of generalization the tendency of individualization or differentiation is remarkable as may be exemplified by the appearance of a system of commercial law separate from the general private law in civil law countries, creation of labour law. The acquisition of independent status by commercial and labour law can be conceived as the conferment of a kind of privilege or special treatment to a merchant or labour class. In the field of criminal law the recent tendency of criminal legislative policy is directed towards the individualization of the penalty.

We can say accordingly that the principle of equality before the law does not mean that absolute equality, namely equal treatment of men without regard to individual, concrete circumstances, but it means the relative equality, namely the principle to treat equally what are equal and un- equally what are unequal.

The question is, in what case equal treatment or different treatment should exist. If we attach importance to the fact that no man is strictly equal to another and he may have some particularities, the principle of equal treatment could be easily evaded by referring to any factual and legal differences and the existence of this principle would be virtually denied. A different treatment comes into question only when and to the extent that it corresponds to the nature of the difference. To treat unequal matters differently according to their inequality is not only permitted but required. The issue is whether the difference exists. Accordingly, not every different treatment can be justified by the existence of differences, but only such as corresponds to the differences themselves, namely that which is called for by the idea of justice—'the principle to treat equal equally and unequal according to its inequality, constitutes an essential content of the idea of justice' (Goetz Hueck, *Der Grundsatz der Gleichmässigen Behandlung in Privatrecht*, 1958, p. 106) [*translation*].

Briefly, a different treatment is permitted when it can be justified by the criterion of justice. One may replace justice by the concept of reasonable- ness generally referred to by the Anglo-American school of law.

Justice or reasonableness as a criterion for the different treatment logically excludes arbitrariness. The arbitrariness which is prohibited, means the purely objective fact and not the subjective condition of those concerned. Accordingly, the arbitrariness can be asserted without regard to his motive or purpose.

There is no doubt that the principle of equality is binding upon admin- istrative organs. The discretionary power exercised on considerations of expediency by the administrative organs is restricted by the norm of equality and the infringement of this norm makes an administrative measure illegal. The judicial power also is subjected to this principle. Then, what about the legislative power? Under the constitutions which express this principle in a form such as 'all citizens are equal before the law', there may be doubt whether or not the legislators also are bound by the principle of equality. From the nature of this principle the answer must be in the affirmative. The legislators cannot be permitted to exercise their power arbitrarily and unreasonably. They are bound not only in exercising the ordinary legislative power but also the power to establish the constitution. The reason therefore is that the principle of equality being in the nature of natural law and therefore of a supra-constitutional character, is placed at the summit of hierarchy of the system of law, and that all positive laws including the constitution shall be in conformity with this principle.

The Respondent for the purpose of justifying its policy of apartheid or separate development quotes many examples of different treatment such as minorities treaties, public conveniences (between man and woman), etc. Nobody would object to the different treatment in these cases as a violation of the norm of non-discrimination or non-separation on the hypothesis that such a norm exists. The Applicants contend for the unqualified application of the norm of non-discrimination or non-separation, but even from their point of view it would be impossible to assert that the above-mentioned cases of different treatment constitute a violation of the norm of non-discrimination.

Then, what is the criterion to distinguish a permissible discrimination from an impermissible one?

In the case of the minorities treaties the norm of non-discrimination as a reverse side of the notion of equality before the law prohibits a State to exclude members of a minority group from participating in rights, interests and opportunities which a majority population group can enjoy. On the other hand, a minority group shall be guaranteed the exercise of their own religious and education activities. This guarantee is conferred on members of a minority group, for the purpose of protection of their interests and not from the motive of discrimination itself. By reason of protection of the minority this protection cannot be imposed upon members of minority groups, and consequently they have the choice to accept it or not.

In any event, in case of a minority, members belonging to this group, enjoying the citizenship on equal terms with members of majority groups, have conferred on them the possibility of cultivating their own religious, educational or linguistic values as a recognition of their fundamental human rights and freedoms.

The spirit of the minorities treaties, therefore, is not negative and pro-hibitive, but positive and permissive.

Whether the spirit of the policy of apartheid or separate development is common with that of minorities treaties to which the Respondent repeatedly refers, whether the different treatment between man and woman concerning the public conveniences can be referred to for the purpose of justifying the policy of apartheid or not, that is the question.

In the case of apartheid, we cannot deny the existence of reasonableness in some matters that diverse ethnic groups should be treated in certain aspects differently from one another. As we have seen above, differentiation in law and politics is one of the most remarkable tendencies of the modern political society. This tendency is in itself derived from the concept of justice, therefore it cannot be judged as wrong. It is an adaptation of the idea of justice to social realities which, as its structure, is going to be more complicated and multiplicate from the viewpoint of economic, occupational, cultural and other elements.

Therefore, different treatment requires reasonableness to justify it as is stated above. The reason may be the protection of some fundamental human rights and freedoms as we have seen in the case of minorities treaties, or of some other nature such as incapacity of minors to conclude contracts, physical differences between man and woman.

In the case of the protection of minorities, what is protected is not the religious or linguistic group as a whole but the individuals belonging to this group, the former being nothing but a name and not a group. In the case of different treatment of minors or between man and woman, it is clear that minors, disabled persons or men or women in a country do not constitute respectively a group. But whether a racial or ethnic group can be treated in the same way as categories such as minors, disabled persons, men and women, is doubtful. Our conclusion on this point is negative. The reasons therefor are that the scientific and clear-cut definition of race is not established; that what man considers as a matter of common-sense as criteria to distinguish one race from the other, are the appearance, particularly physical characteristics such as colour, hair, etc., which do not constitute in themselves relevant factors as the basis for different political or legal treatment; and that, if there exists the necessity to treat one race differently from another, this necessity is not derived from the physical characteristics or other racial qualifications but other factors, namely religious, linguistic, educational, social, etc., which in themselves are not related to race or colour.

Briefly, in these cases it is possible that the different treatment in certain aspects is reasonably required by the differences of religion, language, education, custom, etc., not by reason of race or colour. Therefore, the Respondent tries in some cases to justify the different treatment of population groups by the concept of cultural population groups. The different treatment would be justified if there really existed the need for it by reason of cultural differences. The different treatment, however, should be condemned if cultural reasons are referred to for the purpose of dissimulating the underlying racial intention.

In any case, as we have seen above, all human beings are equal before the law and have equal opportunities without regard to religion, race, language, sex, social groups, etc. As persons they have the dignity to be treated as such. This is the principle of equality which constitutes one of the fundamental human rights and freedoms which are universal to all mankind. On the other hand, human beings, being endowed with individuality, living in different surroundings and circumstances are not all alike, and they need in some aspects politically, legally and socially different treatment. Hence the above-mentioned examples of different treatment are derived. Equal treatment is a principle but its mechanical application ignoring all concrete factors engenders injustice. Accordingly, it requires different treatment, taken into consideration, of concrete circumstances of individual cases. The different treatment is permissible and required by the considerations of justice; it does not mean a disregard of justice.

Equality being a principle and different treatment an exception, those who refer to the different treatment must prove its *raison d'être* and its reasonableness.

The Applicants' norm of non-discrimination or non-separation, being conceived as of a *per se* nature, would appear not to permit any exception. The policy of apartheid or separate development which allots status, rights, duties, privileges or burdens on the basis of membership in a group, class or race rather than on the basis of individual merit, capacity or potential is illegal whether the motive be *bona fide* or *mala fide*, oppressive or benevolent; whether its effect or result be good or bad for the inhabitants. From this viewpoint all protective measures taken in the case of minorities treaties and other matters would be included in the illegal discrimination—a conclusion which might not be expected from the Applicants. These measures, according to the Applicants, would have nothing to do with the question of discrimination. The protection the minorities treaties intended to afford to the inhabitants is concerned with life, liberty and free exercise of religion. On the contrary, the Respondent argues the existence of the same reason in the policy of apartheid—the reason of protective measures in the case of minorities treaties.

We must recognize, on the one hand, the legality of different treatment so far as justice or reasonableness exists in it. On the other hand, we cannot recognize all measures of different treatment as legal, which have been and will be performed in the name of apartheid or separate development. The Respondent tries to prove by the pleadings and the testimony of the witnesses and experts the existence of a trend of differentiation in accordance with different religious, racial, linguistic groups. From the viewpoint of the Applicants, the abundant examples quoted by the Respondent and the testimony of witnesses and experts cannot serve as the justification of the policy of apartheid, because they belong to an entirely different plane from that of apartheid and because they are of a nature quite heterogeneous to the policy of apartheid, which is based on a particular racial philosophy and group sociology.

The important question is whether there exists, from the point of view of the requirements of justice, any necessity for establishing an exception to the principle of equality, and the Respondent must prove this necessity, namely the reasonableness of different treatment.

On the aspect of 'reasonableness' two considerations arise. The one is the consideration whether or not the individual necessity exists to establish an exception to the general principle of equality before the law and equal opportunity. In this sense the necessity may be conceived as of the same nature as in the case of minorities treaties of which the objectives are protective and beneficial. The other is the consideration whether the different treatment does or does not harm the sense of dignity of individual persons.

For instance, if we consider education, on which the Parties argued extensively, we cannot deny the value of vernacular as the medium of instruction and the result thereof would be separate schooling as between children of diverse population groups, particularly between the Whites and the Natives. In this case separate education and schooling may be recognized as reasonable. This is justified by the nature of the matter in question. But even in such a case, by reason of the matter which is related to a delicate racial and ethnic problem, the manner of dealing with this matter should be extremely careful. But, so far as the public use of such facilities as hotels, buses, etc., justification of discriminatory and separate treatment by racial groups cannot be found in the same way as separation between smokers and non-smokers in a train.

We cannot condemn all measures derived from the Respondent's policy of apartheid or separate development, particularly as proposed by the Odendaal Commission, on the ground that they are motivated by the racial concept, and therefore devoid of the reasonableness. There may be some measures which are of the same character as we see in the protection measures in the case of the minorities treaties and others. We cannot approve, however, all measures constituting a kind of different treatment of apartheid policy as reasonable.

One of the characteristics of the policy of apartheid is marked by its restrictive tendency on the basis of racial distinction. The policy includes on the one hand protective measures for the benefit on the Natives as we see in the institutions of reserves and homelands connected with restrictions on land rights; however, on the other hand, several kinds of restrictions of rights and freedoms are alleged to exist regarding those Natives who live and work in the southern sector, namely the White area outside the reserves. These restrictions, if they exist, in many cases presenting themselves as violation of respective human rights and freedoms at the same time, would constitute violation of the principle of equality before the law (particularly concerning the discrimination between the Natives and the Whites).

Here we are not required to give answers exhaustively in respect of the Applicants' allegations of violation by the Respondent of the Mandate concerning the legislation (*largo sensu*) applicable in the Territory. The items enumerated by the Applicants in the Memorials (pp. 118–66) are not included in their submissions. We are not obliged to pronounce our views thereon. By way of illustration we shall examine a few points. What is required from us is a decision on the question of whether the Respondent's policy of apartheid constitutes a violation of Article 2, paragraph 2, of the Mandate or not.

For the purpose of illustration we shall consider freedom of choice of occupations (cf. Memorials, pp. 121, 122 and 136).

In the field of civil service, participation by 'Natives' in the general administration appears, in practice, to be confined to the lowest and least-skilled categories, such as messengers and cleaners. This practice of 'job-reservation' for Natives is exemplified by allusion to the territorial budget, which classifies jobs as between 'European' and 'Natives'.

In the mining industry the Natives are excluded from certain occupations, such as those of prospector for precious and base minerals, dealer in unwrought precious metals, manager, assistant manager, sectional or underground manager, etc., in mines owned by persons of 'European' descent, officer in the Police Force. Concerning these occupations, 'ceilings' are put on the promotion of the Natives. The role of the 'Native' is confined to that of unskilled labourer.

In the fishing industry, the enterprises are essentially 'European' owned and operated. The role of the 'Native' is substantially confined to unskilled labour (Memorials, p. 119).

As regards railways and harbours, all graded posts in the Railway and Harbours Administration are reserved to 'Europeans', subject to temporary exceptions. The official policy appears to be that 'non-Europeans' should not be allowed to occupy graded posts.

The question is whether these restrictions are reasonable or not, whether there is a necessity to establish exceptions to the general application of the principle of equality of non-discrimination or not.

The matter of 'ceilings' was dealt with minutely and at length in the oral proceedings by the Parties. The Respondent's defence against the condemnation of arbitrariness, injustice and unreasonableness on the part of the Applicants may be summarized in two points: the one is the reason of social security and the other is the principle of balance or reciprocity.

The Respondent contends that the Whites in general do not desire to serve under the authority of the Natives in the hierarchy of industrial or bureaucratic systems. If this fact be ignored and the Natives occupy leading positions in which they would be able to supervise Whites friction between the two groups necessarily would occur and the social peace would be disturbed. This argument of the Respondent seems to be based on a pessimistic view of the possibility of harmonious coexistence of diverse racial and ethnic elements in an integrated society.

It is not deniable that there may exist certain causes of friction, conflict and animosity between diverse racial and ethnic groups which produce obstacles to their coexistence and co-operation in a friendly political community. We may recognize this as one aspect of reality of human nature and social life. It is, however, no less true that mankind aspires and strives towards the ideal of the achievement of a harmonious society composed of racially heterogeneous elements overcoming difficulties which may result from the primitive instinctive sentiment of racial prejudice and antagonism. Such sentiment must be overcome and not approved. In modern, democratic societies we have to expect this result mainly from the progress of humanitarian education. But the mission of politics and law cannot be said to be less important in minimizing racial prejudice and antagonism and avoiding collapse and tragedy. The State is obliged to educate the people by means of legislative and administrative measures for the same purpose.

To take into consideration the psychological effect upon the Whites who would be subjected to the supervision of the Natives if a ceiling did not exist, that is nothing else but the justification or official recognition of racial prejudice or sentiment of racial superiority on the part of the White population which does harm to the dignity of man.

Furthermore, individuals who could have advanced by their personal merits if there existed no ceiling are unduly deprived of their opportunity for promotion.

It is contended by the Respondent that those who are excluded from the jobs proportionate to their capacity and ability in the White areas, can find the same jobs in their own homelands where no restriction exists in regard to them. But even if they can find jobs in their homelands the conditions may not be substantially the same and, accordingly, in most cases, they may not be inclined to go back to the northern sector, their homelands, and they cannot be forced to do so.

The Respondent probably being aware of the unreasonableness in such hard cases, tries to explain it as a necessary sacrifice which should be paid by individuals for the maintenance of social security. But it is unjust to require a sacrifice for the sake of social security when this sacrifice is of such importance as humiliation of the dignity of the personality.

The establishment of ceilings in regard to certain jobs violates human rights of the Natives in two respects: one is violation of the principle of equality before the law and equal opportunity; the other is violation of the right of free choice of employment.

The Respondent furthermost advocates the establishment of ceilings by the principle of reciprocity or balance between two legal situations, namely one existing in the White areas where certain rights and freedoms of the Natives are restricted and the other situation existing in the Native areas where the corresponding rights and freedoms of the Whites are restricted. The Respondent seeks to prove by this logic that in such circumstances the principle of equality of the Whites and the Natives is observed. Unequal treatment unfavourable to one population group in area A, however, cannot be justified by similar treatment of the other population group in area B. Each unequal treatment constitutes an independent illegal conduct; the one cannot be counter-balanced by the other, as set-off is not permitted between two obligations resulting from illegal acts.

Besides, from the viewpoint of group interest, those of the Natives living in the White area outside the reserves are, owing to the number of the Native population, far bigger than those of the Whites living in the Native areas, the idea of counter-balance is quantitatively unjust.

It is also maintained, in respect of the restrictive policy as regards study to become an engineer by a non-White person, that the underlying purpose of this policy is to prevent the frustration on the part of the individual which he might experience when he could not find White assistants willing to serve under him. The sentiment of frustration on the part of non-White individuals, however, should not be rightly referred to as a reason for establishing a restriction on the educational opportunity of non-Whites, firstly because the question is that the frustration is caused by the racial prejudice on the part of the Whites which in itself must be eliminated and secondly because a more important matter is to open to the non-Whites the future possibility of social promotion. Therefore, the reason of the frustration of non-Whites cannot be justified.

Finally, we wish to make the following conclusive and supplementary remarks on the matter of the Applicant's Submissions Nos. 3 and 4.

1. The principle of equality before the law requires that what are equal are to be treated equally and what are different are to be treated differently. The question arises: what is equal and what is different.

2. All human beings, notwithstanding the differences in their appearance and other minor points, are equal in their dignity as persons. Accordingly, from the point of view of human rights and fundamental freedoms, they must be treated equally.

3. The principle of equality does not mean absolute equality, but recognizes relative equality, namely different treatment proportionate to concrete individual circumstances. Different treatment must not be given arbitrarily; it requires reasonableness, or must be in conformity with justice, as in the treatment of minorities, different treatment of the sexes regarding public conveniences, etc. In these cases, the differentiation is aimed at the protection of those concerned, and it is not detrimental and therefore not against their will.

4. Discrimination according to the criterion of 'race, colour, national or tribal origin' in establishing the rights and duties of the inhabitants of the territory is not considered reasonable and just. Race, colour, etc., do not constitute in themselves factors which can influence the rights and duties of the inhabitants as in the case of sex, age, language, religion, etc. If differentiation be required, it would be derived from the difference of language, religion, custom, etc., not from the racial difference itself. In the policy of apartheid the necessary logical and material link between difference itself and different treatment, which can justify such treatment in the case of sex, minorities, etc., does not exist.

We cannot imagine in what case the distinction between Natives and Whites, namely racial distinction apart from linguistic, cultural or other differences, may necessarily have an influence on the establishment of the rights and duties of the inhabitants of the territory.

5. Consequently, the practice of apartheid is fundamentally unreasonable

and unjust. The unreasonableness and injustice do not depend upon the intention or motive of the Mandatory, namely its *mala fides*. Distinction on a racial basis is in itself contrary to the principle of equality which is of the character of natural law, and accordingly illegal.

The above-mentioned contention of the Respondent that the policy of apartheid has a neutral character, as a tool to attain a particular end, is not right. If the policy of apartheid is a means, the axiom that the end cannot justify the means can be applied to this policy.

6. As to the alleged violation by the Respondent of the obligations incumbent upon it under Article 2, paragraph 2, of the Mandate, the policy of apartheid, including in itself elements not consistent with the principle of equality before the law, constitutes a violation of the said article, because the observance of the principle of equality before the law must be considered as a necessary condition of the promotion of the material and moral well-being and the social progress of the inhabitants of the territory.

7. As indicated above, so far as the interpretation of Article 2, paragraph 2, of the Mandate is concerned, only questions of a legal nature belong to the matter upon which the Court is competent. Diverse activities which the Respondent as Mandatory carries out as a matter of discretion, to achieve the promotion of the material and moral well-being and the social progress of the inhabitants, fall outside the scope of judicial examination as matters of a political and administrative nature.

Accordingly, questions of whether the ultimate goal of the mandates system should be independence or annexation, and in the first alternative whether a unitary or federal system in regard to the local administration is preferable, whether or in what degree the principle of indirect rule or respect for tribal custom may or must be introduced—such questions, which have been very extensively argued in the written proceedings as well as in the oral proceedings, have, despite their substantial connection with the policy of apartheid, no relevance to a decision on the question of apartheid, from the legal viewpoint.

These questions are of a purely political or administrative character, the study and examination of which might have belonged or may belong to competent organs of the League or the United Nations.

8. The Court cannot examine and pronounce the legality or illegality of the policy of apartheid as a whole; it can decide that there exist some elements in the apartheid policy which are not in conformity with the principle of equality before the law or international standard or international norm of non-discrimination and non-separation. The Court can declare if it is requested to examine the laws, proclamations, ordinances and other governmental measures enacted to implement the policy of apartheid in the light of the principle of equality. For the purpose of the present cases, the foregoing consideration of a few points as illustrations may be sufficient

to establish the Respondent's violation of the principle of equality, and accordingly its obligations incumbent upon it by Article 2, paragraph 2, of the Mandate and Article 22 of the Covenant.

9. Measures complained of by the Applicants appear in themselves to be violations of some of the human rights and fundamental freedoms such as rights concerning the security of the person, rights of residence, freedom of movement, etc., but such measures, being applied to the 'Natives' only and the 'Whites' being excluded therefrom, these violations, if they exist, may constitute, at the same time, violations of the principle of equality and non-discrimination also.

In short, we interpret the Applicants' Submissions Nos. 3 and 4 in such a way that their complaints include the violation by the Respondent of two kinds of human rights, namely individual human rights and rights to equal protection of the law. There is no doubt that the Respondent as Mandatory is obliged to protect all human rights and fundamental freedoms including rights to equal protection of the law as a necessary prerequisite of the material and moral well-being and the social progress of the inhabitants of the Territory. By this reason, what has been explained above about the principle of equality in connection with Article 38, paragraph 1 (c), is applicable to human rights and fundamental freedoms in general.

10. From the procedural viewpoint, two matters must be considered. The one is concerned with the effect of the Applicants' amendment of the Submissions Nos. 3 and 4 (Memorials, 15 April 1961, pp. 197-9) by the submissions of 19 May 1965 (C.R. 65/35). Since the amendment of the submissions is allowed until the stage of oral proceedings, and the amendment was made within the scope of the claim set forth in the Applications, there is no reason to deny its effectiveness. Furthermore, we wish to mention that the Respondent raised no objection during the course of the oral proceedings regarding the amendment.

The other is concerned with the question of choice by the Court of the reasons underlying its decisions.

Concerning this question, we consider that, although the Court is bound by the submissions of the Parties, it is entirely free to choose the reasons for its decisions. The Parties may present and develop their own argument as to the interpretation of the provisions of the Mandate, the Covenant, the Charter, etc., but the Court, so far as legal questions are concerned, quite unfettered by what has been put forward by the Parties, can exercise its power of interpretation in approving or rejecting the submissions of the Parties.

For the foregoing reasons, the Applicants' Submissions Nos. 3 and 4 are well-founded.

PART NINE

# TRADE AND DEVELOPMENT

## INTRODUCTION

THIS Part is intended to present the issues relating to the economic foundations of human rights. Economic inequalities between States are severe and are a chronic feature of international relations. The formal rules and standards concerning the Rule of Law and human rights have little meaning or possibility of effective application in societies in which a substantial proportion of the population are subject to unemployment, malnutrition, starvation, and illiteracy. The present structure of international 'trade and development' is not producing a stable and adequate growth in the underdeveloped countries. This, together with the fact of a considerably faster growth of population in underdeveloped countries, has resulted in a progressive widening of the large gap between the average incomes of the inhabitants of the rich industrial and the poor under-developed countries. See, further, U.N. General Assembly resolutions 2158 (XXI), on Permanent Sovereignty over Natural Resources, adopted on 25 November 1966; 2542 (XXIV), Declaration on Social Progress and Development, adopted on 11 December 1969, especially Articles 7, 17, 23, 24, and 25; 3201 (S–VI), adopted on 1 May 1974, containing a Declaration on the Establishment of a New International Economic Order; and 3281 (XXIX), adopted on 12 December 1974, Charter of Economic Rights and Duties of States. For further references see Brownlie, *Principles of Public International Law*, 4th ed., 1990, pp. 539–43. See also the Declaration on the Right to Development adopted by the United Nations General Assembly on 4 December 1986: on which see the *Yearbook of the United Nations*, 1986, pp. 717–21; and Brownlie, *The Human Right to Development*, Commonwealth Secretariat, London, 1989.

# I. SOME ECONOMIC FOUNDATIONS OF HUMAN RIGHTS: A STUDY PREPARED BY JOSÉ FIGUERES

This paper was published as an official document, U.N. Doc. A/CONF. 32/L.2 (8 February 1968) of the International Conference on Human Rights, held at Tehran in 1968 under the auspices of the United Nations. The author is a specialist in economics, and former President of Costa Rica.

## *TEXT*

### Introduction

1. The Secretary-General of the United Nations, in his statement to the Economic and Social Council at its forty-third session in 1967, declared that *faith in the dignity of man,* and in the equal rights of men and women, is the basic reason for the Organization to promote social progress and better standards of living for all (A/6703, introduction).

2. His statement affirms that *economic and social development* is an indispensable means to the full realization of human rights in the modern world.

3. This theme has been steadily and progressively elaborated by the United Nations and its organs during the twenty-two years of the Organization's growth.

4. There have been numerous pronouncements. The Universal Declaration of Human Rights, Article 22, states that everyone is entitled to the realization of the economic, social and cultural rights indispensable for the full development of his personality. This requires national and international efforts in accordance with the resources of each State.

5. Article 23 of the Declaration recognizes the right of everyone to work, to free choice of employment, to just and favourable conditions of work, to protection against unemployment and to equal pay for equal work.

6. Also affirmed is the right of everyone who works to a remuneration ensuring for his family an existence consistent with human dignity. His income being supplemented, if necessary, by other means of social protection.

7. Another right proclaimed by the Declaration, Article 25, is that of everyone to an adequate standard of health and well-being for himself and his family.

8. Of particular interest for the purposes of this study is Article 28 of the Declaration, which states that everyone is entitled to a *social and international order* in which the rights and freedoms of the Declaration can be fully realized.

9. The Declaration on Permanent Sovereignty over Natural Resources contained in General Assembly resolution 1803 (XVII) of 14 December 1962 (Article 1), provides that the rights of peoples and nations to permanent sovereignty over their natural resources must be exercised in their own interest.

10. It further states (Article 2) that the exploration, development and disposition of such resources, as well as the foreign capital required for these purposes, should conform to the rules that the nations consider to be necessary for the authorization, restriction or prohibition of such activities.

11. It stipulates (Article 6) that international co-operation for development, whether public or private investments, exchange of goods or services, technical assistance or exchange of scientific information shall be so conducted as to further the independent national life and the sovereignty of the developing nations.

12. The International Covenant on Economic, Social and Cultural Rights (a binding legal instrument adopted in 1966 by the General Assembly) not only contains the basic economic and social rights first enunciated in the Universal Declaration, but also in some cases strengthens and supplements them.

13. One right, however, which was omitted in the Declaration but is now included in the Covenant (Article 1) states that all peoples are entitled to self-determination and may therefore freely determine their political status and the pursuit of their economic, social and cultural development. In no case may a people be deprived of its means of subsistence.

14. Article 2 (i) imposes another important obligation. Each State Party shall take steps, individually and internationally, to the maximum of its available resources, to achieve progressively the full realization of the rights recognized in the Covenant. This shall be done by all appropriate means, including particularly the adoption of legislative measures.

15. Article 11 (1) of the International Covenant on Economic, Social and Cultural Rights, after recognizing the right of everyone to an adequate standard of living for himself and his family, goes beyond the Universal Declaration and adds that everyone has the right to the continuous improvement of living conditions.

16. Of interest to the present study is also Article 11 (2) of the Covenant. It provides that the States Parties, recognizing the fundamental right of everyone to be free from hunger, commit themselves to undertake the measures and programmes that may be needed to improve methods of production, conservation and distribution of *food*.

17. Among other things, agrarian systems shall be developed or reformed so as to achieve the highest utilization of natural and human resources.

18. Also, an efficient distribution of the world food supplies should be

ensured, taking into account the problems of both food importing and food exporting nations.

19. Worth noting for this study is also Article 23, which stipulates that international action for the purposes of the Covenant includes such methods as conventions, agreements, recommendations, international assistance, regional meetings and technical consultations organized in conjunction with the Governments concerned.

20. The preceding paragraphs illustrate the unceasing efforts of the United Nations to ensure for everyone the fullest measure of human dignity. These efforts include setting goals and standards in the economic and social spheres, and prescribing means and methods for their attainment.

21. This paper is written by one who fully shares the objectives of the United Nations, and is guided by them in his study. It is intended to serve a dual purpose, broadly speaking: (a) it seeks to identify the obstacles to the full enjoyment of human rights encountered in the economic and social struggles by the peoples of the less developed world; (b) it attempts to suggest some measures that should be taken if economic and social factors are to stop denying to those peoples their full range of human rights.

22. The nature of the subject may help explain why the body of this study contains some of the features of an essay in economics. Indeed, it may be described as a study in 'The Economic Foundations of Human Rights'.

## I. Enunciations

23. We live at a time when human rights have been beautifully enunciated in numerous documents, subscribed to by many nations. These enunciations, in themselves, are no small accomplishment.

24. Ethical codes have always preceded ethical conduct. A certain time is needed for education and adaptation. Even afterwards, perfection is never attained.

25. The Universal Declaration of Human Rights and the Covenants are now in the period of education and adaptation. Actual life in many nations is still far behind the principles. Men tend to be impatient about the apparent slow progress, because they forget that the lives of nations, of institutions, of mankind, are longer than the lives of individuals.

26. The Latin American Republics organized themselves under democratic principles when they won their independence during the first quarter of the nineteenth century.

27. For a hundred and fifty years these societies have been in the process of education and adaptation.

28. Later the principles were vigorously reiterated in the Charter of the

Organization of American States, and in the documents of several sub-sequent conferences. Whatever the remaining shortcomings, these countries are now relatively advanced towards democratic life. It would be in-conceivable to adopt today a non-democratic credo, except by force.

29. If it had not been for the enunciation of principles that were difficult to fulfil, the progress that has been made by these nations would not exist, and probably the vices of dictatorship would be officially sanctioned today.

30. I do not mean that it will take a hundred and fifty years for the Declaration of Human Rights to be implemented throughout the world. All processes move faster in our time. I do mean, however, that we should not be discouraged by differences between principle and fact.

## II. Sovereignty

31. The new nations that have emerged since the Second World War, are still in a state of mind inclined to eradicate the remnants of colonialism and to consolidate political independence or sovereignty. There is a tendency to believe that national sovereignty automatically brings personal liberties. This is not so, as Latin America has well learned through its history.

32. It takes some time to understand that independence, however costly, should really be a means to an end. The end should be the full comprehen-sion and enjoyment of human rights by all the people.

33. Another temporary disillusion that the emerging countries find is that independence, by itself, does not bring about economic development and social well-being.

34. Some socialists of the nineteenth century thought that general welfare was only a matter of equitable distribution of existing wealth and income, not realizing how small wealth and income were. Some of the revolutionary heroes of independence in our time, and their followers, seem to have underestimated the difficulties of development. Abundance for all the people does not come automatically with sovereignty.

35. Human rights, in their economic and social aspects, can only be achieved by a combination of high production and fair distribution. In theory at least, you could even have a society juridically so constituted that everybody enjoys civil rights and everybody is poor.

36. In actual practice, however, aspirations are so high in all modern countries that you cannot maintain political stability in the unrest provoked by the lack of fulfilment of human wants.

## III. Economic Rights

37. The two Covenants of the United Nations correctly equate economic and social rights with civil and political rights.

38. The dignity of man is not respected, by himself or by others, when he is not allowed to earn a decent living. By the same token, in the international field a nation is not sufficiently respected, whatever her political independence, while her work and her trade with other nations do not allow her fully to support all her citizens.

39. The provision of an adequate standard of living for all members of society requires a high degree of economic development.

40. Before the Industrial Revolution such abundance of goods and services would have been unthinkable. It was tacitly agreed, except by some reformers, that the work of the community could only produce the welfare of a privileged minority. Today, for the first time in human history, some countries are producing enough for practically all their citizens.

41. The poorer nations, which still constitute the majority of mankind, want to do likewise. They want to develop.

42. It is of common interest to all peoples, and to the harmony of the human family, that these retarded nations should develop. The economic and social rights cannot be universally fulfilled until the necessary amount of goods and services are produced by all nations.

## IV. Internal Obstacles

43. In their development efforts, poor countries encounter two sets of difficulties: internal and international. The internal obstacles to development are, among others, the following:

44. Lack of capital, which is a consequence of insufficient savings, and in turn, of low income; deficient technology; improper land tenure and tax systems; rapid population growth; poor general education; bad health, largely caused by malnutrition.

45. It would be hard to tell which of these internal deficiencies is more serious. They all cause one another in a series of vicious circles. Some people mention political instability first. I wonder if political instability is not also the effect of the other deficiencies.

## V. International Obstacles

46. The international causes of under-development are less generally recognized. Small nations cannot develop without an intense trade with the

advanced countries, (*a*) because their people want to consume the products of foreign industry or agriculture; (*b*) because industrialization requires capital goods produced in the developed countries; and (*c*) because indispensable services such as communications and transportation are largely the property of the rich countries.

47. The poor countries have to pay for all three—consumer goods, capital goods, services—with their natural resources, such as minerals, and with their agricultural labour turned into a few commodities like coffee, tea, cocoa, bananas and sugar.

48. There is a close association between human rights and the objectives of the United Nations Conference on Trade and Development, established in New York and Geneva in 1964. The Conference was convened for the purpose of studying trade between the rich and poor countries, and to try to find means of correcting the trends that are widening the gap between the two groups.

49. Trade between rich and poor nations *could* be an instrument of uniform world development. If economic and social rights were universally effective, one hour of human work spent in one country would be traded for one hour spent in another. This rule, still a distant goal, would give most retarded countries sufficient foreign income for their development.


## VI. Productivity

50. There are activities in which the product of one hour of work depends largely on the amount of capital investment behind the worker. Also, on the amount of applied technology. A trained driver with a power shovel moves a hundred times more earth than a labourer with a hand shovel.

51. When a poor nation can export products in which investment and technology increase production per man-hour of work, it should be the common interest of both traders, the buying and the selling countries, to make such capital and such knowledge available.

52. The field for improvement of productivity through larger investment is more restricted in agriculture than in industry. Little more could be done to improve the advanced methods already applied in some areas to the production of coffee, tea, cocoa, bananas. Yet, when the coffee farmer buys a truck from an industrial country, he exchanges hours of work at the rate of ten or twenty to one.

53. Internally, in an advanced society, there are activities where productivity per man-hour has increased greatly, like the steel industry. There are other activities where there has been no increased productivity, like the work of the barber, or, for that matter, the teacher or the musician. Logically, the compensation has increased more or less uniformly for the

steel worker and for the barber, thus relating wages to the productivity of the whole economy, and not of a particular activity. The barber who serves the steel worker, indirectly produces steel also. This is in accord with the aspirations of the economic and social rights.

54. In an integrated mankind, the same principles should apply internationally. Fantastic as it may sound in our time, there is no moral reason why the Colombian labourer who supplies the Detroit worker who makes his truck, with his morning cup of coffee, should earn less (sometimes twenty times less) than his northern colleague. The fair rule would be 'equal pay for equal effort'.

## VII. Slave Labour

55. The advanced societies of today abhor even the remnants of slave labour. Minimum wage legislation prevents the economically strong employer from hiring cheap labour, when labour is weak. No low wages for foreign workers are allowed. The United States, with a legal minimum wage of $1.50 an hour, could import millions and millions of labourers for one third that legal wage. Such bargain is prevented not only by the power of the trade unions, but also by the moral sense of the nation, expressed in its legislation. It would be contrary to the economic and social rights of man.

56. Yet, the toil of countless workers at cheap wages is imported to the rich countries in the form of raw materials or primary products, particularly agricultural products. 'Free trade' is allowed between private importers who bargain from the strength of a rich economy, and private exporters who are part of the weakness of a poor economy.

57. Private exporters in poor countries are not responsible for the well-being of their people. Their interest is to have a margin between what they pay to local producers and workers, and the price they get from foreign importers. They continue to do a good business, at any level of prices and wages, unintentionally retarding economic development and social improvement.

58. This shows the need of more study for reasonable regulations of international trade, at least in the relation between rich and poor nations.

59. Such trade might to some extent be entrusted to public institutions with a social responsibility. Or it could be regulated by such means as the International Wheat Agreement which, in times of surplus, has protected the farming communities against undeliberate exploitation in international trade.

60. The goal might be: when two or more countries trade intensely, supply-

ing each other with needed goods and services, their joint economies should provide uniformly adequate standards of living for all their people.

## VIII. Surpluses

61. Surpluses of certain commodities are one of the paradoxes of our time, when two thirds of mankind suffer from scarcities of nearly everything.

62. In the rich countries, agricultural surpluses are the result of market stabilization programmes, without which the development of the rural areas would have been impossible. Large though this problem is sometimes thought to be, it is really small by comparison to the problem of export surpluses in poor countries.

63. For the less developed nations, the prices of a few exports, easily depressed by overproduction, are a question of development or stagnation. And stagnation produces social and political unrest, with all the chain reaction of ill effects.

64. The anomaly is that even at the present (1967) depressed prices, the tendency continues to over-production in coffee and other tropical products. As the economic situation in the producing countries deteriorates, the prices of other crops diminish and the temptation increases to produce more coffee.

65. Furthermore, the tendency to consume imported articles is growing constantly, spurred by the variety of desirable gadgets from the industrial countries, by advertising and by instalment payment sales. All this has negative effects on developing societies.

66. Neither the balance of payments nor the economy as a whole can afford to have too many people rapidly improving their standard of living at the same time. Colour television in one family deprives several families of the bare essentials of life. This is one of the effects of trade between rich and poor nations.

## IX. Diversification

67. The other effect of overstimulated consumption for commercial aims in the poor countries is a tendency to further over-produce coffee, cocoa, tea, as the only possible means of payment for increasing imports. This depresses prices even more, and the vicious circle goes on.

68. It is easy to recommend crop diversification and industrialization. Yet substitute crops for coffee, for example, are extremely difficult to find. Latitude, altitude, the rain system, soil, the local culture of whole societies

that have grown together with coffee culture, all these factors present great obstacles to change. There are some flat areas of Brazil where coffee can be changed for something else at a bearable cost. Over one billion trees have been uprooted there. But on the hills of Colombia, the five Central American countries and others, nobody has found even a half-economical way of substituting crops.

69. Industrialization is going on everywhere at the slow pace permitted by the low prices of exports. It will be a long uphill effort.

## X. Wages and Taxation

70. The 'natural' way to prevent disastrous over-production is, of course, to allow prices to drop. The people who starve will not produce any more coffee.

71. Until recently, this was the only prescription given by some influential groups in the developed countries. One early exception was the International Sugar Agreement, when low prices could hurt the foreign investments in Cuba, or the sugar-beet producers of California or Florida.

72. The first important step to protect the poor economies from free trade exploitation was the International Coffee Agreement of 1962. The difficulties it has encountered, both in the producing and consuming countries, are a measure of the complexity of the problem. In spite of all, the Agreement has saved the numerous coffee countries from an even more serious recession than they are suffering today.

73. In the process of world development, we may expect more trade agreements to come for important commodities. Cocoa is now being negotiated. It would help the cause of economic and social rights, if certain rules were adopted in these agreements:

I. A 'development price' should be established for each important commodity. Perhaps it is too early in human progress to speak of a 'just price'. A just price would be one that would provide equal compensation for equal effort, anywhere in the world. So far this is not realistic.

A development price is a more modest aspiration. It could be defined as a level of compensation that would provide for (a) a certain legal minimum wage for salaried workers in all areas producing the specific commodity, (b) a certain rate of taxation in the country of origin for development purposes, and (c) a reasonable rate of capitalization for the farmer.

I know from experience that a development price is not difficult to determine for each commodity.

II. The developed, importing nations, should not pay less than the development price for those amounts of the commodity that they normally consume. This could be accomplished by the import quota system, as in sugar in the United States and other countries, or by import duties returnable to the producing country, as it is done with Puerto Rican rum in the continental United States.

III. In addition to the effects of the quota system, over-production should be fought by (a) wages, and (b) taxation.

All commodity agreements should include clauses that make it compulsory for the producing countries to enact and to make effective a uniform minimum wage in all areas producing the same article. This would prevent undue competition from the less socially advanced countries, with its depressing effects on prices. It would also increase the cost of production for the individual farmers, with a consequent effect of diminishing surpluses.

The agreement should include a minimum rate of taxation on the commodity in all producing countries. This would be a source of development revenues. Also, by reducing the income left to the farmers, it would discourage over-production.

Allowing prices to drop as a means of avoiding surpluses, diminishes the national income of the developing countries, and makes world problems more complex. Increasing the farmers' costs by wages and taxes has the same effect on surpluses, at the same time maintaining a higher national income.

## XI. More Difficulties

74. Difficult as the commodity price inequities are to remedy, there are other forms of unintended international exploitation which may be even harder to stop.

75. Private foreign investments, even if they were available in the amounts necessary for a relatively rapid development, could create problems for both the investing and the receiving countries. If a large proportion of important decisions affecting the economy of a country are made abroad, they are bound to create frictions, even if only because of psychological reasons.

76. Foreign enterprises would be a greater help to world development, and a normal business for investors, if their ownership and their technology were eventually and gradually transferred to the host countries under honest, mutually agreed terms.

77. In mixed economy nations, some utilities and natural monopolies could be transferred to local public institutions, and some manufacturing facilities to private companies, of local or mixed capital.

78. There are already successful examples of such transactions. An oil refinery, a telephone network, can be paid for in ten or twenty years

(interest and profit to the investors included) by a small surcharge on the gallon or on the call. The capital so withdrawn by the first owners can be profitably re-used for other ventures, simultaneously doing business and helping world development.

79. It is an excess of permanent ownership from abroad that should be avoided, or at least it should not be abused.


## XII. Communications

80. International communications and transportation pose another problem for the developing countries. Both services are indispensable, and both constitute a heavy drain on foreign exchange.

81. Each developed country likes to own as much as possible of the airlines, the shipping companies, the cable and electronic facilities that serve the world. This is due both to commercial and to strategic reasons.

82. Many developing countries have made the effort, perhaps out of proportion to their possibilities, to have their own 'flag airline', or to own a few steamships. As the size and price of aircraft go up, more local companies are turning out to be too small.

83. International ownership of communications and transportation facilities should be encouraged. The Governments of developed countries, which usually subsidize their own companies, could take a broader view and facilitate the proportional ownership of the poor countries, as a step towards an equitable distribution of the world income, and as a psychological satisfaction to smaller nations.


## XIII. Hard Selling

84. Commercial advertising and instalment selling of consumer goods in the poor countries, make the difficulties of development more acute.

85. In the last half century, a country of the size and the political system of the Soviet Union was able to consume internally what it could produce internally.

86. More recently, a short effort was made by a small country, South Korea, at the beginning of General Clark's régime. Foreign 'luxuries' were publicly burnt at the market place. This came close to Plato's ideal location for his modern city: away from the sea, banning outside traders, free from debilitating foreign ideas.

87. Obviously this is not the trend of our world. Our problem is to reconcile the development effort, the need to capitalize, the need to save

foreign exchange to pay for capital goods, with the inordinate consumption of non-essential articles from the developed nations, encouraged by advertising and sales promotions.

88. All consumption is now considered an economic virtue, especially since the Great Depression of the thirties, as a popularization of what people conceive as Keynes' remedy for all ills. The ancient virtue of thrift, which made possible the development of Europe and the United States, has been practically discarded from the moral code.

89. In applying the policies of developed countries, where high consumption is needed to match high production, to the under-developed countries where production is low, we are using Peter's medicine to prevent John's illness.

90. I refer, of course, to high consumption of non-indispensable foreign goods and services, which weakens the balance of payments, lessens the acquisition of capital goods, and retards development.

91. Particularly in a democracy, it is difficult to limit advertising and instalment buying of foreign goods. In spite of high customs duties and exchange restrictions, the balance of payments of poor countries continues to be one of the main obstacles to development. This is one of the most difficult disadvantages of trade with the rich nations.


## XIV. Technology

92. Technology, strangely enough, sometimes poses another obstacle to the retarded countries. Constant technological progress in the developed world brings about rapid obsolescence, which is too costly for the poor nations. Ever more sophisticated machines and gadgets strengthen the demand for foreign exchange, without a corresponding increase in the means of payment.

93. Synthetic products that substitute natural products are another source of worry. At this moment the threat of chemical fibres to abacá, sisal and jute is very serious for many countries in Asia, Africa and Latin America.

94. Research on synthetics is carried on by the large chemical firms which, as private business, are not responsible for world development. In the long run their new products represent progress. But the world is still divided between developed and under-developed nations.

95. For many areas of the world, natural fibres are the only export product, the only means of paying for capital goods, and therefore for development. By custom and by nature, these areas are difficult to cultivate with other crops. And they have the land and the labour to supply any expansion of world demand.

96. Those of us who are in the firing line of the development struggle cannot help but wonder why the admirable chemical companies do not devote their resources instead to find new uses for natural fibres. There must be an interesting field for research in fibre disintegration. This would be a contribution, and not a hindrance, to the fight on poverty in the large sisal, jute and abacá areas of the world.

97. With technological progress unrelated to any plan or orientation of the world economy, companies in the advanced countries are increasing the need for aid and for more taxes.

98. There is even talk of synthetic coffee. If this succeeds, who is going to feed fourteen Latin American nations and an equal number of African countries?

## XV. Aid

99. There are two possible ways of meeting the various disadvantages of international trade to the development of the weak economies. One is to study case by case (commodity prices, different kinds of foreign investments, international services, artificially stimulated consumption, advancing technology, etc.) and find the best possible remedy for each. Another is simply to adopt an over-all compensating policy by that modern invention, foreign aid.

100. Probably the solution will be a combination of both measures, as transitory mechanisms until a world economic balance is attained. On the one side commodity agreements establishing development prices, with clauses concerning wages and taxes. On the other hand direct pecuniary compensation to the developing countries, in amounts that should be much larger than at present, preferably handled by international agencies from contributions of all developed countries, large and small.

101. Commodity agreements will probably become unnecessary in the future, after the poor countries develop to a certain level, because then industrialization and higher wages and salaries will make cheap production of primary articles impossible.

102. Foreign aid, of course, is a temporary measure. As more countries develop, they should also become contributors to the international funds.

## XVI. Food Bank

103. So far I have been dealing with economic and social rights in areas that are partly the concern of UNCTAD. I will now make a reference to a specific contemporary problem on which FAO has shown deep interest: the world food shortage.

104. It is my paradoxical observation that the farmers of the world (of a hungry world) live under the spectre of abundance.

105. The danger of falling food prices under any local or seasonal abundance is such, that many producers are detained by fear of losses. Especially farmers of a certain size who use bank financing for their crops.

106. The risks of nature are bad enough for the farmer: rain or drought, bumper harvests or crop failures. The risks of the market, however, should be run by society.

107. A World Food Bank should be created. Let each agricultural area have surplus buying agencies at guaranteed prices. Establish strategic reserves in the major ports of the world. Be prepared to absorb bumper crops at one end and crop failures at another.

108. Many of the practical difficulties in this plan, such as quality control and proper preservation, have already been met by the internal agricultural programmes of several nations.

109. Experience shows that when the market is guaranteed, the farmer himself goes after technical assistance, to increase production or to reduce costs. On the other hand, in the absence of a guaranteed market, it takes a great educational effort to diffuse better methods, seeds, etc.

110. We might say that the farmers of the world have a right to proper compensation for their work, and the peoples of the world have a right to be fed. A means to fulfil such rights would be a World Food Bank.

111. The World Food Bank could be an instrument of both, FAO and UNCTAD, performing two similar functions with physical reserves: (a) encourage and regulate the world's food supplies; (b) stabilize the market for important commodities that constitute the means of international payment for under-developed countries.

112. The Bank would be a sister institution of the International Monetary Fund and the World Bank. Belatedly this would implement John Maynard Keynes' ideas at the Bretton Woods Conference in 1944.


XVII. More Aid


113. Let me return to foreign aid, as a means of compensating for the weak bargaining position of poor countries, and as an expression of world solidarity.

114. This is the wrong time (1967) to speak about the amounts of aid that would be needed for a satisfactory rate of world development. The largest contributing country, the United States, is presently reducing its participation.

115. In 1964, UNCTAD recommended 1 per cent of the national income of developed countries to go to foreign aid. In 1966 it was found that the

amount given had actually diminished, instead of approaching the goal of 1 per cent. In the meantime, independent scholars have suggested that the total needs are about 2 per cent of the income of the developed world.

116. This would mean, for the United States alone, about 17 billion dollars a year, instead of the two and one-half to three billion which the Congress is debating now. For all advanced nations together, East and West, 2 per cent might [amount][1] to an outlay of about 40 billion dollars a year in aid to the whole under-developed world.


## XVIII. Aid Per Head

117. There are different ways of estimating not only what should be given in aid, in the absence of proper trade regulations, but also what could be effectively used.

118. In 1955, in my speech at the First Conference of Western Hemispheric Presidents held in Panama, I suggested that the Latin American continent could use in the first years of an intensive development programme roughly US$10.00 per inhabitant. Today, in 1967, I doubt if Latin America could do much with less than twenty or twenty-five United States dollars per person.

119. The difference is to be found in the drop of export prices. Twelve yearly crops of coffee and cocoa have been sold at two-thirds of what may be considered as a development price. The backlog of needs has accumulated, in spite of the programmes and financial help of the Alliance for Progress. Without the Alliance, present problems of all kinds would be a great deal worse.

120. Of course, if prices had been fairer there would have been more general consumption, and even some waste, in the small privileged circles that can afford waste. But undoubtedly, capital formation would have gone on at a reasonable rate, as it did during the early fifties when export prices were better.

121. Now it seems that an outside injection of capital of say US$20.00 per inhabitant, as an average for the first few years of an intensive programme, would be needed and could be effectively used in Latin America. With a population of 200 million, this amounts to four billion dollars a year. Current development aid to the whole continent, coming almost exclusively from the United States, is between one half and one billion a year.

[1] Editorial insertion.

## XIX. Aid in Kind

122. If, and when, foreign aid is ever given in the necessary amounts to establish a sound economic world order in a few decades, probably a large proportion of it will have to be given in kind, not in money.

123. So far the developing countries have seriously objected not only to political 'strings attached', but also to policies that would force them to buy the products of the respective aid-giving nation. I do not see why such objection should continue if intensive programmes were undertaken with all the needed aid.

124. In our time, even the strong economies are suffering from balance of payments deficits. This is attributed to defects in the world monetary system. Probably the phenomenon has deeper sources. It may be related to international trade, because the strong economies are simultaneously stimulating and preventing a healthy growth of the weak economies and markets.

125. Of course troops on foreign soil tend to create a deficit at one end and inflation at the other. There may be other causes, and probably other evils, that also cannot be stopped easily.

126. If foreign aid were given in the necessary amounts in money and not in kind, the effects of the balance of payments of the aid-giving countries would be detrimental.

127. On the other hand, if a large part of the aid is given in kind, or, if the recipient nations make most of their purchases in the respective giving country, surpluses in industrial capacity could be utilized, at a low cost to the over-all economy of the developed countries.

128. Overhead costs are currently covered by present production and sales. Any addition in volume, within the capacity of the industrial system, requires relatively small outlays.

129. Aid in kind would present some difficulties to the larger retarded countries, where certain industries like tractor-building are already established. With a certain degree of flexibility in all policies, such obstacles can be surmounted.

130. Besides, if foreign aid is handled by international agencies, goods representing surpluses of industrial capacity could go to a common pool, and would be distributed according to circumstances.

131. Thus the members of the family of nations would be applying the old motto: 'From each according to his possibilities; to each according to his needs'.

## XX. War Expenses

132. What are the probabilities of an all-out effort of development of the retarded world if, in the absence of well-regulated trade, this would require an aid contribution by all developed nations, large and small, of 2 per cent of their income.

133. I am more familiar with the political situation in the United States than in other countries. And, of course, I understand that, as of today, such contribution is politically impossible, even if it is considered to be economically possible and desirable.

134. For our present purpose, we may consider that the national product of the United States is supporting three main kinds of expenditures: (a) the current standard of living; (b) war expenses; and (c) development, both international and internal. Let us not forget internal development; pollution, traffic jams, riot areas, etc.

135. In order to increase one of the three expenditures appreciably, one or the other two must be curtailed. So far it is development that has been sacrificed, because it is politically the weakest. For internal reasons it is difficult to reduce the standard of living or even its rate of growth. And for international reasons it is considered risky to reduce the war expenses.

136. No matter how trite or how unrealistic the suggestion may be, it is the war expenses that should diminish. Now that military forces are largely concentrated in two super-Powers, it ought to be less difficult than in previous centuries to establish civilized relations among the peoples of the world. The military expenses of some poor countries are, if one may use a strong word, preposterous.

137. The arithmetic involved is child's play. If we were to reduce present war expenses by one half, we would still have enough funds to maintain order, and to continue the exploration of space, the atom, the bottom of the sea and the heart of our earth.

138. Not counting the large sums appropriated for war emergencies, the permanent military budgets of the nations of the world now reach a combined total of about US$140 billion.

139. If we are allowed to dream about a better humanity; if as some anthropologists think, mankind is heading toward integration and not to extinction; if we could cut war expenses by half, the more developed countries, without sacrificing their standard of living or their rate of growth, could devote the funds thus released to development, part internal and part international.

140. And if all nations did the same, as they should, perhaps in less than half a century our planet would be embellished by the blossoming of the Great Human Society.

## XXI. Conclusion

141. I have read the documents that tell the story of the accomplishments of the United Nations in the field of human rights.

142. While a long road lies ahead in this field of man's progress, those achievements, that some persons might be tempted to regard as modest, plus the undoubtable greatness and permanency of the Declaration and the Covenants, make the last two decades of initiation in human rights the best spent period in the history of mankind.

143. Much that I have said in this paper belongs to the realm of enunciations. More ideas, more time, more education, more adaptation will be needed. Yet, the rate of progress is an accelerating movement.

144. According to these views, the fulfilment of human rights *requires* economic and social development.

145. Development requires not only corrections to the internal causes of poverty in the retarded nations, but also a full revision of all economic relations with the advanced countries.

146. Since several of these relations are difficult to change, an over-all compensation may have to be given for a time, in the form of increased foreign aid.

147. The increase in foreign aid may be dependent on the reduction of war expenses. This is no surprise. Human rights and world peace dwell side by side in the hearts of men. United Nations is endeavouring to achieve both.

148. Peace will help development. Development will engender peace. They are both causes and effects. They strengthen each other. Their common goal is the reign of human rights.

## II. TOWARDS A NEW TRADE POLICY FOR DEVELOPMENT: REPORT BY THE SECRETARY-GENERAL OF THE UNITED NATIONS CONFERENCE ON TRADE AND DEVELOPMENT, 1964

This Report was prepared by Raul Prebisch, Secretary-General of UNCTAD, and published as a U.N. Document, E/CONF. 46/3 (U.N., Sales No. 64, II.B.4). The excerpts which follow are from pp. 6–10 and 27–31. Reference should also be made to Gunnar Myrdal, *Economic Theory and Under-Developed Regions*, 1957 (published in University Paperbacks, 1963), especially Chapters 1 and 11.

*TEXT*

The potential of modern technology is so enormous that the developing countries should not have to wait as long as the present industrially advanced countries had to wait to develop their technologies step by step and use them for the eradication of poverty and its inherent evils. Indeed, they cannot wait as long, because the acceleration of their development is an absolute necessity that brooks no delay. The pressure exerted by the masses for real improvements in their levels of living has never been as strong as it is now, and in the years to come it will become a growing source of internal and world-wide tension if it is not met by a vigorous policy of economic and social development in which international co-operation must play a decisive role.

The obstacles which the economic and social structures of the peripheral countries place in the way of development policy are well known. It is quite clear that important decisions must be taken to bring about structural changes, as has been indicated in previous reports of the United Nations and its specialized agencies. Suffice it to state here that, without such structural changes, and without a determined political effort to promote development and remove the internal obstacles from its path, measures of international co-operation, however good in themselves, will be very limited in their effect.

### 2. The Old Order

The imposing code of rules and principles, drawn up at Havana and partially embodied in the General Agreement on Tariffs and Trade (GATT), does not reflect a positive conception of economic policy in the sense of a rational and deliberate design for influencing economic forces so as to change their spontaneous course of evolution and attain clear objectives. On the contrary, it seems to be inspired by a conception of policy which implies that the expansion of trade to the mutual advantage of all merely requires the removal of the obstacles which impede the free play of these forces in the world economy. These rules and principles are also based on an abstract notion of economic homogeneity which conceals the great structural differences between industrial centres and peripheral countries with all their important implications. Hence, GATT has not served the developing countries as it has the developed ones. In short, GATT has not helped to create the new order which must meet the needs of development, nor has it been able to fulfil the impossible task of restoring the old order.

In the context of the nineteenth century and the initial decades of the twentieth, as we see it, there was no place for this idea of rationally influencing and so modifying the course of events. The course of events had merely to be followed and anything that obstructed it eliminated. Development in the periphery was a spontaneous phenomenon of limited scope and social depth; it came about under the dynamic influence of a unique combination of external factors which have since ceased to exist.

The situation can be presented simply in the following terms. During the last quarter of the nineteenth century, the United Kingdom, as the world's leading dynamic centre, accounted for 36 per cent of world exports of manufactures and 27 per cent of the imports of primary commodities. Since the historical accident of the industrial revolution happened in the United Kingdom before it did in other parts of the world, that country, with its limited resources and given its level of technology at the time, had to grow outwards and there emerged the classic pattern of exchanging manufactured goods for primary commodities. Imports of primary goods and other commodities by the United Kingdom grew apace, as did their share in the national income: the over-all import coefficient rose from approximately 18 per cent in 1850 to the very high figure of almost 36 per cent in 1880–4, as a result of free trade. This phenomenon influenced the rest of Europe, although not to the same extent, and its effects on the development of countries on the periphery of the world economy were striking.

Actually the process was the opposite of that which has gradually come into existence since the end of the First World War and especially since the great depression: the substitution of imports of food and raw materials for domestic production and not *vice versa*.

There was another factor which encouraged the growth of consumption and primary commodity imports: these imports were not yet subject to the adverse effects of technological progress as they would be in later years. Per capita income was still able to sustain an active demand for foodstuffs, synthetic production of raw materials had not yet begun on a larger scale, and European farmers still clung to their traditional methods.

## 3. The Great Depression and World Trade

It is sufficient to mention these facts to emphasize the radical change which was ushered in during the First World War as a result of political and economic factors and which grew in scope and intensity as a result of the world depression of the 1930s.

The United States displaced the United Kingdom as the leading dynamic centre. This was more than a mere change of hegemony; it had a far-reaching influence on the rest of the world. The enormous natural resources of the vast territory of the United States and the resolutely protectionist policy it pursued from the start of its development were apparent in the steady decline of its import coefficient. In 1929, on the eve of the world depression, this coefficient was barely 5 per cent of total income and the restrictive measures resulting from the depression reduced it still further. In 1939, at the beginning of the Second World War, it had fallen to 3.2 per cent.

The effects of these developments on the rest of the world were of enormous importance. With the advent of the great depression, the order that dated back to the nineteenth century, and which the First World War had seriously shaken, now disintegrated. The trends towards agricultural self-sufficiency were encouraged to an extraordinary degree in the industrial countries, which were striving to cut their imports in order to cope with the violent contraction in their exports. Bilateralism and discrimination emerged as means of mitigating the intensity of this phenomenon. This movement spread throughout the world and forced many developing countries to adopt even more drastic restrictive measures, since the value of primary exports was declining more sharply than that of industrial goods.

The precipitous fall in the import coefficient of the United States, the leading dynamic centre, and the slow recovery in the level of its activity, compelled the other countries of the world to lower their import coefficients too by all kinds of restrictive expedients. Under the most-favoured-nation clause, the restrictions ought to have been applied to all countries alike, but the discrimination fostered by bilateralism allowed them to be directed mainly against the United States, as a means of remedying the acute dollar shortage.

This problem recurred after the Second World War. As in the 1930s, recourse was then had to bilateralism but this phase was very short-lived. Western Europe decided to attack its difficulties boldly, not just by adopting negative and defensive attitudes but by positive action of enormous scope: the modernization of its economy, which boosted its export capacity, and the policy of integration, which promoted its reciprocal trade to the particular detriment of imports paid for in dollars. While this attitude contributed to over-all equilibrium, it had a serious effect on some developing countries. So it was that the European Economic Community (EEC) and the European Free Trade Association (EFTA) came into existence.

Thus ended the long period of structural imbalance vis-à-vis the United States, which not only unreservedly welcomed the formation of the Community but also offered it its firm support.

In their turn, eight socialist countries[1] formed their own grouping, the Council for Mutual Economic Assistance (CMEA), in order to integrate certain important activities, plan them jointly, and import greater fluidity to the reciprocal trade of the participating countries.

A new order is thus emerging among the more advanced industrialized States and the next few years will reveal its ultimate significance more clearly: it remains to be seen whether this new order will be one in which vast regions withdraw into their shells and isolate themselves with a minimum of trade between them, or whether it will be one in which they take advantage of a closer economic link involving new forms of the international division of labour.

Hence the vital significance of the massive cut in tariffs proposed by the late President Kennedy for the next round of GATT negotiations. The success of these negotiations among the advanced countries which conduct their trade relations mainly by means of tariffs will thus have a considerable influence on the future development of the world economy.

The EEC authorities have repeatedly affirmed the outward-looking character of their economic policy, a position which coincides with that of the United States. There has been a gradual relaxation of that country's traditional protectionism and it is to be hoped that this new policy can now enter upon a very broad phase.

The socialist States of CMEA have also repeatedly expressed their support of the principle of the international division of labour. The success of the Kennedy round and the improvement in the international political atmosphere could considerably facilitate the adoption of formulae which would enable the socialist countries to play an active part in world trade by removing the obstacles which obstruct their participation. This refers not only to relations between them and other industrially advanced countries, irrespective of the differences in their economic and social systems, but also to relations with the developing countries, in view of the interdependence of world trade.

### 4. The Disintegration of the Old Pattern and the Developing Countries

All this is highly important for the developing countries, but it is far from enough, as will be seen later. What was happening in those countries after the great depression, while such significant changes were taking place in the industrial countries?

The break-down of the old pattern of trade created new problems for the

---

[1] For the sake of brevity, the term 'socialist countries' in this report refers to the countries designated as 'countries with centrally planned economies' in United Nations publications.

developing countries. The persistent trend towards external imbalance began, first, as a result of the contraction of their exports during the great depression and, later as a result of their slow rate of growth. From the outset, a number of countries tried to counteract this imbalance by means of import substitution, i.e., by inward-looking industrialization, without foreign markets, and later, after the Second World War, by continuing this policy without interruption and by drawing on the international financial resources made available to them.

The external imbalance was thus covered, but in a precarious manner in the countries which at that time were pushing ahead with their industrialization. As time went on, the consequences of this system became increasingly apparent. Industrialization encounters growing difficulties in the countries where it is pursued furthest. These difficulties arise from the smallness of national markets and also from the following peculiar fact. The further substitution proceeds in respect of some imports, the more other imports grow because of the heavier demand for capital goods and, subsequently, because of the effects of higher income. In addition to this pressure, the adverse effects of the decline in the terms of trade in recent years have weakened the effectiveness of financial contributions from international sources.

Furthermore, these contributions entail a heavy burden of servicing which is mounting rapidly, mainly owing to the amount of amortization in respect of relatively short-term credits. Thus servicing competes with an active demand for imports for the relatively scanty supply of foreign exchange earned by exports.

This phenomenon has no historical parallel. The old pattern of international trade, as it existed in the nineteenth century, was characterized, as has already been pointed out, by a strong and steady growth in exports, which provided the means for servicing debts. Any difficulties which arose were due not to structural defects, as now, but rather to financial misbehaviour or short-term cyclical contractions. In addition to all this, there is the mounting burden of external payments for maritime freight and insurance. The developing countries own only 6 per cent of the world maritime tonnage and this creates a series of problems. Moreover, while the system of shipping conferences may be explained by the very nature of sea transport, it involves combines that restrict competition and affects the developing countries as regards both the cost of services and the impact of this cost on various products depending on their degree of processing. The desire to extend import substitution policy to these services is therefore very understandable, but the information so far available in support of this policy is very meagre. All this necessitates further inquiry, and it is to be hoped that the information needed for the purpose will be forthcoming.

This is a characteristic picture of many of the developing countries, especially those where industrialization has made most headway. None of the others, however, is, over the short or long term, immune to the persistent tendency towards imbalance, except in certain exceptional cases; and what is now happening in the more industrialized developing countries foreshadows what will happen in the others unless a conscious and deliberate effort is made to influence the course of economic events and to apply the enlightened policy which those events have made imperative.

## Chapter IV. Gatt and the Developing Countries

### I. THE ACHIEVEMENTS OF GATT

GATT has important achievements to its credit. Following the inter-war period of chaos, it introduced a new concept of a rule of law in world trade. One may criticize the particular character of some of the law that has been applied. But this should not be allowed to obscure the fact that the decision of Governments that world trade should be subject to this law was in itself of vital importance in this field.

In the past, increases in trade restrictions by particular countries have frequently led to a spiral of retaliation in which all have lost and none have gained. The application of a rule of law in world trade has already helped to limit excesses of this type and could do much more if the law itself were made more responsive to contemporary needs.

A second virtue of GATT is its machinery for complaint and consultation. Each member country has an opportunity to bring forward instances in which it feels that it has suffered injury at the hands of another member, and can claim the redress authorized or adequate compensation, although it must be admitted that this procedure has often not been effective in practice.

GATT also provides a forum in which countries can discuss the impact of one another's trade policies, with a view to reaching a satisfactory accommodation.

Within this framework of rules and consultative machinery, GATT has brought about considerable reductions in the tariffs and other restrictions on world trade that were established during the difficult period following the great depression.

It is true, however, that these reductions have been of benefit mainly to the industrial countries and that the developing countries generally have obtained very little direct benefit from this process. But in so far as the reduction of tariffs and restrictions may have created a more favourable basis for growth in the industrial countries, some indirect benefit will have accrued to the developing countries in the form of a higher demand for their exports than would otherwise have occurred.

Finally, since the publication of the report, *Trends in International Trade*, in

October 1958, GATT has been making a serious effort to conduct its activities in a way that would take more adequate account of the unsatisfactory position of developing countries in world trade. Still, it must be admitted that the positive results of these efforts, after more than five years, have been somewhat disappointing. But the problem itself has been recognized, and this recognition led to the consideration of a Programme of Action by a GATT Meeting of Ministers in May 1963, and subsequently to efforts to implement that Programme. The matter now rests with Governments: if this Programme of Action could be fully carried out by all countries concerned, a very important step forward would have been taken. The resolutions relating to the Kennedy round were also adopted at this Meeting of Ministers. The principle of not demanding full reciprocity from the developing countries was accepted, among others, during these negotiations on tariffs and other barriers to trade. In addition, the achievement of satisfactory conditions of access to world markets for agricultural products was set as an objective.

The GATT Tariff Conference of 1960/61 resulted in very limited benefits for the less developed countries; it is to be hoped that the Kennedy round will produce a more favourable balance in view of its significance as crucial evidence of the practical benefits which GATT can offer to the developing countries.

Furthermore, it is acknowledged that GATT has a very efficient secretariat, a fact that is borne out by its studies and the careful preparation of its negotiations; and it has also shown its ability to adapt itself to the changing realities of the times.

The above comments on GATT should be approached within a broad perspective. We can now see clearly things which were still confused and vague in the Havana days. The absolute necessity of industrialization for the peripheral countries had not been recognized or realized nor had the need to intensify this process as advanced techniques permeated into agriculture. Another thing which was not properly understood was the persistent trend towards external imbalance, which was attributed more to the inflationary policy of Governments than to the nature of the growth phenomenon. In addition, the developing countries were still very far from stating their position and defining their aspirations and attitudes. The end of the colonial era was only just in sight. And social tensions in the developing countries were not then so conspicuous or so pressing as they now are. We can now see all this clearly and there is an increasingly strong feeling that a very great effort will have to be made to alleviate and eliminate those tensions, which have such a great impact on world peace.

This effort could no longer take the form of a few rules and principles specifying what must be avoided; it is essential also to determine what must be done and to formulate a policy which meets this need for positive action.

Why has GATT not been as efficacious for the developing countries as for the industrial countries? There are two main reasons. First, the Havana Charter, as has already been said, is based on the classic concept that the free play of international economic forces by itself leads to the optimum expansion of trade and the most efficient utilization of the world's productive resources; rules and principles are therefore established to guarantee this free play. Secondly, the rules and principles in question have not always been strictly complied with and, even though they seem to have been observed in the letter in certain instances, the spirit underlying them has not been restricted.

## 2. The Structural Differences and their Consequences

The free play concept is admissible in relations between countries that are structurally similar, but not between those whose structures are altogether different as are those of the industrially advanced and the developing countries. These structural differences show themselves in various ways which were outlined in the preceding section.

The structural origin of the deterioration in the terms of trade has already been indicated and there is no need to revert to the subject here. It will be recalled that the Havana Charter mentions this phenomenon at one point. Elsewhere, however, in the articles relating to commodity agreements, the predominant idea that ultimately emerges is that basic market trends should not be impeded.

We have also commented on the disparities in international demand, which also derive from structural differences. This is a fundamental point which does not seem to have been given the importance it deserves in the Havana Charter. Thus, in seeking to lower or eliminate tariffs and restrictions with a view to promoting trade, neither the Charter nor the Agreement draws any distinction between developed and developing countries. And since there is an initial assumption of homogeneity, such reductions have to be equivalent everywhere. This is the principle of conventional reciprocity that prevailed until recently. The fact that these disparities place primary and industrial exporting countries in diametrically opposite positions has not been taken into consideration. Hence the importance of the fact that the need to depart from the idea of conventional reciprocity was recognized in the Kennedy round.

The former group of countries, given the relatively slow growth of their primary exports, cannot cope with the intensive demand for industrial imports unless they alter the composition of the imports in question, replacing some of them by domestic production so as to be able to increase others. In the absence of an export trade in manufactured goods, the only alternative left open to the developing countries is to grow at the slow tempo set by their primary exports, or to encourage these substitution activities by means of protectionism so as to develop more rapidly and prevent or correct the external imbalance as they develop.

If protectionism is kept within certain bounds, i.e., if it is applied only to the extent necessary to counteract the disparity in demand, there is no reason why it should have a depressive effect on the dynamics of world trade; on the contrary, it should have a purely balancing influence. Within these limits, not only is industrialization compatible with the development of primary production and exports, but an optimum relation between the two, conducive to intensive economic development, is conceivable. Of course, if a developing country weakens its primary export position by measures which act as disincentives and its place is not filled by other exporting countries, these depressive effects on international trade will be inevitable. But such effects, however we may look at them, are not inherent in the industrialization of the peripheral countries.

On the other hand, protectionism in respect of primary production in the countries exporting manufactured goods does exert a depressive influence, since the disparity in demand, instead of being levelled out, is accentuated, to the obvious detriment of world trade and the growth of the developing countries. In this form, protectionism helps in these centres to slow down still further the growth of the developing countries' primary exports, and hence the expansion of imports of the manufactures needed for their development. In other words, protectionism in respect of primary production in the industrial countries has definitely unfavourable repercussions on international trade and compels the peripheral countries to adopt further import substitution measures so they can continue their development; thus it makes this development even more difficult by curtailing their opportunities for an advantageous international division of labour. The Havana Charter fails to recognize this lack of symmetry and its practical implications for trade policy.

Given the prevailing conception, the objective pursued when that Charter was drawn up could be summed up in the following simple terms. The restrictions and tariffs which had been doing so much to disintegrate the world economy had to be gradually removed and the free play of international economic forces thus restored. The reduction and elimination of restrictions and tariffs would also cover the primary commodities imported by the industrial countries, and, in return, the countries exporting these primary commodities would have to lower their import tariffs on manufactured goods.

Herein lies the concept of the symmetry of a situation that was far from symmetrical: if the peripheral countries wished to reap the benefits of a liberal tariff policy for primary imports in the industrial centres, they likewise had to make equivalent concessions in their own tariffs. This is the serious drawback of such a conception of trade policy: the failure to take account of the fact that those equivalent concessions would intensify the trend towards trade imbalance inherent in the disparity of international demand, instead of helping to correct it.

towards trade imbalance inherent in the disparity of international demand, instead of helping to correct it.

Great strides have been made of late towards recognizing that these rules of reciprocity in trade negotiations must be changed because of the economic inequality between countries. A clear distinction must be made, however, between this conventional reciprocity and real reciprocity.

This is a very important point which must be borne in mind. The request for reciprocity in negotiations between countries which have not structural disparity in their demand is logical. Indeed, it is essential for the stability of the world economy that any expansion of exports which a given country achieves on the basis of concessions from the others should be accompanied by concessions granted to the latter, so that its imports from them can increase.

In the case of trade between the developing and the industrial countries, the situation is different. Since the former tend to import more than they export—owing to the international disparity in demand—concessions granted by the industrial countries tend to rectify this disparity and are soon reflected in an expansion of their exports to the developing countries. In other words, the developing economies, given their great potential demand for imports, can import more than they would otherwise have been able to do had those concessions not been granted. Thus there is a real or implicit reciprocity, independent of the play of conventional concessions. And this is what must be recognized in international trade policy.

This distinction is inherent at the transitional stage through which the developing countries are passing. The disparity in world demand does not have to be a permanent phenomenon. As the structure of production gradually changes with industrialization and industrial exports, this disparity will tend to disappear. Indeed, as such exports, both to advanced and to other developing countries, make headway, the disparity can be levelled out gradually. When this happens—and only then—will the bases have been laid for conventional reciprocity between the industrialized countries and countries that are pressing on along the road of industrialization. But this is a long process for most of the developing countries.

# INDEX